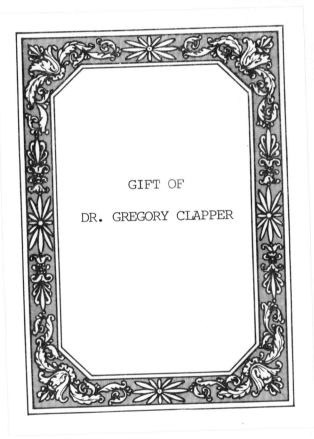

Exploring the
Hebrew Bible

JOHN CARMODY

University of Tulsa

DENISE LARDNER CARMODY

University of Tulsa

ROBERT L. COHN

Lafayette College

90-296

PRENTICE HALL, Englewood Cliffs, New Jersey 07632

Library of Congress Cataloging-in-Publication Data

Carmody, John.
   Exploring the Hebrew Bible / John Carmody, Denise Lardner Carmody,
  Robert L. Cohn.
     p.   cm.
  Bibliography: p. 427
  Includes index.
  ISBN 0-13-297003-1
  1. Bible. O.T.—Textbooks. I. Carmody, Denise Lardner.
  II. Cohn, Robert L. III. Title.
BS1194.C37 1988
221.6′1—dc19   87-29232
                                             CIP

For
Gideon and Maury Cohn
Jessica and Sean Corlett

Editorial/production supervision and
   interior design: Patricia V. Amoroso
Cover design: Lundgren Graphics, Ltd.
Manufacturing buyers: Margaret Rizzi and Peter Havens

 © 1988 by Prentice-Hall, Inc.
A Division of Simon & Schuster
Englewood Cliffs, New Jersey 07632

Printed in the United States of America

10 9 8 7 6 5 4 3 2 1

ISBN 0-13-297003-1 01

Prentice-Hall International (UK) Limited, *London*
Prentice-Hall of Australia Pty. Limited, *Sydney*
Prentice-Hall Canada Inc., *Toronto*
Prentice-Hall Hispanoamericana, S.A., *Mexico*
Prentice-Hall of India Private Limited, *New Delhi*
Prentice-Hall of Japan, Inc., *Tokyo*
Simon & Schuster Asia Pte. Ltd., *Singapore*
Editora Prentice-Hall do Brasil, Ltda., *Rio de Janeiro*

Contents

Charts *xv*

CHART 1: MAJOR PERIODS OF BIBLICAL HISTORY *xv*

CHART 2: CANONS OF THE HEBREW BIBLE/OLD
TESTAMENT *xvi*

CHART 3: CHRONOLOGY OF BIBLICAL WRITINGS *xvii*

Preface *xix*

1 **Introduction** *1*

FRIDAY NIGHT AND SUNDAY MORNING *1*

HABITS OF THE HEART *3*

BETWEEN LITERALISM AND CYNICISM *4*

THE GOALS AND FORMAT OF THIS BOOK *7*

GLOSSARY *7*

STUDY QUESTIONS *8*

NOTES *8*

2   A Brief History of Israel and the Hebrew Bible   9

FROM BEFORE ABRAHAM TO THE END OF THE UNITED
MONARCHY (3000 B. C. E.–922 B. C. E.)   *9*

FROM THE DIVIDED MONARCHY TO THE CLOSE OF THE
CANON (922 B. C. E.–90 C. E.)   *12*

TORAH   *15*

THE PROPHETS   *17*

THE WRITINGS   *19*

GLOSSARY   *21*

STUDY QUESTIONS   *22*

NOTES   *22*

PART ONE: TORAH

3   Genesis   *24*

TEXTUAL ANALYSIS   *24*

    1:1–11:26 Primeval History   *25*
    11:27–50:26 Period of the Ancestors   *31*

HISTORICAL BACKGROUND   *43*

LITERARY INTENT   *45*

LASTING SIGNIFICANCE   *46*

GLOSSARY   *49*

STUDY QUESTIONS   *50*

NOTES   *50*

4   Exodus   *52*

TEXTUAL ANALYSIS   *52*

    1:1–15:21 The Exodus from Egypt   *52*
    15:22–18:27 Israel in the Desert   *56*
    19:1–24:11 Making the Covenant   *57*
    24:12–31:18 Instructions for the Tabernacle   *60*

32:1–34:35 Apostasy and Renewal   *61*
35:1–40:38 Building the Tabernacle   *62*

HISTORICAL BACKGROUND   *63*

LITERARY INTENT   *66*

LASTING SIGNIFICANCE   *68*

GLOSSARY   *70*

STUDY QUESTIONS   *71*

NOTES   *71*

5   **Leviticus**   *73*

TEXTUAL ANALYSIS   *73*
1:1–7:38 The Sacrificial System   *73*
8:1–10:20 Inaugural Services at the Sanctuary   *74*
11:1–15:33 Laws of Uncleanness   *75*
16:1–34 Purification of the Sanctuary and the Nation   *76*
17:1–26:46 The Holiness Code   *77*
27:1–34 Commutation of Votive Gifts   *80*

HISTORICAL BACKGROUND   *81*

LITERARY INTENT   *81*

LASTING SIGNIFICANCE   *82*

GLOSSARY   *83*

STUDY QUESTIONS   *84*

NOTES   *84*

6   **Numbers**   *85*

TEXTUAL ANALYSIS   *85*
1:1–10:10 In the Desert at Sinai   *85*
10:11–22:1 The Journey from Sinai to Moab   *88*
22:2–36:13 Events at Moab   *91*

HISTORICAL BACKGROUND   *93*

LITERARY INTENT   *94*

LASTING SIGNIFICANCE   *94*

GLOSSARY   *96*

STUDY QUESTIONS 96

NOTES 96

7 **Deuteronomy** *98*

TEXTUAL ANALYSIS *98*

    1:1–4:43 First Discourse or Prologue *99*
    4:44–11:25 Second Discourse *99*
    11:26–28:69 Third Discourse *102*
    29:1–32:52 Fourth Discourse or Final Appeal *106*
    33:1–34:12 Fifth Discourse or Blessing and Leaving *109*

HISTORICAL BACKGROUND *109*

LITERARY INTENT *110*

LASTING SIGNIFICANCE *112*

GLOSSARY *115*

STUDY QUESTIONS *116*

NOTES *116*

PART TWO: PROPHETS

8 **Joshua** *118*

TEXTUAL ANALYSIS *118*

    1:1–5:12 Mobilization and Invasion *120*
    5:13–11:23 Warfare *121*
    12:1–19:51 Allotting the Inheritance *123*
    20:1–22:34 Keeping the Peace *125*
    23:1–24:33 The Testament of Joshua *126*

HISTORICAL BACKGROUND *126*

LITERARY INTENT *127*

LASTING SIGNIFICANCE *128*

GLOSSARY *128*

STUDY QUESTIONS *128*

NOTES *129*

9 **Judges** *130*

TEXTUAL ANALYSIS *130*

    1:1–3:6 Prologue *130*
    3:7–16:31 Israel's Liberation by Judges *131*
    17:1–21:25 Supplementary Stories *133*

HISTORICAL BACKGROUND *134*

LITERARY INTENT *134*

LASTING SIGNIFICANCE *135*

GLOSSARY *136*

STUDY QUESTIONS *136*

NOTES *137*

10 **1 and 2 Samuel** *138*

TEXTUAL ANALYSIS *138*

    1 Samuel 1:1–7:17 The Story of Samuel *138*
    8:1–15:35 Saul and the Advent of Kingship *140*
    16:1–2 Samuel 5:10 The Rise of David *143*
    2 Samuel 5:11–20:26 The Reign of David *146*
    21:1–24:25 Miscellaneous Materials *151*

HISTORICAL BACKGROUND *152*

LITERARY INTENT *153*

LASTING SIGNIFICANCE *155*

GLOSSARY *157*

STUDY QUESTIONS *157*

NOTES *158*

11 **1 and 2 Kings** *160*

TEXTUAL ANALYSIS *160*

    1 Kings 1:1–11:43 The Reign of Solomon *160*
    1 Kings 12:1–2 Kings 17:41 The Divided Monarchy *163*
    2 Kings 18:1–25:30 The Kingdom of Judah *169*

HISTORICAL BACKGROUND *171*

LITERARY INTENT *172*

LASTING SIGNIFICANCE *173*

GLOSSARY *174*

STUDY QUESTIONS *174*

NOTES *174*

12 Isaiah *176*

TEXTUAL ANALYSIS *176*

    1:1–39:8 First Isaiah *176*
    40:1–55:13 Second Isaiah *181*
    56:1–66:24 Third Isaiah *184*

HISTORICAL BACKGROUND *186*

LITERARY INTENT *187*

LASTING SIGNIFICANCE *188*

GLOSSARY *189*

STUDY QUESTIONS *189*

NOTES *190*

13 Jeremiah *191*

TEXTUAL ANALYSIS *191*

    1:1–24:10 Visions, Judgments, and Personal Laments *191*
    25:1–45:5 Speeches and Stories *196*
    46:1–51:64 Prophecies Against the Nations *200*
    52:1–34 Historical Appendix *202*

HISTORICAL BACKGROUND *203*

LITERARY INTENT *204*

LASTING SIGNIFICANCE *206*

GLOSSARY *209*

STUDY QUESTIONS   *209*

NOTES   *209*

14   Ezekiel   *211*

TEXTUAL ANALYSIS   *211*

    1:1–24:27 Oracles of Judgment on Judah and Jerusalem   *211*
    25:1–48:35 Oracles on the Restoration of Judah   *216*

HISTORICAL BACKGROUND   *221*

LITERARY INTENT   *221*

LASTING SIGNIFICANCE   *222*

GLOSSARY   *225*

STUDY QUESTIONS   *225*

NOTES   *226*

15   The Twelve   *227*

HOSEA   *227*

JOEL   *230*

AMOS   *232*

OBADIAH   *236*

JONAH   *238*

MICAH   *241*

NAHUM   *244*

HABAKKUK   *246*

ZEPHANIAH   *248*

HAGGAI   *250*

ZECHARIAH   *252*

MALACHAI   *257*

GLOSSARY   *260*

STUDY QUESTIONS   *261*

NOTES   *261*

PART THREE: WRITINGS

16   Psalms   *263*

TEXTUAL ANALYSIS   *263*
    I Psalms 1–41   *264*
    II Psalms 42–72   *270*
    III Psalms 73–89   *274*
    IV Psalms 90–106   *276*
    V Psalms 107–150   *278*

HISTORICAL BACKGROUND   *285*

LITERARY INTENT   *286*

LASTING SIGNIFICANCE   *287*

GLOSSARY   *289*

STUDY QUESTIONS   *290*

NOTES   *290*

17   Job   *292*

TEXTUAL ANALYSIS   *292*
    1–2 Prologue   *292*
    3 Opening Monologue   *293*
    4–27 Dialogues with Friends   *294*
    28–37 Monologues   *300*
    38:1–42:6 Dialogues with God   *303*
    42:7–17 Epilogue   *306*

HISTORICAL BACKGROUND   *306*

LITERARY INTENT   *307*

LASTING SIGNIFICANCE   *308*

GLOSSARY   *308*

STUDY QUESTIONS   *309*

NOTES   *309*

18   Proverbs   *311*

TEXTUAL ANALYSIS   *311*
    1:1–9:18 Teacher's Introduction   *311*
    10:1–22:16 First Collection of Solomonic Sayings   *314*

22:17–24:34 Thirty Precepts of the Sages   *317*
25:1–29:27 Second Collection of Solomonic Sayings   *319*
30:1–31:31 Four Appendices   *320*

HISTORICAL BACKGROUND   *321*

LITERARY INTENT   *322*

LASTING SIGNIFICANCE   *322*

GLOSSARY   *323*

STUDY QUESTIONS   *323*

NOTES   *324*

19   Ruth   *325*

TEXTUAL ANALYSIS   *325*
1:1–5 Sojourners   *325*
1:6–22 Returning Home   *326*
2:1–23 Alien Grain?   *326*
3:1–18 Encounter at the Threshing Floor   *327*
4:1–12 Resolution at the City Gate   *328*
4:13–17 The Birth of a Son   *328*
4:18–22 Appendix: Genealogy   *329*

HISTORICAL BACKGROUND   *329*

LITERARY INTENT   *329*

LASTING SIGNIFICANCE   *330*

GLOSSARY   *331*

STUDY QUESTIONS   *331*

NOTES   *331*

20   Song of Songs   *332*

TEXTUAL ANALYSIS   *332*
1:2–2:6 Prelude and Reverie   *333*
2:7–3:5 First Dream   *333*
3:6–5:1 First Tryst   *334*
5:2–6:3 Second Dream   *335*
6:4–7:9 Second Tryst   *336*
7:10–8:5 Commitment   *336*
8:6–14 Reverie and Postlude   *337*
HISTORICAL BACKGROUND   *338*

LITERARY INTENT   *338*

LASTING SIGNIFICANCE   *339*

GLOSSARY   *340*

STUDY QUESTIONS   *340*

NOTES   *340*

21   Ecclesiastes   *342*

TEXTUAL ANALYSIS   *342*
  1:1- 2 Introduction   *342*
  1:3–6:12 The Vanity of Life   *343*
  7:1–9:16 Realistic Advice   *348*
  9:17–12:8 Concluding Proverbs   *349*
  12:9–14 Postscripts   *350*

HISTORICAL BACKGROUND   *350*

LITERARY INTENT   *351*

LASTING SIGNIFICANCE   *352*

GLOSSARY   *353*

STUDY QUESTIONS   *353*

NOTES   *353*

22   Lamentations   *355*

TEXTUAL ANALYSIS   *355*
  1:1–22 "Is There Any Pain Like My Pain?"   *355*
  2:1–22 "The Lord Became Like an Enemy"   *356*
  3:1–66 Everyman   *357*
  4:1–22 The Account of a Survivor   *358*
  5:1–22 A Prayer   *358*

HISTORICAL BACKGROUND   *359*

LITERARY INTENT   *359*

LASTING SIGNIFICANCE   *360*

GLOSSARY   *361*

STUDY QUESTIONS   *361*

NOTES   *361*

23 Esther *362*

TEXTUAL ANALYSIS *362*

    1:1–22 Introduction to the Persian Court *362*
    2:1–23 Esther Becomes Queen *364*
    3:1–4:17 Haman's Wicked Plot *364*
    5:1–8:2 Esther Thwarts Haman *365*
    8:3–10:3 Happy Ending *366*

HISTORICAL BACKGROUND *367*

LITERARY INTENT *367*

LASTING SIGNIFICANCE *368*

GLOSSARY *368*

STUDY QUESTIONS *369*

NOTES *369*

24 Daniel *370*

TEXTUAL ANALYSIS *370*

    1:1–6:28 Stories of Daniel *370*
    7:1–12:13 Visions of Daniel *374*

HISTORICAL BACKGROUND *377*

LITERARY INTENT *378*

LASTING SIGNIFICANCE *379*

GLOSSARY *379*

STUDY QUESTIONS *380*

NOTES *380*

25 Ezra and Nehemiah *381*

TEXTUAL ANALYSIS *381*

    Ezra 1:1–6:22 The Restoration of the Community *382*
    Ezra 7:1–10:44 The Mission of Ezra *383*
    Nehemiah 1:1–7:73 The Work of Nehemiah *384*
    Nehemiah 8:1–10:39 Responses to the Law *385*
    Nehemiah 11:1–13:31 Organizing the Community *386*

HISTORICAL BACKGROUND *387*

LITERARY INTENT *389*

LASTING SIGNIFICANCE   *390*

GLOSSARY   *391*

STUDY QUESTIONS   *391*

NOTES   *392*

26   **1 and 2 Chronicles**   *393*

TEXTUAL ANALYSIS   *393*

    1 Chronicles 1:1–9:44 From Adam to Saul   *393*
    1 Chronicles 10:1–29:30 The Kingship of David   *395*
    2 Chronicles 1:1–9:31 The Kingship of Solomon   *398*
    2 Chronicles 10:1–36:23 The Davidic Line to the Exile   *400*

HISTORICAL BACKGROUND AND LITERARY INTENT   *403*

LASTING SIGNIFICANCE   *404*

GLOSSARY   *405*

STUDY QUESTIONS   *405*

NOTES   *405*

27   **The World View of the Hebrew Bible**   *407*

THE COVENANTED PEOPLE   *408*

THE BIBLICAL GOD   *410*

THE DYNAMICS OF HISTORICAL REVELATION   *412*

GLOSSARY   *416*

STUDY QUESTIONS   *416*

NOTES   *416*

Glossary   *419*

Bibliography   *427*

TORAH   *427*

PROPHETS   *428*

WRITINGS   *430*

Index   *433*

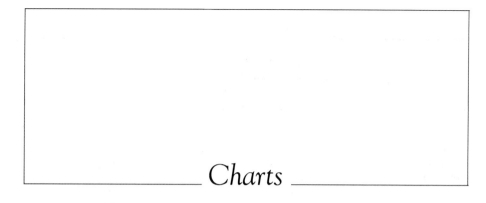

Charts

CHART 1

Major Periods of Biblical History

Period of the Ancestors	ca. 1800–1400 B. C. E.
Moses, Exodus, Covenant	ca. 1300–1200
Conquest of Canaan	ca. 1200–1100
Period of the Judges	ca. 1100–1020
United Monarchy	ca. 1020–922
Divided Monarchy	ca. 922–721
Judah Alone	ca. 721–587
Babylonian Captivity	ca. 597–539
Persian Rule	ca. 539–333
Hellenistic Period	ca. 333–63
Roman Rule	63–end of biblical period

CHART 2

Canons of Hebrew Bible/Old Testament

Jewish	*Catholic/Orthodox*	*Protestant*
Torah		
Genesis	Genesis	Genesis
Exodus	Exodus	Exodus
Leviticus	Leviticus	Leviticus
Numbers	Numbers	Numbers
Deuteronomy	Deuteronomy	Deuteronomy
Prophets		
Joshua	Joshua	Joshua
Judges	Judges	Judges
1 and 2 Samuel	Ruth	Ruth
1 and 2 Kings	1 and 2 Samuel	1 and 2 Samuel
Isaiah	1 and 2 Kings	1 and 2 Kings
Jeremiah	1 and 2 Chronicles	1 and 2 Chronicles
Ezekiel	Ezra/Nehemiah	Ezra/Nehemiah
The Twelve	Tobit*	Esther
	Judith*	
	Esther†	
Writings		
Psalms		
Job	Job	Job
Proverbs	Psalms	Psalms
Ruth	Ecclesiastes	Proverbs
Song of Songs	Song of Songs	Ecclesiastes
Ecclesiastes	Wisdom of Solomon*	Song of Songs
Lamentations	Ben Sirach*	
Esther		Isaiah
Daniel	Isaiah	Jeremiah
Ezra-Nehemiah	Jeremiah	Lamentations
1 and 2 Chronicles	Lamentations	Ezekiel
	Baruch*	Daniel
	Ezekiel	The Twelve
	Daniel†	
	The Twelve	
	1 and 2 Maccabees*	

*Books Protestants consider apocryphal.
†Catholic/Orthodox version has additions not found in Protestant.

CHART 3
Chronology of Biblical Writings

ca. 1100 B. C. E.	Judges 5
ca. 1200–950	Oldest psalms and poems
ca. 950–850	Oldest prose of Torah (J)
ca. 850–750	E
ca. 800–700	Oldest prose of Joshua-Kings
ca. 750	Amos
ca. 730	Hosea
ca. 720	Isaiah
ca. 705	Micah
ca. 630–625	Zephaniah
ca. 625–600	Habakkuk
	Deuteronomic writings
ca. 612	Nahum
ca. 600	Jeremiah
ca. 580	Ezekiel
	Passages of Jeremiah
ca. 550–530	Early P
ca. 550–450	Creation of more psalms
ca. 538–520	Second Isaiah
ca. 520	Haggai
ca. 520–518	Zechariah
ca. 510	Deuteronomistic editing
ca. 500	Collection of ritual psalms
ca. 500–450	Third Isaiah
ca. 490–450	Malachai, Joel, Obadiah
ca. 450–400	Completion of P
ca. 450–375	Compilation of Psalms
ca. 450–350	Job
ca. 425	Jonah, Ruth
ca. 400	Completion of Deuteronomy
	Compilation of Proverbs
ca. 400–300	Canonization of Torah
	Esther
ca. 375–350	Ecclesiastes
ca. 375–200	Ezra/Nehemiah, Chronicles
ca. 250	Greek translation of Torah
ca. 200–100	Canonization of Prophets
	Canonization of Psalms
ca. 165	Daniel
ca. 90–100 C. E.	Compilation of Tanak

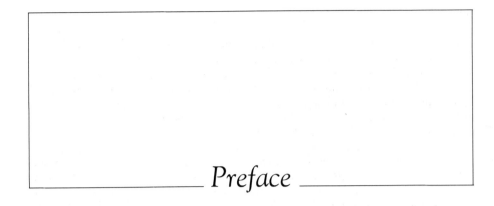

Preface

This book is a text for introductory courses in the Hebrew Bible/Old Testament. It should be suitable for most undergraduates in both four- and two-year colleges. A few suggestions about how best to use the text may prove helpful.

Even though we have limited our exposition to the books of the Hebrew canon, the amount of material we cover remains considerable. We therefore suggest that teachers make judicious selections within each of the three main divisions of the Hebrew canon and that they not try to cover all books. We have covered all twenty-four books. Our aim in so doing has been to free teachers to expose whatever books they themselves wish, and to furnish students with a comprehensive treatment. That means that every chapter of every book of the Hebrew Bible—even every psalm—receives some attention. For larger questions and orientation, we offer an introductory chapter that deals with the place of the Bible in American life and suggests ways for students to approach the text. We also offer a historical overview (the history of Israel and the history of the Bible) and a concluding assessment of the main religious themes we find in the Bible.

The main thrust of our treatment is literary. For each book we provide a textual analysis, discussions of the historical background and literary intent, and a section entitled "Lasting Significance." The sections of textual analysis in effect supply students with chapter by chapter commentaries. They are not meant to substitute for reading the biblical text itself. Indeed, they presuppose that students are reading the text. But they do function as glossings, underscorings, reminders of prior appearances of given themes, indications of historical forces at work, and speculations about the images and arguments being used. The sections on historical background and literary intent are brief, generalized treatments designed to supply the context of the books in question. The sections that deal with lasting significance are probably this textbook's most distinctive feature. In them we take up issues from philosophy and comparative religion, and we place the humanistic wisdom of the Bible in broader context than scriptural exegetes or even biblical theologians usually do. We have found undergraduates to be more intrigued by the grand issues they can treat in this way than by historical or textual detail, and some of their preference has seemed to us praiseworthy.

The scholarly and theological positions that we take are middle-of-the-road; we try to honor both the findings of recent critical scholarship and the traditional views that Jews and Christians have held. Occasionally we indicate what a Christian reading in terms of prophecy and fulfillment has made of a given passage, but our usual approach is to stress what the text likely meant in its original context and on its own terms. Concerning hermeneutics, we have also tried to be centrist, by both admitting that texts can communicate meanings their authors may not have intended and insisting that the original circumstances in which a text arose, along with the probable intentions of its authors and editors, are crucial for a full estimate of its meaning.

Although we have taken the Hebrew canon as our set of parameters, we have used the Revised Standard Version, judging it the best overall translation by such criteria as literalness, availability, and ecumenical acceptability. We offer our work as a modest witness to the collaborative results possible when Jews and Christians are friends—people of the Book who find its words uniting them rather than sparking division.

For those interested in the mechanics of our collaboration, we note that John Carmody has been the principal writer, Denise Lardner Carmody has been a pedagogical and feminist control, and Robert L. Cohn has been the principal scholarly and pedagogical control. We owe a special debt of gratitude to our colleague John G. Gammie, Emma A. Harwell Professor of Biblical Literature at the University of Tulsa, who read the entire manuscript and offered both scholarly advice and much-appreciated encouragement throughout. We would also like to thank our other readers, who furnished much helpful advice: Professor Ronald Modras, Department of Theological Studies, Saint Louis University; Professor Edwin M. Good, Department of Religious Studies, Stanford University; and Professor Sharon Pace, Department of Theology, Marquette University.

CHAPTER 1

Introduction

FRIDAY NIGHT AND SUNDAY MORNING

In the United States, the West, and increasingly throughout the non-Western world, people enjoy weekends set apart from their everyday work. Many such people do little on their weekends that they would call religious, but perhaps equally as many pray, or go to synagogue, or go to church. Only a few, it appears, keep a strict observance of a Sabbath, according to which they would do no secular work. But a great many contemporary people, both religious and unreligious, structure their senses of time by reference to a leisure, a free-zone, that originally came into their culture from the Bible. Even unawares, then, today's Americans continue to be shaped by a biblical heritage. In our common experience of time, as well as in many other areas, we show traces of being "people of the book," as Muslims have long described Christians and Jews.

For pious Jews, Friday evening continues to inaugurate a religious Sabbath. As the sun sets, they feel a call to set aside their secular concerns and assemble to celebrate the creation of the world. When the mother of the family lights the candles, shades her eyes, and blesses God, she calls to mind the centuries of forebears who have acted similarly. Children raised in the tradition of hallowing the Sabbath experience something of the goodness of creation long before they can understand such a notion. The bread and wine shared on the Sabbath stand for a nurture and joy that sustained their ancestors through countless decades, some of them filled with prosperity and many others twisted by suffering.

Something analogous happens in Christian churches on Sunday morning. The people who gather to hear what they consider God's Word and to celebrate

1

the resurrection of Christ punctuate their time and think about their identities differently from those who do not express such faith. Once again biblical religion is setting a horizon against which people are measuring their purpose. As do Jews who assemble Friday evening or gather in the synagogue on Saturday, Christians who dedicate part of Sunday to their God associate themselves with generations of forebears. For both their comfort and their chastening, they are calling to mind an historical template and remembering that millions of their predecessors heard this biblical Word or received this eucharistic bread.

Our first "argument" for studying the Hebrew Bible is the light it sheds on such behavior. If the contemporary United States, despite all of its secularism, sends at least 40 percent of its population to synagogue or church each weekend, one who would understand current American culture had best know something about the Bible. Moreover, many Americans who do not attend synagogue or church regularly think about the world, or about themselves, or about their moral responsibilities in categories much shaped by biblical religion. We reflect more on this matter in the next section, but from the outset it should be clear that the texts we study in this book are not merely historical curios. For better than half of our fellow citizens, they constitute a prime resource for the central human task of making sense out of one's lifetime.

Nonetheless, a second argument leaps to hand when we agree that the Bible is indeed a book laden with history. For thousands of years traditions now collected in the Bible have guided Jews and Christians on their way. Due to the historical fact that Western culture was formed on the basis of biblical religion (although it had other bases, as well), one who would understand European or American art, literature, politics, or even science needs to know at least the main themes of the Bible. Indeed, because modern Western culture was transported to Africa and Asia, students of modern world history are also ill-equipped if they are ignorant of biblical religion. What now happens in numerous homes on Friday evening, in numerous synagogues on Saturday, and in numerous churches on Sunday happened to many of the people who helped shape the current cultures of Africa and Asia. For weal or woe, biblical religion became a world-wide influence, just as Qur'anic religion now has become. And just as one who would understand Muslim culture has to take the Qur'an very seriously, so one who would understand the Western contribution to modern world history has to take the Bible very seriously.

Our third argument for studying biblical religion is more intrinsic. Without deprecating the significance of the cultural or historical arguments, we are more interested in the art, insight, wisdom, and aspiration that the biblical texts themselves continue to provide to any serious reader. No doubt this intrinsic power was the major reason that Jews and Christians kept going back to the Bible, century after century, but past precedent cannot be the whole motivation for studying the Bible today. Unless something happens between present-day readers and the biblical text, the Bible will not be the "classic"[1] that most of its supporters claim it to be. It will not, that is, challenge readers to reassess their assumptions about where their lives are headed, what constitutes genuine human prosperity, how they ought to regard the wonders of physical creation, how they ought to regard the twistedness of social injustice, and so forth.

This last conviction most clearly takes our approach to the Bible beyond the confines of the synagogues and the churches. Although people who do not consider themselves Jews or Christians can profit from cultural or historical appreciations of the Bible and its influence, the crux of a contemporary study of the Bible probably will be whether or not this classical book (somewhat in contrast to "orthodox" assumptions about it or explanations of it) can still communicate to people of good will who are willing to give it a fair hearing. Is the Bible, in fact, a humanistic as well as a religious work? Does it, in fact, so present "religion" that in many ways we cannot be human without having grappled with "religious" questions? Our intrinsic argument assumes that it is and does.

Take, for example, the very first words of Genesis, the first book of the Bible. They deal with "the beginning." Can we be fully human without having pondered "the beginning"? Can we, in fact, be fully human without having pondered "the end"? If not, the Bible continues to be a relevant book. What it says about human life between the beginning and the end will also be significant, of course, but simply by having raised the issue of humanity's whence and whither the Bible inclines its readers to a salutary seriousness.

In the third section of this Introduction we question how to keep biblical literature in balanced perspective, neither approaching it credulously, as though we had to swallow it whole, nor approaching it suspiciously, as though it were bound to invite us to immaturity. Here let our first word be unambiguously welcoming. For cultural, historical, intrinsic, and literary reasons, we find the study of the Bible exhilarating, and therefore we invite you, our readers, to expect an exhilarating experience.

HABITS OF THE HEART

Human beings have always sought exhilarating experiences, of course, and sociological studies of present-day Americans attest that our generation has not changed. We are as concerned with making sense of our lives and gaining prosperity as previous generations have been, although we may be more impoverished than they in our resources for defining what "sense" and "prosperity" ought to mean. Indeed, several recent studies of our contemporary moral consciousness suggest that we are hampered by the pervasive influence of a "therapeutic" language, derived largely from humanistic psychology, that tends to restrict sense and prosperity to what makes the individual self feel good.[2] In comparison with the biblical traditions, which located sense and prosperity in one's relationship to God, and to the republican traditions, which considered civic virtue or citizenship as important as self-promotion, current American culture can seem stunted. Let us consider this possibility.

Using a phrase from Alexis de Tocqueville, a sociological inquiry into these matters recently published by a distinguished team of scholars led by Robert Bellah of the University of California, Berkeley, has spoken of current American "habits of the heart."[3] A synonym for this phrase might be "moral character" or "disposition to civic virtue." De Tocqueville, who wrote an extremely insightful study of American mores in the 1830s, used the phrase to point to the inward dispositions, predilections, assumptions, loves, and the like, by which one might characterize a citizenry. As he observed the then-young American nation, it had a remarkably bright future, because its citizenry thought of their country as an enterprise committed to their common care. Much of this conviction came from their Protestant Christian religious beliefs, especially from the Puritans' notion that God had placed the virgin American lands into their keeping as the site for establishing a people who would live up to the biblical ideals of convenanted holiness and social justice. The great danger that de Tocqueville saw imperiling the future of the United States lay in the individualism that attended many of the people's notions of freedom and citizenship. Were that individualism to lose its healthy, dialectical relationship to a willingness to sacrifice self-interest for the common good, the great American experiment in fashioning a common weal of, by, and for the general populace likely would run aground. The heart of the enterprise would sicken.

The very symbol of the heart as the center of the human personality is characteristically biblical. Other ancient cultures, to be sure, have spoken similarly, using the heart to symbolize the whole person, emotion and feeling as well as intelligence and will. But in our Western culture the Bible has most powerfully inculcated the notion that the most significant laws and judgments are encoded in our hearts. To be heartless toward the widow or the orphan was, in the judgment of the biblical prophets and sages, to show oneself no true worshiper of God. To set one's heart on pleasure, or power, or material gain was to make a foolish choice, one that said, in effect, that there is no God or sovereign mystery that far exceeds the value of any passing human possession.

Of course, the founders of the American experiment in nationhood and citizenship were also influenced by the European Enlightenment, in some cases more than by the biblical text. But on the whole the resource upon which pre-twentieth-century Americans most drew when they pondered the heart of their national enterprise was the Bible. We note, for example, how much of the debate about slavery that sundered the United States in the decades after de Tocqueville's study was transacted in biblical categories. Indeed, many blacks suffering from slavery survived spiritually by taking to heart the biblical stories about an exodus from an oppressive Egypt into a promised land of freedom, milk, and honey. The majestic language of Abraham Lincoln, who gave his life to preserve the union from the sundering sickness of slavery, rings with biblical images and cadences. When we study the habits of the American heart, therefore, we inevitably are led back to the Bible.

BETWEEN LITERALISM AND CYNICISM

Returning to study our American roots in the Bible, however, is only the first step. The second step is determining how we ought to regard the text to which we have betaken ourselves. Ideally, we would make this determination rather explicitly, drawing help from people who have gained expertise in biblical studies. Otherwise, we likely will misperceive the nature of the literature with which we are dealing and so pitch our study at the wrong slant. The Bible certainly is not a literary collection just like those we tend to study in courses on English or American literature. Not only is it far older than all English and American works, it stems from different interests and assumptions. Similarly, the Bible is not comfortably housed in the department called "history," although it certainly has historical interests. If by "history" we mean a narrative (of what happened in the past) that is based on a careful, critical sifting of sources, then the Bible is not historical writing. On the other hand, the Bible is interested in telling what happened in the past, and it does claim to interpret the past truthfully. Although many biblical authors invent speeches and explore motives beyond what they can document, they also aim to convince the reader that what they are reporting depends on trustworthy sources and is to be treated as a precious treasury of memories. Children are to learn these traditions, because in them the next generation will find the lessons about both God and human nature it will need, if it is to survive and prosper. The Bible then is historiographic — concerned with writing "history" in a broad sense — even though it does not pass the tests of modern critical history.

On the whole, we would misread biblical literature were we to take literally its reports about what happened to ancestors such as Abraham and Moses. The intention of the biblical authors, as present-day scholarship can best determine, seldom was simply to report the facts and actions of past events. More regularly, the intent was to preserve or create memories of exemplary or paradigmatic events, confessions of faith, historical personages, and the like, so that readers might form self-conceptions and habits of the heart befitting their relationship with God. In other words, the biblical writers have the general aim of expressing and stirring up people's faith. They assume that readers are interested in such things as the kingship of David, and they characteristically explore the significance of such a happening in terms of what it did for Israel as a people covenanted to God, or in terms of what David suggests about the ideal life of relationship with God.

Our first orientational suggestion, therefore, is that we all come to the biblical texts with a little flexibility. We should be prepared to consider them as literary products — the result of considerable human imagination, editing, and theological judgment — rather than as factual reports about what God or the people of Israel did. Where appropriate we indicate the current scholarly sense of the historical events or conditions that lay behind key biblical texts, but our first concern is with the character of the bare texts themselves. In other words, we are most interested in what directly confronts us on the pages of the individual Bibles that we are using.

On the other hand, we do not want to suggest that the Hebrew Bible is not a reliable record of what happened to Israel. Once we get beyond the literal mentality that reads the Bible as though one were reading *The New York Times*, there often comes a temptation to disregard any claims that the Bible might be an accurate reflection of what happened to the people of Israel 3000 to 2500 years ago. Indeed, the sophisticated historical, literary, and sociological methods that present-day biblical scholars employ can inculcate a certain cynicism about the integrity or unity of the Bible. Because many of these techniques are geared to distinguishing different textual units and stages of editing, they have an atomistic bent. It is useful, therefore, to remind ourselves that the Bible has, after all, been this collection we now have before us for hundreds of years. It was, in fact, edited into its present shape and then used as a canonical expression of Jewish and Christian faith.[4] And if it would be misleading simply to equate the Bible that Jews and Christians have used in their worship and moral education for the past millennia with the collected mentality of the individual biblical authors, it would be perhaps equally misleading to insist that "the Bible" refers only to the product of such a collected mentality, ignoring the fact that any classical text alters its life and reality generation by generation, as it interacts with new readers.

This last point may not be wholly clear, so let us elaborate on it a bit more fully. On the one hand, we do not want to approach the Bible ignoring its peculiar literary character. We do not want, that is, to ignore the aspects of faith and symbolism that separate the Bible from much modern literature. On the other hand, we also do not want to ignore the fact that the vast majority of people who have used the Bible through the centuries have interacted with it in relative innocence of the complicated character that present-day scholars find it to have. For example, most of the great rabbis who commented on biblical texts in the context of talmudic study did so unaware of their complicated editing and unaware, as well, of the many different literary genres that such editing joined together. This is not to say that such rabbis were not keenly attuned to nuances of the Hebrew text and did not frequently come up with ingenious intuitions of what the authors were saying. It is simply to remind ourselves that when we admit that the Bible has been a canonical text, used by generations of believers to set the terms of their relations with God and one another, we admit, as well, the premodern or precontemporary mentality that such believers brought to the biblical text.

For further example, the great Christian commentators on the Bible, such as Origen and Augustine, were quite like the great talmudic rabbis in sensing intuitively the riches of the biblical literary intentions but not having our present-day tools for appreciating the full complexity of either the text or the thought-worlds lying behind it. Certainly neither the rabbis nor the Christian fathers were literalistic in their approach, for they were both keenly aware of symbolism and poetry. But equally they were not cynical about the trustworthiness of the biblical texts, both because they believed God to be the final author of the Bible and because they found verified in their own lives the wisdom of the religious teachings of the Torah or the prophets.

On the whole, the cynicism that would dismiss the Hebrew Bible as not a trustworthy guide to Israelite experience, or as not a trustworthy guide to healthy religious experience, or as not a genuine whole that is more than the sum of its disparate parts is tied up with an interpretational mentality that would bracket deeper questions of human or religious significance. That is, most of the cynicism about the value of the biblical literature is spawned less by the texts themselves than by the limitations that certain present-day methods, when used exclusively or atomistically, rather questionably impose. The critic who would merely separate the different editings of a particular biblical book or block of material, for instance, without attending either to the different visions that the different editings or their combination suggest, let alone attending to the relevance of such visions to the critic's own present-day world, has approached the Bible with what we would consider a truncated appreciation. However necessary and useful it is to narrow our focus to quite precise, delimited textual or historical matters, unless we return from such a narrowed focus to the biblical whole (both the integrity of the Bible as a collection of testimonies from and for faith and the encompassing vision of God, humanity, nature, and the self that various biblical authors generate), we have not done full justice to the biblical literature.

We glimpse, then, the very demanding nature of biblical exposition or interpretation — the several different levels at which the fully adequate expositor has to work. Between a literalism that sticks with the simple surface of the text, and a cynicism that finds no trustworthiness or unity in the complex textual background, we must struggle to let both the individual books and the entire collection express their quite extraordinary range and richness.

THE GOALS AND FORMAT OF THIS BOOK

Our overriding goal in this book is to present an introductory exposition of the Hebrew Bible that will at least suggest its extraordinary range and richness. By "the Hebrew Bible" we mean what Jews often refer to as the Tanak. The word is an acronym derived from the first letters of the three main divisions of the Hebrew Bible: Torah, Nevi'im, Ketuvim (Law, Prophets, and Writings). The first division, Torah, consists of five books (and so is also called the Pentateuch): Genesis, Exodus, Leviticus, Numbers, and Deuteronomy. The second division, the Prophets, subdivides into two main groups. The "former prophets" are represented by the books of Joshua, Judges, 1 and 2 Samuel, and 1 and 2 Kings. The "latter prophets" are represented by the three long books of Isaiah, Jeremiah, and Ezekiel, as well as by the twelve short books of Hosea, Joel, Amos, Obadiah, Jonah, Micah, Nahum, Habakkuk, Zephaniah, Haggai, Zechariah, and Malachi. The third division of the Hebrew Bible, called the Writings, is comprised of eleven works: Psalms, Job, Proverbs, Ruth, Song of Songs, Ecclesiastes (Qoheleth), Lamentations, Esther, Daniel, Ezra-Nehemiah, and 1–2 Chronicles. All in all, therefore, the Hebrew Bible amounts to twenty-four books (several of them in two parts). The main language in which these books were written is Hebrew, although some passages were composed in Aramaic.

Differences between this collection of works and the collection presented in the Christian "Old Testament" derive from several sources, the main one being the dependence of the Old Testament on the Greek translation (Septuagint), which has a different order. Neither the Protestant nor the Roman Catholic canon applies the threefold division of Tanak as the Jewish canon has. In addition, the Roman Catholic canon accepts several other works that the Protestants usually call "apocrypha" ("hidden things") and place in a different, noncanonical collection. Among the apocrypha are the books of Tobit, Judith, Wisdom of Solomon, Ecclesiasticus (Sirach), Baruch, 1 and 2 Maccabees, and additions to the books of Esther and Daniel.

The material with which we deal is only that included in the Hebrew Bible, and we employ the convenient threefold division of the Tanak. Our usual format is to treat each biblical book under four headings: "Textual Analysis," "Historical Background," "Literary Intent," and "Lasting Significance."

GLOSSARY

Canonical Officially accredited or authoritative; entered on the list of approved and directive documents.

Classic A work that later generations use as a measure of their humanity.

Critical Passing judgment or sifting evidence so as to arrive at a reasoned stance about the matter in question.

Dialectical Concerning progress through a clash of opposed elements.

Enlightenment Eighteenth-century European movement that stressed the untrammeled use of reason.

Eucharistic   Pertaining to the Christian sacrament of thanksgiving that recalls the death and resurrection of Christ and offers believers communion with him through consecrated bread and wine.

Faith   Belief; wholehearted commitment or assent beyond factual surety or proof.

Israel   The people descended from Jacob; the Northern Kingdom.

Paradigmatic   Providing a template, a normative pattern.

Qur'an   Muslim scripture; Muhammad's "Recital."

Relativism   The view that there are no binding norms, that all insights and truths are confined to the perspectives that generated them.

Religious   That which pertains to communion with, service of, or concern for ultimate reality.

Secular   Worldly view of life that sometimes tends to depreciate religion.

Talmudic   Concerning the Talmud or main collection of postbiblical Jewish wisdom.

Tanak   The Law-Prophets-Writings that constitute the Hebrew Bible.

Torah   Jewish term for Teaching, Divine Guidance, Law.

STUDY QUESTIONS

1. Sketch two strong arguments for studying biblical literature.
2. What do we mean by "therapeutic" language, and why might we disparage it in comparison with biblical language?
3. Why is the biblical literature not "historical" in the modern critical sense?
4. What is "Tanak?"

NOTES

1. See David Tracy, *The Analogical Imagination.* New York: Crossroad, 1981, pp. 99–338.
2. See Alasdair MacIntyre, *After Virtue.* Notre Dame, Ind.: University of Notre Dame Press, 1981; Robert Bellah et al., *Habits of the Heart.* Berkeley: University of California Press, 1985.
3. See Alexis de Tocqueville, *Democracy in America*, trans. George Lawrence, ed. J. P. Mayer. New York: Doubleday, Anchor Books, 1969, p. 287. This is quoted by Bellah et al., *Habits of the Heart*, on p. viii.
4. See Brevard S. Childs, *Introduction to the Old Testament as Scripture.* Philadelphia: Fortress, 1979; Northrop Frye, *The Great Code.* New York: Harcourt, Brace, Jovanovich, 1982.

CHAPTER 2

A Brief History
of Israel and
the Hebrew Bible

The main interest of our text is the literature of the Bible itself. Most of our space is given to sharpening the reader's eye for what is most typical, important, or interesting in the book under discussion. We also deal briefly with the historical background, literary intent, and lasting significance of the given book, but such discussions follow on the textual analyses and support them. It may be well, therefore, to provide early on an overview of the history of both the people of Israel and the literary components that were sewn into the canonical text. We deal with the history of Israel in two parts: from before Abraham to the end of the united monarchy, and from the divided monarchy to the settling of the present corpus of the Hebrew Bible. Our brief history of the literary components sewn into the canonical text has three parts: Torah, Prophets, and Writings.[1]

FROM BEFORE ABRAHAM TO THE END
OF THE UNITED MONARCHY (3000 B.C.E.–922 B.C.E.)

This period covers what archeologists of the ancient Near East consider the Bronze Ages (Early, Middle, and Late), moving into the Iron Age (after about 1200 B.C.E.). Before Abraham, whom many present-day scholars place around 1800 (his historicity and date are both debated), and serving as the backdrop for early Israelite culture, was the general culture that developed in Mesopotamia and Syro-Palestine. This included such subcultures as the Sumerian, Akkadian, Babylonian, and Assyrian cultures of Mesopotamia and the subcultures of Syro-Palestine suggested by recent archeological discoveries at Mari (on the bank of the Euphrates River, just north of the present frontier between Syria and Iraq), Nuzi (in what is now northeastern Iraq), and Ebla (about forty miles southwest of Aleppo in present-day Syria). Sumerian culture before the year 3000 had only Egypt and China as rivals in splendor. The Akkadians, who conquered Sumeria around 2370, put together one of the first ancient empires. Around 2300 Ebla was an important center for trade in timber, copper, and jewels. The tablets of writings discovered there show a language that presently is one of the best candidates for having sired biblical Hebrew.[2] The overall environment out of which the beginnings of Israel grew is somewhat suggested by the collections of ancient Near Eastern texts that scholars now have available for study.[3] Perhaps their most striking implication, for students of biblical religion, is that different gods presided over most of the important activities of both nature and culture.

From 2000 B.C.E. Egypt was the controlling power in Syro-Palestine. The traditions about Abraham and the other early ancestors of the Israelite people, now collected in Genesis 12–50, suggest a period starting around 2000 to 1500. The people are represented as living a seminomadic life, migrating or following their flocks but also sometimes settling in villages. Michael Grant has suggested that in the centuries prior to Abraham Syria and Palestine had been devastated by climatic changes and waves of invaders:

> During the last centuries of the third millennium the end of the Early Canaanite (Early Bronze) Age came upon the Syrian and Palestinian sites with devastating thoroughness. During the fourth and last phase of that Age (ca. 2400–2000) almost every site in Palestine was either completely abandoned or settled on a greatly reduced scale. For, in the first place, a marked climatic change had produced far drier conditions, resulting in a large-scale supersession of productive agriculture and commercial activities by dry-farming and herding at bare subsistence level. Then, in c. 2200–2000, there arrived waves of invaders, pastoral semi-nomads who, while destroying such settled, urban ways of life as still survived at that time, employed shaft graves and tumulus burials in a manner reminiscent of the Kurgan (tumulus or barrow) culture on the south Russian steppes.[4]

This depiction, like most attempted recreations of the period of Abraham, probably errs on the side of literalness, because many scholars now think that neither what we possess in extrabiblical sources nor what we possess in biblical sources gives us hard information about the ancestors of the people who became Israel. Perhaps, therefore, we better speak of the ancestors of the clans that were to become Israel settling in Canaan and Egypt in the last half of the second millennium B.C.E. At most, the stories of the ancestors may contain some dim recollections of these ancestors. Some clans, escaping from Egypt, saw their escape as miraculous, and the identity forged in the experience of escape apparently became normative for other clans who had not themselves experienced the Exodus but found in it a stimulus to liberate themselves from the Canaanite feudal lords to whom they were bound.

Norman K. Gottwald, following on the work of George Mendendall, has developed this thesis with careful attention to considerable sociological data.[5] We cannot say that the thesis has prevailed in scholarly circles, but it does command respect. At any rate, regardless of how we see the history of the generations from "Abraham," through "Moses," to the establishment of the Israelites in Canaan, two facts seem quite certain. First, only a small part of what later became "Israel" in fact experienced an exodus from Egypt. Second, there was no "Israel" until several tribes confederated in Canaan. We may suspect that this confederation relates to the stories that lie at the base of the Torah as "forming a people" relates to "creating an ideology and a history of national origins."

The Exodus from Egypt and march to Canaan are best located around 1300 to 1250 B.C.E. Pharaoh Raamses II, who ruled from 1290 to 1235, was the one who most likely opposed Moses and the Hebrews in their desire to emigrate. As mentioned, the Exodus and wandering in the desert became the crucible in which Israelite identity was later thought to have been forged. Above all, the imagery of a covenant made with God at Mount Sinai served later generations as their prime paradigm of how the tribes of Israel had been made a people (had been made God's people). This event is reflected and used in many parts of the Hebrew Bible, but the books of Exodus, Numbers, and Joshua bear most directly upon it.

The Conquest of Canaan (the promised land) is depicted in the Bible as having occurred quickly and easily, but most historians now think that it extended over more than two centuries (about 1250 to 1020 B.C.E.). If we follow the "social revolution" model of Gottwald, the "Conquest" of Canaan came about through the revolt of native Canaanites against their overlords. In this revolt they joined forces with a nuclear group that invaded or infiltrated from the desert. This nuclear group took its identity from the Exodus—the experience of escape or deliverance from Egypt. The suggested scenario therefore is that during the fourteenth and thirteenth centuries, when warfare arose among the Canaanite city-states (and, for reasons presently unknown, population declined), peasants, pastoral nomads, and other disaffected groups, including people (the *apiru*) who took their identity from an exodus from bondage in Egypt, came together in at least loose alliances to oppose the city-states. Eventually the ideology of the exodus group, which included religious allegiance to their God YHWH (as some early form of the theology of the Mosaic covenant explained it), became the moving spirit of an effective revolution, through which a rudimentary "Israel" (confederation of tribes) replaced the city-state powers that previously had dominated Canaan (and exacted tribute from the peoples who finally revolted.)[6]

The peak of Israelite history, in terms of secular success, was the monarchic period that ran from Saul to Solomon. Samuel, the last of the judges, and Saul, the first of the kings, probably dominated the period of about 1020 to 1000. David is usually credited with having ruled from about 1000 to 961, and his son Solomon with having ruled from about 961 to 922. Together, David and Solomon mediated the transition of Israel from a loose collection of tribes or clans to a genuine kingdom with a shining capital city and a single ruler. Later history would consider David the ideal king, despite the failings depicted in 2 Samuel and 1 Kings 1–2. David was the warrior who made Israel secure in Jerusalem, and his line became the axis along which later historians, such as the author of 1 and 2 Chronicles, organized the story of the fortunes of the chosen people. Solomon, who became in later judgment and symbolism the premier possessor of wisdom, was the one who carried out the building of the Temple in Jerusalem. Insofar as the Temple was the capital institution of the capital city, it was considered the nerve-center of Israelite life, and Solomon was honored for having erected it.

We consider in the next section the fracture of the united monarchy, which in the time of David and Solomon held together both the northern and the southern tribes. If we reflect here on the course traveled by Israel from its beginnings with Abraham to its acme in David-Solomon, it is apparent that in less than a millennium great changes occurred. In the time of the first ancestors, life was pastoral, and what the God who had spoken to Abraham, promising him a progeny as numerous as the stars in the heavens and the grains of sand along the sea, had in store was quite obscure. The authors who worked up the legends and memories bearing on the time of the patriarchs and matriarchs make these ancestors unique in their geographic area in following the counsel of the God YHWH. This God, who for the ancestors is the only genuine deity, guides Abraham, Isaac, Jacob, and Joseph, making their stories lessons in divine providence. We have no way of knowing to what extent the convictions of the authors of Genesis have altered what the lives of the earliest Israelites depicted there actually were like.

The situation is somewhat similar with Moses, the judges, and David, but it seems safe to assume that the biblical materials dealing with them adequately convey the essentials of Israel's passover from bondage — lack of autonomy — in Egypt to self-rule in Jerusalem. The political history suggests a banding together of tribes, for the sake of exiting Egypt and gaining a land of their own, with a key moment in the desert wanderings (Sinai) when they solemnized their pact with YHWH. With varying degrees of organization and success, they gained control of land in Syro-Palestine near the Jordan River, but their life under the judges continued to be tribal and pastoral, if often quite military. Seeing how their neighbors were more unified and effective for having a warrior-king, the tribes softened the theological tradition that YHWH was their sole warrior-king and chose first Saul, and then David, to lead their forces. David managed to develop a new capital at Jerusalem, and Solomon solemnized it with the Temple. Together, these two rulers of the unified Israel made the children of Abraham a prosperous gem among the nations.

FROM THE DIVIDED MONARCHY TO THE CLOSE OF THE CANON (922 B.C.E.–90 C.E.)

As the Bible tells it, scarcely had Solomon stopped breathing when the northern and southern halves of the monarchy pulled apart. Rehoboam led the southern portion, and Jeroboam I led the northern portion. Their dispute and alienation comprised the first chapter in a sundering that was never to be repaired. In later interpretation, the main cause for both the split and the misfortunes that subsequently afflicted North and South (Israel and Judah) alike was the sins, especially the idolatries, of the kings, who epitomized their people. While the Davidic dynastic line continued in the South, the dynasties of Omri and then Jehu diverted from Jeroboam, giving the North a messier lineage. The North fell captive to Assyria in 722 B.C.E., after which the traditions of the united monarchy lived on only in the South. From the middle of the ninth century prophetic figures such as Elijah fought the injustices and religious infidelities they thought replete in both kingdoms. Amos and Hosea carried on this tradition in the North in the eighth century, prior to the Assyrian victory.

The Southern Kingdom survived until the Babylonian victories early in the

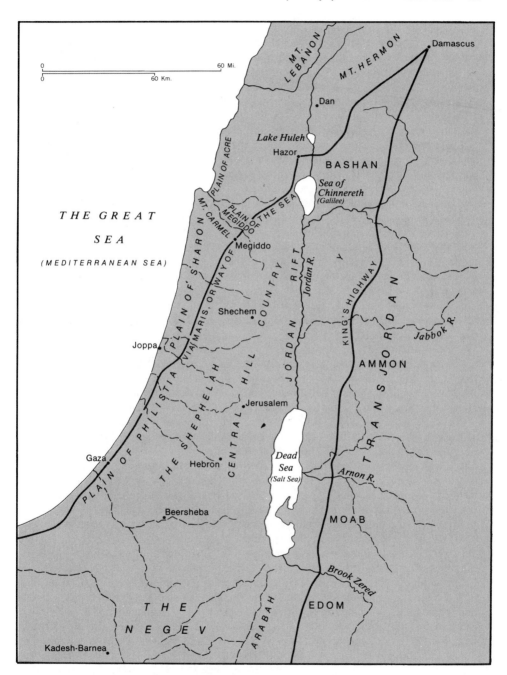

The major geographic divisions of ancient Israel.

sixth century. A first deportation of important citizens from Judah to Babylon occurred in 597 B.C.E. and in 587/586 a larger deportation and conquest, later known as the Exile, occurred. Judah had often paralleled the North in tolerating social injustice and religious infidelity, but kingly reformers, Hezekiah (715–687) and Josiah (640–609), and prophets such as Isaiah and Jeremiah, who worked in these kings' respective eras, kept the Mosaic ideals alive.

The Exile to Babylon lasted about fifty years, until 538, and it created a profound sense of before and after. When Babylon was defeated by Persia, some of the deportees returned to Judah, and the Temple, which had been destroyed at the Babylonian conquest, was rebuilt (around 520 to 515). Israel was now a dependency of Persia, but in the mid-fifth century two returnees from exile, Ezra and Nehemiah, led a reestablishment of its institutions. Alexander the Great defeated the Persians and conquered Israel in 332. This led to a considerable influence of Greek culture (Hellenism). From 323 to 200 the Ptolemies held sway in Palestine, only to be ousted by the Seleucids, who ruled until 142. Both Ptolemy I and Seleucus I were generals of Alexander, so their lines represented warfare within Hellenism and the Alexandrian aftermath. The Ptolemies were centered in Egypt, whereas the Seleucids at one time ruled Persia, Syria, Babylon, and southern Asia Minor.

In 167 the Seleucid ruler Antiochus IV Epiphanes so angered the Jews by his aggressive Hellenization (he profaned the Temple by turning it Greek) that they revolted successfully, under the leadership of a family called the Maccabees. The Hasmonean rule, as the dynasty of the Maccabees is called, lasted until 37 B.C.E., and during it the Temple was rebuilt. From 63 B.C.E. the Romans controlled Jerusalem, due to the conquest by the Roman general Pompey, so from that time the Hasmonean rule was at Roman sufferance. From 40 B.C.E. the Romans backed Herod the Great and thereafter his line, and in 37 Herod defeated Antigonus II, who proved to be the last Hasmonean king. Herod began a reconstruction of the Temple in Jerusalem in 20 B.C.E., and it was finally completed in 62 C.E. The Jews revolted against Roman rule in 66 C.E., but they were crushed in 70 C.E. The Temple was destroyed, and many Jewish institutions were forbidden. The Jewish religious leadership that survived emigrated to sites such as Jamnia, to the northwest of Jerusalem near the Mediterranean coast. There, at the end of the first century C.E., a group of rabbis (Pharisees: the leading party after the defeat by Rome) put the finishing touches on the collection of writings that gradually had been coming to be recognized as authoritative Scripture.

We can see, then, that the majority of the millennium (922 B.C.E. to 90 C.E.) from the death of Solomon to the council at Jamnia produced hard times for Israel. When North and South went to war and gained a permanent separation in 922 B.C.E., the children of Abraham said goodbye to the glory they had known under Solomon. Warfare and injustice marred the reigns of virtually all the Northern kings, as the Bible remembers them, so from 922 to 722 Israel (the Northern Kingdom) mainly knew strife. Southern kings such as Hezekiah and Josiah stand out in the biblical record for piety and reform, but they are the exceptions that prove the rule. Opposed to the usually impious king and the injustice of his realm are the genuine prophets, whom the Bible praises as men (and on occasion women) who upheld the holiness required of a people covenanted to the one true God.[7] Until the Exile to Babylon the Southern prophets mainly inveighed against corruption, but when the punishment (as they saw it) of Exile came the prophets gave eloquent voice to hopes that God one day would restore Judah and Jerusalem.

The deportation of its elite to Babylon for approximately fifty years dealt Israel a blow from which it never fully recovered. When, after 538 B.C.E., the Persians allowed those deportees who wished to return to their native land, by no means all of them did. The reforms of Ezra and Nehemiah recorded in the biblical books that go under their names suggest the labor that was necessary in the fifth century to protect Israel against submergence into the neighboring populations. The sense of separateness, and the necessity for religioethnic purity, that Judaism has regularly manifested in the Common Era got a strong start at that time.

TORAH

The final three sections of this brief history are concerned with (what scholars now opine about) the evolution of the materials we now find in the Hebrew Bible. Generally, all but the most conservative scholars and literal interpreters of revelation (those who hold that God dictated Scripture whole) admit that the Hebrew Bible encloses a great wealth of different traditions, literary units, and editorial strata. We should imagine it not as a work that came off the printing press just as the mind and pen of one writer had composed it (starting at Genesis and ending at 2 Chronicles) but as the end product of a very long process of remembering, recording, creating, rearranging, adding, subtracting, changing emphases, and the like. By about 400 B.C.E. there was general agreement that what are now the first five books (Genesis through Deuteronomy), which as a collection go by various names (Torah, the Law, or the Pentateuch), ought to be considered authoritative (divinely inspired) guidance for Israel. The materials now housed in the second main section of the Hebrew Bible, the Prophets (Joshua through Malachai), had comparable status by about 200 B.C.E. Around 130 B.C.E. these two groupings were together considered Scripture, and some of the materials that we now find in the third biblical section, the Writings (Psalms through 2 Chronicles), were available. By 100 C.E., as we have indicated, the rabbis had authorized what we now find in both the Writings and the whole Bible.

Two more general comments are necessary before we zero in on the specific history of the first five books. The first is that such works as Ezekiel, Song of Songs, Ecclesiastes, and Esther were only accepted into the final canon after considerable dispute and debate. The second point is that the Septuagint translation, from which Christians derived their Old Testament, differed considerably from the Hebrew version and placed the books in a different order. The new works and additional sections in old works that we find in the Septuagint remind us that many other Jewish writings were circulating at the time of closure, offering alternatives that the rabbis finally rejected. Some of these, such as the books of Enoch and 3–4 Maccabees, exerted considerable influence, even though they made it into neither the Hebrew nor the Greek Bible.[8]

Work on the formation and message of the first five books of the Bible has always been a high priority among biblical scholars, and this remains true today.[9] The mainstream opinion today is that all of these books are composite works, pieced together from both originally oral sources and disparate written records and compositions. Such diverse literary genres as sayings, laws, blessings, speeches, sermons, myths, fairy tales, songs, sagas, novellas, and lists appear in the Pentateuch. Some scholars think that the oldest of these sources come from oral traditions passed down from the time of the earliest ancestors (Abraham and Sarah) — the eighteenth century b.c.e. — but more radical historical critics doubt it. It is possible that a common, rather undifferentiated collection of such traditions existed by 1150, after the Exodus from Egypt and Conquest of Canaan. The Yahwist stratum (abbreviated J) that we now find in the Torah perhaps goes back to the late ninth century. It is distinctive for calling the deity "YHWH" and for presenting an earthy view of human nature. The Elohist source (abbreviated E) perhaps goes back to the late eighth century. It is distinctive for calling the deity "Elohim" and for expressing such typically Northern interests as concern about idolatry, worship, and charismatic leadership. (We should note that the isolation and characterization of these sources is quite hypothetical and that no full scholarly consensus about them obtains.)

It is likely that J and E were edited into some sort of unity by 700 b.c.e. or so. A priestly source (abbreviated P), perhaps from about 500 b.c.e., reveals itself through a special concern with ritual and exactness in matters of time and measurement. On one accounting, by about the mid-fifth century these three sources probably were woven together, giving the substance of what we now find in the first four books, Genesis through Numbers.[10] The book of Deuteronomy would seem to have come from another literary process, better treated fully in the next section (because it mainly bears on writings now found in the Prophets). The origins of this other literary process perhaps go back to the ninth century, and an early form of Deuteronomy may well have existed by the late seventh century. (The school that formed Deuteronomy may also have worked on the block Genesis to Numbers, so little is hard and fast in these matters.) Only shortly before 400 b.c.e., however, were the four hypothesized pentateuchal strands (JEPD) edited into anything close to the present Torah, and after 400 b.c.e. this edition seems to have been considered authoritative Scripture.

We must point out that such a sketch of the literary history of the first five books greatly simplifies a process that scholars debate vigorously at virtually every juncture. Although most academic scholars of biblical literature accept a considerable diversity in the sources of the Pentateuch, and some form of the "Documentary Hypothesis" (which holds that JEPD came from four somewhat separate literary works) commands much assent, not all scholars accept this hypothesis even in its broadest form, and so the details of any specification of the hypothesis are sure to be challenged. Moreover, so-called "form criticism" is mainly interested in the oral forms that lay behind the written sources, and it does not place much weight on JEPD. As well, many analysts of the biblical literature are more interested in the final product than in its historical evolution, and they think that we should pay most attention to the form that exerted the greatest subsequent influence. For them the final, canonical arrangement is the thing upon which to focus, and how this final shape arose is of secondary significance. Nonetheless, the work (often described as "historical criticism" and "form criticism") of analyzing the processes and component parts of the evolution of the current canonical text still commands much attention.

To illustrate why such work still commands attention, we may focus briefly on a pentateuchal problem that not only attracts scholarly research but is easily made apparent to any careful reader. The problem occurs in the book of Leviticus. Chapters 17–26 seem to comprise a unit unto itself, because their overriding concern is the laws by which Israel can keep itself holy. These chapters have, in fact, come to be called the "Holiness Code," and as soon as we accept this destion further questions arise about where such materials came from and how they got inserted into Leviticus or the Pentateuch as a whole at this point. Norman K. Gottwald suggests a date of about 620 B.C.E. for the composition or collection of the Holiness Code,[11] which suggests that these materials antedated the priestly source (P), at least as the latter existed in final form. Because the Holiness Code certainly deals with matters of special interest to priests, we would assume that it came from priestly circles, and that assumption in turn reminds us that in considering the historical evolution of the Pentateuch we probably should reckon with interests and "schools" that themselves evolved over numerous generations. We could indicate many more historical questions that the Pentateuch suggests, and all of them would explain why scholars continue to probe and debate about the processes through which what we now hold in our hands got to this present shape.

THE PROPHETS

Jewish tradition divides this second section of the Hebrew Bible, which we have noted was by about 200 B.C.E. a collection considered normative for Jewish faith and so scriptural, into the "former" prophets and the "latter" prophets. In fact, the books grouped as former prophets (Joshua through 2 Kings) are historical works that biblical scholars tend to link with Deuteronomy and consider a single block. The latter prophets subdivide into the books of Isaiah, Jeremiah, and Ezekiel, which are lengthy and carry the prestige of being attributed to some of the greatest of Israel's visionaries, and the (shorter) books of "the twelve" (other visionaries). For all three subgroups — former prophets, major latter prophets, and the twelve — the literary judgment holds that what we now possess are composite works, from several hands and pieced together by editors different from the original sources.

   We have mentioned the view that takes the present Deuteronomy as part of a larger historical writing. Sometimes scholars speak of "the Deuteronomist," meaning by this term the person or persons who shaped the materials we now find in the books Joshua through 2 Kings to express the theological judgment, found in Deuteronomy, that the misfortunes Israel had suffered throughout its history were punishments approved by God because of Israel's wrongdoing.[12] Another term, far from clearly distinguished from "the Deuteronomist," is "the Deuteronomistic history." This second term tends to refer to the framework in which the books Joshua through 2 Kings have been cast, and to the pattern of apostasy, punishment, conversion, and liberation that regularly unfolds in these books.[13] This history is one of several that we find in the Hebrew Bible as a whole. In the Pentateuch, as we have seen, priestly writers gave their view of things past in the stratum called P, as did those responsible for J and E. In the Writings, as we see later, the Chronicler, as the person or persons responsible for 1 and 2 Chronicles (and perhaps also Ezra and Nehemiah) generally is called, offers still another view of the past. These several historical positions and narratives are neither flatly contradictory nor completely agreed. Rather they overlap and turn aside and readjust one another, suggesting both slightly different sources (oral traditions, archives) and slightly different theological standpoints.

At any rate, when we survey the great variety of literary genres that are now represented in the Prophets—a variety at least as rich as what we find in the Pentateuch—we are counseled to suspect that a very complex editorial process lay between the origins of this second portion of Hebrew Scripture and what was basically settled upon as authoritative by 200 B.C.E. Some of the materials that may be the oldest parts of the prophetic materials, such as the Song of Deborah (Judges 5), may go back to about 1125 B.C.E.[14] The sources of what became Deuteronomistic legal sections probably existed in first form by 900 B.C.E., and from that time until the end of the seventh century, when we may opine that materials now present in the block Joshua through Judges 1 merged with the Deuteronomistic historical materials collected in a first form of Deuteronomy-Kings, steady recasting probably occurred. This meant reworking and editing sagas, legends, archival materials, and the like, that bore on the time of the judges, Saul, David, and Solomon. The "book of the law" supposedly discovered in the reign of King Josiah about 620 B.C.E. (see 2 Kings 22) is usually considered to have been some form of what became Deuteronomy. Eventually, this book was joined with the block Genesis through Numbers to make the Torah—the first Scripture or collection of authoritative writings. Such an addition suggests both that Deuteronomy itself was held in great esteem and that the Deuteronomistic school had considerable influence.

The materials we now find in the latter prophets are not as old as the materials of the Deuteronomistic history. Much of what we find in the first part of the book of Isaish (chapters 1–39) probably derives from the prophet of this name, who was active from about 740 to 701 B.C.E. The materials now found in Jeremiah 1–45 probably are similarly tied to the historical prophet whose name they bear, which would place them around 600 B.C.E. Some scholars postulate a Deuteronomistic edition of these Jeremian materials around 535 and the addition of what we now find in Jeremiah 46–52 around 500. Similarly, what is now Isaiah 40–55 perhaps came about 150 years after Isaiah 1–39 (that is, from the time of the Exile), and Isaiah 56–66 came later still, perhaps from about 500. A last refinement of this view of the development of the book of Isaiah would place chapters 32–35 after 400 and chapters 24–27 as late as 225. Needless to say, there is no certainty in this matter, which means that virtually any hypothetical reconstruction will be attacked energetically.

In Ezekiel, the third major latter prophet, some portions of chapters 1–37 and 40–48 seem older than other portions, which suggests that a process of fairly consistent addition went on during the period from the oldest materials (perhaps 540 B.C.E.) to the period of the later materials in these blocks (about 400). Ezekiel 38–39 appears to have been added considerably later. The usual opinion concerning all three major latter prophets is that the oldest materials probably are the sayings put in the prophets' mouths and the reports or biographical materials about them. In the case of Ezekiel, the cultic regulations also may be quite early.

The tendency in treatments of the twelve other prophets is to think of their materials as only having been grouped around 200 B.C.E. into the loose subcollection that all twelve comprise. In other words, the collection of the twelve was virtually simultaneous with the (perhaps still fairly informal, though widely accepted) decision to accredit a second portion of writings as Scriptural. Within the block of the twelve, the oldest source seems to be Amos, and after him Hosea and Micah. Generally, the order in which the twelve are presented in the Hebrew Bible follows the chronology of when they lived and worked. Amos may be dated as early as 750, whereas Zechariah 9–14, which is probably the latest section in the materials of the twelve, perhaps stems from around 260. A good date for the book of Jonah, which differs from the others in being a short story (some would call it a novella, and still others, a parable), is around 400. Hosea and Micah both worked before the Exile, whereas Zephaniah, Nahum, and Habbakuk all seem to stem from right around the time of that victory of the Babylonians. The remaining books (Haggai, Zechariah, Joel, Obad, and Malachi) probably stem from the fifth century, after the return from the Exile.

Even though all of the twelve are short books, the regular tendency is for them, too, to be considered composite works rather than simple, integral creations. They derive from prophets who saw their own times in light of prior history, and so refer back to at least the early years of the divided monarchy. Many of them have been composed by disciples or later interested parties who would not have scrupled to reset the prophets' oracles in light of subsequent events.

The time when the Prophets became canonical coincides with the Jews' existing under threat of Hellenization. This threat is one reason why the Deuteronomistic history and the oracles of the latter prophets could have seemed especially significant. Postexilic Israel felt itself under siege and fighting for its cultural life. The remonstrations of the great prophets who had castigated the people for idolatry, as well as for injustice, and the similar dire warnings of the Deuteronomistic historians, who read past punishments as the just deserts of failure to obey the Mosaic laws, would have sounded very apt. This is not to deny that these materials already had a venerable status, nor that the "canonization" that gilded them around 200 B.C.E. could have been a quite informal affair — mainly a matter of ratifying what most people already felt. It is simply to try to relate the situation around 200 to the materials that then entered the authoritative listing and to muse about what in them might have been most appreciated.[15]

THE WRITINGS

We have noted that some of the pieces that comprise the third section of the canonical Hebrew Bible probably were enjoying full respect by 130 B.C.E., and that the view of the rabbis at Jamnia around 90 C.E. determined the final listing. As was true of Torah and the Prophets, the materials in the Writings exhibit a wide range of literary genres. Many of these materials also probably existed in first or rudimentary forms long before they were formalized in the period from the fourth century B.C.E. to the first century C.E. Among the oldest materials that got into the Writings are probably some of the hymns, laments, thanksgivings, and praises of God as the king of Israel that we find in the Psalms. These could derive from the united monarchy of David and Solomon and the cult of the original Temple. Equally old may be the first form of proverbial sayings, such as those we now find in Proverbs 10–22. Last, the story we now know as the book of Ruth bears some similarities to the stories that have come down from the earliest, ancestral period, and some scholars now place it as early as the tenth century B.C.E.[16]

By the seventh century, at least several of the collections of Psalms we now find mentioned in that work (e.g., the psalms of David, Asaph, and Korah) probably existed. From the eighth century, such proverbs as those we find in Proverbs 25–29 were circulating. At places (for example, Proverbs 22:17–24) scholars can detect Egyptian influence, which may also go back to the eighth century. The earliest parts of Job (1–2, 42:7–17) could come from eighth-century folk literature, but the mid-sixth century seems the best time for such didactic poetry as Job 32–37. The materials of Job 3–31, and 38–42:6 (hymnic songs, laments, and disputes) probably came only slightly earlier. The end of the sixth century (perhaps 520) is a probable dating for Lamentations, and the latest materials in the Psalms, Proverbs (such as 1–9), Ruth, and the Song of Songs take us to around 400. The historical sources upon which the Chronicler drew no doubt existed by shortly after 500, because much in them is identical with what now appears in the books of Samuel and Kings, which existed in nearly final form then. The lists that we find in Chronicles and Ezra-Nehemiah may be dated to about 460, whereas the memoirs of Ezra and Nehemiah probably were in existence only slightly later, perhaps by 440. At any rate, the final version of Chronicles, Ezra, and Nehemiah can be dated to the early fourth century, say 380 B.C.E. Later comes Qoheleth (Ecclesiastes), in view of the peculiar vocabulary, which seems much influenced by Persian, and also in view of Greek influences. The book of Daniel appears determined by the outrages of Antiochus IV Epiphanes in 167, but the stories we now find in chapters 1–6 may be somewhat earlier, although still after the return from exile. The date for the book of Esther, which is perhaps best described as a novella, depends on whether we are stressing the sagas or legends that lie at its base or the final version in which we now have the whole. The basis for the stories would seem to lie in the later Persian period (400–332), and the final version could be as late as 115 B.C.E.

What stands out when we survey the Writings is the disparate character of the materials that were gathered in this third section of Scripture. It seems that these were expressions of praise, wisdom, memory, revelation, and the like that the rabbis felt bound to hold onto and grant authoritative, sacral status. One great influence in the Persian period, during which the bulk of the materials now in the Writings appear to have gained at least a penultimate form (say, by 380 B.C.E., and thinking of 130 B.C.E., the date we have previously used, as a time when most were in virtually final form), was the desire to reconstitute Israel as a liturgically and ethnically pure community that could resist submergence among its neighbors. We see this motivation quite clearly in Ezra and Nehemiah, and it seems to lie behind the Chronicler's history of the Davidic line, which served as the paradigm for how Israel was to think about its future success and failure. Another strong influence surely was the wisdom movement. If Ezra-Nehemiah suggests the motivation for collecting the Psalms, the Wisdom movement suggests the motivation for organizing Proverbs, Job, and Qoheleth. Ruth and Esther portrayed valiant women, one a virtuous foreigner and the other an Israelite patriot. Together they project a balanced, indeed a quite sophisticated, statement about how postexilic Israelites ought to think about the Gentiles. Daniel combines both prophetic and wisdom motifs, but the Song of Songs is something of an anomaly, probably finally accepted into the canon because its (originally quite nonreligious) love poetry could serve as a metaphor for the covenant between Israel and God.[17]

The canonization of the last portion of Scripture, and the organization of the whole, provided a final opportunity to set what Torah, in the sense of the first written form of God's Teaching or Guidance, was to convey. The Pentateuch, which tradition tied closely to Moses, always was the most authoritative part of Torah, and the Prophets had more esteem than the Writings. But the combined effect of the three portions was to give Israel a rich heritage. The overlappings and variations in the books suggested that Torah is living and untidy, rather than static and unmysterious. When the rabbis later spoke of oral tradition, and then developed such collections of written teachings as the Mishnah and the Talmud, they could justify the overspilling, variegated character of these other forms of Torah by saying that the Bible itself was organic and internally argumentative, rather than a precise blueprint that gave all the details and allowed no room for debate.

GLOSSARY

Canon   A list or body of writings that is considered scriptural. The canonization of the Hebrew Scriptures dates from 80 C.E. to 110 C.E.

Covenant   The semicontractual bond between Israel and Yahweh such that Israel would be his people and he would be their God.

Deuteronomist (D)   Concerning the history or theology of the Book of Deuteronomy.

Deuteronomistic history   The narrative that spans from the Book of Deuteronomy through the Books of Kings.

Elohist (E)   The source, found in Genesis through Numbers, that calls God Elohim. The Elohist stems from the eighth or ninth century B.C.E. and supplements the Yahwist in the light of pre-Mosaic theology.

Hellenism   The cultural ideals, derived from Alexander the Great, that dominated the Near East and Eastern Europe in the late centuries B.C.E. and the early centuries C.E.

Mishnah   Code of Jewish law (interpretations of the oral Torah) formally promulgated around 200 C.E.

Talmud   Primary source of Jewish law and rabbinic learning; Mishnah plus Gemara (comments on the Mishnah).

YHWH   The most important personal name for God in the Hebrew Bible. Usually it was represented by the four consonants YHWH but in speech was replaced by Adonai (Lord).

Yahwist (J)   The oldest source in the books Genesis through Numbers, characterized by its use of the name Yahweh (Jahweh in German) for God and dating to the tenth century B.C.E.

STUDY QUESTIONS

1. What are the most important events associated with Abraham, Moses, and David?
2. How does the Bible view the period from Rehoboam to the fall of Judah?
3. What does the contrast between Genesis 1–11 and Genesis 12–50 suggest about the composition of the Pentateuch?
4. Why did the five books of Moses become the preeminent part of Torah?
5. Explain the relation between the Deuteronomistic history and the former prophets.
6. How does the book of Isaiah illustrate the composite character of prophetic authorship?
7. How do the Exile and the problems of the postexilic Jewish community color Chronicles, Ezra, and Nehemiah?
8. Where have Jewish interests in wisdom left their greatest impact?
9. At what approximate dates were the Torah, the Prophets, and the Writings, respectively, canonized?

NOTES

1. See J. Maxwell Miller, "Israelite History," in *The Hebrew Bible and Its Modern Interpreters*, eds. Douglas A. Knight and Gene M. Tucker. Philadelphia: Fortress, 1985, pp. 1–30.

2. See William G. Dever, "Syro-Palestinian and Biblical Archeology," in *The Hebrew Bible and Its Modern Interpreters*, pp. 31–74. See also Michael Grant, *The History of Ancient Israel*. New York: Charles Scribner's Sons, 1984, pp. 7–11.

3. See J. J. M. Roberts, "The Ancient Near Eastern Environment," in *The Hebrew Bible and Its Modern Interpreters*, pp. 75–121. See also *Ancient Near Eastern Texts Relating to the Old Testament*, 3rd ed., ed. James B. Pritchard. Princeton: Princeton University Press, 1968.

4. Grant, *The History of Ancient Israel*, p. 11.

5. See Norman K. Gottwald, *The Tribes of Yahweh: A Sociology of the Religion of Liberated Israel*. Maryknoll, N.Y.: Orbis Books, 1979.

6. See Norman K. Gottwald, *The Hebrew Bible: A Socio-Literary Introduction*. Philadelphia: Fortress, 1985, pp. 272–73.

7. A good general source is *Israel's Prophetic Tradition*, eds. R. Coggins, A. Phillips, and M. Knibb. Cambridge: Cambridge University Press, 1982.

8. See Christian E. Hauer and William A. Young, *An Introduction to the Bible*. Englewood Cliffs, N.J.: Prentice-Hall, 1986, p. 9. See also Gottwald, *The Hebrew Bible*, especially pp. 79–130. Our treatment of the history of the three portions of Scripture is heavily indebted to both Gottwald and the many relevant articles in *Harper's Bible Dictionary*, ed. Paul J. Achtemeier. San Francisco: Harper & Row, 1985.

9. See Gottwald, *The Hebrew Bible*, p. 104.

10. See Douglas A. Knight, "The Pentateuch," in *The Hebrew Bible and Its Modern Interpreters*, pp. 263–96.

11. See Gottwald, *The Hebrew Bible*, p. 104.

12. See Kent H. Richards, "Deuteronomist," in *Harper's Bible Dictionary*, p. 219.

13. See Kent H. Richards, "Deuteronomistic Historian," in *Harper's Bible Dictionary*, p. 219.

14. See J. Cheryl Exum, "Deborah," in *Harper's Bible Dictionary*, p. 214.

15. See Peter R. Ackroyd, "The Historical Literature," and Gene M. Tucker, "Prophecy and the Prophetic Literature," in *The Hebrew Bible and Its Modern Interpreters*, pp. 297–323 and 325–68.

16. See Edward F. Campbell and Paul J. Achtemeier, "Ruth," in *Harper's Bible Dictionary*, p. 886.

17. See James L. Crenshaw, "The Wisdom Literature," Erhard S. Gerstenberger, "The Lyrical Literature," Susan Niditch, "Legends of Wise Heroes and Heroines," and Paul D. Hanson, "Apocalyptic Literature," in *The Hebrew Bible and Its Modern Interpreters*, pp. 369–407, 409–44, 445–63, and 465–88.

CHAPTER 3

Genesis

TEXTUAL ANALYSIS

A first orientation to the books Genesis through Deuteronomy comes from tracing the generations with which the Pentateuch is concerned. Four of the five books focus on the generation of the Exodus. Genesis serves as a prologue to the liberation from Egypt and the giving of the Law that dominates Exodus, Leviticus, and Numbers, while Deuteronomy serves as an epilogue. The Pentateuch itself does not include the story of God's giving the promised land to Israel, only the story of God's promise to do so. Because the texts that we now possess have been shaped by Israel's experience of the Exile in Babylon in the sixth century B.C.E., we may speculate that promise, possession, and dispossession of the land were sensitive matters.

The book of Genesis is one of the richest and most influential in the Hebrew Bible. It is composed of two main textual blocks, a primeval history (1–11) and a history or collection of traditions about the ancestors (12–50) that has three principal subdivisions. The basic editing process seems to have been that priestly editors used the P tradition to provide the final framework, into which they set J and E materials. We discuss the likely history of the text and the proportions of the different textual traditions on later occasions.

In outline Genesis is conveniently broken down as follows:

1:1–11:26   Primeval History
11:27–50:26 Period of the Ancestors
            11:27–25:18 Abraham and Sarah

25:19–37:1   Isaac and Jacob

37:2–50:26   Joseph[1]

1:1–11:26 Primeval History

The basic design or canonical structure of these chapters, in terms of textual traditions and history, is that J traditions, likely first written down in the mid-tenth century, were finally set into a frame based on priestly traditions by priestly editors of the sixth century who were concerned to furnish the exilic community materials that would help it preserve its identity and not simply meld into the Babylonian (or later the Persian) empire.[2]

1:1–2:3 THE PRIESTLY ACCOUNT OF CREATION

The first textual unit in Genesis is the famous account of the creation of the world in six days (after which, on the seventh day, God rests). Two general observations are in order. First, the author does not intend to offer what we today would call a scientific account of how the world came into being. The objective is rather to express the Israelite understanding and conviction that the world owes its being and design to God. Our accepting this verdict of scholarly analyses of Genesis immediately undercuts most of the conflict that sometimes is said to exist between biblical views of creation and modern views derived from natural science.[3]

Second, the priestly account of creation has cast its materials into a repetitive and balanced format. Thus, for each of the six days of creative divine activity there is: (1) an announcement (of what God said); (2) a command (by which God created); (3) an assurance that what God commanded happened; (4) God's evaluation of his work as good; and (5) a statement about when the action concluded. The overall effect is to portray the process of creation as rational, ordered, marching forth neatly. The balance of the "days" of creation deserves fuller comment.

The essential balance is between the first three days and the second three days. Thus, day one, when light appears, is balanced by day four, when the heavenly lights come forth. Day two, when the sky and waters appear, is balanced by day five, when the birds and fish come forth. Day three, on which earth and vegetation appear, is balanced by day six, when the land animals and humanity come forth. Once again, the overall result is orderliness: God has given the world a balanced form, from the very beginnings of its existence.

Beyond these general observations, several particular points deserve comment. Genesis 1:1 depicts the beginning as a chaos that God (had to) put into order. The chaos was characterized by formlessness, a void, and darkness over the "deep." The wind or Spirit of God moved over the face of the waters (of the deep)—a rather feminine figure of brooding. This picture of chaotic beginnings is like that of other ancient Near Eastern creation accounts, except that there is no conflict between the (divine) creative force that brings order and the original materials. In other ancient Near Eastern accounts the materials resist. Indeed, the fact that God creates simply by speaking suggests a transcendence of the original materials that comparative Near Eastern accounts do not accord the creative divinity. The God of Genesis 1 is uniquely sovereign.

The lines 1:26–30, dealing with the creation of humanity, also call for special comment. Human beings are said to be made in the divine image and are given dominion over other creatures, as though our species came as the climax of the creational process. The double-sexedness of humanity is stressed and blessed, and human beings are told to be fruitful, multiply, fill the Earth, and subdue it. Traditional Judaism considered this command both a blessing and the first of the 613 commands of the halachah or religious law. From it derived the notion that marriage is a religious obligation.[4] God's rest on the seventh day, as we have already noted, sanctioned the notion of a human Sabbath. Indeed, it placed the Sabbath rest at the foundations of world order.

2:4–5:32 CREATION, SIN, AND THE GENEALOGY OF ADAM

After the cosmic order has been established, we seem to receive another account of creation. Biblical scholars consider this account to be older than that of the priestly tradition and to have come from the Yahwist school. Among its general characteristics are a greater interest in humankind, a more anthropomorphic depiction of the divinity, and an interpretation of the imperfection of human existence. The style is less solemn, more concrete, earthy, and even humorous.

For the Yahwist theologian of creation, humanity appears at the beginning of the process. The mist referred to in 2:6 probably calls to mind fertility, and the molding of humanity from the dust of the Earth both portrays God as working like a potter and gives humanity very humble beginnings. The name for "man" (adam) is a play on "earth" (adamah). The idea that the breath of life came directly from God became part of a rich complex of notions about the divine "breathing" or "spirit." The word "Eden" appears to have come from the Sumerian and to have originally connoted a place once fertile but later barren. A garden and water were nearly always a delight in the ancient Near East, which generally was quite arid. Other parts of the description of Eden suggest symbols and perhaps myths of vitality and richness. From the outset humanity is portrayed as the worker and keeper of the Earth. The tree of knowledge, when "good and evil" is understood as a synonym for "everything," becomes a symbol of the (divine) fullness of awareness that human beings cannot aspire to attain without forgetting their creaturely status and so denaturing themselves.

For the Yahwist the bisexuality of humanity goes to the center of how men and women ought to understand themselves. The man can find no fit companion ("helper") among nonhuman creation, and his delight with the woman, who as the figure of the rib indicates shares his essence, is quite revealing. When added to the statement that a man therefore leaves his patriarchal loyalties (central to ancient Near Eastern culture) and makes the bond with his woman paramount, the Yahwist depiction of the constitutional relations between the sexes is strikingly egalitarian, as well as strikingly positive about sexual attraction. Thus, a recent commentator, Samuel Terrien, rejects the notion that the central biblical traditions are sexist and depreciate femaleness.[5] The note about the original couple's being naked but not ashamed both supports this interpretation and serves as a foil for the shame that follows on their sin. On the other hand, after Eden we find the male superiority typical of patriarchal societies.

In chapter 3 the serpent appears on the scene, and with it the fertility religion that was a great influence in the ancient Near East. The serpent has phallic

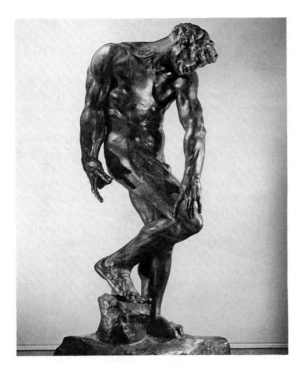

Adam by Auguste Rodin.
*(The Nelson-Atkins Museum of Art,
Kansas City, Missouri [Nelson Fund])*

overtones, which Terrien associates with rituals designed to use sexual ecstasy as a stairway to the divinity. In this view the Yahwist therefore is depicting how people fall away from the faith in God's otherworldliness that was the hallmark of the traditions about YHWH, the God of Abraham, Isaac, and Jacob. However, the serpent also suggested immortality, by the shedding of its skin.

The key to the failure depicted in verses 3:1–7 is the couple's disobedience and lack of trust. Although God has given humanity a generous measure of good things, human beings tend to focus on other things that they think they should have. Whether we stress the ethical dimension of disobedience, or the intellectual dimension of striving for excessive knowledge,[6] or the interpersonal dimension of a lack of trust, or finally the sexual overtones to the biblical "knowledge," the brief account of the awakening of humanity to shame remains a storied, symbolic effort to imagine from where our common intuition that things are not what they might or even ought to be comes.

The details of the fig leaves, the man's blaming the woman, and the woman's blaming the serpent are almost amusing. Quite sober, however, are the depictions of the hardships that humanity suffers in its nonparadisial, everyday life. Women's pain from childbearing and subjugation to men, men's laborious toil after sustenance, and the certainty of both that they will die summarize many of the basic difficulties of the human condition. The Yahwists thought of God as the source of human prosperity and hope. Logically enough, therefore, they thought of being on the outs with God as the likeliest source of human beings' shame and sufferings.

But verses 3:21–22 bring back notes of hope, as Adam names his wife Eve, mother of all living, and God clothes the couple with garments of skin.

It seems clear from other contexts (for example, 1 Kings 8:6–7, Ezekiel 41:18–19, Jeremiah 47:6) that the cherubim and the flaming sword connote the sanctity of the divine precincts. The episode in the garden therefore ends on the sad or at least realistic note that humanity now lives apart from God's holy realm. Still, the Hebrew Bible does not dwell on the couple's fall but rather concentrates on how it carries on and procreates.

Chapter 4 gives us the story of Cain and Abel, who stand for the first successors of primal humanity. Moreover, they stand for the two disparate and often conflicting lifestyles of shepherd and farmer. The story favors Abel, the shepherd, perhaps because ancient Israel remembered its beginnings as pastoral and feared the agricultural life, with its overtones of worshipping nature and fertility. Both the birth of the children and Cain's killing of Abel suggest that humanity (outside the garden) must manage the power of life that God bestowed upon it. If human beings do not create peaceable, cooperative social relations, but fall prey to envy and hatred (to sin, which is like an animal waiting to be roused),[7] they compound their shame, hardship, and sense of being distanced from the holy God. Cain's outcry of near-despair when he hears of the punishment his murder of Abel brings suggests how deeply he appreciates his failure. But just as Adam and Eve received some mercy from God, so does Cain. Although in just two generations humanity has gone from innocence to murder, God does not totally abandon it.

Two further themes worth noting are that of sibling rivalry, which recurs in the story of Jacob and Esau, and that of blood, which is a prime symbol of life. By having spilled blood Cain is liable to a code of revenge (blood for blood). God's giving him a protective "mark" may be read as a rejection of this primitive vindictiveness.

Cain becomes the ancestor of city-dwellers (always suspect as improperly sophisticated), reminding us that the biblical authors drew upon such sources as etiological myths to explain how certain cultural institutions arose. Genesis 4:17–22 continue in this vein. Genesis 4:23–24 seem to be an ancient song, perhaps sewn in here to suggest the continuance of the bloodying and vengeance that started with Cain. The chapter concludes with a suggestion that true worship (of the Lord Yahweh) began in the earliest human generations.

With chapter 5 we get another "generations" (toledot), a term that some scholars see as providing a thread through all of Genesis (see also 2:4, 6:9, 10:1, 11:10, 11:27, 25:12, 25:19, 36:1, 37:2). The first verses recall the priestly account of creation in Genesis 1, repeating the themes of humanity's being an image of God, being composed of two sexes, and having been blessed. The priestly authors say little about a fall from pristine innocence, implying that Adam's original reflection of God was passed on to his son Seth. The genealogical table listing the generations from Adam to Noah perhaps was based on lists of Mesopotamian kings, and the likelihood is that the table in chapter 4:17–26, from Yahwist sources, has been reworked to fit the priestly enumeration, although the ordering in the two lists remains different. Enoch is one of the most interesting figures, and later apocalyptic literature was fascinated by the idea (5:24) that he was so intimate with God that he was finally taken up to heaven by God. That he lived 365 years (one for each day of the solar year) has led some scholars to connect him with worship of a sun god, while his being seventh in the priestly list perhaps reflects the Mesopotamian notion that the seventh king would be taken into the company of the gods. The extremely long lives of the figures in the list symbolically suggest that when humanity was relatively fresh it had great vigor (a common motif in folklore). Overall, the table suggests human fertility abounding, although the last lines of the chapter, referring to the curse of work, link this fertility to humanity's imperfect mode of existence.

6:1–9:29 NOAH AND THE FLOOD

The first verses of chapter 6 reflect the mythological idea of a marriage between sons of God and human daughters — another splinter from the notion that "in the beginning" things were better. Still, human beings remained mortal, even though their span seems vast to us. With verses 5–7 the tone shifts and humanity is depicted as having become so wicked that God repents of having created it. Only Noah finds favor in God's eyes, because of his righteousness "in his generation." The talmudic rabbis were intrigued by this notion. Some of them thought that Noah would have stood out in any age but others thought that the general wickedness made even minimal virtue impressive.[8]

At any rate, God proposes to destroy wicked humanity and the Earth by bringing a flood of waters (a return of primal chaos). Yet he will make a covenant with Noah (6:18, 9:8–17). (Later biblical religion has considered this as expressing the divine bond with righteous Gentiles.) Thereby, God will save Noah (who is like a new Adam) and his family. The story of the building of the ark, the preservation of the different species of animals, and the actual occurrence of the flood draws on Mesopotamian parallels — for instance, the Babylonian epic of Gilgamesh — while the reference to animals that are clean and unclean prefigures later dietary and sacrificial laws.

The account of the flood may draw from ancient memories of great disasters by water, but its main message in Genesis is moral: Natural disasters may be viewed as a punishment for human sins. This is not the only moral outlook in the Hebrew Bible, but, as we see when we study the different understandings of the Mosaic covenant, it is an influential one. Balancing this view is God's rather gracious promise that he will never again so curse the ground or wreak destruction, apparently because he is pleased by Noah's sacrificial worship and realizes that human beings after all are bound to be weak (Genesis 8:21). Genesis 9:1 calls to mind the original blessing of man and woman (1:28), but 9:2 has a stronger note of enmity between humanity and the rest of animal life. Whereas verse 1:29 had allowed Adam only a vegetarian diet, verses 9:3–4 allow the eating of (bloodless) animal flesh. The concern with blood, the prime element of life, continues in 9:5–6, and the reason given for God's sanctions for the shedding of human blood is the image of God that human beings bear. Genesis 9:7 repeats the command to be fruitful, which becomes a key motif.

The covenant with Noah elaborated in Genesis 9:8–17 significantly extends to his descendants and all the animals that came out of the ark. God repeats the promise never again to destroy the Earth, and he sets the rainbow in the clouds as a lovely reminder of his promise. Because it extends to every living creature, the Noachite covenant is the most general or far-reaching. Some commentators consider the bow to be a divine weapon that God has put aside, as though the

Seal of Gilgamesh, heroic
searcher for immortality. Gold
plaque, Persian, about 700
B. C. E.   *(The Nelson-Atkins Museum
of Art, Kansas City, Missouri [Nelson
Fund])*

promise to all living creatures amounted to God's pledge not to make war on his
creation.

Insofar as his three sons Shem, Ham, and Japheth are said to be the source
of the repeopling of the entire Earth (9:19), Noah takes on the outline of a second
Adam. The incident of Ham's gazing at Noah's nakedness, along with his drunkenness itself, suggests both that this righteous progenitor often behaved on a less
than heroic level and that his son committed homosexual incest. Behind the cursing
of Canaan seems to lie an Israelite desire to depreciate the Canaanites, their
neighborly rivals, and to justify Israel's possession of originally Canaanite land.

10:1–11:26 THE NATIONS OF THE WORLD

Chapter 10 is often called "The Table of the Nations," and the author of
the Anchor Bible commentary on Genesis, E. A. Speiser, seems impressed by the
material that it organizes: "The whole is thus noteworthy for its wide scope and
analytical approach. As such, the Table stands out as a pioneering effort among
the ethnographic attempts of the ancient world."[9] Speiser goes on to note, however,
that this does not guarantee that the information in the Table squares with modern
ethnography, because the biblical groupings rely on several criteria—country,
language, ethnic affinities—whereas the modern classifications rely on linguistic
criteria. The effect of the Table is to show that the sons of Noah obeyed the
command to increase and multiply, and to suggest the geographic and ethnic
universe within which Israel, a newcomer on the historical scene, would operate.
The Semitic peoples are considered to be derived from Shem, while "the children
of Eber" probably refers to the Hebrews. In this perspective Israel began as just
one among the many different peoples, with the suggestion that its election by
God rested wholly on God's initiative.

The story of the Tower of Babel in Genesis 11:1–9 is in large part a mythic explanation of the many languages that humankind has developed. Shinar (probably derived from Mount Sinjar) came to be applied to all Mesopotamia, and the brick building described in Genesis 11:3–4 was more characteristic of Mesopotamia than of Palestine. The prideful attempt to build the tower therefore is attributed to Israel's later enemies. The wrongness of this mythic effort seems to stem from two sources. First, it expresses an independence of God and technological self-aggrandizement that could easily become dangerous for a creature. Second, insofar as it was intended to keep humanity unified it could have expressed disobedience to the divine command (Genesis 1:28, 9:1) to fill the Earth (by scattering). The Yahwistic style of the story shows in the anthropomorphic presentation of the deity, who seems jealous or afraid of humanity's technical prowess. Noteworthy is the "us" of Genesis 11:7, which most commentators take as referring to a heavenly court (God and his angels).

Genesis 11:10–26 amount to the genealogy of Abram/Abraham, whose traditions will inaugurate the second portion of Genesis. Whereas the interest of the primeval history was general—the origin and spread of the nations as a whole— the interest of the rest of Genesis will be particularist: the origins and development of Israel. The primeval history shows humanity burdened by the effects of its sins, but the ancestral stories that begin with Abraham appear as narratives about redemption—how God selected a group through whom he might raise humanity to a higher moral level. One link between the two histories occurs in Genesis 11:10, when the announcement that the descendants of Shem are to be enumerated brings echoes of the generations of Adam (5:1), the generations of Noah (6:9), and the generations of the sons of Noah (10:1). The last verses of chapter 11 suggest a migration from Mesopotamia to Canaan and leave the line of Noah, through Shem, focused on the man who will become the starting point of Yahwistic faith. The movement to this point has been centrifugal—out from Eden, closeness to God, and a tight band of just ancestors—but Abraham recenters it.

Recent scholarship has debated the role that the primeval history played in the canonical acceptance of Genesis (how the first eleven chapters were meant to be understood in the context of the fifth century B.C.E. establishment of the Torah as the directive literature of the Jewish people). Trying to mediate between such influential older scholars as Gerhard von Rad and Claus Westermann, Brevard Childs recently has agreed with von Rad and has considered the formula of toledot to be an explicit connector unifying all of Genesis. On the other hand, he agrees with the universalist stress in Westermann's position and concludes that the primeval history did not subordinate creation to redemption. Still, Childs rejects Westermann's downplaying of sin, and so does not see Genesis 2–3 as a depiction of what the human condition always has suggested.[10]

11:27–50:26 Period of the Ancestors

It used to be thought that the stories that comprise the second portion of Genesis referred back to the early centuries of the second millennium B.C.E. Recently, however, scholars have argued that the archeological evidence does not support the view that so early a period is reflected in the text. Rather, they have produced evidence that such supposedly early customs as a woman's being both wife and sister can be found in the tenth century and even later. In general, then, more skepticism reigns nowadays concerning the antiquity of the historical details that we find in the patriarchal stories. Nonetheless, these stories continue to attract literary attention and to be considered some of the most interesting examples of biblical artistry.[11]

11:27–25:18 ABRAHAM AND SARAH

11:27–12:9 The Call of Abraham

The arrival of Abraham is casual or matter of fact, which suggests that, however independent the materials of the primeval history originally were, the final redactors of Genesis believed they could make them flow into the traditions about Israel's beginnings smoothly. As early as Genesis 11:30, though, we are told that Abraham's wife was barren. The story of Abraham begins with a problem or an edge to it. Those who came to Genesis as believing Jews and who thought of Abraham as the father of their nation or peoplehood were reminded from the outset that special things had had to occur for their relation to Abraham to become what it did.

The call of Abraham, as Genesis 12:1–8 are sometimes described, depends for its significance on the background of the Table of the Nations that has preceded it. God, the Lord, gives Abraham a direct command, which literarily makes Abraham like Adam, Eve, Noah, and the few others of his predecessors in Genesis who had direct communication with God. We would distort the form of the story were we to take God's addressing Abraham literally, but there is no reason why we cannot conjecture that "Abraham" includes the notion that the father of the Jews was a person of profound, transforming religious experience.

As well, Abraham was a person of great courage, willing to sacrifice security. He is to go from his country, in a sort of exodus, to a land that God will show him. But this promise and the promise that his descendants will comprise a great nation make Abraham a corporate as well as an individual personality. In other words, his descendants, whom the biblical authors conceived to be present in his loins, were being promised land, national greatness, and blessing along with him. In Abraham God was making a new future. Genesis 12:3, in fact, says that all the nations — not just Israel or the Jews — will find a blessing in Abraham. Abraham responds to the call generously, departing Haran, his current country, and wandering to Canaan, where God promises that his descendants will live. He calls on the name of the Lord — to pray — regularly, and in effect we are witnessing the first phases of Yahwist religion. Such places as Shechem and the oak of Moreh were famous in Canaanite geography, and literarily they serve to tie Abraham to the land quite concretely.

12:10–14:24 Sarah, Lot, and the Four Kings

The story of Sarah's being taken into Pharaoh's harem (12:10–20) mainly serves to portray God as acting on behalf of the ancestress of the Israelites and so keeping alive his promise of a progeny, despite such natural obstacles as famine. Abraham is willing to lie and endanger Sarah and so emerges as a quite human first ancestor. Chapter 12, in fact, anticipates the main pattern of Genesis and Exodus: going to Egypt, encountering Pharaoh, plague, and exodus.

Chapter 13 tells us about the separation of Abraham and his nephew Lot.

Their wealth was so great that the land could not support both their flocks. (The hyperbole suggests that God's blessing has already taken effect.) Lot takes land near Sodom, prefiguring the later stories about Sodom and Gomorrah (Genesis 18:16–19:29). Abraham stays in Canaan, and the Lord repeats and expands his promise to give this land to Abraham's numerous progeny.

Chapter 14 contains materials that interrupt the narrative flow of 13 and 15. In addition, it is replete with historical and geographical details that distinguish it from most of the ancestral legends. The list of kings and warrings may have a historical basis, but current scholarship does not fully trust it. Abraham here departs from his usual role of shepherd and becomes a skillful warrior, caring for his nephew Lot, who had been captured. Thus, he is not only trustful toward God but loyal toward his kin. The blessing that Abraham receives from Melchizedek may serve the editorial interests of those who wanted to make the line of David fuse kingship and priesthood. Later tradition regarded Melchizedek as a righteous Gentile who accepted the God of Abraham. His own "God Most High" may be the paramount deity worshiped in Salem, the pre-Israelite Jerusalem. Bread and wine became key liturgical elements in both Judaism and Christianity. The Hebrew text is not as plain as the Revised Standard Version about who paid tithes to whom. A central effect of the story is to boost the status of Abraham's God and to show Abraham's total dependence on him. Seeing the victory that God gave Abraham, a noble observer such as Melchizedek is moved to admiration, if not indeed acceptance, of this God.

15:1–18:16 Covenants and Offspring

Chapter 15 is important, because it contains another expression of Abraham's faith. Abraham complains about his childlessness — a serious deficiency and sorrow in ancient Near Eastern culture. God renews his promise of progeny, here saying they will be as numerous as the stars. Genesis 15:6 has the influential line, "And he believed the Lord; and he reckoned it to him as righteousness," which admirers of biblical faith often cite. The remainder of the chapter fills out the divine promise in terms of a covenant that God makes. Verses 13 and 14 predict the sojourn in Egypt and Exodus. The sacrifice of animals seems to have been part of ancient protocol for making a treaty or convenantal pact, and fire regularly tokens the divine presence. Verses 18–21 explain how it was that Abraham's descendants, rather than he himself, came to inherit the promised land. One might say that this Abrahamic covenant implies Moses and Joshua, in the guise of Abraham's heirs who make plain the dimensions of God's promise.

Chapter 16 relates the desert tribes to the descendants of Abraham, through Abraham's concubine Hagar, an Egyptian. The customs of the times made Sarah's use of Hagar to obtain children legitimate. The conflict between the two women is another sign of the earthy Yahwistic author, who refuses to glamorize Israel's beginnings. Hagar is abused but receives comfort from God. The description of the child, Ishmael, suggests the free-spiritedness of the desert Bedouins. The story plays on personal and place names. The "messenger" of God mentioned in 16:7 is probably just divinity itself coming to comfort Hagar.

In Chapter 17 Abram has his name changed to Abraham, which signals a change in his destiny, and his covenant with God is redone. God repeats the promise of many offspring and inaugurates circumcision as the sign of the bond between Abraham's people and himself. This helps to particularize the general bond with humanity effected through the Noachite covenant. Circumcision was practiced by some of Israel's neighbors, but probably not as the signal mark of their dedication to their gods.[12]

Sarah, too, has her name changed, from its original Sarai, and she now receives the promise of a son, Isaac. The great ages of Abraham and Sarah only underscore the miraculous character of God's promise, and the laughter of both Abraham and Sarah (Genesis 17:17, 18:12) is winningly bawdy.

Chapter 18 brings another divine visit, this time in the person of three men/ angels. Abraham and Sarah extend the visitors a full hospitality, and the promise of Sarah's conception is specified to the next spring. Sarah denies that she laughed at hearing this, fearing the divinity, but the point is made that nothing is impossible with God.

18:16–19:38 Sodom and Gomorrah

Genesis 18:16–21 contrast the character of the people that God intends through Abraham with the wickedness of Sodom and Gomorrah (who are like humanity before the flood). Genesis 18:22–33 depict Abraham haggling with God on behalf of the righteous of Sodom and Gomorrah. Not only does this scene express the sense of justice that became central in Jewish ethics, it provided later adherents of biblical religion a model for frank personal relations with God. Note-worthy, too, is the willingness of YHWH to be moved from destruction to pres-ervation.

Sodom, however, proves beyond preservation, as the succeeding story in chapter 19 illustrates. Lot, seeming to carry the aura of Abraham, is hospitable to the visiting angels, but when they become the object of the Sodomites' lust he is willing to substitute his virginal daughters, as Abraham, perhaps less offensively, was willing to give Sarah to Pharaoh. The angels can fend for themselves, however, and they try to save Lot and his family from the coming destruction. Sodom and Gomorrah go down under a blaze of volcanic-like fire and brimstone (no watery flood). Lot is portrayed as vacillating, while his wife's becoming a pillar of salt shows the dire consequences of disobedience. The story at the end of chapter 19 confirms the mediocre impression we have received of Lot and gives Israel's neigh-bors, the Moabites and Ammonites, an unflattering beginning.

20:1–22:24 Threats to Sarah and Isaac

At the outset of chapter 20 we encounter a virtual repeat of the story in chapter 12 of Abraham's trying to pass Sarah off as his sister. Following Robert Alter's analysis, we may speak of this story, and other repetitions like it — for example, Hagar's second flight into the wilderness (21:9–21) — as "type-scenes" that reveal the conventional character of some (originally oral) portions of Israelite narrative tradition.[13] The notion is that narrators had certain stock-in-trade scenes or techniques into which they could plug their materials. The variations bring out further nuances — here, for instance, God's protection of Sarah is intensified, and Abraham is depicted as a prophet who has God's ear.

Chapter 21 brings the fulfillment of the divine promise of Isaac's birth. Isaac is circumcised into the Abrahamic covenant, and the elderly Sarah sees herself as an occasion for pleased laughter at God's wonderful powers. The second version of Hagar's being driven off shifts the focus from the previous rivalry between the two women to the potential rivalry between their two sons. The point to God's response to Abraham's displeasure seems to be to underscore the superiority of Isaac's line without denigrating the future of Ishmael. Indeed, God cares for Hagar and Ishmael, preserving their lives. The story of the dispute and covenant between Abraham and Abimelech mainly serves to explain the origin of the famous well at Beersheba, although it also implies Israelite rights to land (later) occupied by the Philistines, their enemies in the time of David.

Chapter 22, on the testing of Abraham and the binding of Isaac, begins with language similar to God's first command to Abraham (Genesis 12:1), which initiated his drama of faith. Whereas previously God asked Abraham to sacrifice his past, now God asks him to sacrifice his future. The rabbis expended much energy commenting on this text, finding in it virtually fathomless depths. Sacrificing human beings, especially children, to gods was acceptable in Abraham's milieu. Still, Abraham is asked to display an extremity of both faith and obedience, as is Isaac. The rabbis noted, however, that God himself also is faithful, in this case to his promise that through Isaac Abraham will have a great progeny, and in other cases to his Law (Torah). The happy outcome of the trial is a renewal of God's promise of a multitudinous progeny. The last verses of the chapter give the descendants of Abraham's brother and introduce Bethuel, a parent of Rebekah.

23:1–25:18 The Advance of the Promise to Abraham

Chapter 23, concerning the burial of Sarah, shows us Abraham's concern for his wife. It also shows how Oriental peoples have long been apt to transact

The binding of Isaac, from *The Sacrifice of Abraham* by Peter Paul Rubens. *(The Nelson-Atkins Museum of Art, Kansas City, Missouri [Nelson Fund])*

business. The cave of Machpelah becomes the ancestral burial site of Abraham's line; Isaac, Rebekah, Jacob, and Leah all come to rest there. Genesis 23:4 has the theme of Abraham's being a stranger and sojourner — his people only will be settled when Joshua leads them into the promised land. The hold on the land, therefore, is fragile.

Chapter 24 begins with Abraham's exacting a promise from his servant that the servant will find Isaac a wife from Abraham's original kinfolk in Haran. The idea is not to corrupt the line with Caananite blood (in view of the later enmity between the peoples). Yet Isaac must stay in the vicinity of the land that God has promised to Abraham, and not return to Haran. To swear an oath by placing one's hand under another's thigh was to solemnize one's word by attaching it to the seat of life.

The story of the securing of Rebekah is another type-scene, repeated when it comes to the securing of Rachel for Jacob (Genesis 29:1–20). Rebekah and Rachel — like Eve, Sarah, and Hagar — are strong women, remarkable for their intelligence, diligence, and wit. The story has a marked motif of providence, God's guiding the progress of the ancestral line. This aspect, in fact, is what convinces Laban and Bethuel that Rebekah should go (24:50). We should note that Rebekah herself is given an important say (24:58), and that the blessing in 24:60 is in keeping with the theme that Abraham will have a multitudinous offspring. The chapter ends on a lovely note, suggesting a tender romance between Rebekah and Isaac (who seems a somewhat passive, sensitive type, led by his father to the brink of death and lonely after his mother's death).

The last portion of the cycle of stories about Abraham includes a note on his further descendants and a confirmation that Isaac was his only full heir. Abraham dies full in years, his role completed, and he is buried with Sarah in the cave of Machpelah. The last note gives us the descendants of Abraham through Ishmael, and these, along with the previously mentioned descendants begotten with Keturah, make Abraham the ancestor of many Arab tribes.

25:19–37:1 ISAAC AND JACOB

This new block of materials begins as a parallel to the brief note on the descendants of Ishmael, but, in fact, the line of Isaac and then Jacob becomes the dominant interest of the next twelve chapters. And whereas the promise to Abraham of numerous offspring unified the tales about the first patriarch, an additional theme — sibling rivalry — unifies the cycle of tales about Jacob.

25:19–26 Jacob and Esau

Isaac, like Abraham, has a barren wife, but his prayers quickly make Rebekah fertile. From the womb her twins battle, prefiguring the struggles between Israel and Edom, the two peoples they shall beget. The text suggests that Rebekah received an oracle, at a sanctuary of God, predicting the submission of Esau to Jacob. The Yahwistic author is again both graphic and unflattering, showing the contrast between the two sons, the different preferences of Isaac and Rebekah, the impulsive nature of Esau, and the wiliness of Jacob. Jacob gets Esau to forfeit the rights he has as the first-born, suggesting how Israel came to prevail over Edom.

26:1–35 Isaac

Chapter 26 gives us rather fragmentary information about Isaac, most of it echoes of Abraham—the command to go forth, the promise of progeny, the attempt to pass his wife off as his sister. Isaac deals with Abimelech, as Abraham had done, similarly prospers and similarly names places later famous. Abimelech sees the good fortune of Isaac, attributes it to his God, and so makes a pact with him and blesses him. The chapter ends on the sour note that Esau and his wives made life bitter for Isaac and Rebekah, which both makes Jacob's coming deceit in stealing Esau's blessing more palatable and sets up Jacob's departure.

27:1–45 Isaac's Blessing

Isaac, old and nearly blind, asks Esau for savory game, that he may eat a last pleasant meal, give his elder son his final blessing (Isaac apparently does not know that Esau has sold his birthright), and die content. Rebekah connives with Jacob to get Isaac to bless Jacob instead of Esau. Both are willing to deceive Isaac and lie, so convinced are they of the (nearly magical) significance or potency of such a departing word. The blessing in verses 27–29 is quite poetic. Esau is anguished, because, according to ancient views of the independent power of the solemn word, the blessing cannot be recalled, and the blessing that he receives is largely a negative mirroring of what Jacob has stolen, except for the final promise that Esau will break free of Jacob's rule. The price of Jacob's gain, however, is the hatred of his brother and the necessity that he flee for his life. Rebekah, too, receives some just deserts, as she realizes that their hatred could cost her both her sons.[14]

27:46–28:22 Jacob's Journey Begins

Rebekah uses her upset with the wives of Esau as a pretext for sending Jacob away: He should find a wife from the land of their ancestors. (At this point the editors seem to have woven in another source.) The blessing from Isaac on which Jacob departs links him to the promises to Abraham. Esau does not pursue Jacob —he may have been somewhat reconciled—and he tries to assuage his mother by marrying wives of different stock (from Ishmael). The dream recorded in Genesis 28:10–22 is famous as "Jacob's Ladder." It confirms the Abrahamic promise and is another revelation of Yahweh. Jacob names the site of the dream *Bethel*: the house of God. The notes of awesomeness and "gate of heaven" reflect a profound religious experience. Jacob vows that in return for a safe prosecution of his mission he will make the Lord his God and tithe to the Lord's shrine. The notion of a revelation coming through a dream is characteristic of the Elohist.

29:1–30:24 Jacob and Rachel

Jacob's meeting with Rachel suggests a type-scene on the order of the servant's meeting with Rebekah in chapter 24. His uncle Laban first cheats him of Rachel (fitting enough treatment for a cheater, as both the motif of blindness—like that of Isaac—and the explicit statement in verse 29:26 about the rights of the elder offspring suggest). Then eventually—after working two terms of seven years— Jacob has both daughters, the elder Leah and the younger Rachel, whom he loves. The sons of Jacob will be the tribes of Israel (Jacob's other name), and the first

four come from Leah. Rachel is barren—as Sarah and Rebekah initially were—
and so gives Jacob her maid Bilhah, by whom two more tribal sons are born. Leah,
now also barren, gives Jacob her maid Zilpah, from whom two further sons are
born. Leah regains fertility with the help of mandrakes, and two more sons come
forth. Having produced six heirs for Jacob, Leah somewhat poignantly thinks that
perhaps now Jacob will honor her. Finally God "remembers" Rachel and answers
her prayers for children, giving her Joseph, who will dominate the last chapters of
Genesis, and Benjamin. By making it necessary for God to open barren wombs,
the stories stress the providential character of Israel's coming into being.

30:25–32:3 Jacob and Laban

Rachel having given him a son, Jacob wants to leave Laban, whom he has
been serving as a profitable laborer. They dicker about the terms of his leaving,
and the wily Jacob resolves to protect himself and get the better of the uncle who
had outsmarted him with Leah. The story of Jacob's getting the flocks to beget
striped, speckled, and spotted offspring relies on ancient views that influences on
parents would be passed on directly to children. Jacob prospers from this practice
but thereby incurs the disfavor of both Laban and his sons. Jacob feels it a divine
call to return to Canaan, the prosperity he has gained is linked to God's favor
(and God's displeasure at Laban's injustices to Jacob), and Leah and Rachel agree
with the plan to return home.

By stealing the household gods Rachel gains power for Jacob over Laban's
household. The way that Jacob flees may indicate that he had been adopted into
Laban's family, and the restraints God puts on Laban continue the motif of a
providential protection of Abraham's line. Rachel's sitting on the household gods
while supposedly menstruating is meant to ridicule such idols. Jacob's anger and
his speech of self-defense seem stronger than Laban's counter-arguments, but the
constraints of God lead Laban to suggest a covenant of peace between them. What
eventuates seems a combination of a peace pact and a boundary agreement. The
upshot is that Jacob gets away.

32:4–33:20 Jacob Reencounters Esau

In deciding to return home, Jacob has to come to grips with the cloud under
which he left. His announcement to Esau of his homecoming is notably deferential.
The enigmatic reply that he gets frightens him with the thought that Esau still
bears him hatred. Jacob is similarly deferential with God, reminding him that the
homegoing was God's idea and also reminding him of the Abrahamic promise that
Jacob carries. Jacob sends plenteous gifts ahead of him and tries to secure the safety
of his immediate family. The incident at Peniel, where Jacob wrestles with the
angel, is meant to explain how Jacob's name was changed to Israel. It shows, as
well, the tenacious character of the great ancestor, who will not let go until he
has gotten the (divine) blessing. He does not get the name of his foe—to possess
the divine name would have implied power over God—and he feels fortunate to
have met divinity face to face and lived (ancient thought frequently held that
perceiving the divine sanctity would bring instant death). The end of chapter 32
explains an Israelite taboo.

Jacob's actual meeting with Esau is something of a (positive) anticlimax,
because Esau fully accepts him (affirming the impression we could get from the

first characterization of them that Esau was the better, if the slower, of the two). Esau is impressed with how Jacob has flourished (although he himself has plenty), and Jacob's gracious speech—probably as much sincere as strategic (he has been changed by his wrestling with God)—has the touching note that seeing the face of his previously estranged brother is like seeing the face of God. Still, Jacob does not place his household into Esau's hands but goes off to settle apart at Shechem, which later became a prime sanctuary for the confederacy of the twelve tribes of Israel.

34:1–31 The Rape of Dinah

The story of the rape of Dinah, which seems mainly from the Yahwist, serves a twofold literary purpose. It explains the later landlessness of the tribes of Simeon and Levi, and it shows the deceitfulness of Jacob extending into the generation of his children. The action of Shechem was mitigated by his love for Dinah, and the Hebrew text does not make it obvious that Dinah was completely unwilling. On the other hand, Hamor and Shechem gloss over this aspect of the proposed wedding when they explain its advantages to their fellow Canaanites. The tactic of attacking the Canaanites when they were still sore from circumcision has its grimly humorous side, but the overall effect of the story is further to call into question the character of Israel's first family, as well as further to explain the enmity between Israel and Canaan.

35:1–37:1 Final Traditions about Jacob and Esau

Chapter 35 gives us some final information about Jacob, most of it from the Elohist. Jacob further consecrates the shrine at Bethel, pilgrimage to which later became customary. The theme of purification from foreign influences is struck and Genesis 35:5 sounds a note of the confusion that God regularly caused when warring on Israel's behalf (see I Samuel 14:15, Exodus 23:27, for example). There follow a repeat of the changing of Jacob's name to Israel and a repeat of the divine promise to Abraham, both of which emphasize the divine guidance of the twelve tribes. Rachel gives birth to Benjamin, the twelfth and youngest of Israel's tribal sons. Reuben commits incest with Jacob's concubine Bilhah, the mother of his brothers Dan and Naphtali, which may explain why, despite his status as the first-born, he did not predominate in Israel. Isaac, who seemed at his last gasp when Jacob originally left home, finally dies in full ripeness, jointly buried by his two sons, who apparently have remained reconciled.

Chapter 36 gives us the genealogy of the line descended from Esau, the first son of Isaac. Throughout, Genesis has been concerned with genealogy, apparently both to explain Israel's relations with other people and to clarify how this singular, chosen people developed. The lineages suggested for different branches of Edom are of questionable historical value. Verses 6–8 tidy up the relations between Esau and Jacob, as though there were no animosity in their original separation, and likely represent interests of the final priestly redactor.

37:2–50:26 JOSEPH

Chapter 37 first appears linked to chapter 36 as the story of the line of Jacob, the second son of Isaac, which understandably would follow on the genealogy of the line of Esau, the elder son. But, in fact, the final chapters of Genesis are a novella, unified around the theme of discord and peace in the family of Jacob,[15] and they stand alone. They also play an important role in the whole of Genesis that the final editing has produced.

37:2–36 Joseph Sold into Slavery in Egypt

The theme of sibling rivalry, which we have seen poisoning relations between Cain and Abel, and between Jacob and Esau, continues in the final chapters of Genesis, and by now we realize that it expresses a perceptive psychology and might, in the authors' eyes, explain much of the discord in later Israelite history. Reuben and Judah play the dominant roles among the elder brothers, Reuben half-heartedly trying to save Joseph and Judah motivated by both greed and fear of an actual murder. Joseph's dreams bespeak his special powers, given him by God. The sons let Jacob infer that the blood on the robe belongs to Joseph, thereby deceiving the one from whom they got their deceitfulness. (Jacob, it appears, is something of a tragic character; earlier his wiliness and here his indulgence seem to be flaws of considerable consequence.) The Ishmaelites, of course, were distant relatives, through Abraham's concubine Hagar. "Midianites" (and "Medianites," in the Hebrew text) were synonymous with "Ishmaelites," with such further overtones as "quarrelsome" and "traders." The text, therefore, brims with suggestive word plays.

38:1–30 Judah and Tamar

Judah, the progenitor of the tribe that eventually prevailed in Israelite/Jewish history, now appears. In the background of the interaction between Judah and Tamar is the custom that a childless widow had the right to gain posterity through a brother of her dead husband. Tamar is clever enough to outwit Judah's denial of this right, both conceiving her desired child and putting Judah embarrassingly in the wrong. The author is likely deliberate in exposing the double standard of sexual morality that held in ancestral times, and there is no doubt that Tamar is to be considered admirable. The twins to whom she gives birth advance the line of Judah, but their uterine struggles, like those of Jacob and Esau, prefigure a later rivalry. It is from Perez, the first-born, that David, the great king, will descend. Once again, the literary tradition of J has provided an earthy, unvarnished account of the people's beginnings, no doubt precisely to make their very mixed or human character clear.

39:1–23 Joseph's Success and Misfortune

The earthiness continues in the J story of Joseph and Potiphar's wife, but here for the purpose of showing Joseph's integrity. The theme of providence enters early on, as Genesis 39:2 attributes Joseph's initial success in Egypt to the Lord's being with him. As with Abraham and Jacob, material prosperity is taken as a sign of God's favoring presence. Potiphar's wife exemplifies both foreign and feminine duplicity. Even in prison, however, God is with Joseph and, therefore, he is relatively prosperous. Literary analysts sometimes use this story to illustrate the careful composition characteristic of many biblical narratives.[16]

40:1–41:57 Joseph Interprets Dreams

Just as Joseph first stood out as gifted with pregnant dreams, incurring his brother's jealousy thereby, so he works his way back into favor through this divine gift. Joseph's interpretations of the dreams of the fortunate chief butler and the unfortunate chief baker are allegorical, seeking a one-to-one correspondence between symbols and events. The same is true of his interpretation of Pharaoh's dreams of cows and corn. Joseph makes it plain that his prophetic power comes from God (implying also that God controls all other events). The repetitiveness of the stories serves to set up a memorable rhythm and enhance an audience's pleasure (it can both follow easily and note significant alterations in the pattern). Joseph prospers beyond even his original status with Pharaoh, and the text gives us the origin from him of the two important peoples Ephraim and Manasseh.

42:1–45:28 Joseph and His Brothers Revisited

Joseph, who had been placed in a pit and then sold into slavery by his brothers, now has his brothers placed in his hands — a vivid reminder of his origins, lest he become fully Egyptianized. Exacting a measure of revenge or justice, he recalls his original dreams that his brothers would bow down to him and resolves to put them through a certain trial. They perceive their imprisonment and testing as just recompense for their treatment of Joseph, whom they continue not to recognize. When they are allowed to return to Jacob, on the condition that they leave Simeon hostage and return with Benjamin, their father's full upset with them waves forth. Jacob/Israel takes the brothers' confession to Joseph that they have a youngest son quite personally, intensifying the motif of "the parent wronged" and so perhaps again recalling his own wrongs toward Isaac. Once again repetition keeps us involved with the main themes of the story.

Returned to Egypt, the brothers bow down to Joseph (Genesis 43:26), fulfilling his original dream. The details about Joseph's emotional reactions to the sight of Benjamin (his full brother, because the two were both born of Rachel), humanize the story, while the details about the Egyptians' desire to stand separate from Jews anticipate the enmities of the Hebrews' slavery in Egypt and their Exodus.

Chapter 44 repeats the motif of money's being put in the brothers' sacks, this time to the point of putting Benjamin into Joseph's hands and sharpening the brothers' guilt before their father. The brothers finally refer to the supposed death of Joseph (still concealing their own having sold him), and finally emotion overcomes Joseph. In revealing himself to them he implicitly forgives them their sins against him and refers the whole nest of happenings to the providence of God. There is an interesting motif of fatherhood, God having made Joseph a father to the Egyptian people who is now able to care for his own father Jacob and his whole family. This Pharaoh seems remarkably generous to Joseph's family, in view of the bad character one of his successors will be assigned in the book of Exodus. So, Joseph gets back his father, in the welcome news that his father still lives, while Israel gets back his beloved son and so feels ready to die.

46:1–47:31 Jacob in Egypt

Israel goes down to Egypt, beginning his journey by sacrificing at Beersheba, the shrine of Isaac. The vision he has blesses this venture and promises an eventual return from Egypt, no doubt implying the Exodus. The genealogy in Genesis 46:8–27 comes from the priestly tradition and seems deliberately designated to total seventy, a number symbolic of fullness. Jacob and Dinah would be the final two. It is remarkable that Jacob blesses Pharaoh, and Jacob's remark about his days being few and evil seems another indication that as humanity progressed it lost

A camel market in Gaza. *(Used with permission of the photographer, Wolfgang Roth)*

vigor and became less than it was in the first generations after Adam, after Noah, and after Abraham. The Egyptians who sell themselves into slavery to Pharaoh through Joseph suggest an ironic preview of the Israelite slaves whom Moses will later free. Joseph's dealings appear both wise and fair, somewhat in contrast to the deceitful shrewdness we are accustomed to find in Jacob. Israel makes Joseph swear formally that he will bury him with his fathers.

48:1–22 The Blessing of Ephraim and Manasseh

Chapter 48 brings together several different traditions about Jacob/Israel's final blessing of Joseph's sons. Genesis 48:8–10 is reminiscent of Isaac's wanting to bless his sons Esau and Jacob before he dies, as witness the motifs of blindness and the younger's receiving the blessing of the elder. The account seems designed to explain the prevalence of Ephraim over Manasseh. The "one mountain slope" of Genesis 48:22 is Shechem.

49:1–33 Jacob's Last Testament

The final legacy of Jacob, spoken forth in all the effective power that ancient people attributed to solemn words, characterizes the twelve tribes, in both their virtues or positive attributes and their defects. Thus we see recalled Reuben's incest, the violence of Simeon and Levi against Shechem, the later preeminence of Judah, and characteristics of all the rest. Clearly, Judah and Joseph rated highest in the eyes of the authors and editors who put together the patriarch Israel's last testament. Jacob charges the sons to bury him with Abraham and Isaac in the cave of Machpelah and dies peacefully.

50:1–26 The Funeral of Jacob and Death of Joseph

Joseph arranges for Jacob to be mourned in all solemnity in Egypt (another remarkable happening), and then he journeys back to Canaan to fulfill his father's charge about the burial. The brothers still feel guilty about their treatment of Joseph, or are afraid of Joseph's power in Egypt, so they try to make it part of Jacob's last testament that Joseph should forgive them. The climax of the entire novella comes in verse 50:20, where Joseph says that what they meant for evil God meant for good — the theme of divine providence nailed down one last time. As Joseph is about to die he predicts that the brothers (in the person of their offspring?) will return to occupy the land promised to Abraham, to Isaac, and to Jacob. According to tradition Joseph finally was buried at Shechem (see Joshua 24:32), but Genesis ends with him placed in a coffin in Egypt.

HISTORICAL BACKGROUND

In the process of exposing the text we have suggested many of the traditions that run through it and some of the historical background that it either presupposes or wants to interpret. Still, it will profit us to ask about the historical background more plainly, so that what we have just studied may fall into its proper context.

Biblical archeologists and historians have labored to elaborate what the cultural conditions likely were in the time of the ancestors, but to date nothing like a full reconstruction is available. The text of Genesis itself is sometimes concerned with interpreting how certain peoples arose or certain lands were gained, but even in these cases descriptions or genealogies have been set in the service of ideological interests. Thus, the overall framework of the primeval history relates the one Creator God to the Gentile nations, while the cycles of ancestral stories focus on how the divine providence moved on to focus on the line of Abraham, Isaac, and Jacob. The history of greatest interest therefore is the beginnings of Israel, the twelve tribes thought to have stemmed from Jacob, with most attention lavished upon Joseph and Judah. Presupposed, certainly, are a wandering early life in Canaan, where the ancestral tribes lived as shepherds. The fact that the major traditions were organized after the Exodus, when the unified tribes possessed the land in Canaan, has shaped the whole conception of what was promised to Abraham and his offspring.

Norman K. Gottwald, distinguishing between the sequence of history-like themes that were preserved in the large block of materials in Law/Former Prophets and the core of the narrative activities that probably generated these materials in cultic situations around 1200 B.C.E., makes the work of Moses and Joshua (the Exodus and Conquest) the original core. That implies, of course, that all of the materials of Genesis were shaped after this original nucleus. Gottwald hypothesizes that first traditions about Jacob, who would have been considered the ancestor of the northern tribes of the then unified confederacy, and second traditions about Abraham and Isaac, to whom the southern tribes would have traced themselves, were added to this original core of Exodus/Conquest. The traditions about Joseph would have entered under the rubric of explaining how Israel had gotten to Egypt (and so subsequently come to fall into slavery and need deliverance). Certain further elaborations on the theme of Exodus and Conquest, which we consider in subsequent chapters, would have expanded the original core "internally" (in terms of its own themes).

Gottwald calls the materials likely assembled to this point of the reconstructed literary process "G" (for *Grundlage*, which means foundation in German), and he thinks of them as a pool of traditions, common to all the tribes, upon which both J and E drew. The Yahwist then added traditions about the creation of the world (the primeval history), which the Elohist further amplified, and thereby "Genesis" came into view (but not final editing) as a preface to the original story of and interest in the Exodus from Egypt and the Conquest of the promised land.[17]

For our present purposes, the point of theories such as this, which (with variations) are now accepted by mainstream academic analysts of the Hebrew Bible, is that they suggest we place Genesis in the historical framework of a people trying to lay a foundation for their national self-conception. "In the beginning" therefore ought to connote not just the creation of the physical world but also the origins of the people of Israel. The two ideas are linked, insofar as the authors and editors of Genesis thought that one God was the main mover in both processes. They are further linked, in that these authors and editors discerned the nature of the one God and judged the purposes of history, both that of primeval times and that of the recent times in which Israel had taken shape, through the lens of their people's experience, especially the experience of Exodus and Conquest.

In other words, Genesis and the other biblical books assume that readers know about the formation of the people under Moses and Joshua. Gottwald himself, following in the footsteps of such prior scholars as Martin Noth and George Mendenhall, has studied extensively the likely social dynamics of the unification of the Israelite tribes, with the result that he tends to read many biblical texts as reflections of a process by which "Israel" arose from a group of sometimes oppressed, sometimes mutually antagonistic tribes.[18]

Most hearers or readers of the biblical traditions, down through the many different stages of their compilation and editing, would instinctively have situated them by reference to the Exodus and Conquest. This would not have diminished the status of Abraham or Jacob, let alone the status of the Creator who dominates Genesis 1 and 2, but it would have cast them all in the light of the people's "founding" through the events of the Exodus, the wandering in the desert, the Mosaic covenant, and the Conquest of the promised land. At still later stages of Israelite or Jewish history, during the monarchy of David and Solomon, or during the Exile in Babylon, or during the postexilic efforts to refashion the people, new overtones would, of course, have been sounding. By the time that Genesis became a canonical text, in the postexilic period, the purposes of God originally sketched in the primeval history or discerned in the experiences of the ancestors would have been extended through numerous later chapters. Similarly, the apparently original traditional axis of Exodus/Conquest would also have been reset, especially through reflection on the painful experiences of the exile to Babylon.

One result of this background, at the least the main outlines of which Israelite and Jewish audiences would always have possessed, was to give the Bible numerous "centers." We only see the fuller meaning of this phenomenon when we have studied the Prophets and the Writings and so surveyed the entire range of Tanak, but even at this point, when we have just begun with Torah, it can profit us to refer to it. The traditional reader of Torah could focus on Genesis, stressing either the original creation of God, or the somewhat historical beginnings of peculiarly biblical faith with Abraham, or the constitution of the actual Israelite people through Jacob. Similarly, traditional readers could meditate on the command of God to be fruitful, multiply, and subdue the Earth, or on the invitation to believe in God's promise of land and progeny, or on the providential unfolding of history with Joseph. Most likely, traditional readers in fact subordinated these themes to the theme of Exodus and Conquest, but both the religious and the historical interests of readers could lead them to rethink the materials of Genesis or of the other books of Torah from different "centers." This is one reason why the Bible has fascinated countless generations, and one reason why today's literary techniques, which often emphasize the variable and independent life that texts can assume as they interact with different readers, are so stimulating in biblical studies.

LITERARY INTENT

It should already be plain that Genesis was not "written" as our present-day assumptions about "books" tend to suggest that writing occurs. Every likelihood is that no single author ever sat down and composed Genesis, beginning at chapter 1 and ending with chapter 50. Even the generalist analysis that we have performed shows that many blocks of material are involved. For example, the main blocks that we distinguished — the primeval history and the three cycles of ancestral traditions — all probably had an originally oral form and were collected in several ways before they were fitted into their present patterns. Moreover, we saw that within each block different sorts of materials — genealogies, stories about the origins of places, type-scenes of betrothal and blessing, and many more — had been woven together.

A comprehensive answer to the question of why Genesis was written would have to include indications of why each of the units that compose Genesis was written, as well as suggestions of what such editors as J, E, and P intended. The most general answer, in such a context, is that the Israelites were keenly interested in their past and their origins. No doubt many other peoples have been similarly interested, as the wealth of the world's traditional literatures, both written and oral, testifies. The desire to define who one is recurs generation after generation, and regularly the accomplishment of this desire turns out to include who one has been in past generations. So each bit of tradition about an ancestor such as Abraham or Sarah begged preservation. For the basic human task of situating themselves in the world, the generations that developed the biblical literature retained what they could of the stories and memories passed down to them.

There are some specifications of this general human tendency when we come to Israelite traditions, however, and it may profit us to preview them here. Whereas virtually all people show some interest in their tribal history and generate stories to preserve it, the people of Israel thought they had a uniquely interesting past. Such a thought, to be sure, occurred to many other peoples, and students of world-historical or world-religious literature are accustomed to finding peoples as diverse as the Japanese and the Greeks depicting their land as the center of the Earth. On the other hand, the Israelite traditions joined the theme of distinctiveness to the theme of a unique deity who had worked singular prodigies to ensure this people's existence. Furthermore, in the Bible both the richness of human historicity — the very concrete, earthy, personal sort of existence that we find in the patriarchal tales — and the nearness of deity gained a clarity unusual, if not unique, in world literature. Whereas the majority of the literatures that we would naturally compare to the Bible are basically mythical, their action taking place outside of ordinary space and time, the biblical literature, largely because of the vividness of the traditional memories (the striking character of the main actors and events) and the link of this vividness to "promises" of God, shows us people recognizably like ourselves the readers. It is hard not to think that the authors and editors of the biblical materials were motivated to compose books such as Genesis not only to preserve tribal memories and aid in the processes of self-definition but also to portray the stunning reality — view of nature, society, self, and divinity —that the traditions either enclosed or on reflection provoked.

A generation ago it was popular to signalize biblical literature as offering the first linear view of human time, in contrast to the cyclical or mythical views dominating other world literatures. Further research has made more nuance necessary, but it remains true that such stories as those of the Yahwist have little parallel in other people's writings. They so illumine human nature — motivation, humor, irony, passion, and the rest — that through them Western peoples took a major step toward the sense of reality that came to prevail in traditional Western culture. Eastern peoples no doubt acted much as Western people did, but a different literary tradition — set of interpretational models — meant that Chinese or Indian reality differed from that of Europe. The biblical authors and editors certainly did not foresee such historical consequences, but they likely did intuit that the way what it meant to be human was being described or proposed in their traditions was alluring, invigorating, deeply challenging, and deeply consoling.

In other words, the story of God's promises to Abraham was not simply a bit of tradition relevant to how the tribes of Israel had come to their present situation. It was also a concrete bit of philosophy or theology or wisdom about how to live. When Abraham believed and it was accredited to him as righteousness, he not only said yes to the process through which Israel believed it had arisen, but he also made present in history, perhaps for the first time articulately, a way of dealing with the mystery of life that was stunning in its depth of implication. Many questions, no doubt, attend the matter of what God's revelations to Abraham might have been — how they might have transpired. We deal with questions such as this later on. But the end result of Abraham's "faith," whether we take it in its historical sense of how a specific patriarch in fact oriented himself in the world or in its literary sense of how a character produced by human art took such a stand and implicitly proposed it to all who read about him, was a very provocative claim: Do this and you will "live" (see also Amos 5:4, 6).

LASTING SIGNIFICANCE

This reflection leads right into the last aspect of our discussion of Genesis. What stands out as the lasting significance of the historical, artistic, and other efforts that we can discern in the process through which this biblical book came to be?

First, Genesis, in fact, has been a main, if not the main, factor in the Western sense of creation. By "creation" we mean both the process by which the world came to be and the span of physical nature. Nowadays the explorations of theoretical physicists such as Stephen Hawking have made the instant at which the universe came to be a matter of intense scientific interest.[19] The methods and conceptual frameworks of such scientists obviously differ dramatically from the approach of the authors of Genesis, but we can find them pursuing the same goal: understanding the beginning. Indeed, perceptive scientists realize that even if they develop equations that make coherent the unfolding of the universe from a primal explosion of hydrogen, questions remain about where the hydrogen "came from" and what caused it to explode. These questions may be of an order that astrophysics, as geniuses such as Hawking now practice it, cannot answer or must consider outside its methodological province. Yet in themselves they certainly are legitimate questions that justify the mythical or commonsensical inquiries into the beginning put forward in the Bible and other world literatures.

Indeed, the basic explanation of the beginning that Genesis provides continues to ground the world views of hundreds of millions of people. Some of them still think in terms of the myths depicting God's speaking the world into being in seven days or placing Adam and Eve in the Garden, whereas others are considerably more differentiated in their understanding of the world's fashioning by God, but the case can be suggested, if not indeed made, that Jews, Christians, and Muslims all have inherited a basic orientation in reality that both owes a great deal to Genesis and sets them apart from other peoples. According to this orientation a divinity free of the world has fashioned the world according to its own designs and good pleasure.

The implications of this orientation include the assumption that the world therefore is intelligible, that the world is purposeful (or teleological), and that all of creation, but especially human beings, have a great dignity, with attendant rights to respect. Certainly present-day science does not accept this assumption, at least in all such entailments, but neither does it provide compelling reasons for rejecting the assumption as irrational. For example, when present-day science refuses to speak of teleology and would want to place considerable qualifications before asserting the intelligibility of nature (as some biblical writers might also want to do), it depends upon an interaction between the data of empirical investigation and the human mind that virtually no epistemologist (student of knowledge) of note would consider clarified definitively.

This first indication of the continuing relevance of Genesis has implicitly focused on the opening chapters. A second relevance appears when we turn our gaze to the ancestral traditions and reflect on the depiction of human nature accomplished there. Abraham, Sarah, Isaac, Rebekah, Jacob, and Esau are all notable "personalities," however limited the manner of their presentation makes our access to them. As we have noted, the authors of Genesis, especially the authors in the J tradition, seem deliberately to have underscored the mixed motivation and flawed character of the leading ancestors. Abraham lies and is willing to imperil Sarah. Sarah's faith in God's promises, like Abraham's faith, falters from time to time. Jacob, especially, is flawed, his deceitfulness leaving us with much ambiguity about the morality by which Israel came to be God's people. Even God himself does things that give us pause, most notably in the binding of Isaac. At the least, therefore, the stories of the ancestors that we find in Genesis prompt us to ask whether our often sanitized, black-and-white views of "religion" and "morality" hold up.

Moreover, some of the descriptions of the experiences of the ancestors reveal a penetrating psychological awareness that even after the rise of psychoanalysis still commands respect. We have noted the theme of sibling rivalry, and we could have added the theme of parental preference, perhaps most notably in the case of Rebekah's meddling on Jacob's behalf. A more stunning example, however, is the incident of Jacob's wrestling with the angel (God) at Peniel (Genesis 32:22–32). This is where Jacob becomes Israel, and shrewd readers will have noted that in addition to the text's providing an explanation for where the clan-founder got his name and whence "Peniel" arose, it also says some remarkable things about religious experience.

Most notably, this experience is presented as occurring when Jacob is quite alone and afraid. He is on the verge of returning to his home, after a long absence, and he does not know how his brother Esau, whose hatred he had to flee, will receive him. He has sent away his family, to ensure their safety, and we may picture him as forced to confront a welter of deep thoughts and emotions. To be sure, the text does not elaborate on any such thoughts. An important part of its disposition, if not of its genius, is to let actions do much of the explaining. But if the Jacob later considered worthy to be the primary ancestor of the united tribes is decisively presented in this incident, and if his best characteristic seems to be his tenacity in struggling for God's blessing, then the psychological juncture at which this episode occurs probably is not incidental or unintended.

It seems quite legitimate, therefore, to point out that much of what a person such as Jacob would be struggling with at a juncture such as his uncertain homegoing would be the meaning of what had happened to him in the first half of his life, including the meaning of the intense early experiences of love and strife that had marked his character in childhood. Jacob is praised by the biblical authors for hanging on, continuing to struggle after such meaning. The mystery of God — no genuine deity ever yields us its name, certainly not the deity queried by Moses (Exodus 3:13) — must be accepted, although not passively. In the figure of Jacob we see a very active struggle to gain a blessing — a sense that one's life is meaningful and good — from the divine mysteriousness in which human beings live, move, and have their being. Moreover, we see the tendency of such "religious" questions to surface not apart from the central issues of our family life or personal destiny but in the midst of them.

The incident of Jacob's wrestling with the angel is but one of numerous cases in which what we earlier called the biblical "humanism" shines forth. In the Bible "God" and "humanity" are correlative terms. Human beings contend with God when they contend with the most significant — fearsome, beautiful, challenging — elements of their own lives. This is not to say that God is only a collection or projection from such elements. Nothing could be farther from the biblical theology, which always stresses the freedom of the creative divinity. But it is to say that the humanity we see displayed in the ancestral traditions of Genesis challenges both most of our present-day humanism and most of our supposedly biblical faith.

A personality such as Jacob wants to prosper, to be fruitful, and to defeat death as long as possible. A personality such as Abraham wants children, has a passion to believe, and feels bound to haggle with God on behalf of just people whom God seems to be treating wrongly. Thus, "God" emerges as the inmost interlocutor of humanity at its most vital. The color purple, rather than the color gray, most befits divinity. Biblical oaths are sworn on the power of procreation, and biblical promises intend great fertility, in numerous children and rich land. The religion of Genesis is amazingly concrete and alive, yet it is bounded by death, as realistic human existence must be. It is mysterious, and it is unsubmissive to tidy human controls, as divine existence must be. And in its correlation of the two, biblical humanism remains perennially significant — a challenge still fresh today.

GLOSSARY

Anthropomorphic   Personifying; treating something nonhuman as though it were human.

Apocalyptic   A supposed revelation about the end of the world or God's coming to render justice; the sort of literature that purports to derive from heavenly visions and usually offers a view of the future consoling to those who suffer for the faith.

Differentiated   Separated, developed. For example, a differentiated consciousness distinguishes myth from history and history from philosophy (without isolating them).

Etiological myths   Stories that employ nonordinary agents or circumstances to explain the origins of something.

Genealogy   A listing of descendants, to establish lineage and personal history.

Grundlage (G)   A source common to J and E and so called (in German) the foundation.

Halachah   Jewish legal tradition; talmudic law.

Heilsgeschichte   Salvation-history (history interpreted as the drama of divine interventions on human beings' behalf).

Mystery   A surplus or excess of meaning; something that has not been explained or cannot be explained.

Noachite covenant   The bond between God and Noah (who came to stand for all Gentiles) established after the flood (see Genesis 9).

Priestly (P)   The source in Genesis through Numbers that is most interested in law and ritual.

Righteous Gentile   A non-Jew who lives a good life and honors God; applied to non-Jews who helped Jews during the Nazi era.

Spirit   The divine breath, animating force, power that gives life, courage, creativity, holiness.

Teleological   Concerning ends, goals, final products, ultimate patterns.

Toledot   The "generations" used in Genesis as a way of periodizing early biblical history.

Transcendence   State of going beyond the usual limits, often going out to the divine.

Type-scene   A term from literary criticism used to describe situations that recur with new actors (for example, how Isaac and Jacob get their wives Rebekah and Rachel).

STUDY QUESTIONS

1. Contrast the priestly and the Yahwistic accounts of creation.
2. What is the significance of the fig leaves of Genesis 2:7?
3. How does blood connect the Cain of Genesis 4:10 and the Noah of Genesis 9:5?
4. Contrast the covenant with Noah and the covenant with Abraham.
5. What does the binding of Isaac suggest about biblical faith?
6. Why does "birthright" figure so prominently in the relation between Jacob and Esau?
7. How does Jacob's wrestling with the angel offset his deceitfulness?
8. Why was it important to make Joseph's sojourn in Egypt providential?
9. What does having the Exodus and the Conquest in the background of Genesis suggest about why it was written?
10. What is the experiential basis for the Bible's correlation of "divinity" and "humanity"?

NOTES

1. See Walter Brueggemann, "Genesis," in *Harper's Bible Dictionary*, ed. Paul S. Achtemeier. San Francisco: Harper & Row, 1985, p. 337. See also Pauline A. Viviano, *Genesis*. Collegeville, Minn.: Liturgical Press, 1985, p. 3. Generally, the textual division follows the main "generations."
2. See Richard J. Clifford, S.J., "The Hebrew Scriptures and the Theology of Creation," *Theological Studies*, 46/3 (September 1985), 520.
3. See Conrad Hyers, *The Meaning of Creation: Genesis and Modern Science*. Atlanta: John Knox, 1984.
4. See Gunther Plaut, ed., *The Torah: A Modern Commentary*. New York: Union of American Hebrew Congregations, 1981, p. 20.
5. See Samuel Terrien, *Till the Heart Sings: A Biblical Theology of Manhood and Womanhood*. Philadelphia: Fortress, 1985.
6. See A. S. Feilschuss-Abir, " '. . . da werden eure Augen geöffnet und ihr werdet sein wie Gott, wissend Gutes und Böses' (Gen 3,5)," *Theologie und Glaube*, 74 (1984), 190–203.
7. For a reading that stresses the improper conception of Cain, see Ulrich Wöller, "Zu Gen 4.7," *Zeitschrift für die alttestamentliche Wissenschaft*, 96 (1984), 271–72.
8. See Plaut, *The Torah: A Modern Commentary*, p. 61.
9. E. A. Speiser, *Genesis*. Garden City, N.Y.: Doubleday Anchor Bible, 1964, p. 71.
10. See Brevard Childs, *Introduction to the Old Testament as Scripture*. Philadelphia: Fortress, 1979, pp. 154–55.
11. See, for example, Robert Alter, *The Art of Biblical Narrative*. New York: Basic Books, 1981; Joel

Rosenberg, "Biblical Narrative," in *Back to the Sources: Reading the Classic Jewish Texts*, ed. Barry W. Holtz. New York: Summit Books, 1984, pp. 31–81; Meir Sternberg, *The Poetics of Biblical Narrative*. Bloomington: Indiana University Press, 1985. On the historicity of the details, see John Van Seters, *Abraham in History and Tradition*. New Haven: Yale University Press, 1975.

12. Terrien, *Till the Heart Sings*, pp. 73–76, explores how circumcision relates to the marginal status of women in priestly Jewish religion.

13. See Alter, *The Art of Biblical Narrative*, p. 49. See also Kenneth T. Aitken, "The Wooing of Rebekah: A Study in the Development of the Tradition," *Journal for the Study of the Old Testament*, 30 (1984), 3–23.

14. See Naomi Steinberg, "Gender Roles in the Rebekah Cycle," *Union Seminary Quarterly Review*, 39 (1984), 175–88.

15. See Viviano, *Genesis*, p. 105.

16. See Alter, *The Art of Biblical Narrative*, pp. 107–11.

17. See Norman K. Gottwald, *The Hebrew Bible: A Socio-Literary Introduction*. Philadelphia: Fortress, 1985, pp. 141–45.

18. See Norman K. Gottwald, *The Tribes of Yahweh: A Sociology of the Religion of Liberated Israel, 1250–1050* B.C.E. Maryknoll, N.Y.: Orbis, 1979.

19. See John Boslough, *Stephen Hawking's Universe*. New York: Morrow, 1984.

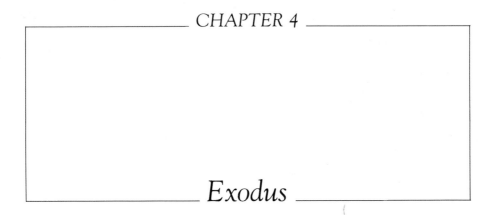

CHAPTER 4

Exodus

TEXTUAL ANALYSIS

Exodus tells the story of how Israel escaped bondage in Egypt, survived in the wilderness, and became covenanted to God at Mount Sinai. It is a crucial book in that Moses, its leading human actor, became for rabbinic Judaism the people's primary founder, the liberation from Egypt became the primary instance of God's effective care, and the covenant of Sinai became the basis for the codification of Torah that determined what being a faithful Jew meant. In terms of thematic content, we may analyze Exodus into six unequal parts:

1:1–15:21	The Exodus from Egypt
15:22–18:27	Israel in the Desert
19:1–24:11	Making the Covenant
24:12–31:18	Instructions for the Tabernacle
32:1–34:35	Apostasy and Renewal
35:1–40:38	Building the Tabernacle[1]

1:1–15:21 The Exodus from Egypt

Exodus begins where Genesis ended, with the sons of Israel/Jacob in Egypt. There they so prospered that they incurred the resentment of a new Pharaoh and were put to hard labor. The opening chapter underscores the strength of the Hebrew women as well as the fear of God that prompted the Egyptian midwives to ignore

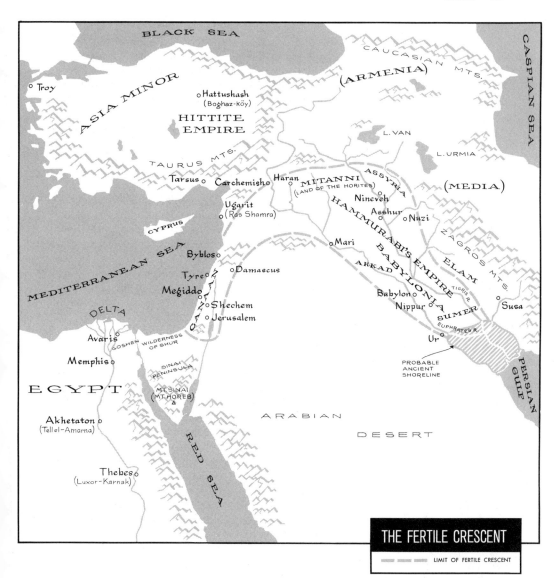

THE FERTILE CRESCENT

LIMIT OF FERTILE CRESCENT

Pharaoh's command to kill the newborn Hebrew males. Chapter 2 rapidly sets up the position and work of Moses: his birth in the line of Levi, his miraculous preservation through Pharaoh's daughter, his defense of his fellow Hebrew, and the resentment (Exodus 2:14) that will dog all his efforts on his people's behalf. We hear of his flight from Pharoah (a miniature of the later Exodus), his coming to Midian, his marriage to Zipporah (after details similar to those in the securing of Rebekah and Rachel), and then of God's hearing the groans of his people and remembering the covenant with Abraham, Isaac, and Jacob.

Chapter 3 is one of the most famous chapters in the Bible. Moses comes to Horeb, one of the significant biblical mountains,[2] experiences the miraculous burning bush, and then encounters the God of the ancestors. All of the overtones are numinous: Moses meets the holy Creator. God promises deliverance from Egypt to a Canaanite land flowing with milk and honey. Moses protests his own unfitness for the role in this that God would have him play and then asks God what name to give to the people of Israel when they ask who has commissioned him. Exodus 3:14 has the famous and enigmatic answer: "I am who I am." This is ambiguous enough not to put God into the power of Moses, but God assures Moses that he is the God of the ancestors and that he will liberate the people despite Pharoah's opposition. The theme of despoiling the Egyptians (Exodus 3:21–22) recurs in Exodus 12:35–36.

In chapter 4 God gives Moses three magical tricks to command the Israelites' respect and the assurance that Moses will have divine help when he has to speak. Moses irritates God by still holding back, but God gives him Aaron as a spokesman. Exodus 4:21 attributes Pharaoh's resistance to the people's leaving Egypt to God's having hardened his heart—another note of divine providence and control. In Exodus 4:22–23 God calls Israel his first-born son and introduces words that are familiar from the spiritual "Let my people go." Exodus 4:24–26 are a strange interpolation, apparently either suggesting a demonic attack before a heroic mission or reporting an ancient tradition about prenuptial circumcision. The "feet" in Exodus 4:25 is usually considered a euphemism for genitals. The chapter ends with Moses' and Aaron's explaining their charge to the people and winning their belief.

In chapter 5 Pharaoh rejects the request for permission to hold a religious festival in the wilderness and increases the people's burdens. The theme is set that the Exodus will be a just, deserved act. Moses complains to God, God repeats the promise of liberation and conquest of Canaan,[3] and the people lose heart. "The people" are somewhat specified by the genealogy of Exodus 6:14–25. The repetitions at the end of chapter 6 and the beginning of chapter 7 summarize the story to this point, adding that Moses was 80 when he spoke to Pharaoh.

The section Exodus 7:8–12:32 amounts to an account of a contest between Moses (or God) and Pharaoh that Moses wins through God's provision of ten plagues. As a prelude, Aaron bests the magicians of Pharaoh in a display of sorcery. When Pharaoh refuses another request to let the people go, Moses turns the water of the Nile (the center of the Egyptian ecology) to blood. Pharaoh's heart remains hardened, so a sequence of nine more requests for freedom, refusals, and plagues unfolds, building tension toward the actual escape. The plagues are of frogs, gnats, flies, affliction of cattle, boils, hail, locusts, darkness, and finally the death of the Egyptian first-born. Throughout Pharaoh remains hard-hearted, although his magicians could replicate the frogs (which gave him some excuse) and after the gnats he tells Moses to have the people sacrifice to their God within Egypt. The boils afflict the magicians (a touch of humor), but still Pharaoh resists. As Exodus 9:16 makes plain, God is declaring his power and making his name known. The Egyptian people start to believe in the plagues and so take protective measures. After the plague of hail Pharaoh confesses his sin, yet he lets go of this confession and again refuses to let the Israelites leave. The theme of Pharaoh's pride (against God) develops, but even when Moses answers Pharaoh's request and drives the locusts off Pharaoh again hardens his heart. By the time of the darkness Pharaoh would

Head of the Egyptian Pharaoh Sesostris III. Sesostris (Sen-Usert) III ruled about 1800–1840 B. C. E. *(The Nelson-Atkins Museum of Art, Kansas City, Missouri [Nelson Fund])*

let the people go, if they left their cattle behind, but Moses will not agree. Chapter 11 predicts the killing of the Egyptian first-born. Chapter 12 sets the Exodus in the context of the feast of Passover, its details being remembered in later ceremonies, especially the eating of unleavened bread and the Passover lamb.

The materials in Exodus 12:33–15:21 depict the actual Exodus. When God smites the first-born of the Egyptians Pharaoh finally relents and send the Israelites off. Exodus 12:40 says that the Israelites had been in Egypt 430 years, and Exodus 12:42 makes the night of the Exodus a night of watching that later generations will commemorate. There follow regulations for Passover (the consecration of the first-born was thought useful for future fertility), notes on the route of the Exodus and Moses' taking the bones of Joseph, and the presence of God in pillars of cloud and fire. In chapter 14 we see Pharaoh's again rebelling against God's will, pursuing the Israelites (who immediately accuse Moses of getting them into worse straits than their previous slavery), Moses' promise that God will fight for the people, the crossing of the sea, and God's routing the hosts of Pharaoh (as the champion/warrior of Israel). This event became the paradigm of later Israelite faith in God's will to protect his people, and the chapter ends with the people's believing in "the Lord, and his servant Moses," a climax its authors seem to have built quite skillfully.[4]

The song of Moses that opens chapter 15 gained special status in the traditional Jewish synagogue, and the people stood out of respect when it was read (a custom also observed for the reading of the ten commandments). God is depicted as Israel's champion, and so as its source of salvation: Who is like unto him? The "steadfast love" (*hesed*) mentioned in 15:13, along with the "redemption," became special hallmarks of the Lord. The terror that the Lord inflicts is the holy fear of ultimate power and sanctity. The segment ends with the prophetess Miriam leading the women in singing and dancing this song (a suggestion that women could lead religious celebrations in early Israel).

15:22–18:27 Israel in the Desert

In this section we witness Israel in a time of what anthropologists call "liminality," a sort of in-between state (here between an old existence in Egypt and a new existence through the covenant and eventually in its own land).[5] The desert itself is something unique and transitional: not like the fleshpots of Egypt and not like the secure prosperity of fertile Canaan. Later tradition thought of Israel's time in the desert as a time of trial. The desert became the proving ground where God acquired a people.[6] Another theme of the entire forty-year period in the desert is the people's grumbling or rebellion. The Yahwist, again, is making sure that readers get no sanitized or varnished impression of the stuff (dust or earth or clay) with which God had to work in this phase of creation.

The grumbling begins as early as Exodus 15:24, when the first minor crisis — no good water — occurs. Moses solves it miraculously, by God's help. The irony, of course, is that God has just liberated the people from Egypt in a much greater display of power. Indeed, God has gone to war on Israel's behalf. But as soon as difficulty — indeed, simple inconvenience — occurs, the people start to hedge their faith. Exodus 15:26 shows the hand of the Deuteronomist, one of whose major themes is that obedience to God's commands brings prosperity, whereas disobedience brings disaster. Because the commands are not specified here, the talmudic rabbis tended to understand them as basic precepts — for example, against adultery or robbery — that could be understood without a written Torah.

Chapter 16 brings the next crisis and murmurings of discontent: scarcity of food. Once again the short memory of the people stands out. They think not of the Exodus but of their days in Egypt when bread was plentiful (although life on the whole was harsh slavery). The answer is another prodigy from God: bread raining down from heaven each day. Exodus 16:4 has another equation of obedience to divine law and material prospering, and 16:5 has in mind the sabbath rest, when one should not work, even at gathering food. When Moses and Aaron gather the people to explain these things to them, they pointedly announce that this prodigy will show that it was the Lord who worked Israel's liberation. (They also suggest that the people should complain to God rather than to their poor human leaders.) God comes in the cloud (divinity is ever an elusive presence)[7] and in effect challenges the people to realize that their meals, morning and evening, demonstrate his sovereign presence with them.

The quail of the evening are plain enough, but the strange bread remains mysterious. "Manna" comes from *man hu* (What is it?). The leveling of the measures is another miraculous element, and the haphazard quality of the people's gathering and the tendency of the manna to melt suggest the imperfections of the scheme. The preservation of the frail manna on the Sabbath testifies to the special powers of that day, a theme of the priestly writer. The disobedience of those who try to gather food on the Sabbath is another indication of the people's lack of trust; they are unwilling to submit to God's mercy (a Deuteronomic concern). (Numbers 11:8 gives a different interpretation of how the manna tasted: like rich cream.) An omer is estimated to have been about 1.6 dry quarts.[8] The suggestion that the manna was placed "before the Lord" (in the ark) contradicts I Kings 8:9, which says that the ark contained only the tablets of the Law. Joshua 5:12 corroborates the statement of Exodus 16:35 that the manna ceased when Israel entered unto the promised land.

With chapter 17 we get more complaining, this time again about a lack of water, and the familiar refrain that it would have been better to stay in Egypt and die comfortably. In Exodus 17:4 Moses complains that the people are ready to stone him (leadership in Israel was no bed of roses). The rock of Horeb from which Moses derives the water combines the sacrality of the mountain with a figure for God's constancy: The Lord is Israel's rock and salvation. Israel's fault finding gives the place its name.

In Exodus 17:8–9 Amalek, probably representing a fierce desert tribe, and Joshua, Israel's military leader who will eventually consummate the Conquest of the promised land, emerge, and Israel engages in another holy war. The figure of Moses with uplifted arms underscores that God is the main warrior on Israel's behalf. The document suggested by Exodus 17:14 is unclear, perhaps "the book of the wars of the Lord" mentioned in Numbers 21:14. To the end of the chapter the text stresses the Lord's warriorship.

In chapter 18 Moses receives back his family, in the person of Jethro, his father-in-law; Zipporah, his wife; and Gershom and Eliezer, his two sons. The implication is that he had sent them from Egypt to Midian to assure their safety. They have heard of Moses' success, and Moses gives Jethro the full details. This narrative leads Jethro to confess his faith in the Lord. He sacrifices to the Lord and shares a (sacred) meal with Aaron and the Israelite elders — solemn signs of his joining their community. Jethro immediately proves useful in helping Moses devise a practical way to handle his heavy burdens of leadership. (The picture of Moses serving as a judge — religious advisor and settler of disputes — makes him like a tribal sheik.)[9] Moses will keep the great tasks of mediating between the people and God, teaching God's statutes, and judging truly significant cases, while the lieutenants he appoints (note the stress in Exodus 18:21 on the moral qualities they should have) will handle lesser matters — a commonsensical delegation of authority. Moses agrees, establishes such a system (the details of which probably reflect administrative structures of the time of the tribes' confederacy after the conquest of Canaan), and (reluctantly? with blessings of peace?) lets Jethro return home to Midian.

19:1–24:11 Making the Covenant

In chapter 19 Israel arrives at Sinai, the mountain (the actual site of which is unknown) where it will receive the crucial Mosaic covenant. The first verses stress that the area was a wilderness. Moses goes up the mountain, to get closer to the divine heaven, and God calls to him, telling him to remind the people of Israel, the house of Jacob, of their deliverance from Egypt. Exodus 19:4 is both poetic and instructive: "I bore you on eagles' wings and brought you to myself." The people to be fashioned through the covenant are uniquely God's own. Exodus 19:5 expands on this theme: If Israel obeys, it will be God's special possession, a kingdom of priests and a holy nation. Christian readers often think that the idea of priesthood implies a ministry to all nations that the whole people, not just their ritual officiants, would perform, and that the idea of a holy nation implies being

View from the top of Jebel Musa, one of the sites suggested as the bibical Mount Sinai. *(Used with permission of the photographer, Robert L. Cohn)*

set apart from other peoples — two striking notions whose relation to one another is intriguing.[10] Moses reports this to the people, and they promise to do all that the Lord commands. God promises to come in a thick cloud, and Moses is to prepare the people for this theophany. The various details of the preparation inculcate a physical sense of the divine holiness: One who is not properly prepared or who comes into wrongful contact will die. The prohibition against sexual intercourse (19:15) had important consequences in the priestly tradition and shows up in the requirements for ritual purity or fittingness to offer sacrifice to God (see Leviticus 15:18). Some commentators consider separation of male priests from sexual contact with women to be a factor in women's disabilities in traditional Judaism.[11]

The manifestation of God is suitably dramatic: The smoke suggests a sacrifice by nature, and the quaking suggests the Earth's entering in. The trumpet is a note of a solemn cultic occasion (see 2 Samuel 2:16), and the thunder reflects God's residence in the heavens. The summons to Moses demonstrates his unique status as mediator. The warning to the people and the priests reenforces the note that the divine holiness is dangerous to human beings. (Christians tend to stress sinfulness at this point, Jews to think of creatureliness.)

Traditional Judaism has looked upon chapter 20 and the giving of the decalogue or ten commandments as the climax of the book of Exodus. The usual scholarly conjecture is that the original form of these commandments was just the short substance, minus the longer explanations. The natural phenomena have set a solemn backdrop, and now God steps forth to center stage and gives the people the words of life. In traditional Jewish interpretation, Exodus 20:2 is a preamble implying the duty to believe in God, which becomes the first commandment. The second commandment forbids idolatry (and introduces the theme of divine jealousy). The third commandment is against swearing falsely. The fourth commandment hallows the sabbath (which it derives from the tradition that after creating in six days God rested on the seventh day). The fifth commandment is to honor one's parents. Commandments six, seven, eight, and nine forbid murder, adultery, theft, and false witness (lying, especially in a solemn or legal context). The tenth commandment forbids coveting anything belonging to one's neighbor: house, wife (who was property, according to Israelite law), servants, or animals. Other traditions divide the materials of the ten commandments slightly differently, but overall the items covered are about the same. Commentators regularly consider these ten commandments to be constructed for easy memory (one for each finger and a similar or repetitive formula). Some commentators also consider the decalogue to be a summary of the covenant tradition fashioned for recitation on public occasions.[12]

The people have been frightened by the awesome manifestation of God so they ask Moses to mediate the divine speech. Moses assuages their fear by assuring them that God only wants to test them and help them not sin. We then enter upon what is called the Covenant Code,[13] the prescriptions of which reflect a settled, agricultural existence in Canaan. The idea is that these rules or laws outline how the people whom God has chosen for himself ought to live. In their very miscellaneousness, they suggest that the whole of life comes under divine guidance. The first concerns in effect elaborate the first commandment's dealing with the Lord's uniqueness. The prescriptions for sacrifice are remarkable for their simplicity, and Exodus 20:21 suggests a presence of God and blessing in every memorable place.

Chapter 21 begins with regulations about slavery, a practice common in the milieu of ancient Israel. Noteworthy are the sabbatical freeing of the slave, the hedged sympathy for the slave's relation to his family, and the procedure for making the slave's service lifelong. This procedure in effect made the slave part of the household and cultic group.[14] The protections prescribed for female slaves express considerable humanity, whereas the restrictions on their going free, along with the assumption that they may be used (sexually) as their masters wish, suggest the liabilities to which female slaves were subject. Exodus 21:13 mitigates the capital punishment for murder prescribed in 21:12 by providing a place of sanctuary or asylum for those who kill unpremeditatedly or unintentionally (they would still be in danger of blood vengeance). Killing one's parents, kidnapping, and cursing one's parents are further deeds deemed worthy of death. They suggest the holiness associated with parents, the source of one's life. From the other legislation of chapter 21 we can: infer that slaves and women were somewhat regarded as property; note the principle of reciprocity (21:24 — eye for eye); and see the principle of an owner's responsibility for the actions of his animals.

Chapter 22 begins with laws about stealing and moves on to responsibility for actions — overgrazing, fire — that injure the property of others. The coming near to God or before God of 22:8 and 22:9 is somewhat obscure: perhaps to swear an oath or be subjected to an ordeal that would prove innocence or guilt. Exodus 22:16 is another window onto the status of women, the understanding being that daughters are (damageable) property of fathers. The severity of 22:18–20 is remarkable and probably expresses deep fears Israel had of being contaminated by Canaanite practices. Equally remarkable is the sensitivity of 22:21–23, which is backed by the wrath of God (the warrior/defender of the vulnerable). Exodus 22:25 stands out for the leniency money lenders should show, the prohibition of usury, and the placing of the welfare of the borrower above the security of the lender. God is compassionate and hears the cries of the afflicted. The rest of the chapter lists incidental regulations, some of them (for instance, not cursing a ruler), rather pregnant in their implications. Giving the first-born to the Lord probably meant consecrating them.

Chapter 23 has more incidental laws, dealing with lying and truthfulness. The prohibition of partiality toward a poor man shows that the ideal was a strict justice. The laws on not oppressing the stranger is a repetition, and the injunction to let the land lie fallow in the seventh year for the sake of the poor is remarkable. It is perhaps linked with the Sabbath rest that all members of the household, including animals, are to enjoy. The three feasts mentioned in Exodus 23:14–17 came to be known as Passover, Shavuot, and Sukkot. Other cultic details follow, and then the code of the covenant concludes with a solemnizing figure of a guardian angel and a promise of protection against enemies—if Israel keeps this code. The last verses speak of a progressive conquest of the promised land and warn against contamination from Canaanite idolatry.

As a conclusion to this exposition of the code that the bond with the Lord entails, in Exodus 24:1–11 Moses obtains the promise of the people that they will obey these commands and then writes them down. Moses then enacts a convenantal ceremony in blood to solemnize the people's acceptance of God's laws. The leaders of the people see the God of Israel and survive to eat and drink (a ceremonial meal). These verses (24:9–11) seem to represent another tradition (J), in which the elders rather than all the people are the principals in the convenantal ceremony.

24:12–31:18 Instructions for the Tabernacle

The concluding verses of chapter 24 place Moses apart with God once more (another textual tradition, most likely P), mentioning the tablets of stone on which the decalogue was inscribed (see, for instance, Exodus 32:15) and stressing the divine glory. With chapter 25 we start the process of God's instructing Moses on how the tabernacle and the ark (which will be its most important artifact) are to be constructed. Both will symbolize God's presence in the midst of people with whom he has convenanted. The central notion regarding the ark is of a throne above which the invisible deity reposed as king. The testimony put into the ark was the tablets of the law. The mercy seat was the cover of the ark and the footstool of the divine throne, where God would meet the priests who represented the people. [15] The cherubim are heavenly presences or angels. The bread of presence was a holy offering. The seven-branched lamp stand became a famous Jewish symbol (the *menorah*).

Throughout this description of the details for the tabernacle the assumption is that sacred precincts constructed on Earth must follow a heavenly pattern or archetype. In chapter 26 many of the details apparently blend the traditions about the tabernacle with aspects of Solomon's temple in Jerusalem (see, for instance, I Kings 6). The effect of the precision and detail of the instructions from God is to give divine sanction to the way that Israel made and thought about its special religious constructions. Throughout, the interest of the priestly tradition prevails, and the line of Aaron is prominent. Aaron belongs to the tribe of Levi, the traditional source of priests. The ephod of Exodus 28:6 is usually considered to have been a linen apron worn by priests, although in the book of Judges it is scorned as something idolatrous. The breastplate of judgment containing the Urim and Thummin served the priest's work of divination or casting lots to determine the divine will. This practice is gilded by the statement (28:30) that Aaron (the priests) should bear the judgment of the people before the Lord continually.

In chapter 29 we witness the instructions for ordaining priests (carried out in Leviticus 8). Noteworthy are the anointing (a suggestion of royalty), sacrifices of animals, use of blood, and mention of the portion of the sacrifice that becomes the property of the priests. The holiness attributed to the ram and the bread derive from their part in a rite that consecrates servants of the holy God who brought the people out of slavery in Egypt.

The opening prescriptions of chapter 31 underscore the holiness of the altar that is to be built. In the background of the census is the idea that counting belongs to God. The offering is both to expiate offenses against God and to support the worship of God. By ritual washing the priests express the purity necessary to serve in the divine presence. The spices, incense, and oil required indicate the Bible's sense that the whole personality, senses as well as mind, ought to honor and enjoy God. Chapter 31 commemorates the workmen responsible for executing the tent of meeting (a third construction, set outside the camp) and the ark. There follow a reinstitution of the Sabbath (a sacralization of time, after the sacralization of space), so that it can be part of the pact of Sinai, and a giving of the tablets of the law, which resume the narrative left in Exodus 24:18, when the block of priestly material (chapters 25–31) on the tabernacle and the ark intruded.

32:1–34:35 Apostasy and Renewal

While Moses is upon the mountain receiving all this instruction from God, the people are on a lower level, becoming restless. The incident of the golden calf became a vivid bit of biblical memory. Among its wealth of implications we may note that the apostasy extended to the ranks of Israel's leaders (Aaron), that the people make their idol their deliverer from Egypt (a special slap at the Lord), that the bull probably is a symbol from Canaanite rites of fertility, and that God's wrath blazes forth against this "stiff-necked" people. Moses intercedes to avert God's wrath, reminding the Lord of the covenant he had sworn with the ancestors. Moses himself is furious with the people, and he breaks the tablets of the convenantal law, as though to show how the people have made it void. The bloody punishment that Moses exacts demonstrates that after the solemn promises of Sinai apostasy from the holy God is a mortal offense.[16] Moses is willing to offer his own life to obtain the people's pardon, but God promises that they themselves will have to bear the consequences and visits them with a plague.

In chapter 33 the Lord instructs Moses to set the people marching toward Canaan again, and they move out as penitents, stripped of their ornaments. Moses uses the tent of meeting for regular contact with God, and the figure (Exodus 33:11) of God's speaking to Moses face to face, as to a friend, became one of highest accolades that tradition associated with Moses. The association of Joshua with the tent anticipates his later succession of Moses. Moses begs God's favoring presence for himself and the people, because this is what makes them distinct from the other nations. God promises to provide this and shows Moses his glory, with suitable protections. Noteworthy here are the divine freedom to show grace and mercy as God pleases and the inevitable mysteriousness of the divinity, whom no one can see. This last notion stands in tension with God's speaking to Moses face to face, but the overall symbolism for the divine-human encounter balances distance or otherness with nearness and communication.

In chapter 34 we witness the renewal of the covenant: new tablets, a new ascent of Moses up Mount Sinai, a new theophany of God in the cloud (Exodus 34:5). The lovely lines of Exodus 34:6–7 express the bonded and faithful love of God, but the last notes of ongoing punishment are a bit ominous. God stresses the singularity of this covenant and how it separates Israel from the other nations. The prescriptions that follow on the renewal of the covenant largely recapitulate items from the code of the covenant (Exodus 20:22–23:33). Moses is with God forty days and nights (a substantial period), oblivious of such earthly matters as eating and drinking. His face shines from this encounter, expressing its unearthly character and the changes in him caused by his interactions with the divine glory. The veil serves to make Moses share in the divine otherness and dangerousness.

35:1–40:38 Building the Tabernacle

In the final chapters of Exodus we have another priestly insertion, concerned with recapitulating the instructions given in Exodus 25–31 and showing the establishment of the Israelite cult. The first verses establish the precedence of the law of the sabbath over all work (including that on the tabernacle). Commentators note that now materials on the tabernacle precede materials on the ark, which is the reverse of the order in Exodus 25–31. Most of the details repeat those of the earlier instructions, and the overall result of the repetition is to lend greater emphasis or significance to this work. The execution of God's orders is depicted as a rather joyous, free-will offering by the people as a whole, who contribute both money and skilled work. Indeed, so generous are the people that Moses has to tell them to bring no more offerings (36:6). The "he" of 36:10 seems to be Bezalel, functioning as the leader and director of the builders (see 37:1). The detail, along with the splendor or richness of the materials, make it plain that things dedicated to the Lord ought to be made with all the excellence that human beings can muster.

The order of construction is from the tabernacle to the ark to the main features or implements of the ark. Stressed for the tabernacle are the frames and the curtains. We note the concern to make the ark mobile, and the prominence of gold. The ark is overlaid with gold, the cherubim are gold, the lamp stand is of pure gold, all the vessels are gold, and the table of incense (horns and all) is of gold. The notion is that the ark is for a kingly being. Chapter 38 continues in the same vein for the altar of burnt offering, and then it stresses the grandeur of the hangings for the court. This latter has been described as "the sacred area surrounding an ancient Semitic sanctuary" and been called synonymous in many parts of the Bible with "temple."[17] The note on the bronze laver and ministering women (Exodus 38:8) does not fit with 40:17, because to this point the tabernacle has not yet been completed. I Samuel 2:22 refers to women who serve at the entrance to the tent of meeting, but the tent described in Exodus 33:7–11 only was attended by Moses and Joshua. Clearly, therefore, we have some mixing of traditions. The likelihood is that the tent was later somewhat assimilated to the

Temple of Jerusalem. Exodus 38:21 repeats that the tabernacle contained the tablets of the law (testimony), and it relates the whole construction to Moses, Aaron, and the priestly line that had responsibility for the cult attendant on the convenant and the law.

The final tally of the materials used in the construction stresses the prodigality of the offering that Israel made, and all the materials and skilled work mentioned in chapter 39 remind us of the craftmanship available in the ancient Near East, at least by the time that the Temple was constructed. Commentators note that, despite this proliferation of constructive materials and skills, Israelite worship was probably less grandly accoutered than that of most of its neighbors, due to the restrictions on representing the divinity. Fear of idolatry was a constant brake, and in Judaism as a whole listening and ethical performance have taken precedence over seeing and aesthetic celebration.[18]

When the construction of the "tabernacle of the tent of meeting" (Exodus 39:32) was finished, it was brought to Moses, who certified that the people had followed God's commands and blessed them. In chapter 40 we witness the erection or installation of the whole construction and priesthood: the cultic mechanism actually being put in place. All the elements are installed, Moses and Aaron wash, and the glory of the Lord fills the tabernacle, coming in the cloud. It is now God's place, the locus of his presence, and the people only march (toward Canaan) when the cloud rises. By day the cloud is on the tabernacle, and by night it houses the divine fire.

HISTORICAL BACKGROUND

Having completed our commentary on the text, let us delve into the background that Exodus presupposes. First, there are the events of harsh residence in Egypt, liberation, and covenanting with God. Although the temporal distance between the composition of the materials that we now have (tenth to sixth centuries B.C.E.) and even the latest date for the Exodus (thirteenth century B.C.E.), to say nothing of the long residence in Egypt (430 years according to Exodus 12:40), suggests that many details probably had become blurred, it seems certain that later Israel was convinced that its ancestors both had suffered grievously in Egypt and had been marvelously delivered by God under Moses. There is no present-day scholarly agreement on the route that the people took, and all that the Pentateuchal sources agree on is that it was located in the northern half of the Sinai, had a stop at Kadesh-barnea, and approached the northern end of the Gulf of Aqaba.[19] Mount Sinai (Horeb) has traditionally been identified with Jebel Musa in the southern Sinai, but this identification is not certain. The details of the wandering, like the details of the plagues and the escape from Egypt, are subordinated to the religious interests, but many of them may be accurate. We just cannot say for certain.

What seems of paramount importance is the tradition that the God of the ancestors Abraham, Isaac, and Jacob was experienced in the Exodus from Egypt as the people's champion. The linked events of being freed from slavery and covenantally bound to this God made a new, Mosaic chapter in Israelite religious history. No doubt the accounts of the covenants with Abraham and Noah were influenced by the more elaborate traditions about the pact struck with God under

Descending Jebel Musa, with the Santa Katerina monastery below.   *(Used with permission of the photographer, Robert L. Cohn)*

the leadership of Moses. Certainly the legal traditions have been woven into the historical narrative,[20] and even though the priestly portion of Exodus has colored these legal materials by reference to the cult, it seems clear that the figure of Moses as the mediator through whom the basic law of the covenanted people arose went back to the sources of J, the earliest tradition. Implicit in the contest of wills with Pharaoh is a conception of Israel as different from the other nations, because of its different God, and this becomes explicit after the liberating event, when the laws governing the people's special relationship with God are elaborated. It is hard to know what historical substance rests at the center of the descriptions of Moses's interactions with God, but clearly the entire presentation of Moses stresses his uniquely intimate relationship.

Indeed, the mediation of Moses lends a thematic, if not a strictly historical, legitimacy to the construction of the tabernacle and the ark, because that mediatorship may be seen as carrying the seeds of the priestly functions that the covenant later was thought to require. Just as Moses is credited with a new experience of the divine name/being, so he is credited with a unique ability to mediate the divine holiness. Both may be theological constructions of later periods, but both suggest a memory of Moses and the origins of the Torah (in the sense of the codification of the behavior incumbent on members of the covenanted people) that connect liberation from Egypt, God's presence in the people's midst, and the laws or mores that Israel developed.

Presupposed also, of course, is the wandering in the desert or the difficult interval between liberation from Egypt and entry into Canaan. How people actually survived in this somewhat nomadic life can only be conjectured from what we know about the past and present nomadism of the Near East, but there is no reason not to picture them as tent dwellers roughly on the model of modern Bedouins. Some historians distinguish between tents made of skin, which likely prevailed prior to the Conquest of Canaan, and tents made of hand-woven goats' hair (both are mentioned in the descriptions of how the tabernacle was made; see, for example, Exodus 35:23, 36). The basic picture that the people for whom Exodus was composed likely would have had was of a rather primitive dwelling erected on poles and containing a modest number of domestic items such as straw mats for sleeping, a piece of leather for a dining table, a few stones for a stove, and a simple array of utensils. Some historians also link the nomadic life of Near Eastern tented groups with an inclination to clan loyalty and a certain democracy or relative equality of members.[21]

The earliest traditions from which Exodus was composed also remember Israel as a rebellious or "stiff-necked" people. Even if this characterization was meant to console later generations, it is so central to the book that claims for historical intentions in Exodus virtually stand or fall with it. From the outset Moses experiences ambiguous reactions from his compatriots: He no sooner intervenes to save one person from a beating (Exodus 2:11–12) than other people are ready to reject

Wadi Firan, an oasis near Jebel Musa.   *(Used with permission of the photographer, Robert L. Cohn)*

him as no prince or judge over them (Exodus 2:14). The people grumble against him right after the Exodus, and the theme of nostalgia for the fleshpots of Egypt, where they might have perished more comfortably, weaves an almost humorous thread through the narrative of the march in the wilderness. The evil inclination of the people comes to a head in the incident of the golden calf, where they receive a deadly punishment. Even though we sense at this point many later cultic notions concerning the holiness of God, something of an earlier dread of the vocation imposed by the experience of liberation from Egypt lingers on. The editors have certainly connected the Abrahamic need to trust in God with a Mosaic need to find the presence of God as God chooses to reveal it and to remember what God did in leading the people out of bondage. Both Exodus 3:14, the famous text on the Mosaic experience of God's nature, and the later descriptions of Moses's meetings with God finally imply that "Israel" thought itself unique because of God's presence with it. The Deuteronomic tradition, as we see later, and the priestly tradition, as the blocks of material on the tabernacle and ark suggest, tackled the problem of this presence by providing mechanisms — the laws that people were to obey and the cult that they were to carry out. Simpler, if not older, was the idea that the people had daily to believe that God would be with them (in cloud by day and fire by night) and would supply their sustenance.

LITERARY INTENT

In addition to the general motives that we have cited in the case of Genesis and biblical history as a whole — for instance, the desire to preserve the traditions that defined where a generation had come from and who therefore it was, and the desire to present a coherent and profound view of reality — we should first note the motives that seem to stand forth in the different textual traditions composing Exodus. The materials of the Yahwist, for instance, seem to have been created or organized as part of a longer narrative stretching from Genesis to Numbers. A prime feature of this narrative is a theological depiction of Israel — an understanding worked out from commitment to the God of the ancestors — that makes the people regularly fail to respond appropriately to the divine goodness. By stressing the distance of the people from God — the moral distance, as much as the ontological gap between Creator and creature — the Yahwist places God in the center of the drama of Exodus.

Moses, consequently, is a secondary character, more a witness or subordinate than an independent initiator. Moses has the unwelcome task of trying to lead a people remarkably self-centered and forgetful. Though chosen, they are indistinguishable from other peoples in their failings and desires. They grumble and suffer bouts of amnesia so regularly that the reader is left to expect little from them. All religious reliance, therefore, must be placed on God, and for the Yahwist God never fails to care for Israel. If this narrative was in fact composed later in the tenth century, shortly after the split of the united kingdom (of David and Solomon) into northern and southern realms, it may have had the goal of assuring people dejected by this misfortune that it was just more of the same old Israelite stupidity or failure to appreciate what God had done for his special people. As well, it could console people with the thought that slavery in some ways was easier than freedom — more predictable, demanding less responsibility.

The Elohistic and Deuteronomistic strains are relatively minor contributors to Exodus, so it is the priestly motivation that we must next consider. Some commentators discern a priestly hand in the episode of the ten plagues (chapters 7–12), insofar as Moses and Aaron are pitted against the magicians of Pharaoh. The description of the lineage of Moses and Aaron (6:14–25) is extended a generation to Phinehas, whom Numbers (25:6–13) assigns an important role in the pristly covenant. For P the events of Sinai focus on God's gift of the instructions for worship, so the extended accounts of how the tabernacle was to be constructed, how the priesthood was to be inaugurated, and the like, are highly important. If we locate the perspective and materials of P in the sixth century, when the Exile and the cult of the Temple in Jerusalem were burning issues, we are inclined to underscore the way that the priestly materials in Exodus establish the cult that went on in the Temple as part of the revelation and covenant of Sinai. This would have had the added effect of relativizing the absence of the Davidic kingship, finally lost in the Exile. P also tends to suggest that God's provision for the people in the wilderness is most illumined by the worship of God commanded to Moses: in effect, God was preserving a people so they eventually could effect the worship befitting the Lord.

The last motives that we should consider are those suggested by the final version of the text that became canonical in the fifth century B.C.E., during the reform of Ezra and Nehemiah. We have mentioned that the canonization of the Pentateuch at this time had the general intent of furnishing the postexilic people reconstituted in the homeland with an authoritative collection of writings that could be as a mirror in which they might read their present success or failure as "Israel." These canonical materials functioned in the cult and became thought of as the Torah or Guidance that God had given the people he wanted to be uniquely his own.

In discussing the effect that the canonical shaping of Exodus has produced, Brevard Childs has focused on the relation of the narrative portions to the portions dealing with legal materials. Even within the legal materials, the final redactors have put together quite varied traditions — interests or understandings of Israelite existence. So, for example, the Decalogue comes at things differently than the Covenant Code, the former being concise and far-reaching, the latter being extended and particularizing. By correlating these materials with historical materials as it has, however, the final editing has put them in illuminating interaction. For example, the Decalogue comes after the liberation from Egypt and some wandering in the desert. It therefore is addressed to a freed but still unfinished people. In addition, the Decalogue now may be seen as a guide to all the succeeding legal materials: an initial summary or overture. Because a purely textual analysis of Exodus would make this positioning of the Decalogue secondary or even incidental, Childs stresses the significance of the final canonical editing and its theological implications, among which the primacy of Moses' interpretation of the covenant stands out.

The materials on the execution of God's instructions for the ark and the tabernacle and the rest (chapters 35–40) also stand in a new light, when we reflect on the canonical positioning of the materials on apostasy and renewal (chapters 32–34) that precede them. Chapters 32–34 are a rather heavy-handed theology of sin and forgiveness. The apostasy in the episode of the golden calf is the low point in the depiction of the people's moral and religious frailty, and the passing by of the Lord and descent in the cloud are striking descriptions of the divine willingness again to draw near. The memorable lines about the Lord's mercy and graciousness, slowness to anger and abounding steadfast love, and his forgiving of iniquity and transgression and sin (34:6–7) have been magnified by the preceding depiction of the people's apostasy. In turn, they set up the concluding materials on the execution of the commands for the tabernacle, making it appear as the obvious way to respond to this generous God — the obvious way to show gratitude for the kindness and avoid his just wrath. Despite all of his mercy and graciousness, he is a jealous God. Exodus was written to express the core of Israelite identity as liberation from slavery by this God and freedom to live in covenant with him.

The canonical redaction manages to suggest that none of these elements of the divine work of liberation, or of the covenant relationship, can be excluded. The final interests in law and worship, certainly, make the ultimate framework or overall design of Exodus priestly. Still, portions such as chapters 32–34 add nuance, so that the priestly laws become linked with a convenantal relationship that derives only from God's generosity. Whereas the people have shown themselves wretchedly faithless, the goodness of God has won out and the covenant has been refashioned. The Law that was broken has been refashioned into new tablets and the work of fashioning the tabernacle and ark that was cast in doubt by the apostasy of the people has been resumed, in fact completed. The end of Exodus therefore is highly positive: The people have constructed the materials for worship generously and joyously, and the Lord stands with the people as they march through the wilderness, in the cloud over the tabernacle by day and in the fire by night, redeeming many of the liabilities and sufferings of a life that is still unsettled (any life?)[22]

LASTING SIGNIFICANCE

No doubt we could find in Exodus many stimuli to rethink current human existence, but perhaps we are wisest to concentrate on the three events that the book itself appears to stress: liberation from Egypt, covenanting with God under Moses, and inaugurating the priestly cult.

The contemporary school of Christian theology that frequently goes under the name "Liberation Theology" embraces diverse groups — Latin Americans, women, blacks, Asians — but all agree that biblical religion means freeing human beings from the bonds that keep them miserable or unfulfilled. These bonds may be economic, political, military, cultural, or religious. Thus, a fully adequate liberation will entail eliminating destructive poverty, powerlessness, warfare, prejudice, and excessive self-concern or sin. Many of the liberation theologians explicitly refer to the account of Exodus as a paradigm for what God wants religious people to believe and collaborate in. Taking a cue from black religion, whose spirituals have long interpreted Exodus as a figure for relief from slavery and oppression wherever found, liberation theologians have been correlating Pharaoh with present-day dictators and the Lord with the mysterious sources of strength and hope that enable people to defeat such oppressors. Indeed, the shrewdest liberation theologians have not neglected the lessons in the portrayal of the Israelite people, whose faith is depicted as less than complete.

Regardless of what we think of the Marxist categories that liberation theology frequently uses to analyze social antagonisms and economic injustices, the story in Exodus of God's intervention to liberate his oppressed people certainly places the Bible alongside socialist and other attempts to free people from debilitating circumstances. It is true enough that the theology of Exodus stresses faith more than secular actions, but the militancy of its God, even after we have made proper provision for the mythological patterns of much of its thinking, should give us pause. Exodus has no trouble with the proposition that those who oppress Israel or stand in the way of its achieving the destiny God has promised it should be fought tooth and nail. As we noted, this raises the troublesome question of "holy war," which Islamic fundamentalists have made only too concrete in our day. We would be misguided to expect Exodus or any other ancient text, however canonical or venerable, to solve our present-day problems. The scenes of God's liberating Israel from Egypt do, however, prompt some intriguing reflections. Just as they suggest that genuine faith will prove liberating, and that the true God is the opponent of all oppression, they also force us to ask about the self-interests we so regularly project onto "the true God" and the impurities or underdevelopments that may afflict even our most treasured canonical texts. Thus, a rabbinic story has God chastize angels who were cheering at the sight of the Egyptians' drowning, saying, "How can you cheer when my people the Egyptians are drowning?"

Similarly, the biblical depiction of God's choosing out a special people and covenanting with it uniquely may well affront the humanist in us, who thinks that this is a partiality or ethnocentrism ill-befitting any adequate "God." Both Jews and Christians have suffered from this charge, all the more so when they have forgotten the other parts of their own biblical tradition that provide for the salvation of the nations and reduce their own roles to those of simple servants of God's universal providence. One counter to the objections to a particularist covenant or chosenness that theologians have made comes from an analysis of human historicity. If the divine is to work in human affairs, some theologians point out, that will mean working through the limitations that space and time impose. Thus, God will have to employ the cultural instruments of language, tradition, and tribal consciousness, even when the ultimate divine intent may be to offer a gracious relationship to all human beings. How we ought to think about the correlation of ethnic specificity and pan-human generality is a very difficult question, of course, and it afflicts us all the more in today's global village. Thus, historians trying to develop models of world history have to struggle with the oneness of homo sapiens and the great many different human societies or cultures. Politicians and economists trying to bring order to a divided, destructive world have to think in terms of both the single whole that we indwell and the very many different political and economic units that we have created. And theologians have to keep at the long-standing problem of overcoming prejudices and stressing the omnipresence of the divine calls to nearness and love, without denaturing the different traditions that people actually have developed and through which they in fact have experienced their God.

Third, although the whole phenomenon of religious law, to say nothing of the particulars of the Decalogue and the Covenant Code, bear us interesting stimuli, perhaps it is the cultic regulations of Exodus that, by their very strangeness, carry the lasting significance most provocative today. The priestly redactors of Exodus thought that ritualistic sacrifice, cleansing, dedication to God, and the rest, were the heartbeat of genuine biblical religion. They saw the Lord less as a warrior bent on the people's liberation than as the sovereign Holiness the people were privileged to worship. The implication of this vision was that worship is the centerpiece of human fulfillment. Even when rabbinic Judaism shifted things somewhat, substituting study of Torah for ritualistic sacrifice, the instinct continued. Christian successors of the Jewish priests thought similarly, as we can discover in the liturgical theologies of both Roman Catholicism and Eastern Orthodoxy. Protestant Christianity focused more on the proclamation of the biblical Word than on cultic sacrifice, but we can make the case that it, too, found worshiping God the most significant religious or even human action.

Virtually by definition, a secular society pays worship little heed. Even when religious psychologists or sociologists can claim to discover transmutations of the urge to worship ultimate reality in such apparently secular activities as the contemplation of natural beauty or sport or the service of scientific truth or even the service of society's most wretched people (who can seem to point beyond themselves, as signs confounding a rationalistic reading of the universe), the common self-understanding of a largely secularized culture like our own shows little commitment to cultic worship and sacrifice. The question therefore presents itself, Are the regulations displayed in Exodus simply antique artifacts—fossils from an earlier evolutionary period to which we can never return—or are they reminders of a better instinct that we would be wise to try to retrieve, all the more so now that our secularism seems on the verge of blowing itself up through nuclear warfare and world-wide social injustice?

GLOSSARY

Ark (of the covenant)   A container or chest, principally used to carry the two tablets of the Mosaic Law; not to be confused with the tabernacle, a larger portable sanctuary within which the ark would be placed for worship services.

Covenant Code   The teaching that lays out the behavioral implications of the covenant.

Divination   Art of discerning future events or God's intentions.

Ḥesed   Steadfast kindness and love, the key attribute of the God of the covenant.

Immanent   Existing or being present within (for example, God is immanent to the world or human experience as well as transcendent); part of Israel's experience of God's action in history.

Liminality   State of in-between existence, experienced at such times as initiation and pilgrimage, when ordinary patterns fall away and people experience a foretaste of the freer community implied by their ideals. Israel's time in the wilderness has liminal ("threshold") characteristics.

Menorah   A lamp stand, usually made of gold, holding seven candles, and used in the cult.

Numinous   Concerning the divine or sacred.

Ontological   Concerning being, existential status, essential makeup.

Passover   The commemoration of the flight from Egypt and escape into freedom.

Shavuot   The Feast of Weeks (Pentecost in Greek) seven weeks after Passover, originally for the wheat harvest but later for the giving of the law on Sinai.

Sukkot   (Feast of Booths or Tabernacles) Autumn harvest festival when huts of branches are erected in memory of the time in the wilderness.

Tabernacle   The portable sanctuary supposedly used in the wilderness (see Exodus 25–30); a rectangular enclosure housing the Holy of Holies, the Ark, the Altar of Incense, the Menorah, and the table for the bread of the presence. The full description of the tabernacle has been influenced by the appearance of Solomon's Temple and probably does not apply to the tent of meeting used in the wilderness.

Tent of meeting   A simple form of the tabernacle probably actually used in the wilderness.

Theophany   A manifestation of the divine.

Usury   Charging interest on money loaned.

Wars of the Lord   Religious battles, supposedly fought by or for God; a source quoted in Numbers 21:14–15.

STUDY QUESTIONS

1. What is the significance of the divine name that Moses receives from God (Exodus 3:14)?
2. What is the cumulative effect of the ten plagues?
3. Why do we find instructions for Passover prior to the actual Exodus from Egypt?
4. How is God depicted in the song of chapter 15?
5. What is the connection between the Decalogue and the Covenant Code?
6. What is the significance of the instructions for the ordaining of priests (chapter 29)?
7. How is Moses presented in chapters 32–34?
8. Explain the symbolism of the cloud filling the tent of meeting and the glory of the Lord filling the tabernacle (40:34).
9. What connection between covenant and law does Exodus presuppose?
10. Why did the priestly writers rework the traditions about the covenant of Sinai?
11. How significant is the inclusion in Exodus of both liberation from oppression and divine commands for cultic worship?

NOTES

1. See John F. Craghan, *Exodus.* Collegeville, Minn.: Liturgical Press, 1985, p. 3.
2. See Robert L. Cohn, *The Shape of Sacred Space: Four Biblical Studies.* Chico, Calif.: Scholars Press, 1981, especially pp. 47–48.

3. See Pierre Auffret, "The Literary Structure of Exodus 6:2–8," *Journal for the Study of the Old Testament*, 27 (1983), 46–54; Jonathan Magonet, "The Rhetoric of God: Exodus 6:2–8," *Journal for the Study of the Old Testament*, 27 (1983), 56–67; Pierre Auffret, "Remarks on J. Magonet's Interpretation of Exodus 6:2–8," *Journal for the Study of the Old Testament*, 27 (1983), 68–71; Jonathan Magonet, "A Response to P. Auffret's 'Literary Structure of Exodus 6:2–8,' " *Journal for the Study of the Old Testament*, 27 (1983) 73–74.

4. See Pierre Auffret, "Essai sur la structure litteraire d'Exodus 14," *Estudios Biblicos*, 41 (1983), 53–82.

5. See Cohn, *The Shape of Sacred Space*, pp. 7–23.

6. See W. Gunther Plaut, ed., *The Torah: A Modern Commentary*. New York: Union of American Hebrew Congregations, 1981, p. 465.

7. See Samuel Terrien, *The Elusive Presence: Toward a New Biblical Theology*. San Francisco: Harper & Row, 1978.

8. See John Gray, "The Book of Exodus," in *The Pentateuch*, ed. Charles M. Laymon. Nashville: Abingdon (Interpreter's Concise Commentary), 1983, p. 134.

9. Ibid., p. 138.

10. See Plaut, *The Torah*, p. 522.

11. See Samuel Terrien, *Till the Heart Sings: A Biblical Theology of Manhood and Womanhood*. Philadelphia: Fortress, 1985, pp. 71–86.

12. See W. Sibley Towner, "Ten Commandments, The," in *Harper's Bible Dictionary*, ed. Paul J. Achtemeier. San Francisco: Harper & Row, 1985, p. 1033.

13. See Anthony Phillips, "A Fresh Look at the Sinai Periscope: Part I," *Vetus Testamentum*, 34 (1984), 39–52.

14. See Anthony Phillips, "The Laws of Slavery: Exodus 21:2–11," *Journal for the Study of the Old Testament*, 30 (1984), 51–66.

15. For a diagram of the tabernacle, see Plaut, *The Torah*, p. 601.

16. See Jay A. Wilcoxen, "Some Anthropocentric Aspects of Israel's Sacred History," *Journal of Religions*, 48 (1968), 344.

17. Gray, "The Book of Exodus," p. 166.

18. See Plaut, *The Torah*, p. 677.

19. See Kevin G. O'Connell, "Exodus," in *Harper's Bible Dictionary*, p. 291. See also Herbert G. May, ed., *Oxford Bible Atlas*, 2nd ed. New York: Oxford University Press, 1974, p. 59.

20. See Calum M. Carmichael, *Law and Narrative in the Bible*. Ithaca, N.Y.: Cornell University Press, 1985.

21. See David H. Scott, "Tents," in *Harper's Encyclopedia of Bible Life*, 3rd rev. ed. San Francisco: Harper & Row, 1978, pp. 27–32.

22 See Brevard Childs, *Introduction to the Old Testament as Scripture*. Philadelphia: Fortress, 1979, pp. 173–76.

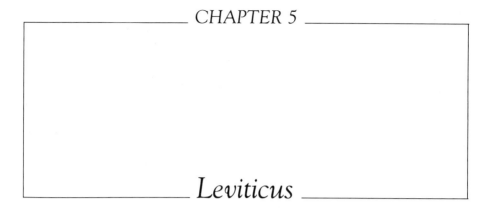

CHAPTER 5

Leviticus

TEXTUAL ANALYSIS

Most analysts of Leviticus consider this book part of the priestly tradition that we find in the first four books of the Pentateuch. The book gets its name from the Latin (Vulgate) rendering of the Greek (Septuagint) translation, which considered it to be concerned with the personnel of the Temple in Jerusalem, who were supposed to be descendants of Levi. The rabbis referred to it as a manual for priests, and perhaps its characteristic note is a concern to distinguish between "the holy and the common, and between the unclean and the clean" (Leviticus 10:10). Jacob Milgrom, one of the foremost scholars of Leviticus, has divided the book into six sections of unequal length.

1:1–7:38	The Sacrificial System
8:1–10:20	Inaugural Services at the Sanctuary
11:1–15:33	Laws of Uncleanness
16:1–34	Purification of the Sanctuary and the Nation
17:1–26:46	The Holiness Code
27:1–34	Commutation of Votive Gifts[1]

1:1–7:38 The Sacrificial System

Leviticus assumes the discussion of Exodus 35–40 on the execution of the prescriptions for the tabernacle and the ark, so it begins with God's commanding

Moses (in the wilderness, at the tent of meeting) to give the people more cultic regulations. The first instructions pertain to the laity and regard voluntary offerings. More often the aim is atonement: trying to make up to God for offenses, involuntary or voluntary, that the individuals have committed. The worshipers are to identify with the gifts being offered, animal or cereal, which come from their possessions and so represent them before God. The stress on blood and destruction in chapter 1 stems from the notion that life is holy to God and so the sacrifice of life will be effective in forgiving sins. With both animals and cereals one is to offer fine, not damaged, specimens.

The mention of a most holy portion (Leviticus 2:10) for the priests means that only they could eat it. Whereas some of Israel's neighbors looked upon foods consumed in sacrifice as supplying nourishment to their gods, most of the Israelite sacrifice went to the priests, both for their support and as a way of uniting them with the offerer. The type of offering burnt was a "holocaust" and signified complete dedication (and so the complete dedication of the one sacrificing) to the praise of God. The idea of another sort of offering for peace included well-being and prosperity, as well as the absence of conflict. It provided the people a way to enjoy meat (a relatively rare occurrence for the poor) and had no overtones of expiation for sin. The restriction in Leviticus 3:17 against eating fat or blood separated these as God's portions of the sacrifice.

Chapter 4 begins with offerings for sins (acts bringing ritual uncleanness) committed involuntarily. It provides for the sins of priests, of the whole congregation, of rulers, and of commoners. There are minor variations (for example, in the animal to be sacrificed — bull or goat — or in the sex), but most of the procedure is the same in each case. Chapter 5 is notable for requiring sacrifices for such disparate matters as refusing to be a witness, swearing a rash oath, and incurring guilt by contact with animal or human uncleanness. There is some confusion between "guilt offering" and "sin offering," which reminds us that the priestly editors were transmitting much older traditions whose terminology they may not have fully understood. The notion that sacrifice may expiate sin differs from that in Numbers 15:30–31, giving analysts a conflict to resolve.[2]

Chapter 6 is interesting for requiring atoning sacrifices for offenses against one's neighbor — robbery, breach of faith, and so forth. This argues that ethics and cult had a mutual influence in ancient Israel, each requiring the other. Indeed, one was not to approach God in worship until one had rectified offenses against one's neighbor. The section 6:8–7:38 shifts the focus from laypeople to priests, distinguishing among burnt offerings, to be rendered to the Lord constantly (as a sign of Israel's constant dedication), cereal offerings, offerings on the day of priestly ordination, sin offerings, guilt offerings, and peace offerings. Throughout, the instructions stress maintaining ritual cleanliness, avoiding eating blood and fat, and taking great care not to do things abominable in God's sight. The reference in 7:38 to Mount Sinai suggests that these laws for priests are different from those in 1:1–6:8, which were given at the tent of meeting.

8:1–10:20 Inaugural Services at the Sanctuary

Chapters 8–10 fit nicely with Exodus 35–40, as though Leviticus 1–7 were a later insertion. Moses predominates over Aaron, which suggests the primacy of prophecy over priesthood. The action of ordaining the priests follows the ritual outlined in Exodus 29. We have seen the significance of blood. Noteworthy also is the fact that the ordination requires seven days in the tent of meeting and that failing this requirement means risking death (Leviticus 8:35), no doubt due to improper relationship with the holiness of God. The priests are to share in the sacrifices brought to the sanctuary (see 1 Samuel 2:13–14). Chapter 9 gives the promise and then the occurrence of the appearance of the glory of the Lord (9:6, 9:23). The logic is that when the rightly ordained priests carry out the sacrifices properly and bless the people, divine revelation occurs. The fire that comes forth to consume this burnt offering is a sign of God's holy presence and acceptance of the sacrifice, as the acclaim and obeisance of the people (9:24) show.

Chapter 10 shows us the sons of Aaron offering an improper (innovative?) sacrifice and perishing from the blazing of the divine fire. Obviously, this is another expression of the holiness of the Lord that priests are bound to respect. Leviticus 10:3 correlates the holiness of God with the demands made of the leaders of the people whom he would have be holy. Traditional Jewish authorities such as Ibn Ezra have correlated this text with Amos 3:2: "You only have I known of all the families of the earth; therefore I will punish you for all your iniquities."[3] The prohibition of expressions of grief from Aaron underscores the justice of the Lord's punishment. Priests are forbidden to drink intoxicants when entering the tent of meeting. We have mentioned the thematic value of Leviticus 10:10, which sets the function of the priesthood as distinguishing between the holy and the common, the unclean and the clean. The things of sacrifice clearly are clean and should not be tainted by intoxicants that could lead to drunken behavior. Aaron's acceptable explanation in 10:19 of why he did not eat the sin offering rests on the symbolism of such eating: It would have implied that through his intercession the people had won forgiveness from God, but the punishment visited on his sons cast his standing with the Lord in doubt (that is, he seemed out of favor with God and so unlikely to be able to intercede successfully).

11:1–15:33 Laws of Uncleanness

Although the main note in these chapters is ritual impurity — dealing with contacts that have something symbolically unsavory about them and so render cultic contact with God unfitting — we also catch signs of ancient Israel's appreciation of the connection between physical hygiene and preventing disease. Thus the washing prescribed for contact with dead bodies (11:25, 28, 40), skin diseases (chapters 13–14), and discharges (chapter 15) would have lessened the chance of infection as well as lessened the ritual impurity. Chapter 11 begins by detailing clean and unclean animals and so stipulating what is acceptable and unacceptable dietary practice. The stipulation had great influence in rabbinic Judaism and the development of the distinction between foods considered pure and foods considered unclean or unfitting.[4] The biblical origin of various of these prohibitions remains obscure, but in some cases the point seems to be to separate Israel from practices of neighboring peoples who threatened to corrupt it. In other cases the basic idea is to promote a desirable wholeness or suitableness. For example, sea creatures should swim rather than crawl.

Commentators note that only animals are in question, and that the rationale

(11:44) is that a holy God demands a holy people (one not associated with repulsive dietary habits). The laws also kept Israelites from many brutalities toward animals and inclined them toward vegetarianism. Chapter 12, concerning the purification required after childbirth, depends on a notion that blood and bodily discharges ill-fit one for cultic contact with God. It does not stigmatize sexual activity, but feminists have argued a connection with a certain religious marginalization of women, who were not eligible for the priesthood, and they have noted the double purification needed for giving birth to a female child[5] (which some say could also be interpreted as honoring the female).

Chapter 13 details regulations for dealing with skin diseases, including leprosy, which rendered one unclean. Assumed here is a connection between physical health and spiritual rightness, for ancient Israel considered the human personality a psychosomatic whole. Priests are shown exercising their responsibility for the cleanness of the people. We catch a glimpse of ancient medical opinions in the different diagnoses, and it becomes clear that the "leprosy" in question is a generic term for "serious skin disease" (including the modern disease called leprosy). The isolation of lepers seems to have had several goals: their own possible healing, the medical safety of those they might infect, and the religious safety of those whom they might render ritually unclean. The washings and burnings of garments no doubt indicate ancient ideas of prophylaxis, and the rituals prescribed in chapter 14 for pronouncing the unclean person cleansed and so restored to the community have archaic elements (including perhaps connection with ancient demonology —getting rid of the evil spirit responsible for the disease) that present-day scholars do not completely understand.[6] The extension of the cleansings at the end of chapter 14 to the house suggests interesting connections in the priestly mind between afflictions of people and afflictions of property or dwellings.

Chapter 15 is concerned with genital discharges ("body" is a euphemism), male and female, pathological and normal, all of which were considered ritualistically unclean or polluting. Any contact with these made people or clothing or equipment unclean, but the solution normally was a simple washing followed by a short period of separation (for example, being considered unclean until evening). Like radiation, this uncleaness was quite impersonal. If the discharge was pathological—for instance, from venereal disease—the assumption was that it had polluted the sanctuary and so required an atoning sacrifice, after a longer separation (see Leviticus 15:13–15). Verses 16–18 had the effect of forbidding sexual intercourse on the eve of worship at the sanctuary (see 31),[7] and verse 19 had the effect of forbidding sexual intercourse during the week of a woman's period. In stringent rabbinic interpretations one had to count the seven days from the cessation of the menstrual period rather than the onset, which considerably influenced marital relations.[8] Verses 25–30 pertain to irregular or pathological bleeding.

16:1–34 Purification of the Sanctuary and the Nation

Chapter 16 probably originally followed on chapter 10. Once again Moses mediates God's words to Aaron. The sons of Aaron have doubly defiled the sanctuary, by their sin and by their deaths, so there has to be a purification. The cloud regularly referred to is a cloud of incense. The point of the ritual is to make the sanctuary and its vessels again holy and befitting God. The incident of sending

The Dome of the Rock (a famous Muslim shrine in Jerusalem) and the fountain for purification, on the site where the Jerusalem Temple once stood. *(Used with permission of the photographer, Robert L. Cohn)*

the goat off into the wilderness is somewhat obscure, but it is the origin of the notion of a "scapegoat" that bears away the sins of the people. Azazel is usually taken to be the name of a demon, and many scholars see parallels with rites of other Near Eastern peoples that were designed to bear away the sins of the people each year and put them on demonic forces. "The holy place" referred to several times came to be known as the "Holy of Holies" or most sacred part of the tabernacle and the Temples of Solomon and Herod in Jerusalem.[9] In 16:29–34 we find instructions for an annual day of atonement (Yom Kippur) that would cleanse the whole people from their sins. This is to be a most solemn sabbath, and the joining of the regulations for it with those for the emergency situation caused by the sin of Aaron's sons suggests that the ritual for Yom Kippur was in effect the application of the emergency measures to Israel's national life as a whole.[10]

17:1–26:46 The Holiness Code

The longest section of Leviticus has come to be known as the Holiness Code, because it contains a wealth of regulations that specify just how Israel is to express in daily life the holiness it must have as a people uniquely covenanted to the holy God. The first regulations, concerning the slaughtering of animals, are intended to preserve Israelites from objectionable rites of their neighbors, who often sacrificed to demons or natural forces (Leviticus 17:7). Israelite sacrifices are to be brought to the door of the tent of meeting. The people are not to eat blood, which carries the life (from God) of the flesh (17:11) and is thus the reason blood can serve in rites of atonement.[11] The harsh penalty of excommunication in many cases testifies to the seriousness of the offenses. Note also the uncleanliness incurred by eating animals that have died naturally or been torn by beasts (17:15).

Chapter 18 begins by distinguishing Israelite ways from those of Egypt and Canaan. Only the Lord should determine what Israel does, and that doing has to be holy as the Lord is holy. The transition to illicit sexual offenses suggests that the ways of Israel's neighbors that are being proscribed are sexual licenses associated with those nations' fertility rites. "Uncover nakedness" means "have sexual relations." The first prohibitions regard incest, and the relations covered include those formed by marriage (that is, with in-laws).[12] Leviticus 18:19–23 cover various practices considered unacceptable. The children devoted to Moloch (the Hebrew text does not have "by fire") may imply either human sacrifice or ritual prostitution. The penalties for homosexuality (male) and bestiality in chapter 20 are death (20:14, 15). The last verses of the chapter suggest a rationale for Israel's possession of its land: The previous possessors behaved abominably and so were unworthy of the property of the holy Lord. If Israel behaves abominably, it will meet the same fate.

Chapter 19 repeats the call to be a holy people, first focusing on the cardinal commands to revere one's parents, keep the sabbaths, and not practice idolatry (compare Exodus 20:2–17 and Deuteronomy 5:6–21). The rest of the chapter interweaves cultic requirements with ethical demands, showing us again the mutuality of the two in ancient Israel. Noteworthy are the command to leave gleanings for the poor, the command to honor the deaf and the blind, the command to judge with strict justice, and the command (sometimes mistakenly thought original with Jesus) to love one's neighbor as oneself (19:18). These commands are spoken forth by the Lord through Moses and so have the force of divine commands. Behind the prohibition of mixing breeds and seeds may lie the idea that God fixed the different species at creation and so their separateness ought to be respected. Many of the other practices that are proscribed likely were practiced by Israel's neighbors —for instance, the use of mediums and wizards. The protections legislated for strangers sojourning in the people's midst reflect the best of ancient Oriental ideas about hospitality. (Note that Leviticus 19:34 commands love of the stranger as oneself.)

Chapter 20 lays out the harsh punishments to be inflicted on those who disobey the laws of holiness. First, those (Israelites or strangers sojourning in Israel) who sacrifice children are to be killed by stoning. Clearly, this practice was considered a special outrage. In cases in which the people do not exact punishment, perhaps because they do not know of the offense, God assures that the guilty persons will be cut off from the divine favor. Adultery, incest, male homosexuality (female homosexuality is not mentioned), and bestiality all warrant death. The excommunication warranted by sexual relations during a woman's menstrual period show the Israelite dread of wrongful contact with blood. The theme is repeated that clean living is required for the rightful possession of the Lord's land, here embellished as flowing with milk and honey: primed to be prosperous, as part and parcel of the blessing of living rightly convenanted to the Lord. In 20:24–26, the separation of Israel from other peoples, like the separation of clean and unclean, completes the work of creation, where God separated out the different elements. "Holy" (*qadosh*) basically means "separate."

Chapters 21 and 22 largely deal with priests and sacrifices: people and deeds required to have a special holiness. Thus the priest is segregated from ordinary death and must stay clear of defilements from sexual irregularities in his household. The various other regulations reflect what ancient Israel found suspect or ill-fitting for those who would have close contact with the holy God. The physical blemishes or defects express once again the holism of ancient notions of both the person and holiness. Like laypeople, priests in a state of uncleanness should not approach the holy sanctuary. Strangers may not share in Israel's sacrificial food. The regulations for sacrificial animals parallel the requirements that priests be physically unblemished. Leviticus 22:26–28 show a kindly regard for mother-child relations among animals.

Chapter 23 is concerned with the religious festivals and its regulations concern all the people. First is the weekly Sabbath, when none is to work. Then comes the annual calendar. The feasts of Passover and unleavened bread apparently were originally separate and ancient observances that became linked after the Exodus and refocused to celebrate that event. The festival mentioned in 23:15–22 came to be known as the Feast of Weeks or in Greek Pentecost (fifty days after the appearance of the first barley). The festival meant in verses 23–25 was the New Year, which translated as the seventh month in the Babylonian and Persian calendar that postexilic Jews followed. After this came Yom Kippur, the Day of Atonement prescribed at the end of chapter 16, and then the Feast of Booths (*Sukkot*), a harvest festival that in preexilic times was the most important observance in the calendar (see Ezekiel 45:25, where it is simply called "the feast").

Chapter 24 seems mainly composed of P material from sources other than the core block of laws concerned with holiness. Verses 1–9 give details for how the tabernacle is to be maintained. The story about blasphemy against the divine name (reality) suggests that that was more likely to occur among people not fully Israelite. Verses 17–21 may have landed here by association with stoning. (Implied in stoning is the idea that the whole community takes part and acts out the judgment on the criminal.)

Chapter 25 contains some remarkable prescriptions that elaborate the important notion and observance of the Sabbath. First there is the command to give the land and animals a sabbatical year (rest every seventh year). Every seventh sabbatical—fiftieth year—was to be a Jubilee, when the land was to lie fallow, all slaves were to be freed, and property was to be returned to its original owner. The rationale for these and the other prescriptions is that the Lord is the true owner of all the land. The Jubilee is to serve as a reference point from which rents can be calculated. It is to help people hold onto their inherited land and provide them all a landed stability. Clearly the text reflects traditions after Israel's entrance upon the promised land.

Equally clearly, it reflects a wonder about the Lord's provision of that land and a faith that, having done such a great thing, the Lord certainly can make the land prosperous enough to make the sabbaticals and Jubilees possible. The instructions about redeeming the land move in this same atmosphere and work against regarding the land as simply property on which human beings may speculate. Milgrom notes that this ancestral system was outmoded by the time of the early monarchy (tenth century B.C.E.), and that the references to city dwelling (25:29 ff.) show emendations in view of later circumstances.[13]

In the canonical redaction, the Jubilee legislation may well have functioned to preserve ancient ideals intimately tied to a vivid sense of the Lord's sovereignty over the land—ideals that later sharp dealing or outright injustice would have made a basis for quite negative judgments about Israelite religious fervor. The limitations on taking interest and accepting slaves are similarly idealistic and similarly related to a vivid sense that the mere possession of the promised land was a wonderous gift from God. The striking refrain is that the people must remember that their Lord brought them out of Egypt, where they had been slaves. Therefore, they should not themselves enslave anyone else. The first verses of chapter 26 tag on a prohibition against idolatry, perhaps occasioned by the foregoing reflections on the land (with its attendant temptations to idolatrous fertility rites).

The conclusion to the Holiness Code is a blend of consequential blessings and punishments: the good that will follow on keeping the precepts and the evil that will follow on disobeying them. Such a cautionary list was common in ancient codes of law, such as the Hittite suzerainty treaty on which the biblical covenants drew (See Exodus 23:20–33, Deuteronomy 28). Among the blessings we should remark are the land's prospering, the people's peace, the people's victory over their enemies, and God's abiding in Israel's midst. The punishments for disobedience, which bulk larger than the blessings for obedience, will include sickness, the land's infertility (the land is a partner to the covenant), defeat by enemies, and all sorts of other calamities—seven times as many as the people's sins. The dominant image is of "walking": either with or contrary to God, who in return will either walk with Israel or walk contrary to it. Although verses 26:34–45 seem to envision exile to a foreign land, differences between them and the conditions of the actual Exile to Babylon (see, for instance, Jeremiah 29:5–7) suggest they may well have been composed before the Exile (at a time, however, when deportation was a live possibility). The figure of the uncircumcised heart (26:41), along with the renewal of the ancestral covenant focused on the land, ties the catalogue of blessings and punishments into God's own unwavering promise. Some commentators therefore see the Holiness Code as the heartbeat of the Torah.[14]

27:1–34 Commutation of Votive Gifts

This last section of Leviticus seems to be an appendix dealing with vows. Feminists note the lower valuation of females. The prevailing idea is that people have promised that if God does such and such for them they will in return render such and such a payment. Perhaps the money was a translation of what service at the shrine by the particular person would have been thought worth. Animals, house, and land also could become means of this sort of exchange. Firstlings (27:26) were already dedicated to God. A "devoted thing" was usually a consequence of holy war and had to be destroyed as an act consummating promises made to God. Verses 30–32 imply that a tenth of one's produce or flocks was automatically consecrated to God's use. As with Leviticus 26:46, which probably refers to the Holiness Code, verse 27:34, which probably refers just to the statutes of chapter

27, concludes by again affirming that these regulations came from God through Moses on Mount Sinai—that is, that they emphatically were part of the original Mosaic covenant.

HISTORICAL BACKGROUND

When we step back to ponder the context of legislation such as what we find in Leviticus, several notions seem presupposed. In addition to the obvious assumption that those addressed knew about the Exodus from Egypt and the giving of the covenant on Mount Sinai, it is clear that they were familiar with religious sacrifice and priesthood in general, as well as with the Levitical form that these had taken in Israel. Edward L. Greenstein, writing about biblical law, goes on, however, to explain some of the key notions or images that give the strictly legal portions of the Torah (itself considered more broadly as overall guidance) their bite. For example, there is the conception that God is a king who naturally would express his will to his subjects and detail the behavior he expected of them. God is also the partner to a covenant—a solemn contract or mutual pact—and so a partner to all of Israel's life. The laws assume that God dwells among the people of Israel and so can be affected by how they behave. Indeed, Greenstein even suggests that God is presented as sensitive to pollution of the environment and inclined to withdraw, as though in an allergic reaction, when the environment becomes tainted. All life derives from God, and God is close to all life, which somewhat explains the many dealings in blood. The holiness of God, as we have seen, produces a call for holiness (cleanness) in the people God has chosen. All of these notions, assumed by the biblical codifiers of the divine law, help to set the stage for the imperative mode in which the laws are given and help to explain why there is so much interest in both cleanliness and justice. The laws reflect the nature of their source.[15] Read at the time of the Exile, they would have strengthened the Israelites' will to stay apart from the Babylonians, an uncircumcised, unclean people.

LITERARY INTENT

Present-day scholarship tends to locate the major responsibility for the present design of Leviticus with the postexilic priesthood interested in the ritual life of the Second Temple built in 515 B.C.E. However, it considers many blocks of material—for instance, chapters 1–7 on sacrifice and the Holiness Code of 17–26—substantially older. Many of the regulations may well have come from religious sanctuaries—shrines or relatively minor places of sacrificial worship—of the monarchical period (about 1050 to 586 B.C.E.). Indeed, we even get glimpses of materials that may bear on premonarchic times close to the founding of the confederacy of the ten tribes.

The primary motivation of the priestly compilers likely was to define holiness in all of its implications and lay out a full, programmatic response to the crises of national life that late sixth-century Israel had relatively recently experienced: the fall of the Northern Kingdom in 721, the fall of the Southern Kingdom in 586, and the Exile to Babylon that lasted until 538. Their idea would have been that if cult and morality could be restored in Israel in full detail and vigor, the life of the people would prosper. Involved here was a conviction that the recent disasters had been the result of apostasy from God. The priestly editors lay special stress on a strict observance of the Sabbath, on the regulations for the Jubilee year, and on the cleanness that a holy people ought to possess. The regular cultic aim of the legislation was to atone for the grievous failures that had brought about the national disasters. Generally speaking, this priestly outlook and laws such as those of Leviticus prevailed as the people's regnant ideal until the destruction of the Temple in 70 C.E. After that there were no actual sacrifices in Judaism, but the rabbis pursued a fascinating study of the laws of sacrifice, while they built on the other laws an ongoing refinement of how the people were to eat, do business, observe the Sabbath, conduct themselves sexually, and so forth.

LASTING SIGNIFICANCE

All of the Hebrew Bible, of course, has a lasting significance as the Scripture that Jews venerate as the primary instance of God's Word. With the slight changes entailed in regarding it as the Old Testment, this corpus of writings has been nearly equally significant for Christians. Both groups tend to think that, when placed in the context of the times when it originated, this body of Scriptural narrative and law is remarkable. We can, of course, note that other cultures were producing remarkable documents nearly simultaneously. Works of the Greek tragedians, the Indian authors of the Upanishads, the earliest Buddhists, and the earliest Confucians come to mind. But in Western cultural history the personal quality of the biblical God, combined with the elevated morality demanded in many of the laws, led to the conviction that Scripture was a unique revelation from the source of all creation. No doubt, this sense of superiority led to considerable arrogance and cultural imperialism, but on some headings comparative research tends to support its claims. There is nothing quite like the transcendent personalism of the Israelite God in the axial period of world history (about 750–250 B.C.E., when the great civilizations were founded and the great ideas about human nature proposed.) Similarly, there is nothing quite like the ethical stringency. Even when we wish to reserve the right to criticize parts of the Mosaic legislation, we should remember that part of its power stemmed from the Israelites' conviction that it amounted to a quantum leap beyond what their Near Eastern neighbors had attained.

The story of how Western religion evolved cultically and ethically from the time when Leviticus was finally redacted to the present would entail some fascinating chapters. Spatial limitations suggest, however, that we conclude our reflections here with annotations on two points. First, the connection that Leviticus establishes between cult and ethics argues that worshiping God and doing right by one's neighbors cannot be separated. The prophets, as we see later, frequently leaned upon this argument, and, in their case, as in the case of Leviticus, the argument ran both ways. That is, those who did not do right by (do justice to) their neighbors were suspect of going to the cult with unclean heart and hands. Equally, however, those who did not worship purely (with proper dispositions, even more than with proper forms) were considered unlikely to prove good neighbors. In present-day religious terms, this suggests reflections about the relations between prayer and praxis, or between love of God and love of neighbor. In present-day secular terms it suggests a certain critique or modification of both terms of the (originally Freudian) criteria for mental health that most of our contemporaries assume: the ability to love and the ability to work. Does such love go to the foundations of the mystery of existence? Does such work express intentions to treat one's neighbors with the justice that one seeks for oneself?

The second point worth annotating concerns the holiness that Leviticus so regularly pursues. In modern times we have tended to shrink "holiness" to an almost genteel sense of being selfless and sweet. Even when a good candidate for sainthood, such as Mother Teresa of Calcutta, breaks such a narrowed framework (if we look closely at how she actually lives), our popular approaches to her in the press or on television underscore her smallness and simplicity. Leviticus reminds us, sometimes in the shocking mode of having God flame forth to consume evil-doers, that the divine holiness must include the power, the raw energy, that made this world of nuclear explosions, of evolutionary violence, of human passions often gone astray. When translators deal with the raw religious experiences that prevail (for woe as well as weal) before people get fully civilized and tidy things up, they find themselves reaching for words such as "awesome" and "terrible," which in their original connotations — before they became popular slang — meant to express hair standing on end and shivers running down the spine. So Jacob, after his dream of the angels' ascending and descending and God's renewing the Abrahamic promise to him, breaks out in these words: "Surely the Lord is in this place; and I did not know it." The text notes that he was afraid and so further said: "How awesome is this place! This is none other than the house of God, and this is the gate of heaven" (Genesis 28:16–17). We cannot try to recapture such experiences artifically, but we can try to appreciate the depths of power and mysteriousness that they broke open, realizing that ancient predecessors often understand far better than we the otherness of the primary forces on which existence and life depend.

GLOSSARY

Holiness Code Chapters 17–27 of Leviticus, which detail the laws for ensuring, protecting, and promoting holiness (nonordinariness, specialness, sacredness).

Holocaust A form of sacrifice in which the victim/gift is burned to symbolize complete giving to God.

Jubilee The fiftieth year (after seven cycles of seven years) when all land was to return to its ancestral owners and slaves were to be freed — a super-Sabbath.

Redaction Editing; reworking.

Sabbath The Jewish day of worship, fashioned in conjunction with the picture of God's rest after creation (Genesis 2:2–3).

Sabbaticals Times of rest and renewal; seventh days or seventh years considered dedicated to God.

Second Temple The temple rebuilt upon return from Exile in 520 to 515 B.C.E. The Babylonians had destroyed the first Temple, built by Solomon.

Suzerain An overlord to whom vassals owe fealty.

STUDY QUESTIONS

1. What is the significance of the requirement that people who have offended against justice to their neighbors must offer atoning sacrifices to God?
2. Why was it just for God to destroy the sons of Aaron by fire?
3. What sort of "cleanliness" do the laws of chapters 11–15 have in mind?
4. Speculate about the psychology involved in the practice of sending the goat off into the wilderness to Azazel.
5. Explain the function of the Jubilee year.
6. What prosperities is walking according to the Holiness Code supposed to bring?
7. How does Leviticus manifest a presupposition that God is like a king?
8. Why did the priestly editors of Leviticus think that obedience to its laws would bring the people a better life?
9. Does a religious program based on cult and social ethics leave out anything of first-rank significance?

NOTES

1. See Jacob Milgrom, "The Book of Leviticus," in *The Pentateuch*, ed. Charles M. Laymon. Nashville: Abingdon (Interpreter's Concise Commentary), 1983, pp. 185–233.
2. See Anthony Phillips, "The Undetectable Offender and the Priestly Legislators," *Journal of Theological Studies*, 36 (1985), 146–50.
3. See Bernard J. Bamberger, "Leviticus," in *The Torah*, ed. W. Gunther Plaut. New York: Union of American Hebrew Congregations, 1981, p. 801.
4. Ibid., pp. 808–13.
5. See Denise Lardner Carmody, *Women and World Religion*. Nashville: Abingdon, 1979, p. 97.
6. See Milgrom, "The Book of Leviticus," p. 210.
7. See G. J. Wenham, "Why Does Sexual Intercourse Defile (Lev 15:18)?," *Zeitschrift für die alttestamentliche Wissenschaft*, 95 (1983), 432–34.
8. See Bamberger, "Leviticus," p. 855.
9. See Carol L. Myers, "The Temple," in *Harper's Bible Dictionary*, ed. Paul J. Achtemeier. San Francisco: Harper & Row, 1985, pp. 1021–29.
10. See Milgrom, "The Book of Leviticus," p. 213.
11. See Adrian Schenker, "Das Zeichen des Blutes und die Gewissenheit der Vergebung im Alten Testament," *Münchener Theologische Zeitschrift*, 34 (1983), 195–213.
12. For nuance on this point, see Angelo Tostato, "The Law of Leviticus 18:18: A Reexamination," *Catholic Biblical Quarterly*, 46 (1984), 199–214.
13. See Milgrom, "The Book of Leviticus," p. 228.
14. See Wayne A. Turner, *Leviticus*. Collegeville, Minn.: Liturgical Press, 1985, p. 80.
15. See Edward L. Greenstein, "Biblical Law," in *Back to the Sources*, ed. Barry W. Holtz. New York: Summit, 1984, pp. 83–103.

CHAPTER 6

Numbers

TEXTUAL ANALYSIS

Numbers is the fourth book of our present Torah or Pentateuch. It derives its name from the Greek (Septuagint) title, which in turn comes from the census or enumeration that the Lord commands Moses to make at the outset of the book. The main traditional sources of Numbers are P, to which most scholars attribute the legal materials, and JE (the Yahwist and Elohist sources are virtually interwoven, or at least very hard to distinguish), which appears in the narrative sections. Numbers concentrates on the wanderings in the wilderness and lays great stress on the murmurings or grumblings of the people, whom the Lord repeatedly must punish. The breakdown of the text favored by most analysts has three major parts:

> 1:1–10:10 In the Desert at Sinai
> 10:11–22:1 The Journey from Sinai to Moab
> 22:2–36:13 Events of Moab[1]

1:1–10:10 In the Desert at Sinai

These materials mainly come from the priestly source and offer miscellaneous laws. The book begins, however, with the Lord ordering Moses to take a census of the people who have come out of Egypt. The time is a month after the construction of the tabernacle, and the organizing principle of the census is to follow families, by fathers' houses. One of the main interests is to estimate the people's military strength, so the focus is on males 20 and older. Each of the twelve tribes of Israel is represented by a named elder. Commentators tend to regard the number of able warriors given for each tribe as unbelievably large, and so either simply exaggerated or representing the strength of Israel at a time much later than the wandering in the wilderness.[2] (The priestly tradition tended to stress the Lord's bounteous fulfillment of the promise to Abraham that he would have a vast progeny, and it also liked to stress the Lord's provision for the multitude throughout the stay in the wilderness.) The Levites were not numbered because their duties at the tabernacle excluded them from military service. Non-Levites approaching the tabernacle were to be put to death, and the purpose of the Levitical guard was to keep the wrath (of the holy God) from striking the community. Here we have the notion, familiar from Leviticus, that improper (unclean or sinful) relationship to the Lord is mortally dangerous.

In chapter 2 we hear of the Lord's arrangement, through Moses, of how the different tribes are to encamp. The tribes are arranged around the tent of meeting and cover all four directions of the compass. Some commentators link this arrangement with the Feast of Booths. Military considerations may also have been a factor, and historians of religion no doubt would note that covering all four directions of the compass is a way of symbolizing wholeness. The tribe of Judah has the first position in the marching order. Insofar as this is honorific, it may represent the fact that Judah later became the site of both the monarchy and the efforts to reconstitute the people after the Exile. The Levites, according to Numbers 2:17, are to be in the middle of both the march and the encampment, and, according to 2:33, they were not counted in the military enumeration.

At the outset of chapter 3 we get another "generations" (toledot), which we know from Genesis is a marker or guiding pattern. Here the focal line is that of Aaron/Levi, which suggests that the authors saw in this priestly tribe an importance parallel to that of Adam, Ham, Abraham, and Jacob: a further specification of where the most significant activity of the Lord was to be located. The fusion of Aaron with the other Levitical people in the priesthood is attributed to God's command, given through Moses. They are to be like first-born, especially consecrated to God. (The danger in this designation is suggested by the reference in 3:13 to the Egyptian first-born whom the Lord slew.)

There follows a nonmilitary census of the Levite males more than a month old (the time of presumed viability and so full humanity). The Levitical census includes subdividing and assigning the different priestly responsibilities—for the tabernacle, the ark, and so forth. As though in miniature of the major encampment of all the tribes, the different subgroups of Levi are ranged around the tabernacle at the different points of the compass. The families of Moses and Aaron get the eastern side of the tabernacle, toward the sunrise (always a marvelous sign of God). The holiness of the area around the tabernacle again is emphasized by the warning that any who approach it illegitimately court death. Another census counts the first-born of all the tribes, repeating that the Levites stand stead as the first-born peculiarly the Lord's. The redemption discussed in 3:46–51 depends on the assumption, which we have seen before, that first-born (first-fruits of the power of life, which in the Bible rather directly comes from God), belong to God. If they are not going wholly to serve God (let alone be sacrificed to God—an instinct that some pagan tribes carried out literally), then something must substitute and buy back their debt.

Chapter 4 shows us still another census, this time of the mature men (aged 30 to 50) of the different subgroups of the tribe of Levi, and it describes the different priestly tasks that the Lord, through Moses, distributed to each subgroup. The Kohathites, who deal with the most holy things (4:4), are the most in danger (4:18–20).

The first four chapters of Numbers, then, display the (ultimately divine) work of census taking that Moses accomplished at Sinai, before the people started marching or wandering toward the promised land. Chapters 5 and 6 contain somewhat miscellaneous materials: laws about holiness, laws about abstinence, and the famous priestly blessing of 6:23–27. First, as though to emphasize the holiness of the encampment commanded by God and centered by God's presence in the tabernacle, such unclean people as lepers, those having genital discharges, and those who have had contact with the dead are put outside the camp. Second, God stipulates that sinners, male or female, must confess their wrongdoing and make restitution (see Exodus 22:7–15, Leviticus 6:1–7).

Third, there is a procedure for dealing with marital infidelity, real or suspected, and the jealousy it can cause. Verses 5:16–22 describe the ordeal that a woman accused of infidelity must undergo. (Feminists note the absence of a parallel rite for males charged with infidelity). The assumption is that through this psychosomatic test God will manifest the woman's guilt or innocence. Part of the affliction following on guilt would be sterility. Numbers 5:31 means that her husband will not be accounted as sharing in the wrongdoing of the woman found guilty.

The details of the Nazirite vow of special consecration to God that we see in chapter 6 are interesting indications of what ancient Israel thought facilitated or went into special nearness to the Lord. Numbers 6:2 implies that women could take this vow. The separation from wine or even grape juice is noteworthy, as is the separation from the corpse of even closest family. The blessing at the end of the chapter has long been loved for its beauty, and we should understand the "peace" with which it concludes as a comprehensive state of well-being based on God's kindly regard.[3]

Chapters 7 and 8 deal with the offerings of princes or tribal leaders and more regulations for Levites. Numbers 7:1 does not square chronologically with 1:1. The offerings — full wagon loads of various valuables — are to (God at) the tabernacle, and the Lord has Moses accept them. They are then made over to the different Levitical servants of the tabernacle, according to the services they perform. The Kohathites, we may note (7:9), have to carry the (most) holy things on their shoulders (during the march). There follow twelve days of offerings, one for each tribe, and this listing is in effect not only another census but another census constructed from interest in the precinct of the priests. Numbers 7:89, on God's speaking to Moses in the tent of meeting, from above the mercy seat that was on the ark, fulfills the promise of Exodus 25:22.

In chapter 8 Aaron sets up the seven lamps and Moses cleanses the Levites. Shaving the hair, like washing one's garments and self, was an expression of purification. The Levites then are to be presented to the people, who will lay hands on them (an indication that the people's need to sacrifice their first-born to the Lord passes onto the Levites, who fulfill it). This became central in priestly "ordination" (a word cognate in Hebrew to "lay their hands"). The Levites are now like a wave offering (a gift set in motion toward God; the motion might be symbolized by hands or body). The implication is that the Levites now stand to Aaron as the waved sacrifices (Exodus 29:24) stand to God. The Lord repeats that the Levites will be like his first-born, and 8:19 relates their service to keeping plague away from the people (who might sinfully have come near the sanctuary). It would not be far-fetched to see the celibacy required of some Christian priests as an interpretation of the possession by God described here, although celibacy was not required of Levitical priests. The chapter concludes by assuring us that these instructions were carried out and stipulating that the period of a Levite's priestly service was from age 25 to age 50. The implication is that the service requires the strength of a man's prime years.

The final section of our first division of Numbers, 9:1–10:10, deals with three final occurrences that precede the actual setting out on march. First, there is the commemoration of Passover. The time is that of Exodus 40:17 (when the tabernacle was erected) rather than that of Numbers 1–6 (a month later). All, even those unclean from contact with the dead, are to keep the Passover, both native Israelites and foreigners sojourning in their midst. Second, the text notes that the cloud of the divine presence was over the tabernacle, and the people would stay when it was stationary and move when it moved. Third, we learn of the two silver trumpets that became a staple in Israelite assemblies and goings-to-war, and we should note (10:10) that they were to help the people remember the Lord their God.

10:11–22:1 The Journey from Sinai to Moab

After these considerable preparations, the march through the wilderness (existence en route to the promised land) begins. The cloud moves out and the people follow. The tribes follow the staged order previously prescribed. In 10:29 we come upon the first bit of material surely from JE, concerning Hobab, an in-law of Moses, whom Moses invites to share in the venture of acceding to the promised land. This seems to reflect a tradition that Midianites were allies of Israel in its early period and helped in the wilderness. Numbers 10:35–36 depends on the belief that the Lord is the people's protective warrior. The two sayings of Moses recorded here have come to be used at the beginning and the end of the traditional Torah service of the synagogue.

With chapter 11 we enter on the theme of the people's murmuring. Lawrence Boadt has noted how this theme connects Numbers with Exodus. As well, he has underscored the more punitive action of the Lord in Numbers. Moses is no uncontested leader, and the sixth-century B.C.E. readers for whom P arranged the whole could look back on recent centuries of rebellion and trial. Perhaps the conjunction of their own time with that of Moses would have offered them some consolation.[4]

The stories of murmuring illustrate the difficulties of being the chosen people, thrown on the mercy of God to survive. In the wilderness the people are ground down, before they can be built up in the promised land. God must provide food and military victory. Neither a wrongful self-sufficiency nor the old slave mentality will suffice. The murmurings of the people show the attractions of this slavish mentality, which lives close to the Earth (from which the leeks and onions come).

The new mentality, oriented to God and heaven (from which the manna comes) makes great demands on Earth-bound, unheroic human beings. In the liminal period of the wilderness, Israel is being initiated into the new form of existence proper to the covenant relationship that ought to flourish in the promised land. Only the new generation will enjoy that phase of the covenant. As in an initiation, the old (here, the old generation) has to die before the new can flourish. Moses, Israel, and even God himself often seem on the verge of discarding the troubled relationship revealed in the desert. Yet despite all the troubles, the Israelites finally persist. Even more important, God finally persists. The unconditional commitment of God to Israel ultimately is much more significant than the flarings of the divine wrath. The murmurings and punishments therefore are bounded, contained, by a gracious, merciful divine love.

It is not clear what the first "misfortunes" of the people were, but it is clear that the Lord dislikes hearing about them, for he makes his fire blaze forth to consume outlying parts of the camp. Soon the complaints become more specific: a hankering after the better diet available in Egypt. The details that follow are roughly familiar from Exodus 16. Moses feels put upon by the discontent of the people and the anger of the Lord, as though unfairly given the burden of being the mother of Israel. There follows, as a solution, something like the division of labor suggested by Jethro in Exodus 18, although here the number of seventy elders is specified. God speaks in amusing hyperbole, promising the people so much meat they will become sick of it, the way a parent might respond to a balky child. Moses doubts that such largesse will be possible, but the Lord's hand is not shortened. (Is Moses, too, forgetting what God did in leading the people out of Egypt?) We note that the elders are able to prophesy because the (divinely inspiring) spirit that was upon Moses was put on them as well. Numbers 11:26–31 display Moses as generous about such divine gifts—he would be happy if all of Israel had God's spirit and could prophesy. The wind that goes forth from the Lord to bring the quail could be another figure for the powerful divine spirit, even though the punishment of plague that eating the quail brings suggests that the miracle was done from spite.

Chapter 12 shows us grumbling in the inner circles of leadership, Miriam's and Aaron's disliking the wife of Moses and the preeminence that Moses has. Verse 12:3, stressing the meekness of Moses, is interesting, because it makes the proclamation of the Lord about the special dignity of Moses the more powerful: God is speaking up for his shy friend. Miriam's leprosy is like an outer affliction befitting her inner disorder. Some commentators argue that Aaron's punishment was the more severe: inner guilt and the need to humble himself before Moses.[5]

Chapter 13 tells of the expedition to reconnoiter the land of Canaan, the good report the scouts make of the fruitfulness of the land, and the mixed counsel they give about the military strength of the inhabitants. Whereas Caleb seems confident of the Israelites' counter-strength (because of his faith in the Lord?), others make a false report about both the value of the land and the power of its inhabitants, to discourage a military expedition.

This false report, we see in chapter 14, throws the ever-volatile people into wails of despair and more complaints. They want to go back to Egypt, but Moses and Aaron fall on their faces before the people (a sign of their weakened leadership?), and Joshua and Caleb express anguish at the people's willingness to forego the promised land and to distrust the power of the Lord. For this faith they win the sentiment of the people that they should be stoned. The glory of the Lord appears, and Moses hears another expression of the divine exasperation. Moses defends the people, arguing rather slyly that destroying them will discredit God's own power to fulfill his promises. Verse 14:18 is a lovely description of the better nature of the Lord, and 14:19 has become part of the ceremony for Yom Kippur, the Day of Atonement.

God agrees to a pardon, yet with the proviso that the grumblers will not see the promised land. Only Caleb, whom the Lord praises for his courage and faith, will go into the land. (The omission of Joshua suggests that this text is from another tradition interested in spotlighting Caleb.) We read a repetition of this judgment of God, with the intriguing bit of irony that God will let the little ones enter in, as if to spite those who thought the children would be like prey. This judgment of God explains the forty years of wandering—the passage of a generation—and links it neatly with the forty days that the reconnoitering of the land (the gathering of the facts necessary to make a good decision) required. Indeed, those who made a false report die of plague. Others only compound the bad situation by now deciding, against the judgment of God that they will have to wait, to try to gain the promised land. Moses warns that, because the Lord is not among them (they are in disgrace), they will only suffer defeat. But they go forth to battle and are defeated.

Chapter 15 lists various cultic laws, as though originally it had been part of what is now chapter 10. Numbers 15:17–21 prescribe the first offering the people are to make after gaining the land. The punishment for breaking the sabbath is worked out to be stoning, and in 15:37–41 we get an explanation of the origin of tassels or fringes that makes them memos—reminders to heed the commandments of the Lord.

Chapter 16 (according to the Septuagint and Christian versions; 16:1–17:15 according to the Hebrew) describes the serious rebellion of Korah, Dathan, and Abiram. They object to the leadership of Moses and accuse him of having brought them from a prosperous Egypt to a threatening wasteland, as well as not having fulfilled the pledge of leading them into the promised land. Moses is angry, but when the Lord threatens to consume the whole people he intercedes so that the punishment falls only on the wicked leaders of the rebellion. (In 16:22 Moses and Aaron are like Abraham in the case of Sodom, defending the just from the punishment of the wicked.) The Sheol of 16:33 is the land of the dead, beneath the earth. Numbers 16:36–40 buttress the notion that the priesthood of Aaron is exclusive and uniquely holy. When the people protest the destruction of the rebels, Moses and Aaron have hastily to intercede lest the wrath of the Lord consume all the rest. Chapter 17, the story of Aaron's budding rod, is but another, miraculous confirmation or defense of the legitimacy of the Aaronic priesthood, but it leaves the precise relation of the Aaronites to the Levites uncertain.

Chapter 18 begins by stressing the responsibilities that Aaron will bear for any cultic improprieties, and then it distinguishes between the Aaronic priests, who are to be the chief officers and will have access to the innermost precincts of the tabernacle, and the Levites, who shall serve the Aaronic priests and work outside the inner precincts. This arrangement clarifies the relations between the two groups and answers the question of the people in 17:13: They will not perish because the Aaronic priests will risk the near contact with the holy Lord that is so dangerous. Numbers 18:8–20 detail the gains of the Aaronites, concluding with a special Aaronic covenant of "salt" (probably everlasting: see Leviticus 2:13) and a striking statement that only the Lord is Aaron's portion of Israel's inheritance. Numbers 18:21–32 are a parallel account of the benefits of the Levites, who receive a tithe from all the people as their inheritance, and who in turn must give a tithe or tenth of their receipts to the Lord.

Chapter 19 has the interesting ritual involving the ashes of the red heifer, which puzzled the early rabbis and probably represents the last vestiges of an ancient, pre-Israelite rite of exorcism that the Israelite understanding of sacrifice had transformed.[6] The intent is to provide a way of cleansing people from the impurity suffered by contact with the dead. Chapter 20 assumes that thirty-eight years have gone by and brings us toward the end of the forty-year drama of wandering. The people arrive at the wilderness of Zin and Miriam, the sister of Moses and Aaron, dies and is buried at Kadesh. The people grumble again about their living conditions, especially their lack of water, and the Lord has Moses work the miracle of getting water from a rock (see Exodus 17:1–7). The Lord's judgment that Moses will not enter the promised land assumes that he did not believe this miracle would occur. Numbers 20:14–21 tell of the refusal of the Edomites to assist Israel. The King's highway of 20:17 went from Damascus to the Gulf of Aqaba. The remainder of the chapter tells of the death of Aaron at Mount Hor. Because of his disbelief about the water from the rock he cannot enter the promised land. The priesthood passes to Eleazar, his son. Numbers 33:38 says that Aaron died in the fortieth year of the march, by which calculation chapter 20 has jumped the narrative forward thirty-eight years, with only silence about what happened in the interval.

Chapter 21 tells of a battle with Canaanites, whom the Israelites defeat (after some initial losses) by the power of the Lord. The people complain again and the Lord afflicts them with fiery serpents. This time the people repent and beg Moses to intercede for them. The rite of the bronze serpent seems to utilize a sympathetic magic for healing (a serpent cult flourished in Egypt — probably for fertility — while in Greece the serpent was associated with Asclepius, the god of healing). The remainder of the chapter is a collection of reports about wanderings, battles, and songs that is hard to organize. By the power of the Lord, the Israelites prevail and come to possess the land of Bashan, a fruitful plain (see Deuteronomy 3). The second portion of Numbers ends at 22:1 with the people settled in the plains of Moab, beyond the Jordan at Jericho. They have concluded a great march, east and north from Kadesh and Mount Hor to Jericho, and now they stand poised to enter the promised land of Canaan to the West.

22:2–36:13 Events at Moab

Chapter 22 is famous for the incident of Balaam's ass. The Moabites, afraid of Israel, engage Balaam, a diviner (wizard, occult figure) to curse Israel. (The assumption is that battles between human armies involve the spiritual forces on which those armies depend.) Balaam, apparently an honest practitioner of his art, consults with God (makes a thoughtful examination of the situation), and gets the judgment that he should not curse Israel. (One of the most interesting implications of this story is an Israelite belief that the one Lord works in the consciousnesses of all people who seek the truth.) The emissaries of the Moabites persist in entreating Balaam, he refuses but again consults the Lord, and the answer that he receives is somewhat vague. Thus it is peculiar that God is angry when Balaam goes with the Moabites (perhaps Baalam should have awaited further instructions; two traditions seem spliced here, a bit ineptly).

The ass can see God's angel (here a good symbol for God's presence and will), but Balaam cannot. The story clearly is meant to be humorous or folkloric (Balaam seems to accept the speech of the ass as quite ordinary). Upon gaining vision of the true situation, Balaam promises to do the divine will. Chapters 23 and 24 show us the further consequences of this conversion to God's will, because the oracles that Balaam pronounces confirm the chosenness of Israel in God's sight. We should note the theme of singularity in Numbers 23:9, the veracity of God and protective blessing of Israel stressed in the second oracle, the symbolism of Israelite military might involved in the third oracle (as well as the inspiration of the Spirit of God, which marks Balaam as a true prophet), and the prediction in the fourth oracle (where the clear vision of Balaam is stressed) that Jacob will crush Moab and gain supremacy over all the neighboring tribes.

Chapter 25 shows Israel's defecting from pure faith and engaging in the pagan rites of its neighbors. (The link between marriage or sexual contact with foreigners and taking on their religious rites is regular in the Bible.) The penalty for this defection is death, at the command of the jealous God. God praises the parallel religious jealousy of Phinehas and blesses his Aaronic line with a covenant of perpetual priesthood. The Lord then directs Moses to have the Israelites harass the Midianites who led them astray.

The census of chapter 26 shows some notable differences from the census of chapter 1, Simeon having appreciably declined and Manasseh appreciably grown. (Scholars dispute whether the census figures should be taken whole or interpreted in terms of "contingents"; the dispute hinges on the meaning of the Hebrew word *elef*: "thousand" or "contingent?")[7]

In chapter 27 we are told how certain laws concerning family inheritance arose, among them the rights of daughters to inherit (when there are no sons). The inheritance is to stay in the family and keep the name of the family alive. Although females clearly were not given rights equal to those of males, the fact that they could inherit property at all was unusual in the ancient Near Eastern world. The rest of chapter 27 portrays the succession of Joshua to the role of leadership that Moses has been carrying. The succession is effected by a priestly laying on of hands in the sight of the whole people.

Chapters 28 and 29 provide regulations for sacrifices by the whole community (see Ezekiel 45:18–46:15) according to the calendar laid out in Leviticus 23. These chapters tend to be accounted material from P and reflective of the cult of the postexilic Temple in Jerusalem.[8] Note that Numbers 28:1–8 deal with sacrifices to be made each day and so effect a constant dedication to God. Chapter 30, which mainly deals with the vows of women, assumes that they are subordinate to the male heads of their households. Thus only widowed or divorced women are held fully responsible for their vows. Chapter 31 shows us the ferocity of Israel at sacral war (the Midianites were considered corrupters of Israelite religion). We note the notion that one becomes unclean by touching the dead,[9] rather than by slaughtering the live. The chapter also discusses the taking and distributing of booty, which easily could become a motive for such war.

In chapter 32 Reuben and Gad want to settle down east of the Jordan, but they gain Moses' permission only by agreeing to fight with the other tribes in the effort to conquer Canaan. Numbers 32:13–15 interprets the forty years of wandering as a punishment for not being willing to fight at the time of Caleb and accuses the new generation of equally angering the Lord. The rest of the chapter credits the holdings of Reuben, Gad, and Manasseh to the distribution of Moses. The recapitulation of the wanderings in the wilderness that we find in chapter 33 lists some forty-two way stations, but it does not square with the order given in Numbers 21. Many of the places cannot now be located. The death of Aaron at Mount Hor is placed in the fortieth year after the Exodus from Egypt. At the end of the chapter the Lord tells the people that their possession of Canaan depends on their willingness to destroy its inhabitants and their idols. Many centuries of battling the Canaanite tribes and their fertility rites echo in this command.

Numbers 34:1–10 give us the boundaries of the Israelite possessions in Canaan, as though the extent and form of the conquest were all foreordained by God. Some fundamentalist interpretations of these boundaries would make them relevant to present-day Israel, but that certainly is anachronistic.[10] In the rest of chapter 34 Eleazar the priest, Joshua the successor of Moses, and the chiefs of the different tribes are to work out the division of the land among the Israelite people.[11]

Chapter 35, contradicting Leviticus 25 and Numbers 18, provides an inheritance for the Levites. Among their cities shall be six that offer sanctuary to people involved in blood-feuds. God again commands the establishment of such cities after the Conquest, suggesting that clan vengeance was a significant social problem. The distinction between murder and manslaughter is interesting, as are the rules that bear on the avenger of blood. At the end of the chapter the explanation for all this concern is that blood pollutes the land (which belongs to the holy God). Chapter 36 stipulates that women who have inherited land must keep it a family possession by marrying within their own tribes. With this final tidying of how the promised land is to be divided and inherited Numbers concludes its rendition of the ordinances given to Moses in the plain of Moab.

HISTORICAL BACKGROUND

Although the final editing of Numbers is quite late, it clearly presents traditions of considerable antiquity and presupposes residual knowledge of the clannish life that preceded the people's establishment in Canaan.[12] The time between the Exodus and the entry into the promised land intrigued later generations, which saw it as a time when Israel received many of the laws on which later social life depended. Numbers presupposes the importance that priestly life had attained in later centuries, as well as the preeminence of the Aaronic line (for which the later editors may be working up some propaganda). It presupposes the election of Israel and the Abrahamic promise both that the people will increase and that it will inherit the Canaanite land. Moses is unquestionably the spokesman or great prophet of God. The spirit of God given to Moses can extend to other people, including such pagans as Balaam.

Finally, the JE strand of Numbers represents interpretive memories of early Israel as a confederacy of tribes housing many grumblers. Although no defection is as outstanding as the apostasy of the Golden Calf (Exodus 32), there are constant withdrawals of faith in God and regularly God blazes back in fury. The God of Numbers, in fact, is harsh, spiteful, and jealous to an extreme: in all likelihood a testimony to the religious threats that the time in the wilderness was remembered as having contained. He commands military slaughter and hands out death penalties left and right. The military adventures of the period in the wilderness are significant, as are the movements of rebellion within the people. Overall, then, Numbers remembers the generation from the Exodus to the Conquest as a spotty bunch, despite their impressive numbers.

LITERARY INTENT

The motives of the different traditional strands that for convenience scholars label J and E continue in Numbers to be what we have previously sensed. The sources used intend to praise the God of the ancestors, for both his fidelity and his con-stancy, and to stress the people's unworthiness of their convenantal election. Numbers may also present Moses as a less than ideal leader, meek and sometimes failing in faith (most crucially at Meribah, when he doubted he would get water from the rock), but it certainly is committed to the primacy of Moses as the spokesman for God. Indeed, in Numbers we see more of the prophetic or inspired aspect of the Mosaic vocation than we had previously. Numbers, probably in an expression of the theology of P, stresses the miracles that God worked on the people's behalf.

P also seems interested in justifying Israel's military ventures as commanded by a God jealous for pure worship. Relatedly, Numbers castigates foreigners as either seducing Israel away from pure cult or opposing the vocation Israel has from God to be unique among the nations and inherit the land of Canaan. Perhaps because the theme of the land bulks so large, Numbers is interested in the laws of inheritance and the sacrifices that the people as a whole are to offer (after Joshua has been commissioned to lead them — that is, in their solidarity as the people of the Conquest and promised land). In terms of its final canonical interests, Numbers shows itself to be a priestly work, concerned with correlating blocks of legal materials with a narrative of the wandering in the wilderness that will make them legislation for a people en route to military conquest of the promised land. [13]

LASTING SIGNIFICANCE

In reflecting on what new themes Numbers has introduced (beyond what we have seen in the Pentateuch thus far), we find that holy war and military ferocity stand out. The first three books certainly have shown us ancestors' doing battle and God's smiting the Egyptians, but in Numbers Israel becomes more aggressive and God becomes more jealous than previously either has been. Whereas Leviticus stressed the holiness, and thereby the dangerousness, of the Lord, Numbers stresses his jealousy and concern that his people not be corrupted by foreigners. We know that after the Exile Israel went through a period of trying to purify itself of ties with foreigners, but here that concern is made part of the theological endowment left by Moses. No doubt many present-day readers will find this theme unattractive, so it bears a bit of reflection.

What our Bible calls the "jealousy" of God is a justification, apparently quite early, for a sense of a special destiny and obligation to holiness that Israel read back into the Abrahamic covenant. To have the relationship with God, and with the promised land, that the religious experiences of Abraham and Moses implied, the people would have to foreswear all other allegiances. Moreover, they would have to elevate their morals — the justice they showed one another — and develop a cultic life that would place them in a clean, fitting, holy relationship with their God. The fact that their God was holy did not completely distinguish the Israelites from other peoples. But the fact that the holiness of their God was transcendent, unearthly, considerably different from the venerable powers that made the Earth flourish and the animals bring forth young set the Israelites apart.

The kindest reading of the rituals for purification, the punishments by God, and the phenomenon of sacred slaughter of one's enemies at God's command is that they were attempts to express the responsibility Israel felt to covenant worthily with God. A fully critical reading, however, has to note the dire consequences this doctrine had in subsequent history (Christian and Muslim history more than Israelite history). The related consequence is that "God" becomes an impossibly flawed reality. Even when we admit that the divine holiness is not peaches and cream, as we tried to explain in the last chapter, the fact remains that unless the divine has a moral status more elevated than human politicians and warmongers it is not much of a God.

We thus tend to consider the savagery depicted in parts of Numbers as the product of underdeveloped religiosity and overdeveloped chauvinism. In blunt terms, it is not God who is commanding slaughter (even though the Scriptures clearly say that it is) but authors at that point too much concerned to promote the interests of their own tribes. Saying this, of course, makes us critics of the whole notion of "Scripture" and intractable enemies of the fundamentalist position that would make Scripture God's simon-pure address from heaven to earthlings below. So be it. We shall have many more occasions to praise the qualities for which the biblical understanding of life has been accounted divine. On this occasion, though, we have to make it plain that we consider the Bible a thoroughly human book (and so we really should not be surprised, let alone scandalized, that on occasion it proposes an ethics we cannot abide). The text itself, as we have noted, has no illusions about human imperfection. It would not surprise the biblical authors, therefore, that they and their later editors now and then missed the mark about the nature of the mysterious God.

Last, we may note that the view of women that we get in Numbers has been part of the ancestral endowment responsible for the second-class status of women in Western history. The Bible does offer enough portraits of strong, respected women to indicate Israel's deep appreciation of its foremothers. But as the inheritance laws of Numbers (like the laws of purity of Leviticus) show, women suffered considerably more liabilities and enjoyed considerably fewer advantages than men when it came to the structural format of Israel in what we may call its constitutional era. Many of these aspects of second-rank status derive from the organization of clannish or tribal life, which stressed rule by mobile military chiefs and male heads of extended families. But the fact remains that in the texts that became scriptural for Western culture women appear under the control of men in ways that call into question their equal worth to the human community.

GLOSSARY

Exorcism The process of trying to cast out evil spirits thought to have possessed a person.

Holy War War sanctioned by God, often supposedly led by God (the prime warrior), and sometimes requiring complete slaughter of the enemy.

Kohathites A Levitical family who had the important function of transporting the Holy of Holies.

Nazirite vow A consecration to God requiring abstaining from wine and other intoxicants, not having one's hair shorn, and not going near a dead body.

STUDY QUESTIONS

1. What is the main function of the tribe of Levi?
2. What implications do you see in the ordeal described in chapter 5 and the Nazirite vow described in chapter 6?
3. Why do so many of the people's grumblings concern food and drink?
4. How does God punish those who disagree with Caleb?
5. What is the significance of the oracles of Balaam and of his prophetic stature?
6. How is the Israelites' possession of Canaan through warfare justified?
7. Explain the establishment of sanctuaries for homicides.
8. On what historical events is the harshness of the God of Numbers perhaps based?
9. What picture of Moses does Numbers want to give?
10. What do the portraits of God and women in Numbers suggest about the authority of this scriptural book?

NOTES

1. See Helen Kenik Mainelli, *Numbers*. Collegeville, Minn.: Liturgical Press, 1985, p. 3; Frederick L. Moriarty, "Numbers," in *The Jerome Biblical Commentary*, ed. R. Brown, J. Fitzmyer, and R. Murphy. Englewood Cliffs, N.J.: Prentice-Hall, 1968, volume 1, p. 87; W. Gunter Plaut, ed., *The Torah: A Modern Commentary*. New York: Union of American Hebrew Congregations, 1981, pp. xv–xvi.
2. See Harvey H. Guthrie, Jr., "The Book of Numbers," in *The Pentateuch*, ed. Charles M. Laymon. Nashville: Abingdon (Interpreter's Concise Commentary), 1983, p. 238.
3. See Michael Fishbane, "Form and Reformulation of the Priestly Blessing," *Journal of the American Oriental Society*, 103 (1983), 115–21.
4. See Lawrence Boadt, *Reading the Old Testament: An Introduction*. New York: Paulist, 1984, pp. 191–93.
5. See Plaut, *The Torah: A Modern Commentary*, pp. 1101–2. Traditionally 248 commands were accounted positive and 365 negative. See B. Martin, "Mitzvah," in *Abingdon Dictionary of Living Religions*, ed. Keith Crim. Nashville: Abingdon, 1981, p. 487.
6. See Jacob Milgrom, *Studies in Cultic Theology and Terminology*. Leiden: E. J. Brill, 1983, pp. 85–95.

7. See Plaut, *The Torah: A Modern Commentary*, p. 1206.

8. See Guthrie, "The Book of Numbers," p. 269.

9. See David P. Wright, "Purification from Corpse-Contamination in Numbers XXXI 19–24," *Vetus Testamentum*, 35 (1985), 213–23.

10. See Plaut, *The Torah: A Modern Commentary*, p. 1239.

11. See A. Graeme Auld, *Joshua, Moses and the Land*. Edinburgh: T. & T. Clark, 1983, pp. 72–87.

12. See Madeline S. Miller and J. Lane Miller, eds., *Harper's Encyclopedia of Bible Life*, 3rd rev. ed. San Francisco: Harper & Row, 1982, pp. 121–232.

13. See Boadt, *Reading the Old Testament: An Introduction*, pp. 190–91. See also Brevard S. Childs, *Introduction to the Old Testament as Scripture*. Philadelphia: Fortress, 1979, p. 200. On the overall significance of the wilderness experience — the murmurings, itinerary, and literary impact — see George W. Coats, *Rebellion in the Wilderness*. New York: Abingdon, 1968. See also George W. Coats, *From Canaan to Egypt*. Washington, D.C.: Catholic Biblical Association, 1976; Frank M. Cross, *Canaanite Myth and Hebrew Epic*. Cambridge, Mass.: Harvard University Press, 1973.

CHAPTER 7

Deuteronomy

TEXTUAL ANALYSIS

Deuteronomy, the fifth and last book of the Torah, derives its name from the Greek for "Second Law." It presents Moses repeating the law — giving it a second time — and exhorting the people to obey it. The setting that Deuteronomy has within the canonical Bible as the capstone of the Torah helps to explain the mode of discourse that we find in it. Because it comes after Genesis, Exodus, Leviticus, and Numbers, it appropriately reflects on the significance of what has happened in those books. Because it presents Israel at the end of the journey in the wilderness, Deuteronomy rightly ponders what the movement from slavery in Egypt to the verge of entry into the promised land means. The Deuteronomic Moses reviews the highlights of the trek, of the trials, and of the law, but his main concern is to elaborate the significance of these experiences. He is about to leave his people, and he wants them to appreciate, to take to heart, what has happened to them. Compared to the prior four books of Torah, Deuteronomy therefore appears more philosophical. T. S. Eliot might have been walking in the footsteps of the Deuteronomic Moses when he pondered the human liability to "have the experience and miss the meaning."

We discuss the historical background of Deuteronomy later, but from the beginning readers should know that it represents a new strand of biblical tradition, probably from the seventh century B.C.E., interested in invigorating the religious and national life of Judah, the Southern Kingdom. The most useful division of the text follows the five speeches of Moses:

1:1–4:43   First Discourse or Prologue

4:44–11:25   Second Discourse

11:26–28:69   Third Discourse

29:1–32:52   Fourth Discourse or Final Appeal

33:1–34:12   Fifth Discourse or Blessing and Leaving[1]

1:1–4:43 First Discourse or Prologue

Deuteronomy begins with Moses' recapitulating the experience of the people in the wilderness. The Israelites are on the verge of crossing the Jordan to conquer the promised land, so their leader offers them a review of the mixed experience — success and failure, faith and unbelief — they have had in the forty years since the experiences on Horeb (Sinai). The narrative repeats incidents we have seen previously (especially in Exodus or Numbers), but with more detail about the enemies fought. The great lure of the whole trek is the good land of Canaan, but the reason that Moses himself is not allowed to pass over and share the Conquest is unclear. Instead of focusing on the incident of unbelief at Meribah (Massah), Deuteronomy gives the impression that God is dissatisfied with Moses' leadership—and his inability to contain the people's grumbling and command their full obedience (3:26). The next chapter of the story belongs not to Moses but to Joshua, who will lead the expedition that will cross the Jordan.

In chapter 4 we start to hear the distinctive tones of the Deuteronomic Moses. He typically exhorts Israel to hear or give heed to the statutes that, in the name of the Lord, he is imposing upon it. The rationale for these statutes is that they lay out the way of life (prosperity, flourishing) that Israel may enjoy in Canaan (4:1). The laws of God, connected with the nearness of God, will make Israel distinguished among the nations (4:6–8). The verses against making graven images, in this introductory context, are best understood as linked with the formlessness (4:12) — the genuine mysteriousness — of the sovereign Lord of Sinai from whom the laws of life derive. Rather than graven images of agricultural deities, the people should remember the historical experiences they have had since the dramatic Exodus from Egypt. Deuteronomy 4:29–31 are especially provocative: The people will find the Lord by searching wholeheartedly, enduring their tribulations in faith, and relying on the covenant God swore with the ancestors (Abraham, Isaac, and Jacob). Moses interprets the revelations of the Lord and his election of Israel as both awesome and unique, and so as a motive for embracing the legislation that the Lord gives. The first address therefore is a rather dramatic, hortatory prologue. More profoundly than in the theologies of Exodus, Leviticus, and Numbers, the God of the Deuteronomic legislation is an elusive presence best tokened by the codes that would form the people in the dispositions of "life": obedience to the mystery that has guided their dramatic history of being freed from bondage, tried in the wilderness, and brought into the possession of the long-promised land.

4:44–11:25 Second Discourse

The second discourse on the Law begins by stressing the present rather than the past: It bears on the covenant that God struck with Moses' generation on

Sinai. One explanation for such a stress on contemporaneity would be liturgical or ceremonial: These words may well have been used in the later cult. The version of the ten commandments that we find in Deuteronomy 5:6–21 may be older than the version we saw in Exodus 20,[2] but it differs little in content. Deuteronomy dwells on the divine fire from which its words of life derive and wraps them in the cloud of the awesome mystery of the Lord. To its mind, the central religious act is obedience: fearing the Lord and walking in the ways of his commands.

Deuteronomy 6:1 begins, "This is the commandment." What follows is a lengthy discourse on the meaning of the first commandment, "I am the Lord your God." Verse 6:4 is a famous passage, named the *Shema* ("Hear") from its first word. The implications of the Shema most significant in later history were monotheism — the utter oneness of the true divinity[3] — and the primacy of religious love. In biblical religion, the one God is the human person's greatest treasure. Indeed, the human personality ought to be erotic about (passionately in pursuit of) the divine beauty and goodness. The overall religious configuration that we find in Deuteronomy may stress obedience, but in the Shema we glimpse the love from which such obedience ought to spring. Verse 6:8 became the basis for wearing *tefillin* ("phylacteries": small boxes, containing parchments with scriptural passages inscribed, that are wrapped around the hand and the head by leather straps and that are used for morning worship). Verse 6:9 led to the *mezuzah* ("doorpost"): the small container and parchment (on which are inscribed Deuteronomy 6:4–9 and 11:13–21) placed on the door of Jewish dwellings.[4] Verse 6:20 has become part of the ritual for Passover, linking the Law to the liberation from Egypt. Note also the theme of teaching one's children: This is a new generation that does not know slavery first-hand.

In chapter 7 we again witness the destructive side of the religion of a jealous God, as the people are commanded to destroy their Canaanite enemies utterly and have no intermarriage with them. Deuteronomy 7:7–10 have been influential in the doctrine of grace that became important in biblical theology, because they make it plain that any distinction Israel has comes from God's free, unmerited love. As well, they offer a thorough assurance of the divine faithfulness, suggesting that the God of the covenant is the one still point in the turning world. The rest of the chapter perhaps taints this elevated doctrine, making the love of God and faith in God the basis for attaining material prosperity and prevailing over one's military enemies, but that is what we have in Deuteronomy: patches of sublime religious instinct in a general quilt of quid pro quo or religious economics (obedience tied to benefits). Alternately, we might say that the unconditional divine passion for Israel stands in tension with the conditional terms of the covenant.

Deuteronomy 8:3, set in the midst of a call to remember all of God's provision for the people through their desert wandering, is familiar to Christians from Jesus' quotation of it during his temptation by Satan in the wilderness (Matthew 4:4; Luke 4:4). In Deuteronomy it is another recommendation of the primacy of the divine Torah over anything material. Deuteronomy 8:5 gives us the interesting symbolism of parental disciplining: God treats Israel like a child in need of stern upbringing (rules and punishments for breaking them). The Deuteronomic theology of the covenant, in fact, interprets the Israelites' misfortunes as punishments they rightly deserve for breaking faith with the Lord and disobeying the Torah.

Indeed, as the remainder of chapter 8 shows, Deuteronomy considers forgetfulness of God and immersion in present material prosperities to be the great bane of Israelite weakness. Whereas memories of the wilderness ought to bring God's gracious provision back to mind, and enjoyment of present prosperities ought to move Israel to bless the Lord, their source, the people are liable to forget from where their wealth comes. In all religions a main reason for liturgical ceremonies is to spark remembrance, anamnesis, and biblical religion is no exception. By reciting the stories of how God formed them and rededicating themselves to their constitutional law, the people might be kept from the most deadly effects of their amnesia (lack of remembrance).

Chapters 9:1–11:25 play variations on these themes. Standing on the verge of conquering the promised land, the people have to have it made unmistakably clear to them that God is the source of all their blessings, and that their past history of dealing with God shows them ever-inclined to forget their source.[5] Deuteronomy 9:4–5 have the theme that the Canaanites are wicked, and so rightly dispossessed — a good example of the biblical writers' search for moral justifications for historical happenings.[6] Indeed, Moses next narrates the stubbornness of Israel in the wilderness and then its infidelity in the incident of the golden calf. The Mosaic intercession for the people gets a boost, as though God only spared the people out of regard for Moses' defense of them. The stone tablets and ark of wood are two powerful symbols of the covenanted life that the Mosaic intercession (and legislation) made possible.

Deuteronomy 10:8–12 actually express several important motifs. First, the commandments appear as prerequisites for possession of the land. Second, Canaan contrasts with Egypt. Whereas Egypt was irrigated by the natural overflow of the Nile, Canaan was irrigated by occasional, irregular, extraordinary waterings by God. God's land, one might say, drinks from heaven, while the land of unsanctified human beings roots after earthly sustenance: leeks, onions, garlic, and the like. The biblical writers were impressed by the dependence of the rich Canaanite agricultural economy on the precarious fall of rain. They saw a special divine providence in this, and it seemed to them symbolic of the entire special relationship Israel had with God.

Deuteronomy 10:12–22 represent the Deuteronomic writers again on the upbeat and lyric about the love of God. All that God requires is obedience and return of love from the heart. This is merely fitting, because the one creator God, purely of his own goodness, has chosen this people. Deuteronomy 10:16 suggests a deeper exploration of the meaning of circumcision: purification or dedication of the heart. Deuteronomy 10:17–18 are memorable testimonies to God's justice and care for the afflicted. The greatest witness to the Lord's stature and goodness was the Exodus from Egypt. The seventy from whom God made the multitude (10:22) seem to be the house of Jacob as calculated in Exodus 1:5. The "terrible" deeds of the Lord are his acts filled with awesome might.

We may note the loving appreciation of the promised land that rings through-out chapter 11, which is one of several biblical passages that could sponsor a better appreciation of ecology in Western culture. Deuteronomy 11:18–25 are virtually a reprise of the last part of the Shema, driving home the value that Israel is to attach to the Torah of God given through Moses. The Deuteronomic code, in its own eyes, is guidance for the best of lives: walking with the one true God and enjoying a beautiful portion of God's creation.

11:26–28:69 Third Discourse

The middle of Deuteronomy is the version of specific Mosaic legislation about the main aspects of Israelite life that this tradition wants to establish as canonical for Israel (and that did in fact become canonical, insofar as the establishment, in the fifth century B.C.E., of Torah as Israel's authoritative Scripture made Deuteronomy the capping book). The closing verses of chapter 11 are a summary: blessing or curse, Israel? Which shall it be? The blessing on Mount Gerizim and curse on Mount Ebal apparently represent an old tradition that regarded Shechem, which lay between them, as the principal site of the divine presence. (The Samaritans claimed that Gerizim was superior to Jerusalem.)

Some commentators have claimed that Deuteronomy 12:2–7 comprise the core of the Deuteronomic legislation, and they read these verses as the most direct expression of the Deuteronomic desire to consolidate the people's cult in Jerusalem.[7] Jerusalem, on this reading, is "the place which the Lord your God will choose, to make his name dwell there" (12:11), to which the people are to bring their sacrifices. They are to forsake other religious shrines, but they may slaughter in the countryside (so that they need not come to Jerusalem to have meat; however, the proscription of eating blood remains in force). The effect of this whole is to make the centralized worship later established in Jerusalem part of the Mosaic endowment. (On the other hand, Jerusalem is not mentioned by name, which may reflect the originally northern origin of this line of thought.) Note the repeated theme that the religious ways of Israel's neighbors (including child sacrifice; see 12:31) are hateful to the Lord and should be avoided at all cost. It seems likely that one of the motives for centralizing the cult in Jerusalem was to move the people's worship away from shrines whose proximity to Canaanite sites was likely to corrupt it.

Perhaps this is a place to suggest the attractions that Canaanite religion would have had for the Israelites and to explain why idolatry and infidelity had such a long-playing career. The naturalistic gods of Canaanite religion put the drama of vegetative life and death, in which farmers and shepherds feel themselves immersed, into vivid, personified form. In the Ugaritic texts concerned with Baal, the most popular Canaanite deity — and also a generic name for "divine lord" — this mightiest of gods triumphs over all challenges until he is undone by death. The Israelite experience of God had to contest this theology in which even divinity was subject to death, and it had, as well, to break the hold of the rituals by which the Canaanites tried to ensure fertility, lest Israelites forget that their God had shown, in the Exodus, that he was free of, more marvelous than, all the forces of nature, all the probabilities of history.

In a word, the attractions of Canaanite religion were the attractions that sensual common sense always exerts. Everywhere people tend to be mesmerized by the forces of sex, fertility, and death. Everywhere they find it hard to live by faith and spirit, which they cannot see and only occasionally can feel. But the Israelite priests and prophets insisted on a God not immanent in nature, not identifiable with the passions of birth and death, because they sensed that only such a God would not ultimately be a prisoner of the natural world. To be a savior, YHWH had to be the ruler of the world, not just part of its remorseless flux.

Chapter 13 legislates out of this background, making fidelity to the God who brought the people out of slavery in Egypt the touchstone of all prophecy and religious leadership. People who propose deserting this God and going over to the gods of the Canaanites deserve stoning (they are like murderers of the people's life). Probably we should both admire the passion of Deuteronomy for the Lord who formed the people and shiver at the abuses to which such extremist legislation could lead.

Chapter 14 is reminiscent of Levitical legislation, in that it seems to express and preserve the holiness that Israel has in virtue of its bonding with the holy Lord. Deuteronomy 14:24–26 are worth noting, both because they again show the concessions that the centralizers of Israelite worship realized their actions necessitated, and because they show that Israelite cult was not conceived in a puritanical or ascetical mode but rather was to be an expression of rejoicing in God — having a feast to God's praise and thanksgiving.

In chapter 15 the authors struggle with the problem of poverty, claiming, in 15:4, that the prosperity of the land (or the fair distribution of the fruits of the land) will eliminate poverty, but conceding, in 15:11, that the land will always have poor people (and so Israelites should be open-handed toward those in need). At the least we are encouraged to think that the Deuteronomic ideal goes against the greed and neglect of suffering neighbors that has made poverty criminal in many societies. Deuteronomy 15:13–15, dealing with the sabbatical release of slaves, is markedly more generous than the legislation of Exodus 21. Note that Deuteronomy 15:17 adds bondswomen to the bondsmen envisioned by Exodus 21:6.

The Deuteronomic twist to the legislation for religious festivals (Deuteronomy 16:1–17; compare with Exodus 23:14–17, Leviticus 23, and Numbers 28–29) is to require their observance in the central sanctuary in Jerusalem. We see that at the time of the Deuteronomic reforms Passover, Weeks, and Booths were the three major religious festivals, and that all were to be celebrated in joyous remembrance of the Lord's bounty. The people were not to come empty-handed, but they were to give back generously, no doubt as an expression of their appreciation of such bounty. Deuteronomy 16:21–22 seem to envision Canaanite practices that the authors wanted to keep apart from the Israelite cult.

Noteworthy in chapter 17 is the evidence that the monarchical form of government into which Israel had grown, after the time of the tribal confederacy and through the prowess of David, had changed the juridical outlook. We find a divine approval of the kingship and the official standing of the Levites, as well as other indications of the significant changes that centuries of settled, nontribal life in Canaan had worked on the original traditions of the people who gathered around Moses in the trek through the wilderness.

For example, Deuteronomy 17:15 speaks of the "gates" (of the city) to which abominable transgressors of the covenant should be brought for stoning. Deuteronomy 17:8 speaks of bringing difficult cases up to the place that the Lord has n (as his capital site). Verses 17:14–17 both give the divine sanction to the kingship (against other, antimonarchical strains that we witness later) and place limits on the extent to which the head of the government should be exalted over the people (verse 17:17 seems expressly directed against the lavish ways of Solomon). The greatest guidance of the king, however, will be the Deuteronomic law itself, in which he is to read all days and learn the fear of the Lord. For Deuteronomy (unlike the royal tradition we see later), the king is subject to the law, not above it.

After sketching some of the rights of Levites in Jerusalem and again warning against the abominable practices of the Canaanites, chapter 18 speaks of "a prophet like me [Moses]." The main intent seems to be to underscore the primacy of Moses in prophetship (as well as in legislation), perhaps in view of the prophetic movement that arose in the monarchic period. This may also be a desire to legitimate such "Mosaic" prophets as Samuel and Jeremiah. At the end of chapter 18, however, the criterion of following in the Mosaic prophetic line is quite pragmatic: If what the prophet says (usually in short-range predictions) comes true, he (or she) is genuine.

Chapter 19 shows us the Deuteronomic tradition putting its own stamp of approval on such disparate laws as those for establishing cities (three rather than the six of Numbers 35) of refuge and those for witnesses in court. The assumptions about court proceedings reflect the more organized situation of the monarchical period, when priests and judges were officials of the realm. The severity of judgment prescribed in 19:21 (see Exodus 21:23–24) could be taken as a symbol of the need to fit the punishment to the crime exactly.

The section 20:1–21:9, dealing with war, has a somewhat sermonic tone. War is construed as a religious event, with the Lord fighting for Israel against its enemies. However, exemptions from military service are possible. Deuteronomy 20:10–14 show that Israel's foreign enemies were to be given only limited options: surrender (and perform forced labor) or fight and, if defeated, have their males put to the sword, their women, children, and possessions taken as booty. The rationale for the slaughter of the Canaanites that the Lord is thought to impose is that the warrior King is to get this tribute, and Israel is to get a land cleansed of abominations. As well, vigorous Canaanites might lead Israel into false religion (20:18). Verses 20:19–20 today have an ecological ring. Originally, the concern probably was to preserve a source of food. The purification rite described in verses 21:1–9 is best explained by the pollution that shedding blood inflicts on both the land and the people.

The remaining legislation of chapter 21 has several remarkable features. We should note the consideration given the female captured as booty in battle, the strength of the Israelite convictions about the rights of the first-born son, the severity of the punishment befitting a rebellious son,[8] and the curse and defilement associated with being hanged. This last judgment figured prominently in early Christian assessments of the crucifixion of Jesus by the Romans.

The laws of chapter 22 offer some interesting glimpses into Israelite social life: the need for thoughtful and honest dealings with one's neighboring farmers, the strength of the need felt to keep the sexes differentiated, the tenderness toward mother birds (or the practical realization that they were the source of more eggs and young), the reluctance to mix kinds of seeds and animals, and the prescription for wearing fringes. Note the severity of the punishment for being an unvirginal bride, the fallibility of the tests (blood-stained sheets) for virginity, and the lack of any sanctions for being an unvirginal groom. Once again the explanation seems to be the patriarchal situation, in which females were like property. The laws against adultery appear fairly even-handed, although the burden of proof put on the betrothed virgin in the city is rather high. The punishment for rape (in open country) of a betrothed woman is more severe than the punishment for rape of an unbetrothed virgin because in the latter case the property can more fittingly be shifted to a new (rapist or fornicating) owner.

The legislation of chapter 23 is best understood as intending the purification of the assembly of Israel. Note the stigma of illegitimacy (22:2), the earthy regulations for keeping the camp of the warrior Lord holy, the proscription of cultic prostitutes (or hierodules), the ban on usury, and the sense Israel had that all people had some rights to an individual's land. The regulations in chapter 24 are meant to control divorce and wife swapping, but they provide women no right to initiate divorce.[9] Women did get some protection through the requirement that they be furnished a bill of divorce. That would both give the reason for the divorce (the "indecency" mentioned in 24:1 was not adultery, because adultery merited stoning) and furnish proof that the woman was free to remarry. Many of the other laws of chapter 24 seek the humane treatment of debtors and servants. Note the capital punishment for kidnapping (24:7), the principle of individual responsibility latent in 24:16, and the requirement that food be left in the vineyards and fields for the sake of the sojourner, the fatherless, and the widow.

Chapter 25, which details the levirate ("husband's brother") law designed to provide a widow and her dead husband with issue, stresses the importance of progeny as a kind of immortality and the obligation to be fruitful. Verses 25:11–12 would be humorous except for the severity of the punishment, which suggests the sacrality that Israel associated with procreative powers. Verse 25:19 is firm in its call not to forget past enemies.

Deuteronomy 26:1–11 carry liturgical overtones (verse 26:5, on the wandering Aramean — Jacob — became part of the Passover Haggadah). The recall of the Exodus links the fruitfulness of the land (being celebrated at harvest) with the liberation from Egypt and conquest of Canaan that were the crucial chapter of Israelite national history. The tithe, in which Levite, sojourner, orphan, and widow were to share, was a way of responding gratefully to the generosity of God. Deuteronomy 26:16–19 have a ceremonial ring, and we note the motif of "this day," which makes the laws and the people's agreement to them contemporary.

In chapter 27 the laws that Moses has been given are incorporated into a ceremony (associated with Shechem) to dramatize the people's coming into possession of the promised land. The use of stone seems to reflect a sense that older, more pristine materials are to be used (in many religious traditions stone symbolizes the changeless existence of the deity). The specific curses in the chapter recapitulate some of the high points of traditional law, but the chapter as a whole has the character of an interpolation that disrupts the flow between chapters 26 and 28. Perhaps the editors wanted to tie the responsibilities of the covenant more closely to the endowment of the land.

The blessings promised for obedience to the covenant law (28:1–14) are rather material. Deuteronomy 28:13, with its promise that Israel will be the head and not the tail, is a wry summary. We realize the problems that this correlation of religious fidelity and material blessing raises, of course, and by the time of the book of Job the problem had become acute: What happens when people are faithful and do not flourish, or when faithless people flourish rather than fail? Either the Deuteronomic theology comes into crisis, or God is found unjust, or people who are afflicted are forced to account themselves unfaithful sinners, even against their own consciences.

The many curses for disobedience to the law essentially mirror the fewer blessings for obedience, although the "curses, confusion, and frustration" of verse 28:20 have no full parallel in "blessings, order, and fulfillment." Some of the lines of the cursing are ironic to the point of humor, and they remind us that cursing (and blessing) on occasion became something of a rhetorical art. Deuteronomy 28:33 and 28:36 seem to reflect at least the fall of the Northern Kingdom to Assyria in 721 and perhaps also the Babylonian captivity of 586.[10] Deuteronomy 28:36–57 suggest in almost loathsome detail the horrors of the attacks, the sieges, and the conquest of the Babylonians. This connection of the punishments of the Exile with violations of the Deuteronomic code, of course, reenforces the final editors' view that obedience and disobedience correlate with prosperity and disaster.

Deuteronomy 28:63 does not hesitate to dress God in very human garb, making him delight in bringing ruin to a disobedient Israel. That image hardly squares with the fidelity of the Lord praised in other texts, and it reveals the unresolved tension at the heart of the Deuteronomic theology of the covenant: Does the covenant finally depend on God's pure grace, or is it essentially a matter of legal justice, such that when Israel fails its part of the bargain, by impure cult or immoral living, it is bound to suffer disaster? As a whole Deuteronomy inclines to the latter position, but it has enough sense of the divine grace to preserve the tension and in effect leave the whole matter of grace and justice mysterious, as no doubt it is always bound to be.

The conclusion of the third discourse, with the figure of Israel's not even being able to regain the wretched status of slave in Egypt, may reflect the depths to which the fall of the Northern Kingdom had taken the Israelite spirit and the way it had cast in doubt the reliability of the previously central metaphor that God finally stood to Israel as he had shown himself to be in the Exodus from Egypt. As we see later, the prophets brooded over these matters and took the question of self-understanding that they imply to remarkable depths.

29:1–32:52 Fourth Discourse or Final Appeal

In this fourth speech of Moses several motifs prevail. God is presented as like a king and Israel as like a vassal — the debts that the covenantal theology owes to ancient Near Eastern treaties between rulers and followers are quite plain.[11] Moreover, this Torah is declared valid for all generations, as a foundation on which Israel can build itself up faithfully. The first verses recall the Exodus from Egypt, and verse 29:4 is remarkable for the assertion that until "this day" the Lord had not given Israel a mind to understand the import of its history. The other great deeds of the Lord, which serve to warrant Israel's complete dedication to him, include his provision for the people in the wilderness and his granting them the victories over their enemies that have opened the Canaanite land to their control. The solemn language of Deuteronomy 29:10–15 has a cultic ring, as well as the note of everlastingness: The covenant begun with Abraham is here being fulfilled (by entry into the promised land) in such a way that all later generations may claim the Lord as their God. This section therefore is like a miniature of the entire Deuteronomic argument.

Deuteronomy 29:16–28 repeat the threat of punishment that infidelity to the responsibilities of the covenant — above all, to the responsibility to serve only the Lord in one's worship — will bring. This is another serving of the jealousy of the Lord, spiced by a detesting of idolatry and an awareness that true fidelity involves much more than merely external agreement to Israel's monotheistic worship. Unless the people are covenanted to the Lord in their hearts, they will not escape the punishments merited by religious desertion. This charge, obviously enough, gave the theologians who wanted to equate hard times with religious infidelity even more ammunition: Hard times would prove interior infidelity, even if no clear exterior infidelities lay to hand. Deuteronomy 29:29, reserving "the secret things" to God, may represent a later appreciation of the dangers involved in trying to make moral assessments about people's interior dispositions. Unless some mystery remains, so that people's consciences finally are surrendered to the adequate justice that God alone can give, a more subtle sort of idolatry has developed, according to which human lawyers, rather than craftspeople, have fashioned things that they would have substitute for the one God.

Deuteronomy 30:1–10 has the tone of harassment or dispossession from the land by enemies. Israel is to remember during its hard times the covenant with God and find in it hope for returning to the blessed land. The figure of regathering the scattered people potentially was very consoling. Deuteronomy 30:6, on the wholehearted love of God, shows the Deuteronomic school at its most appealing. Verses 30:11–14 insist, very appealingly, that the commands of the Lord are near and feasible: a word in the people's mouth and heart. The assurance in verse 30:14 that the word is such that "you can do it" contrasts with the Pauline interpretation of the law that has been very significant in Christianity. In traditional Jewish interpretation, sponsored here by Deuteronomy, the commandments are not impossible but in fact are eminently manageable. They constitute life itself for Israel: Without them Israel has no reason to exist and nothing to hold itself together. Indeed, God formed Israel precisely that this people obey the commandments.

Deuteronomy 30:15–20 resume the Deuteronomic theology in terms of a famous figure: two ways, of death and life, with the stirring command, "therefore choose life." Life means dwelling in the land promised to the ancestors, which makes Zionism, both the general entity (love of the land promised in the ancient covenants) and the modern version (the aspirations that led to the present state of Israel) quite comprehensible.

Chapter 31 shows us the changing of the guard, as Moses, now aged 120 (the 80 he was at the Exodus, plus the forty years of wandering in the desert— both figures of fullness or completion) and forbidden by God from sharing in the actual conquest of Canaan, passes his mantle to Joshua. The people must believe that God will give them the victory. Deuteronomy 31:9–13 offer a rationale for the cultic renewal of the (Deuteronomic version of) the Torah at every sabbatical year, during the Feast of Booths. Note how the cultic occasion is understood as the whole people's "appearing before the Lord." The commissioning of Joshua occurs at the tent of meeting, where the Lord appears in the pillar of cloud (his regular form by day through the march).

The Deuteronomist authors cannot forego one last reference to the infidelity that will arise after Moses, a reference that probably reflects the later disasters of the divided monarchy and perhaps also reflects the sense that the Mosaic period was a golden age compared to which all subsequent ages were bound to seem tarnished. The conception that what Moses has received from God is a "song" is further evidence of the cultic, ceremonial strain that runs throughout Deuteronomy.

Banias, one of the sources of the Jordan river. This picture shows a representative portion of the lovely land.   *(Used with permission of the photographer, Wolfgang Roth)*

Placing the book of the law by the ark of the covenant meant installing it at the heart of Israelite religion. Sometimes this "book" is linked with the text found in the Temple during the reign of Josiah (about 620 B.C.E.), which became the basis for considerable religious reform. The final lines of chapter 31 present Moses as foreseeing the people's later defections and justifying the evils that befall them as their just deserts.

The song or psalm of chapter 32 is a lyric summary of the Deuteronomic thought, with elements of a lawsuit in which the justice of God is vindicated against the infidelity of Israel. The opening verses equate the Torah with rain falling from heaven (it is words of life). The main theme is that God is a rock of fidelity whereas the people are ever wanton, ingrates and amnesiacs. The middle verses of the chapter recall in high poetic style all the benefits God worked in forming the people, liberating them, and guiding them through the wilderness. He is the father of Israel (in other biblical texts maternal imagery prevails, as we see later) who created it. God's jealousy (and the people's sufferings) are presented as spurred by Israel's provocative infidelities. Whatever qualifications we may want to enter about the God of Deuteronomy, we cannot charge the authors with having a God who floats above human affairs, uninvolved with the people to whom he is convenanted.

The imagery of the rock continues, and verse 32:35 gives us the memorable line about vengeance's belonging to God (see Isaiah 61:2): He will deal with both Israel and its enemies. Verse 32:39 stresses the singularity of the Lord, with overtones reminiscent of the Shema (6:4). The militant, vengeful character of Israel's Lord returns, set forth as a basis for his meriting praise from all the nations (32:43).

Moses enjoins the people to take "all these words" (the Torah) to heart—they are no trifle but the life of the people through all their generations. He will die on top of Mount Nebo, able to see the promised land but forbidden from entering into it (because of his infidelity at Meribah, verses 32:51–52 make explicit), and he is gathered to his people (Deuteronomy has little notion of a life after death, except in the sense of joining one's forebears and continuing in one's children.)

33:1–34:12 Fifth Discourse or Blessing and Leaving

Like a symphony that cannot quite bring itself to end but must try for one last finale, Deuteronomy appends to the farewell speech of Moses a last blessing and a reprise of his actual death. In the background seems to be the last blessing or testament of Jacob (Genesis 49), so the literary effect of Deuteronomy 33 is to present Moses as a new ancestor of the twelve tribes who has done for Israel through law what Jacob did through procreation. The style again is poetic, but in this song Israel replaces the Lord as the central reference. The main burden of the blessing is to recount special features of each of the twelve tribes and to have the legislative ancestor of the people beg appropriate blessings for each tribe. The tribes of Levi and Joseph get the most space, but all of the tribes fare quite well. Most of the memories and tributes are positive, and the summary line seems to be Deuteronomy 33:29: "Happy are you, O Israel! Who is like you, a people saved by the Lord, the shield of your help, and the sword of your triumph!"

Chapter 34 presents again the picture of Moses ascending Mount Nebo that we got at the end of chapter 32. No one knows the exact place where he was buried (34:6), and ever afterwards there never arose a prophet like Moses, whom the Lord knew face to face (34:10) and used for the miraculous liberation from Egypt. Joshua stands by, commissioned to continue Moses's work, so the Deuteronomic authors conclude by preparing us for the next part of their narrative.

HISTORICAL BACKGROUND

Clearly, Deuteronomy presupposes knowledge of the ancestral covenant, of the Exodus, of the wandering in the wilderness, and of the origin of the basic Israelite religious code in the period of the desert when Moses was Israel's great leader and link with the Lord. It is impossible for us to retrieve the exact historical experience that lay behind any of these items, but the whole composition of Deuteronomy depends on its readers' finding plausible the picture of Moses and the interpretation of the people's relationship to the Lord that the speeches of Moses exhibit.

When biblical scholars examine the form of Torah developed in Deuteronomy, they tend to stress several explanatory categories. First, comparative studies have made it seem quite likely that the school of writers who began what became Deuteronomy, working in the eighth and seventh centuries B.C.E., self-consciously shaped their covenant by reference to Neo-Assyrian diplomatic conventions, which included laying out the rights and the duties of both parties to a covenant between a king and his vassals and listing blessings and curses that would result from fidelity or infidelity to the covenant. We can see these patterns in Exodus, and they have been altered in view of both the transcendence of the Israelite God and the peculiar history the Israelite people had had with him (especially the promise to Abraham and the liberation from Egypt). But too many standard features of political documents from then-contemporary sources stand out to make the Deuteronomic casting of the Torah as a convenantal quid pro quo accidental. The likelihood, therefore, is that by the time of Deuteronomy Israel had appropriated the political thought of its neighbors and had fused it with its own sense of God.

The features, standard in contemporary Near Eastern political documents, include a preamble dealing with the party accounted the superior (Deuteronomy 5.6a), an indication of the prior history of the relations between the two parties (Deuteronomy 1–3, 5:6b), a stipulation of the obligations of the party to the treaty accounted inferior (Deuteronomy 5:7–12, 12–26), a provision that the text of the treaty be placed in a temple and periodically read aloud to the people (Deuteronomy 10:5, 27:2–3, 31:10–11), and blessings and curses for obedience and disobedience (Deuteronomy 27–28).[12]

Another aspect of Deuteronomy that present-day scholars tend to emphasize is the cultic character of many passages. At the very least the authors of Deuteronomy assume that Israel joined ethics and worship, as we have previously seen. It is likely, as well, that the authors assumed a knowledge of (perhaps an earlier stage of) the priestly legislation represented so fully in Exodus, Leviticus, and Numbers. They, however, were attempting to correlate the fortunes of the nation with its fidelity or infidelity to the God of the ancestors and so to buttress the program to centralize official worship in Jerusalem.

For example, three laws of Deuteronomy 12 suggest that the authors had quite specific incidents from the monarchic period in mind and wanted to ensure that a reformed cult, centralized in Jerusalem, would keep the people more faithful to their God. Deuteronomy 12:2–7, on destroying the places where the neighboring Gentiles worshiped false gods, suggests the entire body of idolatrous kings, from both the Northern Kingdom (Israel) and the Southern Kingdom (Judah), who tolerated such paganism or even succumbed to it. Deuteronomy 12:8–12 suggest the prior period of the judges when Israel was deciding whether to have a king like the other nations (see Judges 17:6, 18:1, 19:1). The refrain is that every man then did what was right in his own eyes, and that many such doings were abominations. Deuteronomy 12:13–28 suggest the disobedience of Saul to Samuel that resulted in Saul's line not gaining the kingship (see I Samuel 13:7–14, 15:10–29).[13] Parts of Deuteronomy also may assume the experience of the Exile to Babylon and the horrors of the siege that preceded it (see verses 28:49–57, 64–68; 29:28–30:5).

LITERARY INTENT

The book of Deuteronomy that we now possess is not only an independent entity and a part of the Pentateuch, it is also a part of a larger block of material, now represented by the swath of biblical literature running from Deuteronomy to 2 Kings. We may say, then, that Deuteronomy establishes the program on which the former prophets are based. The recent tendency of literary historians seems to be to relate the Deuteronomist school to traditionists (keepers of traditions) of the Northern Kingdom who began, nearly from the inception of the Northern Kingdom (from the breakup of the united kingdom of David and Solomon about 930 B.C.E.), to stress obeying the covenant by keeping the (quite old) prescriptions about social justice and pure cult. We see some of this attitude in the Elohist tradition, which apparently predominated in the North. As the Deuteronomists developed it, by reflecting on the period of the judges, of the united kingdom, and then of the divided monarchies, the regular pattern was apostasy and punishment. The theology of Deuteronomy, therefore, is correlated with the history of the former prophets. Theologians of Deuteronomistic persuasion had quite mixed feelings about the value of the monarchy. In their eyes the reliance of kings and court politicians on power plays often detracted from the reliance on God that was the hallmark of Abraham, of the other ancestors, and of Moses: of the formative covenants.

The Northern Kingdom collapsed in 722 B.C.E., the victim of Assyrian assaults, but sympathizers in the South kept its theological outlook alive and influential. When King Josiah inaugurated a reform of the Southern Kingdom around 622, the Deuteronomists stepped forward to provide the rationale. The laws we now find in Deuteronomy 12–26 codified this reform, and many of the other chapters in Deuteronomy amounted to sermonic appeals for fidelity to God by obeying such laws. After Josiah's reform failed, revisionist members of the Deuteronomistic school rethought the history of kingship and clarified a pattern of loyalty and regression. From the experience of the fall of the Southern Kingdom in 586 and exile to Babylon until 538, the Deuteronomistic theology underwent a further refinement, but one that only sharpened its theses about the connection between fidelity to the covenant and national prosperity.[14]

The editors who prepared what became the canonical Torah were much influenced by the reforms of Ezra and Nehemiah, which aimed at repristinating the community that was reestablished in Judah after the Exile. The features of Deuteronomy that Brevard Childs has stressed when searching after the canonical motivations include: (1) a timeless quality (as though the canonical editors wanted to separate Moses and the covenant from the limitations of their own or any other historical period and make the Torah ever-contemporary: the book for all of Israel's generations); (2) an eschatological quality, insofar as the people stand at the verge of entering the promised land, which is a great symbol of consummation; (3) a centralizing tendency, perhaps most clearly seen in the line that runs from one God to one mediator and convenantal law to one people (formed on the basis of the Lord-Moses-Torah); and (4) an interest in making a book — a timeless definitive text — that can be the people's ever-present guide or constitution.[15]

The careful reader, like Childs, will see that these four characteristics of the canonical text present some logical problems. How, for instance, does timelessness square with eschatology (consummation at the Conquest)? How does fashioning the Torah into a book square with constantly renewing the one community in cultic ceremonies? To raise these questions is not to imply that they cannot be answered. It is, however, to suggest that the canonical editors of Deuteronomy themselves brought into being a text that on its own terms demanded ongoing interpretation. We cannot say whether they did this deliberately or inadvertently. Our guess, however, is that they did it somewhat deliberately because they certainly had had many opportunities to learn, from writing and editing, that a text "moves" and so is living whenever one shifts its parts or tries to bend it so that it connects with present-day problems. It is doubtful that the canonical editors of Deuteronomy and the other four books of the Torah foresaw the constant reinterpretation that would become the hallmark of rabbinic Judaism. By fashioning Deuteronomy as they had, however, and by placing it as the fifth book of the Pentateuch, they rounded off the divine Instruction in such a way that they extended to later generations a fairly open invitation to interpretation, reinterpretation, and the other tasks of *aggiornamento* (bringing past tradition up to date) that have preoccupied all serious readers of the Bible.

There is an irony in such an effect of canonization, of course, because frequently canonizers have in the forefront of their minds a desire to settle controversies and eliminate confusions once and for all by laying out a definitive blueprint or articulation of "the faith." But just as making constitutions only begets the discipline of constitutional law, so making canonical texts only begets the works of scriptural interpretation. It is the fashion nowadays to speak rather sophisticatedly and imperialistically about these matters, making "the text" the virtual whole of the phenomenon to be understood and absorbing oneself with its underlying structures, or with deconstructing it, or with its affinities to folkloric (or legal, or sapiential, or other) literary techniques and intents. Deuteronomy both invites and defeats this textual focus, because in its case historical, sociological, and theological forces so clearly joined literary forces in its fashioning.

LASTING SIGNIFICANCE

Deuteronomy offers us a wealth of stimuli, so the problem in this section is deciding upon which lasting implications to focus. Some scriptural scholars, for example, find in the Bible extremely significant calls to liberation. To their mind, the biblical texts speak about freeing people from oppressions of all sorts, so making the Bible contemporary or formulating an angle of interpretation that will disclose the social significance that the texts had in their own times is relatively simple.[16] In the case of Deuteronomy, the laws to stress would be those dealing with the rights of the sojourner, the orphan, the widow, or the indentured servant. As well, we could hearken to the theme of Israel's own liberation from Egypt and interpret the covenantal code as a path of life that would keep the people from the most grievous oppressions: injustice at home and false religion sought abroad.

We have sufficient occasion to pursue these themes, which certainly have not been absent from our previous reflections, when we deal with the major prophets. Here, on Deuteronomy's own terms, the question that seems most pressing is the relation between religious or ethical fidelity and this-worldly prosperity. As we have previously suggested by referring to the continuance of this theme in the book of Job, Deuteronomy's preoccupation with this matter is but one way of dealing with the problem of evil. The problem of evil is never far away in religious studies, so it is a measure of the religious power of Deuteronomy that so many of its pages pressure us to reflect on justice, injustice, goodness, and evil.

First, there is a sense in which the position taken in the majority of the Deuteronomic texts is defensible. This position is that fidelity to the covenant brings prosperity and infidelity brings disaster. On the surface, Deuteronomy seems to tie this equation to the literal observance of the precepts of the Mosaic code that it is announcing, but under the surface lies a more gripping argument: the charge that disasters more often than not at least relate to human failings if indeed they do not stem from such failings. So stated, the argument best fits the negative part of the Deuteronomic equation — punishment or ill-fortune follows on religious defection — and is reminiscent of the negative aspects of the Indian doctrine of karma. Both the Deuteronomic and the Indian view make the connection between vice and ill-fortune intrinsic. Both say that what we do has inevitable consequences, such that the evil we do is bound somehow, somewhere, to come back to haunt us.

In the Deuteronomic case, an Israel that went after the gods of the surrounding peoples was forgetting its own genius or special character. That special character, in turn, inclined it to stay away from the common political, military, and religious ways of other peoples, who again and again did business by the rule that might makes right. One way of phrasing the Deuteronomic proposition, then, is that Israel was not to base its life or action on such a rule of power politics. The prophets frequently pushed forward this proposition, and we can find amidst their many other convictions a rather shrewd assessment of how likely it was that a small nation such as Israel would only come to grief if it tried to play by the rules of much stronger nations.

To be sure, we are overlooking many other ingredients of both the prophetic and the Deuteronomic theologies. The prophets speak as though their judgments come not from human shrewdness but from revelations by God, while the Deuteronomic authors not only make God the author of their counsel but also make such counsel itself startlingly brutal: Slaughter foreigners who get in your way or might seduce you, and eliminate as well your own people who fancy foreignness. To say that Deuteronomy grapples with a profoundly significant problem, close to the heart of what we mean by "evil," is not to say that we have to accept all of the paraphernalia of its answer.

We have been trying to think the thoughts of the Deuteronomic theologians after them, working up the best case we can for their equation of disaster and human culpability or sin. But even though we can see some merit in the equation, we must confess that on the whole it does not balance. This may be somewhat mitigated by the fact that Deuteronomy is more interested in the collectivity of Israel than in the fate of individuals, but ultimately we cannot separate the two. A God just to the nation but careless of individuals remains an unjust God. Not only, then, is the human factor secondary in such cases as earthquakes, tidal waves, and cancer, which remain effects of ecological systems much greater than human control, the picture of the divine factor given in Deuteronomy is also highly questionable.

Does divinity, in fact, come to us with expressions of punishment when we suffer natural, or medical, or economic, or social afflictions? Conversely, does divinity come to us with rewards when we enjoy good fortune and prosperity? The best way to read the biblical presentation of these matters may well go against the apparent sense of the text itself. Although the text seems to be saying yes to both of these questions, what it in all likelihood ought to be saying is that in all cases, good or bad, of prosperity or disaster, we can find a meaning by connecting what we experience to the mysterious source of our lives and all creation.

Such meaning often cannot be a strict equation. (Deuteronomy itself sometimes sings hymns to the divine grace.) Often there is no obvious evil or good we have done that we can connect with what eventuates. But it may well be that blessing God or the mystery of our lives when good fortune comes proves to be good mental and religious health, just as it may well be that taking ill-fortune as a occasion to recognize our frailty and cast aside our foolish pride is an act of wisdom. This is translating Deuteronomy considerably, of course, and trying to soften the hard edges of its effrontery. On its own terms it makes far more of the nation than of the individual. Unless we accomplish some such translation, however, many of us will find the Deuteronomic Word of God impossibly compromised or allied with unacceptable injustices.

Indeed, there is no sense pretending that some evils do not call into question the very possibility of the good Creator of Genesis or the covenanted Lord of Deuteronomy. Massive cruelty and slaughter, whether ancient or recent, make us wonder whether any ultimate mystery so silent could meaningfully be called God. Even smaller scenarios — the sudden death of a child or the explosion of a space shuttle while millions of children are watching — puncture people's faith. Ultimately evil and destructiveness are mysterious: beyond our capacity ever to understand. To be sure, goodness and creativity are also mysterious, so both those who deny divinity and those who affirm it are speaking more than rationally. The issues that Deuteronomy raises, therefore, take us in the direction of an attentive silence, suggesting that the wisest religious posture finally may be waiting and asking for understanding.

This posture perhaps explains the passages in Deuteronomy in which the Torah or Law clearly is more than a protocol by which the divinity would handle the nuisance-ridden business of organizing human affairs. Periodically Deuteronomy steps back from its predominant conception of the covenant as a compact of rights and duties to delight in it as grace and revelation. The Word of God is not far away or difficult. It is near and loving. Just as God chose Israel freely, rather than because of its merits, so God communicates the Torah freely, more as a Word of life than a Word of judgment.

Consequently, the Torah joins other ancient codes in being revelation as well as jurisprudence. It is like the Indian *Dharma* or the Muslim *Qur'an*. As Indian tradition associated the Dharma with the visions of ancient holy men, or with the great enlightenment of the Buddha, and Muslim tradition associated the Qur'an with disclosures that God made to Muhammad through the angel Gabriel, so Judaism looked upon the Torah given through Moses as the lovely address of the Creator and Lord to the representative of his people whom he could treat like a friend. All three traditions tended with time to reify their Guidance and place it at the foundations of creation or make it coeternal with God. For each tradition "Law" became the expression of ultimate reality and holiness and an address to human beings for the sake of their right relation to sacrality and so their flourishing.

Pursuing very far the changes that Christianity rang on Torah would take us afield, but we should note that they produced an understanding of the Gospel, the divine Word, and revelation that was more like than unlike what Judaism, Indian religion, and Islam produced in their understanding of their religious Guidance. The Christian belief in the divinity of Jesus, of course, colored all of its central categories, but in Christianity, too, the Way or Guidance possessed a gracious, revealed core that was finally much more important than its external legal letters. The difference would be that in Judaism the core is known through the Law and the Law remains more central.

It is noteworthy, though, that the Deuteronomic code contained no provision for an afterlife. Whereas Hinduism, Buddhism, Islam, and Christianity all rather quickly set the relationship between divinity and humanity that their Law was to mediate in a framework larger than human mortality, space, and time, Deuteronomy focused on the mortal span of the human generations. We noted the allusions to being gathered to one's people and the sort of immortality that procreation implied. But Deuteronomy virtually never uses these extensions of the span between an individual's birth and death as a safety value or escape hatch by which it might ease the problem of the divine justice. With great courage, it takes the covenant to bear on what people enjoy and suffer in the short while that they take breath and have light in their eyes. Once again, the centrality of peoplehood steps forth. Torah is distinctive, if not unique, in world religion for being content that the people continue on.

GLOSSARY

Aggiornamento   Pope John XXIII's Italian word for bringing Roman Catholicism up to date.

Anamnesis   Recollection, remembrance, deliberately making the past inform present consciousness.

Baal   A general Canaanite name for "lord," "owner," "husband," as well as for "god." Also the name of a specific Canaanite god (of the storm).

Booths   (Feast of Sukkot.) Festival commemorating life in the wilderness.

Canaanite religion   The polytheistic cult of Israel's most important neighbors. It was greatly concerned with fertility.

Canonization   Process of drawing up a list of officially approved writings.

Election   Selection to special status (as the unique people of God).

Eschatological   Pertaining to the last things (end of world, judgment, heaven, hell) or final age.

Grace   Divine favor, help, blessing, benevolence.

Hierodules   Slaves attached to temples; sacred prostitutes.

Ideology   Positively, ideas or doctrines that strongly influence or shape behavior; negatively, such ideas or doctrines that substitute for primary reality and commonsensical honesty.

Levirate law   (see Deuteronomy 25:5–10) the law that the brother of a man who died without a son had the obligation to marry the widow and try to give her a son in the dead man's name.

Levites   Members of the tribe of Levi (the third son of Jacob) who had priestly duties of both sacrificing and administering the divine law.

Mezuzah   The doorpost, and so the container affixed to the doorpost that holds scriptural passages (see Deuteronomy 6:9).

Tefillin   Phylacteries; a pair of small black boxes that contain scriptural passages in parchment and that are wrapped by straps around the upper left arm and forehead during morning prayer.

Weeks   (Feast of Shavuot.) The Feast of Pentecost.

Zionism   Jewish movement to secure a state in Palestine; centralizing focus on Mount Zion as the holiest place (site of the Temple) in the holiest city (Jerusalem).

STUDY QUESTIONS

1. What is the "life" that Deuteronomy wants to foster?

2. Why has the Shema been considered so significant?

3. Explain the appreciation of divine grace in verses 10:12–22.

4. What is the significance of "the place which the Lord your God will choose" (verse 12:11)?

5. How do women fare in the Deuteronomic legislation?

6. What is the significance of the phrase "this day" (for example, in verses 26:16–19)?

7. Explain the phenomenon of blessing and cursing (for example, chapter 28).

8. How does the song of Moses depict God?

9. How does chapter 33 make Moses an ancestor like Jacob?

10. What features of an ancient Near Eastern treaty do we find in the Deuteronomic covenant?

11. Why did the authors of Deuteronomy want to make a book (that would merit being placed by the ark of the covenant)?

12. What are the advantages and disadvantages of the Deuteronomic equation of infidelity and worldly misfortune?

13. What is the significance of the fact that Deuteronomy appears unconcerned about immortality?

NOTES

1. See Leslie J. Hoppe, *Deuteronomy*. Collegeville, Minn.: Liturgical Press, 1985, p. 3. See also W. Gunter Plaut, ed., *The Torah: A Modern Commentary*. New York: Union of American Hebrew Congregations, 1981, pp. xvi-xvii. More generally, see Moshe Weinfeld, *Deuteronomy and the Deuteronomic School*. Oxford: Oxford University Press, 1972; and Gerhard Von Rad, *Deuteronomy*. Philadelphia: Westminster, 1966.

2. See Bernhard Lang, "Neues über den Dekalog," *Theologische Quartalschrift*, 164 (1984), 58–65.

3. See Peter Hoffken, "Eine Bermerkung zum religionsgeschichtlichen hintergrund von Dtn 6, 4," *Biblische Zeitschrift* 28 (1984), 88–93.

4. See Plaut, *The Torah: A Modern Commentary*, p. 1367.

5. See Georg Braulik, "Law as Gospel: Justification and Pardon According to the Deuteronomic Torah," *Interpretation*, 38 (1984), 5–14.

6. On the lack of historical evidence of special Canaanite wrongdoing, see Norman K. Gottwald, "The Book of Deuteronomy," in *The Pentateuch*, ed. Charles M. Laymon. Nashville: Abingdon (Interpreter's Concise Commentary), 1983, p. 302.

7. Ibid., p. 304.

8. See Phillip R. Callaway, "Deut 21:18–21: Proverbial Wisdom and Law," *Journal of Biblical Literature*, 103 (1984), 341–52.

9. See Plaut, *The Torah: A Modern Commentary*, pp. 1501–2.

10. See Gottwald, "The Book of Deuteronomy," p. 332.

11. See William W. Hallo, "Deuteronomy and Ancient Near Eastern Literature," in Plaut, *The Torah: A Modern Commentary*, pp. 1297–1306.

12. See Norman K. Gottwald, *The Hebrew Bible*. Philadelphia: Fortress, 1985, pp. 205–6.

13. See Calum M. Carmichael, *Law and Narrative in the Bible*. Ithaca, N.Y.: Cornell University Press, 1985, p. 26.

14. See Gottwald, *The Hebrew Bible*, pp. 138–39.

15. See Brevard Childs, *Introduction to the Old Testament as Scripture*. Philadelphia: Fortress, 1979, pp. 222–23.

16. See Norman K. Gottwald, ed., *The Bible and Liberation*. Maryknoll, N.Y.: Orbis, 1983.

CHAPTER 8

Joshua

TEXTUAL ANALYSIS

The books that comprise the former prophets display an interesting thematic balance. In Joshua, for instance, the Israelites enter the land, whereas at the end of 2 Kings they are exiled from the land. If Joshua depicts the creation of the people and its land, 2 Kings depicts its destruction. Joshua displays the inheritance that Israel entered upon, whereas 2 Kings amounts to a disinheritance. Moreover, despite the historical cast of these books the viewpoint throughout is prophetic. That is, in addition to the individual prophecies of such spokespeople as Elijah and Elisha, we find the basic narrative voice or perspective to be the prophetic view that human leaders and institutions always are liable to the judgment of the Word of God. Perhaps this explains why 1 and 2 Samuel are not named "The Book of David." Although David is the central figure, the point of view is not that of a king given rule but that of a prophet commissioned to pass judgment on kingly rule according to divine standards of justice.

Joshua normally is associated with the Deuteronomic materials in the books Deuteronomy–2 Kings. Although some scholars consider its relationship to the Pentateuch, as well as to Judges-Samuel-Kings,[1] many scholars limit their analysis to its distinctiveness within the Deuteronomistic materials and note, for instance, that whereas the book of Deuteronomy has the literary form of a series of discourses by Moses, Joshua shifts to a quasi-historical narrative.[2] Following is a useful division of the text:

1:1–5:12	Mobilization and Invasion
5:13–11:23	Warfare

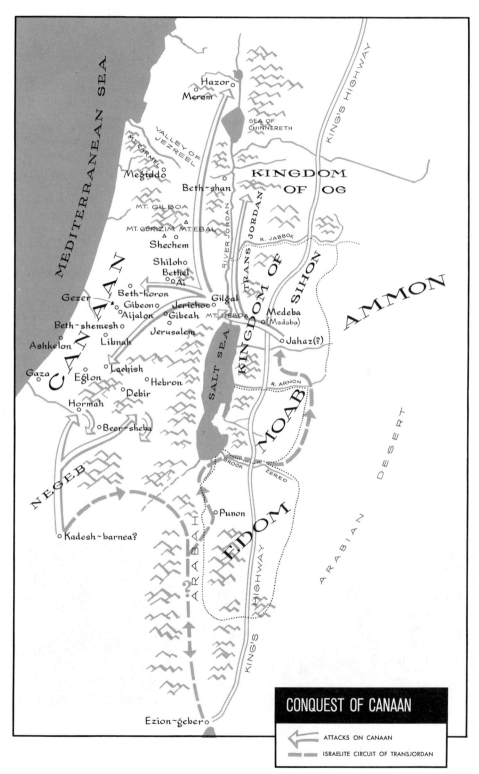

CONQUEST OF CANAAN

← ATTACKS ON CANAAN

▬▬ ISRAELITE CIRCUIT OF TRANSJORDAN

12:1–19:51	Alloting the Inheritance
20:1–22:34	Keeping the Peace
23:1–24:33	The Testament of Joshua[3]

1:1–5:12 Mobilization and Invasion

The book of Joshua begins where the book of Deuteronomy ends: Moses has died and Israel is poised to conquer the promised land in Canaan, to the west of the Jordan. As befits the successor of Moses, Joshua receives directions from the Lord, the first of which amount to a reprise of the promise that the Lord will deliver the land that he had promised as far back as the ancestors. The land itself is the focal point in the drama of the book of Joshua, along with the people's success and failure in believing in the Lord's promises and so fighting courageously. Joshua 1:8 refers to the (Deuteronomic) book of the law, but on the whole this portion of the Deuteronomistic work is less concerned with fidelity to the precepts for pure cult or social justice than with the regulations for holy war. Chapter 1 ends with Joshua's readying the people for the coming battle.

Chapter 2 has the well-known incident of Rahab the harlot, who serves, somewhat as Balaam did in the book of Numbers, to "prove" that righteous Gentiles recognized the holiness of Israel's God and so saw the Conquest as properly inevitable. The story probably comes from old traditions about the tactics of the Conquest,[4] and it suggests that some Canaanites joined the Israelites in the Conquest. The fidelity to their word of both Rahab and the Israelite spies gives a shine of probity to the enterprise of capturing Jericho (a settlement that some archeologists number among the oldest of humanity's cities).

In chapter 3 the people march out of their camp, following the priests who carry the ark of the covenant (which bears the Lord who will be the main warrior). Chapter 4 is like a miniature of the Exodus from Egypt, as the Lord makes the Jordan river dry so that his people can cross it. This is but one of numerous miracles that the book of Joshua narrates (clearly its intent is to depict the Conquest as a

Jericho, city of palms.   *(Used with permission of the photographer, Wolfgang Roth)*

marvel wrought more by God than by human agents and to cast Joshua as the successor of Moses: crossing the Jordan is like crossing the Reed Sea, although the Reed Sea was an entrance into the wilderness while the Jordan was an exit from the wilderness). The stone memorial is to keep the miracle fresh in Israel's mind.[5] Chapter 5 tells us that the kings of the Amorites and the Canaanites—the people who possessed the land that Israel was invading—lost spirit when they heard of this miracle. Joshua then initiates into the convenant the generation that had grown up in the wilderness. Their parents had proved unworthy of entering the promised land, so perhaps the hitherto delayed circumcision of the new generation was to link the Conquest with an unsullied covenantal faith. The first phase of the Conquest ends with explicit ties to the experience in the wilderness, as the people keep the Passover and change from a diet of manna to a diet based on the produce of their new land (5:10–12).

5:13–11:23 Warfare

At the end of chapter 5 Joshua encounters the angel (the divine presence) that will make successful the holy warfare necessary to secure the promised land. (Note the similarity to the experience of Balaam in Numbers 22:23.) This divine presence makes the ground where Joshua stands holy (note the imitation of Moses at the burning bush), as all of the conquered land later could be considered to be. Chapter 6 shows us the siege of Jericho, worked out according to a pattern of sevens (the number of wholeness). Clearly the ark and the trumpeting of God's presence are the focus of the action. The people are instructed in the central precept of holy war—people and booty conquered are to be destroyed, because they are the portion of the chief warrior, the Lord—and Jericho falls.

(Perhaps this is a good point at which to introduce the sociological theory of the Conquest associated with the work of Norman K. Gottwald, especially in his book *The Tribes of Yahweh*. Gottwald believes the data make most sense if we hypothesize (1) that the "Israelite" forces who entered upon the Conquest of the promised land in fact were composed in considerable part of native Canaanites who revolted against their oppressive overlords; (2) that the nucleus of the conquering group was Israelites formed in the desert experience of YHWH; and (3) that the ideology motivating the nucleus and catching the imagination of the native Canaanites who joined them amounted to a revolutionary understanding of Yahwism: a political or liberational theology.

We deal with this last point momentarily. Prior to doing so, however, we should note that this sociological reading of the Conquest finds support in such other biblical data as the traditions that suggest, on the one hand, that "Israel" was composed of more than simply a band of former Egyptian slaves, and, on the other hand, that "Israel" was not just diverse immigrants but owed a great deal to the band of former Egyptian slaves and their memories. In other words, both people who came into Canaan from without and diverse other native or at least non-Egyptian peoples are recalled in the welter of traditions about the desert and the Conquest.

The conditions that Gottwald assumes prevailed in Canaan at the time of the Conquest and that made revolt attractive amounted to an oppressive, feudal rule that had two levels. Immediately over the Canaanites were their native, local rulers, but over these, as the ultimate lords and profiteers, were the Egyptians, who had hegemony over both Canaan and Syria. The Egyptian system vacillated between tight and loose oversight, with a correspondingly heavy or light burden in such matters as taxation. Even in times of loose oversight, however, taxation in kind (produce) and forced labor was the rule, if not for the benefit of Egypt then for the benefit of the local overlords. The burdens of forced labor, of being pawns in military skirmishes, and of being forced to satisfy the various appetites of royal and military bureaucracies could well have made the native population ripe for uprising. The genius and attraction of Yahwism would have been its celebration of liberation (in Egypt) from precisely such an enslaving set of circumstances. "YHWH," the nuclear group promoting this ideology would have said, "is a God who frees his people from oppression, a God who makes tremble all pharaohs and chieftains who would ride roughshod over those who place their trust in him. [So place your trust in him and join us.]"

The revolt of the Israelite-Canaanite alliance led to a different form of government: by tribal elders rather than centralized kings. The political theology used to buttress this shift away from the form of government found most oppressive would have stressed the sole kingship of YHWH and the idolatry of being asked to pay great homage to earthly rulers. The religious system that propped up the prior, oppressive rule also would have come in for theological critique. If the Egyptian pharoah and the local Canaanite kings had profited from being considered part of the system of baals and fertility forces that focused the Canaanite cult, then that cult would have become doubly (politically as well as religiously) repugnant. Insofar as it was the cult of mortal enemies, the psychological move to "holy warfare" — battle to oppose stark evil and defend divine truth — would have been eased by the conviction that in tearing down Canaanite shrines one was destroying places of ill-fame, just as by slaughtering Canaanite enemies one was justly punishing idolaters (worshipers of evil powers, of dark forces that supported injustice). None of this finally justifies holy warfare, but, as a complex of ideas, it makes more sense out of holy warfare and the ongoing Israelite polemic against idolatry. [As well, it further explains the initial resistance to Israel's establishing a kingship under Saul.] Just as the French and Russian revolutions of modern times went from hatred of injustice to an at-times bloody atheism, anticlericalism, and antiroyalism, so the same psychodynamics may well have been at work in religious ideology of the Conquest and its theological aftermath. If the Conquest originally was a sort of guerilla movement or peasants' revolt that only in retrospect got its patina of ideological [theological] justification as the command of YHWH, it comes closer to politico-ideological movements we find in other phases of history. Gottwald's sociological model of the Conquest certainly has not prevailed in scholarly circles, but it does now command considerable attention and respect.)

In chapter 7 the disobedience of the people to this central precept of holy war leads to the Lord's not being with them, so initially they suffer defeat at Ai. Joshua determines who has offended, and the people stone him. Chapter 8 tells of the clever stratagem by which Israel captured Ai, and then of the ceremonial renewal of the law of Moses that served as a celebration of the victory.[6] Chapter 9 shows that enemies can be as clever as Israel itself, as the Gibeonites win security by their deception. (The chapter depends on the ancient notion that holy words, such as an oath, have a force that cannot be retracted [recall the blessing of the disguised Jacob by the blind Isaac]. It also explains how the Gibeonites came to be menials in Israel.) Chapter 10 contains the famous miracle of the sun's standing still, as the Lord gave Israel victory over the King of Jerusalem and his fellow Amorites, who wanted to punish the Gibeonites. Note that the king and the Amorites, like the other peoples whose conquest is narrated in this chapter and in chapter 11, fell foul of Israel's divinely given destiny: "For it was the Lord's doing to harden their hearts that they should come against Israel in battle, in order that they should be utterly destroyed, and should receive no mercy but be exterminated, as the Lord commanded Moses" (11:20).

12:1–19:51 Alloting the Inheritance

The great concern in this long middle section of the book of Joshua is apportioning the land that Israel had gained by the Conquest. Chapter 12 describes the land in terms of the kings who used to rule its different portions, and chapter 13 considers further land that was to be possessed and how it was to be alloted to different of the Israelite groups. Scholars consider that Joshua 13:13, on the continuance of the Geshurites and the Maacathites, indicates that the Conquest was in fact less than complete. As the warfare described in Joshua begs comparison with the instructions for holy war given in Deuteronomy 20, so the distribution of the land begs comparison with the distribution described in Numbers.[7] The apportionments to the different tribes, described in Joshua 14–19, are noteworthy for the detail of their information about both people and places. Caleb stands out

Tel Beth Shean, an artificial hill formed by repeated settlement over the water source. The land to be conquered was quite varied. *(Used with permission of the photographer, Wolfgang Roth)*

Traditional locations of the tribes of Israel.

as especially important, the incident of Achsah (15:17–19) suggests the wealth of tribal memories atop which the account sits, the continuance of the Canaanites of Gezer (16:10) is another indication that the Conquest was not exhaustive, and the power of Joseph (17:14–18) is remarkable. The Levites continue to get no portion, because the Lord is their portion, but in chapter 21 they finally end up with forty-eight cities and their surrounding pasturage (something of a compromise). The seven tribes who get their territories by lot have their holdings described with a care that only surveyors could wish, and finally, as a sort of climax, Joshua receives his own inheritance at Timnathserah in the hill country of Ephraim (19:50).

20:1–22:34 Keeping the Peace

Chapter 20 shows us the execution of the prescription for cities of refuge laid down in Deuteronomy 19 (reminding us that in many ways Joshua stands to Deuteronomy as execution to prescription). The intent, once again, is to defuse the lethal potential of blood-feuds. Chapter 21 lists the levitical cities, in a manner similar to the prior allotment of land to the other tribes, and it concludes with an assurance (21:43, 45) that all the promises of the Lord had come to pass. In chapter 22 we see the inheritance given Reuben, Gad, and Manasseh, who stay to the east of the Jordan. They are accused of idolatry but successfully defend themselves as true followers of the one God of Israel. The implication is that had their worship

The ancient wall of Shechem, with Mount Gerizim in the background. *(Used with permission of the photographer, Robert L. Cohn)*

been impure, the other tribes would have had to wage war against them. The section thus ends on a note of peace, perhaps so that the allotment of the land might contrast with the militancy that was necessary to gain it.

23:1–24:33 The Testament of Joshua

Somewhat like Moses in Deuteronomy 31, Joshua, grown old, summons the people for a last instruction or bequeathment. He reviews what the Lord has done for Israel and the allotment of the land, both that which has already been gained and that which is still to be gained. His command is that the people keep to the law of Moses and maintain themselves without corruption from their pagan neighbors — for example, through intermarriage. Chapter 23 ends with the familiar Deuteronomic equation of blessings with obedience and punishments with disobedience. In chapter 24 Joshua gathers the tribes at Shechem, reviews the history of God's providential care for them, and gets them to pledge fealty to their God, who is jealous and exclusive. Joshua makes of this promise a covenant, imitating Moses in writing its terms in the book of law, and he sets a commemorative marker near the sanctuary of the Lord. Joshua dies at the age of 110 (ten years younger than Moses was when he died), and his time is remembered as one when Israel was faithful to its God. The last verses of the book, 24:32–33, which refer to the bones of Joseph, suggest that Shechem became a cultic center where the Joshuan covenant of the Conquest regularly was renewed.

HISTORICAL BACKGROUND

The book of Joshua obviously presupposes that its readers know about Moses, Joshua, and the Conquest of the promised land. Small conflicts in the text suggest a discrepancy between the assumptions or propaganda of the final editors, who stress the complete fulfillment of God's promises, and the original military or political reality, which was that several Canaanite peoples continued to hold their possessions. The extended descriptions of the territorial allotments of the different tribes suggest not only a general familiarity with which tribes had come to settle in which areas, but also a love of thinking about their allotments, partly because the land was the most concrete form of God's blessing to Israel, and partly because prosperity is something that human beings generally like to contemplate in their mind's eye. "Tribe" may have been an anachronism by the time Joshua was written, but it lingered in Israelite memory.

Joshua also presupposes a familiarity with the concept and rules for holy war, and considerable acceptance of both. Little sympathy is wasted on the enemies whom Israel has to exterminate, and in fact the worst problems arise when Israel fails to destroy the booty that ought to be made over to the Lord. The presumption of Israel's unique destiny under the guidance of its God runs throughout the narrative as its implicit rationale. Indeed, the peoples who oppose the Conquest are, like Pharaoh in Egypt, considered to have had their hearts hardened by God so that they might fulfill their fated roles. Without trying to justify the exterminations of holy war, Gottwald, as we noted, has argued that Israel's sense of singularity and election makes more than simply ideological or self-serving sense if we relate it to a democratic form of political organization that was virtually unique in its ancient Near Eastern milieu. Then God, destiny, and political organization would comprise a trio of reasons for staying apart from the Gentiles and thinking itself unique.[8] This argument at least has the merit of suggesting an empirical referent for the theological convictions about uniqueness, and in Joshua we could link it with the fairly democratic way that the land was distributed and the tribes covenanted with God at Shechem.

The last presupposition in the text of Joshua is that, despite their perhaps remarkable democracy, the tribes were keenly aware of who got which portions of the promised land and so are presented in Joshua as fertile ground for discontent. By the time of the Deuteronomistic redactions not only had the people established a monarchy in which some of the tribes (for instance, Judah) were more prominent than others, but they had also shown themselves unable to keep their monarchy together and so were more vulnerable to outside enemies than they need have been. This suggests that readers would have assumed, as a matter of course, that "Israel" was always more an ideal than an actual historical unity. The symbolism of common descent from Jacob and common covenanting to God through Moses and Joshua notwithstanding, there was always something centrifugal in Israel's existence that threatened to shatter its unity and scatter its tribes.

LITERARY INTENT

The book of Joshua partakes of the general motivation of the Deuteronomistic history, which, as we have seen, was largely to reinterpret the Mosaic covenant according to its own "economic" sense of the relationship between obedience to the legal codes and prosperity. In this book Israel on the whole is faithful or obedient, so on the whole the Conquest and allotment of the land go forward quite successfully.

Generally, the book of Joshua explains how God fulfilled his promise to Abraham and how the land was cleansed of the Canaanites and their abominations. This latter action allowed the chosen people to get off to a fresh start. The supposedly quick conquest of the land emphasizes the providential character of the Israelites' possession of it, but it also conflicts with the evidence presented in Judges 1, to say nothing of Joshua 23:4 (see also Joshua 21:44–45). This suggests a certain ideological requirement: The Canaanites had to be destroyed as an offering to God that cleansed both the land and the new people entering into a divinely promised possession of it. We can see the extension of this ideology in certain justifications attempted for Christian crusades and Muslim "holy wars" (*jihads*), so it is worth underscoring that the actual conquest may not have been a bloody extermination, however much the authors of Joshua wished it had been.

More particularly, Joshua wants to celebrate the deeds of the man who succeeded Moses and to make him, like Moses, a model of faith. Some commentators have suggested that the authors thus depicted Joshua as a rather regal figure who might be a model for the role of later kings such as Josiah.[9] The aura of authority and sanctity that Joshua carries helps to accredit the distribution of the land that he oversees and to make the relations among the tribes divinely sanctioned. Commentators such as Gerhard von Rad and Robert Boling have seen a motive of confessing the Conquest to be a great act of the Lord, using as primary evidence such texts as Joshua 24:2–13. Relatedly, they have noted a desire to present the Lord as a divine warrior.[10] Brevard Childs, emphasizing the final, canonical shape of Joshua, has found a theology of the Conquest, such that the Deuteronomic Torah gets a considerable boost and Joshua's successes are seen as deriving from his obedience to the law.[11] Summarily, therefore, we may say that the authors of Joshua have shaped memories of the Conquest so as to justify it as a work not only sanctioned but also mainly carried out by the Lord who is so jealous for Israel's covenant with him.

LASTING SIGNIFICANCE

The theme of the land that is so central in the book of Joshua certainly is with us in full force nowadays, due to both the ecological crisis and the establishment of the contemporary state of Israel. Indeed, literalists in both the Jewish and the Christian camps sometimes regard the contemporary state of Israel as justified by biblical materials such as what we find in Joshua, and environmentalists who wish to link land with a stewardship imposed by God can find some provocative hints (although certainly not a creation-centered theology) in Joshua.

Certainly there are difficulties lying in wait for any who wish to pursue either of these two topics, but they are nothing compared to the difficulties raised by the doctrine of holy war that gives Joshua much of its rationale. We have been over some of this ground before, so let us simply suggest that here we find in scripture a negative example: The treatment of Israel's neighbors/enemies reflects the chauvinism of the human authors more than it reflects the deepest instincts of the best biblical theologians. Such chauvinism may, in practice, have been virtually necessary if a people was to wage war courageously in a time of tribal existence such as that which Joshua depicts. Life was holistic in such a way that if a people went to war, for what we would consider good reasons or bad, its gods went marching with it. If we consider the history of modern warfare, we can see that this phenomenon was much with our own fathers and grandfathers, and that we today are not above assassinating the character of our opponents and making them people God might command us to eliminate. "Civil religion," as recent sociologists and students of religion sometimes call the fusion of national culture and theology, is nearly as much in our midst as it was in the midst of the tribes whom Joshua led across the Jordan.

GLOSSARY

Apostasy   Renouncing one's faith or professed allegiance.

STUDY QUESTIONS

1. How does Joshua compare with Moses?
2. Why does Joshua enact a mass circumcision?

3. What is the function of Rahab the harlot?

4. How does the book of Joshua show that the Lord is the main agent of the Conquest?

5. Why is so much space given over to the allotment of the land?

NOTES

1. See Otto Eissfeldt, *Hexateuch-Synopse*. Darmstadt, Germany: Wissenschaftliche Buchgesellschaft, 1983, pp. 66–84.

2. See Robert Polzin, *Moses and the Deuteronomist*. New York: Seabury, 1980, p. 73.

3. See Robert G. Boling and G. Ernest Wright, *Joshua*. Garden City, N.Y.: Doubleday Anchor Bible, 1982, pp. vii–x.

4. See Robert Huston Smith, "The Book of Joshua," in *Old Testament History*, ed. Charles M. Laymon. Nashville: Abingdon (Interpreter's Concise Commentary), 1983, p. 11.

5. See Brian Peckham, "The Composition of Joshua 3–4," *Catholic Biblical Quarterly*, 46 (1984), 413–31.

6. See Ziony Zevit, "Archeological and Literary Statigraphy in Joshua 7–8," *Bulletin of the American Schools of Oriental Research*, 251 (1983), 23–35.

7. See A. Graeme Auld, *Joshua, Moses, and the Land*. Edinburgh: T. & T. Clark, 1983; pp. 52–87. On the many documents from which the lists and borders of Joshua 13–21 derive, see Boling and Wright, *Joshua*, p. 70.

8. See Norman K. Gottwald, *The Tribes of Israel*. Maryknoll, N.Y.: Orbis, 1979, pp. 702–3.

9. See Simon B. Parker, "Joshua, the Book of," in *Harper's Bible Dictionary*, ed. Paul J. Achtemeier. San Francisco: Harper & Row, 1985, p. 509.

10. See Boling and Wright, *Joshua*, pp. 5–37.

11. See Brevard Childs, *Introduction to the Old Testament as Scripture*. Philadelphia: Fortress, 1979, pp. 244–52.

CHAPTER 9

Judges

TEXTUAL ANALYSIS

The book of Judges is a collection of somewhat disparate stories, most of them about people who led particular tribes during the period between the Conquest and the monarchy of Saul, that became part of the Deuteronomistic history of the nation (probably in the late seventh century B.C.E.), and then was edited into its present form after the Exile.[1] In terms of literary units, the book is conveniently divided as follows:

1:1–3:6	Prologue
3:7–16:31	Israel's Liberation by Judges
17:1–21:25	Supplementary Stories[2]

1:1–3:6 Prologue

The beginning of the book of Judges links it with the book of Joshua, but the annalistic character of the materials in 1:1–2:5 suggest pre-Deuteronomistic sources.[3] Judah is the featured tribe, cutting off thumbs and toes is a grisly epitome of what was at stake in tribal warfare, Jerusalem is of great interest because of its later prominence as the seat of the monarchy, the incident of Achsah (1:12–15) is a repeat of Joshua 15:16–19, Caleb and Joseph have featured roles, and the faithful treatment of the friendly Gentile (1:24–25) is reminiscent of the treatment of Rahab, the harlot of Jericho.

In both chapter 1 and chapter 2 we receive more evidence that the Conquest met with considerable resistance and was less than complete. The angel of the Lord (2:1–3) explains this situation as caused by the people's failure to obey the requirements of the covenant, especially those regarding separation from pagan neighbors. We again witness the death of Joshua, after which the people fall into infidelity and so are victimized by their neighbors. This leads to the practice of God's raising up judges — leaders who exercise both military and governing roles — and to what the authors see, in typically Deuteronomistic fashion, as a regular rhythm of apostasy, subjugation, and then liberation. The prologue concludes with a list of the foreign tribes into whose hand the Lord delivered Israel, to test the generation (after Joshua) who had no experience of war (and so, presumably, did not realize the implications of fidelity to the Lord or the cost of the Conquest).

3:7–16:31 Israel's Liberation by Judges

Judges 3:7, echoing Judges 2:11, gives us the thread through the stories about the judges whom God raised up: "And the people of Israel did what was evil in the sight of the Lord," prompting the need for liberation. The evil that they do, in most cases, is to worship pagan deities concerned with fertility. The deliverers, beginning with Othniel, are charismatic people empowered by the Spirit of the Lord. Thus, Othniel frees the people (perhaps originally just his own tribe, but all of Israel in the later redaction) from the oppression of Cushan-rishathaim and gives them forty years (a sizable time, like the epoch in the wilderness) of peace. With the incident of Ehud (3:15–30), we come to some of the imaginary vigor for which Judges is prized by literary analysts,[4] as well as to a solid indication that the later editors have pieced together much older folkloric materials.

Shamgar follows Ehud as a deliverer, but the focus of chapters 4 and 5 is Deborah. With Jael, Deborah is hearty proof that in the culture of ancient Israel and its environs, women could be formidable creatures. Deborah seems to have been a prophetess to whom the people brought their concerns. The juxtaposition in chapters 4 and 5 of prose and poetic versions of the battle that she and Barak led against Sisera has long intrigued literary analysts.[5] Note the vividness of detail in chapter 4, the roster of the tribes in chapter 5, and the brilliant, if cruel, touch at the end of the song (5:28–30), where the mother of Sisera tries to stifle her foreboding.

The first verses of chapter 6 prepare us for Gideon, the next judge, by indicating what Robert Boling calls "the evil" and "the menace" that Israel faced.[6] The appealing story of Gideon underscores his modesty and his courtesy (a formulaic feature of the prophets' calls), as well as the striking experience he has of the divine presence and acceptance of his gift. Gideon has to oppose the paganism of even his own family, and his asking for signs makes us consider him prudent, even cautious. The details of how he is to whittle down his force and what his dreams mean suggest the folkloric character of the memories about him. His modesty about his victories bespeaks not only his realization that God was his strength but also his shrewd sense of how to get along with stronger tribes such as Ephraim.

Gideon is firm enough, or has matured enough, however, to deal decisively with detractors like the men of Succoth, and with enemies such as Zebah and Zalmunna, who had slain his kin. His refusal of kingship may reflect the anti-monarchical strain of the Deuteronomistic history, which often presents the time

Judith with the Head of Holofernes by Simon Vouet. Judith, a valiant woman, clearly followed in the footsteps of Jael (see the Book of Judith). *(The Nelson-Atkins Museum of Art, Kansas City, Missouri [Nelson Fund])*

of the judges, when leadership came directly from the Spirit of the Lord, as purer. The only stain on Gideon's reputation comes in Judges 8:27, when he apparently falls into idolatry (and so suggests the seductiveness of the foreign cults). His seventy sons represent the blessings God heaped upon him, but after his death there is little memory of the faith he championed or the service he rendered. (However, the bad rule of Abimelech, Gideon's son, shows the wisdom of Gideon's refusal to be king.)

Chapter 9 shows the brutal and follied kingship of Abimelech. The fable or parable of Jotham effectively portrays Abimelech through indirection, so we are prepared for the insurrection of the men of Shechem and consider it deserved. The incident of Gaal seems designed to show how Shechem had become rife with opportunists, in this case one who made no pretense of serving the Lord or being close to Gideon/Jerubbal. For a while Abimelech prevails, but finally his treachery in killing his seventy brothers is requited and, like Sisera, he is killed by a woman.[7]

The cycle of stories about Gideon and his line completed, we enter a cycle, in chapter 11, about the next great judge, Jephthah. Here the enemy is the Ammonites, and the lowly beginnings of Jephthah suggest the depths to which Israel has sunk in punishment for its infidelities. The rehearsal of Israel's right to its land raises the status of Jephthah by associating him with a righteous cause. He is seized by the spirit but rashly vows the sacrifice that costs him his daughter (note the solemnity accredited to a vow, and also the grief attending virginity or child-lessness, which was like living only half a life). In chapter 12 the battles with the Ephraimites, who had bothered Gideon, confirm their quarrelsome character, and the story about the telltale "Shibboleth" (verse 12:6) has a folkloric specificity.

More minor judges appear, but after Jephthah the next noteworthy figure is Samson. Samson's exploits are more self-serving than altruistic, and probably their literary quality was a major reason for their preservation. Samson, like a child of the ancestors, comes to a previously barren mother, under the sign of a Nazirite vow that makes him special to the Lord. The encounter with the angel of the Lord is like Gideon's. Manoah's wife, whose name never appears, clearly is a stronger believer than her husband. Samson's desire for a Philistine wife indicates that he will be a flawed hero, whatever his final utility against the oppressive Philistines.

The first descriptions of Samson present him as a somewhat sensual, unreflective man of brute strength and courage. His wife clearly has mixed loyalties, and the tension between the champion of Israel and the Philistines builds through the story of the riddle, until he kills thirty of her compatriots to get the prize he deserved. Samson's further killings are presented as somewhat justified, because in all of them he is but retaliating for wrongs done to him. The legend of his slaying 1000 with the jawbone of an ass stresses his possession of the Lord's spirit; his finding water also demonstrates God's favor. We have already seen that Samson has a weakness for women, so through the incident of the harlot and the first traps contrived by Delilah we feel foreboding build. Finally Samson betrays the secret of his strength, which chapter 13 has prepared us to link with his consecration to God by Nazirite vow, and the Lord leaves him. His final destructiveness against the Philistines comes from his return to the Lord through prayer, and the cycle of stories ends by associating Samson with the others who had judged Israel and helped it against its enemies.[8]

17:1–21:25 Supplementary Stories

The story about Micah and the 1100 pieces of silver seems designed to show the paganism into which Israel again had fallen. The acquisition of a Levite for his shrine represents a step back toward fidelity, and the description of the Danites illustrates the lawlessness and migration that having no king allowed. (Here we see some of the rationale for a centralized authority.) The Danites are impure in their cult, worshiping with graven images, and the story of the Benjaminites in chapter 19 shows even worse evidence of the corruption in premonarchic times.

Mount Tabor, where the battle won by Deborah and Barak began. *(Used with permission of the photographer, Robert L. Cohn)*

The story of the concubine raped to death is in part an inversion of the story in Genesis 19, the point being that the evil previously ascribed to Sodom was now being exceeded in Israel.[9] Chapter 20 shows justice done to Benjamin, despite that tribe's formidable powers. The evil of the times has now reached the point of intertribal warfare or fratricide. Yet Benjamin cannot fall into extinction, so in chapter 21 the (disloyal) people of Jabesh-gilead are made a sacrifice to secure Benjamin wives, as though in a holy war for the sake of offspring. The further device of snatching brides from among the dancers at Shiloh skirts the curse laid on whoever would give Benjamin a wife, but the final judgment on Benjamin and the whole period at the end of the book of Judges comes in the concluding lines: "In those days there was no king in Israel; every man did what was right in his own eyes" (21:25).

HISTORICAL BACKGROUND

We can seldom assume, let alone prove, that the typical reader of a book such as Judges had the historical awareness that present-day scholars can achieve, even when such scholars mainly depend on the biblical text itself.[10] We can expect, however, that its readers would have found the text plausible, either as a presentation of what had happened to Israel in the period under discussion or as a theological interpretation that tipped its hand by obviously slanting commonly held memories in a particular direction. In the present case, the likelihood seems to be that the final authors both utilized previously existing and well-known folkloric materials about heroes such as Gideon and Samson, and that they impressed upon these materials a pattern of apostasy, subjugation, and deliverance through a judge that found some receptivity for its theological message. If we read the stories apart from the Deuteronomistic framework in which they have finally been cast, the period of the judges is presented quite positively. It was a time of heroes whom God empowered to defend his chosen people. The final editing therefore leaves us with a complex presentation, which perhaps is the richer for leaving a clash between the positive traditional stories about the judges and the negative theological framework into which they were later fitted.

LITERARY INTENT

In light of the foregoing analysis, Judges was written not simply to extend the Deuteronomistic interpretation of history forward into another significant epoch but also to spotlight the question of leadership that would come to a head with the matter of whether Samuel ought to anoint Saul king. The Lord had been the great warrior of Israel in the book of Joshua, securing the land for the people, and during the period of the judges the best leadership came from those who possessed the divine spirit: Deborah, Gideon, and Samson. A decline in national fortunes was, in the eyes of the Deuteronomistic theologians, the result of Israel's failure to keep the covenantal law, but the most pointed expression of this failure came in the military terms that the situation of constant friction with the Canaanite tribes spotlighted: a lack of stable peace. The "judge" that we see in the book of

Judges is less an interpreter of the Deuteronomistic code than a person divinely gifted with the capacity to lead Israel in battle. That such leadership was as much a matter of (spirit-given) trust in God as a matter of military savvy is obvious not only from a case such as Gideon, who apparently had no prior military training and no militancy in his character (and who, indeed, has to reduce the number of his soldiers, so that the fact that victory came from the Lord would be obvious), but also from the fact that when the spirit leaves a judge he is left empty and impotent: no leader. The theme that the Lord was the great warrior of Israel thus continues in Judges, through more devices than the most obvious one of angels' coming to lead Israel's forces. The point is made at every level of the culture represented that without living fidelity to the source of their covenant the people can only decline.

LASTING SIGNIFICANCE

Charismatic, spirit-given leadership and prowess concern us more fully when we discuss the latter prophets, who speak of the Word and the Spirit at great length. Here let us simply anticipate these issues by noting that the history of religion and simple psychology conspire to make the matter of inspiration, confidence, having "heart," and the like, a constant preoccupation. If scholars and theologians do not always make it central, ordinary people, believers and unbelievers alike, are nearly obsessed with it. They all battle with and are intrigued by their experiences of

Gan ha-Sheloshah, Israeli national park in the eastern Jezreel valley formed by three natural pools. Present-day Israelis enjoy the land. *(Used with permission of the photographer, Wolfgang Roth)*

being uplifted and being cast down, being encouraged and being discouraged or depressed. When this matter gets full and careful attention, religious analysts realize that some sophistication is required to interpret what emotional states likely reveal about the divine presence. But at both the beginning and the end of such analyses, the predominant impression is precisely that given by the Bible in books such as Judges: the desolation that renders one ineffective is a mark of the divine absence. That absence may be interpreted as pedagogical — allowed so as to teach those who experience it a salutary if painful lesson. But in itself it is a negative indicator, because the biblical God is a giver of life and effective power.

The second significance of Judges that it seems well to mention here is the humanity that Israel is made to display. We are probably wise to interpret much of the lamenting about the evil-doing of the people as simply an expression of human weakness, such that the generations of the judges were like most generations in human history: filled with people who were venal, self-serving, and not deep enough to realize what treasures they ought to set their hearts upon. That the people emerge as extremely derelict in their obligation to respond generously to the great gifts of the Lord is due as much to the high standards set by the authors as to what the people themselves actually did. With the exception of the concluding materials on the Benjaminites (which, to be sure, may be read as the consummation of an overall decline), we receive few instances of egregious wrong-doing, and these are rather flatly narrated rather than dramatized. Most of the slaughters come in warfare apparently commonly accepted at the time, and the cultic infidelities that the authors stress did not, by the implication of their own account, impress the people as obviously wrong, like murder or adultery. So Judges gives the present-day reader no valid grounds for stigmatizing the people of its period as nonpareil sinners, and of course to use it as a basis for depicting Jews or Judaism as depraved and so rightly cast off by God at the time of Jesus is bigotry pure and simple.

GLOSSARY

Shibboleth   Catchword or slogan thought to distinguish true adherents (native speakers) of a tradition.

STUDY QUESTIONS

1. What were the main functions of Israel's judges?
2. What details and devices make the story of Ehud so gripping?
3. What is the gain of having a second, poetic account of the victory of Deborah and Barak over Sisera?
4. What features make Gideon several-dimensioned?
5. Is the story of Samson a polemic against women?
6. What is the overall tally of comings and goings of the divine Spirit in Judges, and what does this suggest about the author's overall assessment of that period of Israelite history?

NOTES

1. See Robert B. Boling, "Judges, the Book of," in *Harper's Bible Dictionary*, ed. Paul J. Achtemeier. San Francisco: Harper & Row, 1985, p. 515.

2. Ibid. See also Robert Huston Smith, "The Book of Judges," in *Old Testament History*, ed. Charles M. Laymon. Nashville: Abingdon (Interpreter's Concise Commentary), 1983, pp. 39–80.

3. See Norman K. Gottwald, *The Tribes of Israel*, Maryknoll, N.Y.: Orbis, 1979, pp. 163–75.

4. See Robert Alter, *The Art of Biblical Narrative*. New York: Basic Books, 1981, pp. 37–41.

5. See Barnabas Lindars, "Deborah's Song: Women in the Old Testament," *Bulletin of the John Rylands University Library of Manchester*, 65 (1983), 158–75.

6. See Robert G. Boling, *Judges*. Garden City, N.Y.: Doubleday Anchor Bible, 1975, pp. 122–27.

7. See Harmut N. Rösel, "Überlegungen zu Abimelech und Sichem im Jdc. ix," *Vetus Testamentum*, 33 (1983), 500–503.

8. See Stanislav Segert, "Paronomasia in the Samson Narrative in Judges xiii–xvi," *Vetus Testamentum*, 34 (1984), 454–61.

9. See Stuart Lasine, "Guest and Host in Judges 19: Lot's Hospitality in an Inverted World," *Journal for the Study of the Old Testament*, 29 (1984), 37–59.

10. See Michael Grant, *The History of Ancient Israel*. New York: Charles Scribner's Sons, 1984, pp. 49–63.

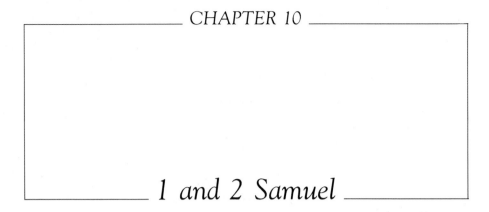

CHAPTER 10

1 and 2 Samuel

TEXTUAL ANALYSIS

The books 1 and 2 Samuel appear originally to have been a single "book" (and are so enumerated in the Hebrew) and part of the Deuteronomistic history that spans the volumes Deuteronomy-2 Kings. They depict the interesting and important time when Israel became a monarchy, and their most famous materials bear on David, who became Israel's ideal king. We treat the two books as running consecutively, using the following breakdown of the text:

1 Samuel	1:1 – 7:17	The Story of Samuel
	8:1 – 15:35	Saul and the Advent of Kingship
	16:1 – 2 Samuel 5:10	The Rise of David
2 Samuel	5:11 – 20:26	The Reign of David
	21:1 – 24:25	Miscellaneous Materials[1]

1 Samuel 1:1–7:17 The Story of Samuel

The conclusion of the book of Judges left the impression that Israel had fallen into evil times because there was no king and so all individuals did what they thought right. The book of Samuel sets out to show how God raised up another judge, this time a holy prophet, who had to deal with the people's desire for a king. The tale of Samuel's birth uses the familiar motif of a mother long-barren finally conceiving a special son. As with Samson, the most recent instance of this pattern, we find a Nazirite vow involved (1:11). Hannah has the double dose of troubles familiar to us from the conflict between Sarah and Hagar: Her husband's other wife, who is fertile, mocks her barrenness. The text goes out of its way to emphasize the depth of both Hannah's affliction and her piety. Indeed, in his study of prose prayer in the Bible, Moshe Greenberg has used Hannah as an example of the sincerity that genuine worship requires.[2] Her dedication of Samuel to the Lord goes beyond the requirements of the first fruits of the womb, in keeping with her vow prior to conception. The first chapter, therefore, leads us to expect special things of Samuel.

Verses 2:1–10 comprise the well-known "song" of Hannah, which is notable not only for itself but also because it was the model for the "Magnificat" of Mary, the mother of Jesus (Luke 1:46–55). Hannah's song praises the Lord, her rock, but it also stresses his paradoxical ways: The mighty are broken and the feeble gird on strength, the barren becomes fruitful and she who bore many becomes forlorn, and so forth. Such paradox is a fine way of confessing that God can have purposes in history that human agents do not descry. Here it foreshadows the fall of Saul and the rise of David.

The sons of Eli strike any reader as offensive, but priestly readers would have been especially offended by their flouting the laws regarding the priestly portion of the sacrifice (see, for example, Leviticus 7:28–36). The point seems to be to show the low estate to which the cult of YHWH at Shiloh had fallen.[3] The narrator makes their evil providential (2:25), in view of the future rise of Samuel, who functions as their replacement. In verses 2:27–36 "a man of God" or charismatic figure predicts the fall of the sons of Eli and the rise of Samuel, in the process giving us an oblique look at what the priesthood was supposed to be and how it could miscarry.

Verse 1 Samuel 3:1 builds on the prophetic character of the prediction of the man of God, noting that receiving the word of God and experiencing (divine) vision had become rare. Samuel experiences a call that turns out to be from God, and his eagerness to respond is our tipoff to the religious fervor that he has developed (see also 2:26). Eli interprets this call (which some scholars consider a dream),[4] and Eli's willingness to hear the fearsome oracle against his own sons suggests that his earlier reproaches of his sons were heartfelt. By the end of chapter 3 we thus have prophecy or the word of the Lord again well established at Shiloh, reinvigorating that hallowed shrine.

The capture of the ark of the covenant by the Philistines is the final blow to Eli, more powerful even than the news of the death of his sons, so he dies, at the nadir of Israel's religious fortunes: The divine presence has gone over to the enemy. The story of the birth of Ichabod seems sewn in at this juncture to underscore the dire situation, because his name means "no glory." Chapter 5 is contrived to exhibit the power of the Lord over the pagan divinity of the Philistines, and its humor, as well as its conviction that being out of sorts with the divine power is bound to bring disease and misfortune, gives it the flavor of an old folktale. The guilt offering that the Philistines prepare in chapter 6 (golden tumors and golden mice) continues in this vein, and the idea that they were afflicted as with a plague calls for comparison with the situation in Egypt, where the Lord prepared for the great deliverance of the Exodus by afflicting Pharaoh and the Egyptians ten times over. The use of the mice and tumors probably indicates a practice of "sympathetic magic," according to which one tries to influence real events by working on models or dummies. The entire story is miraculous in the manner we have seen typical of the Deuteronomist, down to the details of the cows' pulling the ark back to Bethshemesh. The deadly power of the ark, which results in killing seventy men (the Hebrew also says 50,000), is reminiscent of Leviticus. The theological punch line apparently is verse 6:20: "Who is able to stand before the Lord, this holy God?" Certainly not the Philistines, as any who truly trusted in the Lord would have been sure.[5]

At Samuel's insistence the people finally (twenty years later) follow up on this realization and quit their foreign gods to return to the Lord. The penitential ritual described in 1 Samuel 7:6 has no equivalent in other biblical sources,[6] but the thunder of the Lord recalls the pristine days of the appearances to Moses, as if to signify that with Samuel another intimate of God had appeared at whose intercession the great force of the Lord could express itself. The use of memorial stones, as we have previously seen, was a common early Israelite practice. The concluding portrayal of Samuel as a circuit rider suggests that his judgeship did contain some of the administration of justice that we now associate with that term. In general, though, our first sense of the career of Samuel is that he was the foremost leader of Israel in the period after Samson, and that his leadership was more priestly or formally religious than that of Samson and the other judges, who were essentially military chiefs.

8:1–15:35 Saul and the Advent of Kingship

Like his patron Eli, Samuel suffers the fate of having impious sons who corrupt their father's work. Samuel's initial dislike of Israel's having a king no doubt is linked to the people's desire to be like the other nations, because, associated with this desire, we may think, is a temptation toward fertility rites that (in the eyes of the Deuteronomistic history) has been the people's fatal flaw. Verse 8:7 gives us the theological implications: The people are rejecting the kingship of their God (who has been their great warrior; perhaps the leading function of a king was to lead the people in battle). This rejection implies a negation of the covenant. Samuel warns the people of what a king will mean (here the text no doubt draws on grievances that the people had from the actual exercise of kingship in later times), beginning with such military consequences as a draft. But the people will not be dissuaded, and the Lord has Samuel let them have their way, as though he were washing his hands of them.

Chapters 9–11 show the selection of Saul as Israel's first king. We get the sense that Saul's physique made him a standout, and the story about his search for his father's lost asses is a rather transparent means of explaining how (providentially) he came into contact with Samuel. The note in verse 9:9 about the shift in terminology from "seer" to "prophet" probably reflects the consciousness of the editors that in their later times prophecy had become a fairly well-defined activity. The implication of the answer of the girls who draw water is that Samuel has continued to go round the district to supervise religious functions.

Samuel learns by extraordinary means that Saul is the Lord's choice for the ruler (here called prince) whom the people have been desiring. Verse 9:16, in fact, recalls Exodus 3:7: God is sending Saul as a savior like Moses. Samuel's knowledge that the asses have been found serves to confirm his status as a seer. His somewhat obscure prediction of Saul's high future (verse 9:20: "And for whom is all that is desirable in Israel? Is it not for you and for all your father's house?"), when made to override Saul's denial or unbelief, recalls the paradoxical ways of God praised by Hannah, the seer's insightful mother. The anointing that Samuel performs was a solemn rite of consecration usually performed most publicly as a great moment. The secrecy of this consecration is not explained, so it stands as a pregnant silence. One likely connotation is that although the Lord accedes to the wishes of the people, he does so minimally, according to terms known only to himself.

The instructions that Samuel gives to Saul, all cast in the forseeing mode of the prophet, brim with symbols of Saul's secret election by God: sacrificial animals and materials (bread and wine). The ecstatic prophets are another indication that the phenomena of the inspiring spirit are much on the editors' minds, either in view of their reflections about the ideal, fairly sober prophecy that Samuel exemplified, or in view of their intuitions about the charismatic side of a kingship that grew on the soil of a judgeship dependent on the spirit (recall Gideon and Samson). 1 Samuel 10:6 is a key verse, speaking of Saul's becoming another man when the spirit of the Lord comes mightily upon him, and implying that when he does not have that spirit he is but a tall man fit for tracking lost asses. Relatedly, verse 10:9 has Saul receive from God a new heart when he leaves Samuel, as though his contact with the holy man has changed his inmost personality. The prediction comes true, so much so that Saul is accounted spirit-filled like the wandering prophets whom he joins. Like Samson's keeping secret from his parents his slaying of the lion (his first experience of his extraordinary destiny), Saul keeps silent about Samuel's revelations to him.

The ceremony at Mizpah that makes Saul king by lot is prefaced by Samuel's gloomy assessment that it represents the people's rejection of the Lord. We readers are bound to anticipate that this ceremony will somehow realize the divine intent that first Samuel and then Saul have had revealed to them. The lottery proceeds inexorably to single out Saul, and the incident of his hiding may be meant either to dramatize his eventual appearance and acclamation by the people or to signify his unease with his fated role. Samuel's explication of the rights and duties of kingship is meant to suggest that from the beginning it had a legal or quasi-covenantal status (and so was bounded, as well as legitimated). By being placed in a book and laid up before the Lord (verse 10:25), the rights and duties of kingship partook of the sacrality of the Deuteronomic Torah. But few matters are simple in the Deuteronomistic history, so we hear that from the outset (worthless) people doubted Saul's (and by implication any king's) ability to save them. Again and again the kingship is presented as a two-edged sword — a highly ambiguous institution and symbol. Note, however, that Saul, holding his peace, seems confident that he has a reply for such doubters.

In chapter 11 we see this confidence to be well justified, as Saul, in the power of the spirit, both leads Israel to victory over the fearsome Ammonites and demonstrates the restraint befitting a king. His installation as king at Gilgal therefore seems to set the kingship off on a good note.[7] Chapter 12 is both a justification of the judgeship of Samuel, whom no one can convict of wrongdoing, and another blast from the group within the Deuteronomistic camp who see the rise of kingship as an expression of faithlessness toward the Lord. Samuel's rehearsal of the Lord's mighty acts in the past is meant to highlight the people's lack of trust. His assurances that if they repent they will not be cast off by God reminds us of the grace that always counters a narrowly economic reading of the covenantal relationship.

The ritual misdeed of Saul that we witness in chapter 13 strikes us as punished excessively and so alerts us to the editors' intent to down play the priestly rights of kings (contrast this with verses 14:31–35). God seems to have stacked the deck against Saul, assuring his failure. The prediction that Saul's kingdom will not continue, because of his sin in offering sacrifice, serves both to explain his later failures and to justify the succession of David. In terms of the personal relationship between Saul and Samuel, the author suggests that Samuel was looking for a pretext to punish the man who inaugurated the kingship that he himself so greatly disliked.

Chapter 14 shows Jonathan, Saul's son, in an attractive light, because it makes him a bold and courageous soldier, a man who trusts in the Lord, and a man who inspires dedication (the commitment of his armor bearer makes the later friendship of Jonathan and David quite credible). Saul's behavior turns somewhat erratic or irascible, as though Samuel's prediction of his failure is starting to take hold, and the criticism of Saul by Jonathan, whom we have come to respect, seriously injures our estimate of Saul's character. Indeed, the ritualistic sin that the people commit by eating blood can be laid to the account of Saul's harsh demand that they fast. The silence of God is another portent of Saul's fall from divine favor, and the casting of lots (the use of the Urim and Thummim) reminds us that the early Israelite priesthood engaged in divination (which could be considered God's speech). Saul's willingness to sacrifice Jonathan (even though this was directed by God) further blackens his character, as the opposition of the people testifies. Those opposed to Saul would consider his heeding the people to indicate weakness and disobedience to God—he cannot win. Yet, as though other voices from the tradition are now allowed to speak, chapter 14 concludes with testimonies to Saul's military valor.

Samuel seems to be concurring with this estimate when he gives Saul the divine command to punish Amalek, but the negative soundings about Saul are verified when Saul disobeys the laws of holy warfare and spares Agag. We do not know whether or not to believe Saul when he protests that he has kept back the best of the Amalekite booty for a sacrifice to the Lord, but because the authors have established Samuel as the authentic interpreter of the divine judgments, chapter 15 clearly places Saul in the wrong. In addition, the failure of the narrator to corroborate Saul's self-defense tells against him. The judgment that obedience is better than sacrifice suggests the superiority of prophetic to priestly religion and is another in the line of markers that indicate the prophetic sympathies and interests behind 1 and 2 Samuel. Saul confesses that he has sinned, through fear of the opinion of the people (which suggests a lack of the self-confidence a good leader must have; see verses 15:13, 14, 15), but, in a scene that prefigures many later confrontations in Western history between crozier and crown, Samuel rejects him harshly, until finally Saul wins forgiveness by almost craven pleading. The rigorism in the figure of Samuel at this point, along with the fanaticism of the precepts of holy war that Saul has flouted, make the entire exchange taut with pulls and counter-pulls. Chapter 15 concludes with the grisly scene of Samuel's hacking Agag into pieces, and then Samuel departs from Saul definitively, grieving over what Saul and kingship have become.

16:1–2 Samuel 5:10 The Rise of David

Saul's demise having become a foregone conclusion, attention shifts to his successor, David (who does not know that Saul is doomed—the author retains the dramatic tension). The future bitterness between the two is anticipated in Samuel's response to the Lord's command that he go with oil to (anoint a son of) Jesse: If Saul hears of it he will kill Samuel. Apparently Saul is not accepting Samuel's interpretation of the divine will that Saul not continue in the kingship. The nervousness of the elders of Bethlehem confirms our sense that tensions are running high. The advice that Samuel gets (verse 16:7) that the Lord considers the heart rather than the outward appearance is both in keeping with the paradox sung by Samuel's mother at his consecration to the Lord and in contrast to the characters of Saul (who was chosen for his outward appearance) and David (who, though handsome, was apparently not tall). As soon as Samuel anoints David the spirit of the Lord departs from Saul, and henceforth he is tormented by an evil spirit. We may consider the relief that Saul finds in David's music to be a balm for the kingship whose well-being now controls Israel's fortunes. It in ironic in the extreme, however, that Saul is soothed by the one who will replace him.

The story of David and Goliath has been embellished with folkloric exaggerations (Goliath is made the equivalent of ten feet tall), and the way that David is introduced (verses 17:12–15) indicates that at this point the editors have woven in another source. David's supposed prowess in killing lions and bears calls Samson

A shepherd and sheep near Jerusalem. *(Used with permission of the photographer, Wolfgang Roth)*

to mind,[8] and the rather full story as a whole expresses both legendary materials about David and praise for the shepherd's life. The speech put in David's mouth affirms that the Lord is Israel's main warrior (the theme of the Exodus), and his victory with sling and stone (verse 17:50) has the rhythm of a summarizing religious chant. The chapter ends with an identification of David that does not fit with chapter 16, and thus adds more evidence that the materials on David come from several sources.

Chapter 18 shows the deep attraction Jonathan feels toward David,[9] and then the growth of Saul's jealousy at David's increasing fame. The text makes it plain that the spirit of kingship, if not the trappings, has now passed over to David. Saul acts murderously and deceitfully toward David, reneging on the gift of Merab and trying to set up David's death in battle. The foreskins that David supplies are emblematic of the paganism of Israel's enemy. Saul's unstable character, and the continuing presence of goodness in him, are revealed when he hearkens to Jonathan's admonitions not to kill David. The episode in verses 19:9–10 repeats that in verses 18:10–11 and confirms Saul's instability. At first we read Michal's help to David as like that of Jonathan: evidence that even Saul's own children sided with David. The love of Saul's children for David epitomizes the love of Israel (18:28). The reference to Saul's prophesying (verse 19:24) occasions a second mention of his prophetic character, and it suggests both that it lay in the storehouse of memories about Saul and that it needs explanation.

The conversation between Jonathan and David in chapter 20 highlights not only their personal friendship but the intertwining of Saul's kingly line with David. Some commentators consider Saul's cursing of Jonathan to be an accusation of sexual misdeeds between Jonathan and David,[10] but at least equally likely as the source is Saul's bitterness that David is supplanting Jonathan as the heir to the throne. Jonathan, however, keeps faith with David, assuring the reader that those with good hearts found David in the right and Saul in the wrong. David's use of the bread of the Presence associates him with the divinity in a priestly way. We might contrast the madness that David feigns before Achish with the madness that is now running Saul.

Quickly the tension between Saul and David divides the people, as those disgruntled with Saul's regime join themselves to David. David departs for Judah, where he will establish his kingdom, and Saul begins to indulge in the self-pity that later will disfigure David's kingship as well. That he turns to the Benjaminites, whom Judges left us regarding as the lowest of Israel's low, hardly relieves our bad judgment of Saul. Saul and Doeg then convict themselves by killing the honest priest of the Lord Ahimelech, and we note that when David takes in Abiathar he takes to himself some of the guilt, presumably because he did not act on his intuition and slay Doeg when he could have.

David's conquest of the Philistines on behalf of afflicted Keilah reminds us that he is continuing to function as Israel's champion.[11] In chapter 23 David is forced to live as an outlaw (another of the paradoxes that pervade the literary work of Samuel), but Jonathan's renewal of their covenantal bond keeps us convinced of David's rectitude. The pursuit of David that we witness in chapter 23 becomes comic in chapter 24, when Saul relieves himself in the cave where David is hiding. David's guilt at cutting off the skirt of Saul's royal robe is meant to assure us of his pious respect for the kingship. It reflects as well a school that rated the kingship higher than did the prophet Samuel's speeches (although those may be read as opposing Saul as much as kingship). The interview between David and Saul, in which David asks God to judge between them, mainly shows the instability of Saul. In his honesty at this moment, though, Saul becomes the mouthpiece for the author's high esteem for David.

The incident of Nabal, David, and Abigail in chapter 25 plays on the significance of Nabal's name: "Foolish." Abigail keeps David from a bloodshed that superficially would be justified but at a deeper level would displease the Lord of life. On the other hand, we see hints of the dark side of David's character, which comes out in the murder of Uriah the Hittite in 2 Samuel 11. In both cases, David is moved by desire for another man's wife. The justice comes in the better way of the Lord's own smiting of Nabal, and the whole incident confirms both David's innocence and the Lord's presence with him. When David successfully wooes Abigail we judge it a victory for womanly peace-keeping and rhetorical skill. As David weds, we are notified that Saul, for the second time, has taken away a daughter he promised David, and this time one David actually had wedded.

Chapter 26 gives more games in the king's pursuit of David, and more expressions of David's reverence for the Lord's anointed leader. The spear and jar of water, in fact, are the equivalent of the cut portion of the king's skirt. David repeats his request that the king judge which of them is innocent, and Saul again condemns himself and convinces us that he has become radically unstable, unable to decide whether David is his hated enemy or his beloved son. The irony of the whole situation is sharpened when David can only find peace among the Philistines, the hated enemies of Israel whom he has been fighting so long. David is growing increasingly wily, however, because he deals with Achish deceitfully.

How low Saul has fallen religiously is conveyed by his consulting the witch of Endor, a practice proscribed both by Leviticus 19:26 and by Saul's own law (1 Samuel 28:9). The whole scene of the woman's bringing up Samuel may strike today's readers as absurd, but the authors make even this occult form of religion serve the purposes of the Lord. The ghost of Samuel repeats that failure to slay Amalek (chapter 15) was the crux of Saul's downfall. Samuel predicts Saul's coming death, and the woman provides an ironic bit of sanity by prevailing upon Saul to eat (verse 28:22). When Samuel repeats God's rejection of Saul in favor of David, nothing is left for Saul but death.

In chapter 29 Achish gives David credit for an honesty David did not in fact fully practice. David is put back in the right, however, by the capture of his wives at Ziklag, and his pursuit of the Amalekites is justified by the answer of the Lord. The story of David's recovery of what had been taken is in good part an explanation of the later statute about the equality of the baggage minders with the warriors proper. In all of his doings in Judah David has been diplomatic and politic, and he has won favor with the local tribes. Chapter 31 brings the conclusion to Saul that the ghost of Samuel had predicted, but it brings the death of Jonathan as well, reminding us that despite his friendship for David, Jonathan had kept a proper loyalty to his father and king. Saul's falling on his own sword may be read as a last failure of nerve. The end of the first book of Samuel shows a ritual that gives the passing of Saul and Jonathan some dignity (note that Saul had saved the men of Jabesh-gilead at the beginning of his career, in 1 Samuel 11).

An account of Saul's ending is offered in 2 Samuel 1 that differs slightly from the previous one, the point apparently being to get the crown to David. The hapless (but, in virtue of 1 Samuel 31, lying) Amalekite who acceded to Saul's request is made a victim of David's respect for the dignity of God's anointed (the strength of this theme leads us to suspect that David's party had to counter the accusation that he had wished Saul's death).[12] The lament of David over Saul and Jonathan also counteracts such an accusation, and it stands as a poignant testimony to what might have been, had the better feelings of Saul for David won out. The last lines of the lament in 2 Samuel 1 show the deep bond between David and Jonathan, and the refrain, "How are the mighty fallen" (another echo of Hannah's song), has become a staple expression of Western appreciation of the fragility of power and the reversals that history so often brings.

Chapter 2 shows the conflict between the North (Israel) and the South (Judah) that arose after the death of Saul. David is anointed king over Judah but Saul's son Ishbosheth, championed by Saul's general Abner, rules over the North. The Benjaminites figure prominently in the forces of the North, hardly to their credit, and the question arises why David is not himself present in the fight between Abner and Joab (perhaps so that he will not have to dirty his hands). Saul and David seem to be continuing to clash through their representatives.

At the opening of chapter 3 we realize that David has taken to himself a royal harem and is raising up sons by many different wives. The negotiations between Abner and David, especially that regarding the return of Michal, show the political considerations involved in uniting the Northern and Southern Kingdoms. The murder of Abner reveals David's lack of control over Joab, as well as Joab's willingness to do what has to be done if David is to secure the throne (see verse 4:1). That David is able to pacify the northern tribes by his show of regret over the death of Abner testifies to his political skills. The place that women have in this chapter (including the indications latent in the conflict between Abner and Ishbosheth) shows how easily they could become pawns. The weeping of Paltiel over the loss of Michal is one of the sad little gems that make the biblical humanism so affecting.

The murder of Ishbosheth in chapter 4 no doubt further complicated David's relations with the North, but his punishment of the murderers appears motivated by more than political considerations: As he lamented Saul and was deeply offended by the slaying of God's anointed, so he is deeply offended by this further regicide. Note how quickly the author, interested in the human story of David, passes by the key event of the capture of Zion (2 Samuel 5:7), which henceforth will be the capital and crown property. Chapter 5, as several of the preceding chapters, depends on the prediction, supposedly from the time of Samuel and David's first victories over the Philistines, that David would one day rule all Israel. David must move his capital from Hebron to Jerusalem because he needs a central place between the North and the South. Commentators do not know what to make of the obscure sayings in verses 5:6–8 (which may refer to David's infiltrating the city through a water shaft) and usually consider the text corrupt at this point.[13]

2 Samuel 5:11–20:26 The Reign of David

David's prosperity at the beginning of his reign in Jerusalem is tokened by both his procreation and his victories over the Philistines: The Lord clearly is with

THE EMPIRE OF DAVID

him. Bringing the ark to Jerusalem therefore but solemnizes the reality of the divine presence already granted. The death of Uzzah (2 Samuel 6:7) reminds us of the dangers that the holy presence of God carries, as well as of the priestly concern for propriety in all ritualistic dealings with the Lord.[14] David's dancing before the ark of the Lord (2 Samuel 6:14) has become a much celebrated scene in Western art. It is indeed one of numerous biblical memories that paint David as profoundly religious. (The attribution of much of the book of Psalms to David is another indication of this traditional judgment.) David acts like a priest in making offerings to the ark and blessing the people. Note how distribution of the ceremonial cakes and meat allows the people to share in the sense of communion with the Lord. The bitterness of Michal consummates what began with her lie in 1 Samuel 19:17, and the paradox in David's response fits the literary character we have noted from the beginning of the history centered around Samuel. Perhaps Michal has long resented being merely a pawn in the relations between Saul and David. At this point we recall the pathetic weeping of her former husband Paltiel, who apparently loved her for herself. At any rate, David cuts her off from his progeny, and his response has the vindictive tone of a victor who is glad enough to see an irritating enemy put by fate at his mercy.

The discussion that focuses around the prophet Nathan in chapter 7 brings us to the high point of David's career. It elevates the house of David as especially blessed by God (like Abraham, David is promised a "great name," in verse 7:9, and his rule of the land fulfills God's promise to Abraham). However, chapter 7 also expresses the ambivalence that Israel felt about building the Temple that became a permanent house for the divine presence. The conservative strain that preferred the simple, wandering presence in the ark relates to the preference for the simpler, charismatic days when the Lord ruled Israel through judges raised up as the occasion demanded. On the other hand, the blessings of stability through the kingdom that unified the northern and southern tribes seems fittingly enough to call forth the construction of a stable dwelling for the Lord. The chapter ends with an eloquent prayer of David that gives all praise to God for the upraising of the Davidic line and justifies the Temple (and, by implication, the priestly worship that transpired there) on the highest religious grounds.[15]

Chapters 8–10 show David's consolidating his realm with numerous victories over Israel's neighboring enemies and his picking up the remains of the house of Saul. He and those loyal to him are now completely in control. Chapter 9 burnishes the character of David by showing him mindful of his friendship with Jonathan and therefore generous to Jonathan's crippled son Mephibosheth. Chapter 10 further indicates that the Lord is with David, as David's armies continue to triumph in holy war. Some recent commentators use these chapters to counteract the negative portrait that begins in chapter 11.[16]

Chapter 11 is, by general consensus, a high-water mark in biblical narrative. Meir Sternberg's recent literary analysis shows the great skill with which the narrator uses silences — what we are not told about the motives of David and Uriah — to make us ponder the interactions more deeply and so to finally realize the flaws in David's character.[17] (By the end of the "court history," as 2 Samuel 9–20, 1 Kings 1–2 is sometimes called, David seems all too like Saul in being emotionally unstable.)[18] The incident of David and Bathsheba beginning in verse 11:2 has also entered Western artistic memory, but the murder of Uriah the Hittite (verse 11:17) most powerfully discloses that the Davidic kingship is becoming rotten. David lounges in Jerusalem, free to have adulterous affairs, while Joab and his army fight against the Ammonites and besiege Rabbah. Uriah is made so noble a figure that we suspect he knows what the king has done with his wife and is choosing non-cooperation as the most dignified and vexing response. There is irony upon irony in the speeches of David, Uriah, Joab, and the messenger, but throughout the narrator keeps the posture of the simple reporter, until, at the end of the chapter, the verdict crashes down: "But the thing that David had done displeased the Lord."

Chapter 12 plays like a melodrama,[19] representing David as inordinately moved by the parable of Nathan and little touched by the reality of what he has done with Bathsheba and to Uriah. In the fashion of good Deuteronomistic theology David's sin is punished by blight on his house. The touches that lighten David's dark character include his willingness to repent upon his realizing the point of Nathan's story and his realism about the ways of the Lord after his intercessions for the sake of his child and his lamentations at the child's death have left him empty. The note that the Lord loved Solomon, David's next son by Bathsheba (verse 12:24), indicates a movement of grace and forgiveness, and it prepares us, as well, to look upon the golden age of Solomon, when the Davidic kingdom was at its height, as a sign that despite all David continued to be beloved by God. Although it is Joab who wins the battle at Rabbah, and David's part is largely ceremonial, David's taking the great crown there is something of a recoronation.

Chapter 13 begins the story of Absalom, which has become a classic account of the degeneration of father-son relations. As well, it shows the political crises to which such flaws of David as inaction and insensitivity led. The rape of Tamar by Amnon triggers the rage of Absalom (like father, like son). But we should not miss the insight of the story itself, especially the note that Amnon hated Tamar after the rape, no doubt because she stood as a living testimony to his diseased spirit. David has to carry some of the blame for Absalom's murder of Amnon, because for two years he did nothing to punish Amnon, and even though chapter 13 makes it plain that David greatly loved Absalom, we do not see David doing anything to reach out to Absalom and reconcile him to the royal family.

Chapter 14 has the intriguing incident of the woman of Tekoa, who at the instance of Joab, David's loyal general, gives David a story in which he might read his own situation more insightfully, somewhat the way that the prophet Nathan gave David the parable in which he finally saw the significance of what he had done to Uriah. The story depends on the practice of the king's granting audience (like a judge) to commoners to hear their needs. In the background also is the institution of blood vengeance, which we have noted several times in the past. The woman's speech is both wise and eloquent (especially in verse 14:14: "We must all die, we are like water spilt on the ground"), which inclines us to add her to the line of strong biblical women we have previously noted. David wins our respect for hearing the woman's message, but once again a curious inaction or failure to follow through mars his situation and character: He invites Absalom back but for two years will not meet with him to be reconciled. Absalom himself is flawed, despite his physical beauty, but in the beginning most of his wrongdoing seems the impetuousness of youth. As well, we get the sense that he would do anything to win his father's attention and praise.

By chapter 15, however, Absalom enters on darker days, manifesting an ambition to supplant David that casts all of his prior doings in a new light. David seems rather dignified in verse 15:14, the scene of his departure from Jerusalem (although his granting Absalom four years in which to plot his overthrow makes us question his astuteness), and his concern to keep the ark in Jerusalem would have appeared as a deeply religious touch. David goes into mourning, as much for the way the favor of the Lord has departed from him and put Absalom in the wrong (by violating the sacrality of the truly anointed king) as for the physical threats to his person and rule. The scene suggests sufficient discontent with David's rule in the land to make Absalom's coup possible. But by the end of chapter 15 we see the wiliness of David resurrecting, almost as though he only needed a stiff challenge to get his combative juices flowing again.

Some of the discontents with David surface in chapter 16, as Ziba and Shimei illustrate the bitterness of old partisans of Saul against the Davidic rule. David's enduring the cursing of Shimei is made penance and surrender to whatever the Lord has in store for him, and the Benjaminites again are cast in a bad light. That Ahithophel, the revered counselor, is siding with Absalom lends credence to the charge that David's rule ought to have been overthrown, but we know that Hushai, David's plant in Absalom's camp, is working to undermine Ahithophel's influence. The counsel that Absalom should take over David's harem (a right of the new king) strikes close to the nerve of the relationship between father and son and seems remarkably Freudian in its insight into the sexual portion of the contest between parent and child.

The victory, in chapter 17, of the counsel of Hushai, which appeals to Absalom's vanity, over the counsel of Ahithophel is attributed to divine providence. Also, if we examine God's preference for David rather than Absalom in Deuteronomistic terms we are bound to conclude that, on the whole, David was the better man. The suicide of Ahithophel in verse 17:23 may symbolize either his despair at falling out of royal influence or his realization that the counsel of Hushai will lead to disaster and so his own death later at David's hand. David picks up support, and, at the end of chapter 17, his people are like Israel in the wilderness, besieged but on a holy mission. Absalom shows poor judgment in removing Joab, who goes over to David, just as he showed poor judgment in rejecting the counsel of Ahithophel. We are tempted to speculate that Absalom's ambivalence toward his father has continued to cripple him: He wants the allegiance of his father's counselors but he also wants a fresh start with his own people dominating the inner circles of government.

In verse 18:5 David counsels Joab to deal gently with Absalom, but the story of Absalom's death displays Joab's following his own judgment about where David's best interests lie, in ways mindful of the murder of Uriah the Hittite. In this case it seems that Joab knew that David would not have been able to deal with Absalom as the military realities of the situation dictated. Joab in fact has replaced David as the fighting head of Judah (note that in this battle "Israel" stands for the forces of Absalom) since the time of Uriah and the siege of Rabbah. Absalom's funereal heap of stones stands in ironic contrast to the monument he built for himself, and even though David's grief-stricken response to the news of Absalom's death strikes us as heart-felt, we cannot but wonder why such professed love could not have dealt with the young man more wisely and headed off his parricidal revolt. The speech of Joab, whom we have come to respect as a loyal and realistic, if brutal, man, pins the matter to the board: "You love those who hate you and hate those who love you" (verse 19:6). David, like Saul, has become so confused emotionally that good judgment has left him. He can govern the nation better than he can govern his own family. We are almost forced to ask whether kingship necessarily unbalances those who must negotiate its burdens and sift out all the false responses it generates from the people.

The aftermath of David's victory over Absalom shows the different portions of the kingdom outdoing one another in false flattery and desire to win back the restored king's favor. David handles all of this masterfully, indicating that he is better at dealing with wily, dishonest people than with honest brokers such as Joab, whom he demotes from the generalship. The strains between North and South that will fracture the kingdom forever in two generations show plainly in the rivalry of the factions competing for closeness to David. Sheba, the Benjaminite who leads Israel away from David (see verse 20:2), speaks out of tribal pride and is condemned by the southern authors of this memoir as a worthless fellow. Joab rather ruthlessly regains command of David's forces and gains the head of Sheba, through the wise counsel of the woman of Abel who will not let her whole city suffer for the worthless life of Sheba. The account of David's warfare with Absalom and its aftermath concludes with David and Joab again well in control.

21:1–24:25 Miscellaneous Materials

David's grant of vengeance to the Gibeonites for what they had suffered under Saul implies that the divinity was blessing the old tribal ways of blood vengeance. The action of Rizpah in verse 21:10 symbolizes the popular feeling that David had

A mountain goat in the wilderness of Ein-Gedi, where David hid from Saul. *(Used with permission of the photographer, Wolfgang Roth)*

overdone this vengeance, so the reburying of the bones of Saul and Jonathan amounts to an honoring of them meant to reset the balance. David has become ineffectual in battle, as the request of his men in verse 21:17 that he not accompany them indicates. Indeed, since the incident of Uriah the Hittite David has not been much of a soldier. The descriptions of the giant Philistines at the end of chapter 21 are miscellaneous materials no doubt thought pertinent to the whole saga of David, which began with his victory over Goliath.

The song of David in chapter 22 shows figures familiar from the song of Moses, but many of the poetic turns refer to David's exploits and sufferings as a warrior and king. There is noteworthy propaganda on behalf of David's blame-lessness, and a noteworthy conclusion that links the steadfast love of the Lord to the line of David forever. Indeed, verse 23:5 exalts this love into an everlasting covenant between the Lord and the house of David. The last words of David are quite military; they depict the righteous man as arming himself against the godless, who are like thorns.[20] The remainder of chapter 23 reads like a collection of tributes to fighting men that their relatives or scrupulous archivists insisted be entered on the canonical record of David's battles with the Philistines.

Chapter 24 is a rather confused account that many commentators think belongs before chapter 9. We recall from Numbers that a census was a divine prerogative, so the story might make sense if David ordered the census on his own initiative, but verse 24:1 makes the Lord the initiator and sounds the note that the census was to be an occasion for punishing Israel. The reader gets a sense of the relative strengths of Judah and Israel, as well as a sense of the ambivalence of the David who, on the one hand, does not want to risk his own hide (verse 24:14) but, on the other hand, grieves for the suffering of the innocent people (verse 24:17). Perhaps the best explanation for the chapter is that the final editors wanted the portrait of the David associated with Samuel to end with some complexity. The final word, however, is that the Lord heeded the supplications of David for the land and averted the plague from Israel.

HISTORICAL BACKGROUND

The books 1 and 2 Samuel obviously suppose widespread memories of the time when kingship arose in Israel and great interest in the person of David, the man who became Israel's ideal ruler. The final text comes from a time when kingship had faltered considerably, as we see in both 1 and 2 Kings and the writings of the latter prophets. David is notably enhanced in the later literature, so we may suspect that 1 and 2 Samuel are supposed to keep the pans of judgment balanced. As we noted, Samuel is made the mouthpiece for a prophetic view in which kingship arose from a lack of faith in the Lord's ability to furnish the people effective leadership through charismatic judges. This part of the history of the rise of kingship was undoubedly somewhat influenced by later theological perspectives, but the most plausible scenario suggests that the recorded memories in fact provided evidence that at the time of the anointing of Saul the people were divided about the wisdom of becoming like the other nations.

That the Philistines figure prominently in the historical reports of 1 and 2 Samuel means that the authors could presuppose that they most resisted Israel's presence in the chosen land. The materials about Goliath reveal the folkloric and perhaps quite ancient character of the deeper strata of the memories about David. As well, they indicate the considerable change from David's being a simple shepherd boy to his becoming the ruler of a unified kingdom in Jerusalem. Obliquely, we are instructed in such matters as the military tactics of the times and the political maneuverings. We note too that on the one hand some women are used as pawns and are added to the royal harem virtually at the king's will, while on the other hand stronger women, such as the one from Tekoa and the wise one from Abel, continued to wield influence at the time that the monarchy was being founded.

Certainly the most celebrated materials in 1 and 2 Samuel come from the court history of 2 Samuel 9–20. Some scholars think that this history presupposes an eyewitness to the events of David's early years as king, whereas others think that archival materials and a good artistic imagination would have sufficed. Either way, the result is a portrait of the king that is unmatched in the world literature of the time for its psychological acumen. The minimal presupposition of the story is a general memory of David that considered him a complicated and flawed (if ultimately divinely blessed) human being and ruler. The incident of David and Bathsheba associated David with Samson and other powerful leaders who were undone by their untoward love of women; the story of David and Absalom is a case study in how not to deal with a talented but troubled son.

Similarly, the authors assume that the reversals that David suffered, above all those that came when Absalom drove him from the capital, were justified by his sins. Not only did he sin grievously against Uriah, and so merit the death of the first child that Bathsheba conceived, he sinned as well in not acting against Amnon to avenge the rape of Tamar. Moreover, his inaction or even petulance regarding Absalom is presented as the direct cause of his troubles from Absalom. The presupposition of the portrait of David is thus Deuteronomistic in the manner that we have come to expect: David received justice for both his good deeds and his bad deeds, but on the whole the Lord dealt more graciously with him than he was entitled to expect (because this is the way the Lord deals with most human beings).

LITERARY INTENT

The different traditions from which 1 and 2 Samuel were composed furnish a disparate and conflicting series of motivations. The first desire was certainly to recall the wisdom and power of Samuel. A related desire was to elevate prophecy or judgeship such as that of Samuel and to contrast the monarchy with it unfavorably. Thus, the earliest sense we get of kingship is Samuel's quite negative attitude toward what the Lord is letting happen by acceding to the people's wishes and having the prophet anoint Saul king.

The second, contrasting desire was to present the monarchy as something providential: the way that the people came to be centered in Jerusalem under David and to enjoy what turned out to be a troubled, flawed, yet still glorious time of independence and prosperity as a realm unto themselves. The refrain about the sacrality of the Lord's anointed is one indication of this motivation, and the pride in the subjugation of the Philistines is another. The coming of the ark of the covenant to Jerusalem symbolizes the consecration of the city of David as the site of the special presence of the Lord. The approvals for building the Temple, even though they are contested, indicate a desire to make the monarchy and the priesthood institutions blessed by God.

The canonical redactors appear to have deliberately kept the tension between these two views of the monarchy,[21] and that reinforces the sense we have been gathering that the final edition of the Deuteronomistic history, or indeed of the Hebrew Bible as a whole, consciously wants to represent the life of Israel as a very human, mixed entity. So, for example, we are shown Samuel, Saul, and David, three major figures, whose relationships are such that nothing simplistic may rightly be said about Israelite prophecy or monarchy. Samuel is exalted, to be sure, and with him is exalted the prophetic side of Israelite life, but Saul and David have enough grandeur about them, and enough sanction from God, to warrant the view that kingship also could be excellent.

The materials on David show us a third reason why 1 and 2 Samuel were written: artistic and humanistic interest. Those who wrote and edited the stories of the court history no doubt wanted to preserve such materials for the national endowment. No doubt they also wanted to preach certain theological lessons. But what most strikes many readers is the psychological interest of the cycle of stories about David. Clearly David was sufficiently large in both his virtues and his vices to be read as an object lesson. For instance, he committed two of the worst sins or crimes that one could commit: murder and adultery. Yet he also humbled himself, confessed his sins, and went on with the business of trying to serve his God and his people. He was a warrior courageous and wily, yet he became a king who divided the people by his inaction. He loved his son Absalom more passionately than wisely, showing any with eyes to see what happens when emotion upsets judgment or ego predominates over selflessness. Because David had successes far beyond the ordinary and was blessed with gifts of which most people can only dream — military and regal rule, wonderful friendship, beautiful sexual partners, the love of his people, and presumably the best material riches his times had to offer — he shows the peaks of human achievement: what they do for, and what they do to, one's key relationship to God.

David was not the man that Moses was, able to speak with God face to face like a friend (in part because he was a king, rather than a prophet). As often as not, David came to the Lord in the garb and posture of the penitent sinner, again forced to confess that he had forgotten himself and wandered away into foul vices. Yet he seems never to have abandoned his bedrock reliance upon God, nor to have doubted that honesty before God was the final measure of his self-respect. Equally and relatedly, he seems never to have been seriously tempted to idolatry, because we get no record of his having left the Lord for the fertility deities or rites of the Canaanites.

Legends we may have about David, but myths seem remarkably absent. By the art of the biblical narrators, David stands forth as a truly historical personage: a man like us in all things including flaws. The care with which his portrait has been constructed is so obvious that this result cannot have been unintended. The canonical editors of 1 and 2 Samuel sought our identification with David, as though they felt that when we drew close to him we would see how vibrant, intense, or fully rounded life riveted onto the Lord of Israel could be.

The City of David, the original Jerusalem captured by David. *(Used with permission of the photographer, Robert L. Cohn)*

LASTING SIGNIFICANCE

Let us continue this line of reflection, because, although current biblical scholarship rejects the black and white contrast that once was made between the historical attitudes of Israel and the mythological attitudes of the peoples contemporary with Israel, our Western inclinations to think about time as linear rather than circular do owe a great deal to the Hebrew Bible. The characters who appear in 1 and 2 Samuel, as we have particularly noted in the case of David, are not just players in type-scenes that always have been and always will be. They are remembered to have arisen, performed, and declined at particular times and places and with specific consequences for later generations. Indeed, and connectedly, they are remembered to have acted freely and responsibly, although, of course, within the orbit of divine providence, so that what they became and what rippled out from their actions could be laid to their own accounts.

This historicity, coupled with this stress on personal responsibility, goes to the heart of what we have been calling biblical "humanism." Without in any way detracting from the biblical convictions about a transcendent God, it gives us a focus on humankind that wonderfully illumines our dramatic possibilities. We are not just puppets directed by capricious gods. Although we do not finally determine our own measure, and our existence always has a mysterious depth that we cannot fathom, there are valid senses in which we determine our own destinies. This means that what we choose to do and what we refrain from doing, what we prize and what we despise, are not casual but serious. It means that a figure such as

David or Saul, Samuel or Jonathan, is presented as exemplary: as a person whose seriousness ought to teach us the choices clamoring for attention in our own lives. On the biblical interpretation, historicity and existential seriousness are but two sides of the same coin. The past that has shaped the present juncture at which we stand was fashioned by individuals like ourselves whose final wisdom or folly should be lessons to us.

If any of this rightly expresses something central to the nature of the biblical narratives, or something accurately reflecting the intentions of the authors who composed the Hebrew Bible, then the nature of what we are dealing with in books such as 1 and 2 Samuel comes into a new and perhaps clearer configuration. We said at the outset of this textbook that the biblical authors were not writing "history" in the critical manner that scholars nowadays associate with that term. But we did say then, and we must repeat now, that the biblical authors were attempting an accurate report or interpretation of the past. Unless what we read of David and Saul in 1 and 2 Samuel is the truest representation of what they were that the biblical authors could muster, the entire biblical project wastes away. Certainly every episode that we have studied has been shaped by the authors' and editors' intentions, and certainly we have the right, perhaps even the duty, to puzzle out what those intentions were and how they have married or come to misfit. But in and through such intentions the Bible stands as an account of Israelite experience that asks us to accept it as true. Indeed, it asks us to take it as God's own guidance, by which we are to set our course.

This means that David, Saul, and the rest are accorded the basic yet also supreme respect of being taken seriously and rendered for later generations under the watchful eye of the Lord. It means that the texts are not just circles of linguistic games, referring only to other texts and juggling hypothetical possibilities for the fun of it. Despite the complexity that they, like any significant texts, assume when we begin to penetrate their world, they remain writings that patently are trying to say something objective, other-oriented, or simply true about history and human nature, about the singular entity called Israel and the primordial mystery called God.

Not to be too subtle about it, such reflections as these have the lasting significance of calling into question any one-sided interpretational theory that would fail to honor the objective intentionality, as well as the self-referential linguistic quality, of the biblical narratives. Alternatively, no school of textual interpretation, or historical reconstruction, or sociological analysis, or theological rendering can claim hegemony over the Bible and dictate what the Bible may and may not have been signifying. Whether to counter the critics from Yale University who are currently bemused by deconstructionism,[22] or the traditionalist theologians who think that the rabbis or the church fathers said the last word about the meaning of the Bible, the biblical texts themselves have a winning way of delivering an effective comeuppance.

This, of course, is just another way of saying that the Bible is a classic, a work that is as much a norm by which to measure ourselves as something we can subject to our norms and measures. If we are misguided to surrender to the Bible our critical faculties and insist that what we get from the pages by reading most literally is the best indicator of the divine Word, we are equally misguided to take a superior attitude and lay the Bible on the rack of our dogmas about invariant structures or the independent life that a text leads apart from the time and the agents who begot it. Someplace in the middle stands the position of the virtuous interpreter, just as someplace in the middle stands the Bible's own overall interpretation of such Israelite phenomena as kingship and prophecy, or such human regularities as stupidity and repentance.

We should also note that this virtuous balance of the Bible is not pressed or artificial. It comes from several sources—the multiplicity of the traditions and points of view that the Bible enfolds, the many centuries of painful human experience at the authors' and editors' disposal, the very manifold of the ways of being wise or religious or human that followers of the Lord displayed—and it moves with an animal grace, trying this and that, probing here and there, before settling down and accepting the life meted out to it.

Finally, we show our appreciation of the classical status of the Bible by distrusting any know-it-all who pontificates about what a given text has to mean. Even more, we show our appreciation by refusing to follow any reductionism that would dilute the biblical humanism by taking away the transcendence of its divinity, or the freedom of its human actors, or the historical intentions of its authors, or the literary genius of some of its narrators, or the sociological and political traces embedded in its sources, or . . . on and on. What is in the Bible is not the summary of all human wisdom or of all divine self-expression. The Bible is not the only book by which human beings have or could set their course. But it is more significant than the fashions of any particular generation of its interpreters, and we are only the poorer if we do not let its own polytraditional character teach us this lesson.

GLOSSARY

Biblical humanism   The appreciation of human existence—grandeur, depravity—we find in the Bible.

Hegemony   Preponderant influence or authority; leadership.

Historicity   The quality of existing in time, developing in epochs, and being liable to narrative description.

Utopianism   The tendency to project ideal states in which one's hopes and convictions may be contemplated as though realized.

STUDY QUESTIONS

1. How might the paradoxes in the song of Hannah prefigure the stories of Saul and David?
2. Explain how the ark is related to the Philistines.
3. Why does the Lord accede to Israel's desire to have a king and be like the other nations?
4. What role does the spirit play in Saul's life?
5. Describe the character of Jonathan.
6. How does David show himself reverent toward God's anointed king?

7. What does the figure of David dancing before the ark suggest about the religion of the early monarchy?

8. How does David's murder of Uriah square with his behavior at the death of his first child by Bathsheba?

9. How does 2 Samuel render David responsible for the revolution led by Absalom?

10. Should we consider Joab a good interpreter of the character of King David?

11. How significant to the background of 1 and 2 Samuel was David's unification of the North and South and his establishment of Jerusalem?

12. Do the authors of 1 and 2 Samuel present the pros and cons of kingship evenhandedly?

13. What is the lasting significance of the historical reality and psychological complexity in the portrait of David?

NOTES

1. See P. Kyle McCarter, Jr., "Samuel, the First and Second Books of," in *Harper's Bible Dictionary*, ed. Paul J. Achtemeier. San Francisco: Harper & Row, 1985, p. 903.

2. See Moshe Greenberg, *Biblical Prose Prayer*. Berkeley: University of California Press, 1983, p. 49.

3. See P. Kyle McCarter, Jr., *I Samuel*. Garden City, N.Y.: Doubleday Anchor Bible, 1980, p. 84.

4. See Wilfrid G.E. Watson, "The Structure of 1 Sam 3," *Biblische Zeitschrift*, 29 (1985), 90–93.

5. See G. W. Ahlström, "The Travels of the Ark: A Religio-Political Composition," *Journal of Near Eastern Studies*, 43 (1984), 141–49.

6. See McCarter, *I Samuel*, p. 144. 1 Kings 18:33 does have an offering of water.

7. See Diana Edelman, "Saul's Rescue of Jabesh-gilead (I Sam 11: 1–11): Sorting Story from History," *Zeitschrift für die alttestamentliche Wissenschaft*, 96 (1984), 195–209.

8. See Anthony R. Ceresko, "A Rhetorical Analysis of David's 'Boast' (1 Sam 17:34–37): Some Reflections on Method," *Catholic Biblical Quarterly*, 47 (1985), 58–74.

9. See Katharine Doob Sakenfeld, *Faithfulness in Action: Loyalty in Biblical Perspective*. Philadelphia: Fortress, 1985, pp. 8–16.

10. See Samuel Terrien, *Till the Heart Sings*. Philadelphia: Fortress, 1985, p. 169.

11. See Timo Veijola, "David in Keila," *Revue Biblique*, 91 (1984), 51–87.

12. See J. Fokkelman, "A Lie, Born of Truth, Too Weak to Contain It: A Structural Reading of 2 Sam 1:1–16," *Oudtestamentische Studien*, 23 (1984), 39–55.

13. See John William Wevers, "The First Book of Samuel," in *Old Testament History*, ed. Charles M. Laymon. Nashville: Abingdon (Interpreter's Concise Commentary), 1983, pp. 144–45.

14. See P. Kyle McCarter, Jr., *II Samuel*. Garden City, N.Y.: Doubleday Anchor Bible, 1984, pp. 169–70.

15. Ibid., pp. 190–241.

16. See Keith W. Whitelam, "The Defence of David," *Journal for the Study of the Old Testament*, 29 (1984), 61–87.

17. See Meir Sternberg, *The Poetics of Biblical Narrative*. Bloomington: Indiana University Press, 1985, pp. 190–222.

18. See Stuart Lasine, "Melodrama as Parable: The Story of the Poor Man's Ewe-Lamb and the Unmasking of David's Topsy-Turvey Emotions," *Hebrew Annual Review*, 8 (1984), 101–24.

19. Ibid.

20. See G. Del Olmo Lete, "David's Farewell Oracle (2 Samuel xxiii 1–7): A Literary Analysis," *Vetus Testamentum*, 34 (1984), 414–37.

21. See Brevard Childs, *Introduction to the Old Testament as Scripture*. Philadelphia: Fortress, 1979, pp. 277–78.

22. See Colin Campbell, "The Tyranny of the Yale Critics," *The New York Times Magazine* (February 9, 1986), 20 ff.

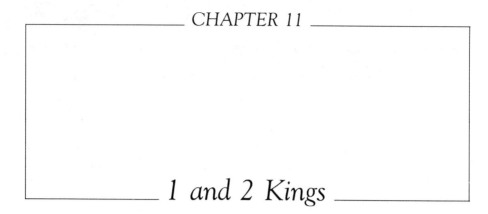

CHAPTER 11

1 and 2 Kings

TEXTUAL ANALYSIS

The books 1 and 2 Kings comprise the final portion of the Former Prophets. Most scholars consider them the conclusion of the Deuteronomistic history. They were originally an undivided whole that traced the devolution of kingship and history from the death of David and the golden age of Solomon to the fall of the Southern Kingdom to Babylon—a temporal frame of almost 400 years (about 965 to 586 B.C.E.). As do many other parts of the Bible, these books present a history that is as much paradigmatic as factual—as much a template of God's action as a literal report of what happened. For our purposes, the following threefold division of the two books is useful:

1 Kings	1:1–11:43	The Reign of Solomon
1 Kings	12:1–2 Kings 17:41	The Divided Monarchy
2 Kings	18:1–25:30	The Kingdom of Judah[1]

1 Kings 1:1–11:43 The Reign of Solomon

At the end of 2 Samuel, David had resumed control of the kingdom and, however diminished his stature because of his failings, he is portrayed to be in favor with the Lord, as the aversion of the plague symbolizes. At the opening of 1 Kings David is old, in need of warmth at night and perhaps senile, and his eldest living son, Adonijah, is preparing to succeed him. However, although some powerful people such as Joab and the priest Abiathar supported Adonijah, another party favored the younger son Solomon. The prophet Nathan and Bathsheba, the mother of Solomon, play on a reputed promise that David had made that Solomon would succeed him, as well as on David's offense that Adonijah would be so ambitious and unseemly as to exalt himself to the kingship before his father's death, to get David to establish Solomon as king. Adonijah does not contest this action but trembles in fear (with good reason, it turns out) that Solomon will slay him as a dangerous rival. Bathsheba is presented artfully: able to stir David to action when the younger Abishag apparently fails, and more ambitious than what Nathan counseled. She is finally getting her just deserts.

Chapter 2 gives us David's dying counsel to Solomon, which amounts to a Deuteronomistic homily: Keep the laws of Moses and you will prosper. David assigns Solomon several pieces of unfinished business, most notably punishing Joab, and in this moment of transition David twice alludes to Solomon's wisdom (verses 2:6,9), prefiguring the theme of wisdom that came to be associated with Solomon. Solomon is presented as the first installment of the promise to David (2 Samuel 7:16) that his line would be established forever. Solomon expresses offense at Adonijah's request for Abishag, using it as an occasion to eliminate his brotherly rival, and then he banishes the priest Abiathar, one of Adonijah's most powerful supporters. The text seems to favor these decisive actions by which Solomon consolidated his power, as it seems to justify the murder of Joab in the tent of the Lord and the murder of Shimei. The promise to David, the supposed wickedness of these victims, and David's dying testament (verses 2:5–9) are the justification for Solomon's ruthlessness.

In chapter 3 Solomon strikes an alliance with Pharaoh and prays for wisdom — "an understanding mind to govern thy people" (verse 3:9). We may suspect that the final edition of 1 Kings has been influenced at this point by the views of a quite late school interested in the wisdom of the Lord. The Deuteronomistic theology is invoked, so that Solomon's wisdom and riches become the reward for his and David's piety. Immediately after the dream in which Solomon receives the gift of wisdom we see him exercising it in the famous case of the two women's disputing about the one child, which begins in verse 3:16. This story, like the preceding story of the dream, bolsters Solomon's reputation for wisdom and links his wisdom with rendering justice. Chapter 4 details Solomon's administration and paints a picture of a kingdom greatly flourishing, because it has the wisest man of his time administer it. Just as Moses became associated with all Law, so Solomon became the personification of all wisdom.[2]

Solomon begins building the Temple in Jerusalem, a monument much prized by later generations, but chapter 5 contains a conscription of labor that starts to fulfill Samuel's prophecy (1 Samuel 8:11–18) of the toll that kingship would exact. Chapter 6 not only describes the sacred house that Solomon was building but also renews the Lord's promise to dwell (there) with his people Israel. Chapter 7 begins on the ominous note that Solomon spent thirteen years building his own palace (whereas the Temple had only taken seven years). His palace is also a grander construction (although many of the details in chapter 7 appear to apply to the Temple rather than to Solomon's palace). The whole description stresses the lavishness of the constructions and the great prosperity of Solomon's reign, and it implies that this prosperity first of all went for the praise of the Lord.

The dedication of the Temple described in chapter 8 adds details of a marvelous coming of the Lord in a cloud that, along with the reference to the tablets of Moses, makes the Temple the fulfillment of the housing for the Lord that began with the ark of the Mosaic covenant made in the wilderness. The speech of Solomon exalts the city of David (Jerusalem), and the building of the Temple by Solomon rather than David is likened to the entry into the promised land under Joshua rather than Moses. The line of David is sanctified in Solomon's prayer and made the inheritor of the Deuteronomistic covenant. Solomon does indicate that the Temple cannot contain the Lord, but the entire ceremony is an obvious effort to exalt the religion of the Temple and make it the heir or fulfillment of prior Israelite religion. The God who judges (by Deuteronomistic standards) from heaven is the same God who blesses the Temple in Jerusalem with his presence. The chapter is a masterpiece of synthesis: The piety of Solomon, the Davidic covenant, the religion of the Temple, the Mosaic law, and the transcendence of the Lord are all expressed in terms that gild the Temple, justify the priestly religion, and buttress the Deuteronomistic theology.

Chapter 9 gives us a second appearance of the Lord, which is apparently designed to explain the later fate of the people and ruin of the Temple as caused by defections from pure worship. The rest of chapter 9 indicates some of the consequences of the expenditures that Solomon's building projects had necessitated: ceding twenty cities of Galilee to King Hiram of Tyre and conscripting many workers as slave labor. The coming of the Queen of Sheba in chapter 10 is another plank in the platform supporting Solomon's reputation for wisdom. The chapter tends to equate the wealth of Solomon's era with his wisdom and to combine the two into a lyric reminiscence of the time when Israel most prospered by pleasing its God.

Chapter 11, however, shows us cracks in this shining edifice and prepares us for the demise of Solomon's achievements. The root of Solomon's errors lay partly in his excessive love of women, but more crucially in his willingness to indulge the religious desires of his foreign wives. By contrast, David never wandered from the true cult, so David was the greater ruler, despite his personal failings. As the rest of 1 and 2 Kings will make plain, proper worship of the Lord, in contrast to idolatrous worship of foreign deities, became for the Deuteronomistic theologians the razor's edge. The foreign deities that Solomon honored in his old age are called "abominations" (verse 11:5), and serving them is accounted "evil in the sight of the Lord" (verse 11:6). The kingdom of Solomon will shatter, because of this evil. The adversary Haddad rises up as something of an avenger, and verse 11:22 likens him to Moses in asking Pharaoh to be let go.

With the advent of Jeroboam in verse 11:26 we enter on a theme of prophecy and fulfillment that dominates the middle portion of 1 and 2 Kings.[3] The tearing of Ahijah's garment into twelve pieces, ten of which are given to Jeroboam, symbolizes the fracture of the united twelve tribes. Solomon will be left only Judah (which, since it had incorporated Simeon, could be rated as one or two tribes). The cause of Solomon's loss is, no doubt retrospectively, made his turning to false gods. The loss will occur or come to fruition with his son, but the cause will be Solomon's own behavior. Jeroboam is given the chance to rule Israel, the North, and to prosper if he keeps the Mosaic commands and walks in the ways of the Lord. Verse 11:41, which refers to a "book of the acts of Solomon," is one of several texts (verses 14:19, 14:29) that suggest that the editors of 1 and 2 Kings had access to archival materials and wove their narrative from several sources. Solomon finally dies, after a rule of forty years (a round figure and the equal of David's rule). He is buried in the city of his father, and his son Rehoboam succeeds to the throne.

1 Kings 12:1–2 Kings 17:41 The Divided Monarchy

The first act of Rehoboam is a folly completely contrasting with the wisdom of his father Solomon. Forsaking the advice of age and listening to the advice of youth, he rejects the petition of Jeroboam and the North for gentler treatment. This petition calls into question the justice of Solomon's reign, and the crudeness of verse 12:10 ("my little thing") symbolizes Rehoboam's unfitness for the delicate tasks of kingly politics. To this point Jeroboam and Israel have justice on their side, so the split of the unified kingdom lies on Rehoboam's head. But when Rehoboam follows the counsel of Shemaiah and refrains from fratricidal war against Israel the ball passes to Jeroboam's court. He flubs it, forsaking true worship (centered in Jerusalem) and reestablishing false worship at two shrines in the North. (This perspective is retrojected from the time of Josiah almost 300 years later.) This is the sin that will beget his undoing, and the author connects it with the idolatry of the golden calf in Exodus 32. Verses 13:1–32 are the center of the paralleled structure of the story of Jeroboam. The unnamed man of God who gives the oracle in favor of Josiah and pure cult bests Jeroboam by miraculous power. The further stories of the man of God and the old prophet demonstrate the power of the Word of the Lord and prepare us to expect the fulfillment of prophecy in the chapters ahead. The conclusion of the incident, verse 13:33, thus predicts the fulfillment of the prophecy of the man of God against the pagan shrines of the high places.

Jeroboam, however, far from repenting, keeps up his idolatrous ways. In chapter 14 the prophet Ahijah utters a second prophecy, balancing that of verses 11:29–40, and this time it foretells the destruction of Jeroboam's line. The scene in which Jeroboam's wife receives not healing but destruction from Ahijah is carefully wrought, with contrasts between seeing and blindness and action carried forward by the word "feet." Clearly David's great virtue was his purity of religion, and Jeroboam has failed, and so deserves to lose the Israel given him, because of his impurity. Verse 14:19 refers to another of the authors' sources, the "Book of the Chronicles of the Kings of Israel." Jeroboam dies a failure whose line has no good future, as we see later.

Rehoboam and Judah, however, also sin idolatrously, and they are punished by the despoiling of the Temple and royal palace carried out by Shishak of Egypt. Verse 14:29 tells us of an archival source for the history of the kings of Judah, reminding us that the authors self-consciously linked the ongoing fates of Israel and Judah. The last impression we get of Rehoboam is that he was coresponsible for the continuous warfare between North and South that marred both his reign and Jeroboam's.

Chapter 15 introduces both Abijam and the formulaic presentation of lineage and religious estimate that will punctuate the following history of the divided kingdom. The key line is 15:3: "And he walked in all the sins which his father did before him; and his heart was not wholly true to the Lord his God, as the heart of David his father." David, then, has become the standard (for the Kings of Judah; Jeroboam is the [bad] standard for Israel), and the critical question to ask of any king is how pure his religion was. Again and again the kings (especially those of the North) fail this test and provide the cause for the troubles of both North and South. (Note, however, that verse 15:5 admits David's failure with Uriah the Hittite.)

Asa, son of Abijam, does better than his father, putting away the cult prostitutes and idols (verse 15:12). His only failure, in fact, lay in not removing utterly the "high places" where idolatrous worship occurred. Still, the continuous warfare between Israel and Judah, which necessitated Asa's league with Syria, shows the rottenness of the overall situation. Thus Nadab, son of Jeroboam, continued his father's sinful ways, making Israel a place of false worship (verse 15:26). Within two years Baasha has murdered him and fulfilled the prophecy of Ahijah that the line of Jeroboam would perish. Baasha, however, is equally idolatrous, so Israel continues to sin. This reaps the prophecy of Jehu that Baasha's house will be swept away.

In chapter 16 the general Zimri destroys Elah, the son of Baasha, and Israel continues to flow with blood. Zimri in turn comes to grief, destroys the palace at Tirzah, and commits suicide because of the assaults of the military commander Omri (see verse 16:18).

Omri overcomes his rival Tibni, but he too does evil in the sight of the Lord. Indeed, he is labeled the worst of the wicked northern kings, until his son Ahab comes on the scene to best him. The tension in fact has been building to the reign of Ahab and Jezebel, where the cult of the baals reached its peak, as though setting the stage for the arrival of the great prophet Elijah.

The passages in 1 Kings 17–2 Kings 10 concern the contest in the North between prophecy (Elijah, Elisha) and wicked kingship (the line of Omri). Elijah appears from nowhere, predicts a drought, and is nourished miraculously by God, somewhat like Israel in the wilderness. The miracle that Elijah works, in 1 Kings 17, for the widow of Zarephath and her son symbolizes that all life lies in God's hands. The resuscitation of the woman's dying son has the same message, and we should note that whereas the widow is first (verse 17:18) bitter and accusatory toward Elijah, she finally acknowledges (verse 17:24) that Elijah is indeed God's mouthpiece.[4]

Chapter 18, which brings Elijah to Ahab, contrasts Jezebel's cutting off the prophets of the Lord and Ahab's seeking provision for his animals. So wicked has Israelite kingship become that horses and mules rate higher than God's spokespeople. The meeting of Obadiah and Elijah skillfully presents the righteousness of Obadiah, the tendency of Elijah to disappear, and the campaign of Ahab to get his hands on Elijah. When Elijah confronts Ahab he rejects Ahab's charge that he, Elijah, has brought the drought, hurling the responsibility back upon Ahab, because of his apostasy. To demonstrate the supremacy of YHWH, Elijah arranges a contest between the Lord and Baal. Elijah challenges the people to stop "limping" (crippling themselves) on a divided faith. (Note that verse 18:26 has the priests of Baal appropriately "limping" about their ineffectual sacrifice.) Elijah's mockery will recur in the latter prophets' ridicule of pagan idols. The successful conclusion of Elijah's dramatic counter-sacrifice shows the superiority of the Lord, and the slaughter of the priests of Baal shows the seriousness of false cult (it is the same

Excavation of King Ahab's palace in Samaria. *(Used with permission of the photographer, Wolfgang Roth)*

as an enemy in holy war). Elijah then secures a rain to break the drought (showing, in verse 17:2, that it was a punishment from God), and his running ahead of Ahab symbolizes the priority of prophecy over kingship.

Despite this impressive victory, Elijah fears the wrath of Jezebel, who in chapter 19 appears as the true power in the realm. Fleeing the kingdom, Elijah begs to die, but he is nourished by the angel of the Lord and journeys to Horeb — more symbolic associations with Moses and the wilderness. The famous scene in verses 19:9–18 is reminiscent of encounters that Moses had with the Lord, but the notion that the Lord was not in the wind or the earthquake or the fire but in the still small voice suggests a touching shift toward interiority: the essence of the prophetic vocation is not the miracles but the quiet communication. Elisha receives the mantle of prophecy from Elijah, and we know that Hazael and Jehu will avenge the Lord for the evil done in Israel.[5]

The victories that God promises Ahab through the mouth of the unnamed prophet are delivered, in proof of who real deity is. But Ahab violates the rules of holy war by not killing Benhadad and so, like Saul (1 Samuel 15), dooms himself to destruction. Chapter 21 shows the childishness and greed of Ahab, who would violate the Levitical laws of inheritance to secure land that he wishes. (The conflict is between ancestral laws of inheritance and royal despotism.) By contrast Jezebel is ruthless and arranges a legal fiction by which to secure the vineyard of Naboth. For her, royal power is everything. Elijah is commissioned to deliver the Lord's oracle of vengeance on Ahab (being given to dogs, as we have previously seen — for example, in verse 14:11 — is a symbol of ruinous ending), and, somewhat surprisingly, Ahab repents.

Statue of Elijah, on Mount Carmel. *(Used with permission of the photographer, Robert L. Cohn)*

Chapter 22 concerns the contest between false prophecy and true, as only Micaiah seeks what the Lord says rather than what the kings want. Ahab dies in fulfillment of Micaiah's prophecy, driving home the truism that kings may propose but only God disposes. He ends in ignominy, the dogs licking his blood and the harlots washing in it. Jehoshaphat, like his father Asa, is a righteous king of Judah, not himself worshiping idolatrously (but too lenient concerning the high places in Judah where pagan rites continued) and making peace with Israel. The remainder of 1 Kings 22 lists incidental information, most importantly the wickedness of the offspring of Ahab and Jezebel.

Another dying monarch is discussed in 2 Kings 1, in a scenario that current literary interpretation considers somewhat typical.[6] The context continues to be the struggle between true prophecy deriving from the Lord and false prophecy or pagan worship, but here Elijah takes the initiative. The fire's coming down again shows the sovereignty of the Lord, and the king's death, in fulfillment of Elijah's prophecy, is attributed to his idolatries.

Kings 2 chapter 2 has stylized predictions of Elijah's rapture and affirmations of Elijah's loyalty. When Elijah parts the Jordan we are reminded of both the Exodus and Joshua's leading the passage at the Conquest. Elijah's being taken up in the whirlwind symbolizes his special status with God. Elisha receives the vision that guarantees him a double share of Elijah's spirit, and with Elijah's mantle he too is able to part the waters of the Jordan. All of this suggests that prophecy is being proposed as the inheritor of Mosaic power and authority. That the fifty prophets cannot find Elijah is in keeping with his tendency to appear and disappear mysteriously during his lifetime. Their failure, which Elisha predicted, establishes Elisha's authority. Elisha's making the water wholesome is reminiscent of Elijah's miracles with meal, oil, and rain (1 Kings 17:16, 18:45), but it is less dramatic. Elisha's cursing the boys who jeered at his baldness is both amusing and grisly: One is not to mock the spokesperson of the Lord.

Chapter 3, a war story like 1 Kings 20 and 22, informs us of the mixed relations between North and South. Elisha's prophecy deals in a symbolism of water, as Elijah's sometimes had. The degradation of Moab is epitomized by the king's willingness to sacrifice his own son, and this enormity paralyzes Israel, indicating its susceptibility to being awed by the supposed powers of the pagan gods. By verse 3:11 Elisha is recognized publicly as Elijah's successor. Elisha's miracle in chapter 4 recalls Elijah's similar provision of oil. He gives the Shunnamite woman her son, and then restores him to life, as Elijah had done for the widow of Zarephath. The other miracles of chapter 4 confirm the power of Elisha, and likely indicate a desire to exalt him above Elijah.

Another episode occurs in 2 Kings 5 that present-day literary analysis finds to be carefully wrought.[7] The text suggests that Naaman has to be cleansed of his inner pride before he can be cleansed of his leprosy. This Syrian's confession of faith, of course, contrasts ironically with the failure of so many Israelite kings to honor the true God. The deception of Gehazi merits the reception of Naaman's leprosy, and it testifies to the knowledge God gives a true prophet.

Chapter 6 magnifies the power of Elisha and illustrates the spiritual forces (verse 6:17) supporting a great prophet. The theme that a prophet sees and ordinary people are blind is quite common (recall 1 Kings 14, where the blind prophet Ahijah was the true seer). Elisha is blamed for the siege of the Syrians, because earlier he had gotten them let go, and the story of the two women's agreeing to eat their children but one's holding back is reminiscent of Solomon's case of the two mothers with the one child. The lepers who despoil the Syrians (who have been routed by the Lord's deception) turn out to be spiritually whole and honest, and their information serves the fulfillment of Elisha's prophecy that the famine would be overcome. The captain who doubted Elisha's promise is considered justly trampled for his unbelief.[8]

The vision of Elisha's regarding the death of Benhadad and the succession of Hazael in chapter 8 shows that prophecy sometimes means seeing unwelcome things. It appears that Hazael in fact murders the king to make the prophecy come true, which could make us think that at this stage Israelite prophecy was an amoral force, operating like a physical phenomenon. God continues to preserve Judah, despite the evil of kings such as Jehoram, because of the divine promise to David. We learn of Edom's liberation and of an alliance between Israel and Judah against Hazael and Syria. Elisha has Jehu anointed king of Israel, to wreak the long-announced vengeance on the house of Ahab. This is executed on the very land for which Jezebel had murdered Naboth. Jezebel comes to her appointed end, eaten by dogs.

As the cycle of stories about Elijah and Elisha concludes, we should note that it represents a major intrusion into the stylized, formulaic account of the royal reigns. This collection of Northern stories about the prophets is unique: No other prophets are depicted as wonder workers (except Moses). The point to the stories is twofold: to offer evidence of the uncompromising Yahwism that remained strong in the North and to explain the fall of the apostate dynasty of Omri. The stories about Elisha express traditions about local miracles that he worked, but their larger significance derives from his intervention in politics. Elisha carries out the mission of his master Elijah to foment revolution in Syria and Israel by provoking Hazael and Jehu. The climax is the ignominious death of Jezebel (predicted by Elijah). There the instigator of apostasy (1 Kings 9) and its main source receives her just punishment. What follow are mainly clean-up operations. Summarily, Elijah and Elisha, the only instance of prophetic succession, successfully fight YHWH's war against Baal by defeating Baal's royal agents. Their remarkable work is the highlight of the history of the divided monarchy.

In chapter 10, Jehu carries out a great purge of Ahab's line, of Ahaziah's people, and of the priests of Baal, purifying the land of those who had polluted it by false worship. Still, Jehu inexplicably does not walk in the law of the Lord wholeheartedly, so the healing of Israel is not complete. The result is that parts of Israel fall to its enemies.

In chapter 11 royal slaughter continues as the wicked queen-mother Athaliah slays all the heirs and gains the throne. She in turn is slain, however, after the Lord shows the priest Jehoiada the one son who had been sequestered. The covenants of Jehoiada have the ring of a renewal of faith in Judah. Jehoash, the boy-king, comes to be a pure ruler, following the counsel of the priest Jehoiada. The black mark of not removing the high places reminds us that the Deuteronomistic theology wanted all cult centralized in Jerusalem.

The priestly interests displayed in chapter 12 remind us that this party played a significant role in the editing of the Deuteronomistic history, and it is interesting that the priests come off as irresponsible, having failed to use the money to repair the house of the Lord honestly. Jehoash's giving the gifts of the house of the Lord to Hazael apparently is considered legitimate, unless we read the murder of Joash as a punishment for that action. Meanwhile oppression continues in the North, because of the continued idolatry, until the Lord hears the prayers of Jehoahaz. Elisha dies, having been acclaimed, as was Elijah, as the chariots of Israel and its horsemen (verse 13:14) and having given a last prophecy. The resuscitation of the dead man thrown on Elisha's grave shows that the power of the prophet even extends to his corpse.

In Judah Amaziah wins praise for his righteousness and justice (chapter 14). He overreaches himself in challenging Israel, however, and suffers defeat, including Israel's seizure of the treasures of the Temple. The Lord preserves Israel despite the wicked rule of Jeroboam, son of Joash, which suggests some leeway in the Deuteronomistic correlation of national sin and punishment. In chapter 15 Azariah of Judah does what is right, but by not razing the high places he lays himself open to the charge that his leprosy was a punishment from the Lord. The rest of chapter 15 is an uninspiring record of evil-doing, incidental warfare, and slaughter. Ahaz brings Judah to the pit of child sacrifice in chapter 16, and then he replicates the pagan altar of Damascus, but apparently he suffers no direct punishment for these sins. Despite the negative characterization by the Deuteronomistic author, Ahaz seems to have saved Judah by accommodating to Assyria.

Chapter 17 brings us to the end of the kingdom of Israel, as Assyria crushes the Northern Kingdom, in part because of its intrigues with Egypt.[9] Verses 17:7–18 read like a brief from the Lord explaining the justice of this punishment of

Israel's idolatries. Verses 17:24–28 claim that the power of the Lord continued to be in the land and forced Assyria to honor it. The foreigners, despite their allegiance to their own gods, feared the Lord, but Israel was subjugated because of its infidelities — that is the final reading of the fall of the Northern Kingdom to Assyria in 721. The land of Israel demands life lived in accord with the "fear of the Lord," so a priest of the Lord must be sent from exile to teach those who should have known better. Verse 17:34 ("to this day") identifies the imported people as Samaritans.

2 Kings 18:1–25:30 The Kingdom of Judah

Chapter 18 shows one of the few kingly heroes of 1 and 2 Kings, Hezekiah, who was faithful to the model of David (see verse 18:3). Notably, Hezekiah removed the high places, and he even purged Mosaic religion of traces of paganism (verse 18:4). For the purity of his faith, the Lord made him prosper, and so Judah escaped the Assyrians. The text approves Hezekiah's using the riches of the house of the Lord to buy Judah's freedom, which implies that the welfare of the people was more important than the adornment of the Temple. The prophet Isaiah defends Hezekiah against the threats of Rabshakeh, representative of Assyria, and verses 19:14–19 show Hezekiah at prayer, begging salvation from the Lord and the manifestation of the Lord's sole sovereignty over all the kingdoms of the Earth. The word of the Lord spoken through Isaiah confirms this prayer and Hezekiah's conviction of the Lord's sovereignty. In verses 19:30–31 we first hear of the "remnant" of Judah that will survive — perhaps a retrojection from the postexilic period.

Assyria departs, afflicted by the Lord (and by other military problems). Hezekiah is saved from mortal illness by his piety (another use of the type-scene of the dying king),[10] and Isaiah is now the heir of Elijah and Elisha, bearing kings the prophetic word. Isaiah predicts the coming exile of Judah to Babylon, but Hezekiah seems rather self-centered in not caring about this as long as it will not occur during his rule (see verse 20:19).

Manasseh, the son of Hezekiah, departs from his father's pious ways and so shows the evil that exile to Babylon will rightly punish. Not even child sacrifice is beyond him (verse 21:6). Therefore, even the remnant of the old unified kingdom will fall, when the Lord wipes Jerusalem like a dish. Amon, the son of Manasseh, also is an evil ruler, so his murder seems well merited. Josiah, by contrast, is another good king, deserving to be ranked with Hezekiah. The collection of money mentioned in verses 22:3–7 is reminiscent of the episode with Jehoash (see verses 12:4–16). Verses 22:8–10 tell of the discovery of the book of the Law in the Temple. (Most scholars believe that this book was an early form of Deuteronomy, because Josiah's reforms, especially the centralization of the cult in Jerusalem, reflect Deuteronomy's concerns.) Josiah takes this as a stimulus to repentance from the disobedience that has run riot in Judah, so the entire symbolism is that the rediscovered Law may bring Judah back to the Lord and prosperity. Huldah, the woman who is now carrying the mantle of prophecy, interprets this happening so as both to foretell the people's coming punishment and to shield Josiah from it.

In chapter 23 the king hears the Law read and promises to follow it with all his heart. The first fruits of this promise are his purification of Jerusalem from all the idolatries that had grown up.[11] Then he spreads his purification outside of the

SENNACHERIB'S INVASION AS IN ISAIAH 10:28-32

holy city, defiling the pagan shrines. Josiah restores the celebration of Passover, which had fallen into abeyance (a striking sign of religious decay). Clearly this king impressed the authors of the Deuteronomistic history as a king after their own heart, zealous for the Mosaic law. Still, in verses 23:26–27 the Lord says that Josiah's reform will not save Judah from punishment (exile).

Josiah's sons do evil in the sight of the Lord and are controlled by Pharaoh. Egypt proves to be no protection against Babylon, however, so Jehoiakim's rebellion against Babylon proves short-lived. After a rule of only three months his son Jehoiachin surrenders to Nebuchadnezzar, king of Babylon, who is besieging Jerusalem. Nebuchadnezzar carries off the cream of the population and makes Zedekiah his ruler in Judah. Zedekiah follows his brother Jehoiakim in doing evil, so his punishment for rebelling against Babylon befits his immorality. First famine afflicts the besieged Jerusalem, and then during the Babylonians' triumph the Temple is burned down — traumatic events indeed. Only the poorest inhabitants of Judah are left to dress the vines and plow the soil.[12] The Babylonians carry off the riches of the Temple. Gedaliah, appointed native governor, is slain by Ishmael, a member of the deposed royal family, which destroys any chance for a peaceful regime in Judah. (Note the designation of the Judean natives as "Jews" in verse 25:25.) The people flee to Egypt from fear of retribution. As 2 Kings ends, Jehoiachin, king of Judah, is being released from prison in Babylon, and he is being treated kindly by the king of Babylon, as though to presage better days when God would be able to deal more kindly with Judah.[13]

HISTORICAL BACKGROUND

The books 1 and 2 Kings presuppose archival materials about the reigns of the kings who followed David, as we have already indicated. Some records of both the northern and southern realms obviously served in the construction of the Deuteronomistic history, but all materials have been set in the framework of the theological reading that the final authors and editors want to convey.[14] This reading is consistent to the point of being repetitive: Israel and Judah did evil in the sight of the Lord by forsaking the ways of the Lord. Therefore, their difficulties, punishments by foreign forces, and eventual subjugation by Assyria and Babylon were well merited.

To have been accepted as plausible, let alone as the canonical interpretation of this period of Israelite history, the accounts we find in 1 and 2 Kings would have had to show themselves faithful to their annalistic sources. The assessment of the piety or impiety of the different kings might be more debated, but the polemic against the high places and the various abominations most likely had some objective warrant.

These books also develop the theme of prophecy and so presuppose both the background we have seen in 1 and 2 Samuel and the continuance of charismatic power in such figures as Elijah and Elisha. Many of the materials about these two great prophets are legends and miracle stories collected by disciples, but the theological use of even such miracle stories is patent: The prophets were the great defenders of the rights of the Lord against the baals and the sinful kings who conspired to betray the Israelite tradition.

The many stories of regicide and slaughter would be mere vilification if kings had not actually arisen and declined by the sword during this period. The fall of the North to Assyria in 721 and the fall of the South to Babylon in 586 were bitterly remembered, especially the more recent Exile to Babylon. The most significant assumption of 1 and 2 Kings is that the audience to whom these books finally were directed were ripe for an explanation of what had gone wrong in Israelite history and kingship. With both North and South brought to their knees, what lessons ought the people to learn? For the authors of these materials, clearly, they ought to learn that falling away from the Lord was the path to disaster. The books 1 and 2 Kings therefore presupposed a realization that after David pagan rites flourished in Israel and Judah, and that the evils done in both kingdoms, as well as the evils of both kingdoms' fall, could not be separated from the betrayal of the people's Mosaic heritage that such rites represented.

LITERARY INTENT

The books 1 and 2 Kings were written as the final portions of an interpretation of what happened to Israel after Moses and the fulfillment of the Mosaic covenant by the Conquest of the promised land. The book of Deuteronomy itself reset the terms of the Mosaic covenant and reexpressed the Law by which the people were to live. Joshua through 2 Kings interpreted how the people fared with this covenant, increasingly setting pure religion over-against idolatry and judgeship/prophecy over-against kingship. The focus on doing evil by indulging in false cult that predominates in 1 and 2 Kings suggests the axial line that had emerged by the conclusion of the Deuteronomistic historiography. The program of reform initiated by Josiah lay in the minds of the final authors and editors as the model for what they needed after the Exile to Babylon, if they were truly to take to heart the lessons of the period from Moses to the Exile (especially the lesson of the fall of Israel in 721).

We could say, then, that 1 and 2 Kings were written not only to preserve the history of kingship in Israel and Judah, but also to make that history undergird the reforms that, after the Exile, were proposed as the way for the Jewish people to avoid such catastrophe in the future. The authors were undoubtedly sufficiently sophisticated to realize that "history" always remains open-ended, so that no program of reform can guarantee a brighter future. Indeed, their own sensitivity to the ironies of history is quite sharp. But at the center of their interpretive intuition was the instinct that the true heritage of their people was their special relationship with their special God. There was only one God, who was sovereign over all nations. Yet it was one thing to find this fact in Deuteronomy 6 and another thing to live it out, maintaining a purity of worship and a fidelity to covenantal law that made the people eccentric to their neighbors.

The writers of 1 and 2 Kings go out of their way to underscore the many demonstrations of the reality and power of the Lord that holy prophets and righteous kings received. The issue was not that the Lord had not left traces of his power and did not make his presence in the people's midst known. It was that the people, largely for lack of good kingly leadership, were not drawn to the centralized cult in Jerusalem and defended against the seductions of their pagan neighbors. When the people worshiped the baals and other fertility deities, they were succumbing to the understandable human desire to bring divinity under control or to find it

palpably present in such comforting regularities as spring fertility and winter fal-
lowness. The Lord remembered as revealed to Abraham, covenanted with Moses,
and favoring toward David was more demanding than the lords of the neighboring
peoples. Like Elijah, he came and went as he chose. His Torah was a secure
guidance, but to animate this Torah people had to have a lively spiritual experience,
and that in turn depended on gifted prophets and priests. The books 1 and 2 Kings,
we might finally say, were written to rouse trust in the traditional God, assuring
people that he was powerful and able to save them from the never-failing threats
of war and famine.

LASTING SIGNIFICANCE

The books 1 and 2 Kings supply much of our knowledge of the period between
the death of David and the fall of Judah. Beyond this bare historical significance,
however, they also provide a most provocative interpretation of kingship and
national life. We should note, for example, that the activity of the former prophets
and the books that reflect on their struggles with different kings testify to a remarkable tolerance for self-criticism. (This continues in the latter prophets.) Rather
than blaming God, these books blame the people of God themselves. God is
portrayed as always remaining faithful to his side of the covenant. It is the people
who fail to hold up their side, and the writers of the historical books are unsparing
in their criticism of this infidelity. Implied in such self-criticism, of course, is the
capacity to reform and change. The goal of the former prophets was not merely
destructive or negative. They hoped that a strict criticism of the past would lead
to better performance in the future. The latter prophets develop this theme, insisting that the people have the freedom and God gives the help to make justice
and mercy practicable goals. Thus the overall theology of the prophetic books
places great power and responsibility in human hands. The fault is not with God
or with the stars. The fault is with ourselves.

We have previously reflected on the Deuteronomistic theology, with its
conviction that fidelity to God brings prosperity and infidelity brings punishment.
By and large this theology prevails in 1 and 2 Kings, although we noted that several
sizable sinners do not receive their expected punishments. So it is more the character of the leadership presented in 1 and 2 Kings that draws our attention and
that causes us to wonder what we should make of such a sorry succession of kings.

The books themselves apparently make this succession cause for considerable
lament and reason to judge that what Israel and Judah received was well deserved.
But beneath this obvious line of interpretation lies a second level, at which the
authors suggest that God is willing to keep doing business with humanity, even
when it fails consistently and evilly. Despite the punishments visited on the evil
kings and their people, and despite such negative verses as 2 Kings 17:20, there
are many indications that Israel and Judah continued to be the portion of the Lord.
Not only did the Lord keep sending prophets who contested the backsliding and
evildoing of the worst kings, the chosen people itself survived, even through the
fall of the two kingdoms. Indeed, one American scholar has argued that Kings
went through two editings, to explain first the prospects latent in Josiah's reform
and then the causes of the Exile of Judah to Babylon.[15]

So in 1 and 2 Kings the bedrock questions of a theology of history are never far away. As soon as we enter into the process of wondering about the vagaries of Israelite experience during the divided monarchy, we start pulling at threads that take us into the mysteries of time, providence, election, and preservation. Any philosophy of history of course ought to deal with these matters, but in fact most philosophies that do not take nourishment from the Hebrew Bible rather neglect them. Thereby, they neglect an inexhaustible source of contemplative growth and political hope: If past generations have been able to make even their worst disasters meaningful, perhaps we too can wring significance from our shabby times.

GLOSSARY

Historiography   The writing of history; narrative reconstruction of the past.

Remnant   The portion left over after a part has been removed; the portion of the covenant community that would remain after defection and chastisement.

STUDY QUESTIONS

1. How does David's final counsel to Solomon set the plot line of 1 and 2 Kings?
2. What evidence are we given of Solomon's wisdom?
3. Analyze the symbolism of the Lord's presence in the Temple.
4. How does the interaction of Ahijah and Jeroboam draw the battlelines between prophecy and kingship?
5. What is the significance of king slaughtering king slaughtering king?
6. Describe the religious experience of Elijah in 1 Kings 19.
7. Describe the religious experience of Elisha in 2 Kings 2.
8. Why do the authors show Elisha to be a miracle worker on the model of Elijah?
9. Compare the good kings Hezekiah and Josiah.
10. What is the significance of the prophet Isaiah?
11. Why is Israel painted as more wicked than Judah?
12. Why do the authors find false cult so great a failing?
13. What is the significance of the Lord's not breaking the covenant and writing wicked Israel and Judah off?

NOTES

1. See Mordechai Cogan, "Kings, the First and Second Books of the," in *Harper's Bible Dictionary*, ed. Paul J. Achtemeier. San Francisco: Harper & Row, 1985, p. 530.
2. See Lawrence Boadt, *Reading the Old Testament: An Introduction*. New York: Paulist, 1984, p. 237.
3. See Robert L. Cohn, "Literary Technique in the Jeroboam Narrative," *Zeitschrift für die Alttestamentliche Wissenschaft*, 97 (1985), 23–35.
4. See Robert L. Cohn, "The Literary Logic of 1 Kings 17–19," *Journal of Biblical Literature*, 101 (1983), 333–50.

5. See Denise Dick Herr, "Variations of a Pattern: 1 Kings 19," *Journal of Biblical Literature*, 104 (1985), 292–94.

6. See Robert L. Cohn, "Convention and Creativity in the Book of Kings: The Case of the Dying Monarch," *Catholic Biblical Quarterly*, 47 (1985), 603–16.

7. See Robert L. Cohn, "Form and Perspective in 2 Kings V," *Vetus Testamentum*, 33 (1983), 171–84.

8. See Robert LaBarbera, "The Man of War and the Man of God: Social Satire in 2 Kings 6:8–7:20," *Catholic Biblical Quarterly*, 46 (1984), 637–51.

9. See Arie van der Kooij, "Zür Exegese von II Reg 17:2," *Zeitschrift für die alttestamentliche Wissenschaft*, 96 (1984), 109–12.

10. See Cohn, "Convention and Creativity in the Book of Kings: The Case of the Dying Monarch," 612–14.

11. See Christoph Levin, "Joschija im deuteronomistischen Geschichtswerk," *Zeitschrift für die alttestamentliche Wissenschaft*, 96 (1984), 351–71.

12. See J. N. Graham, "Enigmatic Bible Passages: 'Vinedressers and Plowmen': 2 Kings 25:12 and Jeremiah 52:16," *Biblical Archeologist*, 47 (1984), 55–58.

13. See Jon D. Levenson, "The Last Four Verses in Kings," *Journal of Biblical Literature*, 103 (1984), 353–61.

14. For details on the annalistic sources of 1 and 2 Kings, see John Grey, *I and II Kings*. Philadelphia: Westminster, 1977.

15. See Frank Moore Cross, *Canaanite Myth and Hebrew Epic*. Cambridge, Mass.: Harvard University Press, 1973, especially pp. 274–89.

CHAPTER 12

Isaiah

TEXTUAL ANALYSIS

With Isaiah we come to the "major" prophets whose writings give the Hebrew Bible some of its most poetic and insightful theology. Isaiah of Jerusalem, the prophet who gives this book its name, was active in the latter half of the eighth century B.C.E. Scholars generally assign only the first thirty-nine chapters of the current book of Isaiah to him, and they tend to refer his work to two major crises, the Syro-Ephramite war of 734 to 733 and the Assyrian threats to Judah from 734 to 701. (We noted the relation between Isaiah and King Hezekiah in 2 Kings 20, where Isaiah both healed and consoled the king.) We deal with the book of Isaiah in three textual divisions, and we discuss the differences among them as we go:

1:1–39:8	First Isaiah
40:1–55:13	Second Isaiah
56:1–66:24	Third Isaiah[1]

1:1–39:8 First Isaiah

The bulk of the first portion of the book of Isaiah concerns oracles and prophecies that Isaiah of Jerusalem uttered in the context of the turmoils and threats of foreign invasion that dominated the last third of the eighth century B.C.E. The first twelve chapters are prophecies against Judah and Jerusalem that envision the punishments merited by Judah's defection from its covenant with the Lord. Verse 1:1 tells us that Isaiah worked through the reigns of four kings, from

Uzziah (783 to 742) to Hezekiah (715 to 687). At the least, therefore, he had a career of thirty years. Some scholars consider the first pericope or textual unit to be verses 1:2–20, which is literarily like a lawsuit.[2] Note the theme that the people do not know or understand—culpable ignorance—and that their God is "the Holy One of Israel." The sorry state of the Southern Kingdom is due to dereliction of its religious duty, which the prophet describes with affecting poetry. Note that the cult being offered is rejected as false: not correlated with social justice (as verse 1:17 makes plain).

Isaiah 1:18 is a famous line; the imagery conjures up God's winning the people back to reason and thereby becoming able to cleanse it of its sins. Verses 1:21–23 further detail the lack of righteousness and justice that prevails. This will bring the wrath of God, but those who are righteous will redeem Zion (Jerusalem). Chapter 2 paints a scene of a peaceful future when all nations recognize the God of Israel and come to Jerusalem to learn Torah. The mood shifts in verse 2:6, offering an oracle about divine vengeance against the idolaters and the high and mighty.

Chapter 3 foresees how present disorders will run their course, but note that Isaiah expects the righteous to fare well in God's judgment. The injustice of men and the vanity of women will cost the whole people dearly. Indeed, verse 4:1 imagines such a slaughter of the male population that women will outnumber men seven to one. The rest of the chapter, however, speaks of a blessed aftermath, when the presence of the Lord on Zion will be like the divine manifestations on Sinai and through the time of the wandering in the wilderness.

Chapter 5 introduces the famous imagery of Israel (the whole covenanted people, North and South) as a vineyard that the Lord would husband to rich growth. For its bitter fruits of injustice and bloodshed, though, the people will merit desolation. Verse 5:13 seems to refer to the Exile afflicted on the North by Assyria, a fate that Isaiah attributes to "want of knowledge."[3] Verse 5:19 again refers to the coming judgment of the Holy One of Israel, and verse 5:20 summarizes the moral perversion that Isaiah hated: calling evil good and good evil. Verse 5:26 sounds the note that the Lord will use foreigners to execute his judgments.

One of the most famous texts in Isaiah is the vision of the Lord (chapter 6), which many scholars have considered to be an account of Isaiah's prophetic "call." In various ways the prophet proclaims the holiness of the Lord (verse 6:3 has had a great liturgical impact, and the imagery of the burning coal in verse 6:7 has become a staple in reflections on the prophetic vocation). The paradoxes of verse 6:9–10 reflect the prophetic experience of giving the people messages they could not or would not understand (and so could not or would not be turned [converted] and healed). The rest of the chapter employs figures all too fully realized in the actual history of Israel's devastating wars.

Chapter 7 refers to the league of Syria and Ephraim (the Northern Kingdom) against Judah. Isaiah and his son Shearjashub ("a remnant shall return") assure king Ahaz that this threat will not crush Judah. Isaiah counsels trust in God and offers a sign to assure Ahaz that God will defeat the alliance of enemies. The sign is that a young woman (the queen?) will give birth to a scion of the line of David in whom God's presence will be felt.[4] Before he grows up, Syria-Israel will fall. Isaiah 7:17–25 refer to the Assyrian invasion that came after the threat from the league of Syria and Ephraim (Israel) abated.

Chapter 8 begins with a dramatic signing (Isaiah and other prophets sometimes acted out their oracles). The symbolic name of another of Isaiah's sons, "the spoil speeds, the prey hastens" relates to the coming invasion of Assyria and its defeat of Syria and Israel. Note the call to consider the holy Lord one's sole fear.[5] Verses 16–22 may provide evidence for the preservation of Isaiah's oracles among his disciples. Chapter 9 moves to more pleasing scenarios, looking to the imminent coming of a Davidic king who will be a prince of peace. The language in Isaiah 9:2–7 suggests cultic use and certainly is idealized or visionary. The rest of the chapter deals with the judgments to be wreaked on the North, which Judah should take as object lessons.

Chapter 10 returns us to the theme of chastisement for injustice, and verse 10:5 is notable for the Lord's calling Assyria "the rod of my anger, the staff of my fury." To Isaiah's mind, the nations subserve the Lord's purposes, and verses 10:13–19 carry the assurance that Assyria, too, will be punished for its pride and excesses. The "remnant" mentioned in verses 10:20–23 is the survivors of Assyria's assaults on the North, and their survival is linked with their leaning on the Holy One of Israel in truth. The rest of the chapter promises Judah safety against Assyria.

Chapter 11 takes us back to the visionary or utopian mood of Isaiah 9:2–7 and is another imagining of the ideal Davidic king who might lead Judah to a flowering of religious and material prosperity. Verse 11:2 is reminiscent of the imagery associated with the wisdom of Solomon. Verses 11:6–9 have become famous as a picture of the peaceable kingdom in which all of nature would be harmonious. Isaiah lovingly imagines reconciliation between Ephraim and Judah and their union against their common enemies. Chapter 12 concludes the first collection of Isaian oracles with a psalm of trust, thanksgiving, and prayer.

In chapters 13–23 the focus shifts from Judah to the foreign nations, whose fate also falls within a prophet's purview (see also Jeremiah 46–51, Ezekiel 25–32, and Amos 1–2). Chapter 13 again speaks of the day of the Lord as a time of fierce, military judgment. Such scenes as infants' being dashed to pieces and wives' being ravished remind us that in Isaiah's day people knew war to be a brutal, hand-to-hand destructiveness. Babylon, threatening to smaller kingdoms like Judah, will be smashed by the Medes, as if to remind Judah that all powers are small to the Lord. Chapter 14 seems to envision the return of Israelites captured by Assyria and their regaining sovereignty over their original land. Alternatively, the passage has perhaps been influenced by the later experience of exile to Babylon and return. (We discuss the literary complexities of the book of Isaiah later.) The rest of chapter 14 describes the humbling of the mighty Babylon and Assyria, in proof that they are nothing compared to the Holy One of Israel. Note that here, beginning in verse 14:22, Isaiah favors the epithet "the Lord of hosts": the fullness of heavenly powers, who rules over all creation. The oracle against the Philistines apparently came in 715, and the desolation predicted for Moab in chapter 15 moves even a Judean prophet to pity (verse 15:5). Chapter 16 seems to counsel kindness and mercy toward Moabite refugees coming to Judah.[6]

The oracle against Damascus in chapter 17 is another demonstration that foreign nations, too, come under the Lord's chastisement. Note the reference in verses 17:7–8 to idolatry. Although the book of Isaiah does not beat this theme to death, the way that the books of the former prophets do, it agrees that going over to the fertility deities is an epitome of the nation's loss of soul: It has forgotten the rock of its refuge (verse 17:10). Chapters 18 and 19 concern Ethiopia and Egypt. Historians sometimes suggest that behind these oracles lies the effort of the twenty-fifth Egyptian Dynasty, run by Ethiopia, to recruit Hezekiah and Judah in a plot against Assyria.[7] Isaiah would then be warning that all such things lie in God's hands.

The civil turmoil predicted for Egypt in chapter 19 seems historically factual, and the satire of Egyptian gods and the denigration of Egyptian wisdom express Isaiah's own sense of theological superiority. The rest of the chapter makes Israel and its God a saving if chastening force for Egypt and a party to the reconciliation of Egypt and Assyria, envisioning a time when hated Egypt will acknowledge the God of Israel. Chapter 20 gives another dramatic sign that the prophet felt called to act out in front of the people. Clearly, the import of his nakedness was the fate that would come to Egypt from Assyria and the folly of relying on Egypt for protection against Assyria. Chapter 21, concerning Babylon, has often been assumed to be postexilic.[8] The prophet's vision brings him great suffering, and he feels like a watchman, posted to descry what is coming upon the people, who mainly sees the advent of horrors. Isaiah 21:11–12 may be saying that the future simply is uncertain.

Chapter 22 may reflect the time, after 701, when the Assyrian Sennacherib had lifted the siege of Jerusalem. Isaiah was not impressed by the people's courage when under assault, and he foresees impending disaster. Verses 22:8–11 criticize the dependence on human constructions that neglects trust in God. When the people should have repented they gave themselves over to pagan pleasure-taking instead. Isaiah lays much of the blame on Shebna, steward of Hezekiah, who opposed the prophet's advice of noninvolvement in the struggle between Assyria and Egypt, trying to get the king to join with Egypt. According to Isaiah 36:3–22, Eliakim did replace Shebna as steward. The key verse in chapter 23 is 23:9, which explains the fall of Tyre and Sidon as the Lord's dishonoring of the honored.

Chapters 24–27, which are often regarded as an Isaian apocalypse (no earlier than the Exile), stress a coming universal judgment of the Lord against all sinful nations and reflect on what that will mean for Judah. The cause of the coming general suffering will be transgressing the laws—the general canons of decency and justice—through which God, holy light and truth, is known and obeyed. Verses 24:14–16 suggest songs generated by suffering and repentance. Verses 25:1–2 praise the certain, foreordained justice of the Lord in bringing widespread punishment. Verse 25:4 beautifully expresses the piety that monotheism can bring out of suffering: confession that God is a solid defense against all creaturely enemies and causes for depression. The rest of the chapter bespeaks encouragement and the joy of feeling assured that God's salvation one day will come. Even though "First Isaiah" lashes sinful humanity, it offers equally powerful consolations. Chapter 26 continues in this vein, offering psalm-like praise of God and expressions of trust. Note the feminine imagery of miscarriage in verses 26:17–18.

Leviathan, the Canaanite monster of the sea mentioned in Isaiah 27:1, symbolizes creation potentially chaotic and resistant to the divine will. Verses 27:2–6 repeat the imagery of a vineyard, and verse 27:9 calls for the destruction of idolatry. Note the return of culpable ignorance ("without discernment") as a summary judgment in verse 27:11.

Chapters 28–33 bend judgment back upon Israel and Judah again. In verses

28:1–4 the garland of the drunkards of Ephraim comes in for scorn, and verses 28:5–6 delight in the Lord's diadem of beauty, which the remnant faithful to him will enjoy. Yet the people will be taught the harsh lessons they need by foreigners. (The Northern Kingdom, often called Ephraim, did fall to Assyria in 722.) Verses 28:16–18 foresee a Jerusalem reconstructed on justice, recovenanted to a living God rather than a dead immorality. Those who scoff at religious trust and wisdom are the hardest cases: what can God do with the cynical? Chapter 29 poetically describes the punishment of Jerusalem and its cause, without giving the enemies of Jerusalem full hope. Note the symbols of stupor, sleep, and covered eyes (no prophets), which express spiritual obtuseness. Verses 29:13–16 deal with the irony or paradox of insincere or superficial religion. There and in the rest of the chapter the prophet is impressed by the shakeup that the return of divine presence and justice would have to entail.

Chapter 30 pillories dependence upon Egypt and perverting prophecy so that it becomes a tool of state policy. In different language, we are back to Elijah and Ahab. Verse 30:15 is notable religious poetry: "In returning and rest you shall be saved; in quietness and in trust shall be your strength." Taken either corporately or individualistically, it is provocative, like the poet T. S. Eliot's notion that our greatest action is our passion. Verse 30:18 offers assurance of the Lord's grace and justice, which should be Judah's deepest cultural foundation. Note the image of Teacher (the Lord or his prophets) in verse 30:20, which counter-balances the negative imagery of ignorance that Isaiah employs. The remainder of the chapter is quite positive, promising both a use for Judah's sufferings and the smiting of Assyria.

Chapter 31 begins on the familiar note of the prophet's complaining that the people rely on Egypt more than on the Holy One of Israel (their victorious champion against Egypt in the Exodus that made them God's people). The defeat of Assyria (Judah in fact did not fall) will be accomplished by God rather than by human swords. Verses 32:1–8 link the coming of better leadership with a turning from rashness to good judgment and from foolishness to wisdom. Verses 32:9–14 would rock the complacent and have them prepare for hard times. The final scenario in this chapter is positive, though, as the divine spirit gives renewed life to the land and justice to the people.[9]

The last of these chapters giving oracles against Jerusalem may begin by referring to Assyria (verse 33:1), but it soon turns to a quasi-liturgical petition of the Lord on Judah's behalf. The alternation between praising God and criticizing the impious seems stylized. Verses 33:14–15 condense the prophet's program: Walk righteously and speak uprightly. Verse 33:22 links the flourishing of Jerusalem with its truly having the Lord for its judge, ruler, and king.

The mood turns upbeat in chapters 34–35, which foresee better times when Jerusalem will be restored. Chapter 34 predicts harsh vindictive ruin for the foreign nations that have been oppressing Judah. Verse 34:16 refers to a book containing the divine plan and a roster of the saved. Verses 35:1–4 further develop imagery of the time of restoration. Verse 35:5 has become famous in English through its use in Handel's *Messiah* (see also Matthew 11:5).

The final chapters of First Isaiah, 36–39, offer an historical account of the relations between the prophet and the king Hezekiah (mainly repeating 2 Kings 18:13–20:19). Note that Rabshakeh interprets Assyrian power as derived from the

Lord (36:10), and that he in effect is challenging Hezekiah's and Judah's interpretation of what the Lord can or will do for Judah. In chapter 37 Hezekiah gets
Isaiah to pray that the Lord will rebuke Assyria and its interpretation of the divine
plan. Isaiah promises that Assyria will be diverted. Hezekiah's prayer in the Temple
is like the prayers of Moses, asking God not to besmirch the divine reputation by
bringing the faith of his people into mockery. Isaiah gives the oracle that we have
previously seen (37:22–29; compare 2 Kings 19:21–28). The Lord delivers Judah
from Assyria as Isaiah promised, and in chapter 38 Isaiah heals the king, after
Hezekiah's repentance has overturned the oracle predicting his death. The "writing"
of Hezekiah (verses 38:9–20) is the only new material in chapters 36–39. It
expresses the gloom that going to Sheol or the land of the dead could create and
offers praise of divinity as a cause for God to preserve the living. Chapter 39
completes First Isaiah on the note that Babylon will take away all the treasures of
Judah. Overall, this narrative appendix offers so different a picture of the prophet
and his functions that we wonder if it originally described someone other than
Isaiah.

40:1–55:13 Second Isaiah

By general scholarly consensus, chapters 40–55 of the book of Isaiah deal
with events — notably, the Exile to Babylon — that occurred long after the period
of Isaiah of Jerusalem. Yet the book of Isaiah as a whole displays sufficient thematic
and stylistic unity to "justify" the final editorial combination of these chapters
(along with 56–66).[10] It is debated whether Second (or "Deutero") Isaiah was a
member of an Isaian prophetic circle, and whether chapters 40–55 derive from a
period before Judah's release from Babylonian captivity (538 B.C.E.) or after it.[11]
It is not debated that Second Isaiah writes principally to console those who have
suffered from the fall of Judah to Babylon in 586, which entailed the deportation
of much of the community and the destruction of the Temple. Neither is it debated
that Second Isaiah is a peak experience within the Hebrew Bible and creates some
of its loftiest poetry and theology.

Chapters 40–48 focus on the salvation that God will give captive Judah,
through the fall of Babylon and the coming of Cyrus of Persia as God's anointed
deliverer. The very first words of this prophecy are thematic and memorable:
"Comfort, comfort my people, says your God. Speak tenderly to Jerusalem, and
cry to her that her warfare is ended, that her inquity is pardoned" (verses 40:1–
2). Judah has suffered enough. It is time for relief and restoration. Verses 40:3–4
have the famous figure of valleys' being filled and mountains' and hills' being made
low. Verses 40:6–8 are equally famous: All flesh is grass, but the word of God
stands for ever. We could scarcely overestimate the historical effect of these words,
which have been cherished for millennia. Verses 40:9–11 take us to a high place
of vantage, from which we may imagine God's coming in deliverance.[12] The rest
of chapter 40 is a powerful theological argument for trusting that history, like
creation, rests in God's hands, and it rings with a poet's appropriation of monotheism. The refrain "Have you not known? Have you not heard?" (in verses
40:21, 28) is characteristically Isaian in marveling at the people's ignorance. The
Judahites have been in exile for over forty years — long enough for a new generation
to have grown up and faith in a long-absent God to have atrophied. Second Isaiah

is challenging his audience to keep the traditional faith. He is trying to rouse his people to remember the God who formed them, saying in effect that the recent experience of exile has not vitiated God's power or care. Rhetorically, he wants to attack the claims made for the Babylonian gods and demonstrate the exclusive power of the Holy One of Israel. Indeed, few theologians of the Hebrew Bible rival Second Isaiah in appreciating that only God created the world (so independently as in later centuries to intimate the doctrine of "creation from nothingness").

With chapter 41 Cyrus of Persia enters on the scene, the one from the east (verse 41:2) that God has stirred up, ultimately, Second Isaiah contends, for the sake of Israel, his servant, whom he has not forgotten. The "fear not" that punctuates this chapter is like the "comfort, comfort" of chapter 40: prophecy nearly wholly positive and consoling. Verse 41:14, speaking of God as "Redeemer," depicts the Lord as the people's champion and liberator, who protects the poor and waters the parched land. Verses 41:21–24 have the form of a legal challenge to the foreign nations and their idolatrous gods. Verse 41:24 makes such idols "nothing." The rest of the chapter looks to the coming of Cyrus and dismisses the power of the nations or their gods.

In verses 42:1–4 we get the first of what many scholars consider four famous songs about the "servant" of God (see also Isaiah 49:1–6, 50:4–11, and 52:13–53:12). There has been enormous debate about the identity of this servant.[13] The safest assumption probably is that the author had in mind the restored nation, whose way will be a gentleness and justice given by the divine Spirit. Indeed, on several occasions (for example, verses 44:1, 45:4) he names Israel as the servant. Verses 42:5–9 present another ringing declaration of the divine creativity, which links physical creation to the creation of the people of Israel, as a warrant for the newness promised in verse 42:9. (This appeal to the role of YHWH in creation does not appear before the Exile.) The praise from nature and the imagery of the Lord as a warrior give way in verse 42:14 to imagery of God as a mother in labor to bring forth a new people and era.[14] The rest of the chapter deals with the overturnings that the divine creativity will entail, again mentions God's servant, and reminds us of the infidelities that the Exile punishes.

In chapter 43 we are back in the midst of consolation: redemption and promises of deliverance. Verses 43:4–5 are remarkable for their promise of love and presence. The special servanthood of Israel among the nations (verse 43:10) leads on to a ringing declaration of monotheism and singular redeemership: No other than the Holy One of Israel is God and savior. Note how verses 43:15–19 link the new thing that is promised with the old redemption at the Exodus, implying that the new will be as unlikely and splendid as the old. The divine voice does not deny Jacob's lack of worship, but verse 43:25 emphasizes instead forgetting the people's sins. The alternation of accusation and more significant forgiveness continues to verse 44:8, assuring the people that they belong to the only God and have nothing to fear. Verses 44:9–20 comprise a devastating critique of idolatry and those foolish enough to be enticed by it. Verses 44:21–23 assure readers that despite its past idolatries Israel is offered forgiveness and a new start. The rest of the chapter builds up the value of the promise of the Lord, noting his power in the womb and in creation, and again making Cyrus an agent of providence.

This motif continues in chapter 45, where the only God uses Cyrus despite the Persian's ignorance. The prophet gives Cyrus the title "Messiah" to emphasize this use. Second Isaiah is so convinced of the singularity or onlyness of the Lord that divine providence is a nearly automatic deduction: Whatever happens happens only as the sole God wishes. Verse 45:8 is marvelous poetry that has shaped the Christian liturgy for Advent. Verses 45:9–13 variously symbolize the priority of the maker over the made, thereby encouraging confidence and acquiescence. In verse 45:15 we note the hiddenness of God, which is another symbol for the divine transcendence and freedom. This hidden God makes salvation rather than chaos. He is the only source of salvation, and verse 45:22 invites all the ends of the Earth to turn to him and be saved—a remarkable universalism. The conviction that only in the Lord are righteousness and strength (verse 45:24) is another corollary of the uniqueness, the onlyness, of the Holy One of Israel.

Following the satire of pagan idols in verses 46:1–2 (and 5–7), verse 46:3 has another maternal figure for God: carrying Israel from its conception. There is none to compare with God, no other genuine deity. What he proposes is accomplished, what he speaks comes to pass. If he says salvation will come to Zion, the logic runs, so it shall be. Alternately, if he foresees Babylon's being brought low (as in verse 47:1), so it shall be. Verse 47:6 has the striking phrase that the Lord himself, out of anger, profaned his inheritance (Israel). The punishment of the punisher Babylon therefore assumes the aspect of the Lord's correcting a mistake on his part. Note the contrast between Babylonian pretensions to immunity and the sole sovereignty of the Lord. Babylon itself is depicted in chapter 47 as a false god. Chapter 48 reviews the history of punishment and promised deliverance as wholly in God's hands. The religious lesson is that both punishment and prosperity are divine instruction, to those who draw near and harken. The word now, though, is redemption.

The second portion of Second Isaiah, chapters 49–55, deals with the restoration of Zion or Jerusalem, the holiest of God's presences. Verses 49:1–6 are for many scholars the second servant song, depicting the predestined vocation of Israel. Here, the motif is reconstituting the people of Jacob and serving the nations as a light, for the sake of universal salvation. Verses 49:7–13 contrast Israel's despised status with what the Lord shall do for it, and verses 49:14–21 offer moving assurances that God has not, never could, forget Zion—no more than a nursing mother could forget her child. By exalting Israel higher than it was brought low, God will show the nations that Israel's savior is the sole Lord. Note that verse 49:8 addresses the exiles as potential returnees to the promised land.

The imagery at the outset of chapter 50, divorce and slavery, runs to the same conclusion: Israel has not been cast off. The punishment of Exile stems from failing to hear the call addressed through the prophets. Note the repetition of the theme of teaching (here stronger than in First Isaiah) in verses 50:4–5, the beginning of the third servant song. The mark of the servant in this song is patient endurance of taunts. The rest of the chapter stresses blind trust of (the hidden) God. Chapter 51 offers the example of Abraham and Sarah, the prime models of faith, for trusting that Zion will be restored. Verse 51:7 encourages the righteous to fear no human reproaches. Verses 51:9–11 plead with God to show himself a deliverer (Rahab is like Leviathan). The rest of the chapter offers variations on the theme that the Creator is uniquely trustworthy (because uniquely powerful), as well as a promise that the drunken stupor of suffering will end for Judah and pass over to its enemies.

Verses 52:1–12 weave together various assurances that Zion will be renewed and should recleanse itself and notes (in verse 52:7) the beauty of this good news and those who announce it (the image of the watchman again). Verse 52:11 suggests the priestly concern with ritual cleanness. Verses 52:13–53:12 comprise the fourth servant song, which begins on the note that what has been marred will be wondrously lifted up. Verses 53:1–12 movingly interpret the sufferings of the servant people as effective or expiatory for the failings of all, and they consider the Exile as finally providential: "Yet it was the will of the Lord to bruise him; he has put him to grief; when he makes himself an offering for sin, he shall see his offspring, he shall prolong his days" (verse 53:10). It is understandable that Christian exegesis would apply this to Jesus, but, of course, Deutero-Isaiah was writing about 600 years before the gospels.

Chapter 54 depicts Israel's present barrenness in Exile as but transitional, in view of the fruitfulness to come. Verse 54:1 is reminiscent of Hannah's song (in 1 Samuel 2:5), and verse 54:5 makes the divine Maker Israel's husband (source of fertility). This marital imagery continues in verses 54:6–8, and it culminates with a remarkable assurance of everlasting love. Note the explicit parallel with the Noachite covenant (Genesis 8:21–22) in verse 54:9—"never again!" The scene has aspects of the reconciliation of bruised spouses who realize at the end of their suffering and discord how deep their love remains. Verse 54:13 gives us another figure of teaching, and 54:14 promises an establishment (foundation, stabilization) in righteousness. The chapter ends with assurances of protection from future foes.

The conclusion of the materials usually ascribed to Second Isaiah rings like a hymn celebrating the graciousness of the Lord that the prophet has discovered or has had revealed to him. The everlasting covenant in the tracks of the promise to David takes us beyond the Deuteronomistic instinct, and the universalism of the prophet becomes very explicit: Nations shall run to Israel because of its God. Verses 55:6–7 are a classical call for serious religious attention and conversion. Verses 55:8–9 comprise perhaps the most famous statement in the Hebrew Bible of the transcendence of the divine ways and ring as a permanent rebuke to the human pride that likes to think itself all-knowing or in control. Verses 55:10–11, on the effectiveness of the prophetic divine word, recall the creative divine word of Genesis. The chapter and Second Isaiah end with a last assurance that deliverance (being led out, another exodus) will come (soon) in joy.

56:1–66:24 Third Isaiah

A majority of scriptural scholars distinguish these final chapters of the book of Isaiah from chapters 40–55, but conviction seems less on this point than on the distinction between First and Second Isaiah. Generally the feeling is that the final materials reflect a period considerably later than the return from Exile, perhaps in the fifth century B.C.E., under Ezra and/or Nehemiah. The main interests are ritualistic, as though priestly writers were at work, but the rejection of the proposal to rebuild the Temple (Isaiah 66:1–4) clashes with the view of such prophets of the sixth century as Haggai and Zechariah. Second Isaiah or others of his time were perhaps the dominant influences on chapter 56–66 after all.[15]

Chapter 56 immediately stresses observance of the Sabbath and shows great interest in foreigners who would cling to the Lord.[16] Verse 56:7 speaks of the

Temple and opens it to all peoples. Verses 56:9–12 strongly condemn corrupt leadership, as though postexilic Israel were more mundane than Second Isaiah's visionary establishment. Chapter 57 bitterly laments the suffering of the righteous and the prospering of the wicked. Verses 5–13 focus on the old abominable fertility sacrifices and idolatries. Verses 57:14–21 have some of the comforts of Second Isaiah, but more prominent are the disjunctions between the righteous and the wicked. Chapter 58 includes a penetrating analysis of inauthentic religion, whose worshipers seek themselves more than God. Verses 58:6–7 exhibit the social conscience (somewhat in contrast to the priestly concern for ritualistic proprieties) for which the Hebrew prophets are famous. The rest of the chapter continues in this vein, linking social justice (and keeping the Sabbath) with pleasing the Lord. Most of chapter 59 is a diatribe against the wicked, in the spirit of First Isaiah at his most biting.[17] Verses 59:21–22, however, have positive promises mindful of Second Isaiah. Chapter 60 celebrates the exaltation of Zion, which will become a lodestone for the nations, because of the presence of the Lord. The implication is that what was laid low will be greatly raised up. Note the symbolism in verses 60:19–20 that the Lord will be the light of Zion (source of splendor, guidance, wisdom, and so on).

In chapter 61 the prophet is poetic in the mood of the servant songs of Second Isaiah, and he stresses the benefits to come to the afflicted. Verses 61:1–2 call to mind a Jubilee year (Leviticus 25:41, 54). Verses 61:6–7 seem to make Israel the priestly tribe among the confederacy of nations. Other interesting features of the chapter are the Lord's love of justice and the idea that salvation is clothed like nuptials. Verses 62:4–5 continue this nuptial theme, in the course of promising the vindication of downtrodden Zion by the God who delights in her. The imagery of watchmen and the promise of "not again" recur, along with the idea that Zion will be an ensign (flag) over the other peoples, honored and exemplary for its holiness. Chapter 63 depicts the deliverance of the Lord as vengeance upon the wicked, creating the famous imagery of the grapes of wrath. The mood shifts in verse 63:7 to love and mercy, as though the guidance of the theology of Second Isaiah had returned. Note in verse 63:9 the Lord's share in Zion's affliction. Verses 63:11–14 paint the deliverance from Babylon in colors of the Exodus. Verses 63:15–19 comprise a call of the living, present generation upon the living God.

Isaiah 64 deals with the terrible or awesome side of the sole God, and then it bemoans the people's sinfulness, wondering whether any salvation is possible. This leads to a remembrance of God's formation of the people and a plea that this Father not be angry forever. Zion is depicted as though still in captivity, and the divine silence is the people's great burden.

As though fearing that attributing silence to the Lord distorts the reality, chapter 65 has the Lord affirm his availability to those who truly wanted him. Verses 65:3–4 contain accusations of ritualistic sins or pagan practices. These would bring the Lord to speak, but in judgment rather than mercy. The motif of silence and speaking reverses in the middle of the chapter, when it is Zion that does not respond. Here the theology seems Deuteronomistic: just desserts to righteous and wicked alike. Verse 65:17 has been picked up by Revelation 21. The close of the chapter is a utopian future for Zion, where speech between Lord and people will flourish and wolf and lamb will feed together (see also Isaiah 11:6–9).

Chapter 66, which concludes the book of Isaiah, opens with imagery somewhat mindful of First Isaiah's vision (in verse 6:1), but apparently to the purpose of opposing the Temple and its sacrificial cult. The imagery of Zion's giving birth probably expresses the wonders of postexilic restoration. Notice the strength of the maternal imagery that succeeds to the imagery of birth: Zion is the mother of Israelite faith. The fiery judgment of Isaiah 66:15–16 shows the divine warrior's afflicting the wicked. Verse 66:17 castigates idolaters, and verses 18–20 impressively sketch a universal judgment centered on Mount Zion. The conclusion of the book promises the endurance of the newly remade people, bending all worship away from false gods and back to the Lord. Verse 66:24 is rather harsh, as though the final editors wanted to make the book end on a note of dire warning.

HISTORICAL BACKGROUND

The book of Isaiah most centrally presupposes the threats that both the Northern and the Southern Kingdoms suffered in the eighth century, the Exile that Judah suffered in the sixth century, and the social function that prophecy enjoyed during those centuries.[18] During the span of time through which the Isaiahs wrote, Israel was a pawn in the power struggles between such giants as Egypt and Assyria. Later redactors clearly found the lessons that the prophets drew from this experience

The Damascus Gate to Jerusalem above and a gate from the Second Temple times below.
(Used with permission of the photographer, Robert L. Cohn)

revelatory of the problems and possibilities in the nation's faith. The greatest problem, according to the former prophets, was idolatry. Here, in the first of the major latter prophets, we see an interesting shift. The worship of idols and fertility forces continues to be castigated, but probably more central is the idolatry of political and military power.

First Isaiah has clarified the dangers of joining political intrigues between greater secular powers—primarily, turning away from the divine power that formed the people in the Exodus. Second Isaiah has clarified the positive side of monotheistic faith: No secular power is ultimate, and God can always make new beginnings. The book of Isaiah as a whole presupposes a time when these lessons were being learned most painfully. We can sympathize with the problems of kings and ministers, who have to make political decisions, but the editors of Isaiah, wanting to make prophecy an important part of the canonical interpretation of the nature of Israelite faith, had more sympathy for the insights of the prophets who fought to keep the people's vision greater than secular politics.

When the smoke of the incursions of Assyria and Babylon had blown away, the Isaian prophets were judged to have shown great wisdom about what really had been at stake. The reception of their prophecy therefore presupposes that their allegations of false worship and lack of trust in the Lord had a solid foundation. Even though Second Isaiah goes considerably deeper than the Deuteronomistic instincts about the covenant, and stresses the power of the divine creativity to make new beginnings, he assumes that the Exile was punishment well merited.[19]

LITERARY INTENT

The prophecies recorded in the book of Isaiah originally were written to circulate or preserve the prophet's assessment of his times. In contrast to the nonwriting prophets Elijah and Elisha of the ninth century, later prophets or their discipular scribes recorded the word of God given to them. Whereas the Deuteronomistic history preserved tales, often miraculous, about early prophets, the collections bearing the names of later prophets claim to preserve their words. The shift, then, is from tales about to words of. After the events that the prophets were concerned to interpret had run their course, later students or disciples had the chance to reflect on the validity of the masters' interpretations. A book such as Isaiah clearly is a composite of many different textual units, and the final canonical redaction took place hundreds of years after the earliest of the events and prophecies represented. The text frequently tempts us to think that the final editors have arranged it so that the words of the prophets seem vindicated by history. (Note that this does not imply fraud. On the other hand, many predictions are not fulfilled, which implies that accurate prediction was not considered the essence of prophecy.)

The better reading is that the final editors wanted to leave an interpretation of the disasters associated with the names Assyria and Babylon that would make them permanent lessons. As well, they wanted to preserve the memory and work of the profound spirits who had fought most courageously against the policies and religious failings that figured in those disasters. First and Third Isaiah no doubt commended themselves by the astringent quality of their religious criticisms, as well as by their moving poetic passages. Second Isaiah, the centerpiece of the book, represented unequaled poetry and theological depth, taking the sense of the Lord to the foundational level of *the* creative force responsible for all of nature and history and making Israel's God a loving redeemer almost pathetically moved by the sufferings of his people, his espoused, during the Exile. This theology was a new chapter in the history of interpreting national disasters. The servant that it features could be for later generations a touchstone and template, implicitly asking them whether they had the faith and grit to put themselves at the Lord's disposal, as Second Isaiah had seen the exilic community put. The comfort that Second Isaiah originally offered the exiles was thus taken into the national treasury and canonized as relevant to any time. If God had shown the divine nature able to be compassionate to the sufferers of the Exile, why could God not be gentle, encouraging, recreative for any later time?

The book of Isaiah therefore became paradigmatic, serving somewhat as Genesis and Exodus had. If the Lord's action in leading the people out of Egypt was a valid paradigm for later periods when trust was being put to the test, so was the Lord's action at the time of the Exile — both his allowing the punishment for the people's defections and his producing a return and restoration. The book of Isaiah was preserved in its present form because discerning canonical editors found it a marvelous resource for the clarification of Israel's past experiences and the nourishment of Israel's future faith.

LASTING SIGNIFICANCE

We have several times mused about the utilities of significant interpretations of national history, dealing with the themes of providence and evil, so we need not gloss the Isaian contributions to this dimension of biblical religion. More specific or distinctive are the themes of the divine holiness, the divine uniqueness and creativity, and the divine tenderness that we find in Isaiah.

The divine holiness certainly has not been neglected previously, as merely recalling the priestly theology of Leviticus reminds us. But in First Isaiah we have a poetic and prophetic sensibility that can express such holiness more adequately than the legal and somewhat mechanistic views of the priestly theology allow. The vision recorded in chapter 6, for example, draws on some traditional imagery of the divine presence or theophany, but the awesome holiness of the Lord convinces the prophet that he is lost: No mortal is not rendered sinful, impure, and unequal to the task of expressing the divine communication, when vision is given of just who and what the divine communicator is. The prophet has his lips cleansed by a burning coal, because only fire could purify the distortions that make human speech unfit for divine service. And as soon as he has the vision of the true nature and stature of the Lord, he has the innermost core of his proclamation: The people forget, ignore, do not know the Holy One of Israel, so it is no wonder that they behave badly, need punishment, stumble and blunder at every turn.

As we noted, this in turn leads to the paradoxical themes of increasing people's guilt by prophesying to them and sharpening the edges of "hearing" and "turning." An audience comes into crisis when the one speaking to it does not so much impart new information as demand a new vision or mode of communication that implies a wholesale reinterpretation of the situation. The problem that First Isaiah, like all visionaries, faces is the disparity or incommensurability between what he sees and what his audience can appreciate. His reading of the times depends on his sense of the Lord's sitting high above the Temple enthroned. Until his audience enters into a similar vision, his castigation of their reliance on anything but the power of this Holiness will seem to them but folly, utopianism, or harassment like that for which Elijah earned the epithet, "Troubler of Israel."

So First Isaiah reminds us of the perennial problems of religious communication. Second Isaiah carries the no doubt greater significance of fusing the holiness of the Lord with the unique divine creativity and making trust in the power of God to make new beginnings the bedrock of the national faith. The consolations of Second Isaiah are inseparable from his convictions about the divine uniqueness.

His further insights into the compassion of the divinity may be anthropomorphic, but certainly they draw on some of our keenest intuitions of what God would "have" to be like if divinity were not to fall below the standard of humanity at its best. With Second Isaiah's imagery of redemption and expiatory suffering we get a new handle on the problem of evil and the repair of flawed history. The heavens are far above the Earth, so the divine power to repair, buy back, remake flawed human experience cannot be limited. The God people want to believe in says "Comfort" to his people, because this God is a caring, nursing mother as much as a creative, chastising father. The force that made the world and called forth the people has vanished or become inert unless it can inspire hope that all things can be made new and every tear can be wiped from our eyes. It is, as we mentioned, hard to overestimate the impact this imagery of comfort has exercised in Western history, and it is hard to overestimate the challenge it sets theological reflection. Second Isaiah is saying that a genuine divinity always can redo history and redeem it, because "history," in both its natural and its cultural aspects, is the work of creatures who depend on divinity for every breath they ever draw (as Third Isaiah underscores).

GLOSSARY

Oracle An expression of divine revelation, usually enigmatic and given through a prophet or diviner.

STUDY QUESTIONS

1. What are the reasons for dividing the book of Isaiah into three distinct portions?
2. Explain the imagery of the prophet's vision in chapter 6.
3. What are the implications of calling Assyria the rod of the Lord's anger?
4. Explain the images of vineyard and watchman.
5. How does Second Isaiah depict the comfort that Judah will experience?
6. What are the main motifs of the four servant songs (verses 42:1–4, 49:1–6, 50:4–11, and 52:13–53:12)?
7. Explain the correlations among monotheism, antiidolatry, and redemption.

8. How is the God of Second Isaiah maternal?

9. Illustrate the ritualistic interests of Third Isaiah.

10. How is the imagery of chapter 61 like that of Leviticus 25?

11. What does the relation between Isaiah of Jerusalem and king Hezekiah suggest about prophecy in eighth-century Judah?

12. Why did the final editors link First and Second Isaiah?

13. What is the lasting significance of the prophetic notions of redemption and suffering servanthood?

NOTES

1. See Yehoshua Gitay, "Isaiah, the Book of," in *Harper's Bible Dictionary*, ed. Paul J. Achtemeier. San Francisco: Harper & Row, 1985, pp. 426–32.

2. See John T. Willis, "The First Pericope in the Book of Isaiah," *Vetus Testamentum*, 34 (1984), 63–77.

3. See Peter Machinist, "Assyria and Its Image in First Isaiah," *Journal of the American Oriental Society*, 103 (1983), 719–37.

4. See Rüdiger Bartelmus, "Jes 7:1–17 und das Stilprinzip des Kontrastes," *Zeitschrift für die alttestamentliche Wissenschaft*, 96 (1984), 50–66.

5. See Wolfgang Werner, "Vom Prophetenwort zur Prophetentheologie," *Biblische Zeitschrift*, 29 (1985), 1–30.

6. See Frederick L. Moriarty, S. J., "Isaiah 1–39," in *The Jerome Biblical Commentary*, ed. R. Brown, J. Fitzmyer, and R. Murphy. Englewood Cliffs, N.J.: Prentice-Hall, 1968, Volume 1, p. 274.

7. Ibid., p. 275.

8. See Peter R. Ackroyd, "The Book of Isaiah," in *The Major Prophets*, ed. Charles M. Laymon. Nashville: Abingdon (Interpreter's Concise Commentary), 1983, pp. 45–46.

9. See Richard J. Sklba, " 'Until the Spirit from on High Is Poured Out on Us,' " *Catholic Biblical Quarterly*, 46 (1984), 1–17.

10. See Rolf Rendtorff, "Zur Komposition des Buches Jesaja," *Vetus Testamentum*, 34 (1984), 295–320. See also Millard C. Lind, "Monotheism, Power, and Justice: A Study in Isaiah 40–55," *Catholic Biblical Quarterly*, 46 (1984), 432–46.

11. See Gitay, "Isaiah, the Book of," p. 430.

12. See Oswald Loretz, "Die Gattung des Prologs zum Buch Deuterojesaja (Jes 40: 1–11)," *Zeitschrift für die alttestamentliche Wissenschaft*, 96 (1984), 210–20. See also Oswald Loretz, "Mesopotamische und ugaritisch-kanaanäische Elemente im Prolog des Buches Deuterojesaja (Jes 40, 1–11), *Orientalia*, 53 (1984), 284–96.

13. See John L. McKenzie, *Second Isaiah*. Garden City, N.Y.: Doubleday Anchor Bible, 1968, pp. xxxviii–lv. See also James D. Newsome, Jr., *The Hebrew Prophets*. Atlanta: John Knox, 1984, pp. 154–56.

14. See M. I. Gruber, "The Motherhood of God in Second Isaiah," *Revue Biblique*, 90 (1983), 351–59.

15. See Leslie J. Hoppe, "The School of Isaiah," *The Bible Today*, 23 (1985), 85–89.

16. See Christopher T. Begg, "Foreigners in Third Isaiah," *The Bible Today*, 23 (1985), 90–108. See also Gregory J. Polan, O. S. B., "Salvation in the Midst of Struggle," *The Bible Today*, 23 (1985), 90–97.

17. See Daniel Kendall, "The Use of Mispat in Isaiah 59," *Zeitschrift für die alttestamentliche Wissenschaft*, 96 (1984), 391–405.

18. See Robert R. Wilson, *Prophecy and Society in Ancient Israel*. Philadelphia: Fortress, 1980, pp. 297–308.

19. See Ralph W. Klein, *Israel in Exile*. Philadelphia: Fortress, 1979, pp. 97–124.

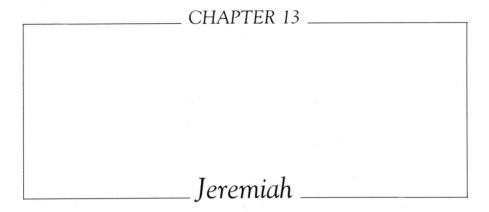

CHAPTER 13

Jeremiah

TEXTUAL ANALYSIS

The book of Jeremiah is another composite work, the product of considerable revision, but unlike the book of Isaiah its central source is a single prophet, Jeremiah of Anathoth, a town of Judah about 2.5 miles from Jerusalem. Current scholars estimate that Jeremiah was born about 645–640 B.C.E. and that he died in Egypt shortly after the fall of Judah to Babylon in 586 B.C.E. We treat the book of Jeremiah in four unequal parts:

1:1–24:10	Visions, Judgments, and Personal Laments
25:1–45:5	Speeches and Stories
46:1–51:64	Prophecies against the Nations
52:1–34	Historical Appendix[1]

1:1–24:10 Visions, Judgments, and Personal Laments

The "words" or historical legacy of Jeremiah begins by situating the prophet in terms of his family line (the priests related to Abiathar, David's man, and the shrine of Anathoth, which succeeded to fallen Shiloh) and his personal career: prophetic work from the thirteenth year of Josiah (627 B.C.E.) to the eleventh year of Zedekiah (586 B.C.E.). Josiah, as we have seen, spearheaded the Deuteronomistic reform, and Zedekiah was the unfortunate ruler during the final Babylonian onslaught. Jeremiah therefore lived through years that proved crucial both religiously and politically.

Verses 1:4–10, portraying Jeremiah's call, is a famous example of the self-understanding that Israelite prophecy developed. Jeremiah's life is determined by the word of the Lord. From the womb God had purposes for him. When Jeremiah, who in fact probably was quite young (less than 20), protested his unfitness, he got no relief: God would be his resource. Note how the psychology and the theology dovetail: Both the prophet's strength and his message come from the Lord. He is to be a mouthpiece of God.[2]

The visions of the rest of chapter 1, balanced by the visions of chapter 24, form what literary analysts call an "inclusion" that brackets the materials of chapters 1–24 as a discernible unit. The pun at work in verses 1:11–12 ties the "almond" (*shaqed*) that the prophet sees to the "watching" (*shoqed*) of the Lord. The vision of the pot symbolizes trouble coming from the North to set Jerusalem aboil. Note how the Lord's assurances set Jeremiah up as a realm unto himself, able to stand against the rest of Judah.[3]

Chapter 2 introduces the theme that Israel has defected from its religious beginnings. The early time of the covenant was like an espousal; the trek in the wilderness, before agricultural settlement, was a time when Israel was God's own holy portion.[4] But for his many good deeds, including both the Exodus and the Conquest, the Lord received only abuse. Like the Deuteronomists (who may have greatly influenced the editing of parts of Jeremiah), Jeremiah focuses on the idolatries that came with settlement. This defection strikes the prophet as a new thing in history (verse 2:11), a stupidity without parallel. All of the people's misfortunes stem from this folly. The variety of images in chapter 2 convinces us that we are dealing with a gifted poet. The people's defilement makes his skin crawl, and he uses both physical imagery (washing, soap) and erotic imagery (heat, lust) to castigate it. Like the book of Isaiah, Jeremiah satirizes the no-gods of the nations to which Israel has turned. The overall charge, argued this way and that, is that the nation is guilty of having forgotten its God.

Chapter 3 develops the imagery of marital failure. Verse 3:1 assumes Deuteronomy 24:1–4 on divorce. Verses 3:2–3 extend the symbolic line of equating the nation's apostasy with female infidelity or wantonness. Verses 6–10, which make the fall of Israel in 721 B.C.E. an object lesson that Judah has failed to learn, are a good example of what some scholars consider Deuteronomistic editors' supplementing Jeremiah's own work. Indeed, the Lord is better disposed toward Israel than toward Judah. Note in verse 3:15 the image of feeding with knowledge and understanding. Verses 16–18 seem to envision a return of Israel from Assyrian bondage and a reunion of North and South. Jerusalem will be the holy attraction (a Deuteronomistic theme). The rest of the chapter weaves together two somewhat disparate images: God as the father of ungrateful children and God as the spouse of an unfaithful wife.

Verse 4:4, gathering momentum about how Israel ought to return to the Lord, has the figure of spiritual circumcision (it is characteristic of Jeremiah to stress the inner meaning of outward ritual acts). In verses 4:5–8 the Lord's anger makes use of military punishment coming from the North. This punishment will befit the people's apostasy, yet verse 4:22, in which the Lord laments their stupidity, has the ring of a parent's feeling compassion for the hurt of a still-loved child. The rest of the imagery in this chapter seems histrionic. Note, however, how Jeremiah involves the land in the desolation to be visited on the people. Indeed, verses

4:23–26 suggest a reversal of creation (Genesis 1:2), and verses 4:19–22 indicate the prophet's suffering at Israel's prospects.

Chapter 5 accuses the people of having grown hard in their injustice, unwilling to repent. First the prophet thinks this senselessness only afflicts the lower classes, but then he finds it among the great.[5] After more images of infidelity and senselessness, we find a note of professional pique (in verse 5:13): The words of the prophets have been dismissed as merely wind. The word that Jeremiah brings will be fire devouring the people like wood. Note in verses 5:18–19 the parallel between serving foreign gods and being forced to serve foreign masters. The senselessness of the people shows in their inability to see the obvious fact of the Lord's creative power in nature. The injustice and wickedness that prevail must bring the Lord's punishment, if he is to be true to himself. How bad has a people become, when it loves false prophecy and dishonest priesthood?

Chapter 6 describes the destruction facing the comely and delicate (pampered?) daughter of Zion. Jerusalem's wickedness will bring her low, unless she swiftly repents (verse 6:8). Note the image of the vine in verse 6:9, and the imagery of deafness (to the word of God) in verse 6:10 — two prophetic staples. Verse 6:14 is a famous image for false consolation and religion: "peace, peace, when there is no peace." Verse 6:15 suggests that lack of shame bespeaks profound moral sickness. In his poetic creativity, the prophet tosses off image after image: not walking the good way, not heeding the watchman who outlines the moral imperatives. Therefore, the destroyer from the North will sweep down. In verses 6:27–30 the prophet becomes the assayer who tests the people's mettle. They fail. Verse 6:30 attributes this to the Lord's rejection of them and raises the knotty question of whether people sin because divinity has not sufficiently enlightened or endowed them. On the whole the Bible certainly absolves God and makes human beings responsible for their own moral failings, but on occasion the mystery of how human freedom reposes in divine grace comes into view.

Jeremiah 7:1–15 (see also 26:1–6) are called by scholars "The Temple Sermon." The prophet stands at the gate of the Temple in Jerusalem and announces a word from God warning worshipers not to assume that the sacrificial cult of the Temple will save them. (The "temple of the Lord" is chanted like a mantra or magical phrase.) God can and will destroy his own house, as the fate of Shiloh, vivid to Jeremiah because of his priestly family line, makes clear. In contrast, right religion includes strict social justice: "if you do not oppress the alien, the fatherless or the widow, or shed innocent blood in this place . . . ." To visit the Temple and live contrary to God's laws is hypocrisy. Shiloh was destroyed, Jeremiah says, because of the people's wickedness. Because the final editors of the book of Jeremiah knew that the Temple was destroyed in 586, they could cast this sermon as visionary. Verses 7:16–20 whirl with provocative theological implications: Do not pray for people whose actions show them unwilling to consider repentance; consider the moral effects of sins such as idolatry on the idolaters themselves the first "provocation" or affront. Jeremiah quickly resumes his more usual anthropomorphic view of God, according to which God is affronted by sin the way that a sensitive or abused human being would be. But here we get a splinter of the divine transcendence, suggesting that sin injures the sinner, not God.

The middle of chapter 7 accuses Israel of having always disregarded the prophets and been stiff-necked—a common Deuteronomistic theme (see, for example, 2 Kings 17:23). The harvest that this hardness of heart will reap is mourning and desolation. (Compare Jeremiah 7:34 with 33:11: Silence will token mourning and speech will token restoration.) Chapter 8 has the strong figure of the bones of the leading citizens' being exposed to the elements they have worshiped to their peril. God seems to have taken to himself a people unique in creation, the one entity not knowing its natural law. It is as though the inner apparatus of the people were disordered and its wisdom and judgment perverted (more "peace, peace" where there is no peace). The vineyard bears no fruit. The times prepare destructive war. In verse 8:18 the prophet laments, grief-stricken at the news he must bear to this city. Verse 8:22 famously asks, "Is there no balm in Gilead?" This line of lamentation continues in chapter 9, as the prophet details the defects for which Israel will be punished. Jerusalem will become a heap of ruins (as indeed Babylon made it). Again the reason, clear to any wise enough to understand, is Israel's having forsaken the law of the Lord. Verse 9:19 seems to reflect actual deportation. The prophet sees corpses everywhere. Verses 9:23–24 sound like a theorem from a circle where axioms of religious wisdom were coined: Knowledge of the Lord is the only thing in which one ought to glory. Israel has become like the unclean nations, uncircumcised at heart.

Chapter 10 brings back the theme of the nothingness of the nations' idols, contrasting them with the greatness of the Lord. Verse 10:12 is reminiscent of the monotheism of Second Isaiah, who was so impressed by the uniqueness of the divine Creator. Some commentators consider Jeremiah 10:17–25 editorial fragments,[6] but they have the powerful literary effect of identifying the prophet with the coming sufferings of Judah. Verses 10:18–20 comprise the first of the so-called "confessions" of Jeremiah, which are very similar to Psalms. Verses 23 and 24 provocatively refer good living to God's correction rather than to anything in the virtuous person. The shift of word in verses 10:23–25, from lament to intercession, bears noting as well. Chapter 11, which proposes Jeremiah's prophecy as a covenant, expresses the straight Deuteronomistic line: Obey the Torah of the covenant or be punished. The idolatrous disobedience is a form of stubborn revolt. The people have taken themselves beyond the reach of prayer. By their misdeeds they have forfeited the rights they had as God's beloved. The rest of chapter 11 has a personal tone: The prophet feels that his life is threatened, because of the prophecies he had been giving.

Verse 12:1 puts succinctly the case that suffering people have ever felt: Why does the way of the wicked prosper? Jeremiah gets no straightforward reply to his personal sufferings, though he prays that the wicked receive the punishment they merit for afflicting him. The voice seems to shift in verse 12:7 from Jeremiah to the Lord, who feels the pain of having to forsake his people. Verse 12:15 may have in mind the punishment of Exile and then the return. Jeremiah has to be content with a reaffirmation of faith that the Lord will bring justice. The dramatic symbolism of the loincloth in chapter 13 is explained by reference to how Israel ought to have clung to the Lord but has become spoiled. Some commentators see a reference to King Jehoiakim's pro-Babylonian policies, which the prophet saw as a lack of faith in the Lord. Verses 13:12–13 have the Isaian figure of drunkenness. The chapter brims with images of coming destruction: crowns lost, birth pangs, rape. Judah will be abused because its idolatries have been lewd and abusive to the Lord.

Chapter 14 opens with images of desolation, as the very land suffers from the people's punishment. Verses 14:8–9, however, mount another prayer of intercession to the God who used to be the hope of Israel. Verses 14:13–16 reveal that Jeremiah has had to contend with false prophets who were offering false consolations. This begets more genuine attitudes placed in the people's mouths: acknowledgment of wickedness and prayers that the Lord not spurn Israel, for his own name's sake. In chapter 15 the Lord is stony faced: Moses and Samuel (the two greatest prophetic intercessors) would not be able to gain forgiveness for this wicked people. God is weary of relenting from the justice he ought to deliver. Verses 15:10–21 have the flavor of another personal lament.[7] The prophet rues his birth and marvels that, without having borrowed or lent, he has become a center of strife. Verse 15:14 clearly focuses on the deportation to Babylon. Verse 15:16 has the interesting figure of the prophet's eating and delighting in the words of the Lord, which are like a physical presence that Jeremiah could consume. The following verses express the loneliness of the prophetic vocation. The rest of the chapter reads like a concession that Jeremiah has wrung from God: If the people return to God they may be restored to favor and their land.

The degree to which his prophetic vocation determined Jeremiah's life is made starkly clear in chapter 16. He received a word not to marry or beget children, so as to testify to the destruction coming upon Judah. He is neither to mourn nor to rejoice — all normal reactions are suspended, because normalcy itself will soon be suspended. When the people ask what they have done to deserve this woeful future, the prophet is to show them the idolatries of their ancestors, which they themselves have surpassed. Verses 16:19–20 sound like an interpolated prayer, to the theme that the nations will come to the true God, realizing that their own idols are nothing. The effect is to assure Israel that those who punish it themselves need its God.

Chapter 17 flatly asserts that the sin of Judah is known to all. Verse 17:5 gets to the religious bottom line: Those who trust in human power rather than God are cursed. Jeremiah 17:5–8 correlate with Psalm 1. Verses 9–10 reveal the Jeremian inclination to focus on the human heart and wonder at its unfathomable ways. Verse 17:10, in fact, makes the Lord the descryer of the heart, with the assurance that this means justice. The following verses amount to a prayer for this justice. Striking is the end of verse 17:14: "for thou art my praise." In verse 17:19 Jeremiah receives another pointed command, like the earlier one to go to the Temple. Here he is to tell the kings and others who pass through one of the gates of Jerusalem that they are to keep the Sabbath laws. Obedience to these laws will bring Davidic prosperity; disobedience will bring the destruction of Jerusalem. All readers of the canonical text knew what had happened to Jerusalem and could make their own inferences.

Chapter 18 has another symbolic revelation. The potter shows the prophet how God deals with the house of Israel. As the potter can reshape what is on the wheel, so can God reshape the destiny of any nation, depending upon its behavior. Israel, which ought to be associated with the Lord the way the snow is associated with the mountain, has done the unnatural thing of leaving its God. So it will be scattered and will see only God's back. In verse 18:18 the prophet is again lamenting the personal abuse he suffers for his message, and again he wonders about the divine justice: What sort of recompense for his fidelity is having his life threatened? His response is to curse his enemies and beg the Lord to bring their overthrow.

Chapter 19 shows another stipulated sermon, this time at the Potsherd Gate.

Jeremiah is to proclaim that the evil to come will make the people's ears tingle. The spot will be known as the valley of slaughter. He is to break the potter's vessel to show how Jerusalem will be broken. He does this, making it plain that the people get this sign because they have stiffened their neck in idolatry. Chapter 20 shows Jeremiah beaten and put in the stocks for delivering this message. The language even suggests that Jeremiah was raped by God — a powerful description of the prophetic vocation. Jeremiah tells Pashur, the priest who does this to him, that the future will make the priest a terror to his friends (because he helped them avoid the hearing that might have brought them back to the Lord). For his false prophecy, the priest will be buried an exile in Babylon. The rest of chapter 20, another "confession," depicts the price that Jeremiah's vocation has cost him: He has become a laughingstock and an object of derision, because of the gloomy words of judgment given to him.[8] For this Jeremiah curses the day he was born.

In chapter 21 King Zedekiah sends a delegation to Jeremiah to inquire about the future that Babylon will determine for Jerusalem. The prophet foresees complete destruction. Verse 21:8 adapts the Deuteronomistic notion that obedience to the Torah is the way of life. The rest of the chapter condemns Judah as meriting full punishment. Chapter 22 continues in this vein, calling for a return to social justice and a rule worthy of David. Verse 22:9 describes idolatry as the cause of the nation's coming destruction, and verse 22:10 explicitly foresees deportation. Verses 22:13–19 comprise one of the classical denunciations of regal injustice; they end with the prediction that none shall mourn when Jehoiakim dies. Coniah (Jehoiachin), the son of Jehoiakim, will fare no better, being like a broken pot that no one cares about.

In chapter 23 the prophet expands the range of those he castigates by accusing all the people responsible for the nation (shepherds) of having botched their care. Verse 23:5 can be read as a messianic oracle. The prophet is looking ahead to a descendant of David who will save Judah. The restoration of Judah then will be like the Exodus. Verses 23:9–40 comprise one of the most withering attacks on false prophecy that we find in the Bible.[9] The comforts Jeremiah's contemporaries were offering did not come from God. True prophecy would detail the honest truth that the people itself has become the burden of the Lord.

Chapter 24, the conclusion of this first portion of the book of Jeremiah, has a vision paralleling the opening vision of the almond tree. The two baskets of figs stand for the exiles to Babylon and the unjust remnant who stayed behind and expropriated the property of the exiles. The former will be blessed with restoration, but the latter will be severely punished.

25:1–45:5 Speeches and Stories

The central portion of the book of Jeremiah contains speeches and stories gathered in memory of the prophet's work. The opening theme is that the prophet regularly called the people to repentance, and regularly they did not listen. Therefore, punishment will come to the land, in the form of Babylonian oppression, and the guilty generation will die before Judah gets any relief.[10] Verses 25:15–29 develop the figure of the cup of the wine of the Lord's wrath, which all the peoples involved in the destruction of Judah will have to drink. The rest of the chapter threatens a universal judgment on all peoples, because all have shown themselves wicked. Here Jeremiah portrays a God very angry and intent on exacting fierce punishment.

Chapter 26 probably gives another account of the Temple Sermon of chapter 7. At the beginning of the reign of Jehoiakim, son of Josiah, the people might have made a new beginning and turned back to a justice that could have won them God's favor. But for delivering the word of God Jeremiah wins only the wrath of all the people, priests, prophets, and commoners. Certainly, Jeremiah is a striking illustration of the pattern that those who bring unwanted judgments or news are likely to receive abuse rather than gratitude. His charge is that the disorder aı d wickedness of the people were manifest, and that the disastrous consequences of their policy of scheming against mighty Babylon were plain to any who could see. But his contemporaries had no will to know the truth, because he prophesied the destruction of their city. They thus abused the word and its bearer, who might have saved them from destruction. Those who clamor for Jeremiah's death make cheerleading for Jerusalem, never speaking or entertaining a discouraging word, into loyalty and patriotism. The prophet, far from desisting, tells those who seize him that his blood will be on their heads. This sobers them into recalling that a good king like Hezekiah did not slay the prophet Micah when Micah brought oracles of a dark future. Jehoiakim, however, slew the prophet Uriah (the only such execution of a prophet, as far as we know), so clearly kings were not always as honest as Hezekiah. That Jeremiah survived was due to the patronage of Ahikam. Verses 26:20–24 are often considered an addition by the prophet's secretary Baruch.

Chapter 27 describes the dramatic symbolism of the thongs and yoke bars that the Lord directed Jeremiah to act out. The Lord has given Israel and the surrounding territories into the hands of Nebuchadnezzar of Babylon.[11] This is the yoke to which the people have to submit themselves, if they are to survive. Prophecy to any other effect is false, so Jeremiah urges Zedekiah and the people to submit themselves. We might say that the prophet is asking his contemporaries to believe that God can have a future for them despite their loss of political sovereignty. Apparently, prophets whom Jeremiah thought false were assuring the king and the people that the booty taken by Nebuchadnezzar in 597 would be returned. Chapter 28 puts this argument in the mouth of Hananiah, who predicts a return of the booty and the exiles taken in 597. He breaks the yoke bars of Jeremiah, who, however, receives God's assurance that his symbolism of yokedom will prove valid — indeed, that the yoke will be iron rather than wood. As Jeremiah prophesies, Hanmiah dies because of his false prophecy.

The episodic character of the middle of the book of Jeremiah continues in chapter 29, where we hear of a letter written by the prophet to the first group of exiles. The letter contains a new note: Exile is not death, because God transcends the land of Israel. The implication is that the exiles should accept their situation, go on with daily life, and not be misled by false promises of a speedy return. Only after the present generation will the Lord's plan to return the people be executed. Jeremiah details the failings and punishments of those given over to false prophets promising consolation.[12] The end of the chapter shows the contest between Shemaiah and Jeremiah, which ends when Zephaniah, Jeremiah's priestly friend, will not rebuke the prophet as a madman.

Chapter 30, like verses 29:10–14, offers prophecies of restoration. Merited though the punishment of exile has been, the Lord will bring the people healing.

Part of the reason given is the nations' mockery of Zion and so disrespect for the Lord. The nations will learn that the whirling tempest of the divine wrath can burst upon their wicked heads. Chapter 31 continues in this spirit, speaking of the everlasting love of the Lord for Israel and evoking images of the privileged time in the wilderness. Note that Israel is now virginal, in contrast to its previous adultcrousness. God will be a father to Judah and Ephraim, the exiled people of the North, in restoring and reunifying them. Mourning will change into joy, as the nations learn that the same power that led Judah into captivity can lead it back into prosperity. Verse 31:15 has Rachel's lament over the North, but the preponderance of the imagery continues to be positive. Note the intimate parental love expressed in verse 31:20, whose imagery is of the visceral or womb-like emotion that God feels for the people.[13] Jeremiah wakes from this dream of restoration (verse 31:26) and feels good about it. Verses 31:29–30 deny that hereditary sins will continue, and thus express a morality based more on individual responsibility. Indeed, the famous passage in verses 31:31–34 interiorizes the covenant, speaking of a renewal that will make the Torah written on the people's hearts. Knowledge of the Lord — a major prophetic theme — will be from the heart, shortcircuiting the possibility of false prophecy and aberrant rule. And concommitant with this new, interiorized covenant will be the Lord's forgiveness of Israel's iniquity. Jeremiah foresees not only restoration from Exile, but also religious advance to a new stage of intimacy between the Lord and his special people.[14] Verses 31:35–37 take the lastingness of nature as a pledge of God's commitment to Israel. The chapter ends with imagery of a rebuilt Jerusalem and assurances of a sacred, rooted relationship with God.

The scene in chapter 32 is Jeremiah in prison for predicting the victory of Babylon and greatly irritating the king, Zedekiah. The business transacted between Jeremiah and his cousin Hanamel symbolizes the reality of the promised restoration of Judah, without which the land would have been worthless. Jeremiah's prayer rehearses the many reasons for believing in the power and good will of the Lord, and it shows how Israelite religion interpreted the great events of the past as religious paradigms. The present punishment by Nebuchadrezzar (an alternate rendering of Nebuchadnezzar) is in keeping with the justice of punishment for immoral conduct or infidelity to the covenant. In verse 32:38, however, the prophet foresees the restoration of Jerusalem, at which time the Lord will again say, "they shall be my people, and I will be their God." This throwback to the new covenant described in verse 31:31 stimulates more reflection on interiority: The people will have one heart, and the Lord will make an everlasting covenant with them, raising up a proper fear of his divine holiness and doing good to them. At the end of the chapter a buying of fields (like Jeremiah's own symbolic action of buying land from his cousin Hanamel) stands for the time when normalcy will return to Jerusalem.

Chapter 33, detailing another word from God that came to Jeremiah while the prophet was imprisoned, again predicts both punishment and restoration, the latter including God's cleansing the people of their sins and forgiving their guilt. In the future Jerusalem will be a name summoning praise of the Lord for his generosity. Verse 33:11 parallels Psalm 136:1. Note also the return of the voices silenced at the time of desolation and death (Jeremiah 7:34). Verses 33:14–16 carry messianic overtones and lay a new stress on righteousness. Verses 17–18 seem to depend on the notion that the Davidic covenant would be everlasting, and they add that the Levites have a sort of covenant or undying promise, too. The poetry of verses 33:19–22 reenforces the Davidic covenant: It is as constant as the Lord's commitment to day and night. Verses 33:23–26 make David and Jacob equivalent in having a firm promise of continuance from the Lord. It is hard to know how to square this stress on the Davidic monarchy with the time of the canonical editing of the text. By then kingship clearly had shown its fragility, so perhaps the final editors had in mind a simpler pledge that the people of Jacob and David or the city of David would survive.

In chapter 34 Jeremiah is back troubling King Zedekiah with gloomy prophecies of the fall of Judah to Babylon, but he can assure the king that the king will not die by the sword. The discussion in the middle of the chapter about freeing slaves refers to legislation in Exodus 21:2 and Deuteronomy 15:12. Apparently, the king and people first intended to do the right thing, perhaps as a show of good will that would lead the Lord to protect them against Babylon, but then (typically) they slid back and retracted their generosity.[15] The Lord will therefore free the sword and pestilence to ravage the people, making them like the animals whose ritualistic slaughter in covenant ceremonies the people's sins have rendered useless. The Rechabites mentioned in chapter 35 were a rigorist group in whose fidelity to principle Jeremiah saw the attitude that might have made Jerusalem worthy of the Lord's protection.[16]

Chapter 36 shows Baruch's reading the scroll that summarized the prophecies the Lord had given Jeremiah. The reaction of the king demonstrates the unconcern for the word of God that had developed by the time of the threat from Babylon. Robert Alter has used the passage Jeremiah 36:27–31 to illustrate the prophets' preference for prose, rather than poetry, when they wanted to report a word given more for their own instruction than to be immediately passed on to the people. (Poetry, on the other hand, seems to have been considered more appropriate to the prophets' role as mouthpieces of God.) Note also the literary complexity of this passage (the indirection), which would be hard to render in poetry.[17]

The prophecy that the descendant of Jehoiakim would not gain the throne is fulfilled, but Zedekiah, the replacement, is no better at listening to the word given through Jeremiah (chapter 37). When the king inquires about the future, Jeremiah can give him only a promise of Babylonian victory. This brings the prophet arrest (on suspicion of desertion), beating, and imprisonment. The king apparently respects Jeremiah's prophecy, because he asks whether there is any word from the Lord, and he honors the prophet's request not to be returned to the dungeon. The next threat, reported in chapter 38, is death on the charge of weakening the people's will to resist Babylon. The king has Jeremiah rescued from the cistern — another indication that he either respects or fears the prophet as a man of God.

In their next exchange, Jeremiah forces the king to grant him assurances that telling the truth will not do him in (verse 38:15). Jeremiah can only counsel surrender to Babylon, and although Zedekiah is not strong enough to let this counsel become public knowledge, he does keep his pledge not to harm Jeremiah. Chapter 39 shows the aftermath of the king's apparent decision not to take Jeremiah's advice and sue for peace: Zedekiah sees his sons slain and then has his own eyes put out. Verse 39:10 tells us that some poor people were left in Judah, apparently to till the land, but most of the inhabitants of Jerusalem were carried off to Babylon.[18] Jeremiah apparently had gotten a good reputation among the

Babylonians, because he is spared and remanded to the custody of Gedaliah, the governor set up by the Babylonians. The oracle in verses 39:15–18 seems to belong after verse 38:13, in which Ebedmelech saves Jeremiah from the cistern.

In chapter 40 Jeremiah's commission into the care of Gedaliah is made a matter of his own choice—Nebuzaradan would have taken him to Babylon, had he wanted. Gedaliah seems in tune with Jeremiah's interpretation of the providential quality of the fall to Babylon. In chapter 41 Johanan and his followers drive the would-be assassin Ishmael off, but they plan to go to Egypt for fear of the reprisals from the Babylonians that Ishmael's slaying of the governor could bring. Jeremiah, however, receives from the Lord instruction that they should remain in Judah and not fear the king of the Babylonians (verse 42:11). Babylon clearly has become the righteous agent of the Lord's designs. Chapter 43 shows that Jeremiah's oracle against going to Egypt was not well received (note verse 43:2: "all the insolent men"). Indeed, Johanan marches the people back into Egypt (a reverse Exodus). At Tahpanhes Jeremiah carries out the instructions about the stones that will serve the throne that Nebuchadrezzar will erect—another bit of dramatic symbolism.

Chapter 44 equates the people's disobedience of the prophets that resulted in the destruction of Jerusalem with the disobedience that brought them to Tahpanhes. Verse 44:8 tells us that in Egypt the people worshiped idolatrously. Despite the punishment foretold, the people boldly tell Jeremiah that they will persist in their paganism. Jeremiah clearly equates present punishments with past infidelities. Pharaoh Hophra, mentioned in verse 44:30, in fact was assassinated in 569 B.C.E. Chapter 45, which ends this middle section of speeches and stories, is a dictation to Baruch that summarizes the themes concerning the Egyptian sojourn: "The Lord is bringing evil on all flesh." Overall, then, the middle chapters of Jeremiah amount to narrative biography, from the siege of Jerusalem by Babylon to the prophet's exile to Egypt.

46:1–51:64 Prophecies Against the Nations

In these chapters the prophet turns from Judah to the Gentile nations, announcing what the Lord has told him about their fate. Egypt will suffer much from Babylon. Note in verse 46:15 the fleeing of Apis, the divine Egyptian bull, who is thrust down by the Lord. In verse 46:25 Amon, god of Thebes, fares little better. Babylon is functioning as the Lord's agent against Egypt, as well as against false Judah. But the conclusion of chapter 46 is that Judah/Jacob should not fear these clashes of the nations, for the people will be restored from captivity into quiet and ease.

In chapter 47 the prophet envisions the dark future in store for the Philistines, whom the Babylonians will destroy. The oracles against Moab in chapter 48 reflect "the age-old rivalry of Israel and Moab. They are jingoistic saber-rattlings in which Moab is told that Yahweh is going to punish it so that it will never recover. These pieces rely heavily on two literary forms, the lament and the taunt song."[19] Chemosh, mentioned in verses 48:7 and 48:13, was a leading Moabite god. Verses 48:26 and 48:29 imply that Moab is being punished for its pride, and perhaps also for times past when it derided Judah. The length of the chapter of woes that Moab will suffer no doubt reflects the satisfaction that the prophet and his editors took in contemplating the downfall of this long-time and bitter foe.

Chapter 49 opens with oracles against the Ammonites, who seem to have been resented because of their claim to Transjordanian territory that Israel relished. The restoration promised in verse 49:6 softens the punishment predicted, however. The oracles against Edom reflect a similar resentment. (The Edomites were pushed by Arab tribes into southern Judah, where they conflicted with the Jews. Also, after the fall of Jerusalem in 586 they looted the city.) Note that the passage considers Esau the ancestor of the Edomites, which gives them the status of half-siblings or cousins to the descendants of Jacob. Scholars assume that Edom, too, had to submit to Babylonian rule, which extended throughout southern Judah. These oracles, which probably came from later editors rather than Jeremiah himself, reflect Obadiah 1–9.

Damascus is another city brought low by Babylon, although in fact it had lost its independence in the eighth century, when Assyria took control of the North. The book of Jeremiah emotes about its sufferings but does not ascribe them to religious or moral failings. The same holds for Kedar and Hazor, and also for Elam, which lay to the East of Babylonia and was captured in 596.

In chapter 50 Babylon itself comes in for destruction. Babylon actually fell to Persia in 539, but whether Persia is the nation from the North mentioned in verse 50:3 is uncertain. The editors of this chapter, which seems not to be from Jeremiah himself, may have sought a parallel with his prophecy in Jeremiah 4:6. Verses 50:4–5 foresee a repentance of Israel and a desire for an everlasting covenant with the Lord. Note that verse 50:7 claims innocence for the Gentile nations that have afflicted Israel, making the sins of the people the true cause of their sufferings. On the other hand, the prophecies against Babylon that follow seem to make its downfall a just punishment for its having plundered Israel's inheritance from God and sinned against the Lord (verse 50:14). (This chapter as a whole is somewhat confused and disorganized.) Verses 17 and 18 draw a parallel between Assyria and Babylon, both conquerers who themselves later were conquered. Note that verse 50:20 finds no sin in (restored) Israel or Judah and thinks that the Lord will have forgiven the remnant not taken into captivity.

The following verses depict the fall of Babylon as divine vengeance. Verse 50:29 even speaks of "her" having defiled the Lord. This charge obviously counters the many Jeremiah passages that make Babylon the predestined and so sanctioned instrument of the Lord's punishment of Judah. Verse 50:34 employs the figure of God as redeemer that we noted in Second Isaiah (for example, in verse 47:4). The figure of the sword employed in verses 50:35–38 is vivid and effective. The reference to Sodom and Gomorrah (see also Jeremiah 49:18) is meant to impute wickedness to Babylon and so justify its coming desolation. The rest of the chapter continues the theme of Babylon's punishment, effectively using the figures of childbirth and lion's attack to increase the tension.

Chapter 51 continues the oracles against Babylon, which suggests that we are in the midst of materials that seemed germane to Jeremiah's overall work but in themselves were rather disparate. The variety of figures eases the monotony of this prophecy, however, as first winnowers and then archers and soldiers pass across the poet's mind. Verse 51:7 has the striking figure of a gold cup in the Lord's hand making all the nations drunk with Babylonian prosperity. The tone is of exiles' witnessing the downfall of Babylon and being glad enough to interpret it as the work of the Lord according to his own justice. The Medes of verse 51:11 may be an oblique reference to Persia. Verse 51:13 suggests the figure of a life line that

God severs at the time appointed by the inscrutable divine counsel. Verses 15–19 are in the style of the Deutero-Isaian appreciation of the divine Creator who makes the idols of the nations naught.

The image of Babylon as the hammer of God (verses 51:20–23) is developed in the rhythms of an independent fragment of poetry. Verse 24 takes us back to a Babylon meriting punishment, and by now we are so inured to the illogic or inconsistency of the oracles against Babylon that we may think the author is using the "coincidence of opposites" (simultaneous presence of contrasting attributes) to say that Babylon was both an agent of the Lord and tainted or wrongly oppressive. Some ideas that cannot be expressed in straight logic can be communicated holistically through contradictory assertions or images.

The description of Babylon's fall is vivid enough to suggest composition after the fact. In verse 51:34 Nebuchadrezzar is made the personal antagonist of the Lord—hardly the role he played previously. Here, the author is identifying the Lord with a suffering Judah deserving release and vindication. Verse 51:44 adds the precisely theological notion that the fall of Babylon is the fall of the realm of an alien, false god (Bel). Verse 51:47, speaking of the punishment of Babylonian "images," is in the same vein, reminding us of the ancient Israelite notion that the Lord is the main warrior of Israel and that the main combat is between contesting divinities. We can read verse 51:56 as the coming of the Lord upon Babylon, as well as the coming of Persia. The close of chapter 51 situates the foregoing oracles in the time of Jeremiah's visit to Babylon with Zedekiah (594), but we have no external corroboration of such a visit. However, the sinking of the book of oracles in the Euphrates is a dramatic act in the style of others that we have seen the prophet carry out.

52:1–34 Historical Appendix

The final chapter of the book of Jeremiah largely duplicates materials in 2 Kings 24:18–25:30. The theological assessment of Zedekiah is swift and negative, blaming the fall of Jerusalem on the evil that he did in the sight of the Lord. The siege of Jerusalem obviously had etched itself deeply into the consciousness of Judah, especially the severe famine. Jeremiah 39:1–10 also describe the attempt of Zedekiah to escape, making us wonder whether the final redactors considered this episode so significant that it deserved repetition. In terms of literary effect, the slaying of Zedekiah's sons and putting out of his eyes do serve as a powerful if grisly summary symbol of the disinheritance and blindness associated with the Exile. Note the burning of the Temple and the palace, along with the other great houses of Jerusalem. The details of the booty carried off serve to concretize what the fall of Jerusalem in fact meant. Verses 52:24–27 indicate that the Babylonians did not scruple to kill those who had some military force to oppose them, or who might have become rallying points for uprisings. The numbers given for those carried off actually seem rather small, perhaps indicating that only key people were selected.

Indeed, the depth of the trauma that "Exile" later connoted is hard to understand unless those influential in shaping the canonical biblical text felt that people and/or institutions critical to the nation's religio-cultural life had been seriously imperiled. The fall of the Temple, for example, certainly symbolized the destruction of established priestly power, just as the fall of the palace symbolized the destruction of Davidic rule. Priests and royalists therefore probably found the fall of the Southern Kingdom especially disturbing. The famine and other sufferings of the common people were bad enough, but they could be written off as mainly physical: the sort of hardship that the warfare of the times made all too common. In the fall of the Temple and the palace, however, the Judean spirit suffered grievous blows, for the constancy of the Lord could easily seem cast in doubt.

Part of the therapeutic response, certainly evident in the composition of the book of Jeremiah, was to make these traumatic events simply the long-overdue punishment that idolatry and other violations of the covenant had merited. But another part was to linger in memory over the events themselves and to associate them with the spirit of prophets such as Jeremiah who had endured them. The prophet was remembered not only to have predicted the victory of Babylon, but also to have found a depth of spirit that undercut the basis of the badly broken old covenant and intimated a new covenant written on the heart.

HISTORICAL BACKGROUND

The book of Jeremiah first of all presupposes the events of the prophet's lifetime. Northern Israel had long been in bondage to foreign power, but Jeremiah and such other prophets as Nahum and Habakkuk lived through the fall of Judah. This was the greater tragedy, if only because after the fall of Israel in 721 B.C.E. all of the hopes of the twelve tribes rested in Judah. The death of the Assyrian king Ashurbanipal in 627 had signaled the end of Assyrian dominance. Babylon and Judah immediately asserted their independence, the former by expelling Assyrians and the latter by claiming cities of Israel. Babylon, in coalition with the Medes and the Scythians, captured the Assyrian capital of Nineveh in 612.

From 622 the reform of King Josiah had reinvigorated Judah. But Josiah was killed in a skirmish with the Egyptians in 609, and his son Jehoiakim proved a feeble successor. Under Nebuchadnezzar the Babylonians defeated Egypt in 605, which gave them claim to Judah as well. Jehoiakim continued to rule, but only as a puppet of Babylon. Unlike his father, he aggrandized himself more than the people, rebuilding the royal palace and forcing many of his people to work under harsh conditions. His religion also was suspect, so the Deuteronomistic historians listed him among the rulers who had done evil in the sight of the Lord and who had worshiped idolatrously (2 Kings 23:37).

Egypt enjoyed a resurgence around 601 and managed to push Babylon back. This encouraged Jehoiakim to think of allying himself with Egypt and throwing off Babylonian dominance, a line of thought that Jeremiah considered madness. The son of Jehoiakim, Jehoiachin, had little stomach for trying to resist Babylon, but when Jerusalem fell in 597 he was replaced by his uncle Zedekiah. At that time a contingent of leading citizens, including Jehoiachin, was carried off to Babylon, but Judah continued to enjoy some self-rule under Zedekiah. Babylon took booty in 597 and kept Zedekiah on a short leash, but prophets such as Jeremiah knew that the situation could have been much worse.

However, Zedekiah participated with Egypt in intrigues preparatory to mounting a rebellion against Babylon. Eventually Zedekiah decided to revolt against

Babylon, but after a year and a half of opposition, including a deadly siege of Jerusalem that brought the city to the point of famine, Babylon crushed the revolt. This time Babylon showed little leniency, killing Zedekiah's sons, blinding the king himself, ravaging the city, destroying the Temple and palace, and carrying off a significant portion of the population. This was the great disaster that Jeremiah had feared and predicted. When the regent Gedaliah was assassinated, Jeremiah was carried off to Egypt by those who feared Babylonian retaliation. There is some indication that the prophet's high standing in Babylonian eyes caused those who were fleeing to take him as a hostage.[20]

Second, the poetry of Jeremiah suggests a literary background that we do well to ponder. Certainly this prophet entered the canonical lists as much for the brilliance of his imagery as for the politico-religious clarifications that his prophecies wrought. Jeremiah is another instance of the creativity that comes when a personality is forced into the divine mysteries of creation, providence, suffering, and renewal. His theology does not delve as deeply into these bedrock matters as the theology of Second Isaiah, and we would not argue that he is a greater poet. But we have more historical information about Jeremiah than we have about the other major prophets, so he better personifies the prophetic vocation. In addition, he worked at the crucial time of the decisions and failures that led to the destruction of Jerusalem and the Exile to Babylon, and his imprisonment brought home even more dramatically than the threats on the life of Elijah the price that fidelity to the divine word could exact.

It is extraordinary that a culture would allow Jeremiah to function, let alone later canonize his message as an important part of divine instruction. We should not let the fact that he was threatened and imprisoned blind us to the more significant fact that he had sufficient support and credibility to survive. In our day a person crying out at the gates by which the movers and shakers of the land enter and leave would merely be dismissed as a lunatic, or carted off for violating the ordinances against creating a public nuisance. In Jeremiah's day a person who claimed to be delivering a word from the Lord commanded attention. To be sure, this word would be tested, and battles between true and false prophets so raged that "prophecy" itself became tarnished. But the highly unpopular things that Jeremiah was saying to the Judean establishment either had such support among other portions of the community or were so accredited by their depth and the rest of the prophet's life that people took full notice. Indeed, later people found them a dazzling interpretation of the fall of Jerusalem and so entered them in the record of wisdom from the past that might make the future less follied.

LITERARY INTENT

Interpreting the book of Jeremiah, Norman K. Gottwald has first stressed the burden of the prophet's own historical message. This he takes to be the charge that the internal order of Judah had become corrupt and so left the country ripe for takeover by Babylon.[21] The main form that this corruption took was a lack of social justice. Underneath the social injustice, however, lay an abandonment, in both spirit and detail, of the covenantal relationship with the Lord that gave the people their distinctive identity. Jeremiah likely thought that under Babylonian rule the priesthood and the monarchy would have at best only reduced roles, and he was thus willing to stay in Judah to help ensure the people's cultural survival. This detachment from the religious institutions of his day was not shared by the later editors of the book of Jeremiah, however, so we find what seem to be later additions that blacken the Babylonian victors, reassert the Davidic promises, and plump for a renewed dedication to the ethics and cult of the Mosaic covenant by blaming the Exile on injustice and idolatry.

The context usually assumed for the final redaction of the book of Jeremiah is a Deuteronomistic circle interested in reestablishing the monarchy and cultic life along the lines of the reforms of Ezra and Nehemiah after the return from Exile. It seems unlikely that these final editors would have created all of the oracles of restoration and placed them under Jeremiah's name, but it makes sense that they would have stressed this stratum of the prophet's work and perhaps given it more play than he himself had. When commenting on the final editing, Gottwald underscores the effect of the narrative materials in chapters 26–45. These emphasize the opposition that the prophet had to endure, the advance warning that he gave Judah, and so the value that his life — both his message and his example — had in the aftermath of Exile, when people were pondering what lessons they ought to draw from this painful period of national history.

Brevard Childs, who is principally interested in the canonical or final shape of the book of Jeremiah, includes such motivations for the final shape as: (1) a desire to validate the two forms of prophecy (oral and written) that the prophet used; (2) a desire to square the prophet's interpretation of contemporary events with the Deuteronomistic interpretation of the covenant and history (that is, with a basic equation between punishment and infidelity); (3) a desire (shown most clearly by the addition of the historical appendix in chapter 52) to square the prophet's judgments with 2 Kings; (4) a desire to show, through the biographical materials that dramatize the rejection of the prophet and his message, the opposition that the word of God faced at the critical juncture prior to the disaster of the Exile; and (5) a desire to stress the elements of promise and salvation in Jeremiah's message, especially in the famous chapters 30–33 that speak of a new, interior covenant. By placing this positive aspect of the prophet's work prior to the account of the fall of Jerusalem (chapter 39), the canonical editors implied that Jeremiah spoke of restoration from the outset and so foresaw the Exile within a larger and more hopeful framework.[22]

We ourselves have alluded to the desire to contemplate the events of the fall and Exile through the profile, if not the eyes, of a prophetic contemporary like Jeremiah. In the overall context of the Hebrew Bible, he somewhat resembles the suffering servant of Second Isaiah, a person whose life became a sacrifice for the common good of the nation. Indeed, like the suffering servant Jeremiah was despised and rejected, and much of the abuse that he bore was on behalf of the word given him and the benefits to the people that it carried. In contrast to the faithless leadership of the people, if not in fact to the people as a whole, the prophet is shown clinging to the Lord, even when his vocation caused him to lament the day he was born. Unlike Jonah, who tried to escape his vocational destiny, Jeremiah never turned his complaints into flight or apostasy. Even when he found the word that he had to announce bitter and bound to bring him grief, he never failed to deliver it. We may suspect that at times he took a perverse pride in such stubborn integrity, but overall the text presents Jeremiah as a man of duty rather than sadism or masochism. As such, he could serve later times as a fine religious model.

Last, we should point out the utilities of preserving poetry like that of Jeremiah and so of offering the later Jewish imagination both solid food and encouraging example. In the book of Jeremiah we encounter a religious intelligence discernibly different from that of the historians, or the writers of law, or the sapiential writers. Of course Jeremiah dealt with themes treated by all three of these other mentalities or schools. But his own distinctive voice and sensibility are different. For him the image is less separable from the word of God. As much as the historical narrative of what happened and what it might teach us, or as the conduct that the word of God ought to inspire, or as the prudential maxims that we could draw from an experience and use to honor the wisdom of the Lord, the prophetic imagery of Jeremiah attached to the essence of what divine revelation denoted.

Such imagery, first, was an invitation to an encounter or an engagement with the address of God. It grasped the faculty we have to picture and feel a communication, and thereby it moved the affections. At times Jeremiah must have made his readers come close to weeping, when they let themselves dwell within the imagery of the fallen, suffering Judah. At times he could have sent shivers of repulsion at the harlotry that the false cult entailed. And his oracles of salvation could have reverberated equally profoundly, helping to lance the hearts infected with woe. Often we fail to appreciate the significance of what a people is able to imagine. Present-day philosophers have coined the dictum that the limits of our language are the limits of our world. It is equally true that the limits of what we can imagine nearly define what we may hope or propose to ourselves as curative action.

LASTING SIGNIFICANCE

The lasting significance of the book of Jeremiah is intimately bound up with the alternatives suggested by its poetic imagery. Its first significance is in the imagery that portrays religion, or one's deepest allegiance, as a marital venture. For Jeremiah Israel is the bride of the Lord and so Israel's infidelities take on the aura of adultery. We have previously hinted at the dangers in such imagery. The feminization of wanton Israel tends to stigmatize women more than men, even though any commentator would quickly point out that "Israel" not only included men but was more run by men than by women. In addition, the use of erotic imagery nearly always should set readers on guard, not because the erotic dimension of the psyche is intrinsically tainted but because such powerful factors are at work that special balance is needed if one is to serve both good theology and good taste. Granted these cautions, however, we should appreciate the depth of implication in Jeremiah's imagery.

For example, we should appreciate the psycho-religious fact that we all are romanced by the mystery of human existence, beguiled and solicited if not seduced, and that conceiving of our time as a chance for a love affair with the mystery of human existence can be highly positive and energizing. The Israelite sense that covenantal existence meant going forward in time with an unknown God, who would only be revealed through shared experience or sojourning, could easily lead

A monastery in Wadi Qelt, in
the wilderness of Judea. *(Used
by permission of the photographer, Wolfgang
Roth)*

to marital symbolism. Today we often still use "for better, for worse; for richer,
for poorer; in sickness, in health" to express the union of two people seeking to
become one flesh. People of significant and articulate religious experience often
think the same way about their relationship with God. They are wedded to, welded
to, ineluctibly defined by their reference to God. What stands at the beginning,
at the end, at the height, and at the depth of their lives and consciousnesses, they
realize, has everything to do with how they finally estimate the significance of
their time and themselves.

Jeremiah is well aware of what the Lord has done for Israel. Like the Deuteronomistic historians, he knows the drumroll of favors, from exodus from Egypt
to establishment in the land. But his special genius is to feel the betrayal in Israel's
failings, the wounds to the love that God has offered. Hosea perhaps dramatizes
this marital theme more effectively, and Ezekiel is more extreme about harlotry,
but Jeremiah's prophecy can hold its own when it comes to romantic insight. The
people have tarnished something beautiful. They have taken religious love and
made it pornographic: a matter of itchy excitement rather than holy gentleness
and self-giving. Beneath his anger at this Jeremiah is hurt. He senses the beauty,
the fragility, the gratuitousness of what the Lord has offered and can only weep
that clods, sensual dullards, so predominated in the nation that Israel missed its
chance.

A second lasting significance of the book of Jeremiah relates to this feeling
for the depths of love that religion ought to imply, and it also relates to our prior
reflections about the utilities of the prophetic imagination. Without biblical writings like those of Jeremiah, we could think either that the word of God was a

complete illusion, or that such a word, born of divine love, was bound to resound clearly and be embraced by all. Jeremiah is eloquent witness that neither of these two alternatives accurately describes how things tend to go.

The word of God is not an illusion, because equivalents of Jeremiah, some of whom have read his prophecy and many of whom have not, arise generation after generation to call their times to account and give fresh reports about the possibilities that the divine mystery keeps lively. Martin Luther King, Jr., for example, who certainly had thought much about Jeremiah, gave the past generation of Americans ample stimulus not only to face their sins, to acknowledge the racism that was warping the whole fabric of American society, but also to feel sources of change, of repentance, forgiveness, and renewal. These sources, he suggested, were as near as a few moments of honest examination of conscience. They only required the courage to name what was occurring and own up to one's own responsibility for it. Thus King's preaching differed little from Jeremiah's preaching, and in his preaching the word of God showed itself as vibrant as it had been 2500 years earlier, when Jeremiah was trying to deal with the quickening crisis of the fall of Judah.

Jeremiah, Martin Luther King, Jr., and many other prophets also keep us from the naive assumption that, because the word of God is alive and kicking, all will unfold according to its imperatives. Jeremiah was thrown into the cistern, Martin Luther King, Jr., was murdered, and a high percentage of the other people who have borne the word of God forth to their people have suffered greatly for their mission. The theology of the prophets, based in painful experience, is quite different from the smiley theology of optimists. The prophets have looked into the human heart, their own included, and seen the puzzle, the absurdity, of sin. How can people reject the light for which they have been made? How can they not surrender themselves to the love they most crave? They rush after no-gods, idols of stone and wood, when they could fall into the embrace of the love that moves the stars. They become besotted with pleasure, wealth, status, and other spiritual idols, when either death or religious ecstasy could assure them that the heart of the human matter is very much more. The Isaiahs boggle at the ignorance, the not knowing, that all such foolish self-ruin expresses. Jeremiah is equally astounded and saddened, but he comes virtually to expect that his message will be rejected.

Things have changed very little since Jeremiah's day, when we get down to the bedrock mysteries of the human heart. We remain creatures of a day whom nature solicits at sunrise and sunset to appreciate our very small place in the total scheme of things. Yet most days and nights, nature labors in vain. Either because we would rather rush and struggle than rest and attend, or because we fear the unknowns lurking in contemplative silence, we abet the many-sided conspiracy against reflection and so become part of the problem racking our society. Jeremiah and the other prophets saw very well that the fault, the crack running through human affairs, lies neither with the stars nor with God. The fault lies with, in, ourselves. The machinery we have for hearing the word of God is flawed, so unless we labor heroically we mainly catch only muffles and scratches. Like the prisoners of sensuality trapped in Plato's cave, we need prophets, people whom God has dramatically given new eyes to see with and lips cleansed to speak, to drag us out of what we have become convinced is "reality" and to show us a much braver new world.

GLOSSARY

Agape   The sort of love that can be predicated of God—selfless, pure, willing to suffer.

Jingoism   Belligerent chauvinism, aggressive nationalism or ethnocentricity.

STUDY QUESTIONS

1. How does the description of Jeremiah's call (verses 1:4–10) prepare us for the work and message we shall see displayed?
2. Discuss Jeremiah's images of defilement and marital infidelity.
3. Why does Jeremiah oppose those who say, "peace, peace"?
4. Compare the two versions of the Temple Sermon (chapters 7 and 26).
5. How significant is Jeremiah's not marrying?
6. How does the figure of the potter relate to the question of redemption?
7. Summarize the relations between Jeremiah and Zedekiah.
8. Analyze two of Jeremiah's symbolic dramatizations.
9. Apart from Christian interpretations, are verses 31:31–34 especially significant?
10. Explain the ambivalent status of Babylon.
11. What is the symbolic message in the disastrous end of Zedekiah?
12. Is it possible to account for most of Jeremiah's prophecy without calling upon miraculous revelations from the Lord?
13. What does the final arrangement of the book of Jeremiah suggest about the canonical editors' views of historical suffering and Jeremiah's weighting of punishment and restoration?
14. Explain the significance of the prophetic poetry that likens biblical religion to a love affair between God and his people.

NOTES

1. See Alexander Rofé, "Jeremiah, the Book of," in *Harper's Bible Dictionary*, ed. Paul J. Achtemeier. San Francisco: Harper & Row, 1985, p. 457.
2. See Peter R. Ackroyd, "The Book of Jeremiah—Some Recent Studies," *Journal for the Study of the Old Testament*, 28 (1984), 47–59.
3. See Robert M. Patterson, "Reinterpretation in the Book of Jeremiah," *Journal for the Study of the Old Testament*, 28 (1984), 37–46. See also Felix Garcia Lopez, "Élection-vocation d'Israel et de Jérémie: Deutéronome vii et Jérémie i," *Vetus Testamentum*, 35 (1985), 1–12; and Scott L. Harris, "The Second Vision of Jeremiah: Jer 1:13–15," *Journal of Biblical Literature*, 102 (1983), 281–82.
4. See Michael DeRoche, "Jeremiah 2:2–3 and Israel's Love for God during the Wilderness Wanderings," *Catholic Biblical Quarterly*, 45 (1983), 364–76.
5. See R. Carroll, "Theodicy and the Community: The Text and Subtext of Jeremiah 5:1–6," *Oudtestamentische Studien*, 23 (1984), 19–39.

6. See Stanley Brice Frost, "The Book of Jeremiah," in *The Major Prophets*, ed. Charles M. Laymon. Nashville: Abingdon (Interpreter's Concise Commentary), 1983, p. 152.

7. See Patterson, "Reinterpretation in the Book of Jeremiah," pp. 37–46.

8. See Jon D. Levenson, "Some Unnoticed Connotations in Jeremiah 20:9," *Catholic Biblical Quarterly*, 46 (1984), 223–25.

9. See Wolfram Hermann, "Jeremiah 23,23f. als Zeugnis der Gotteserfahrung im babylonischen Zeitalter," *Biblische Zeitschrift*, 27 (1983), 155–66.

10. See Léo Laberge, O. M. I., "Jérémie 25, 1–14: Dieu et Juda ou Jérémie et tous les peuples," *Science et Esprit*, 36 (1984), 45–66.

11. See Berhard Lang, "Ein babylonisches Motiv in Israels Schöpfungsmythologie (Jer 27,5–6)," *Biblische Zeitschrift*, 27 (1983), 236–37.

12. See William L. Holladay, "Enigmatic Bible Passages: God Writes a Rude Letter," *Biblical Archeologist*, 46 (1983), 145–46.

13. See Phyllis Trible, *God and the Rhetoric of Sexuality*. Philadelphia: Fortress, 1978, pp. 39–53.

14. See Meindert Dijkstra, "Prophecy by Letter (Jeremiah xxix 24–32)," *Vetus Testamentum*, 33 (1983), 319–22.

15. See Patrick D. Miller, Jr., "Sin and Judgment in Jeremiah 34:17–19," *Journal of Biblical Literature*, 103 (1984), 611–13.

16. See Karlheinz H. Keukens, "Die rekabitschen Haussklaven in Jeremia 35," *Biblische Zeitschrift*, 27 (1983), 228–35.

17. See Robert Alter, *The Art of Biblical Poetry*. New York: Basic Books, 1985, p. 138.

18. For an opinion that only a fraction of the population of Judah was exiled to Babylonia, see Norman K. Gottwald, *The Hebrew Bible*. Philadelphia: Fortress, 1985, p. 420.

19. Frost, "The Book of Jeremiah," p. 204.

20. See James D. Newsome, Jr., *The Hebrew Prophets*. Atlanta: John Knox, 1984, pp. 101–4.

21. See Gottwald, *The Hebrew Bible*, p. 396.

22. See Brevard Childs, *Introduction to the Old Testament as Scripture*. Philadelphia: Fortress, 1979, pp. 345–52.

CHAPTER 14

Ezekiel

TEXTUAL ANALYSIS

Ezekiel is the third of the three "major" prophets canonized in the second portion of the Hebrew Bible. Like the books of Isaiah and Jeremiah, the book of Ezekiel is a composite work that both draws together oracles from numerous different occasions and shows signs of considerable editorial revision. A representative chronology places Isaiah of Jerusalem in the eighth century B.C.E., Jeremiah of Anatoth in the seventh and sixth centuries, and Ezekiel of Chebar (in Babylonia) in the sixth century. Jeremiah and Ezekiel, in fact, overlapped, both prophesying after 598 B.C.E. The rabbinic commentators sometimes disputed this chronology, however. Similarly, there is no complete agreement about the best division of the text. We divide the book in half, considering chapters 1–24 as oracles focused on the doom of Judah and chapters 25–48 as oracles focused on Judah's restoration. As we proceed, we note the further groupings that particular scholars suggest.[1]

1:1–24:27 Oracles of Judgment on Judah and Jerusalem

Ezekiel 1:1–3 situate the work we are about to read. The speaker is in the thirtieth year of some temporal framework, most likely that of his prophetic career, and he is located by the river (canal) Chebar in Babylonia, among the Jewish exiles carted off with Jehoiachin in 598 B.C.E. The usual interpretation is that verse 1:3 gives the date for the beginning of Ezekiel's prophetic work (593), so verse 1:1 refers to visions experienced in 563, thirty years later. Most of the first three chapters of Ezekiel describe what we may consider his call from God,[2] the first episode of which is typically fantastic. The opening vision of the divine throne and chariot exerted enormous influence on later Jewish mysticism, because these became privileged symbols for the divine mystery and presence. It also shaped Revelation and Christian imagery for the four evangelists. Note the many natural elements associated with the divine majesty: wind, cloud, light, fire, and gleaming bronze. The general effect is to express the splendor or glory of the Lord God, as well as to stress the divine mysteriousness.

The living creatures are guardians of the divine throne — images of how the holy power that runs the world and directs the fortunes of Israel would be attended. Quick movement, intelligence, strength, purity, and other attributes are implied. In Ezekiel we have a highly impressionable mentality, which at times (for instance, the mention of lightning) reminds us of the power that basic natural phenomena had to shock and structure the archaic human consciousness. The imagery of the chariot also relates to the design of the ark that housed the divine presence and was incorporated into the Temple in Jerusalem. Ezekiel's God is a holy power attended by an impressive throng — a very different ultimacy from the serene one of later Greek philosophy or of high Hindu speculation. Ezekiel can only bow low in the total surrender and adoration proper to the creature when the splendid glory on which it depends for every fiber of its existence appears.

In chapter 2 the spirit of God sets Ezekiel on his feet and, calling him "son of man" (an emphatically nondivine person), gives him his charge. The keynote of this charge is that he is to speak the word of God fearlessly to a rebellious, stubborn people or house. As in Jeremiah 15:16, the word of God is likened to a scroll that the prophet must eat. Although it contains words of lamentation and woe, the prophet finds it sweet (the divine truth, however apparently harsh, is pleasing nourishment to the genuine prophet or religious personality). Verses 3:4–11 repeat the charge that exilic Israel is stubborn, but God will make Ezekiel stronger or harder. (In Hebrew "Ezekiel" means "God will make strong.") The spirit takes Ezekiel away — he is rapt by the glory — and for seven days he is overwhelmed (one of many hints that the book of Ezekiel comes from an abnormal psyche). Ezekiel is to be a watchman (see also Jeremiah 6:17), commissioned to warn the house of Israel. The binding and dumbness that come upon him are certainly symbolic of the traumatic effect of his charge to preach woe, but they may also describe physical symptoms of stroke or seizure.[3] Clearly, the word Ezekiel has received has taken over his life and personality. He has become like a psychic experiment in which God will elaborate the causes, effects, and implications of the Exile to Babylon.

In chapter 4 the prophet dramatizes the siege of Jerusalem. The iron plate in verse 4:3 presumably is Babylon as the agent of the divine punishment for the infidelities of Judah. The days that the prophet must lie on his sides symbolize (how exactly is not clear) the punishments of Israel and Judah by foreign powers. The diet that Ezekiel is given symbolizes the scarcity and religious impurity into which siege and captivity cast Judah. Recall that Deuteronomy 23:12–14 accounted human excrement unclean. The symbolic use of hair in chapter 5 seems designed to denote the three woes of death, doom for the defenders, and dispersement into exile, and the shaving itself is an act of mourning. The small portion bound in the prophet's skirts (verse 5:3) may indicate those who survive, and their fate, in turn, may be either to perish (Jerusalem was burned) or to be radically purified.

The word of God to Ezekiel makes it plain that the sufferings of the siege are God's punishment on Jerusalem, and such details as cannibalism convey the extremity of what actually occurred. Jerusalem is being made an object lesson to the nations of what happens when the chosen defile their inheritance.

The mountains castigated in chapter 6 are wicked for having hosted idolatrous worship. The sufferings of the survivors are to show the nations the holy justice of the Lord. The stamping and clapping of 6:11 presumably are to get the people's attention (or to mock their false worship). Ezekiel, described in verse 1:3 as a priest, has the priest's hatred for false (rival) cult. Chapter 7 continues the mood of dire warning, speaking of a terminal judgment. Few prophets equal Ezekiel in stressing the divine wrath. Symbols of slaughter, weakening, uncleanness, blood, and anguish abound.

Chapters 8–11 mainly deal with visions of the abominations that have defiled the Temple. In chapter 8 the prophet is carried in spirit by a flaming spirit back to Jerusalem (note the structural parallel to chapter 1). The guiding notion of the tour of the Temple that Ezekiel takes is that everywhere false cult had defiled what ought to have been God's holy house. Making images of divinity was repulsive to Jewish monotheism, and the fact that many such images were borrowed from the polytheistic cults of the nations only compounded the offense. Tammuz was originally a Sumerian vegetative deity who died and rose annually. The general picture painted in chapter 8 is of a Temple invaded by foreign fertility rites or worship of the sun.

The avengers who come in chapter 9 are clothed in priestly linen (a pure material). Those in the city who lament the abominations of the Temple are marked for preservation (see also Genesis 4:15, Exodus 12:22–23). A city of blood, injustice, and idolatry is being purged (in the siege and exile) of its defilements by the pure, priestly arm of the Lord. The strewing of burning coals (from the pure fire of the divine presence among the cherubim or holy spirits attending the Lord) in chapter 10 is reminiscent of the destruction of Sodom and Gomorrah in Genesis 19. The glory of the Lord and cloud that fill the Temple ring with traditional associations with the march in the wilderness and the ark of the Lord. Ezekiel is bedazzled by the wheels (verses 10:11–12) that move without turning and are full of eyes (symbolizing omniscience). The imagery shouts that the regal proto-power and holiness, quick as spirit and blazingly pure, have come to repossess the Temple. Ezekiel identifies this imagery with the vision he had by the river Chebar, saying in effect that to God Babylon and Jerusalem are one — the Lord holds sway everywhere.

Many commentators think that verses 11:1–13 are out of place (they would logically follow after verse 8:18). Ezekiel castigates the leaders of faithless Jerusalem, using imagery that suggests that their whole conception of themselves as the area (cauldron) of God's action will be reset by the Exile. Verses 11:14–21 are directed against those who used the Exile to aggrandize themselves with the exiles' property. Note the Jeremiah imagery of the new covenant and the promise of restoration from Exile. Verses 11:22–25 stress the exit of God's glory from Jerusalem and Ezekiel's (shaman-like) spiritual return to Babylon.[4]

Chapter 12 begins with the familiar prophetic lament that the people have eyes but do not see, ears but do not hear. What is distinctively Ezekielian is the stress on Israel's rebellion. The symbolic action imposed on the prophet in chapter

12 seems to have been fitted to Zedekiah's effort to escape Jerusalem (see Jeremiah 52). The time would be between the deportation of the first group of exiles in 598 and the definitive deportation in 586. Verses 12:21–28 assure that the visions of the true prophets will soon come true, but they suggest the confusion or opposition between true and false prophecy that we see in the book of Jeremiah. As well, verse 27 shows the sort of popular sentiment with which the prophets had to contend.

Verses 13:1–7 develop this theme, castigating the false prophets as spokespeople who deliver only their own words. The " 'peace,' when there is no peace" of verse 13:10 is familiar from Jeremiah. The wall of verses 13:10–15 seems best understood as Jewish society. The women castigated in verses 13:17–23 had roles in pagan divinations or cults that they could not play in approved Israelite worship.

Chapter 14 blasts the idols ("balls of dung") being worshipped in Jerusalem, promising that the Lord will cut off from his people those who bow to them. The Noah, Daniel, and Job of verse 14:14 stand for paragons of righteousness, but the times are so bad that they would not be able to save the land. (How much Ezekiel knew of the stories underlying the Daniel and Job treated in the Writings is uncertain.) One implication may be that things are even worse than they were in the time of Sodom and Gomorrah, when Abraham could wring from God the promise that the presence of a few righteous people would save the whole city from condemnation (see Genesis 18:22–33). At the end of the chapter the Lord assures the prophet that those who escape the four acts of judgment—sword, famine, evil beasts, and pestilence—will justify his punishments.

In chapter 15 the inhabitants of Jerusalem are likened to the wood of the vine, fit only for the fire. Chapter 16 excoriates the city of Jerusalem as unclean in its birth (from the land of Canaan), as though none had given the young city a proper washing and upbringing (guidance in true religion). Verses 16:6–14 rather brilliantly develop some of the feminine imagery for Judah that we found in Jeremiah, although the stress on blood makes Ezekiel's depiction more vivid and perhaps more offensive. Verses 16:15–19 seem rather routine developments of the charge of idolatry, but verses 16:20–21 bring us up short with an accusation of sacrificing children to pagan gods. Along with the strictly religious charge in these verses may run the political charge of coveting alliances with foreign powers. The prophets ultimately abhorred these alliances because they imperiled true worship but also because of the stupidity they evidenced and the suffering they brought. The Egyptians, Philistines, Assyrians, and Chaldeans (Babylonians) thus seduced Israel on several levels.

As he moves into the logic of this imagery, Ezekiel finds an apostasy worse than harlotry. The better figure is adultery, and a profitless one at that. Verses 16:35–43 depict a divorce and stoning in keeping with Deuteronomy 22:21–24. All the nations whose worship Ezekiel wishes to criticize, from Samaria to Sodom, are associated with Judah in a feminized wantonness. Judah, though, has been the worst (no doubt because Ezekiel thought Judah should have known better). Despite the harsh punishments the chapter parcels out, it ends with some notes of mercy: restoration of fortunes (verse 16:53) and an everlasting (Davidic?) covenant (verses 16:60–63).

The allegory of chapter 17 explains recent happenings in Judah.[5] Nebuchadrezzar is the eagle, taking the top of the house of David. King Jehoiachin is the topmost of the young twigs. The seed of the land is probably Zedekiah, and the second great eagle is Psammetichus II, pharaoh of Egypt from 594 to 588. The east wind is also Nebuchadrezzar of Babylon, who quickly crushed the alliance between Judah and Egypt. Ezekiel himself explains the allegory, assuring Judah that Zedekiah's cabals will prove disastrous, and that its sufferings from Babylon will be punishment for having broken the covenant with the Lord. The end of the chapter, when the Lord becomes the eagle, can be interpreted as an oracle of restoration, and certainly Ezekiel makes plain his conviction that only God plants and uproots.

Chapter 18 opens with a famous statement that seems to individualize responsibility (see Jeremiah 31:27–30), or at least to insist that each generation bears responsibility for what it becomes. The details of sin and righteousness that follow express a priestly concern for legal or ritualistic probity. Note the echoes of Deuteronomic laws and ideals of social justice, as well as the explicit assurance that a just child will not be condemned for the sins of its parent. In a situation of exile, Ezekiel would have had much occasion to remind people that they were responsible for their own morality. They might be in harsh circumstances, due to the wrongs of their parents, but they still had a say in what they themselves would become. Verse 18:23 is an encouraging assurance from God that he desires the conversion of the sinner rather than the satisfaction of punishing the sinner. Conversion — turning from wickedness to good — is, in fact, depicted as the death of sin (verse 18:24). The charge against God that the Lord is unjust (for allowing Judah to go into exile?) boomerangs: Each person will get just deserts. Note the reference to a new heart and a new spirit (verse 18:31), reminiscent of the new interior covenant. The uplifting end of the chapter is a reaffirmation that God wants people to turn and live (sin is death, virtue is life — on several levels; we do not have here a doctrine of immortality, however).

Chapter 19 features poetic lamenting. The first imagery plays off the figure that Judah was a lion. Ezekiel, unlike Jeremiah, moves along more allegorically than truly poetically, speaking of Kings Jehoahaz and Jechoiachin as whelps. The imagery of Judah as the maternal vine also is somewhat belabored, with Nebuchadrezzar again appearing as the east wind and stems again equated with rulers.

In chapter 20 we get another indication that Ezekiel wants to reverse a tendency in exilic Judah to call God into judgment. Rather, God is judging Judah, and Ezekiel is the instrument by which heaven's standards will be reasserted. First, God reminds the people of the Exodus and the conditions for enjoying the promised land. They violated this trust, rejected this goodness, by their idolatries. This was in keeping with the rebellions in the wilderness and the rejection of the kindly guidance offered in the Torah. Note in verses 20:23–26 the paradoxical turn that the divine accusation takes: God inspired the people to wrongdoing, so as finally to horrify them and reveal the depravity that had settled in their hearts. Ezekiel's totally negative reading of Israelite history is distinctive.

Verse 20:32 rejects the notion that Israel ever could become like the nations, allowed an idolatrous way of life. Throughout this chapter Ezekiel is building a case that the people ever have been rebellious and so have no platform whatsoever for questioning the justice of God. If only in pain and solitary judgment, Israel will know that only the Lord is its king. The gathering and worship described in verses 20:40–44 is bittersweet, in that God forces the people to be what they ought to be. After the oracle against the south (Judah) at the end of the chapter, Ezekiel somewhat ironically laments that the people have come to consider him a maker of (bad) allegories.

In chapter 21 the initial imagery is straightforward: God will come upon Jerusalem with the sword. Ezekiel, the son of man who has to carry this prophecy, sighs because of its burden. This punishment will be more than the spanking received previously. It will be a sword rather than a rod. By verse 21:17 Ezekiel has worked himself up to the point at which the Lord is wielding the sword in fury. Babylon will be divine punishment for Judah. The suffering of people and king (Zedekiah) alike will be well merited by their guilt. In the rest of the chapter Ezekiel receives still more visions of coming disasters.

Chapter 22 details the sins of Judah under the twin headings of shedding blood and worshiping idols. The listing combines a prophetic hatred of injustice with a priestly aversion from ritual uncleanness. Verses 22:15–16 use the figures of the Lord's consuming the filthiness of Judah, through his punishments of it, and of the Lord's himself being profaned—having his reputation mottled—among the nations by the immoral conduct of the people he has chosen. These lead on to the figure of purifying an Israel composed mainly of dross metals. All ranks of society—priests, princes, prophets, and commoners—have participated in the injustice and uncleanness.

In chapter 23 Ezekiel is back to the theme of harlotry, depicting the apostasies of Samaria and Jerusalem in sexual imagery. The various nations with which Samaria and Jerusalem had consorted—Assyria, Babylon, and Egypt—are assimilated to paramours. Fittingly, these false lovers will be the agents of the Lord's punishment. The two names Oholah and Oholibah suggest the tent of the Samaritan sanctuary for the Lord and the Temple in Jerusalem: two places where holiness ought to have obtained but instead infidelity flourished. Note the charge of child sacrifice in verse 23:39. Like Jeremiah, Ezekiel has the intuition that pure religion is a marital love affair with God and so false religion is adultery.

Verse 24:1 gives us one of Ezekiel's precise datings: January 15, 588. The first figure for the punishment of the siege and burning of Jerusalem is of a scalding cauldron in which good citizens and bad alike are boiled. Verses 24:15–18 have the affecting oracle about the death of Ezekiel's wife and his inability to mourn. So would the people of Jerusalem be unable to mourn at the enormity of the suffering to come. The loosening of Ezekiel's tongue would be a sign that his burdensome prophecy had been fulfilled and a new stage could begin.

25:1–48:35 Oracles on the Restoration of Judah

In chapters 25–32 Ezekiel turns from casting woes upon Jerusalem to prophesying against the foreign nations (a theme common to all the major prophetic collections), as a first step in portraying better times to come.[6] The Ammonites will be overrun by easterners (Bedouins), because of their delight in Judah's miseries. The same with Moab, which wanted to reduce Judah to the level of other, unchosen nations, and with Edom, which treated the house of Judah badly. The Philistines, too, will get their just deserts for having abused Judah.

In chapter 26 the prophet delights in foreseeing the punishment of Tyre, which also had taken pleasure in Israel's misfortunes. Note that Ezekiel's interpretation of history is completely ethnocentric, because he equates the fortunes of Israel's neighbors with their treatment of it. Like Jeremiah, Ezekiel sees Nebuchadrezzar as a providential agent of the Lord, and his main, if not only, category for understanding the woes that Babylon inflicts is just punishment for immorality or other rebellion against the Lord. The length of the imaginative musings about the fall of Tyre suggests a special interest, perhaps provoked by Tyre's prosperity as a great port or by Tyre's failure to support Israel as an ally. Chapter 27 continues in this vein, building up the prosperity of Tyre so as the better to celebrate its fall. The maritime basis of Tyre's greatness suggests that its fall will be a drowning in the primeval waters, as though the times had reverted to the chaos of precreation when God gave no order to the world.

Chapter 28 interestingly equates the pride of Tyre with self-exaltation to divinity — the "inflation" that modern psychology often finds in those who forget their humble origins in the earth. The prudential wisdom that brought Tyre its great trade and wealth is no match for the divine cunning that runs history. So, like all others who run afoul of history and come to grief, Tyre will learn its mortality and finitude painfully. Its cries of grief will be confessions that it is no God. Verse 28:12 has the effective figure of the king of Tyre's considering himself the signet of perfection. Verses 13–15 liken flourishing Tyre to humanity's enjoying Eden, prior to the fall. Verse 28:17 has the ring of a sapiential saying capable of wider application: "You corrupted your wisdom for the sake of your splendor." The fire of verse 28:18 is like that which consumed those who profaned the sanctuary of the Lord (see Leviticus 10:2).

The next city-state to fall under Ezekiel's baleful eye is Sidon, which will learn in its punishment that only the Lord is God. Verse 28:24 explains the upshot for Israel of all this suffering of the nations: Its enemies will be reduced to the status of briers and thorns, capable only of scratching it. Verses 28:25–26 pivot from this review of the nations' fallings to the good future that restored, reconstituted Israel will enjoy.

In chapter 29 Ezekiel goes to work against Egypt, proclaiming the word that the Lord has given him about that great nation's fate. The pride of Egypt is turned against it, using imagery of the Nile, the center of Egypt's self-conception. Verses 29:6–9 make the reason for Egypt's sufferings its failure to be a strong ally to Judah. After forty years — a sizable period — of desolation Egypt will be restored, but only to the status of a petty kingdom so lowly that Israel will have no temptation to rely upon it. Egypt will recompense Babylon for the smallness of its gains against Tyre. Most commentators consider verse 29:21 to be a symbol of royal, possibly messianic restoration for Israel.[7]

Chapter 30 deals in the imagery of the day of the Lord that had become a staple of prophetic figures for divine judgment (see Amos 5:18–20, Isaiah 2:12, Jeremiah 30:7). Here it is coming upon Egypt and its supporters. Note in verse 30:13 the fall of both idols and prince — the centers of Egyptian religious culture. Ezekiel seems to think of Egypt as an age-old antagonist whose religious impressiveness caused Israel significant temptation. The fall of pharaoh is the fall of power dangerous precisely because of its effectiveness in centering a systematic understanding of divine force that strongly contested Israelite monotheism.[8] Chapter 31 is reminiscent of the earlier chapters that prophesied against Tyre. Ezekiel beautifully builds up the splendor of Egypt, in order to make its fall — like the crash of a mighty, towering cedar—the more impressive. Egypt, with its tops among the divine clouds, has offended against the right order of monotheism and contested the transcendence of the true God. The sin for which it is most being punished therefore is its pride and self-deification. The mourning of the nations is like a dirge at the funeral of the most splendid attempt to divinize human culture. The note of consolation that runs through the depiction of Sheol is interesting, as though Ezekiel found a touch of pathos in the shattering of Egypt's grand illusion.

Chapter 32 describes the fall of pharaoh in less profound but still effective imagery, making nature—beasts and heavenly elements—turn against this foremost human player in the cosmos. As the chapter continues, the fall of Egypt brings the dread of having to watch a central portion of what had come to be considered the natural order of things shift. Egypt had so long held power in the region—better than 2000 years of hegemony, now greater and now less—that its fall forced people to gaze into the abyss of power politics (the nothingness revealed by finally meaningless shifts of merely pragmatic conquest and dominion). As uncircumcised, Egypt falls outside Ezekiel's priestly sense of those who rightly enjoy intimacy with the holy, true God, so the significance that his imagery attaches to the fall of Egypt is the more striking. With Assyria, Elam, and all the other unclean peoples who have experienced Sheol, the death of historical prospects, Egypt will have only the fundamental consolation of realizing the truth of its creaturely fragility.

The next section of the second portion of Ezekiel, chapters 33–39, offers many oracles of the restoration of Judah.[9] Chapter 33 renews the imagery of the watchman, according to which Ezekiel must utter the Lord's words of warning or himself bear the responsibility for Israel's wickedness. The middle of the chapter promises forgiveness and renewal, if people will turn from their wickedness. Chapter 33 thus becomes an important witness to the prophetic convictions about individual responsibility and divine forgiveness. Ezekiel again defends the justice of the Lord, and in verse 33:22 we learn that, virtually coincident with the fall of Jerusalem, he receives back his speech. The desolation to follow is interpreted as punishment for Israelite idolatry, and Ezekiel makes it plain that the covenant with Abraham concerning the land depends on good morals. The final verses of the chapter explore the difference between saying and doing—between the religion of words and the religion of action.

The diatribe of chapter 34 against the false shepherds (leaders) of Israel is a high-water mark in the history of religious self-criticism. Few passages make it clearer that biblical religion was no simple "civil religion" concerned to prop up the status quo. Note how the failure of the shepherds prompts the Lord to take the care of the sheep into his own hands. This latter imagery points in the direction of a restoration after the Exile. Ezekiel elaborates the basic metaphor to almost painful length and detail, but by verse 34:23 it is plain that the sheep, too, have to live virtuously, even though the Lord is to be the (gracious) agent of a Davidic restoration that will unify the flock. The end of the chapter approximates the peaceable kingdom of Isaiah 11.

Chapter 35 opens with an oracle against Mount Seir, which stands for Edom. The reason for the coming destruction of Edom is its mistreatment of Israel. Verse 35:11 could be read as a divine encouragement of international amity. The prophecies to the mountains of Israel in chapter 36 depend on the double significance of the mountain as a holy place of encounter with God and a place profaned by idolatrous worship. The mountains of Seir and Israel, therefore, are addressed as contrasts—the first as a place of destruction and the second as a place of restoration. The oracle foresees the restoration of Israel and a time of flourishing for both nature and society. The middle verses of the chapter revive the imagery of uncleanness, and verse 36:22 is interesting for making the motive of restoration God's own holy name or reputation. The prophet is moving from the economic equation between evil-doing and punishment to musings about what God owes himself. Note in verse 36:26 an Ezekielian version of the new, interior covenant, with the effective figure of replacing the heart of stone with a heart of flesh. Like Jeremiah, Ezekiel has realized that renovation has to be from the wellsprings of moral action (though the statutes that Ezekiel has in mind in verse 36:27 concern more than morality). Nature shares in the restoration to come, and throughout restoration will be a matter of grace—God's free, unmerited blessing.

Chapter 37 contains the famous vision of the dry bones.[10] The symbol is encouraging: The spirit of the Lord can revive even what seemed skeletal—dead to the bone. The pessimistic view of Israel-in-Exile that the exiles themselves have (in verse 37:11) is thus not the final word. Consequently, this passage is a major resource for theological reflection on the breath or quickening spirit of the Lord. The logic that may be implied is that when the breath of the deathless divinity comes over human substance it revivifies or resurrects that substance and makes it participate in deathlessness. Ezekiel's accent falls on the social body of Israel, but later Western speculation extended the logic to the individual human being. The word and dramatic enactment of verses 37:15–23 look to the reunification of the northern and southern tribes, who always remained one in the biblical theologians' sense of God's people. The rest of the chapter is fully messianic, anticipating a Davidic ruler who will unify the people and lead them to enjoy the everlasting covenant of peace and blessing thought promised to David and his line.

Chapter 38 develops somewhat obscure, and certainly symbolic, language in prophesying against nations of the north that were afflicting Judah prior to the fall of Jerusalem. Apparently the prophet (or one of his successors) wants to paint with a wider or more vivid brush than just "Babylon." The main notion is that God will defend restored Israel against its foes and bring Gog to ruin. Chapter 39 continues in this vein. Note the divine fire (lightning?) to be sent on Magog (verse 39:6), and the theme of preserving the holiness of the divine name (verse 39:7). The birds and beasts will feast on Israel's destroyed enemies. The final verses of the chapter make the restoration of Judah the great manifestation of the divine holiness and outpouring of the divine spirit.

The last section of the book of Ezekiel, chapters 40–48, presents Ezekiel as a second Moses, legislating for the restored Israel that he foresees.[11] The prophet first receives a vision in which an emissary of God measures out the area of the Temple. In the background are I Kings 6–7, where Solomon's Temple is described. After twenty-five years in Exile, the prophet, whose priestly vocation would have made him especially interested in the Temple, envisions what the house of God will be like after Judah's restoration. (There are numerous small differences in the enumerations of the Hebrew and the Greek texts.) There is no indication that Ezekiel's vision became prescriptive (or that it was an exact retrojection by editors after the rebuilding of the Temple in 520 to 515 B.C.E.). As we see when we treat

Zechariah, the role of the priesthood in national life expanded after the restoration, so the Second Temple was less dominated by the political leadership than the Temple of Solomon had been.

After three chapters of architectural details, we get in chapter 43 a vision of the glory of the God of Israel coming from the east. Ezekiel is explicit that this vision dovetails with his earlier visions of the divine glory, and that, whereas the point of the earlier visions had been the Lord's forsaking of Israel, that of this vision is the glory of the Lord's returning to take possession of his house. Note that the new Temple is to be more strictly reserved for religious use than the first Temple was. As verse 43:12 makes explicit, the whole precinct of the Temple is to be considered holy ground, the mountain of the Lord. The prescriptions for consecrating the altar reflect Exodus (29:36–37, 40:1–38) and Leviticus (8:14–15). Chapter 44 continues directions for purifying the Temple and assuring its properly religious use. The proscription of foreigners squares with the general trend of postexilic Judah to try to purge Gentile influences. Note the signs of contest between Levites and priests of Zadok. The regulations for the dress and behavior of those who minister in the Temple express the nearly fanatical priestly concern for purity (for example, verse 44:18 frowns on sweat). The priests are again being considered a tribe whose inheritance is the Lord (see Numbers 18:20–32, Joshua 13:14).

Chapter 45 imagines an ideal division of the (repossessed) land. Verse 45:9 is a powerful call for the end of violence and oppression. The remaining legislation is reminiscent of legal materials we have seen previously, blending a concern for justice with a concern for purity and ritual exactitude. Chapter 46 sketches what behavior in the Temple ought to be on the Sabbath and such festivals as that of the new moon. Ezekiel imagines the sacrifices and the role that the prince should play. Note in verse 46:18 the controls on the prince's use of the common property. The prophet's tour of the Temple, which takes him to its different sides, amounts to a mandala or sacral form, in which the holiness due to the Lord in his divine house is physically displayed.

Chapter 47 describes a sacred river flowing from the Temple, perhaps on the model of the waters of life common to ancient Near Eastern religious mythology. At this point the restored, idealized Temple has become like Eden and other paradisic realms. The division of the land resumes, as though in foreseeing the restoration of Judah Ezekiel has to redo the apportionment of Joshua after the Conquest. Note that the priests and Levites get special consideration, and that aliens are to be like native-born children (verse 47:22).

Chapter 48 runs through the twelve tribes, describing the portion that each is to have in the repossessed land. Imagining the exiles' return has given Ezekiel the chance to repicture the great gift from the Lord of the promised land. Note that the sanctuary of the Lord is to be in the midst of Judah (verse 48:8). Verse 48:19 says that workers of Jerusalem from all the tribes are to till the land near the Lord's holy portion for food. Clearly Judah and Jerusalem are the centerpiece of the reallotment, because the tribes treated both before and after Judah are dispatched quite quickly. Each of the tribes gets a gate to the holy city, signifying its portion in the holy center. The last line of the book of Ezekiel summarizes both the visions of chapters 40–48 and the conviction about the renewed holy city that the entire oracular process of condemning and consoling has produced: "The Lord is there."

HISTORICAL BACKGROUND

The book of Ezekiel presupposes the events of the years 593 to 571 B.C.E. (the period in which Ezekiel's various oracles seem to fall), as well as the prior history of threats by Babylon and alliances with Egypt, and, for the final editors, the subsequent history of return to the land under the Persians. The prophet himself would have been most concerned with the victory of Babylon in 597 and the first deportation of Jews that followed shortly afterwards. He himself was taken away with King Jehoiachin at that time, and he spent the first part of his career anticipating the definitive fall of 586. The prophet was thus greatly concerned first to explain why Judah had lost control of its own destiny through defeat by the Babylonians. Then, probably after 586, he was concerned to console the people, by teaching them how to turn their sufferings to good account, and to help them believe God had a new future in store for Judah.

We have frequently noted the assumption of all of the prophets that Israel had sufficiently flouted the laws of the covenant and indulged in false cult to warrant punishment from the Lord. Thinking that God was at work in history guiding all events according to the divine purposes, the prophets rather logically concluded that the fall of Israel and Judah alike was providential. If it would teach the people what the wages of sin or infidelity were, such suffering could in the long run prove beneficial. Ezekiel especially singles out the failures of the leaders, who should have guided the people to better love of the Lord and kept them away from reliance upon either foreign political powers or foreign deities. One of his dominant figures, as we have seen, is that of harlotry: The people have spurned their true spouse and defiled their marital compact. Ezekiel is the heir of Jeremiah, especially, in thinking about the deep renovation that return to the Lord and the land should entail. The covenant must be renewed on a more interior basis, with a fresh spirit and a heart of flesh that will feel its obligations to the Lord.

LITERARY INTENT

Ezekiel obviously was written to collect the oracles of a famous prophet thought to have proffered the word of the Lord about the situation of exile. The later editors who arranged these oracles into prophecies of first woe and then restoration were following a logic doubly justified. First, they were thinking of the history of exile and restoration through which Judah actually passed. Second, they were thinking about the psychology of penance or conversion (a major theme in Ezekiel, as we have seen), which tends initially to spotlight an awareness of guilt, and so a need for change, and then to spotlight sources of a hopeful future.

The book of Ezekiel, like its prophetic predecessors, sought to rouse its readers to understand and reject their past sinfulness. At the least, it wanted the painful experience of the Exile to serve the people's purification. In addition, the book of Ezekiel displays priestly interests not so prominent in Isaiah and Jeremiah. The clearest indication of these priestly interests comes in the final chapters, where the editors have made the climax of the prophet's view of restoration the reestablishment of the Temple as the center of the land. As well, they have detailed many moral and ritualistic reforms in the punctilious spirit of the priestly legislators, more than a few times evincing a special concern for purity. If we retroject from this conclusion, we can read many of the prior oracles about defilement as priestly interpretations of immorality and exilic punishment.

The priests were concerned to make Israel a people holy to the Lord. Their rituals made sense only if the God intended in worship was incomparably holy — pure, powerful, free of imperfection. Such holiness, as we have previously seen, was what we might call physico-moral. It affected both body and mind, both physical actions and interior dispositions. Some of this holism comes through in Ezekiel's imagery of harlotry. If the people were intimately bonded with the Lord, as in a marriage, and if their injustices and idolatries were affronts to the holiness of the Lord, then it made sense to depict their failures as harlotry or adultery. The vision of God with which the book of Ezekiel begins only reenforces this line of thought. Like Isaiah, Ezekiel felt himself summoned by a heavenly power that existed on a level of purity far beyond him. The symbolism of the chariot and the cherubim is like the symbolism of Isaiah 6 in stressing the moral transcendence or otherness of the Lord. The book of Ezekiel wants to convince both its first readers, who were suffering in exile, and its later readers, who were trying to ponder the historical lessons of this remarkable prior patch of national history, of the sovereignty of the one who held the nation's fate.

Brevard Childs, interested in the canonical shape of Ezekiel and the dominant feature of the book as a whole, stresses theocentricity.[12] He understands the liberties that the book takes with ordinary conceptions of space and time as flowing from a central sense of the utter primacy of the divine (which, of course, can be thought to escape the spatial and temporal limitations that human beings suffer). If it is genuinely the word of God that the prophet is experiencing and expressing, then there is little problem in the fact that the prophecy treats past, present, and future as a unity. Similarly, there is little problem with the shifts that the prophecy makes between a location in Babylon and a location (either past or future) in Jerusalem. "Israel" and "Judah" both become more than historical entities: the people of past-present-future who enjoy those names by covenantal reference to the transcendent God. The prophet regularly moves to a level of generalization that takes him apart from historical events and lets him play with the interaction of symbols or ideas about God that stand free of time. This is not to deny that Ezekiel was deeply influenced by the specific event of exile to Babylon, any more than it is to imply that the death of his wife had little significance for him. It is simply to suggest that the visions that the book itself makes most impressive are the key to his conception of reality — are the main guides to his symbolic universe. These visions were of the holy God. Having glimpsed the divine splendor, Ezekiel had to recast everything else in its light.

LASTING SIGNIFICANCE

Let us reflect on Ezekiel's glimpse of the divine splendor in light, first, of the mysticism that later focused on his symbolism of the divine chariot, and then, second, of his leading notions of personal responsibility and divine forgiveness or regeneration.

During the late Second Temple period (first century B.C.E. to first century c.e.), a literature called *apocalyptic* dwelt on disclosures thought to come from God. Angels played a large role in these apocalyptic revelations, and the basic imaginative framework for the angels and the deity they served often came from Ezekiel's vision. The earliest phase of rabbinic mysticism regularly went under the name *merkabah* ("chariot") and described ecstatic ascents to heaven, encounters with the angels who attend the Lord, and the like in terms of the symbols of Ezekiel's vision in verses 1:4–28. Some historians of Jewish mysticism imply that later developments of merkabah mysticism departed from the rabbinic mainstream. K. P. Bland, for example, has written:

> Rabbinic Judaism tempered its transcendental image of God with a loving appreciation for God's intimacy and presence (*Shekhina*) and emphasized the study of Torah and its interpretation as the ideal of religious life. Merkabah mysticism, on the other hand, sought religious experiences independent of the study of scripture. It evacuated the divine from this world and located it at the farthest possible remove from ordinary human experience, emphasizing God's awesome grandeur, otherworldly majesty, and numinous quality.[13]

Ezekiel's own vision certainly is heavily symbolic, and it pays enough attention to heavenly creatures to make understandable the later fascination with angels. But the chariot or throne of God is also intriguing for its symbolism of movement and rest, which it develops by speaking of the wheels that can go in any direction without turning and that stop or start with the living creatures. Any interpretation of these images is speculative, but they do suggest a fascination with the motility of spirit — its capacity to move instantly, like the flash of a thought or the outburst of an ardent emotion. The prophet might be thinking that the divine is like the quicksilver movements of his own (highly charged) mind, will, and imagination. Yet, on the other hand, the divine in whom he believes is covenanted to Israel: God has chosen to "stop" at certain moments in history, to be present to places and people that, by comparison with the motility of highest spirit, seem arrested. To be sure, the imagery is also an extrapolation from the regalia that kings and warriors of the time enjoyed: thrones, chariots, attendants. But Ezekiel's heavenly king is instantaneous or lightning-quick. The cherubim shield him from creaturely sight, as befits the tradition of the hidden God, but they themselves can move in a flash, keeping pace with divinity and being animated by the fiery spirit at the center of their formations.

Ezekiel certainly was shaped in his entire prophetic career by his intuition of the divine holiness, but he was also concerned to make divine power bear on the renewal of human spirit or consciousness. It was not enough simply to condemn the people for their past apostasies and interpret the exile as a fitting punishment. It was not enough even to call the people back to the morality of the Deuteronomistic covenant. Like Jeremiah, who no doubt greatly influenced him, Ezekiel was concerned to assure the people of the divine will that they be converted and live. As we saw, he not only rejects the people's claims that God is unjust, he also spotlights the arena of individual conscience and promises that those who turn from sin will be forgiven. God desires the people's life, not the pleasure of condemning them. That so holy a God as Ezekiel's should finally express himself as more gracious than judgmental is remarkable. Ezekiel the prophetic visionary somewhat broke the bonds of Ezekiel the scrupulous priest. Even though the priestly thought made provision for cleansing and forgiveness, it did not instinctively think of replacing a heart of stone with a heart of flesh.

Equally, the priestly thought that we find in Ezekiel, especially in chapters 40–48, is not so appreciative of the divine spirit that can work such a transformation as is the prophetic visionary we find in chapters 1 and 37. Chapter 1 has sufficiently concerned us already: Ezekiel was formed by a blazing vision of the holy divine king. Chapter 37 has the famous vision of the valley of dry bones that the breath of the Lord brings back to life. The "word" of God, like the "spirit" of God, stands for the divinity addressing its creatures and acting to transform them. In later biblical thought, both Jewish and Christian, these divine attributes became hypostasized (made into independent entities), but at this stage they mainly seem symbolic expressions of the divine interaction with creation.

In the vision of the dry bones breathed back to flesh and vitality, Ezekiel is saying that the divine force is its own law. When God chooses to oppose the ordinary inertia or entropy of either nature or morality, which tend to decree that physical life will run down and moral probity will grow dull, neither can resist. Let a human being be so dead as to have become a skeleton, and the divine creativity is still not defeated. Let a people become so forgetful or perverted that they throw over their holy spouse and play the harlot with despicable foreign gods ("dung balls"), and the divine creativity is still not defeated.

Perhaps now the link between Ezekiel's vision of the divine splendor and his confidence of the Lord's power to revivify or resurrect Israel is apparent. The fire of the heavenly divine presence is primal power that can either create or destroy.

Jerusalem "in the midst of the nations with countries round about her" (Ezekiel 5:5). *(Used with permission of the photographer, Wolfgang Roth)*

Apart from the graciousness of the Lord and Israel's many historical reasons for believing in his plighted troth, the people would only be able to quake in expectation of the divine fury. Ezekiel is well aware of this divine fury or wrath, because he threatens Israel with it frequently. But his larger theology is structured by the divine creativity and fidelity: God wants life for his people, not death. God takes no delight in the sinners' self-chosen perdition. What gladdens the divine heart is turning people around, giving them new possibilities, replacing hearts of flesh with hearts of stone, giving old bones new flesh, blood, and spirit. The divine holiness, then, is inseparable from the divine creativity and the divine forgiveness. The Lord, Israel's God, is one in all perfections.

GLOSSARY

Allegory   A literary form that makes point-by-point correspondences between two different situations.

Mandala   Visual form, often of wholeness, useful for meditation.

Merkabah   The divine chariot featured in the vision of Ezekiel (verses 1:22–28) that became a central symbol in Jewish mysticism.

Mysticism   Experience of or direct communion with ultimate reality.

Shekinah   The glorious divine presence (considered feminine); seen in the cloud that accompanied the marchers in the wilderness.

Sheol   The shadowy underworld to which the departed spirits of the dead go.

Theocentricity   God-centeredness.

STUDY QUESTIONS

1. How does the vision of chapter 1 express the divine glory?
2. What impact did the siege of Jerusalem have on the prophet?
3. Explain the symbolism and role of the avengers of chapter 9.
4. How does Ezekiel clarify the zone of individual conscience?
5. What are the gains and the dangers in the imagery of harlotry?
6. Compare the fall of Tyre to the fall of Egypt.
7. How does the criticism of the false shepherds (chapter 34) qualify the notion that religion and culture were fused in biblical religion?
8. Explain the implications of the work of the divine spirit depicted in chapter 37.
9. How does the prophet's tour of the Temple make a mandala?
10. What characteristics of the book of Ezekiel suggest a priestly background?
11. Why did the authors of Ezekiel place the vision of the chariot and the cherubim at the beginning?

12. How does the view of the divine breath in Ezekiel justify the book's view of personal responsibility, conversion, and renewal?

NOTES

1. See Moshe Greenberg, *Ezekiel 1–20*. Garden City, N. Y.: Doubleday Anchor Bible, 1983; Walter Zimmerli, *Ezekiel 1*. Philadelphia: Fortress, 1979; Werner E. Lemke, "Ezekiel, the Book of," in *Harper's Bible Dictionary*, ed. Paul J. Achtemeier. San Francisco: Harper & Row, 1985, pp. 293–94; William Hugh Brownlee, "The Book of Ezekiel," in *The Major Prophets*, ed. Charles M. Laymon. Nashville: Abingdon (Interpreter's Concise Commentary), 1983, pp. 233–306.

2. See Robert C. Wilson, "Prophecy in Crisis: The Call of Ezekiel," *Interpretation*, 38 (1984), 117–30.

3. See John C. Marshall, "In the Region of Lost Minds," *The New York Times Book Review* (March 2, 1986), 3 (reviewing Oliver Sacks, *The Man Who Mistook His Wife for a Hat*. New York: Summit Books, 1986).

4. See Moshe Greenberg, "The Vision of Jerusalem in Ezekiel 8–11: A Holistic Interpretation," in *The Divine Helmsman*, ed. I. Crenshaw and S. Sandmel. New York: KTAV, 1980, pp. 143–63.

5. See Moshe Greenberg, "Ezekiel 17: A Holistic Interpretation," *Journal of the American Oriental Society*, 103 (1983), 149–154.

6. See Carol A. Newsom, "A Maker of Metaphors—Ezekiel's Oracles Against Tyre," *Interpretation*, 38 (1984), 151–64.

7. See Arnold J. Tkracik, "Ezekiel," in *The Jerome Biblical Commentary*, ed. R. Brown, J. Fitzmyer, and R. Murphy. Englewood Cliffs, N.J.: Prentice-Hall, 1968, Volume 1, p. 359.

8. Eric Voegelin has contrasted the "cosmological" cultures, such as Egypt, which lived with a sense that nature was a single, comprehensive vitality, with the monotheistic culture produced by Israelite revelation. In the eyes of the prophets, the idols of the nations were part and parcel of the mortality intrinsic to cultures that did not know the living God. See Denise Lardner Carmody and John Tully Carmody, *Interpreting the Religious Experience*. Englewood Cliffs, N.J.: Prentice-Hall, 1986.

9. See Werner E. Lemke, "Life in the Present and Hope for the Future," *Interpretation*, 38 (1984), 165–80.

10. See Marco Nobile, "Ez 37,1–14 come costitutivo di una schema cultuale," *Biblica*, 65 (1984), 476–89.

11. See Moshe Greenberg, "The Design and Themes of Ezekiel's Program of Restoration," *Interpretation*, 38 (1984), 181–208. See also Jon Douglas Levenson, *Theology of the Program of Restoration of Ezekiel 40–48*. Missoula, Mont.: Scholars Press, 1976.

12. See Brevard Childs, *Introduction to the Old Testament as Scripture*. Philadelphia: Fortress, 1979, pp.

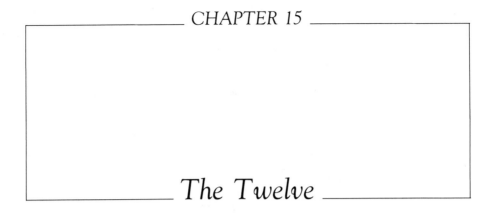

CHAPTER 15

The Twelve

The short prophetic collections that we find in the book of the Hebrew Bible called "The Twelve" perhaps were grouped together because, collectively, they approximated the length of the books of each of the major latter prophets (Isaiah, Jeremiah, and Ezekiel) and thus, filled what probably was a standardized length of scroll. The number twelve recalls the twelve tribes of Israel and so may be symbolic. The order in which the twelve prophets now stand is roughly chronological. Hosea and Amos are the oldest, and Haggai, Zechariah, and Malachai come at the end. Canonically, the editors of the Hebrew Bible seem to have been more interested in shaping the individual books than in working with the twelve as a malleable unit. The twelve also functioned as a solid final contribution to the prophetic block of materials that the editors seem to have envisioned as a unit usefully set over and against the Torah. Although our treatments are necessarily brief, for each prophet we still discuss the same four topics we have for all the others.

HOSEA

The majority of commentators divide the book of Hosea into two unequal parts. Chapters 1–3 concern Hosea's marriage, which serves as a symbol of Israel's relation to God. Chapters 4–14 comprise prophecies, mainly of judgment, stemming from Israel's infidelity and threat from Assyria (the general historical context is the mid-eighth century B.C.E., when the Northern Kingdom obviously was imperiled).[1]

Chapter 1 gives a chronological reference (from the beginning of Uzziah to the end of Hezekiah was about 783 to 687; Jeroboam ruled from about 786 to 746) and then plunges into the symbolism of the prophet's marriage. Like Isaiah's children, Hosea's children are given names symbolic of the prophet's reading of the times. Gomer, the prophet's wife, comes to stand for Israel, beloved but a harlot. Despite the warnings of punishment in the first verses, verses 1:10–11 (2:1–2 in the Hebrew) echo the covenantal promise to Abraham and foresee a good future.

Chapter 2 shows the theme of harlotry and adultery that was greatly elaborated by Ezekiel. Hosea is evidence that the imagery that Ezekiel used was part of a prophetic tradition more than 150 years old. God is the aggrieved husband, and the source of Israel's many blessings, who has been shamed and angered by the people's idolatries (we might think of a play between "adultery" and "idolatry"). Note in verses 2:14–16 touches of tenderness that soften the divine anger and recall the pristine relationship of the Exodus. Many of Hosea's references are to Exodus (for example, Exodus 19–24). Verses 2:16–17 suggest that once it was considered legitimate to call Israel's Lord "Baal" ("Master"). Verses 2:19–23 are a high point in the biblical expression of God's covenanted love, scarcely equaled for their expression of the stable marriage that God has contracted. Although most of the imagery makes Israel feminine, verse 2:23 suggests some nuance. Throughout chapter 2 an extended metaphor presents the lovers of the harlot as failing to provide the goods that the husband alone can provide.

In chapter 3 the prophet buys back his adulterous wife (scholars debate whether Hosea's marriage is completely symbolic or was historically factual in the main details). Verses 3:3–5 appear to predict a fall of kingship and then a later, Davidic restoration.[2]

Chapter 4 begins the second section of the book, where the main burden is accusations against Israel and prophecies of well-merited suffering. Verse 4:1 sounds the note of God's grievance with the people and employs the regular prophetic figure of the people's having no knowledge of God. Note also the charge that faithfulness and kindness have left. The catalogue of sins that follows is so full that even nature enters into the mourning and bad results that the prophet, given the word and viewpoint of the Lord, discerns (verse 4:3). Priests and prophets alike lack knowledge of the Lord. Note that some of the punishment this immorality begets is intrinsic: In verse 4:10 the people can get no (spiritual) nourishment or fertility. Images of harlotry abound, castigating the false cult. Verse 4:15 seems to want to shield or separate Judah from these sins of Israel. Overall, chapter 4, like chapters 2, 5, and 11, has the shape of a covenantal lawsuit that God, the aggrieved party, brings against Israel, the offender.

By verse 5:5, however, Judah is included in the harlotry that will bring stumbling. With verse 5:8 we enter on a series of threats of what will come if Israel does not repent. Note in verse 5:12 the figures of moth and dry rot: The Lord will wither the faithless people. Verse 5:13 is explicit that Assyria is not the answer. Only return to the Lord can help, and verse 6:2 assures that the Lord can bring Israel out of its sufferings. Verse 6:3 is another call to knowledge of the Lord. Verse 6:4 has the effective figure of love as insubstantial as the morning dew. Verse 6:6 has a famous ring: steadfast love ("mercy," in other translations) rather than sacrifice, knowledge of God instead of burnt offerings—heartfelt morality rather than superficial ritual. The rest of the chapter details how the people have failed to meet this ideal.[3]

Chapter 7 offers further analysis of the people's failings, many of them couched in brilliant imagery (for instance, the overheated oven of verse 7:4). Note how Hosea uses "Ephraim" to refer to the Northern Kingdom, no doubt because of the strength of that tribe. The burden of the chapter is the sins that the Lord will punish and would redeem, were the people to deal honestly with him (verse 7:13).

Chapter 8 rehearses such divine grievances as transgressions of Torah, a faithless kingship, and impure cult. Israel's faithless works will fall and it will stand among the pagan nations as a useless vessel (verse 8:8). The destructions to come will be judgment on the people's resort to the ways of the nations and neglect of their true treasure, the Lord.

Chapter 9 has more on harlotry. Domination by Egypt and Assyria serve both symbolic and historical duty as punishment. Notice the criticism of (defective) prophecy in verses 9:7–8. As both vineyard and mother, Ephraim has no good yield. Chapter 10 makes Israel a luxurious vineyard with an inner falsity. Verse 10:6 shows the shadow of Assyria threatening the times. Verse 10:11 has Ephraim as a heifer suborned to the yoke of punishment. Verse 10:13 describes the just yield that Israel's wickedness has brought it. As it trusted in weapons, so shall it be punished by war.

Hosea 11:1 is a famous and tender line, harkening back to the Exodus. God would have been a kindly parent but the child became wayward. The cruelties of Assyria will redress this waywardness. Yet in verse 11:8 the Lord is lamenting like a grief-stricken parent, unable to cast off the foolish child who has done so much injury. Note the images of restoration at the end of the chapter, and also the opinion that Judah, in contrast, has remained faithful.

Chapter 12 suggests Israel's fascination with things Eastern (Assyrian). Hosea 12:2–6 play off the career of Jacob, apparently to urge imitation of his stubborn clinging. Hosea reviews the time in the wilderness and the gifts to the prophets, the better to display Israel's ingratitude. Chapter 13 laments the idolatries of Ephraim, which have made him like a filmy mist. Verses 13:4–5 are a strong statement of the identity and rights of Israel's one God. His anger will express his sense of injustice. Verses 13:10–11 comprise one of several expressions of Hosea's disdain for kingship. Note the imagery of stillbirth in verse 13:13, and the use of Sheol in 13:14 to symbolize the mercy of annihilation. Verse 13:16 is a brutal prediction of how Israel will be punished.

The final chapter of the book of Hosea, however, looks beyond punishment or judgment to a better future. If Israel would heed the Lord's call and return, it could find genuine religion and healing (verse 14:4). The Lord will moisten the people and make it flower. The conclusion stresses true worship, which the final verse, Hosea 14:9, equates with the wisdom to walk uprightly in the ways of the Lord (a central theme of the sapiential literature).

The book of Hosea clearly presupposes the situation of threat from Assyria, skepticism about Israelite kingship and dabbling in power politics, a history of hankering after the fertility gods of the nations, and a sense that the inmost vocation of the people is to marital fidelity to the Lord. The Lord is understood to be both punishing, on the model of a parental disciplinarian, and loving beyond the people's deserts. We do not find the strict, Deuteronomistic slant on the covenant but rather a perception of the love, even the vulnerability, from which God's choice and provision for Israel spring. Hosea himself was the only literary prophet native to the North (where anti-establishment prophecy began with Elijah), and so, presumably, the only one fully involved, emotionally, in the Assyrian threats to Israel. The final redactors of the text clearly knew of the fall of Israel and the sufferings wrought by Assyria. As the very last verse (14:9) suggests, they had some desire to draw out the lessons, the potential wisdom, that the prophet was reading in his times. The viewpoint of both Hosea himself and his later disciples apparently was that Israel should have known better, and this assumed as generally accepted a judgment that Israel had not lived up to the grace offered it by the Lord.

The book of Hosea was written to express and preserve these judgments and no doubt as well to communicate the poetic depths and creativity that reflection on the Lord's emotional bonds with the people could reveal. Hosea is unsurpassed at imagining the hurt and tenderness of the Lord, and this anthropomorphism, instructively, brings us some of the most provocative theology. The knowledge of God that the people lack is like the knowledge between Adam and Eve: sexual, whole, necessary to life and fertility. The many other figures of the book often deal in fertility/sterility, flourishing/withering, and the like. God is variously a spouse, a father, a mother (Hosea 11:8), and by implication a tiller and ruler who would have things go better for his charge. The priests and prophets who are castigated should have been the teachers of Israel, and their failure means that even the elite of Israel have not known the Lord. The seductions of the surrounding nations — religious, military, and cultural — have proved stronger than the weakness, the itchy adulterousness, mottling the people's heart. The book of Hosea was written to express the counter-imagery and counter-vision that might give Israel both a shock into repentance and a reason to hope that its return to the Lord would revive it.

The lasting significance of Hosea, beyond doubt, attaches to its marital symbolism and central theme of intimate knowledge of God. We have reflected on this theme previously, and so need not belabor it here. Because Hosea is the most explicit and moving of the prophetic depicters of Israel's marriage with the Lord, this book has a certain pride of place among the resources for appreciating the romantic, even vulnerable, love of the divinity for its wayward, flawed creature called "humanity." Hosea bears, with Jeremiah and Ezekiel, some responsibility for stigmatizing femininity as the symbol of unfaithful humankind, but in his case the marital symbolism rather quickly shows itself more positive than negative. Hosea leaves no doubt that the Lord loves humankind almost despite himself, and that nothing it (we) can do will ever fully destroy that love.

JOEL

The short book of Joel is an historical puzzle, as we see later. In the Hebrew text it has four chapters, but the English text, following the arrangement of the Septuagint, combines chapters 2 and 3 of the Hebrew and so has only three chapters. Chapter 1 focuses on a plague of locusts, chapter 2 focuses on the day of the Lord as judgment on Judah, and chapter 3 focuses on the day of the Lord as judgment on the enemies of Judah.[4]

Chapter 1 begins with the formulaic "word of the Lord." There are several

Joels in the Hebrew Bible, and we know nothing about the Pethuel who fathered this one. Verses 1:2–3 assert the uniqueness of the event that the prophet is going to contemplate. In verse 1:4 we learn that this event was a devastating plague of locusts. Most likely this was an historical occurrence, but clearly the prophet also saw it as a harbinger of the wider destruction coming with the day of the Lord. Many readers probably thought of the plagues with which the Lord afflicted Egypt prior to the Exodus. The "nation" described in verses 1:5–7 is probably the horde of locusts. Those lulled by drink should be shocked awake. That priests and farmers alike should mourn suggests both the extent of the agricultural tragedy[5] and the overall cultural depression it might symbolize. The withholding of cereal and drink from the house of the Lord (there were no materials with which to offer sacrifice) suggests both the prophet's interest in the Temple (many commentators consider him to have been a priest) and a criticism of the Lord: For having allowed the plague he will see his cult diminish. In verse 1:15 the prophet makes his main transition: This plague prefigures the day of the Lord that will wreak more wide-spread punishment upon Judah. The last verses of the chapter make the natural devastations occasion for crying to the Lord for help (if not also to confess the misdeeds that the plague could be punishing).

Chapter 2 concentrates on the coming day of judgment itself. Note the theophanous imagery of dark, thick clouds. Verse 2:2 still seems to have in mind the "people" of the locusts, although other earthly or spiritual enemies may be symbolized. Verse 2:3 effectively describes the result of the locusts' march: What was fertile, even Edenic, before them stands desolate in their wake. Verses 2:4–5 liken the insects to an enemy's advancing in the gear of battle. The prophet is impressed by the orderliness and efficiency of this natural wrecking crew. Verses 2:10–11 associate the Lord with this army, suggesting the familiar theme that everything that happens in nature or history finally serves the divine purposes. These purposes stand clear in verses 2:12–13: the return or repentance of the people. Note the call to rend hearts rather than garments, which recalls the interiorization of the covenant in Jeremiah and Ezekiel. Verse 2:13 beautifully transmits the center of the prophetic theology: The Lord is gracious and merciful, slow to anger, and abounding in steadfast love (see also Exodus 34:6). In Joel 2:14 the carrot is held out: The Lord might himself repent of the evil he is allowing to afflict Judah, if the people rend their hearts. What this might mean is sketched in verses 2:15–17: fasting, religious assembly, and rededication of all ranks of Jewish society. The happy result is described in the rest of the chapter: The Lord will free the people of their enemies and restore the prosperity of the land. This will be an assurance of the Lord's presence among his people again. Joel 2:28–29 comprise a famous passage in which the prophetic spirit is universalized, as a sign of the abundance of blessings that the positive side or aftermath of the day of the Lord will bring. Note the evenhandedness of the distribution of the spirit: Women share along with men. Verses 2:30–32, completing the description of what the day of the Lord will mean for Judah, speaks of both portents of doom and sure deliverance.

Chapter 3 depicts the judgment on the nations, and the related benefits for Judah, that the day of the Lord will entail. Note the implications of a diaspora or scattering of Jewish people in verses 3:2–3, as well as the indications of the servitude (prostitution) that conquest could entail. Israel's neighbors are castigated for selling Jerusalem to the Greeks. (Gentiles? Some commentators take this to indicate a very late postexilic date of composition.) Joel 3:10 reverses the figure of Isaiah 2:4 and has the future portending war rather than peace. The previous images of natural devastation are replaced in verse 3:13 by naturalistic symbols of how wickedness has flourished. Note the dwelling of the Lord on Mount Zion in Jerusalem in verses 3:16–17. By this period Zion had become the parallel of Sinai as the place where the Lord centered Israelite life.[6] The chapter and book conclude with pictures of Judah flourishing, but its enemies, such as Egypt and Edom, growing desolate. Joel 3:21, the last verse, associates divine vengeance for harm done to Judah with the Lord's inhabiting Zion.

The book of Joel presupposes a situation after the Exile, when the Temple has been rebuilt (after 515 B.C.E.). Most commentators therefore favor a date between 500 and 450. We know nothing about a dramatic plague of locusts in that period. The references to the enemies of Judah are not very clear either. Judah was under Persian dominance until the last part of the fourth century, when Alexander the Great won control for Greece. The references to the priests and the sacrifices of the Temple suggest that Joel was familiar with a functioning cult at the Temple in Jerusalem. The prominence given to Mount Zion dovetails with this note, suggesting a time when Judah again could think of itself as fairly well resettled in its privilege as the special locale of the Lord. Apart from these historical intimations, the text assumes the usual fertility of the land, the prophetic imagery associated with the day of the Lord, and the traditional reference of whatever happened to the will and judgment of the Lord.

The book of Joel was probably written and entered in the canonical lists because it supplemented other prophetic treatments of the pattern or rhythm of divine judgment and restoration. The plague of locusts could stand symbolic duty for natural or cultural disaster generally. The prophet does not dwell very much on the people's sins, in contrast to forebears of his whom we have studied, but he does vividly portray the judgments of the Lord and eloquently call for conversion back to the Lord's graciousness. His vision of the day when the prophetic spirit would be poured forth on all flesh entered the treasury of images for the day of messianic fulfillment. Note in Acts 2:16–21 that the interpretation of Pentecost put in the mouth of Peter explicitly depends on this passage from Joel.

Joel does not have any obviously special lasting significance. Without the book we would not have this passage on universal prophesying, nor the references to the plague of locusts, but certainly we would have from the other prophets most of the book's gist. Probably we should best consider Joel to be another (very significant) indication that Israel continually experienced people of charismatic gifts interpreting the signs of its times as a call for both repentance and hopeful renewal.

AMOS

Amos of Tekoa has the honor of being considered the first of the prophets a number of whose oracles were preserved in written form. Although he came from Judah, Amos worked in Israel around 750 B.C.E., during the reign of Jeroboam II, a time of considerable prosperity. Scholars debate the best division of the book of Amos. We treat chapters 1 and 2 as dominated by oracles against the neighbors of Israel, chapters 3–6 as indictments of Israel itself (note that these chapters are also united by such catch words as "hear" and "woe"), and chapters 7–9 as featuring the prophet's dismal visions.[7]

The opening verses of chapter 1 identify Amos as a shepherd from Tekoa who received a threatening word from the Lord against Israel in the days of Jeroboam. Note in verse 1:2 that Zion and Jerusalem have become the accepted dwelling of the Lord. The first foreign locale set aside for coming punishment is Damascus, which will suffer for its ill-treatment of Gilead (northeastern Israel). Similarly Gaza, Asdod, Ekron, the remnant of Philistia, Tyre, and other foreign nations will receive punishments well merited by their ill-treatments, presumably of Israel (see verse 1:13). Although these nations should have lived in peace with the Israelites who were like their kin, they behaved violently. Amos, typically, describes their fate in vigorous imagery.

We should note that all the nations listed prior to Judah are condemned for international crimes and brutalities, whereas Judah and (especially) Israel are judged for their social sins. The "oracles against the nations" here become a dramatic litany, as the nations surrounding Israel are condemned. But just as the Israelites might be cheering at these attacks on their enemies, Amos turns his sword against his own people and levels any pretensions they might have to innocence.

Chapter 2 denounces Moab for outrages against the king of Edom, making it clear that the Lord demands justice of the nations. Judah, too, comes under the divine wrath, being subjected to the same formula, "for three transgressions . . . and for four, I will not revoke the punishment." In other words, the people have done sufficient evil to have put themselves irremovably in the path of divine vengeance. Note that Judah is denounced for having violated the statutes of Torah (verse 2:4). Amos 2:6–8 turn the spotlight on Israel, discovering harshness toward the righteous, the needy, the poor, and the afflicted, much of it for the sake of profit. Amos has few betters among the prophets when it comes to anger at social injustice. Note that verses 2:7–8 equate idolatrous worship and debauchery in a spirit of incest. Verses 2:9–10 are a reminder of what the Lord had done for Israel in the Exodus and the Conquest, and 2:11 seems to make the raising up of prophets and Nazirites a special favor from the Lord. But Israel perverted this favor, and so days are coming when even the stoutest of heart will try to flee.

The indictment of Israel previously interspersed with indictments of the nations (2:4–16) continues apace in chapters 3–6. Note in verse 3:2 the prophet's expression of Israel's unique election, with the implication that it should have offered unique fidelity. The images of Amos 3:3–6 build a picture of consequence: When affairs get to a certain state, certain results are sure to follow. Verse 3:7 is a famous line that expresses Amos's conviction that the prophets serve Israel as God's means of announcing his purposes. Verse 3:8 likens the word of the Lord to the roar of a lion, and the fear of the lion's roar to the prophets' inevitable necessity to announce the divine roar.[8] In verse 3:10 we catch a glimpse of the familiar prophetic theme that the people have become morally stupid, not knowing how to do right (not knowing the Lord). Verse 3:11 would have struck later readers as a prediction of the fall of Israel that occurred in 721. Verse 3:12 rather dramatically pictures the rescue of only a remnant. Amos is remarkably given to images of devouring lions, as though he had a fierce, hunter's imagination. The end of the chapter leaves no doubt that the prophet is promising harsh punishment for Israel. In a time of peace and prosperity, this must have been an irksome message.

In chapter 4 the imagery becomes, if anything, more offensive. The women of Israel hardly would have been pleased to be described as oppressive cows.[9] Note that the evil inciting the prophet's wrath is crushing the needy. Amos 4:3–4 mock, almost satirize, the insincere cult of Israel, and 4:6–8 paint Israel as an ingrate, unappreciative that its blessings were gifts from the Lord. On the other hand, misfortune also did not bring the people back to the Lord. Amos seems to be playing both sides of the theology we have associated with Deuteronomy, asking the people to join blessings to gratitude and to make curses an occasion of conversion. Whether the woes pictured in verses 4:10–11 are symbolic or reflect later sufferings, perhaps during the fall of Israel, is uncertain. The "prepare to meet your God" of verse 4:12 is nothing pleasant to contemplate. Most commentators consider the hymnic verse 4:13 a late addition. It is reminiscent of the psalms that deal with creation, and also of sapiential piety. Note the similarity to Amos 5:8–9 and Amos 9:5–6.

Chapter 5 assures the fall of Israel and Israel's grim diminishment. Verse 5:2 is a funeral song, applied to the nation as a whole. The prophet's overall message could not be clearer than verse 5:4: "Seek me [God] and live." This is repeated in verse 5:6, and only a little reflection is needed to make us realize that the God of Amos is nothing if not vital, powerful, the sole source of energetic being. Verse 5:7 is a vintage piece of the prophet's wrath at injustice. Verses 5:8–9, as noted earlier, move in the hymnic and sapiential train of verse 4:13, showing deep appreciation for the Creator. Indeed, we might conjecture that they come from a time after Second Isaiah, when the radical depths of monotheism had been well probed. Verse 5:10 contains this prophet's version of the frequent prophetic theme that bearing forth the word of the Lord only brings one contempt. The prudence suggested in verse 5:13 sounds like a wisdom that Amos himself never would have been able to practice. Indeed, the social evils described in verses 5:11–12 make it seem inevitable that a genuine prophet would be hated by all who sat atop ill-gotten riches. Verses 5:14–15 comprise a biblical version of the most fundamental ethical precept: Do good, and avoid evil. The peculiarly biblical intonation is the ring "that you may live" (with the living God). The wailing described in verses 5:16–17 coalesces into judgment in verses 5:18–20, which are perhaps the classical interpretation of the day of the Lord as a time when injustice will receive severe punishment. Note the vigor of verse 5:19, and the overall motif of darkness and gloom. Amos 5:21 is one of the strongest denunciations of false cult in the Bible. The image in verse 5:24 concluding the diatribe is deservedly famous. In place of cult the God of Amos wants justice to "roll down like waters, and righteousness like an ever-flowing stream." The generally arid geography of Israel only made this image the more powerful. (Recall Hosea 6:6: steadfast love [or mercy] rather than sacrifice.) Amos 5:25, focused on idolatrous cult, further distances Amos from priestly religion.

In Amos 6:1 we catch reflections of the indolence and self-satisfaction that Israel was enjoying in Amos's time. The implication of verse 6:2 is that nations more prosperous than Israel have tumbled and should be an object lesson. Verses 6:3–7 intimate the luxury that certain classes of Israelites were enjoying, apparently while neglecting concern for others who were suffering. Amos foresees grim punishment coming upon this injustice. Note in verse 6:12 the naturalistic figures used to convey the distortion involved in perverting social justice.

Chapter 7 begins to describe the prophet's visions. Note the formulaic pattern in the first two: Amos sees a woe to come, intercedes for Jacob, and wins exemption. Locusts and fire add to Amos's reputation for strong imagery, and the plaintive "He is so small" introduces a new, rather mothering note. The figure of the plumb line in verses 7:7–8 is meant to suggest that Israel is warped in its foundations. The confrontation between Amos and the priest Amaziah suggests the opposition that the prophet received. Verse 7:10 suggests the weightiness of the prophetic word, oppressing the land. In verse 7:14 Amos argues that his prophecy lies out of his hands: He has no choice but to deliver the word the Lord unexpectedly gave him. We see, then, that in the time of Amos prophecy was far from institutionalized. The response Amos gives Amaziah is in keeping with the testy character we have seen thus far: He increases the intensity of his denunciations and predictions of coming punishment. Whether the prediction in verse 7:17 is meant for Amaziah himself or, more likely, for Israel as a whole, it is insulting as well as frightful.

Chapter 8 opens with a vision reminiscent of Jeremiah's baskets of figs (Jeremiah 24:1–3). The prophet, we may say, sees the world through God's eye and so finds everyday objects revelatory. The symbolism seems to be that Israel is like ripe, summer fruit, come to term and sure to decline. Verses 8:4–6 are another vivid picture of the injustice that caused Amos's wrath to flame. The merchants resent the holy days and can hardly wait to get back to their profiteering. Note in verse 8:9 the familiar figure of darkness approaching. Ritual mourning will be the only suitable response to the woes the Lord's justice will entail. The famine of hearing the words of the Lord predicted in verses 8:11–12 is more serious than threats to crops: God will stop giving Israel what it needs to be his people.

The vision of Amos 9:1 may be an ironic contrast with the false priestly religion that Amos has been castigating: When you see the Lord at the altar, you will find him full of fury. Verses 9:2–4 are a peculiar expression of the Creator's omnipotence: No place can hide those whom he pursues to punish. Verses 9:5–6 are another hymnic interlude, setting the prophet's diatribe in the context of the serene governance of the Creator. Verses 9:7–8 carry double dosage: Israel is as much subject to the divine power as other nations are, and because of its injustices Israel has failed to honor its distinction as God's especially responsible people. Note, though, that verse 9:8 promises the preservation of at least a portion of Jacob. The shaking of the sieve in verse 9:9 is an effective image for judgment. Sinners will find their confidence of avoiding a reckoning ill-placed. The last verses of the book are so positive, and therefore so great a contrast with most of the foregoing prophecies, that many commentators consider them a later addition.[10] The imagery is quite agricultural, which fits the outlook of Amos well enough, but we might expect animals rather than vines to carry the message. At any rate, the canonical Amos foresees blessing and restoration on the other side of the tunnel of the harsh judgments to come, and therefore he fits the general profile of the writing prophets, which always makes the creativity and restorative love of the Lord greater than either Israel's sins or the Lord's own wrath.

The book of Amos presupposes the social conditions of the reign of Jeroboam II, when Israel was enjoying an interlude of significant prosperity. Assyria certainly was on the horizon as a threatening presence, but the punishments that Amos predicts seem more the nearly inevitable consequence of the injustices rife in the land than the probable result of political or military incursions by powerful enemies from without. The prophet definitely assumes a general understanding of the relationship between the Lord and Israel that makes social justice obligatory. As well, he assumes that those who claim to have received the word of the Lord have an inalienable commission to preach it. The mood of the book fits a time, prior to subjugation by foreign powers, when the glow of the Kingdom of David and Solomon still lingered. Although North and South had separated, neither Israel nor Judah had yet fallen.

The book of Amos was written and edited into its present shape mainly to retain the vigorous, trenchant critique of injustice that the prophet had developed. His main target is the rich and powerful who gouge the poor. The oracles describing the punishments to come upon Israel because of its religious failings outweigh the descriptions of injustice, but when we ask why Amos prophesied such punishments, and why the canonical editors thought his prophesies a revelation of the divine instruction worth considering permanently regulative, the descriptions of injustice stand forth. To their great credit, Judah and Israel developed a theology that demanded more of their people, and ultimately more of all people, than what was standard among the nations of its time. Prickly, crusty Amos contributed significantly to this theology, serving all later generations as a strict father figure.

The lasting significance of Amos derives from these characteristics. For our characterization of the biblical God, Amos supplies perhaps the most biting descriptions of the Lord's insistence that people treat one another fairly, humanely, kindly. Having read Amos, we could never in good conscience subordinate people to profits or efficiency. Two dozen centuries before Kant, Amos had the conviction that genuine ethics always depends on treating people as ends rather than means. The Israel of his time thought it was enjoying the blessings of God-given prosperity. Amos slashed at that complacency, because the people had blinded themselves to the toll such "prosperity" was exacting from the poor. The Puritan reading of history that equated prosperity with election by God had some foundation in the Deuteronomistic theology, but it must have shielded its eyes from the vision of Amos of Tekoa. For Amos, no election was valid unless justice rolled down like waters and righteousness cascaded like an ever-flowing stream.

Overall, Amos furnishes us a remarkable portrait of the severity and unimpeachable integrity that those who would speak for God ought to present. Unlike Jeremiah and Ezekiel, Amos does not bemoan the costs of his vocation. A simple, straightforward man, he lives by a logic of one-two-three: God gave me a word, I spoke it, what happened happened. It may be that Amos enjoys being a curmudgeon, delivering a word harsh and full of woe. But that is secondary. First is the fact that God has sent him to denounce injustice, and he has fulfilled his commission. The rest is epilogue, out of his hands and anticlimactic.

OBADIAH

The book of Obadiah, only twenty-one verses long, is the shortest in the Hebrew Bible. We know nothing about the author, but the focus on Edom suggests a time shortly after Edom's participation in the sack of Jerusalem (586 B.C.E.). In three brief movements, the book describes the destruction of Edom (verses 1–9), the sins of Edom against Israel (verses 10–14), and the restoration of Israel (verses 15–21).

Verses 1–6 echo Jeremiah 49. Obadiah is described as both a visionary and one bearing the word of God. He first sees the destruction of Edom, which in fact occurred in the fifth century B.C.E. Note the main motif: Pride that flew aloft will crash down to Earth. Verse 6 considers Edom the offspring of Esau, which explains the bitterness Israel felt: It had been pillaged by kinfolk. The not-understanding of verse 7 seems rhetorical: What rot or injustice caused allies to turn against Edom? Israel knows full well.

Verses 10–14 make this plain. Esau did violence to Jacob, so its fall will be fully just. The prophet seems oblivious to the ambiguity that attends all the relations between Jacob and Esau in Genesis. By his time these kinfolk shared a geographical context among the nations that underscored what they had in common. The litany of the offenses of Edom is negative: such things a cousin should not have done. Most of them suggest a desire to please foreigners, and share in foreigners' spoils, although certainly Edom's gloating at the fall of Judah (verses 12,13) is also a bitter memory.

Verses 15–21 predict a change of events, such that Israel will again flourish and those who punished her will come crashing down. Note the references to Mount Zion in verses 16–17, and the figure of drunkenness (spiritual mindlessness). Verse 18 foresees Jacob's flaming up in renewed prosperity. In the process it will burn Edom like stubble. The final verses of Obadiah gladly contemplate the fall of Edom, as the nations rumble in to possess that land. Verse 21 concludes the short book by strongly affirming that rule and salvation completely belong to the Lord of Israel.

The book of Obadiah presupposes the vivid memory of a recent fall of Judah and Judah's mistreatment by Edom. As we noted, this best fits the historical situation shortly after the fall of Judah in 586. However, final redactions of the text may have occurred after the return from Exile, when the positive prophecies would have seemed amply fulfilled.

The book of Obadiah was probably written to preserve the memory of betrayal by Edom, and to add to the store of oracles and warnings that bore on the fall of Israel, Judah, and various nations. Obadiah is like Ezekiel in stressing the pride of the nations that the Lord will bring low. The fundamental theological insight that rules this book is the fragility of all political or military power, which is as nothing (verse 16) compared to the power of the Lord. Only the power of the Lord is trustworthy, and Israel is favored for having its identity rooted in a covenant with that power.

Obadiah has no unique lasting significance. Like Joel, it mainly exemplifies prophetic themes that others have displayed more fully and profoundly. The bitterness and hurt that the condemnations of Edom express are distinctive, although not unique in biblical literature. They suggest that Israel long maintained its sense of clan and so its expectations of clannish loyalty. We could say, then, that, like Amos, Obadiah is most interested in social justice, in this case the justice that ought to obtain between groups that shared a common lineage. Were we to generalize such an interest it no doubt would lose the intensity that clannish emotions tend to have, but it would suggest that, in the eyes of God, all peoples have the responsibility to treat others decently and sympathetically, because all peoples are subject to the same God and ultimately to the same mortality and vulnerability.

Trees in Bethel, an important city of the Northern Kingdom.   *(Used with permission of the photographer, Wolfgang Roth)*

JONAH

The book of Jonah is unique among the writings attributed to the prophets in that it is less a collection of oracles than a parable[11] or a short story.[12] The historical personage to whom the story is attached seems to be a prophet who worked in the eighth century B.C.E. and, according to 2 Kings 14:25, counseled King Jeroboam II (786–746). The book itself, however, better fits a postexilic situation, such as the middle of the fifth century B.C.E., when Israel's relations to the Gentiles was a subject of considerable debate. Scholars also debate the rhythm of the four chapters, but we can note that chapters 1 and 3 focus on the prophet's relations with the Gentiles, and that chapters 2 and 4 focus on his relations with the Lord.

Verse 1:2 gives Jonah a divine commission to preach to Nineveh, in Assyria, and call its pagan people to repent. This is somewhat unusual, because Israel's prophets preach only to Israel; even their oracles against the nations are addressed to an Israelite audience. Equally unusual is the prophet's response: He flees from this assignment upon the sea. No one can escape the will of God, however, so in verse 1:4 we find the Lord's pursuing Jonah through storm (a traditional imagery for the divine power, but one usually set over land). Note in verse 1:5 the indication that the sailors were poor pagans trusting in useless idols—reason for both the Lord and the reader to take pity on them. Verse 1:6 implies that the captain thought of Jonah as just another passenger and was irritated that he did not join the others and petition his god (that is, help them try anything that might work). When the casting of lots points to Jonah (and therefore serves the Lord's truth), the fear that comes over all the crew expresses a general religiosity: It is dangerous to be on the outs with the divine. (Although in verse 1:9 Jonah formulaically says that he fears the Lord, his actions belie his words. The sailors, in contrast, pray fervently to the Lord—in verse 1:14—and the narrator confirms their sincerity in verse 1:16.) Jonah seems to accept his fate and rather gallantly urges the crew to throw him overboard. Note that they only do this after having tried to row back to land and failed. Jonah splashes into the sea (there is no reason not to think that the biblical writers meant us to enjoy their story). The fish that swallows him up no doubt suggested Leviathan, the great beast of the depths, who now is put into service by the Lord. At this point the story clearly has become legendary, and all attempts to deal with it literally run the danger of badly misconstruing it.

Chapter 2 begins with Jonah's praying to the Lord from the belly of the big fish—an amusing *mis en scène*. Note that his prayer is confident, and that it assimilates his situation to death, the belly of Sheol. It could thus serve individuals as a model for prayer in dark times. (This portion of Jonah is like a psalm.) The core of the negativity is expressed in verse 2:4: being cast out of the divine presence, which the prophet interestingly immediately associates with the Temple. Jonah promises thanksgiving for the deliverance he has received. The Lord has the great fish vomit Jonah out onto dry land—another quite amusing picture, and a rather ambiguous response to his prayer.[13]

In chapter 3 the Lord again commands Jonah to preach to Nineveh, and this time Jonah obeys quickly. At his first preaching the people of Nineveh repent (more indication that many pagans were well disposed). Even the king and the beasts do penance (everything is exaggerated in this book), hoping that their repentance from sin will bring the Lord to repent of the punishments he has in store for them (an interesting mirroring or parallelism). God is in fact converted from the punishment he has in store, testifying to the truth of Ezekiel that the Lord delights in people's life rather than in punishing them to death.[14]

The book of Jonah becomes most interesting in chapter 4, where the response of the prophet is described with an artistic brevity and a biting wit. Jonah grumbles to God, muttering that, from the beginning, when he first objected to his mission to Nineveh, he knew that something like the conversion of the Ninevites would occur. His description of God in verse 4:2 is the standard praise (Exodus 34:6–7) that stresses the divine ḥesed or steadfast enduring love (another formula). That the Lord's show of this better divine nature to pagan Nineveh so greatly displeases the prophet—he asks God to take his life—may be a satiric commentary on the harshness that the prophetic personality in general, or the reforms going ahead in postexilic Judah in particular, could show. These reforms wanted to separate Jews from Gentiles as much as possible, and they risked compromising the status of the Lord as God of all peoples. Note the divine response in verse 4:4: The Lord rather gently questions the prophet whether his anger is justified and becoming. In a sulk, Jonah goes outside Nineveh, obtains some shade, and waits to see what will happen.

The touch of the shade plant is more mischief on the part of the authors and the God they want to praise. God is out to teach Jonah a gentle lesson. Once again Jonah wants to die, this time to escape the heat. Again God questions the prophet—now he would throw his life away in pique over a plant? Like a small child, face wrinkled up in a stubborn pout, Jonah affirms that he is certainly right to be angry, but we know that he knows that he is acting badly. Verse 4:10 expresses the bottom line of which the Bible so frequently reminds us: God makes all that lives, and no creature finally has any rights against God (except those that God graciously grants), because all creatures are sprung from nothingness. The last verse of the book carries the punch line: Is not the Lord indeed a God of graciousness and pity, thinking kindly of the poor, dumb creatures he has made and always hoping to give them mercy?

The book of Jonah presupposes that Assyria is the feared, perhaps hated, enemy of Israel, who conquered Israel in 721 B.C.E. As well, it presupposes a balanced view of God's relations with both Israel and the nations: Although he is uniquely covenanted to Israel, the Lord remains the Creator of all. Finally, the book presupposes some debate or controversy about the status that the nations should have in Israel's eyes. Jonah does not develop any extensive critique of Assyria, but we get the impression that he stands for those who considered the nations unclean, pure and simple. In resenting the nature of the Lord to be gracious and merciful, Jonah stands for all people who want a "justice" less than what divinity wants. Like the book of Ruth, the book of Jonah therefore opposes ethnocentrism and xenophobia (which were dangers in the postexilic era). The parallel between Jonah and the elder son of the parable of the prodigal son (Luke 15:11–32) is quite striking.

The book of Jonah was written to present these issues in entertaining, provocative garb. The author wished to show the Lord of Israel to be precisely as Exodus 34:6–7 had proclaimed. The Lord may command Jonah to preach a word that the prophet dislikes, and he may create the storm that occasions the descent into the belly of the big fish, but throughout he is a God who preserves human life (that of the crew, Jonah, and Nineveh). Indeed, in the final analysis he is a gentle God, playing with Jonah and teaching him by dexterous questions and the cameo episode of the shade plant that the Lord loves all his creatures.

The lasting significance of Jonah is greater than its brevity suggests. First, it is one of several striking testimonies to the humor of the authors of the Hebrew Bible, and so to the finally comic view that they have of the human situation. In the final analysis, human beings tend to be a rather dim, stubborn, childish lot, and the best stance to take toward this fact is laughter. The Bible does not blink at the evil that human beings can do, but it defangs much of such evil by introducing a God slow to anger and abounding in steadfast love. In this parable, God is a patient parent, waiting for his immature child to grow up. Second, when we reflect on the human condition, as time after time and place after place display it, God is often put in precisely this position. Either the divine mystery, the ultimate norm and judge, laughs at our human follies and pityingly devises ways to clean up our messes, or it writes us off as too stupid to be borne. The majority of the prophets exhibit the divine impatience and anger. The book of Jonah, in contrast, shows a kindlier, more hopeful possibility: God gently, smilingly nudges us along, making us do what we should, feel what we should, more frequently than we initially like. Philosophers can debate the final pros and cons of the comic and tragic understandings of human existence. Psychologists (in the broad sense of those concerned with mental health) tend to realize that humor is healing, and that thinking about human foibles as the God of Jonah does is both the part of sanity and a strong component in the ability to enjoy human time.[15]

MICAH

The book of Micah takes us back to the oracular style that is the predominant literary characteristic of the minor prophets. The historical personage round whom these oracles have been gathered worked in Judah during the reign of Hezekiah, toward the end of the eighth century B.C.E. As we see, however, later editors of the postexilic period may have added some of the materials. The book divides into two unequal sections. Chapters 1–5 focus on Samaria and Jerusalem, the capital cities of North and South, predicting first punishments and then restoration. Chapters 6–7, reminiscent of Hosea, amount to a trial of Israel by God that first announces judgment and then holds out hopes for restoration.

Verse 1:1 locates Micah as from Moresheth, about twenty-five miles southwest of Jerusalem, and working during the reigns of the southern kings Jotham, Ahaz, and Hezekiah (742–687). Generally, Micah is considered to have been a younger contemporary of Isaiah. Jeremiah 26:18 places him in Jerusalem during the reign of Hezekiah (715–687) and notes his prophecy that Jerusalem would become a heap of ruins. In the oracles that Micah derives from the divine word given him the Lord comes from his Temple to render judgment on the mountains (that housed idolatrous worship). Note that Micah 1:5 makes Samaria the sin of Israel and Jerusalem the sin of Judah. The idols of Samaria will be stripped and laid waste, and the evil (the punishing judgment) of the Lord will roll to the gates of Jerusalem. Verse 1:16 concludes the vision of fallen cities by having Jerusalem mourn like a mother for her lost children.[16]

In chapter 2 the wickedness that first draws the prophet's ire is social injustice: taking others' land. The taunt of Micah 2:4 is an ironic song, put in the mouth of Israel's oppressors, that reverses the unjust state of affairs and takes Israel's land (or privilege from God) away. In verse 2:7 the prophet defends himself and God, on the grounds that those who are just need not fear the Lord's judgments. Injustice and (ritual or moral) uncleanness dominate the next verses, and in verse 2:11 Micah sketches the kind of prophet the people would like to have: an utterer of wind and lies, an advocate of wine and strong drink. Verses 2:12–13, however, seem to describe a restoration of Jacob, after the flock has been scattered by conquest.

Micah 3:1–3, a slashing criticism of the rulers and leaders, accuse them of devouring the people by their injustices. The Lord will turn a deaf ear when such leaders cry out for help. (Micah is probably envisioning conquest by Assyria, which had taken over Damascus in 731/732 and was threatening Samaria or the North, and also Judah, thereafter.) The prophets criticized in verse 3:5 are time-servers, supporting whoever feeds them. Because of this they shall lose all vision of the divine. Verse 3:8, contrasting Micah himself with these false prophets, seems boastful, but it indicates the confidence that genuine convictions about the word of the Lord could give. The concluding verses of chapter 3 detail more species of injustice and corruption, and imply (in verse 3:11) that such behavior removes any basis for trusting in the Lord's favor. Note that Micah 3:12 squares with what Jeremiah 26:18 reports about the preaching of Micah.

With chapter 4 the mood changes, however, and Jerusalem receives happier oracles. Note the imagery of the mountain (Zion) raised up and become a drawing card for the nations. There one will find the law (Torah) of the Lord, and so guidance on the path that pleases God. Verse 4:3 has the familiar Isaianic figure of swords beaten into plowshares; in fact, Micah 4:1–3 exactly reproduce Isaiah 2:2–4. Verse 4:4 has a nice image for peace. Verse 4:5 reminds us that "walk," active moving toward the Lord or in the ways of the Lord, was a very common metaphor for religious existence. Perhaps the lame remnant of Micah 4:6 come to mind as the group that wanted to walk but could not. As with many oracles of restoration, a certain paradox or overturning of past and worldly ways intrigues the prophet's mind. Verses 9–10 may be late additions, because they would better fit the sixth century, when Judah was facing punishment by Babylon. Verse 4:12 recalls Second Isaiah (55:8–11) on the transcendence of the divine thoughts. In Micah 4:13 the people are like the heifer of Hosea 4:11, but here their threshing will mean the defeat of their enemies.

Micah 5:1 (4:14 in the Hebrew) recalls the siege of Jerusalem described with dread by Jeremiah and Ezekiel. Verses 5:2–3 have a messianic ring, and the ruler from Bethlehem fits the profile of David. The travail of the people or the land that restoration will end could later be read as either the sufferings of the North or the exile of Judah. Current commentary on this section of Micah tends to stress the Davidic imagery,[17] but in fact it simply is not clear what the seven shepherds and eight princes (in verse 5:5) symbolize. Perhaps we simply have the familiar poetic pattern of X and X + 1 (see, for example, Amos, chapters 1 and 2). The main point, however, is clear: The prophet wants to cheer Judah with assurances that the Lord will deliver it from Assyria. Verses 5:10–15 describe the purifications that will accompany such deliverance.

In chapter 6, as we noted, the opening motif is of a legal contest. Verse 6:3 is a ringing challenge to the people to find fault with their God and has been taken into the Christian liturgy for Good Friday. The Lord lists all the good things done for the people and by implication asks why such grace has been answered only with the abuses of idolatry and injustice. Verses 6:6–8 imagine the response that proper religion would make: not sacrifices (including human children), but ethical performance from the heart: "to do justice, and to love kindness, and to walk humbly with your God." (Micah 6:8 rivals the best summaries of Amos and the major prophets on the heart of the religious matter.) Verse 6:9 bears overtones of the wisdom literature: rightful fear of the Lord. Verses 6:9–16 list the flaws of Judah in a manner reminiscent of many other prophets: unjust deals and false cult. Note in verses 6:14–15 the message that this sort of immorality is parasitic on the people's genuine spiritual life: They eat and get no nourishment, sow but do not reap.

The images of fecklessness continue in chapter 7: Harvest has passed Israel by. Virtue has fled the land, and the worst predications of the prophetic watchmen (verse 7:4) have come true. Note in verses 7:5–6 the strong depiction of distrust. Micah sees no familial confidence, no friendship, the breakdown of the most intimate relationships upon which human stability and joy depend. The conclusion of this description, however, is not despair but pivoting to the Lord, who by contrast is completely trustworthy. Here again we catch overtones of the later wisdom literature, which made the unreliability of human beings cause for relying completely on God.[18]

With verse 7:7 the mood shifts and the oracles promise deliverance. Verses

Bethlehem in the morning mist. *(Used with permission of the photographer, Wolfgang Roth)*

7:8–9, in fact, make the phase of suffering like a necessary prelude to bright deliverance. The prophet expresses a willingness to suffer, if that be the price exacted by the justice of God for the deliverance to come. Verse 7:10 is not admirable, gloating over the fall of enemies who enjoyed Israel's apparent desertion by God, but it is very human. Verses 7:11–12 could be read as bearing on the reconstruction of Jerusalem. The following verses make the restoration of Judah cause for the nations to wonder and shrivel their pride. Micah 7:18 is a striking praise for the Lord's tendency to forgive transgressions, as though that were unique among the gods of the Earth, and the final portion of the verse shows that in the background is the theology of Exodus 34:6–7 that we found central in Jonah 4. In Micah 7:19 God treads iniquities, rather than sinners, underfoot, and the book of Micah ends with a firm profession of faith in the fidelity of the Lord of the covenant.

The book of Micah presupposes threats from foreign nations, as so many other prophetic books do. Often its references are obscure, but it certainly depends on the conviction that Israel was covenanted to the Lord, could expect punishment for its sins, and had a God finally more gracious than punitive. Christian commentators have tended to stress the messianic possibilities of Micah 5:3–5, referring them to the birth of Jesus, but the general use of Davidic themes to express hopes for God's future deliverance suffices to explain what Micah himself probably had in mind.

These prophecies were apparently written to augment the treatments of Israel's (the Northern Kingdom's) fall to Assyria and to amplify the prophetic repertoire of images on the theme of judgment and restoration. Micah has some images of restoration that work well, but the most memorable and famous images bear on justice, the corrosion of human trust, and the Lord's case against his faithless people. The final editors have given chapter 7 a liturgical cast, creating a dialogue between God and the people, and Brevard Childs finds Micah so correlated with Isaiah that the two prophets become interpreters of one another.[19] We can say, therefore, that Micah gained its present shape because the final editors wanted to vindicate the Lord in the fall of Israel and stir later generations to trust that the divine nature was best expressed as faithful love (*ḥesed*).

Micah's lasting significance is its suggesting the social breakdown from which genuine faith in God can deliver people. As well, this book joins many other biblical writings in challenging us to consider the ultimate nature of the divine mystery to be steadfast love. The social breakdown hinted in verses 7:2–6 is reminiscent of the much older Egyptian dialogue between a man about to commit suicide and his soul.[20] The marked difference is the faith of Micah that recourse to the God of Israel can supply for such defects of fallible human beings. Indeed, Micah uses human fraility to show people that the part of wisdom is placing their ultimate reliance only upon God. In Egypt there was no such articulate monotheism, and so no such obvious answer to the problem—the soul threat—of social breakdown.

Micah clearly offers nothing dramatically new about the ultimate nature of the divine mystery, but the faith in the final graciousness of God that shines through in the last chapter of this book is a small gem. For example, note "When I sit in darkness, the Lord will be a light to me" (verse 7:8). With only a bit of conceptual juggling, this confession of faith becomes the carte blanche urged upon us by some of the most profound mystics. In their eyes, we must finally trust that no matter what befalls us, even our own sins, God is always greater. In all circumstances, God can work some good or redemption. Clearly this is not an easy doctrine to accept, and when we are suffering evils we do not understand—for instance, the sudden death of a child—it can seem offensive pap. But when we have the peace to look unblinkingly into the depths of our condition of ignorance and dependency (none of us ever knows, experientially, the most basic things: where we come from and where we are going), the mystics' call for a carte blanche can make great sense. Indeed, it can come to seem obvious: What other choice do we have? The universe is there, immense and immeasurable. We are here, tiny and sure to die. If we choose to rebel against these facts, denying them or shaking our fists in impotent fury, we become figures of fun, absurd in our self-centeredness. A Sisyphus constantly rolling his rock up the hill, or a Sartre bitter to the quick that he is not God, can show aspects of tragic grandeur, but in the perspective of the billions of years through which the universe has rolled such figures soon become ridiculous. Micah would have us consider the initially strange but before long almost obvious alternative of accepting our creaturely limitations and testing the proposition that the mystery that holds our fate is stronger and better than we imagine.

NAHUM

The short book of Nahum is situated by its own reference (verse 3:8) to the fall of Thebes (663 B.C.E.) and by the fall of Nineveh (612 B.C.E.) that it anticipates. We know nothing about the prophet other than what we are told in verse 1:1: He came from Elkosh in southwest Judah. Chapter 1 praises God in hymnic style, and chapters 2 and 3 give oracles against Nineveh.

Nahum 1:1 warns us that this book concerns Nineveh, which was the capital of Israel's conquerer during the seventh century B.C.E. But whereas Jonah two centuries later used Nineveh to epitomize the Gentiles for whom God has a care, Nahum's memories of Assyrian brutality are fresher and he therefore makes Nineveh the symbol of the foreign power that the Lord will harshly judge. Thus verse 1:2 immediately characterizes the Lord as jealous, avenging, and wrathful. Verse 1:3 almost grudgingly recalls that the Lord is slow to anger, but it insists that the guilty will get what they deserve. Verses 1:2–14 and 1:15–3:19 appear to have originally been poems, the former an acrostic, but in their present state they are somewhat fragmentary or disordered. Verse 1:3 depicts the Lord in the theophanous imagery of the whirlwind and storm that we have come to consider almost staple. The point of this verse and verses 1:4–5 is to establish the Lord's credentials. As creator, he has full right to vent anger at the nations who violate his elementary laws of justice. Verses 1:7 makes explicit the contrast between what the Lord shows those who take refuge in him (that is, Judah, his covenanted favorite) and those who oppose his will (primarily, the enemies, such as Assyria, who had afflicted Israel and Judah, for four and three generations respectively). Those who do evil are bound to perish — for Nahum (1:8–11) this is almost a law of the divine nature. Verses 1:12–13 appear directed to Israel, for its consolation, but verse 1:14 again predicts woe for Assyria. Verse 1:15 (2:1 in the Hebrew) has a lovely ring and has entered the store of messianic images (it is repeated in Isaiah 40:9). If Judah obeys the Torah, it will find its foe cut off.

Nineveh is the apparent focus of attention in chapter 2. The prophet foresees the destruction of Nineveh that will restore the majesty of Jacob. The assumption of verses 2:3–9 is that the Lord's purposes are being realized in the sack of Nineveh. Verse 2:8 implies that once the process begins, stopping it will be like trying to catch water in one's hands. (Once again we are reminded of the commonplace brutality of biblical times, when sack and counter-sack was an accepted historical rhythm.) Verse 2:11 has a strong figure: Nineveh was a lion who filled his cave with prey. Against the Lord, however, the lion will fall at a stroke.

Chapter 3 continues the play of military imagery. Verse 3:1 accuses Nineveh of blood, lies, and plunder, establishing the justice of its fall. Verse 3:4 speaks of harlotries, perhaps to connote the seductions of pagan cults. Note that both the plunder and the harlotry of Nineveh receive fitting punishments. Verses 3:8–9 compare Nineveh with other pagan powers that have fallen, insinuating the true weakness of nations that can seem great. The image of little ones dashed in pieces (verse 3:10) epitomizes the barbarism of even petty warfare. Verse 3:14 sketches a frantic yet useless activity against siege. The figure of locusts in verses 3:15–17 appears satiric: Assyria devoured other nations, but soon it will melt away. The final verse of the book, 3:19, supplies the prophet's basic rationale: Assyria has done unceasing evil to many peoples, so many will applaud the news of its fall.

The book of Nahum presupposes the conditions of the late seventh century B.C.E., when Israel was ruled by Assyria and Judah was on a tight leash. The prophet nurses his grudge against this state of affairs and the evils that accomplished it, but he is confident that the days of Nineveh are numbered. The theological assumption is that the Lord guides all of history, but in this book the application of this assumption deals more with punishing the oppressor of Israel and Judah than with explaining their sufferings as merited by their sins.

Nahum appears to have been written and preserved principally to offer evidence against Assyria and to assure Israel that the Lord has a liberation in store. Such a prophecy would have bolstered the people's confidence in the divine justice and provided them energy to endure and hope. The imagery of warfare that the book employs is quite vivid, and its messianic figure of good tidings of peace (verse 1:15) is quite memorable. Apart from these literary virtues, its intent is somewhat questionable, because the face of God it praises is vindictive, as is the elation it raises. No doubt people suffering oppression need to gain strength wherever they can find it, but revenge can easily leave victims as deformed as their oppressors.

The lasting significance of Nahum is probably its testimony to the imperfection that the Bible, and so perhaps any wise estimate of human nature, is willing to tolerate. Nahum says that a people oppressed may be excused its dreams of bloody vengeance. More questionable is the projection of such vengeance onto the divine mystery that is the final fullness and measure of reality. If God is no better than the vindictive anger we may need to survive when we are hard pressed, then the world and history are much as Hobbes and other cynics depicted them: a theater of wolves. Xenophanes, and after him many other analysts of religion, made the always-relevant observation that people tend to mold their divinities according to their own image and likeness. If we had only Nahum, representing humanity as hard pressed and disfigured by suffering, we would have only a hurtful and partisan God. But Nahum reminds us that sometimes people do in fact seethe with a sense of injustice, and it suggests that this reality, too, has its place.

HABAKKUK

With Nahum (and Jeremiah), Habakkuk worked toward the end of the seventh century B.C.E., when hints of the fall of Assyria were in the air and Babylon was emerging on the horizon as the next great foreign power with which Judah would have to contend. The book contains a searching probe of the divine justice, and its response that Israel has to hang on in trust has made it more significant than its brevity would suggest.[21] Three subunits stand out: Verses 1:2–2:5 comprise a dialogue between the prophet and God, verses 2:6–20 pile up oracles in the classically prophetic style, and verses 3:1–19 are a hymn, complete with liturgical directions.

The theodicy for which Habakkuk is famous appears from the outset. The prophet asks in verse 1:2 why his cry for help goes unheard. The wrongs that prompt this cry are variants of the violence that social injustice creates. In a word (verse 1:4), "justice goes forth perverted." The religious question implied clearly is, How can a just God tolerate this state of affairs and not act to deliver his suffering people? The Lord's reply begins in verse 1:5: The history occurring among the nations (mainly, the conflict between Assyria and Babylon) is serving his plan of redress. Verses 1:6–11 are a splendid, if frightening, description of the fierce power of Babylon that the Lord is deploying.

The prophet's next speech in the dialogue, in verses 1:12–17, at first seems an acceptance of this divine promise. God is eternal and holy, so his people must have confidence that they will not die. If Babylon comes in chastisement, God has ordained it. But in verse 1:13 Habakkuk wavers: How can a pure God look on evil, why does a holy God let the wicked triumph over the good? The imagery of fishing in verses 1:14–17 pretends to an historical realism—human beings are no more sorted out (according to their moral deserts) than fish in a huge net—but actually accuses the Lord of a cruel carelessness. Indeed, it even suggests that God may live off this situation (from the many sacrifices that desperate people offer?) and luxuriate. Having unburdened himself of this dark suspicion, the prophet seems to take a deep breath at his own audacity and prepare himself for the Lord's answer.

This comes in verses 2:2–5: Hang on, justice may seem slow but it surely is coming. Note in verse 2:3 the figure of providence: literally, the vision God has of how history will unfold. Verse 2:4 goes to the religious core: The upright can endure this testing by time. The righteous person lives by faith that nothing can finally contest God's dispensation, and that this dispensation has to be just. Correlatively, the wicked are sure finally to collapse and go down to Sheol. Note in verse 2:5 the lyric expression of the universality of the divine sovereignty: "He gathers for himself all nations, and collects as his own all peoples."

The oracles of verses 2:6–20 are similar to predictions of just retribution that we have found in most of the biblical prophets. The first image is of a financial reckoning: Those who accumulated great moral debts will soon become booty. Those who have plundered will soon be plundered. Throughout this section it is not clear whether Habakkuk principally has in mind the foreign power (Assyria) occupying Israel or unjust Israelites themselves. Part of the book's effectiveness is the breadth of its relevance. Verses 2:13–14 contrast the useless labor of the nations with the coming success of the Lord, which Habakkuk describes as a time when the Earth will be filled with knowledge of (the glory of) the Lord—a familiar prophetic motif. Verses 2:15–17 make most sense if directed against Babylon. Verses 2:18–19 are a classical prophetic mockery of idolatry. Note how "breath" comes to stand for life, effectiveness, and worth. Verse 2:20 suggests that Habakkuk, or a later editor, had priestly sympathies, because it associates the presence of the Lord with the Temple in Jerusalem. The silence of the Earth that the prophet enjoins is not lifeless or craven; rather, it is the awe and respect of those who appreciate the divine splendor.

Chapter 3 is a psalm intended for liturgical performance. The direct address of the Lord reminds us of the right Judahites had to speak with their God as though face to face. The "fear" of verse 3:2 might better be translated "respect" or even "admire." Note the conflation of images that recall God's work as both redeemer and creator. The prophet is especially sensitive to the response that the divine power elicits from nature. Verse 3:13 is explicit that the Lord worked salvation for his people, who have been anointed (like kings). The military exploits of the Lord at the Exodus may lie in the depths of this imagery. Verse 3:16 shows the prophet weakened and physically shaken by the contemplation of the Lord's fierce justice that is to come. Verses 3:17–18 echo the unqualified commitment that prophetic faith most admired. Here there is no human equivalent of the Deuteronomistic view of the divine justice but a carte blanche. At the finale, the psalm makes God the vitality of the prophet's life, his source of courage and animal vigor.

Habakkuk presupposes the traditions of the Exodus and the covenant of Sinai, which gave Israel the right to expect God's provision. It also presupposes a situation in which injustice and threat flourished sufficiently to call such provision into question. As we noted, scholars tend to postulate the historical situation at the end of the seventh century, when Babylon was on the verge of subjugating Assyria — and Judah. Chapter 3 shows that the prophet could assume a liturgical acceptance of his work. The dialogue between the prophet and God in chapters 1 and 2 depends on a theology in which God tolerates, indeed invites, the frank reactions of his followers.

Habakkuk was probably written to incorporate into the Hebrew Bible the poetry and sentiments well expressed in chapter 3, and its oracles against injustice in chapter 2 measure up to similar prophecies that the canonical editors found perennially useful. But the main intent of the book, in all likelihood, was to preserve the challenge to the divine justice that the dialogue of chapters 1 and 2 mounts. As though anticipating Job, Habakkuk asks the divine mystery to defend itself, because the history that it supposedly controls presently is rotten. Why does God not answer the cries of the just, who call upon him for redress? Ultimately, no one knows, and the answer that the prophet receives spotlights the need to establish one's soul in bedrock, adamant trust. We now tend to read such texts as Habakkuk 2:4 individualistically, thinking about the personal aspects of the life of faith. In the prophet's day the first instinct would have been social: This is the attitude Judah needs if it is to keep its psychic balance and prove worthy of the overall treatment it has received from the Lord of the covenant (who again and again has shown himself trustworthy).

The lasting significance of Habakkuk derives from these issues of theodicy. In more times than not, the divine justice can be questioned, and easily indeed does the mystery of evil blind our eyes to the mystery of goodness. When injustice flourishes, most people stop seeing the thousands of small acts of fairness that keep life going in the family, in the village, on the job. When expectations, valid or quite presumptuous, that we have come to cherish are not met, we can shield ourselves from such apparently stark but actually comforting realities as the gratuity of our birth and the omnipresent possibility of our death.

Habakkuk does not develop this line of defending God very much. His divinity rather asks for a bare hanging on. The book does suggest the theology of history that such counsel implies — a conviction, finally based upon some evidence, that God, not chaos, is running time. But we sense that the delight of the prophet, anticipated in verse 2:4 and elaborated in chapter 3, is rather to contemplate the glory of God. Such contemplation amounts to a holistic response to the problem of evil, in that it takes all the actions of creatures, however tawdry or hurtful, up into the comprehensive and so more adequate perspective of the divine creator. If God chooses to tarry, that is God's business. The business of people such as Habakkuk, who have glimpsed the divine glory, is to remember the splendor they have seen and to let it become their strength (verse 3:19).

ZEPHANIAH

The book of Zephaniah appears, on the basis of internal evidence (especially verse 1:1), to come from the period 640 to 609 B.C.E., during the reign of King Josiah. The prophet's work probably intersected with the Deuteronomistic reform, and his interest in purifying the cult of Jerusalem suggests priestly affiliations. He has less interest in social justice than some of his fellow prophets. The three chapters of the book deal, respectively, with the doom coming upon Jerusalem, the judgment coming upon the nations, and the comforts available to those who wait upon the Lord. [22]

The word that Zephaniah receives from God begins like a blast from a fiery furnace: God will sweep everything away from the face of the Earth. We seem back in the days of Noah, when primeval humanity caused God to repent of creation and want to destroy the wicked life he had sponsored. Verses 1:4–6 describe a profanation of cult, through worship of Baal or the heavenly elements, and a failure to keep the Torah or seek the Lord (pursue knowledge of God). The day of the Lord described in verses 1:7–18 is in the spirit of Amos: darkness rather than light, wrath rather than consolation. Verse 1:9 singles out violence and fraud as reasons for punishment. Verse 1:12 takes a figure from wine making, indicating that Judah has gone bad. Zephaniah probably does not have Assyria or Babylon in mind as the likely punisher of Judah; enough hostile foreign tribes were around to cause anxiety. Verse 1:15 is the biblical text responsible for the *dies irae* (day of wrath) that became a staple Western image for divine judgment at either death or the end of the world. The very extremity and universality of the imagery that Zephaniah uses distinguish this book as the most fierce or cataclysmic of the prophecies of divine judgment.

Zephaniah 2:1–3 seem addressed to Judah, as an exhortation to reassemble itself and ward off the Lord's wrath. Verse 2:3 exalts humility, suggesting that it may hide believers from the wrath to come. The rest of chapter 2 hurls oracles of woe against the nations, promising them a full measure of the divine judgment. Note the special concern with the sea coast, and the promise (in verse 2:7) that the remnant of the house of Israel (a theme of Isaiah) will gain possession of it. Verse 2:8 foresees the vindication of Judah against the taunts of neighbors such as the Moabites and the Ammonites, who enjoyed its misfortunes. The overthrow of these Gentiles has the motif of holy war, in that the true God is "famishing" (verse 2:11) the idols on which they depend. Ethiopia, Assyria, and even the animals of such nations will suffer the Lord's devastations. The exultant city of verse 2:15 is probably Nineveh, which we recall was the special target of Nahum. [23]

In chapter 3 Zephaniah applies the lash to Jerusalem, which he calls "the oppressing city" (in verse 3:1). Jerusalem neither trusts in the Lord nor draws near to him (for worship). Officials, judges, prophets, and priests all fail their responsibilities — the roster of condemnation we have seen in other of Israel's self-criticizers. Zephaniah 3:5 absolves the Lord of any injustices that might excuse this bad response by his people. Despite the lessons available in the Lord's punishment of the nations, Judah has not repented of its corruption. The transition to verse 3:8, in which this state of affairs seems to propel the Lord into forensic action, so that he takes the stand as a witness and initiates a process of resolution, is peculiar. We might read this verse, and the following sketch of a juridical assembly that finally will put pure speech and righteous action into the nations, as the prophet's intuition that only gratuitous action by God can remedy the diseased state of affairs. For Judah, the result will be a humble people's seeking refuge in the Lord. In verse 3:13 the tone is utopian: a people finally worthy of their holy God. Verse 3:14 proclaims a festival: exultation for Zion at the good news of the Lord's forgiveness and liberation. Note in verse 3:15 the explicit assertion that God is Israel's king. This is the warrior God remembered from as far back as the

Exodus. The last verses could be read as messianic: promises of a coming ruler who will free Judah and make its estate blessed.

Zephaniah presupposes the state of affairs in Judah prior to the Babylonian Conquest, when many in the land thought reform was long overdue. The Lord is assumed to be a God who demands righteousness of his people and who, not finding it, flames into wrath. Zephaniah draws on the altered sense of the "day of the Lord" that had come into the prophetic tradition with Amos. Whereas the earliest sense of this time of divine intervention had the positive connotation of Israel's warrior coming to its rescue, after Amos the prophets realized that the presence of the holy God was bound to mean judgment and punishment for a sinful people. Zephaniah assumes that Judah had foreign enemies worth fearing, and that its Lord also had to dispense justice to them. Last, this prophet, like the majority, assumes that ultimately the Lord will prove a God more gracious than punitive, and so his word from God conveys more reason for hope than for fear.

Zephaniah was written and preserved to testify to the inadequacies of religion in Judah at the end of the seventh century B.C.E., and to leave all later readers of the canonical text no doubt that God accomplishes a severe reckoning for all sinners. By the final edition of the text apocalyptic attitudes were about, and editors interested in a final revelation and accounting from the heavenly Lord could have found the universality of Zephaniah's judgments congenial. Finally, this text overtly wants to exonerate God of any injustices. All fault lies on human beings' side, and therefore the primary stance that human beings ought to take toward God is one of humility.

The lasting significance of Zephaniah derives from this counsel to humility, as well as from its dramatic depictions of justice and its final messianic verses. Judgment and restoration are staple prophetic themes, as we have seen. Zephaniah stands out for the strength of its promise that the day of the Lord will be grim, but this notion itself is not novel. The counsel to humility derives from the prophet's unusual sensitivity to the gap between what God's people ought to have done and what in fact they tend to do. If the nations fall because of their pride, Judah falls because of its weakness. It simply cannot seem to measure up to the grace and depth of existence offered it through the covenant. But Zephaniah sees that God is creative enough to turn this situation around. Weakness need not be a cul-de-sac condemning Judah to pure inadequacy. If the people will confess their sins to God, will repent of their wrongdoing and ask for help, they will find God forgiving and restorative. Humility, then, becomes salvific. Facing the realities of its moral situation, Judah can ask God to accomplish the renewal that it realizes it needs but seems unable to achieve on its own.

HAGGAI

The short book of Haggai relates to the situation in Jerusalem around 520 B.C.E., when the people had returned from the Exile in Babylon and were faced with reassembling their national life. The prophet's great theme is the rebuilding of the Temple. Chapter 1 deals with God's call to this task, and chapter 2 contemplates the benefits that accomplishing it will bring. Note that the style is more prosaic and historical than poetic and oracular.

The second year of the rule of the Persian king Darius was 520 B.C.E. Upon conquering Babylonia in 538, Cyrus had decreed that the Jews could return to their homeland and rebuild their Temple. So the conjoined issues of rebuilding the Temple and reestablishing the nation's cultural (religious) life had been simmering for more than a decade. Haggai becomes God's mouthpiece for a message to Zerubbabel, the political ruler, and Joshua, the religious leader, and tells them to get moving. Note in 1:3 the rejection of the people's excuses: They have had time to build themselves houses, but they have let the house of the Lord lie in ruins. Verse 1:6 correlates the agricultural and economic problems that the people are experiencing with their failure to honor their God by restoring his Temple. The notion is that God is absent because he has no decent place in which to dwell. To this point the text operates on a rather primitive theological assumption: God is not giving because God is not getting. Verse 1:12 tells us that this message had its intended effect on Zerubbabel and Joshua, and they agreed to what the prophet had asked. God then draws near and stirs up a will to work so that the reconstruction of the Temple gets under way.

In chapter 2 the word of God that Haggai speaks is less a threatening instruction and more an encouragement. First, should the leaders think that what they are building is embarrassingly plain, compared to the prior Temple of Solomon, they must not lose heart. The Lord, remembered as powerful from the time of the Exodus (Haggai 2:5), is with them in this work. Verse 2:6 seems to predict a future enrichment of Judah, at the expense of the nations, that will allow it to embellish the Temple. Verses 2:10–14 employ a priestly sense of cleanliness to argue that the cult of the Temple will be useless unless the people cleanse themselves. Haggai then contrasts the hard times that preceded the building of the Temple with a prosperity to come. From henceforth, Judah will know the Lord's blessing. The final word that Haggai hands on concerns Zerubbabel himself. The prophet predicts that Zerubbabel will become a messianic ruler, presiding over the fall of many nations and the exaltation of Judah. Verse 2:23 recalls Jeremiah 22:24, making the king God's signet ring (official authority). The short book ends on an upbeat note, having linked the rebuilding of the Temple with a restoration of prosperity like that of David and Solomon.

The historical assumptions of Haggai are clear enough. The prophet worked at a time when those who returned to Jerusalem needed a spur to get their priorities straight and refurbish the traditional center of their national life. The book assumes that both king and high priest have an obligation to listen to a prophet who is announcing the word of God. It can plausibly interpret depressed times as an effect of God's absence, and it can link the temple with royal imagery to create a vision of a renewed Judah in which cult, kingship, and economy all flourish together.

Haggai was probably written and preserved to endorse the rebuilding of the Temple and to strengthen the hand of the (priestly) party, which wanted to reconstitute the returned community along theocratic lines. In its present form it is as much historical as prophetic, purporting to present not just the word that Haggai received but the story of how king and high priest received it.

The lasting significance of the book is its testimony to the strength that the Temple, with its implications of priestly religion, had on Judahite imagination. Unless God had a fitting house in the center of Judah, things could not go well for the people. This institutionalization of the divine presence may strike us as quaint, just as the book's correlation of Temple and prosperity may strike us as questionable. Both can nonetheless stimulate useful reflections about what sort of incarnations a religious tradition needs, if it is to serve adherents of flesh and blood, and what sort of "benefits" a people can rightly expect from the supposed presence of God in its midst. For all the differences between Judah of 2500 years ago and the present-day United States, such questions come into view whenever we debate prayer in the public schools or the path to economic renewal. If we generalize some of Haggai's claims for the Temple, then, we can find him lastingly significant.[24]

ZECHARIAH

The book of Zechariah generally is considered to be a composite work. The first eight chapters derive from a contemporary of Haggai, who worked from 520 to 518 B.C.E. and shared many of Haggai's convictions, and the remaining six chapters collect materials from considerably later, perhaps the fourth and third centuries B.C.E.

The word of the Lord that comes to Zechariah in verse 1:1 is precisely dated to the year 520. The cry is for repentance, on the model of the past returns to God that prior prophets provoked. Beginning with verse 1:7 we get the first of eight visions that are the core of the prophet's message. The man riding the red horse, as interpreted by the angel, is one of the presences that patrol the Earth. This imagery is reminiscent of later apocalyptic, wherein heavenly intermediaries interpret visions that feature God's forces marshaled for judgment upon evil-doers and relief of the just. The seventy years mentioned in verse 1:12 approximate the time of the subjection of Jerusalem to foreign rule and echo the prophecy of Jeremiah 29:10. (From 586, the year of the fall of Jerusalem to Babylon, to 516, the year of the rebuilding of the Temple, equals seventy years.) The answer from God promises compassion for Jerusalem, apparently largely in the form of the Lord's resuming residence in the Temple. The measuring line of verse 1:17 probably symbolizes God's again judging the people, in the sense of again effectively being the norm of their life, no doubt through their renewed observance of Torah.

The second vision, of the horns and the smiths, begins in verse 1:18. It represents the powers of the Earth that have afflicted Israel and Judah and the agents who will work the Lord's destruction of such oppressors. Note that for Zechariah "business" between heaven and Earth is transacted through angelic intermediaries. Sometimes commentators link the priestly interests of Zechariah to the theology of Ezekiel, which greatly emphasized the transcendence of the Lord. The intermediaries then would compensate for the otherness of the Lord and provide a mechanism for mediating the divine will to Earth.

The third vision, which occurs at the start of chapter 2, is heavily indebted to Ezekiel 40:3–4. In addition to the implication of God's overseeing control, this vision adds the promise that the Lord will protect the city like fire and so make it open to rich increase. Verses 2:6–13 appear to be an interpolated appeal to exiles who have remained in Babylon. Note in verse 2:8 the figure of Judah as the apple of God's eye. Verse 2:10 seems to sweeten the appeal to return by promising the Lord's dwelling in Zion (in the rebuilt Temple). The call ends with a promise of

Judah's renewed status as the Lord's chosen portion, and verse 2:13 sounds Eze-kielian in suggesting the splendor of God that silences all flesh.

The vision of chapter 3 presents Joshua, the same high priest addressed by Haggai, being accused by "the Satan." The basic meaning of this name, in fact, is "the accuser," and here the assumption is that an officer of the heavenly court is named. God clearly opposes the Satan and defends Joshua, with imagery of the priest's restoration to good standing (apparently some in Jerusalem were contesting his authority or virtue). Note that the angel of the Lord does more talking than God himself. Joshua's leadership is conditioned upon his walking in God's ways and fulfilling his charge. The "branch" of verse 3:8 is a sprout from the tree of David. Joshua is accredited through the seven-faceted stone of verse 3:9, which is probably meant to symbolize a stable foundation from God that is all-comprehensive (seven is the number of fullness). With the priestly rule settled, and, by implication, the Temple well served, the people can look forward to peace and prosperity: inviting their neighbors to relax under their vines and fig trees.

In chapter 4 Zechariah's angel wakes him for what proves to be his fifth vision, this time of the sevenfold lampstand (symbolic at once of the tree of life — note its shape — light, and the divine presence everywhere).[25] The two olive trees usually are understood to be Zerubbabel and Joshua, the political and religious leaders. Note that the word to Zerubbabel in verse 4:6 enjoins him to rely on the spirit of God (again especially significant to Ezekiel) rather than worldly might or power. The following verses foresee the completion of the Temple. The seven eyes of the Lord in verse 4:10 are another figure of fullness, this time signifying the divine omniscience. Because the two rulers stand on each side of the lampstand, the lampstand within the Temple signifies the true source of life and light for the unified community and its leaders.

The sixth vision, which occurs in verses 5:1–4, is of a flying scroll. The function of the scroll seems to be that of Torah, judging all evils such as thievery. The seventh vision, in verses 5:5–11, personifies the sin of Judah as a woman sitting in a container. The female angels who take the woman away to Shinar (Babylon) are more indications of an apocalyptic mentality, and the feminization of sin is in keeping with priestly theology. Apparently the wickedness being spirited away is false cult, which naturally would be appropriate in pagan Babylon.

The eighth and last vision occurs in Zechariah 6:1–8. The chariots remain obscure but probably represent military forces coming to God to report and be reassigned. Note in verse 6:7 the imagery again of patroling the Earth: God's creation has become filled with intermediary powers that effect the divine governance. At the end of this vision, in which the "winds" (breath of the Lord) have played so significant a role, is peace: The divine spirit has accomplished an international pacification (by rendering judgment?).[26] Overall, the visions blend judgment with stronger imagery of the Lord's reestablishing the divine presence in Jerusalem and preparing an age of cleansed religion and peace.

The word developed in verses 6:9–15 is somewhat confusing, but the general intent seems to be to sanction the rule of Joshua and make his control of the Temple part of the Davidic, messianic dispensation about to unfold. Perhaps the role of Zerubbabel has been dropped, to make it plainer that the Lord is the true king of Judah and the one whom the high priest directly serves. At the end of the passage, the building of the Temple has occasioned the drawing near of those

(exiles and Gentiles?) from afar and so has reasserted the centrality of Jerusalem as the prime cultic shrine on Earth.

Chapter 7 takes us off on a tangent about fasting. The inquiry of the people of Bethel seems to occasion a criticism of the motives that underlay the penance Judah did for the sins that led to the Exile. Verse 7:6 extends this criticism to both the present and the time prior to the Exile, when Jerusalem enjoyed prosperity. The result is to make all fasting, eating, and drinking suspect, and so to remind Judah that joy and sorrow alike only gain significance by reference to God. This rather vague draft on the prior prophetic tradition then leads to a clearer statement of the prophetic sense of the heart of the matter: justice, kindness, mercy, and the other social virtues that Amos, Hosea, and others have impressed upon us. Verse 7:12 paints the people as resisting the heartfelt covenant called for by Jeremiah and Ezekiel. Note in verse 7:13 the creative use of the prophetic theme of not hearing: God himself finally turned a deaf ear. The passage interprets the Exile as punishment for Judah's hardness of heart and religious deafness, and so by implication says that the next generation ought to resolve to listen.

In chapter 8 we encounter the Pentateuchal theme of the divine jealousy, here applied to the Lord's return to Jerusalem (in the Temple). As though Israel's lover has been away, now that Jerusalem is being reestablished the Lord wants all competitors brushed aside. Verses 8:4–5 paint a happy picture of restoration: old people and youths enjoying the streets of Jerusalem. Verses 8:7–8 promise restoration and the flourishing of the old intimacy, when Israel was God's unique people and the Lord was Israel's only God. Verses 8:9–10 refer to the state described by Haggai, when Judah was desolate prior to the rebuilding of the Temple. The remnant returned from Exile will experience great prosperity. What previously was a byword for cursing among the nations will all the more become a blessing. The cause for not fearing, for trusting, is the Lord's promise to rebalance the scales. Zechariah foresees a prosperity equal to the punishments of Exile. Verses 8:14–15 make this explicit, and verses 8:16–17, in rather Deuteronomistic fashion, supply the recipe: speaking and doing the truth. Verses 8:18–19 sound like an affirmative answer to the question about fasting posed in verse 7:3. What had been times of sorrow will become occasions for celebration. Verse 8:19 is not a bad summary of the morality suitable in a time of divine favor: "Love truth and peace." At the end of this first portion of the book of Zechariah, the nations flock to Jerusalem and entreat the Jews to let them share in the favor of hosting the presence of the true God.

The oracles of chapters 9–14 jar with the positive expectations of chapter 8 and so, as noted, most commentators place them considerably later, perhaps around 333 B.C.E., when Alexander the Great became the focal point of Jewish hopes for deliverance from Persian rule and fears of further foreign oppression. The oracles against the nations that we find in chapter 9 are in the style of the major prophets, castigating these peoples for their pride and thoughtless opulence. Verse 9:8 seems to promise protection for Judah. Verse 9:9 is a messianic prophecy, picked up by the New Testament (see Matthew 21:5, Luke 19:35–36, and John 12:14–15). Zechariah 9:11–12 promise the release of Jewish captives. Verse 9:13 seems to depict the Lord using Judah and Ephraim to oppose Greece. The chapter ends, in verses 16–17, with a ringing prediction of Israel, the Lord's flock and jewel, shining in the land and enjoying the bounties of nature.

Chapter 10 rebuts the worship of nature and the use of pagan tricks of worship, urging the people to take their petitions to the Lord. Verse 10:3 has the figure, familiar from Ezekiel, of false shepherds who rouse the wrath of God. The imagery turns martial, suggesting battle and victory against pagan rulers. Verse 10:6 has the Lord's virtually repenting of the punishments he had laid on Judah and deciding to remember that he is the people's God, obliged to answer them. The great ingathering depicted in the rest of the chapter would reverse the dispersion among the nations produced by the falls to Assyria and Babylon. In the background is the first liberation, from Egypt.

In chapter 11 Lebanon is the victim, its fall epitomized by the felling of its glorious cypresses and cedars. Verses 11:4–6 again deploy the image of cruel shepherds, apparently to explain the sufferings Judah presently undergoes. The great power hinted in the background may be the the Ptolemaic dynasty that arose in Egypt after Alexander.[27] Verses 11:7–14 extend the metaphor of shepherding to portray the Lord's unsuccessful efforts to reestablish a decent rule in Judah. Frustrated, he says, What will be, will be, and annuls the covenant. Indeed, he likens himself to a slave who has labored on Israel's behalf and now only wants to get his measly wages and call it quits. The gesture of throwing the thirty shekels into the treasury seems ironic: Take your silver and put it where the sun does not shine. The staff of grace has already been broken, when the Lord annulled the covenant, but the second staff, symbolizing the union of Judah and Israel, is also to be broken. In the disorder that the oracles are either interpreting or predicting, North and South stand apart. In the last verses of chapter 11 the prophet plays a false shepherd, to dramatize (whether just in writing or through some acting out is not clear) the low estate to which leadership in Israel has fallen. The imagery is roughly the opposite of the messianic notes given in Isaiah 61, where the most needy are given the most help.

Chapter 12 begins with a dismal oracle of coming judgment, wherein Jerusalem will become like a source of drunkenness to the surrounding nations. Alternately (verse 12:3), Jerusalem will be a stone crushing those who try to take it over. The general tenor, then, is that the Lord will bring wrath upon the enemies of Judah. Realizing this, the clans of Judah will rejoice in the strength given them by their God. Verse 12:6 beams the same message through another image: Jerusalem will be a blazing pot in the midst of wood — more woe to the nations afflicting it. Verse 12:7 hints at tensions between Jerusalem and the rest of Judah, and the stress on Davidic imagery may be meant to downplay the privileges of the priesthood and upgrade the status of the Judean rulers. The figure of verse 12:10 is obscure, but the gain of gazing at the victim is clear: greater compassion in the land. The mourning alluded to in verse 12:11 is for a fertility god whose death symbolized the cyclical perishing of nature. All of the great families of the nation will execute this mourning, which in the literary reality of the oracle is for a victim of great moment.

In chapter 13 the first figure is of water to cleanse the house of David and Jerusalem of their sins. Then idols are to go, and then (false?) prophets. The implication is that prophecy had fallen on hard times and become rife with charlatans or uncontrolled visionaries. Verse 13:6 suggests that in their frenzies these ecstatics would wound themselves. The rest of the chapter plays variations on the theme of shepherding, apparently on the way to predicting a coming purge of Israel.

In chapter 14 this purge becomes more explicit and graphic: Jerusalem taken, its houses plundered, and its women raped. The temper here is as much apocalyptic or eschatological as predictive of historical happenings. The coming of the Lord in verse 14:5, after the earthquake, brings a train of angels. Verses 14:6–7 confirm that this is a special day, of the Lord's judgment, when the ordinary processes of nature will be suspended. The living waters that will flow symbolize the life and renewal that the presence of divinity brings. Verse 14:9 makes the kingship of the Lord universal, as though an enthronement ceremony exalted him in the sight of all the nations. Jerusalem will be secure in this decisive hour, but its enemies will suffer plague. Verse 14:14 again implies antagonism between Jerusalem and Judah. In verse 14:16 all of this final judgment gets somewhat domesticated, as the survivors neatly go up to Jerusalem to worship each year and observe the Feast of Booths. (We suspect that a priestly hand has now entered and completely taken over the apocalyptic mind.) The Feast of Booths gets more attention, and the plagues in store for a disobedient Egypt recall the plagues of Moses that originally got the people free. The rest of the chapter continues in a priestly vein, as even the bells of the horses proclaim dedication to the holy God.

The different parts of the book of Zechariah have different presuppositions. The first eight chapters, dominated by the prophet's visions, presuppose the time when the Temple was being rebuilt and the theological legitimacy of apocalyptic imagery and mechanisms for calling the people to renew their covenantal bond was accepted. The Lord is coming to judge Israel and reestablish it. The authors and editors presuppose the validity of this scenario, including the prominent place it gives to angels. In the second portion of the present book, chapters 9–14, the historical assumption is of a later time, when Israel was groaning for freedom from pagan overlords. The assumption is that God rules the nations, has afflicted them in the past, and will afflict them in the future for Israel's benefit. The editors assume the traditional figure of shepherds, true and false, and the final chapter develops the traditional imagery of the day of the Lord in the direction of an eschatological judgment on the nations and an enthronement of the Lord.

The book apparently was written and edited into its present shape to preserve the striking visions of the prophet and to tie them to later interest in apocalyptic reckonings. Whether it simply assumed the importance of angelic intermediaries or wanted to promote this doctrine is not clear. Perhaps by its time the influence of Ezekiel had become such that the cherubim of his key visions had taken on wider roles. The final chapters seem designed to console people chafing under later foreign rule, promising that Jerusalem would come into its own as the center of the Earth and that the nations would either honor Israel's God or suffer dire plagues.

The lasting significance of Zechariah is its evidence about the development of the prophetic imagination in postexilic times. The text shows many signs of priestly shaping, as we noted, but the speculations about angelic patrolers and the coming universal judgment strike a new, previously unsounded note. We see more of this mentality when we deal with Daniel and apocalyptic more fully. Generally, however, this kind of imagination springs from frustration. People despair of effecting the changes they desire through earthly means and begin to long for heavenly interventions. The history of millennial movements, right through to the twentieth century c.e., shows many examples of these psychodynamics. Generally, biblical religion is rather cautious or even cold toward them, wanting to preserve the

Excavations at Qumran, where the Dead Sea Scrolls were found. *(Used with permission of the photographer, Robert L. Cohn)*

mystery and freedom of God to control history as God wishes. Zechariah might remind us, then, of the difficulty of keeping psychic balance, neither trying to peer into the inscrutable mysteries of God nor giving up on the hope that God somehow will make history bearable.

MALACHAI

This last book of the minor prophets is from an anonymous priestly prophet of the period 500 to 450 B.C.E., when it was clear that the rebuilt Temple had not spurred the religious revival that Haggai foresaw. The "oracles" of the book are in the style of the final chapters of Zechariah, and the distinctive format is one of question and answer. The traditional division of the brief text is into eight sections (1:1, 1:2–5, 1:6–2:9, 2:10–16, 2:17–3:5, 3:6–12, 3:13–4:3, 4:4–6).[28]

Malachai 1:1 simply provides the assurance that this book follows the prophetic conventions and may be trusted as the word of the Lord. The name "Malachai" appears derived from verse 3:1, because it means "my messenger."

Verses 1:2–5 provide a somewhat disturbing argument on behalf of God's love for Israel. If Israel will consider the fate of its brotherly neighbor Edom (Esau), it will see that the Lord has loved it (Jacob) and hated Esau. Edom lies in ruins, and the prophet is assured that the Lord will resist all its efforts to rebuild itself. Apparently the enmity against Edom that we saw in Obadiah was still strong in this prophet's day. Israel, then, should take heart from its own rebuilt state and account this a sign of God's love (realize it is nothing to take for granted).

Verses 1:6–2:9 question the treatment the Lord has received from Israel. Note in verse 1:6 the designation of the Lord as father and master of Israel. The priests have failed to honor this relationship, offering maimed animals for sacrifice instead of the perfect animals required by Leviticus (22:17–25) and Deuteronomy (15:21). Verse 1:8 ironically suggests that the earthly governor would reject such sorry gifts. How much more, then, must the Lord despise them? Verse 1:10 seems a gentler version of Amos 5:21. Verse 1:11 might be read as a liberal interpretation of the cults of the nations, inspired by a strong faith that there is only one God, however various his or her names. Verse 1:13 somewhat inadvertently reveals the burden that priestly, sacrificial religion can become when people have come to question its utility. Verse 1:14 strongly affirms the divine kingship and is another suggestion that, by the time of the final edition of the prophetic books, Israel had developed a considerable awareness of the Lord's positive appreciation among the pagan nations (perhaps due to the Hellenistic culture that stressed the common humanity of all peoples). In chapter 2 the laxity of the priests wins them strong curses from God. The Lord is so affronted by their irreligion that he considers their sacrifices dung. Originally, the priestly covenant with Levi was a thing of life and peace. Malachai 2:5–7, in fact, sketch the profile of the ideal priest: fearful of the Lord, learned, honest, upright, and mindful that he is the messenger of God. In contrast, the priests of this prophet's day have perverted the Torah, not keeping it themselves and showing partiality in their instruction of others.

Malachai 2:10–16 bear on the faithlessness that Judah shows through intermarriage with foreigners. Verse 10 might be read in a universalistic spirit, as the praise of the single parenthood of God and so the sibling status of all Jews or even all people. In the postexilic period, a strong movement existed to purify the Jewish people of foreign taint, and the reforms of Ezra and Nehemiah proscribed intermarriage with Gentiles. Verse 2:13 expresses a feeling of rejection, the cause of which it finds in the tainting of progeny that comes through intermarriage. Verse 2:16, on the Lord's hatred of divorce and violence, should be taken symbolically as well as literally: infidelity to one's covenantal commitments.

In Malachai 2:17–3:5 the motif is the Lord's weariness with unfaithful Israel and so his determination to come in judgment. The two offenses first singled out are moral corruption and questioning the justice of God. Verse 3:1 speaks of a messenger-forerunner, perhaps drawing on the interest in angels that we saw in Zechariah. The messenger and God will come to the Temple, but it will be a day of judgment more than rejoicing. Verse 3:2 may be familiar from Handel's "Messiah." The next imagery is of refining a tarnished people and accusing sorcerers, adulterers, oppressors, and various other sinners.

The next section, Malachai 3:6–12, begins by extolling the fidelity and permanence of the Lord, implicitly contrasting him with the unstable, fickle Israelites just depicted. Only the stability of the Lord's goodness has kept Jacob from being consumed in judgment. Note the image of mutual returning or conversion in verse 3:7. The "robbing" of God described next is surely symbolic, but it may also indicate tampering with the tithes that the people were to provide. Verse 3:11 may refer to locusts, which were the great devourers of Israel's crops. Verse 3:12 betrays another interest in how Israel is related to the nations or is regarded by them.

The next section, verses 3:13–4:3, rebukes those who have spoken against the Lord, questioning his faithfulness. Verse 3:15 vividly exemplifies what happens when people lose faith: The arrogant are deemed blessed, evil-doers are judged to prosper (and so are considered shrewd). In later times "Godfearers" became a synonym for the properly pious. Verse 3:16 has the figure, frequent in apocalyptic literature, of a book (of "life") in which the names of the faithful are inscribed (often by an angel). The Lord promises to spare the Godfearers and treat them like his children. Verse 3:18 is a strong charge to distinguish between the wicked and the good, letting the chips fall where they may. The sense of verse 4:1 is that the day of the Lord foretold in Malachai 3:1–2 is certainly coming, burning like an oven. (Verses 4:1–6 are 3:19–24 in the Hebrew.) The Godfearers need not worry: The day of the Lord will dawn for them with healing (note the solar symbolism of verse 4:2). In verse 4:3, the righteous become the punishers of the wicked, tramping them down like ashes (after they have been burned by the wrath of the Lord).

The conclusion of Malachai, verses 4:4–6, features a call to rededicate Israel to the Torah of Moses, and a promise that Elijah will come to herald the terrible day of the Lord. This promise had great influence in later Jewish speculation about both judgment and the messianic age. Note in verse 4:6 the image of a family, reconciled and united in love. The other choice is the Lord's smiting the land with a curse — hardly a desirable alternative.

Malachai assumes a situation when priestly religion was depressed. The priests themselves displeased the Lord, and the people failed to receive effective instruction. The most probable historical occasion for its messages of reform, as we noted, would be the mid-fifth century, when the Temple had been rebuilt but piety had not reflamed. This also fits what we know from the later historical books (Ezra to Nehemiah and Chronicles), especially in the concern to prohibit intermarriage with Gentiles. The book displays priestly concerns and priestly judgments, although they are thoroughly informed by the prophetic convictions about the day of the Lord. Lastly, we can again mention the awareness of the nations, which suggests a more positive appreciation of their service of the one true God than what we tend to find in earlier biblical writings.

Malachai probably was written and preserved because of its priestly critiques of irreligion. Both positively and negatively, it concisely indicates how Torah and cultic sacrifice ought to have provided Israel a healthy center. The dialogical format of the book supports the right to address God as though face to face that we noted when dealing with Habakkuk. The imagery of the messenger fits the apocalyptic interest in angelic intermediaries, and the addition of Elijah to the scenario of the day of the Lord has the effect of making a proto-prophet the most decisive messenger. Parental imagery for God provides a basis for relations warmer than what we usually find in priestly religion. Last, the status given the Godfearers would seem strongly to support humble, traditional piety.

The lasting significance of Malachai is probably its enrichment of the imagery we have for the day of the Lord and its interpretation of priestly religion. The format of questions and answers supports frank, even challenging, approaches to the divine mystery, although, as we find in other biblical works that employ such a format (for example, Job), the dialogues usually turn accusation back on the human questioner. The disparate character of the book — eight different sections in only four chapters (three in the Hebrew) — keeps it from having the powerful effect that concentration can produce, but its images are sufficiently strong to make Elijah and the day of the Lord memorable. Indeed, they remind us that history

The village of Silwan, south of the Mount of Olives.   *(Used with permission of the photographer, Robert L. Cohn)*

does need divine judgment, if we are not to lose confidence in the separation of sinners from the Godfearing and so become moral cripples.

GLOSSARY

Acrostic   An arrangement in which stipulated letters (for example, the first) of the words in question (often of a poem or psalm) themselves form a word or regular pattern.

Anthropomorphism   Personification; treating something nonhuman as though it were human.

Carte blanche   A blank check, free rein.

Dies irae   The day of wrath (judgment), especially as contemplated liturgically.

Godfearers   Gentiles who accepted the biblical God and the biblical ethics and perhaps were considering conversion.

Millennial movements   Tendencies to expect the end of the world or Judgment Day after 1000 years or at the turn of a millennium.

Mis en scène   Stage setting; context for a given action or speech.

Sapiential   Concerning wisdom.

Theodicy   The attempt to justify God in the face of evil.

Theophanous   Manifesting or bearing God.

Xenophobia   Fear of foreigners, usually to the point of hostility.

STUDY QUESTIONS

1. What is the significance of Hosea's marriage to Gomer?
2. Explain the criticism of ritual implicit in Hosea 6:6.
3. How does Joel relate locusts to the day of the Lord?
4. How does Amos 3:7 understand the role of Israel's prophets?
5. Explain the place of justice in Amos.
6. How does Amos understand "The day of the Lord"?
7. What lasting significance do you find in Obadiah?
8. Exemplify the humor of the book of Jonah.
9. Evaluate Micah 6:8.
10. Why was Nahum entered in the canonical Bible?
11. Describe the theodicy of Habakkuk.
12. What background does the universal judgment of Zephaniah presuppose?
13. What are the main theological assumptions of Haggai?
14. What are the functions of angels in Zechariah?
15. Explain the symbolism of the lamp stand in Zechariah 4.
16. Evaluate the ideal priest of Malachai 2:5–7.

NOTES

1. See Frederick E. Greenspahn, "Hosea, the Book of," in *Harper's Bible Dictionary*, ed. Paul J. Achtemeier. San Francisco: Harper & Row, 1985, pp. 407–8; Francis I. Andersen and David Noel Freedman, *Hosea*. Garden City, N.Y.: Doubleday Anchor Bible, 1980; Charles F. Kraft, "The Book of Hosea," in *The Minor Prophets*, ed. Charles M. Laymon. Nashville: Abingdon (Interpreter's Concise Commentary), 1983, pp. 1–27.
2. See Walter Vogels, "Diachronic and Synchronic Studies of Hosea 1–3," *Biblische Zeitschrift*, 28 (1984), 94–98.
3. See Millard C. Lind, "Hosea 5:8–6:6," *Interpretation*, 38 (1984), 398–403.
4. See Marc Z. Brettler, "Joel, the Book of," in *Harper's Bible Dictionary*, pp. 495–96.
5. See Elias D. Mallon, "A Stylistic Analysis of Joel 1:10–12," *Catholic Biblical Quarterly*, 45 (1983), 537–48.
6. See Jon D. Levenson, *Sinai and Zion*. Minneapolis: Winston, 1985.
7. See Herbert G. May, ed., *The New Oxford Annotated Bible with the Apocrypha*. New York: Oxford University Press, 1977, p. 1107.
8. See Gerhard Pfeifer, "Unausweichliche Konsequenzen: Denkformenanalyse von Amos iii 3–8," *Vetus Testamentum*, 33 (1983), 341–47.
9. See Paul F. Jacobs, " 'Cows of Bashan' — A Note on the Interpretation of Amos 4:1," *Journal of Biblical Literature*, 104 (1985), 109–10.
10. See Charles F. Kraft, "The Book of Amos," *The Minor Prophets*, p. 70.
11. See Joel W. Rosenberg, "Jonah, the Book of," *Harper's Bible Dictionary*, p. 503.
12. See Norman K. Gottwald, *The Hebrew Bible: A Socio-Literary Introduction*. Philadelphia: Fortress, 1985, p. 558.

13. See Duane L. Christensen, "The Song of Jonah: A Metrical Analysis," *Journal of Biblical Literature*, 104 (1985), 217–31.

14. See Allan John Hauser, "Jonah: In Pursuit of the Dove," *Journal of Biblical Literature*, 104 (1985), 21–37.

15. See Etan Levine, "Jonah as a Philosophical Book," *Zeitschrift für die Alttestamentliche Wissenschaft*, 96 (1984), 235–45.

16. See James Luther Mays, *Micah*. Philadelphia: Westminster (The Old Testament Library), 1976, p. 60.

17. See Bruce T. Dahlberg, "The Book of Micah," *The Minor Prophets*, p. 98.

18. See Hans Walter Wolff, "Michah the Moreshite — The Prophet and His Background," in *Israelite Wisdom*, ed. J. Gammie et al. Missoula, Mont.: Scholars Press, 1978, pp. 82–83.

19. See Brevard S. Childs, *Introduction to the Old Testament as Scripture*. Philadelphia: Fortress, 1979, pp. 437–38.

20. See James B. Pritchard, ed., *Ancient Near Eastern Texts Relating to the Old Testament*, 3rd ed. Princeton: Princeton University Press, 1969, pp. 405–7.

21. See Abraham J. Heschel, *The Prophets*. New York: Harper & Row, 1962, pp. 140–44.

22. See Norbert Lohfink, "Zefanja und das Israel der Armen," *Bibel und Kirche*, 39 (1984), 100–108.

23. See Duane L. Christensen, "Zephaniah 2:4–15: A Theological Basis for Josiah's Program of Political Expansion," *Catholic Biblical Quarterly*, 46 (1984), 669–82.

24. See Peter C. Craigie, *Twelve Prophets*, Volume 2. Philadelphia: Westminster, 1985, pp. 133–53. See also David L. Petersen, *Haggai and Zechariah 1–8*. Philadelphia: Westminster (The Old Testament Library), 1984, pp. 17–106.

25. See Carol L. Meyers, "Lampstand," in *Harper's Bible Dictionary*, p. 546.

26. See Petersen, *Haggai and Zechariah 1–8*, p. 271.

27. See May, *The New Oxford Annotated Bible with the Apocrypha*, p. 1156.

28. See Eric M. Meyers, "Malachai, the Book of," *Harper's Bible Dictionary*, p. 598.

CHAPTER 16

Psalms

TEXTUAL ANALYSIS

The third portion of the Hebrew Bible is a disparate collection of materials known as the "Writings." Traditionally the rabbis grouped these materials into the large works (Psalms, Proverbs, and Job), the works used at religious festivals (Songs, Ruth, Lamentations, Ecclesiastes, and Esther), and the historical works (Daniel, Ezra-Nehemiah, and Chronicles). Present-day scholarship makes further distinctions, noting that Psalms is often hymnody; Proverbs, Job, and Ecclesiastes are mainly wisdom literature; Ruth is much like a short story; Daniel is apocalyptic literature; and so forth. In fact, the study of the genres and subgenres composing the books of the Writings has now become quite sophisticated.

The Book of Psalms is the closest thing to a biblical prayerbook or psalter that either early Judaism or early Christianity ever sanctioned. As we see, Psalms contains many different types of prayer, but all of them have functioned through the ages after the canonization of this book as authoritative models of how the community or the individual might address the Lord. By longstanding consensus the present work is divided into five subunits or "books" (which perhaps were meant by the canonical editors to recall the five books of Torah):

    I Psalms 1 – 41
    II Psalms 42 – 72
    III Psalms 73 – 89

IV Psalms 90 – 106

V Psalms 107 – 150

I Psalms 1–41

We do not have the space to comment extensively on all the psalms, so we have decided to concentrate on four psalms that are both instrinsically significant and also illustrate main genres within the Psalter: Psalms 1, 51, 110, and 145. Respectively, they represent the genres of the wisdom psalm, the individual lament, the royal psalm, and the hymn (of praise or thanksgiving).

Psalm 1 is generally regarded as both an introduction to the entire collection and an example of the genre "wisdom psalm" or "psalm about the law." (The pioneering work of classifying the Psalms according to different genres was inaugurated by Herman Gunkel in the first decades of the twentieth century and was forwarded by his pupil Sigmund Mowinckel. Subsequent scholars have generally accepted this foundational work, as well as its main assumption that most of the Psalms arose in the context of the cultic life of the Israelite community, but they have added qualifications and nuances as further research has suggested.)[1] As a celebration of wisdom, which it correlates with walking according to the Torah of God, Psalm 1 orients the entire Psalter toward religious obedience. Thereby, it suggests that Israel's existence should center in a prayerful, wholehearted fidelity to the covenant (first, the Mosaic covenant but, as we see, the kingly Davidic covenant frequently comes into play as well). Note the correlation between fidelity to the Torah and prospering.

Psalm 1 proposes a model of the ideal Israelite, as the editors of the Psalter conceive it. Such a person meditates on the Torah day and night. By comparison with Deuteronomy 30 and Joshua 1, it seems plain that the Mosaic Law has become the spiritual food of the ideal Israelite personality. The further implication is that human meditation and prayer constitute a response to God's prior speaking. What Israel does at prayer, communal or private, is the second moment in a dialogue. Taking the Torah as God's initiating address of the chosen people, the editors of the Psalter conceive of the various sorts of prayers in their book, from hymns of praise and thanksgiving to painful laments and cries for help, as the people's answer. Worship or prayer, therefore, should be the habitual medium of national life. What the theology of the covenant puts in reflective form the Psalter puts in direct, spontaneous form. When Israel is what it should be, national life is an ongoing conversation with God, an ongoing exchange (heart to heart) in which the holy Lord speaks forth the words of life and then listens to the chorus of positive and negative responses his words have provoked.

Psalm 1 also holds the seeds of a notion of sacred scripture. What Israelites are to delight in, are constantly to meditate upon, virtually had, in the psychology of such intense usage, to become a privileged text, a unique source of guidance. The sapiential outlook of Psalm 1 and the canonical editors ensured that the Torah would become the basis of distinguishing the righteous from the wicked. A person is blessed for not following the counsel of the wicked, not going as sinners go, not taking the position of scoffers, but the reason why such an ideal Israelite is able to refrain from wrongdoing is the greater allure of Torah. Because Torah gives delight, the precepts of the Law, the holy behavior demanded by Moses and the prophets, and a stance of thanksgiving and trust are not only possible but obvious, easy. We could say that Psalm 1 gives to Torah the enabling function that other aspects of biblical theology, both Jewish and Christian, give to the divine Spirit. When Torah (by divine gift and grace) delights the believer's spirit, and so plants the believer like a sturdy tree, the radical prosperity of being where one ought to be, being oriented as one has been made to be, inevitably occurs. The psalmist may have material prosperity in mind, but further reflection shows that the only prosperity outside human vagaries is the prosperity of wisdom and holiness that comes when the human personality is rightly ordered. For the psalmist, such right ordering is a spirit open to God, beholden only to God, in both good times and bad. Genuine worship, in contrast to idolatry, takes aim at the sovereign mystery of God, knowing this is the only absolute in human life.

The matter of religious delight and disgust, to be sure, is elusive. Whether and how people find nourishment, fulfillment, in some version of the divine law is part of the strictly mysterious matter of divine providence. What the psalmist here seems to rely upon is both the historical experience of Israel (the Torah of Moses kept the people in good overall health, while disobedience — following the ways of the nations — brought manifold sickness) and the intuition that human beings can only be fulfilled by the true, living God. The argument from historical experience is familiar to us as the crux of Deuteronomistic theology. The argument from the requirements for human fulfillment tends to spotlight the significance of worship, and so to increase the significance of the rest of the psalter.

Nowadays, we may say that worship tends to be the act separating the formally religious from the irreligious or secular. In the days of the psalmist, virtually all people worshiped, so the question was which worship was genuine — that is, directed to the true God. Israel was convinced, by the mighty acts of God on its behalf, that its God was the sole true divinity. The coin of this argument was experiential: what happened when Israel believed in God, prayed to God, set its heart only on the one revealed to it through the ancestors and Moses. "Open to this Lord, make this Lord your treasure," the argument ran, "and you will know the best of human portions." In our translation, the best of human portions is not lording it over other people, not having more flocks and stocks, but being in love with the love that moves the stars, having one's heart overflow with joy in realizing that the ultimate, creative force is better than one ever could have hoped. This is the sort of promise we find Psalm 1 making and the rest of the Psalter insinuating. In the hymns of praise, the promise seems completely fulfilled. In the psalms of lament, the fulfillment is muted, pained, groping. There the touch of grace is having a place to go when one feels forsaken, having a final defense against despair and meaninglessness. But always the "answer" is turning to God.

Psalm 2 also has introductory or orientational value. It recalls the covenant with David and sets Israel among the nations as God's elected people who center at Zion under God's kingly son. The nations oppose the destiny of Israel, to their frustration, because it is established in the immutable decrees of the Lord. Psalm 2 is usually considered a "royal ceremonial song" — a psalm that was performed, if not originally composed, for the coronation of the king.[2]

Psalm 3 is usually considered an "individual lament." Note the ascription of the song to David at the time he was fleeing from Absalom. As the Torah was attributed to Moses, so the Psalms were attributed to David and the wisdom literature was attributed to Solomon. Modern scholarship takes these attributions as symbolic or associative (a Psalm could be for David or to David as well as of David or by David) rather than literal or univocal. The word "selah" that occurs after verse 3:2 puzzles scholars, who do not know its precise significance. Sometimes this word and others that, like it, seem to be marginal notations are taken as musical directives.[3] Note how the psalm expresses both distress at troubled circumstances and trust that God will see the one praying through the hard time. The very vagueness or generalized quality of both the distress and the confidence make this psalm, like many others, suitable for use in a variety of different physical or emotional circumstances.

Psalm 4 tends to be considered a "psalm of confidence," here both anonymous and written for an individual person (rather than for the community as a whole, although there is no reason that a group of people could not all use it together). The hallmark of this genre is the surety of receiving a hearing from God that it expresses and the trust it shows that God will effect deliverance. Verse 4:4 sanctions expressing one's anger (and by implication one's other emotions) forthrightly. Verse 4:8 suggests the trust of a child, who goes to sleep feeling secure in the strength and love of its parents.

Psalm 5 is another individual lament, anonymous and written for the individual voice. It counsels trusting God and doing right as the proper responses to hard times (groaning). Note the implicit call to worship in the Temple and the association of enemies with wrongdoing and so eventual doom.

Psalms 6 and 7 are further examples of the "individual lament." Verse 6:3 has become a famous cry of distress at troubles that have brought the petitioner to the breaking point. Note in verse 6:4 the reference to the divine *ḥesed* or steadfast love. Verse 6:5 shows that at the time of this psalm's composition Israel had no strong confidence about an afterlife. Psalm 7:3–5 express the petitioner's sense of innocence, which translates into a readiness to accept even death if guilt should be proved. Note the imagery that makes God both a warrior and a judge. Righteousness becomes human beings' best hope for help from God.

Psalm 8 exemplifies still another genre, usually classified as a "hymn of descriptive praise." The hallmark of this sort of psalm is the praise of God with which it begins and ends. We might also stress wonder and the engendering of faith in God. Verses 8:3–4 comprise a famous expression of God's control of nature and humanity's consequent smallness. Verses 8:5–6 are equally famous for marveling at the dominion and glory that God nonetheless has lavished on human beings.[4]

Psalms 9 and 10 are related (in the Septuagint they are a single psalm), and they are composed as an acrostic (every second verse begins with a different succeeding letter of the Hebrew alphabet). Generically, they are individual laments, although Psalm 9 opens with thanks and praise of God. Note the kingship accorded God in Psalm 9, and the implication in verses 9:13–14 that life is best used for praise of God. Verse 9:18 spotlights the plight of the poor in the tradition of the prophets, as does verse 10:2. The description of the wicked in Psalm 10 is classic. In addition, the prayer to God for justice, and the expectation that God does work for justice, go to the marrow of Israelite faith (all the more remarkably so after the Exile).

Psalm 11 is an individual psalm of confidence. It stresses the oversight of the

God who rules in both the Temple and heaven and emphasizes the Lord's love of righteousness.

Psalm 12 brings us a new genre: "communal lament." The characteristic feature of this type of psalm is an expression of the whole community's grief and need due to such afflictions as famine, military disaster, economic hard times, and the like. Such psalms also likely were used on days of fast and penance, when the community ceremonialized its expression of lament for the perennial hardship of its life or for its moral failings. Note in verses 12:1–2 the near-despair about human morality, which makes God like a last or sole resort. God is depicted as rising up to defend the poor and as pure in his own promises.

Psalm 13 is an individual lament, again sounding the refrain "How long?" It shows a dread of being defeated by the enemy (whether military or social), and a tendency to link such defeat with the humiliation or detraction of God himself. The last line, though, is a winning expression of gratitude for God's bounty.

Psalm 14 introduces the genre known as "prophetic oracles of judgment or admonition." Verse 14:1 is a famous line, later taken as a condemnation of atheism but in its own day probably an implication of the practical disregard of God (especially as judge) that wicked behavior carries. Verse 14:2 confirms the initial impression that folly and wisdom are at issue. Verse 14:4 reminds us of the prophetic lament that knowledge of God has fled from the land. The concluding verses suggest a time when deliverance from oppression was desperately needed.

Psalm 15 introduces the new category "entrance and processional liturgies." The list of virtues amounts to the passport needed by those who would ascend to the holy hill of Zion and enter into the Lord's house.[5]

Psalm 16 is another individual psalm of confidence. Among the interesting notes are the way that God becomes the believer's chosen portion (treasure) (verse 16:5), the stress on counsel and instruction (verse 16:7), and the joy that fidelity entails (verse 16:9, 11).[6]

Psalm 17 is another individual lament. The petitioner seeks vindication and claims righteousness. Note the figure of "the apple of the eye" in verse 17:8, as well as the figure of divine wings. As usual, the lamentor asks the destruction of the wicked, as though that were the right of the innocent.

Psalm 18 is a "royal thanksgiving song or declarative praise," and it is a doublet of 2 Samuel 22. The king gives thanks for deliverance from a military foe, but the expression is general enough to celebrate any victory. Note the figures of the Lord as rock, of the theophanic smoke and fire, and of the divine deliverance. The one offering praise stresses keeping the divine ordinances, the Lord's loyalty and help for the humble, and the confidence that God gives the religious warrior. Verses 18:43–45 suggest a king of an Israel in charge of other nations. The imagery of the conclusion is especially dependent on the royal Davidic covenant.[7]

Scholarly commentary tends to divide Psalm 19 into two portions: verses 19:1–6 and 19:7–14. The first portion is a hymn, and the second portion is usually considered a wisdom psalm. The first verses employ naturalistic figures that have come to be well known and loved. The underlying notion is that natural phenomena, especially those of the heavens, express the glory and governance of God. The second portion of the psalm has some of the most confident praise of the divine law that we find in the whole Psalter. The generality of the benefits of obeying the Torah suggests that a good conscience is its own reward.

Gottwald considers Psalm 20, like Psalm 2, to be a royal ceremonial song, connected either with the coronation of a king or with the annual celebration of his accession to rule. A leading scholar of the Psalms, the late Mitchell Dahood, rather speaks of "a prayer of the congregation for the king setting out for battle (vss. 2–6), and the answer to the prayer announced by a priest or prophet (7–10)."[8] The overall impression created is that God deals with his people through his anointed king, so that the fate of the king epitomizes the fate of the people.

Psalm 21 is another royal ceremonial song, this one celebrating a king's victory (perhaps in the battle assumed by Psalm 20). The effect is to make kingly power, both military and administrative, derivative from God's anointing and support. The God in the background is himself the great warrior on Israel's behalf (a theme as old as the Exodus). Note that enemies are to be destroyed forthrightly, without much pause for scruples.

Psalm 22 is an individual lament. It begins with a sense of forsakenness, moves to a recall of God's holiness and trustworthiness, and then dialectically alternates between the low estate of the petitioner and the many reasons the divine nature gives for trusting that it will help. The final verses are a great expression of faith and praise, with the motif that God has dominion over whatever happens on Earth (divine providence). In Matthew 27:46 and Mark 15:34 Jesus quotes the beginning of Psalm 22 from the cross, just prior to his death.

Psalm 23 is an individual psalm that expresses confidence in God. Certainly it is one of the most famous psalms in the whole psalter. God is the shepherd who takes full care of the people who are his sheep. Confident of this, the psalmist fears no evil and expects a feast of goodness and mercy. Note the rod and staff of verse 23:4—shepherd's implements that in the context of Torah and wisdom suggest the discipline of the covenantal law.

Psalm 24 may be a song for a liturgical entrance or procession. The first motif is the Lord's rule of natural creation, and the second motif is the moral cleanliness required of those who would ascend to the Lord's Mount Zion or Temple. Verses 24:7–10 are quite famous, praising the King of glory for whom the gates of all sanctuaries stand guard.

Psalm 25 is an individual lament in acrostic form. The petitioner asks deliverance from enemies and seeks to walk in God's ways. Note the request for pardon of guilt in verse 25:11 and the correlation of holy fear with friendship with God in verse 25:14. Verse 25:22 seems designed to generalize the psalm for communal use. Psalm 26 is an individual lament as well. The petitioner would establish his or her innocence and love of the Temple, because of which deliverance from personal enemies would be fitting.[9]

Psalm 27 expresses an individual's confidence in the Lord. Note the surety that trust in God brings, and the desire to dwell in the Lord's house. Verse 27:11 has the familiar motif of learning the Lord's way or path. The concluding "Wait for the Lord" is sufficiently general to be relevant at virtually all times.

The individual lament of Psalm 28:1–5 gives way in verses 28:6–9 to a song of thanksgiving. The "pit" of 28:1 is Sheol, the underworld. Note the opening request that sinners be requited for their evil-doing. The blessing offered in verse 28:6 apparently is provoked by the petitioner's having been heard and answered. Note also the images of strength, refuge, and shepherd in the concluding verses.

Psalm 29 is a hymn that descriptively praises the Lord. The psalmist fixes on the voice of the Lord (perhaps echoing the creative word of Genesis). The proper response (verse 29:9) is "glory," and the concluding imagery is of the Lord's being enthroned as king over the flood (of chaos) and his giving strength to his people.[10]

Psalm 30 is the first example of an "anonymous individual thanksgiving song." Typically, psalms in this category include a call to give thanks, an account of past distress, a confession that Yahweh has given deliverance, and perhaps a mention of a sacrifice or an expression of blessings. Here the petitioner feels as though he or she had descended to Sheol, the underworld of the dead, and had been raised up. Verse 30:5b is an effective line: "Weeping may tarry for the night, but joy comes with the morning." The effect of the psalm is to strengthen confidence that God does help his people turn mourning into rejoicing.

Psalm 31 is an individual lament. Note the parallel between verses 1–8 and 9–24: two similarly structured cries for help. God is a rock, calling people away from trust in idols. Wicked enemies are the menace, and the psalmist clearly suffers from their scorn, plotting, and whispering.

Psalm 32 tends to be classified as an anonymous individual song of thanksgiving, like Psalm 30. Here the motif is gratitude for the forgiveness of sin, and the noteworthy feature is the psalmist's insight into the psychology of guilt. Verses 32:8–9 suggest the wisdom motifs of teaching and understanding. The finale argues that a good conscience brings singular joy.

Psalm 33 is a hymn proper, because it mainly expresses descriptive praise of God. Note that the praise can be musical and that one of its main subjects is the creative word of the Lord. Verse 33:6 is a famous verse on this theme. Further imagery includes the oversight of God from heaven, especially his eye upon those who fear him and hope in his steadfast love (verse 33:18).

Psalm 34 is an individual thanksgiving song, concerned with "magnifying" (making great) the name of the Lord. Verse 34:4 suggests a foundation in the experience of being answered and delivered, as does verse 34:6. From verse 34:11 on, the tone becomes that of a wisdom psalm, whose motif is learning the fear of the Lord and the pathway to the good life. The last half of the psalm also is reminiscent of the prophetic theme that God takes special care of the poor and the downtrodden.[11]

Psalm 35 is an anonymous individual lament (the category with the most psalms: forty-four). Here the enemies are presented as military foes, and the petitioner is concerned to profess innocence. Verse 35:13 suggests that the petitioner did such enemies good, when they were on hard times. Putting them to shame, now that they rejoice at the petitioner's misfortunes, would be an act vindicating justice and right order.

Psalm 36 is also an anonymous individual lament. The opening verses sketch a grim portrait of the wicked, by contrast with which the righteousness of the Lord shines like light dispelling darkness. Note how the steadfast love of God is this psalmist's bedrock and how it could make possible the endurance of wickedness.[12]

Psalm 37, which deals with wisdom and the law, has an acrostic form. The main instruction is to do good and wait patiently for God to reward it. Lawrence E. Toombs has commented that "the terms righteous, meek, poor, needy, upright, blameless, and saints mean the same thing. They refer to the faithful adherents to Israel's covenant faith whose chief characteristic is unshakable confidence in the God of the covenant (they trust in and wait for the Lord)."[13]

Psalm 38 takes us back to individual lamenting. The petitioner equates present sufferings with punishment by God and is eloquent in cataloguing the trials that have come. The solution suggested for problems like this is waiting for the Lord with longing and confessing one's iniquities.

Psalm 39 is but variation on the theme of pouring out one's lament. Verses 4–6 have the overtones of a sapiential musing about the futility of fleeting human life. Present sufferings are again interpreted as the Lord's chastisement, and the petitioner rather movingly asks merely to know gladness before death comes.

Gottwald considers Psalm 40 to be another individual lament, but Dahood thinks it is composed of two distinct parts. Verses 2–11 express thanksgiving for healing, and verses 12–17, which are nearly identical to Psalm 70, are a lament. Note the linking of pride and idolatry in verse 40:4 and the depreciation of sacrifice in verse 40:6. The conclusion expresses faith in God's deliverance, but quite humanly it asks God not to tarry.

Psalm 41, which concludes the first book of the Psalter, has elements of thanksgiving and petition for healing. First the psalmist praises those who are generous to the poor. Then the motif shifts to a plea for healing and relief from the delight enemies are taking in the petitioner's misfortune. The rather solemn blessing ("doxology") with which the psalm concludes is usually interpreted as a way of indicating and solemnizing the end of the first book of the Psalter.

II Psalms 42–72

Psalm 42 is the first of several psalms (see also Psalms 44–49, 84–85, 87–88) that refer to the sons of Korah. (For the sorry end that came to Korah, see Numbers 16–17.) According to 2 Chronicles 20:19 the Korahites were a major guild of Temple singers. A "maskil" is a "skillful song." Many scholars consider Psalm 42 and Psalm 43 individual laments that in fact constitute one Psalm (note the refrain of verses 42:5, 42:11, and 43:5). Psalm 42 is famous for the opening lines poetically expressing longing for God. As a whole, it depicts well the emotional prosperities and sufferings that the presence or absence of God tends to bring to the devout. Psalm 43 covers some of the same ground, although the mourning it describes seems owed to human enemies. It is best known in Christian circles for verse 3: "Oh send out thy light and thy truth."

Psalm 44 is a communal lament. Note the opening recital of God's great deeds on Israel's behalf in the Exodus and Conquest of the promised land. After this faith-bolstering recall, however, the psalm dips into lament about present downtroddenness. The tone suggests the defeats of the Exile. We should not miss the protestations of fidelity to the covenant (verses 44:17–18, 20) nor the call to God to rouse himself (and be the warrior-protector he was of old).

Psalm 45 has been taken to be a royal wedding song. Note the almost fulsome praise of the king, the reference to the Davidic covenant (45:6, picked up by Hebrews 1:8). From verse 9 to verse 15 focus shifts to the bride and her attendants. The conclusion foresees a fruitful progeny for the regal pair (and so the extension of the Davidic covenant).

Psalm 46 is the first that Gottwald classifies as a "hymn of Zion." Characteristically, such psalms picture God as dwelling on Mount Zion and overpowering Israel's enemies. Whereas Herman Gunkel stressed an eschatological reference to a future day of salvation, Sigmund Mowinckel found in these hymns overtones of

Jerusalem, the Old City in the foreground and the New City in the background, as seen from the Mount of Olives. *(Used with permission of the photographer, Wolfgang Roth)*

a cultic affirmation that God was present to resecure the foundations of Israelite life. Either way, Psalm 46 stresses the stability that God gives Israel. Its most famous line is probably 46:10: "Be still, and know that I am God."

Psalm 47 is also the first instance of a genre we have not yet encountered. Like Psalms 93, 96, 97, and 99, Psalm 47 celebrates the kingship of Yahweh (again either hoped for in the future or affirmed cultically as shaping the present). Perhaps the most remarkable feature of Psalm 47 is the unmitigated joy and praise that burst out of it.

Psalm 48 is another hymn of Zion. Here, the presence of God strikes fear in Israel's enemies. The implication is that Mount Zion had come to function, symbolically, as a fortress guaranteeing Israel's security in its land.

Psalm 49 returns to sapiential interests. From the certainty of death the psalmist would gain proper perspective. Note in verse 49:15 the faith that God can ransom the soul of the faithful person from death and "receive" that person (take him or her into the divine presence?).[14]

Psalm 50 is the first of a group (see also Psalms 73–83) credited to Asaph. According to 1 Chronicles 6:39 an Asaph was appointed by David to oversee music in worship; according to 2 Chronicles 5:12 a man of this name sang at the dedication of Solomon's Temple. Gottwald considers Psalm 50 a prophetic oracle of judgment, and Dahood largely agrees, speaking of a prophetic liturgy of divine judgment. Note the qualifications placed on sacrificial offerings and the call for observance of the code of the covenant. The general effect is a sobering reminder that God's judgment is the only one that his people have to pass.

Psalm 51 is the second we treat fully. Whereas Psalm 1 exemplified the wisdom psalm and had to be estimated in terms of its introducing the entire Psalter, Psalm 51 represents the lament, the outpouring of the soul in need. Scholars sometimes distinguish between laments of individuals and communal laments expressed in the voice of the entire nation. Here the individual accents prevail.

The distinguishing feature of Psalm 51 is the consciousness of sin it reveals. When biblical theologians discuss the sense of sin manifested in either the psalms in particular or the Hebrew Bible in general, this is one of the texts to which they tend to refer. The cry to God is for mercy: overlooking, not dealing harshly with, the person's wrongdoing and guilt. The steadfast love mentioned in verse 1, we recall, is the prime attribute of the God of the covenant. The context of this confession of sin and plea for mercy, then, is the relationship established on Sinai. God has graciously offered guidance of the people, presence with them as their fellow traveler. The people in return have pledged fidelity. Almost always, we can translate the sins lamented in the psalms as ruptures of this covenantal relationship. They are not so essentially violations of an ethical code as personal offenses against God. Thus, we might say that the crux of biblical ethics is maintaining personal relationships with God. "Sin" is the commission or omission that breaks contact and sunders the bond of communion and fellow traveling. It is the active unwillingness to maintain the reflection of God's own justice and love intrinsically necessary if we are to be related to God.

Verse 2 asks God for cleansing and implies that God can give such cleansing, which would be like being washed of one's filth. Verse 1, which speaks of blotting out transgression, achieves the same effect through slightly different imagery: a clean slate. Verses 3–5 appear to go deeper, making sin habitual, even constitutional. The lamenter is not simply repenting of individual transgressions. A constant tendency toward transgression, a regular weakness and so inability to be and act as one ought, seems in question. Religious people, in fact, do usually develop this sort of sensitivity. They examine their consciences regularly and find themselves far distant from the purity they feel God desires of them. Note the personal tone in verse 4: sin is against God — against God alone. Certainly we would have to say that some sins are social and wound specific fellow human beings. But here the lament is more concerned with how wrongdoing and bad conscience reject calls from God, intimacies God held out. Here "God" covers "truth" and "justice," with the result that all dishonesty and injustice can be considered personal offenses against God. Verse 5 makes sinfulness congenital, suggesting that the generations pass on their liability to disorder, their itch to evil, like a noxious gene. In one sense relationship with God is more than human beings can sustain. The holiness of God condemns them always to be somewhat in the wrong. Consequently, the divine mercy is always a need and a blessing. If God were not willing to covenant with weak, sinful human beings who regularly fail to hold up their side of the compact, the very notion of a divine-human bonding would be impossible.

Verses 6–9 conjoin wisdom, cleansing, renewal, healing, and forgiveness. The faith is that God can work reform, regeneration of the sinner, from within. Here we think of the new covenant of Jeremiah or the refleshed bones of Ezekiel. The spirit of God, moving in the depths of the personality, can turn what was disordered into order, can replace a heart of flesh (wayward desire) with a heart of spirit (purified love).

Verses 10–12 make this longed-for renewal explicit: a clean heart, a new and right spirit, a sense of the holy spirit that brings joy. Peace and joy, the two marks that spiritual masters regularly use to discern the presence of divine inspiration, are here in abundance, with the added motif that forgiveness, return from waywardness, has special joys. Restored, the sinner pledges to help others back to righteousness. The restoration will become another title by which to praise God.

In verses 15–17 the dominant imagery contrasts animal sacrifices with the sacrifice of a broken (repentant) spirit. This is in keeping with the spiritualizing of the covenant we have seen in the prophets: mercy rather than sacrifice. The point seems to be that sin requires much more than guilt offerings, which are external rituals. It requires inner breakup of the sinful patterns and restoration to habits of righteousness. Verses 18–19 have the note of a later addition by a priestly editor fearful that the spiritual note struck in verses 16 and 17 would denigrate the official cult.

Psalm 52 qualifies as an individual's song of thanksgiving. The opening verses threaten the wicked, but from verse 6 on the threats merely become background for the praise that the righteous direct to the steadfast love of God.

Psalm 53 brings more admonition in the style of a prophetic oracle. The psalmist first attacks atheism, whether practical or speculative, and then correlates lack of wisdom and falling away into depravity. The final themes are the sure punishment that will come upon the wicked and Israel's hopes for deliverance.

Psalms 54–57 qualify as individual laments. Psalm 54 is not distinctive, but Psalm 55 has interesting naturalistic imagery. Note also in verses 55:13–14 the special suffering the psalmist finds in being ill-used by friends. (See also verses 55:20–21.) Verse 55:22 provides the bottom line: "Cast your burden on the Lord, and he will sustain you." Psalm 56 opens with rather standard complaints about afflictions from enemies, but its concluding trust that God both notes every happening and is on the psalmist's side is distinctive. Psalm 57 opens with a winning description of gaining shelter from God. The imagery of the middle verses — lions and hunters' snares — is both strong and archaic. The concluding music to God seems both realistic and symbolic: Israel worshiped with song, and the spirit of the believer regularly proclaims the goodness of God.

Psalm 58 continues the mood of lament but shifts it into a communal voice. The language is especially harsh, in both its accusations against enemies and the punishments it asks God to exact. Verse 58:10 summarizes this dark mood: "The righteous will rejoice when he sees the vengeance; he will bathe his feet in the blood of the wicked."

Psalm 59 expresses more lament, this time in the first person. The psalmist's hopes for deliverance dovetail with God's derision of the (antagonistic) nations. The steadfast love of God stands in counterpoint with the prowling and howling of the enemies, who are like vicious dogs.

Psalm 60 seems to be a communal lament that perhaps dates to the time of David or Solomon.[15] Noteworthy is the connection made between military distress and God's rejection (as though he would not fight on behalf of his king and people).

Psalm 61 also expresses lament, but more individualistically. The psalmist first thinks of the refuge God could offer, but then, in verses 7–8, prays for the king.[16]

Psalm 62 breaks the mood of lament with expressions of confidence. God alone offers security in a world full of enemies and troubles. The concluding verse sketches a justice in terms of which all people would receive from God what their deeds merited.

Psalms 63 and 64 are more individual laments. Psalm 63 mainly deals in religious experience, describing the effect of the presence or absence of God. Verses 9–11 seem to be add-ons because they throw in opponents and the king. By now the "enemy" of verse 64:1 seems to be a stylistic device, capable of application to any sort of foe. Note that scheming and backbiting seem to injure the psalmist as much as physical assaults.

Psalm 65 qualifies as a song of communal thanksgiving or declarative praise. The psalm begins by praising the God who grants forgiveness. Then it uses naturalistic imagery to express the grandeur of this God, who is the creator and governor of all that exists.

Psalm 66 is mainly declarative praise in an individual voice. The words "glory," "terrible," and "power" show that the psalmist is facing the God who is both the creator of the world and Israel's savior from its enemies. The first verses intimate the history of God's mighty deeds on Israel's behalf and focus on the entire people, but the last half of the psalm focuses on an individual's worship and sense of having been heard by God.

Psalm 67 offers praise in a communal voice. Verse 67:1 recalls the blessing of Numbers 6:25. The main reason given for blessing God is his judgment over all the nations (over all history).

Psalm 68 alters the mood by suggesting a liturgical procession. God is the cosmic king who scatters his (and Israel's) enemies merely by arising. Note the tender figure of verse 68:5: "father of the fatherless and protector of widows." Verses 15–16 place this great king on Mount Zion. Verses 19–20 unqualifiedly make God Israel's salvation. The suggestion of a liturgical procession is strongest in verses 24–27. Verses 28–31 seem to have Egypt in mind. The overall effect is a great tribute to the awesome rule of Yahweh, conceived as a cosmic warrior.

Psalms 69–71 are individual laments. Psalm 69 is a quite extended description of the petitioner's sufferings. Note the theme that piety brought reproach. The imagery of drowning recurs, and the revenge sought against enemies nearly exceeds the bounds of justice. Verse 69:31 is interesting because it makes thanksgiving more pleasing to God than sacrifice. Psalm 70 is an unexceptional or typical lament, except that it reproduces parts of Psalm 40. Psalm 71 is equally typical, although verses 71:9 and 71:17–18 suggest the special sufferings of old age. A touch of sapiential interest in verse 71:17 makes the concluding praise of God seem like the consummation of wisdom.

Psalm 72 is a royal ceremonial song. Its opening verses suggest a parallelism between God and the righteous king, and the rest of the psalm spells out the prosperities that a righteous kingship would entail. The blessings at the end of the psalm are like a doxology. Verse 72:20 makes it explicit that this collection of psalms, attributed to David, is ended.

III Psalms 73–89

Psalm 73 deals with wisdom, which here clearly is practical knowledge of how to prosper in ultimate perspective. The psalmist urges purity of heart, which contrasts with the pride of the wicked (who may prosper materially). Note in verses 73:10–14 the entrance into theodicy: The prosperity of the wicked tempts people to say that God does not know what is happening. Wisdom, however, means finding in prayer (in the sanctuary of God) a proper perspective, according to which the wicked are sure to come to ruin. God is the refuge of the wise, and following God's counsel will bring one to glory (verse 73:24).

Psalm 74 qualifies as a communal lament. The scene described suggests the conquest by Babylon in 587 to 586 B.C.E. (except for verse 9, which complains of a lack of prophets). Most of the reasons given in the middle of the psalm for trusting in God stem from his lordship over nature. Verse 74:19 interestingly makes Israel God's dove. Throughout the assumption is that Israel's defeats reflect badly on its God.

Psalm 75 deals in judgment or admonition. God speaks in the first person, promising a judgment on the wicked that will make the Earth steady.

Psalm 76 is a hymn of Zion, typical in locating a theophanous deity on the mountain of Jerusalem. The hymn of verses 76:4–9 recalls the exploits of the divine warrior who accomplished the Exodus.

Psalm 77 is an individual lament, mainly about the absence or punishment of God that troubled times signify. Verses 77:11–12 suggest that remembering God's past actions on Israel's behalf might import him into the present. The closing verses carry imagery first of creation and then of the Exodus.

Psalm 78 is the first of a genre called "historical psalms," into which Psalms 105 and 106 also fall. The opening verses have the sapiential tone of a teaching, but the bulk of the psalm is a recital of salient facts from Israelite history, especially from the time of the Exodus and the wandering in the wilderness. The main point is the championship of Israel that God has exercised, despite its infidelities. This suggests that wisdom is remembering that the Lord is the great defender of the people's prosperity.

Psalm 79 is a lament in a communal voice. The time clearly is one of defeat, and the greatest offense Israel takes is at the pollution of God's Temple by foreigners. Compassion and deliverance will mean the abating of God's anger, as suffering has meant its flaming forth. The desire for vengeance is clear in verse 79:12: "Return sevenfold into the bosom of our neighbors the taunts with which they have taunted thee, O Lord."

Psalm 80 also qualifies as a communal lament. The shining face petitioned in verses 80:3 and 80:7 is imagery associated with the divine glory. Verses 80:8 and following develop the imagery of Israel as God's vine. By the logic of the psalm, the shining of God's face itself is the substance of salvation.

Psalm 81 expresses judgment or admonition. After an initial call to praise God (liturgical imagery), the divine voice speaks in prophet-like tones, castigating the people for their idolatries and infidelities. Verse 81:13 strikes the motif of walking according to Torah, and verse 81:16 recalls the feeding in the wilderness.

Psalm 82, which also expresses admonition, recalls the prophetic themes of justice for the weak and knowledge of God. Verse 82:1 is interesting for the figure of the deity in council. Verses 82:6–7 strip lesser deities or idols of their immortality (and so deny that they are truly divine).

Psalm 83 is a communal lament that names several national enemies. Note the references to Gideon's victory over Midian (Judges 6–8) and to Deborah's and

Barak's victory over Sisera and Jabin (Judges 4–5). The God of the wind and flame is asked to shame Israel's enemies, for the honor of his own name.

The first verses of Psalm 84, another hymn of Zion, are well known. The psalm as a whole glorifies a life centered on divine worship, which this writer associates with God's mountain in Jerusalem.

Psalm 85 shifts the mood back to communal lament. The opening verses recall that in the past God has acted favorably toward his land and people. Surely then his present anger (expressed in the hard times his people are suffering) can abate and "salvation" (restoration to wholeness and felicity) can return. The psalmist is confident that God will speak peace to his people, and the concluding verses anticipate the blessing that the return of God's favor will entail.

In Psalm 86 the voice of lament is more individual. The petitioner claims justice and deals with God as his or her sole reliance. Although verse 86:11 speaks in sapiential tones, the lamentation does not gather fullest momentum until the final verses. Note that verse 86:15 depends on the famous description of God in Exodus 34:6.

Psalm 87 qualifies as another hymn of Zion. For this psalmist the center of Israelite worship is without peer.

The individual lamenting of Psalm 88 first deals in the familiar imagery of a spirit depressed unto Sheol. Verse 88:7 probably conflates the psalmist's sufferings with an assumed rejection by God. The argument of verses 88:10–12 is that the living are the ones who deserve God's help. The mood of this psalm continues grim to the end, with little of the customary outbreak of hope, although certainly we can interpret persevering in asking for help as an expression of considerable trust or hope.

Psalm 89 is a royal prayer in which the king mainly asks for deliverance from his enemies. One division of the psalm considers verses 1–37 to comprise covenantal promises to the king and verses 38–51 to lament the fall of the king. The initial verses, which praise at length God's wonderful attributes as creator and savior, lean heavily on the Davidic covenant. Note the qualification entered in verses 89:30–32, where fidelity to the covenantal law is required, and also the counter-assertion of verses 89:33–37 that the promise to David is inviolable. Verses 89:38–45 finally bring us to the royal lament over the hard times upon which the Davidic rule has fallen. (Perhaps the historical occasion is the fall of Jehoiachin in 597. See 2 Kings 24:8–15.) Verses 89:47–48 express wisdom convictions about the relativities introduced by death. The final argument is that God's anointed should not be mocked and that the enemies of the king are the enemies of God.[17] Verse 89:52 functions as the doxology that we have come to expect at the end of a book of psalms.

IV Psalms 90–106

Psalm 90 may be classified as a communal lament. Note the attribution of the psalm to Moses. The opening verses establish the long view dear to the wisdom literature, using the Isaianic figure (Isaiah 40:6) that all flesh is like grass. Verse 90:8 makes it plain that no sins are secret to God. Verse 90:12 is explicit about the desire to be taught and to gain wisdom. The lamenting comes mainly in the concluding verses, which buttress an overall impression that the psalmist here basically is contemplating the deeper sufferings brought by such intrinsic human limitations as mortality, ignorance, and moral weakness.

Gottwald classifies Psalm 91 as a wisdom psalm. Dwelling with God, who is like a great overshadowing angel, is the best protection against the terrors of either night or day. Verses 91:9–10 rather dangerously promise that making God one's refuge guarantees protection against evil. Verses 91:11–12 appear in the accounts of Jesus' temptation by Satan (Matthew 4:6, Luke 4:10–11). The divine voice enters in the concluding verses, ratifying the psalmist's previous assurances that cleaving to God brings sure protection.

Psalm 92 offers thanksgiving or declarative praise in the first person. The initial mood is strikingly joyous, even grateful, at the chance to offer praise to God, and so the psalm first shows an impressive purity or exalted character (the self-interest it expresses is more elevated than what we find in laments or petitions). The middle verses express sapiential convictions: The stupid do not know that the wicked are bound to perish. By the end we realize that the psalmist has more in mind than the pure praise of God, but his or her benefits remain framed by the virtue of God.

Psalm 93 hymns the kingship of God. It deals mainly in cosmic imagery (the creator is a king, and the king of the world is its creator).

Psalm 94 is another individual lament, but it begins especially bitterly. Verses 94:8–12 manifestly express wisdom convictions, and verses 94:14–15 vote confidence in the Lord. The final convictions link the comfort of God's steadfast love with the overthrow of the psalmist's enemies.

Psalm 95 has two parts. Verses 1–7 celebrate God's kingship, and verses 8–11 deliver an admonition. The "joyful noise" of verses 1–2 is familiar to liturgists. Verses 6–7 are a warm commendation of worship. The admonitory verses at the end recall the hardheartedness of Israel in the desert, implying that those who do not harken to the divine voice (perhaps as proclaimed in the cult) will feel the divine wrath as the generation of the Exodus did.

Psalms 96 and 97 are hymns celebrating the kingship of Yahweh. Psalm 96 can hardly be equaled for the joy it expresses in the simple grandeur of God and for the purity of its praise. The opening imagery of Psalm 97 is theophanic, recalling the God who struck the covenant on Sinai. This God judges all nations, supporting the good, punishing the wicked, and upholding moral sanity.

Gottwald classifies Psalm 98 as a hymn of descriptive praise (this second largest category numbers twenty psalms). Verse 98:1 echoes verse 96:1 in speaking of "a new song." The victory par excellence was the Exodus, but verses 1–3 also imply all of God's later defenses of Israel. Verses 98:4–6 call to mind lively liturgical celebrations with energetic music. The concluding invitation to nature to join in the celebration unites the God of historical salvation with the God who created and sustains the cosmos.

Psalm 99 is another celebration of the divine kingship. The dominant motif is the divine holiness, which probably explains the explicit mention of Moses, Aaron, and Samuel as priests.

Psalm 100 is a hymn of especially pure praise. For this psalmist God more than merits joyous worship from the heart. Note in verse 3 the several images for the people's belonging to God as his special portion.[18]

Psalm 101 qualifies as a royal ceremonial song (see Psalm 2). As such its sapiential concerns may be read as those of a king pledging himself (perhaps on the day of his accession) to rule justly. A parallel is established, such that the rule of the king would reflect on Earth the justice that God dispenses from heaven.

Psalm 102 is an individual lament, notable for its vivid description of the the psalmist's dejection. Typically, hard times are taken to express the divine wrath. Yet the stable kingship of God gives reason for hope. Verses 102:18–22 strike the novel note of asking that future generations may read the record of God's having delivered the psalmist's generation of "prisoners" (exiles?). The concluding verses make the permanence of the Creator reason for hoping that present trials will prove passing.

Psalm 103 returns to praising and blessing God. The figure of the eagle recalls Isaiah 40:31. Few psalms surpass this one in celebrating the graciousness of the Lord. Verse 103:15 also recalls Second Isaiah (40:6–8), reminding us of the wonderful poetry of that great prophet. Verse 103:18 introduces a touch of sobriety: We must keep the covenantal law. The final verses, however, again sublimely praise the divine king and intimate the glories of his heavenly court.

Psalm 104 continues this mood of hymnic praise. The opening verses celebrate the grandeur of the heavenly creator, Lord of all the winds. Through the middle verses God appears as the provident Lord who cares for all the creatures of his Earth. Note the sapiential touch in verse 104:24: All of the works of God have been made in wisdom (and so, by implication, the study of creation reveals something of the divine nature). By the end, the psalmist has powerfully made the point that everything depends on God for its breath and life. The pivot of the whole psalm takes us from wonder at creation to awe-touched praise of the divine glory.

Psalm 105 is another historical psalm, like Psalm 78. The opening verses establish the theme: God deserves great thanks and praise because of his divine deeds on Israel's behalf. For this psalmist the high points of Israelite history have been the covenant with Abraham and Jacob, the gift of the promised land, and the liberation from Egypt under Moses, who gets the most attention. Note the concluding verse: All of these divine benefactions were "to the end that they [Israel] should keep his [God's] statutes, and observe his laws" (verse 105:45).

Psalm 106 also remembers the history of salvation, with special stress on the failings of the Israelites (and so greater magnification of God's graciousness). The concluding doxology (verse 106:48) seems to punctuate not only the end of book IV but also the entire history of Israel's transgressions and God's patience.

V Psalms 107–150

Psalm 107 seems to be a communal declaration of thanksgiving and praise of God. Again and again, the psalm declares, the steadfast love of God has delivered his people. The catalogue of the Lord's good deeds is not so much historical as topical: the great variety of afflictions from which Israelites asked deliverance and received it. Note the sapiential conclusion in verse 107:43: "Whoever is wise, let him give heed to these things; let men [people] consider the steadfast love of the Lord."

In Psalm 108, the mood shifts from an opening praise of God to a concluding communal lament. This psalm shows signs of borrowing from Psalm 57:8–11 and

Psalm 60:7–12. The objective petitioned seems to be military conquest, although in verse 9 revenge also peeks through ("Moab is my washbasin; upon Edom I cast my shoe; over Philistia I shout in triumph").

Psalm 109 is an individual lament. The psalmist complains of receiving evil from those to whom he or she did good and so asks God to punish the evil-doers. The litany of punishments proposed reads like a string of curses, and we recall that the curse was an established literary form in the ancient Near East. Verse 109:17 makes this explicit: "He loved to curse; let curses come on him!" (See also verses 109:18–19.) The final verses describe the psalmist as poor, needy, afflicted—and so as meriting God's intervention and blessing.

Psalm 110, the third we treat fully, is a royal ceremonial song: something to be sung at the coronation or other festival of the king. Sigmund Mowinckel, the scholar who argued most strongly for the cultic setting of the psalms, discusses Psalm 110 in the following terms:

> Several of the traditional royal psalms have their place within the framework of the anointment ritual. This applies, e.g., to Ps. 110. It evidently belongs to the moment when the king is led forth to ascend his throne. The king's throne was in the East, looked upon as a symbol of the throne of the deity. It is on a throne flanked by winged lions (cherubs), like that of Solomon, that the deity himself sits in Syro-Canaanite pictures. Such a winged lion throne (empty!) stood in the Temple in Jerusalem also, and it was supposed that "Yahweh who sits upon the cherubim" was seated on it invisibly. When the king as the "son of Yahweh" seats himself on his throne, this is a symbolic expression of the fact that he, as Yahweh's appointed governor, sits on the Lord's own throne, i.e. wields sovereign power in the name of Yahweh. That is the background of the oracle in Ps. 110. There reference is made to the holy robe in which the king has been arrayed for the anointing, to the life-giving water from the holy spring—probably the waters of Gihon—with which he has been purified and strengthened, and to the procession from the brook to the king's palace. And at the moment when he ascends the throne, the temple prophet stands forth and proclaims for him in the name of Yahweh that to the king belongs the seat of honour on the right hand of Yahweh, and the priest kingdom "after the order of Melchizedek"—or, for Melchizedek's sake . . .
>
> The union of royal and priestly power was the main characteristic of El Elyon's kings in ancient Jerusalem, whose realm David and Solomon had inherited and maintained as the foundation of their position of power. But the increased influence of the priests soon threatened the ecclesiastical power of the king. So it was important to have Yahweh's promise of the old right. Apart from this the warrior-ideal is strongly marked in this psalm. By the eternal "youthful force" which the king—like the Canaanite fertility god *Tal*, "Dew"— in that day receives from Yahweh, he shall "strike through" his enemies.[19]

Detached from this original cultic setting, the psalm no doubt mainly served to stir up the hopes of the people at large (whether or not they were then enjoying good kingly rule) that God would continue to bless their national enterprise. Whatever the ambiguities that kingship always retained in Israelite memory, the time of David and Solomon qualified as a golden era, giving Israel its own version of the assurances of the cosmological myth that rule on Earth went best when it was a microcosmic reflection of the divine rule in heaven. The individual's interest was in contemplating the head of the nation raised to intimacy with God (sitting at God's right hand), and in remembering that the true holder of the Israelite throne was YHWH himself. Notice how Zion functions as the site of divinely sanctioned rule (mountains often are the dwelling place of the divinity, who most dramatically descends in the cloud that obscures the mountain's top). Verse 3 has the overtones of fertility that Mowinckel mentions, and verse 4 expresses the royal claims to priestly status. Melchizedek stands for the pre-Davidic line of Jerusalem's kings, and the author of the psalm may well have had in mind the meeting between Abraham, father of the people, and Melchizedek, king of the city that was to be the people's capital, recorded in Genesis 14. The final verses of the psalm are rather bloodthirsty, assuring the king, and thereby the people, that God will stand by him in battle.

The New Testament placed great weight on Psalm 110. Matthew 22:44, Acts 2:34, I Corinthians 15:25, and Ephesians 1:20–22 all employ the first verse as a prefigurement of the ascension of Jesus to heaven, after he has triumphed over death. The Epistle to the Hebrews may be read as an extended commentary on the psalm, in that it uses verses 1 and 4 as a proof-text for its dominant imagery of Christ the high priest's presiding at the heavenly liturgy at the right hand of the Father.

On its own terms, the psalm reminds us that worship was the place where king and people together celebrated their divine constitution. The powers of the king had their legitimacy from the divine anointing carried out at his consecration. The people were enjoined to look upon the king as the representative of YHWH in their midst. Although this representation was originally strongly military, in that the king stood at the head of the Israelite forces as the visible embodiment of the leadership of YHWH, the people's great champion, later it became broader. The fact that priests did the anointing, like the fact that prophets challenged kings with God's word, provided checks and balances.

Psalm 111 qualifies as a hymn, concerned to declare God's titles to praise. Wisdom motifs are also strong, as the psalmist speaks of study, fear, mindfulness of the covenant, trustworthy precepts, and finally wisdom and good understanding.

Psalm 112 even more explicitly deals with wisdom and may have landed after Psalm 111 because it would continue the concluding mood of Psalm 111. (Both psalms are also acrostics.) In both psalms the "fear" of the Lord that is praised is not craven or cringing but it is expressive of the awe that the power and holiness of God ought to stir. Psalm 112 correlates material prosperity with wisdom (with fidelity to the Torah), but verses 6–8 suggest that the deepest prosperity is the peace of soul that delighting in the Lord's commandments brings.

Psalm 113 is another hymn. Its opening verses praise the cosmic powers of the creator and the concluding verses focus on the graces that the savior extends to the poor and needy.[20]

Psalm 114 continues the mood of hymnic praise. Here the memories that occasion such praise are more specific: what God did at the Exodus. Notice the literary conceit of having the sea and the mountains move to accommodate Israel.

Psalm 115 is the first example of a genre (small in scope: three psalms) that Gottwald calls "communal psalms of confidence." The characteristic of this genre is that the community expresses its full certainty that God will give it a good hearing. The first motif of Psalm 115 is the vitality of Israel's God, in contrast to the inertness of the idols of the nations. The second note is a call to trust the Lord, who has always been mindful of his people and blessed them. Verse 115:16

strikingly claims the Earth as the God-given province of human beings, suggesting that they rule there as God rules in the heavens.

Psalm 116 is an individual's song of praise and thanksgiving. The psalmist testifies to deliverance received from God, which becomes a bedrock foundation for asserting the divine graciousness. In return for the Lord's favors, he or she promises faithful worship and service.[21]

Psalm 117 is another (very brief) hymn of praise. It increases our impression that this stretch of psalms is one of the most affirmative or laudatory in the Psalter.

Psalm 118 shifts to the mood of a processional liturgy. The opening verses praise the steadfast love of the Lord, who is a sure refuge. In the middle verses the psalmist testifies to help that the Lord has provided. The "right hand" of the Lord suggests his military prowess and kingly rule. The "gates" of verses 19 and 20 suggest the liturgical procession. The original significance of verse 22 was probably that Israel, a small nation, had become the foundation of God's multinational empire.[22] The New Testament applied this verse to Jesus (Matthew 21:42, Acts 4:11, I Peter 2:7). Verse 118:27 supports the interpretation that this psalm originally had a ceremonial occasion in view. (Gottwald also lists this psalm as a communal song of thanksgiving; Dahood prefers this latter designation as well.)

Psalm 119 is sapiential and an acrostic. Walking according to the command of Torah is extolled as the way to blessedness. Verse 119:9 suggests that the psalmist is an older man having in mind the instruction of youth. The continual delight that the Law of God affords the author throughout is the psalm's most striking feature. By the end of the psalm all good things have come from the Torah, and no suffering or hardship has caused the psalmist to abandon it. Psalm 119 is by far the longest in the Psalter (176 verses), and its extolling of the Law significantly fills out the ethical implications of Psalms. Wisdom is walking according to God's precepts, and such walking should flow back and forth with prayer (praise and petition of God). An outstanding feature of this psalm is that every verse mentions the Law or a synonym.

Psalms 120–134 as a group are called "songs of ascent" and perhaps were sung in processions to the Temple. Psalm 120 itself is an individual lament, rather obscure in some of its imagery. The psalmist may be speaking as an exile, beset by liars and military foes.

Psalm 121 mainly expresses an individual's confidence in God. It has become famous through liturgical blessings that are adaptations of verses 2–8. In this lovely imagery, God presides over every moment of Israel's life, always functioning as its protector.

Psalm 122 is a hymn of Zion. Noteworthy are the motifs of pilgrimage to Jerusalem, the throne of David, and peace for the city of peace.

Gottwald qualifies Psalm 123 as a communal lament. The dominant image is a servant looking to his master for mercy and deliverance.

Psalm 124 comes across as a communal thanksgiving and praise to God. The dominant motif is the Lord's deliverance of Israel from its enemies (the Egyptians and the Exodus seem most in mind).

Psalm 125 is the second example of a communal psalm of confidence (see Psalm 115). Note the assimilation of both those who trust and the Lord who surrounds to Mount Zion. Jerusalem centers the land of the righteous, and the final petition asks the heavenly king to treat both good and evil as they deserve.

Psalm 126 is classified as a communal lament. The opening verses would fit the time of the return from Exile, and the concluding verses may reflect the difficulties of later postexilic years.

Psalm 127 is a sapiential psalm. The opening verses confess the primacy of God's action in all that befalls human beings. The concluding verses make children the greatest of the divine blessings.

Psalm 128 is the first example of a "blessing" (see also Psalms 133 and 134). The first verses sound the sapiential note that fear of the Lord brings prosperity. The final verses beg the Lord's favor for the person held in mind.

Psalm 129 qualifies as a communal psalm of confidence. Although the people have suffered many afflictions, the psalmist trusts that God will punish their enemies.

Psalm 130 is one of the most famous individual laments. The "depths" no doubt are Sheol, considered as a psychological state. The psalmist hopes for forgiveness, which he or she implies that all people need. Verses 5 and 6 speak of waiting for the Lord in a way that blends patience with longing. At the finale hope surges to the fore, stimulated by the steadfast love the Lord has shown in the past.

The brief Psalm 131 speaks in tones of an individual confident that God will offer help. The opening verses carry the mood of the wisdom literature: humility and self-control. At the end the psalmist is a child reposing on the bosom of its divine mother.

Gottwald lists Psalm 132 in two categories. Although the whole falls into the group of psalms suggesting processional liturgies, verses 11–18 appear to be derived from a royal ceremonial song. The royal note appears with David in verse 1, and verses 7 and 8 suggest the movement of a liturgical procession. The overall constellation of images calls to mind the king, the priests, and the people gathered in the Temple on Mount Zion to worship the heavenly king in their midst.[23]

Psalms 133 and 134 qualify as blessings. Psalm 133 envisions the goodness of communal peace, which is an unction for all. Psalm 134 briefly exchanges blessings for God and for the people that God rules from Zion.

Psalm 135 is a hymn whose first verses burst with praise for the Lord, who has been so good to Israel and so gracious. The middle verses celebrate both the powers of the heavenly creator and the mighty deeds of the savior who led the people out of Egypt and gave them the promised land. This Lord is everlasting, and the idols of the nations are like inert toys. Recalling its God, all of Israel should bless him fivefold, very grateful that he condescends to dwell on Zion.

Psalm 136 is a communal song of thanksgiving. The distinctive feature is the refrain, "for his steadfast love endures forever." The first verses celebrate the divine control of nature, in the spirit of a sapiential appreciation of whence natural order and beauty derive. The middle verses recall and bless the historical actions of the Lord on Israel's behalf, stressing the Exodus, the time in the wilderness, and the extended Conquest of Canaan. Verses 23–25 generalize the many reasons why the refrain is merited.

Psalm 137, a communal lament, is perhaps the most famous expression of the desolation that came with the Exile. It reminds us how integral the promised land became to Israelite faith. The concluding verse, 137:9, has become infamous as the nadir of biblical vengeance, but even its hyperbole testifies to the abandonment Israel felt when Babylon dispossessed it.

Psalm 138 is an individual's song of thanksgiving. Verses 2 and 3 join the general steadfast love of God with specific answers this psalmist has received. The middle verses foresee the homage of the nations to the universal Lord. At the end we are reminded of Psalm 23, for the psalmist again walks through troubles unafraid.

Psalm 139 is the last classified as a wisdom psalm. The opening motif is that the Lord is omniscient, knowing everything about the psalmist's life, thought, and action. Verses 7–11 shift only slightly to the divine omnipresence. Verses 139:13–16 make God the main agent in human conception, forming the new person with his or her specific destiny in mind. Verse 139:17 is a good indication of the piety that sapiential inclinations could develop: "How precious to me are thy thoughts, O God! How vast is the sum of them!" At the end, the request is for justice: a divine ordering of the moral sphere (that it might equal the order of nature).

Psalms 140–143 qualify as individual laments. The opening verses of Psalm 140 are remarkable for the violence they call to mind. The rest of the psalm asks the justice of seeing the psalmist's enemies overthrown. Psalm 141 would have petition rise like incense before God. The psalmist prays to be kept free of the ways and the company of the wicked, that God may serve as his or her sole refuge.[24] Psalm 142 is more emotional; the petitioner is quite frankly lamenting to the Lord. The mood is one of being hedged in or trapped and having no one but God to give a care or lend a helping hand. In Psalm 143 the first concern is a divine answer that does not depend on the psalmist's righteousness (no one is righteous before God). Presently enemies appall his spirit, and by contrast former days seem like a golden era. Verse 8 asks for both a sense of the divine *ḥesed* and practical insight about the path to take, and verse 10 expresses a willingness to do the divine will. The final affirmation is that the psalmist is God's servant (who deserves his king's help).

Psalm 144 ends as a communal lament, but verses 1–11 sound like the lament of an individual king. God is the shield of the warrior, whom he has trained. Verse 3 expresses the appreciation of human insignificance prominent in many wisdom writings, and verses 4 and 5 recall the theophanic imagery of Sinai. The image of the lyre in verse 9 perhaps stimulates the mention of David in verse 10. From verse 12 to the end, the mood shifts to a petition for manifold fertility, no doubt as a sign of the divine blessing.[25]

The last six psalms of the Psalter are all hymns that praise the Lord. Collectively, they make Psalms end on a high note of pure laud of the one who was the center of Israelite life. Psalm 145, an acrostic in form, has cadences and images that have made it well known and well loved. We thus treat it fully here, as we have Psalms 1, 51, and 110. The opening verses celebrate (rather vaguely or generally) the greatness of God that merits human praise. Gerhard von Rad, perhaps the leading Old Testament theologian of the past generation, has pondered the significance of Israel's commitment to praise God:

> We have thus stumbled on one of the strangest propositions in the Old Testament's doctrine of man. Praise is man's most characteristic mode of existence: praising and not praising stand over against one another like life and death: praise becomes the most elementary "token of being alive" that exists: from generation to generation the hymns of the thanksgiving community flow on ("bubble"!) (Ps. CXLV. 4ff.). How one-sidedly praise had its home in life and in life alone can be seen in the fact that

the people of God at praise regarded itself as standing shoulder to shoulder with the community of the divine beings before the throne of Jahweh — to such an extent was it in antiphony with the community above that the command to strike up praise could even be issued to those above by those below. In this presumptuous order to praise the community on earth appears as "the leader of the praising universe."[26]

The voice of Psalm 145 therefore can ring confidently, as though it were executing a commission of great dignity. Verse 1 bespeaks a commitment — to extoll YHWH — that brims with pride: "In doing this," the voice implies, "I am acting on the heights of human achievement." The rationale given for the praise is most general and opaque, as though simply to say "my God and king" is to summon the command, "Praise him!" The distinction between blessing and praising no doubt is not sharp, but each word has slightly different overtones. In blessing one consecrates and implicitly prays for a good use or outcome. Obviously, human beings can only bless God in a derivative sense, because God is the source of all consecration and good outcome. Praising carries less problematic overtones and seems precisely what a creature ought to do in the presence of its creator. God may be praised for any of the divine works, but the core of religious praise will always be the divine excellence (holiness, goodness) itself. Verse 2 suggests that the vocation to bless and praise God is a daily affair. Every time the sun rises more titles by which God deserves praise come to light. Verse 3 seems the semantic parallel of verse 1: simply another way of saying the same thing (but by repetition intensifying the effect).

In his study of biblical poetry, Robert Alter has noted that such semantic parallelism is a recurrent feature, and he has used Psalm 145 as an example of how the biblical poets managed, despite static linear balancing such as we have seen in verses 1–3, to achieve development in the entire body of the work:

> There would seem to be differences between one poet and the next and one poem and the next, and perhaps also between different periods, in regard to the preference for heightening and focusing within semantic parallelism. In some texts, such as Moses' valedictory song and the Book of Job, this intensifying tendency of biblical verse is entirely dominant; elsewhere, as in some of the Psalms, the poet seems to have preferred relatively static semantic parallelism. Interestingly, however, where static parallelism prevails, one may discover that developmental movement is projected from the line to the larger structure of the poem, as in Psalm 145, where the poet moves through a series of relatively synonymous lines in a progression from the general praise of God to an affirmation of His compassion, His kingship, His daily providing for those who truly call unto Him.[27]

The first seven verses of Psalm 145 remain quite general, praising God for such attributes as his mighty acts (perhaps the Exodus would have come to mind, but it is not specified), his greatness, his goodness, his righteousness. Something of the divine nonspecificity, of the way that God's mystery escapes the defining characteristics that provoke poets to concrete and so gripping images, hovers in these generalities. Verses 8 and 9 summon the divine *hesed*, extending the outreach of the divine goodness to the whole of creation.

Indeed, the works of nature are allied with the saints (the members of God's holy people) in the task of thanking and blessing the Lord. But still they mainly

tell of abstract qualities: divine glory, power, splendor, and dominion. Perhaps because of the inclusion of natural works, the poet stresses the everlasting character of God's reign. Because of the regularity of nature, as well as his covenantal word, God should be praised as faithful. Because of his universal concern, he should be called the upholder of all who fall down. Verses 15–16 are the most famous and are used in monastic grace before meals: "The eyes of all look to thee, and thou givest them their food in due season. Thou openest thy hand, thou satisfiest the desire of every living thing." In the final verses, more titles for praising God pass review, making the whole psalm completely laudatory.

In Hebrew Psalms 146–150 all begin and end with "Hallelujah!" Verse 146:3 contrasts earthly princes with the heavenly king, showing that only the latter merits complete trust and praise. In Psalm 146 the Lord is both the maker of heaven and Earth and the comfort of the sojourner and the widow.

Psalm 147 also blends references to the savior of human beings from their troubles with references to the ruler of the heavens and the fields. Verse 147:11 praises fear of the Lord as a signal virtue. The material prosperity lavished on Zion is impressive, but the singularity of Israel (see verse 147:20: "He has not dealt thus with any other nation") stems from the Torah God has declared.

Psalm 148 invites the heavens and the angels into its praise of God. The "establishment" of the natural forces praised in verse 148:6 is one of the delights of the wisdom writers. The overall imagery is of an entire creation united in praising its source. In verse 148:14 Israel stands out as the people near to God—a nice image for election.

Psalm 149 wants a new song sent to God, one sung and danced with liturgical instrumentation and joy. The mood is one of celebrating a victory, and the joy includes getting vengeance on the nations who have been Israel's enemies.

The final psalm of the Psalter is like a full-length doxology. All of creation is invited to praise God, who rules in the heavens. Every instrument shows its best purpose—praise of God—and the Psalter ends in a mood of purest religion: God is all in all, and the best human vocation is to praise God for this primacy.

HISTORICAL BACKGROUND

Scholars of the Psalms tend to agree that the present collection contains works from a considerable temporal span and that the Israelite cult was a strong factor in shaping many psalms. Gunkel thought that most of the genres we now find were started in the preexilic cult, were further shaped (often in the direction of suitability for private use) by the prophetic critiques of the cult that were influential after the eighth century B.C.E., and finally were collected into a hymnbook used in the Second Temple (the Temple rebuilt after the return from the Exile). Mowinckel, on the other hand, thought that many of the actual psalms we now possess, and not just the genres they represent, derive from the preexilic cult. He also down-played individualistic usage thought to have derived from the prophets and posited a cultic context for the majority of the psalms, underscoring such hypothetical liturgical dramas as the enthronement of YHWH as king and the celebration of an annual New Year festival. Last, Mowinckel theorized that after the Israelite

monarchy collapsed many of the psalms were given an eschatological interpretation that pointed to a future in which Israel would again prosper.

Mitchell Dahood has accepted much of Mowinckel's case for a cultic setting for most of the psalms, arguing that this makes the dating of individual psalms problematic. On the whole, however, he finds studies of Ugaritic literature, and the realization that often the translators who rendered the Hebrew Bible into Greek in the third century B.C.E. did not understand the original biblical idiom very well, tending to suggest quite early dates for some of the psalmic material.

Accordingly, Dahood comments:

> The tendency in recent years to assign earlier rather than later dates to the composition of the psalms comports with the evidence of the Ras Shamra [Ugaritic] texts. These show that much of the phraseology in the Psalter was current in Palestine long before the writing prophets, so the criterion of literary dependence becomes much too delicate to be serviceable. On the other hand, the inadequate knowledge of biblical poetic idiom and, more importantly, of biblical images and metaphors displayed by the third-century B.C. translators of the LXX, bespeaks a long chronological gap between the original composition of the psalms and their translation into Greek. Even the admittedly later poems in the Psalter are considerably older than the Hodayot (hymns of praise) from Qumran, which freely borrowed the phraseology, the imagery, and the central ideas of the Book of Psalms. These considerations thus point to a pre-Exilic date for most of the psalms, and not a few of them (e.g., Pss ii, xvi, xviii, xxix, lx, lxviii, lxxxii, cviii, cx) may well have been composed in the Davidic period.[28]

More theologically, the psalms presuppose the great themes of Israelite faith: the work of God as creator of the world, the great deeds of creating and saving Israel through the Exodus and the Mosaic covenant, the establishment of the Davidic kingship, the presence of God to Israel as Lord and king, the right of Israel to ask for help against its foes, the primacy of the Torah as the guide to wisdom and prosperity, the moral weakness of human beings, and the assurances the divine nature holds out that justice finally will prevail.

In addition, the Psalter itself brings out the praiseworthiness of the Lord — how the holiness and goodness of God ought to stimulate human acclaim. The many psalms of lament reveal that Israel felt licensed, perhaps even urged, to bring its sufferings and needs before its God and ask for relief. What Moshe Greenberg has found in the prose prayers of the Bible — the right of the individual to address God person to person — the Psalter expresses for the community as a whole.[29] In terms of antiquity, cultic setting, theology, and religious rights, therefore, the Psalter unveils a deep background of passionate, urgent orientation to God. From its inception, Israel had been emotionally as well as legally bonded to its God. The psalms suggest that praying to God, whether in petition or in praise, was to Israelite faith what breathing was to its bodily existence.

LITERARY INTENT

The individual psalms manifestly were written for various reasons. Each of the different genres that we have noted suggests a different compositional purpose: individual lament, communal lament, royal ceremony, solemn and prayerful re-

flection about wisdom, praise and thanksgiving, and so forth. The Psalter taken as a whole gives a few statistical clues to the final editors' intentions. For instance, individualistic prayers predominate in the first half of the book (Psalms 1–75) whereas communal prayers predominate in the second half (Psalms 76–150). This could mean that individualistic interests were older, if the editors were following an historical or antiquarian principle of arrangement, but it is more likely that psalms were grouped, roughly but still significantly, by similarity of theme. The final editors may deliberately have introduced alternations in mood, so that one using the book as a totality would encounter some variety. If the Psalter was in fact a handbook or hymnal for use in the Second Temple, an interpretation that remains tenable, and if the division into five books was meant to mirror the Pentateuch, then the five collections probably were formed through a combination of practical interests (some thematic grouping) and theological concerns.

When we look at the five collections, we note that Book I assigns its contents to David and uses the name YHWH for God. Books II and III (up to Psalm 78) employ Elohim for God, and the psalms that are attributed to David are surrounded by psalms attributed to Korah and Asaph, leaving the "Davidic" psalms in the middle (roughly, Psalms 51–72, if we connect those specifically assigned to David and those without assignment). Books IV and V may well have been added to Books I–III at a later date. They use the name YHWH and generally lack an assignment to a source. We have noted the orientational value of Psalms 1 and 2, which set themes of wisdom and Davidic kingship. Psalm 150 seems to be a deliberate effort to bring the Psalter to climax on a note of purest praise.

Taken together, these editorial characteristics suggest that the Psalter was meant to guide a prayer, both communal and individual, that was formed by Torah. Such prayer, as well, thought of Israel as most itself when ruled by God's Davidic son, and it passed through the workaday, expectable business of suffering (being beset by enemies, needing correction, trying to celebrate the seasonal festivals, and the like) to emerge chastened for the holiday, especially sacral "business" of appreciating the great beauty and splendor of God. To the great beauty and splendor of God, the only fitting response was pure praise. The Psalter, on this reading, came into being because those concerned for Israel's soul (over a long period of time) wanted to have at hand, in a form useful for both communal cult and private prayer, hallowed, consecrated expressions of faith and religious emotion. If the fate of the Psalms in Jewish and Christian religious life of the Common Era is any indication, the project was a great success.

LASTING SIGNIFICANCE

Our last lines have suggested the significance that the Psalter had in Jewish and Christian religious life of the Common Era: It became a treasury of prayer forms, which both individuals and communities used to pour forth petition and praise to their God. In the Christian case, the significance of the Psalter also derived from the influence it had in Christology (the interpretation of Jesus as the Messiah), through the application of psalms such as Psalm 110.

In more general and humanistic perspective, the Psalter provokes such questions as, What is prayer?, Why do people pray?, and Does prayer remain valid or intellectually respectable in our present age? These questions are no less useful because raising them may cause embarrassment to college students or their professors. Indeed, perhaps such embarrassment is a good first clue to where the lasting significance of the Psalter lies.

One of the major ways in which we citizens of modern Western culture differ from our predecessors, East and West, is in our secularism. Whereas they assumed as a matter of course that the world of nature and human events was surrounded by or immersed in a sacral mystery, we are not so sure. Modern science, psychology, and social theory have all suggested that a great deal of what people consider to be "reality" is the product of human imagination and human convention. Because such modern thought uses an empirical criterion to determine its own "reality," the divinities and mysteries that bulked very large in premodern cultures have become problematic. This holds for the God of the Psalms as well as the divinity whose help the Eskimo shaman seeks. The Lord of Israel, like the Hindu Krishna or the Muslim Allah, cannot be measured or interviewed. To say that he is real and influential is to interpret beyond the significance that either natural phenomena or human experiences surely, unambiguously, incontrovertibly carry.

On the other hand, much the same can be said of many other things that virtually all people, premodern and modern alike, consider real and immensely important. These include human love, fidelity, wisdom, justice, and much more. Whenever virtues and values are at issue, empiricism shows itself to be a paltry philosophy. Our present time, which many commentators call "postmodern," has been greatly enriched by the modern search for critical understanding, but it has also found reasons to call modern secularism inadequate. If critical understanding — the demand for hard evidence and solid reasoning, before one accredits an hypothesis — has proved to be a great boon in combating superstition, emotionalism, and the pseudo-reasons behind which bigotry likes to hide, it has also proved to be less than the philosophy (the love of wisdom) that human beings require if they are to be fully creative, ecstatic, and surprised by joy. The link between this line of criticism and the lines that run through modern warmaking, ecological pollution, economic injustice, and the like, is not always clear, but few proponents of a new, postmodern humanism doubt that it exists.

What has all of this to do with the Book of Psalms? Perhaps a great deal. The psalms assume, without doubt or argument, that the treasure of Israelite existence is the divine power and love. From time to time they linger over what we would call secondary causes, thinking about the phenomena of nature or human social life that provoke pain or provide pleasure, but the main thrust of the psalms is toward the creator and savior who to their authors' minds gives nature and human social life their full significance. Were there no God who made the world "in the beginning," as Genesis claims, the phenomena of nature would shrink considerably in interest. For the psalmist, the beauty of the stars, the fury of the storm, and even the destruction of the flood or the famine are interesting, significant, portentous because they mediate the power and purpose of the creator. Sometimes they may suggest that the creator is angry, or careless, or even malevolent. Other times they may suggest that the creator is provident toward Israel and beautiful beyond compare. Always, however, they take their interest and significance from the "other," the mysterious divinity, that the psalmist intuits or trusts moves in their depths, directs their patterns, and enfolds their goals or final meanings.

The same holds for the psalmist's view of human affairs, whereby intelligence and freedom only make the story more complex and fascinating. As we see in the laments of individuals, the God of the Psalter is approached as one who can and should rescue sufferers from enemies or circumstances that afflict them. As we see in the royal psalms, the pivotal figure of Israelite society owes his significance to the one who had him anointed and would have him continue the covenantal promises to David. The historical psalms make it plain that Israel organized its memory and periodized its past in terms of such "mighty acts" of the divine mystery on its behalf as the Exodus and the Conquest of Canaan. The hymns of thanksgiving and praise go even farther, equating the peak experiences of the Israelite spirit, the richest feelings of peace and joy, with acclamations of God and rivetings of the soul to God's beauty, goodness, and grace.

"Prayer" is probably the best name for the manifold address of the living God that the Psalter exemplifies. As such, prayer is at the heart of biblical religion, if not indeed of all world religions. (The heart of any tradition, we may argue quite well, is the place where it deals with ultimate reality passionately, holistically, with full interest and existential involvement. This "place," were we to generalize from the full span of the data of the world religions, is usually best called "prayer" or "worship.") Prayer undoubtedly labors under several severe liabilities nowadays, because we can find many dubious specimens of it flooding the electronic airwaves. Some of these probably are quite sincere, but many others manifestly are impure: tied to fundraising, antiintellectualism, emotional excess, and smarmy self-satisfaction. Nonetheless, there is wisdom in the old dictum that "abuse does not take away use." Merely because prayer, like sex, love, and power, can be abused and become degenerate does not prove that better specimens could not be dazzlingly significant and valuable.

The Psalter shows few signs of mysticism (in the sense of wordless interiority), where some of the best fruits of prayer flourish. It shows many signs of "mysticism" if the traditional definition, "experience of the divine," is employed. Biblical religionists, perhaps especially Talmudic Jews and Protestant Christians, have tended to focus on the first, quietistic significance of "mysticism" and to have neglected the second significance. Other Jews and Christians have narrowed the distance between the psalms and other literatures of prayer, thinking that the petitions and praises of the psalms do not pretend to be the whole story.

GLOSSARY

Cosmological myth   The notion that the whole of reality is an ordered (usually living) unity composed finally of a single stuff.

Doxology   An expression of praise and giving glory.

Hodayot   Songs of praise used at Qumran (the Essene community of separatists) at the end of the biblical period.

Parallelism, semantic   Symmetry of meaning, repetition of denotation.

Parallelism, static   A duplication or mirroring with little movement of thought or imagery.

STUDY QUESTIONS

1. What is the significance of the fact that many of the psalms in the Psalter only roughly or approximately fit the genre to which scholars tend to assign them?

2. What are the usual characteristics of a "wisdom psalm," and how does Psalm 1 exemplify them?

3. How does Psalm 2 relate to the traditional attribution of the Book of Psalms to King David?

4. Give an example of a psalm that shows signs of having been composed for a public liturgy.

5. What implications do you see in the fact that the largest psalmic category is the individual lament?

6. Evaluate Psalm 150 as a hymn and comment on the fact that the last six psalms of the Psalter fall into this category.

7. How closely does the assumption, found in many laments, that suffering tokens the Lord's anger correlate with the Deuteronomistic theology?

8. What are the psychological or theological warnings that a close reading of the Psalter ought to occasion?

9. In what humanistic sense could a life without prayer be stunted and two-dimensional?

NOTES

1. See Brevard S. Childs, *Introduction to the Old Testament as Scripture*. Philadelphia: Fortress, 1979, pp. 508–11.

2. See Norman K. Gottwald, *The Hebrew Bible: A Socio-Literary Introduction*. Philadelphia: Fortress, 1985, p. 531. Our descriptions of the psalms are greatly indebted to Gottwald's classification.

3. See *Harper's Bible Dictionary*, ed. Paul J. Achtemeier. San Francisco: Harper & Row, 1985, p. 922.

4. See Pierre Auffret, "Essai sur la structure littéraire du Psaume viii," *Vetus Testamentum*, 34 (1984), 257–69.

5. See Lloyd M. Barré, "Recovering the Literary Structure of Psalm 15," *Vetus Testamentum*, 34 (1984), 205–10.

6. See Klaus Seybold, "Der Weg des Lebens. Eine Studie zu Psalm 16," *Theologische Zeitschrift*, 40 (1984), 121–29.

7. See Kenneth Kuntz, "Psalm 18: A Rhetorical-Critical Analysis," *Journal for the Study of the Old Testament*, 26 (1983), 3–31.

8. See Mitchell Dahood, S. J., *Psalms I*. Garden City, N. Y.: Doubleday Anchor Bible, 1966, p. 127.

9. See Paul G. Mosca, "Psalm 26: Poetic Structure and the Form-Critical Task," *Catholic Biblical Quarterly*, 47 (1985), 212–37.

10. See James L. Mays, "Psalm 29," *Interpretation*, 39 (1985), 60–64.

11. See Anthony R. Ceresko, "The ABCs of Wisdom in Psalm xxxiv," *Vetus Testamentum*, 35 (1985), 99–104.

12. See R. J. Tournay, "Le Psaume XXXVI, structure et doctrine," *Revue Biblique*, 90 (1983), 5–22.

13. See Lawrence E. Toombs, "The Book of Psalms," in *Wisdom Literature and Poetry*, ed. Charles M. Laymon. Nashville: Abingdon, 1983, p. 108.

14. See Dahood, *Psalms I*, p. 301. See also Bruce Vanter, "Intimations of Immortality and the Old Testament," *Journal of Biblical Literature*, 91 (1972), 158–71.

15. See Mitchell Dahood, S. J., *Psalms II*. Garden City, N.Y.: Doubleday Anchor Bible, 1968, p. 76. See also Graham S. Ogden, "Psalm 60: Its Rhetoric, Form, and Function," *Journal for the Study of the Old Testament*, 31 (1985), 83–94.

16. See Pierre Auffret, " 'Alors je jouerai sans fin pour ton nom.' Étude structurelle du psaume 61," *Science et Esprit*, 36 (1984), 169–77.

17. See Timo Veijola, "Davidverheissung und Staatsvertrag. Beobachtungen zum Einfluss altorientalischer Staatsverträge auf biblische Sprache am Beispiel von Psalm 89," *Zeitschrift für die Alttestamentliche Wissenschaft*, 95 (1983), 9–31. See also E. Theodore Mullen, Jr., "The Divine Witness and the David Royal Grant: Ps. 89:37–38," *Journal of Biblical Literature*, 102 (1983), 207–18.

18. See Walter Brueggemann, "Psalm 100," *Interpretation*, 39 (1985), 65–69.

19. Sigmund Mowinckel, *The Psalms in Israel's Worship*, Volume 1. Nashville: Abingdon, 1962, pp. 63–64. On Christian use see John D. Zizioulas, "The Early Christian Community," in *Christian Spirituality: Origins to the Twelfth Century*, ed. Bernard McGinn, John Meyendorff, and Jean Leclerq. New York: Crossroad, 1985, p. 26.

20. See Peter C. Craigie, "Psalm 113," *Interpretation*, 39 (1985), 70–74.

21. See Pierre Auffret, " 'Je marcherei à la face de Yahvé.' Étude structurelle du Psaume 116," *Nouvelle Revue Théologique*, 106 (1984), 383–96.

22. See Mitchell Dahood, S.J., *Psalms III*. Garden City, N.Y.: Doubleday Anchor Bible, 1970, p. 159.

23. See Heinz Kruse, "Psalm cxxxii and the Royal Zion Festival," *Vetus Testamentum*, 33 (1983), 279–97.

24. See R. J. Tournay, "Psaume cxlii nouvelle interprétation," *Revue Biblique*, 90 (1983), 321–33.

25. See R. J. Tournay, "Le Psaume CXLI. Structure et Interprétation," *Revue Biblique*, 91 (1984), 520–30.

26. Gerhard von Rad, *Old Testament Theology*, Volume 1. New York: Harper & Row, 1962, pp. 369–70.

27. Robert Alter, *The Art of Biblical Poetry*. New York: Basic Books 1985, pp. 22–23.

28. See Dahood, *Psalms I*, p. xxx.

29. See Moshe Greenberg, *Biblical Prose Prayer*. Berkeley: University of California Press, 1983.

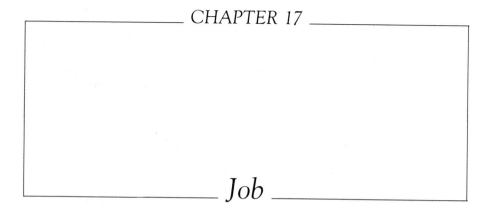

CHAPTER 17

Job

TEXTUAL ANALYSIS

The Book of Job is an important specimen of biblical reflection on wisdom. Probably the main portion of the present text was composed after the Exile to Babylon in 586 B.C.E. Allusions to Canaanite and Mesopotamian myths give the book a cosmopolitan flavor, and signs of later additions suggest editorial reworking over a considerable period of time. As we see, interpreters debate virtually all of the questions crucial to determining the message of the book, and some interpreters conclude that the final version is deliberately ambiguous. We divide the text into six unequal parts:

1–2	Prologue
3	Opening Monologue
4–27	Dialogues with Friends
28–37	Monologues
38:1–42:6	Dialogues with God
42:7–17	Epilogue[1]

1–2 Prologue

The first two chapters of the Book of Job and the epilogue in chapter 42 are written in prose, but the rest of the work is written in poetry. We thus immediately question the function of the prose passages. One persuasive possibility is that the whole work is a "framework poem," for which Egyptian and Sumerian models existed, in which the prose sections give the plot and the long poetic section allows for the development of character. This hypothesis would unify the total work and diminish the apparent contradiction between the docility predicated of Job in the prose sections and the rebelliousness exhibited in the poetic section.[2]

Chapter 1:1–5 would establish that Job was devout, blameless, and blessed by God. The picture represents the ideal of biblical prosperity. The "sons of God" of verse 1:6 most likely are angels. Note that Satan is not the rebellious and wicked figure we find in later Jewish and Christian theology. He is simply, as his name suggests, "the adversary" who presents the other set of possibilities. Here the first other possibility is that Job is pious simply because things are going well and he has no reason not to be. The first test of both this possibility and Job himself focuses on what will happen if misfortune afflicts Job's possessions (which include his children). Not so subtly, then, the author is introducing the possibility that Job, and human beings generally, are but pawns in the hands of God — pieces that may be moved around to make an interesting game. Job passes this first test, not cursing God or becoming bitter but rather accepting whatever God chooses to dispose. Verse 1:21 has the ring of sober biblical wisdom: whatever human beings have is completely the gift of God and nothing to which they may lay permanent claim.

Chapter 2 begins as a reprise of the scene in heaven laid out in chapter 1. The motif of cruel playing with Job continues, as the Satan (The Adversary) gets permission to afflict him bodily. Note in verses 2:5 and 2:9 the cursing of God,[3] and recall the ritual uncleanness that the Torah associated with skin diseases. It is hard to tell whether Job's wife thinks he has committed some sin meriting this suffering or whether she wishes to shorten his pain through death. But Job continues to be docile and accepts evil and good with equanimity. The friends who come to condole with Job and comfort him will serve as mouthpieces for various interpretations (many of them insidious[4]) of his situation. At this juncture, however, they mainly serve to confirm that Job has become a striking, provocative example of suffering.

3 Opening Monologue

Chapter 3 shifts the literary form to poetry. From the outset the religious mood also shifts strikingly, because Job immediately bursts out with bitterness. Here Job is quite willing to curse, and even though the object of his curse is the day he was born, quite clearly the One who made that day (and by Israelite conviction had guided Job's development in the womb to that day) comes under a cloud. The argument is that not having been born or death would be preferable to the life of suffering that Job epitomizes. This argument of course could be considered to support suicide, and it represents a frontal challenge to the theme of Genesis that creation and life are thoroughly good. Already, then, we see that Job is functioning as a spokesperson for the shadows of the Israelite psyche. He is presented as a foreigner, and the tone of his speech is reminiscent of foreign wisdom literature. But he has been brought into contest with the biblical God, no doubt so that the unbelief and despair that always threaten a mature faith and hope (that is, a religion that realizes the complexity of human psychology, moods, and motivations) can be brought out into the open.

4–27 Dialogues with Friends

The central portion of the Book of Job moves with some of the strophic rhythms of an epic or dramatic poem.[5] Chapters 4–14 comprise a first cycle of dialogues, which begin to analyze Job's situation and evaluate his bitterness. Eliphaz the Temanite initiates what becomes the trial of Job (and so from the beginning has overtones of blaming the victim) by noting that whereas Job was a support to others when they were suffering, he is impatient at his own suffering. Indeed, his suffering has threatened his confidence in God and has called his integrity into question. Further, Eliphaz puts forth the (rather Deuteronomistic) opinion that suffering comes to the wicked, which implies that if one is suffering one must have been wicked. Eliphaz authenticates this opinion with a numinous dream, in which he received a revelation that made his hair stand on end[6] and convinced him that human beings are always unrighteous before the holy God. (The rhetorical questions in this and other speeches are interesting, because they suggest that in fact the author of Job does not agree with the position being put forth and hopes that the reader, struck by a bout of common sense or independent faith, will answer, "No!" Interpreters who follow this analytical line read Job as an ironic work, full of invitations to the reader to resist the outer evaluations in the text and probe beneath to find a more lively and challenging religion. In this religion human beings would interact with God not as slaves to their Lord but as free spirits who demand that God be just and finally trust that God's love does make him just.)

Chapter 5 moves forward in the didactic, observational style that we found in some wisdom psalms and see more of in Proverbs and Ecclesiastes. Many of the lines are like maxims from sober, dour reflections on the sufferings and waywardness of unimpressive humanity.[7] Although they may be persuasive in themselves, on the hypothesis that the author intends us to hear ironic overtones throughout they ring as suspiciously pat and self-serving. We have no reason to think that Eliphaz has gained his wisdom admirably, by himself having suffered and clung fast to God. So the whole can seem to be cheap wisdom, the sort of impure advice offered to the poor by the rich over cocktails. This does not mean that the author rejects the meditations on divine providence and reliability that Eliphaz proffers, any more than it means that the rich may not be insightful about the poor. But it does mean that the Book of Job is richer than a manual of prudential maxims. And it does mean that the Book of Job challenges all parties—God, characters, readers, and no doubt author—to study how well words and deeds, professed faith and lived faith, actually square.

By the end of Eliphaz's speech we are well situated in the cosmological context dear to many biblical treatments of wisdom, and we realize that Job and all other human beings can only be properly estimated by reference to the whole of God's creative and providential activity. Eliphaz apparently means this as comfort for Job, but from the outset of chapter 6 we find that Job is not satisfied. He still prefers death to the miserable existence he is enduring. The new notes are his sense that he has done nothing to deserve this punishment (verses 6:10, 30) and his bitterness toward his friends, who are proving themselves no real friends or comforters (verses 6:14–15, 24–29).

Chapter 7 continues Job's bilious complaint, reiterating the wretchedness of his life, which is slavish (the common human fate), empty, hopeless, leprous, and mortal. Job might as well give vent to his spleen: He has nothing to lose. From verse 7:12 the anguish seems directed to God, who has become oppressive to Job and overbearing. The "watcher of men" in verse 7:20 is angry and accusative, and the conclusion of Job's first response is black humor and triumph: God will look for him even in the grave, but then at least he will not exist (to be troubled and hounded).

In chapter 8 a second "friend," Bildad the Shuhite, takes up the task of responding to Job, supposedly in condolence and comfort but actually in accusation. Taking the high ground, Bildad simply asserts that God is just and answers those who entreat him. He claims that this is the wisdom of the ancients (which Job ought to know). The general message of chapter 8 is that the evil and impious merit their sufferings. (The Book of Job is putting views such as this on trial, as much as it is trying to assess the innocence or guilt of a man such as Job.) Verses 20–22 do, however, attempt a consoling application to Job: Surely God will return an innocent man like him to prosperity (which, as in the Psalms, will include seeing his enemies brought low).

Job's answer to Bildad (perhaps actually to Eliphaz, compare verse 9:2 with verse 4:17) begins accommodatingly (or ironically): Such traditional wisdom must be true. But immediately thereafter Job moves to deeper ground: Can anyone be just before the holy God (and so merit prosperity)? We should note the cosmological imagery dear to the wisdom writers and realize that for them the divine wisdom and holiness dovetail with the divine creative power. Verse 9:11 is worth remarking, as a hint of the biblical appreciation of the divine mystery: "Lo, he passes by me, and I see him not; he moves on, but I do not perceive him." The logic of Job's depression is that even though he feels himself innocent there is nothing that he, a tiny fragment of creation, can do to oppose the might of God. By verses 9:22–24 Job has tentatively concluded that the world and so its source are amoral: "He destroys both the blameless and the wicked." Yet in the final verses of the chapter a winning poignancy emerges. No matter what he suffers or how he tries to cleanse himself, Job feels he will end up condemned. He cannot win fair judgment (who could arbitrate between him and God?), and, somewhat like a small child hurt that the game is being played unfairly, he moves the reader to want to comfort him.

In this mood, the reader can find chapter 10 encouraging. Job summons the courage to fight back, even though the bully is God, and the solidarity we feel with him in the vulnerabilities of being but limited creatures can make us cheer. Why has God made him (note the reference to conception in verses 10:10–11),[8] if he is only destined to suffer? Note in verse 10:12 the confession of faith in God's *hesed*, which seems to emerge despite Job's bitterness, as if to suggest that when one confronts God in angry honesty one may meet a more complex reality (in oneself as well as in God) than one anticipated. Still, most of chapter 10 beats the drum of "I cannot win." By the end, Job is again persuaded that death would be a relief.

Chapter 11 introduces a third friendly accusator or accusatory friend. (The more Job gives vent to his anguish the less sympathetic his "friends" become. They would rather hear "correct" answers in which he does not believe than his honest emotions—a constant danger for "orthodox" piety of any tradition.) Zophar "knows" that Job in fact must be getting less punishment than he deserves (verse 11:6).

God is greater than creation, which dwarfs Job, and so God's wisdom is bound to exceed Job's understanding. (True enough, but not precisely to the point: Can God's justice utterly contradict what human beings feel "has" to be right?) In full rhetorical flourish, Zophar argues that if Job will set his heart aright all good things will return to him.

By now Job has had a bellyful of his pious (unafflicted) friends, and his reply at the outset of chapter 12 is sarcastic. Verse 12:5 is worth pondering: The fortunate easily condemn the misfortunate (and think that their own fortune is deserved). Verse 12:6 implies that idolatry is not far from (ill-gotten) prosperity. Job himself then produces the most traditional, even winning tribute to the wisdom and power of God, to prove that he knows at least as much as his self-important friends. But the implication in Job's layout of the traditional convictions about the divine omnipotence is that *therefore* injustices should be laid right at God's door.

In chapter 13 Job also implies that (any worthwhile) God will devastate the arguments so far put forward by his friends, because they are "proverbs of ashes" (the remains of a religion once full of fire and vitality, which would let the problem of evil rage, in all its existential ardor). Verse 13:15 rather famously shows the extremity of Job's own religious vitality. Verse 13:18 contains imagery from the courtroom, and the reference in verse 13:24 to the hiddenness of God sounds a theme very influential in Western theology. In the final verses of the chapter Job addresses God directly (and so shows his strong desire that God really be God for him). He wants to know what his sins have been, where he has gone wrong. The implication is that if he could see his errors he would gladly repent of them.

By putting Job's "case" in this way, the Book both clarifies the state of soul that innocent suffering can induce and questions whether this sort of "justice," this equation of suffering with wrongdoing, is an adequate framework. Suppose there is unmerited suffering (and unmerited worldly prosperity). What does that do to the calculus that even most religious people instinctively employ? (In many religious traditions, the notion of an afterlife arises at this point: Even though there is no sure justice in "this" life, after death God or the gods will separate the wicked and the good into realms of suffering [hell] and happiness [heaven]. As we see in Chapter 14, Job rejects this notion.)

Chapter 14 opens with straightforward, traditional sapiential reflection, rooted in the manifest mortality of human beings and the unknowable reaches of the divine mystery. Verses 14:7–10 explicitly separate humankind from plant life, because plant life regenerates itself but human beings do not. Where it has a novel or singular note is in Job's yearning to be relieved of both his mortality and his vulnerability to divine judgment (he can never be impeccable). The petition in this chapter is one of the most profound in the Bible, if not in world literature as a whole (we can think of the Sumerian epic of Gilgamesh as comparable), because it asks for a life with God that would defeat the death that withers everything human. Greece and India thought they had found such a life in the imperishability of the spiritual component of the human being, but the Bible thought of human nature more holistically. So when the Bible did begin to intuit a divine answer to this petition, it came as a resurrection and restitution (beyond mortal corruption) of the embodied human personality. Job, however, only implies such a solution, by presenting acutely the need that must be met, if human beings are to have a truly open, hopeful future.

Chapters 15–21 compose a second cycle of speeches, and Eliphaz the Temanite again leads off. He asserts, rather than proves, that Job's words are mere wind, and then he accuses Job of "doing away with the fear of God, and hindering meditation before God" (verses 15:2,4) — two virtues that we saw (in the Psalms) were dear to Israelite seekers after wisdom. The burden of Eliphaz's second speech is that Job is wrong (self-centered) to go on as he does, because his situation is of minor importance and not at all unique. God is the only one who is pure. The wicked surely suffer, and their suffering is just. Neither of these themes is new, and both carry the old cruelty of implying that Job simply has to be suffering because of his sins. (If Eliphaz intends to stress all people's impurity, why is he himself not suffering like Job? Or why, at least, does he not confess that it is merely accidental, and no credit to himself, that he has not been brought equally low?)

Job's response in chapter 16 shows that we are beyond witnessing pleasant rhetorical exchanges and are now hearing positions that are deadly serious. Job dismisses Eliphaz's contribution as but windy words (the very charge that his friends have brought against him; by having this charge made against both Job and his friends, the author of Job invites the reader to judge who in fact does speak substantially and who speaks only wind). Verses 16:6–17 directly attribute Job's sufferings to God, and they are effective for the force of their imagery. Because his earthly friends dismiss any possibility that Job might be in the right, Job turns to heaven for a hearing. The same God who afflicts him might be the defender of his justice.[9] Note in verse 16:21 the plea that human beings have a right (to complain or bring suit) with God like the right they have with their fellow human beings.

The logic of chapter 17 is not always clear, but Job's continuing lamentation certainly is. He seems to be asking God to show him the appreciation that his friends do not, and now he throws himself against the barrier of death, which fences the way against his hope of winning justice and vindication.

Bildad the Shuhite returns for another speech in chapter 18, and the tenor of his first words suggests that he has been stung by Job's dismissal of the friends' reasonings. Yet Bildad has nothing new to offer, merely the old assertions that God brings the wicked to destruction.

Job's reply to this speech in chapter 19 seems to come from beyond anger. The tone is one of desolation at the wrong he feels his friends have done him. Still, Job feels that God is the one whom he must most deeply accuse: "Know then that God has put me in the wrong, and closed his net about me" (verse 19:6). The image is of an animal caught by a hunter. Job receives no more justice than a rabbit snared and carted off. The further description of his desolation brings Job to stress how suffering has isolated him from the fellow human beings who ought to be close and comforting. God has touched and withered him, but why have his friends, wife, and servants also cut him off from sympathy? Verses 19:23–24 are amusing, in the context of Job's being a literary figure, whose existence in fact depends on his being inscribed in a book.

Verse 19:25, which a Buddhist might say rises like a lotus from what previously was only mud, is a famous line. The word translated "Redeemer" (*Goel*) means one who vindicates, and it was applied to God's various deliverances of his people (see for example, Exodus 6:6 and Psalm 103:4). The thought expressed here is a good specimen of the hope against hope, or the belief because it is absurd, that biblical faith can generate. The psychology here seems to be that although the upper mind finds only blocks and hindrances to trusting in God, the depths of the soul finally revolt and say, "Nonetheless, it has to be — and so it will be." God will show himself to be Job's redeemer, buying him back from the opprobrium he has suffered and rendering him justice against his enemies (which include God himself: Job is implying that God will defeat God, which obviously means that "God" admits of several different understandings).

Chapter 20 contains the second speech of Zophar the Naamathite, who, like his colleague accusers, first thinks in terms of the personal insult that Job's expostulations have carried. (This may well imply that Job's friends are too self-concerned to be genuinely wise.) Once again the main theme is the surety of the sufferings and punishments that will come upon the wicked — a significant theme, but hardly the depths of religion. Zophar neither applies this theme directly to Job, to interpret Job's sufferings as well-merited, nor makes the theme carry the comfort that Job is sure to see his enemies (Who are they? Job mainly accuses God.) overthrown. The impression left is that Zophar is too unimaginative or banal a thinker to do anything but keep repeating, as if by rote (although the poetic imagery does vary from speech to speech), the hackneyed argument that the wicked will get their just deserts.

Perhaps sensing this, the Job of chapter 21 seems gentler (although no more in agreement) with his useless friend. Indeed, he wants Zophar and the others to listen for the consolation this speech will carry, as though they were the party afflicted and infirm (as they may in fact be, because banal religion and smallness of soul are quite significant afflictions). Job assures them that his complaint is not against the human order (verse 21:4), but rather against the divine ordering of things. If one looks to what actually happens, rather than to what thoughtless piety asserts has to happen, one sees many wicked people prospering. Their children sing and dance, and they are not hounded by the "watcher of men," for they have told God to take a hike. Job rejects the answer that even when one generation of the wicked are not punished their children get it in the neck. Like Ezekiel and other prophets who clarified the notion of individual responsibility, Job wants the very ones who do evil to get evil recompense (verse 21:20). Death levels all people, those who have been enjoying life and those who have been miserable. It is important, therefore, that justice come while people are still living. The satisfactions that Job's friends claim to find in the punishment of the wicked in fact are "empty nothings" (verse 21:34). Until the friends deal with what actually happens, they will never be accounted wise, just as until God manifestly punishes the wicked, the divine justice will be highly questionable. We therefore have reached a high point in Job's argument that retribution doesn't work out, that it is not pragmatic.

The third and final cycle of Job's dialogues with his friends occurs in chapters 22–27. Eliphaz the Temanite, back for his third venture, starts off on a new tack. Wisdom, he proposes, is for the sake of the human being who possesses it. God is so far beyond the human realm that neither the presence nor the absence of human wisdom or fear concerns him — a view that virtually destroys the notion that God has a personal care for creatures. Then Eliphaz presumes to convict Job of actual wrongdoing, to justify the afflictions that have come upon him. The rest of Eliphaz's speech in chapter 22 is just another stanza in the by now monotonous refrain that God rewards the pious and afflicts the impious.

Job virtually disregards this piece of mediocrity and lets his voice fly directly to God in chapter 23. He wants to be quit of these human lawyers, we infer, and deal with the divine judge (who is also both the one who accuses Job and the one whom Job accuses) face to face. The pathos is that Job cannot find God to conduct this interview. Job has grown more confident (perhaps because he has grown more desperate) that God would give him a hearing, but whether he looks ahead or behind, he cannot find God. The middle verses of this chapter contain a noteworthy assurance that Job has kept to the path of Torah. Yet this is no final defense against the power and plan of God, who does whatever he wants whenever he wants. So Job realizes that traditional righteousness is small protection against divine judgment, and with a truly religious fear he dreads the darkness of uncertainty in which the divinity conceals all ultimate assessments.

In chapter 24 Job first rather touchingly wishes that God kept office hours, so that one might do business with him and rout some of the obscurity under which all moral matters seem to labor. The "those who know him" of verse 24:1 are probably those accounted the friends of God, who also have to fly blind. The following verses make it plain that Job is most interested in the opacity of the ethical realm: why the innocent suffer and the wicked are not punished. The wrongs listed in this chapter are some of the worst crimes human beings can commit. The poetry is distinctive as well. Note, for instance, verse 24:17: "For deep darkness is morning to all of them; for they are friends with the terrors of deep darkness." Darkness can, of course, symbolize the divine mystery, which is too bright for human understanding and so comes as an obscuring cloud. But its simpler symbolic valence in the moral life is to connote the realm of evil. Whereas the light of conscience and following the path of light symbolize trying to discern what is right and accomplish it, love of the night, the dark, or the depths tends to symbolize the way of criminals and those whose consciences have died. Job wants the realm of God and the realm of human righteousness manifestly to coincide. Much of his anguish comes from the apparent confusion of righteousness and criminality, the apparent amorality of what God allows human beings to do. Lurking in this disorder is the horrible possibility that there is no final meaning but only divine absurdity, chance, or caprice.

Bildad the Shuhite responds briefly in chapter 25, but confusedly and to little profit. His view is that God rules with complete sovereignty and that nothing is righteous before God, least of all human beings, who are maggots and worms.

Job responds to this irrelevance with acidic sarcasm: "How you have helped him who has no power!" The rest of Job's speech in chapter 26 magnifies the cosmic creator (and so foreshadows the speech that God himself will give), whose very omnipotence exacerbates the problem of evil.

The conclusion to the exchanges between Job and his friends occurs in chapter 27, where Job insists that to his last breath (as long as the spirit of God is in him) he will not agree with his accusers that he deserves what he is suffering. Strangely, though, the rest of the chapter puts into the mouth of Job the assurance (that the wicked will be destroyed) that we have come to expect from the accusers. If we lean heavily on verse 27:7, we may interpret this speech as applying to the accusers, who have become Job's enemies. However, some scholars solve the problem of the apparent illogic of the speech by positing textual irregularities. Marvin Pope, for example, writes of verses 27:7–23:

> 7. This malediction implies that the wicked are punished, whereas Job has argued that the wicked often prosper. It may be that this is merely a stereotype curse which Job uses to pay his respects to the friends who assert the doctrine that the wicked are

always punished. 8–23. These verses present the point of view of the friends and cannot be attributed to Job. We take them as part of Zophar's missing speech. . . .[10]

28–37 Monologues

The three cycles of dialogues with Job's friends are concluded, and from here until Job meets God (chapter 38) the genre is monologue. (We may also consider chapters 28–31 to be Job's last reply to his friends—see verse 32:1.) Chapter 28 is quite famous and is usually considered a meditation or a hymn on the inaccessibility of wisdom. As such it is a high point in the biblical reflection on wisdom. Verses 28:1–11 prepare the way by noting that ordinary things like silver and gold can be searched out and found. As verses 12–22 reflect, wisdom is not the same: "But where shall wisdom be found? And where is the place of understanding?" Only God knows, because only God has the wisdom to carry out the work of creation.[11] The somewhat moralistic conclusion in verse 28:28 fits well with the regular sapiential tendency to try to link the cosmological expression of divine wisdom with an ethical uprightness that would be the parallel expression of wisdom in the human realm: "Behold, the fear of the Lord, that is wisdom; and to depart from evil is understanding."

Chapters 29–31 comprise a concluding soliloquy and solemn oath that round out Job's position.[12] In chapter 29 Job reviews the prosperity that he once enjoyed, prior to his present sufferings. It is remarkable that he most stresses the good works he did and the high reputation he possessed. In contrast, chapter 30 describes the low estate to which he has fallen. This, too, is mainly a matter of low reputation: being the sport of vulgar people whom previously he would have despised. Verse 30:11 attributes this to God's having loosed the cord by which previously he guided Job to prosperity. Verses 30:9–31, overall, sound like a psalm of lament. Interestingly, verses 24–25 claim that Job himself sympathized with compatriots who were suffering. Unlike most of the psalms, however, the chapter ends with no upsurge of hope that God will grant deliverance. Job is in the dark night of the soul, when everything looks black.

The oaths of innocence offered in chapter 31 are reminiscent of the swearings of Egyptian texts, such as the Book of the Dead,[13] by which dead people would defend themselves before the god of the underworld who needed assurances of their having lived good lives. Among the virtues that Job claims are chastity; honesty; justice with his servants; generosity to sufferers such as poor people, widows, and orphans; freedom from greed; freedom from idolatry (verses 31:26–27); not having rejoiced in the ruin of his enemies (which many of the psalms suggest was allowable); not having cursed; hospitality; and openness or publicity (made possible by a good conscience). Job is willing to sign his name to this list, as though it were a formal document by which God might judge him. He would be able to bring it up to the king of heaven feeling like a prince. Indeed, Earth itself has no valid claims against him, because he has dealt righteously with the land and its owners.

The monologues of Job therefore end with a self-description that makes Job the ideal that the moralistic sages wanted to achieve. As such, Job 31 joins Ezekiel 18 and Psalms 15, 24, and 51 as high points of biblical ethics. If Job is indeed as this self-description paints him, it affronts all justice that he has fallen so low. Thereby, it calls into question the entire theology that based the covenant on appropriate recompense (for individuals as well as the nation) for both evil-doing and goodness, and if that theology goes, the credibility of the God of the covenant cannot be far behind.[14]

Chapters 32–37 express the discourses of Elihu, a character not previously heard. The singularities of these chapters (for example, many Aramaic words occur) suggest that they come from a different source than the rest of the Book (which itself is quite idiosyncratic, compared to the rest of the Hebrew Bible).[15] At any rate, the first verses of chapter 32, which are in prose, introduce this new character. He comes on stage having been described as angry that Job justified himself rather than God, and as angry as well that the three friends had found no effective answer to Job. Thus he appears like a young Turk eager to succeed where his elders (and so presumed betters in wisdom) have failed.

First, Elihu rebuts the easy equation of age and wisdom, noting that it is the breath of God that gives anyone, old or young, understanding. Elihu cannot restrain the spirit in him any longer, and he promises that what he has to say will not be deflected by any need to produce flattery.

Second, in chapter 33 Elihu launches his address by claiming uprightness of heart and inspiration from God (for which he offers no behavioral proofs). Job has spoken in his hearing, and he itches to take issue with the innocence that Job has claimed. To begin with, Elihu rejects Job's presumed right to contend with God. Next, he expresses the opinion that God speaks variously, in dreams (as well as in the Torah?). Verses 19–28 may imply still another form of divine revelation: a message given through human suffering.[16] Note the angel of verse 33:23, and the quite traditional theological assumption (prayer to God will win God's acceptance and thereby a return to vigor and joy).

Elihu would therefore have Job confess his sin, missing the point of Job's anguish: Job cannot find in himself sins to confess. To this point, the young accuser is doing no better than his elders did, not hearing what Job is saying and being shaped by ideology (convictions that live a life of their own, little touched by actual human experience). Elihu claims that God gives people two or three chances to learn through suffering the wisdom of repentance. His pretense to teach Job wisdom (verse 33:33) would be humorous, were it not so arrogant. Especially offensive to a person in Job's situation, we presume, is Elihu's lack of any experience of suffering. Nothing we know about him indicates that he has ever been brought low by God, and the fact that this does not stop his headlong rush to preach to Job marks him as sophomoric: a wise fool.

In chapter 34 Elihu accuses Job of scoffing, going with evil-doers, and depreciating delight in God (verses 34:7–9). We have no evidence that Job displayed any of these vices before being afflicted by the Satan by God's permission. Even after his fall into suffering, he has not walked with the wicked, and his scoffing and scepticism seem, in kindly interpretation, more probes for understanding or calls for fully satisfying explanation (theodicy) than attacks on genuine religion. Elihu then merely marches along, reasoning that the Lord of creation has to be just. To verse 34:28 the speech of Elihu is but fine piety. Verse 34:29 might be interpreted as profound, based on insight into the freedom to reveal or not reveal itself that a genuine divinity always would retain, but we have little reason to think that Elihu is a profound thinker. Verses 34:31–32 seem quite cynical in positing that repentance and humility are rare. The rest of the chapter accuses Job of making rebellion the capstone of his sins.

Chapter 35 opens with a fine testimony to God's independence of human behavior, whether sin or righteousness. The problem with proposing this as a response to Job is that, on its own, this proposition makes God careless of human fate and so a God very different from the God of the covenant. Moreover, a God so removed from human behavior logically should not take pains to judge human affairs, and the whole assumption of Job's friends that suffering inevitably points to moral failure thereby sluices down the drain. Verses 35:9–11 offer an interesting commentary on popular religion, which Elihu depicts as turning to God only when things are going badly and seldom offering the Creator of the world disinterested praise. The Psalms, of course, dispute this reading of Israelite religion, because they regularly break out in pure praise of the divine beauty or the divine power or the divine goodness.

Verse 35:14 implies that Job's confession that he does not see God and is waiting for God to hear his case are an "empty cry" and so rightly are not heard by God. How does Elihu know this? By what title does he so presume to pass judgment on Job's motivation? At the end, Job is again convicted of foolishness: He is said not to realize the grandeur of God or the utter freedom of the creator to do what he wishes. The prior speeches of Job certainly call this judgment into question.

Chapter 36 offers more of the same: variations on the assumption or the dogmatic faith that God is mighty, good, and just (according to Elihu's quite standard, even prosaic definitions). Verse 36:13, perhaps by Elihu's inadvertance (presumably the author of the book, however, is writing deliberately), seems to vindicate Job: "The godless in heart cherish anger; they do not cry for help when he binds them." Job certainly expresses anger, although it is debatable whether he cherishes it. Clearly, however, he has done little else than cry for help from the bind in which God has put him. On Elihu's own terms, therefore, Job is not godless in heart. More positively, his crying out for help might establish that he is full of genuine religion. Verse 36:23 is a stronger argument that makes the irrefutable point that no one has the stature to judge God. However, Job has not been unqualified in his judgments against God. The main thrust of his complaint is that he cannot find in his life wrongdoing sufficient to justify the sufferings he is experiencing. If God would make plain why he is suffering, and so vindicate the traditional equation of suffering and sin, he would shut his mouth. Job does not assert that God could not do that. He simply says that God has not done that, and that the arguments of his friends fail to convince him that he has merited what has befallen him. The rest of chapter 36 is fine sapiential poetry, but it wanders afield from the crossroads of Job's argument.

Chapter 37 rumbles along in this vein, winningly extolling the wisdom of the creator and exhibiting the marvels of his cosmic rule. Even in our time of greatly expanded scientific knowledge, the freezing of the waters and the thickening of the clouds are wonders we do not fully comprehend. (For example, why should water freeze at 32 degrees Fahrenheit?) Elihu quite correctly infers that no creature, neither he nor Job, has the stature to contest with God. He does not prove, however, that God has been just in his dealings with Job (according to the standard ethical view that sufferings bespeak wrongdoing), and he does not prove that this standard ethics flows from the cosmic transcendence of the creator.

In other words, the sapiential convictions quite poetically expressed by Elihu provide a fine context for probing what the divine transcendence might mean in the moral sphere, but Elihu does not carry out this probe. Had he taken a symbol such as the Isaian figure of the divine ways being as far from human ways as the heavens are above the Earth (Isaiah 55:8–9), he might have done first-rate ethical reflection. Failing that, his conclusions seem postulated rather than argued, seem matters of dogma and prejudice rather than matters of genuine moral insight and helpfulness. So although Elihu's conclusion (verse 37:24: "He does not regard any who are wise in their own conceit") certainly seems to follow from the grandeur of the creator, it begs the question pertinent here and assumes rather than proves that Job holds the conceit that he is wise.

38:1–42:6 Dialogues with God

One who accepts our rather harsh impression of Elihu can read the abrupt out-break of divine speech from the whirlwind (see verse 38:1) as an expression of God's own irritation, as though God himself said, "With a babbler like this for a friend, I don't need any enemies. Get this sprout off the stage. I'll speak for myself." That God completely disregards Elihu and speaks directly to Job supports the notion that Elihu's speeches have been interpolated into a prior text in which the present chapter 38 followed on the end of Job's self-defense in chapter 31. That God speaks out of the whirlwind adorns his speech with the theophanous overtones of the God of the Mosaic covenant. Indeed, it conveys the vigor of the ancient storm god that probably underlay the YHWH in whom Israel came to believe through the ancestors.

God takes the core of the cosmological argument that the friends and Elihu have been pushing and shoves it directly at Job. Dramatically, the argument gains considerably because God himself is now making it in the first person. God's own description of the processes of creation comes across in splendid poetry, convincing us that the sapiential writers greatly loved the theme of cosmic wisdom and were moved by it to great creativity. The assumption throughout is that the one behind cosmic phenomena must know how and why they occur, and that one who does not know how and why they occur stands so far below this one that his or her passing judgment on heavenly things is supreme arrogance.

Verse 38:21 seems sarcastic, skewering Job with the implication of his lawsuit (that he knows the proportions of creation and so must have been at the first day). But has Job in fact claimed anything like such a competence? As God marvelously parades through the wonders of the stars and the heavens, we continue to wonder whether this is fully relevant. Certainly it will silence Job, and reduce him to dust and ashes, but will it meet the small still voice of his moral probing? And if it does not, is not the God expostulating from the whirlwind exactly the bully that Job has implied the injustice he is suffering proves God to be? Here God would only be a rhetorical bully, whereas there he is singeing Job's flesh, but in both instances his character would be the same and so Job's charge would only gain in plausibility.

In chapter 39 (from verse 38:39) God's examples shift to the realm of animal life, but his argument continues simply to demonstrate the transcendence of the divine creator (and so, by inference, to demonstrate that the creator is beyond the moral judgment of human beings). Note the theme of divine knowledge (wisdom): God is the only one who knows when the goats bring forth and how long it takes the hinds to calve. The examples paraded before Job stress the uncanniness of animal habits, and thus suggest that the world is a far stranger place than Job thinks. Verse 39:17 implies that God may give wisdom to his creatures or withhold it. Verses 39:26–27 are rhetorical questions that Job cannot answer affirmatively. So by arguing from the orderly and uncanny phenomena of nature, God has backed Job into the corner of creatureliness and beaten him over the head with his ignorance and impotence.[17]

Chapter 40 begins with a question that initially seems to be rhetorical but bears further examination. God asks Job whether he, a "faultfinder" who would contend with God, can answer "it" (apparently, the question we might generalize from the descriptions of chapters 38 and 39: Do you understand how the world runs?). Job is cowed, well impressed with the smallness of his significance. He has nothing more to say: "I lay my hand on my mouth" (verse 40:4). But God will not let him off so easily. From the whirlwind the divine voice challenges Job to gird up his loins like a man and get back into the rhetorical ring. The key question occurs in verse 40:8: "Will you even, put me in the wrong? Will you condemn me that you may be justified?" Certainly we may interpret Job's prior feistiness as having this intention. Yet on a sympathetic reading he need not appear so arrogant. It is unfortunate that God immediately returns to the physical disparity between Job the creature and himself the creator. We would like to hear what God himself might make of Job's plea for ethical explanation, what God's own sense is of how doing evil and doing good are recompensed.

Verses 40:10–14 do deal with the moral realm, but not completely seriously. God challenges Job to put on the raiment of the kingly judge and to carry out the divine business of punishing the wicked. Of course, Job cannot do this. Unanswered, however, is Job's charge that the wicked often are not punished (that God does not always show himself a careful king who renders exact justice). It would clarify things if God assured Job that, according to some higher, heavenly calculus, justice in fact always is done. God tells Job to tread down the wicked, but God does not guarantee that heaven will tread them down.

Verses 40:15–24 describe behemoth, a huge animal perhaps modeled on the hippopotamus but here swollen to mythical proportions. Scholars debate the purpose of introducing behemoth (and leviathan, in chapter 41).[18] Perhaps these great beings are meant to console Job as examples of creatures for whom things do seem to go well. Another interpretation notes that behemoth is a land monster, leviathan is a sea monster, and each is the mightiest creature in its realm. Yet both are mere playthings for God, even though Job is no match for them. Still a third possibility in this imagery is that leviathan represents the primeval chaos that God defeated at the beginning of creation. Such chaos, including moral evil and social breakdown, remain poised to take over, should God ever lose his grip. Perhaps Job's challenge to God therefore threatens to spring leviathan from the deep and overturn creation.

The reference to a covenant in verse 41:4 could be meant to remind Job that human beings are the only creatures whom God has singled out for special (free, intelligent) service. Verses 41:9–11 move from leviathan, who certainly dwarfs Job, to God. If Job could not stand up to leviathan (the crocodile or whale, also swollen to mythical proportions), how could he ever think of standing up to God? Once again the ratio or scale being used is physical, whereas the order in which

Job wished to compete was moral, so the argument does not quite meet the point, and God can continue to seem a bully.

On the other hand, we realize by now that the wisdom writers tend to conjoin the physical and moral realms more than we moderns, that their religio-cultural outlook was less differentiated and more holistic than ours. Indeed, we might regard the Book of Job as a prime example of the pressures and probes that Israelite experience was exerting to introduce more distinctions and gain better differentiation. So even though the bottom line enunciated in verse 41:11 is impressive ("Whatever is under the whole heaven is mine"), it still leaves us dissatisfied. If we have identified with Job (and the text provides many clues that the author hopes we will identify with Job — for example, the probity with which Job is credited prior to his affliction, and the honesty and courage he displays in challenging God), we will be impressed but not wholly persuaded. In times of trouble we will feel it proper to surrender to a cosmic creator whose ways we can never fathom, but we will continue to wish for greater clarity and parity in the moral order and more persuasive evidence that the creator is controlling evil-doers and supporting those who do good as wisely as he is controlling the stars and the great beasts.

The remainder of chapter 41 extols the construction of leviathan, certainly to the praise of God his creator but perhaps also for the consolation of human beings, who might reflect on their singular rationality and so account themselves the leviathans of the moral order. Echoing verse 41:33, human beings could say, "Upon earth there is not our like." Whether they could go on to call their kind "a creature without fear" is more debatable. If we get rather subtle, we can think that the author of Job might be trying to bring about this conclusion. Having contemplated the heights of divine power and the depths of human misery, the reader might conclude that trust in the creator can cast out fear of whatever happens in creation. By sapiential standards, this would be a consummation devoutly to be hoped, although it would take us beyond the holy fear of the Lord that much sapiential literature suggests is the beginning of human wisdom.

The second response of Job, in verses 42:1–6, confesses what the entire poetic bulk of the book has been structured to produce. Job responds to the creator of the universe (whether he responds to the God of Abraham, Isaac, and Jacob is less certain), and he asserts that he accepts the proposition that God can do all things and never is thwarted. Moreover, Job accepts the charge that he "hid counsel without knowledge" and spoke of things he could not understand. We should note, however, that God does not endorse the view of Job's friends, which would have tied suffering to sin, and that Job repents of sins committed *after* his suffering and so not its cause. Verse 42:5 is enigmatic, perhaps implying that Job used to know God through echoes of the divine speech (for example, in the Torah or traditional mores or from the friends' speeches) but now "sees" with the light of understanding (has had his mind stretched by the demonstrations of the divine creative power). The conclusion we find in verse 42:6 is a fitting symbol for the service that radical monotheism encourages. Like a good Muslim, persuaded to the bone that God is the absolute sovereign before whom the believer (the creature) has no rights, Job "despises" (belittles) himself and repents (of his presumption or pride in challenging God). The text gives Job no particular posture here, but it is hard not to picture him bowed low in obeisance. (Note, however, that verse 42:6 can also be translated in such a way that Job does not give in.)

42:7–17 Epilogue

The poetic sections of Job are not the whole story, however, so just as scholars have had to estimate the orientational significance of the prose introduction, they have had to ask whether the prose epilogue does not reset the whole. In verse 42:7, for example, God blasts Eliphaz the Temanite, saying that his wrong speech has incited the divine wrath and that "my servant Job," in contrast, has spoken what is right. This correct speech of Job might be his response to God in chapters 40 and 42, but it could also apply to the whole of Job's utterance and so put a seal of approval on Job's search for the divine justice.

Either way, Job becomes a priestly figure, commissioned by God to intercede for Eliphaz and the other friends (who by implication also spoke wrongly) that God might avert his wrath from them. Job has his fortunes restored to him in double measure, and his family and friends come back to comfort and reward him. From this time forth Job's whole family flourishes, clearly enjoying the divine blessing, and Job lives to the ripe age of 140 years (double the normal good span), dying full of days (verse 42:17). Does he gain this good end simply because he confessed God's supremacy over him, or does he gain it as well because he had the courage to pursue ethical understanding and justice, even to the point of challenging God? Although the Book of Job allows the reader either choice, it may in fact want to sanction both choices.

HISTORICAL BACKGROUND

At the outset we suggested that the Book of Job probably was written after the Babylonian Exile, which would mean that it presupposed that national trauma. This suggestion runs into difficulty, however, because the Book of Job pays no attention to the Exile and so has to be related to it through perhaps too subtle analogies. For this reason, as well as archaic features that the Book presents (Job is quite like an ancient ancestor and in his [admittedly non-Israelite] milieu there is no Temple or priesthood), scholars have proposed a wide range of dates, from the second millennium B.C.E. (when extra-Israelite literature presenting some parallels to Job flourished) to the fourth century B.C.E. (when Persian rule encouraged a cosmopolitan culture).[19]

James L. Crenshaw, who favors a date in the sixth century, has stressed the international background and spirit that applies for the biblical wisdom literature as a whole:

> Both Egypt and Mesopotamia had a flourishing wisdom tradition, consisting of professional sages who composed extensive literary works which manifest remarkable thematic and formal coherence. In Egypt those writings included instructions and reflections upon life's deeper mysteries. Such texts functioned within the royal court as a means of educating future courtiers, and in time produced a scribal profession that looked upon other vocations as inferior to their own exalted one. Similarly, Mesopotamian wisdom texts preserve valiant gropings with the problem of human suffering, but also contain numerous collections of popular proverbs.[20]

Crenshaw goes on to credit ancient Near Eastern wisdom literature with an international spirit, with speaking of problems that transcended particular historical circumstances, with a strongly humanistic outlook, with optimism based in a conviction that God had made an orderly universe, with self-interest (seeking the path that would bring prosperity and avoiding the path that would bring disaster), and with looking to the physical world (rather than to special revelations from God) for the secrets that would make one wise. We can see that these characteristics largely apply to Job, because even the speech of God from the whirlwind deals with the structure of the cosmos and says little about special revelations or covenants in the tradition of the God of the ancestors, Moses, and the prophets.

LITERARY INTENT

Certainly the different portions of the Book of Job may have been composed for different reasons, and we have already noted some of the tensions between such portions as the prose framework and the poetic bulk. The speech of Elihu does not fit the rest of the structure neatly, and the speeches of God, as well as the monologues of Job, are certainly somewhat different from the cycles of dialogues between Job and his friends. Yet the book was, after all, edited into the form in which we now find it today, and that form has carried the stamp of canonical approval. After noting that appreciating a canonical integrity need not mean denying the tensions within the book, nor failing to see how such tensions force readers to reflect about the choices solicited by the interplay of positions and counter-positions, Brevard Childs finally describes the Book of Job as concerned with the limits of wisdom. As well, he finds that it serves as a corrective to Proverbs and Ecclesiastes (where the horizon is less profound).[21] These are not the most lucid or helpful observations, but they do confirm the opinion, developed in our commentary, that the Book of Job can be read from several different perspectives and seems richest when taken as a quite ironic approach to such questions as justice, ethical uprightness, the wisdom of the typical elder or friend, and even the divine goodness or concern for human beings.

In contrast to the prophetic concern with the catastrophes that had afflicted the community, the Book of Job struggles with the problem of individual suffering.[22] For this problem, the Deuteronomistic notion that sin brings suffering proved highly debatable. We might in fact consider the speeches of the friends of Job as evidence of the extremes to which orthodox Israelite thought was willing to go to try to make the Deuteronomistic view apply to individuals. The result, however, is that the friends become a parody of orthodoxy: right words but unpersuasive applications and dubious motivations. In their mouths the orthodox formula has become "sin causes suffering" (a stricter nexus than Deuteronomy proposed), and the individual is thought bound by this formula. Deuteronomy, by contrast, focused on national sins. By rejecting the counsel of the friends, and keeping the Deuteronomistic theology questionable, Job offered its readers a great stimulus to rethink the whole question of individual suffering and reach higher ground.

In our view, Job is most impressive when taken not as a didactic text, written to convey wisdom like a tract or a homily, but as a teasing, indirect, dialectical, ruminative work that would challenge the reader to break out of the narrow legalistic framework in which Israelite religion, like all other religions, was tempted to squat and confront the genuine puzzles, if not mysteries, of moral existence. The poetry in the book testifies to literary artistry of high rank. The themes do credit to wisdom speculation on the order of the cosmos and the transcendence of the creator. But the peculiar genius of the work is the inner debating occasioned by the friction between the cosmological order that the friends, Elihu, and God himself tend to consider and the precisely moral order that troubles Job. We therefore prefer to think that Job was written to challenge Israel and all readers to come to their own judgments about what sort of justice is likely to occur in their experience and how they will relate suffering, especially that which is personal and apparently unmerited, with their senses of God.

LASTING SIGNIFICANCE

Job has intrigued and delighted readers for centuries, and it continues to receive much attention today, because the questions about human justice and theodicy (the justice of God) that it raises are always relevant. We have noted most of these questions in the course of our textual commentary, so we do not belabor them here. Summarily, Job shines a spotlight on the disparity between virtue and reward, or between vice and punishment, that tends to obtain in every age and asks what this says about God and the constitution of the order (moral as well as physical) that human beings indwell.

What seems worth adding at this juncture is the significance that the Book of Job has for our understanding of biblical religion and, by extension, for our understanding of the human condition that applies always and everywhere. In this book the tentative, self-critical, argumentative character of the Bible and Israelite religion is very obvious, so reading it can help us appreciate that other books of the Bible share these characteristics, and that biblical religion as a whole is much more provisional than dogmatic, much more tolerant of conflict and diversity than concerned to lay down a single party line. This appreciation will be all the more valuable if our experience of the people who profess to follow biblical religion, be they Jews, Christians, or Muslims, has suggested that biblical religionists are not always tentative and tolerant but, on the contrary, often seem sure of themselves to the point of simplemindedness.

One thing the Book of Job clearly is not is simpleminded. Even if we accept the position laid out in all the speeches of those who oppose Job and agree that the splendors of creation place the creator beyond all accusations of injustice, we have to admit that the authors write Job a sufficiently attractive personality and a sufficiently cogent intellectual position to create a genuine tension and make the debate that unfolds far from determined from the outset. Moreover, the text grapples with notions that lie at the border of all comparison of the ways of God with the ways of human beings, and thereby it suggests to all with ears to hear that such staples as "justice," "innocence," "righteousness," "punishment," "prosperity," and "wisdom" itself are far from obvious in their significance.

GLOSSARY

Agnosticism   Not knowing one's position, especially on ultimate matters such as the existence of God.

Didactic   Teaching, lecturing, explaining.

Dogmatic   Pertaining to official doctrine, set forth by a religious group's duly constituted authorities, that is considered binding on all orthodox members.

STUDY QUESTIONS

1. Do chapters 1 and 2 support the charge that God plays with human beings as with pawns on a chessboard?
2. What is the significance of Job's longing for death?
3. What are the assets and the liabilities in the friends' assurance that misfortune must be tied to wrongdoing?
4. How valid is the argument that God's control of nature assures justice in the moral realm?
5. Does the Book of Job allow the conclusion that God is a bully?
6. Why is Job restored to good fortune, and why are the friends finally condemned by God?
7. How valid today are the poetic appreciations of nature that we find in the Book of Job?
8. Does Job justify describing biblical religion as tentative, several-layered, ironic, and challenging interlocutors to decide for themselves whether God is just?

NOTES

1. See J. Gerald Janzen, "Job, the Book of," in *Harper's Bible Dictionary*, ed. Paul J. Achtemeier. San Francisco: Harper & Row, 1985, p. 493.

2. See Hugh Anderson, "The Book of Job," in *Wisdom Literature and Poetry*, ed. Charles M. Laymon. Nashville: Abingdon (Interpreter's Concise Commentary), 1983, p. 7.

3. See Paul-E. Dion, "Un nouvel éclairage sur le context cultural des malheurs de Job," *Vetus Testamentum*, 34 (1984), 213–15.

4. See René Girard, "Job et le bouc émissaire," *Bulletin du Centre Protestant D'Études*, 35 (1983), 3–33.

5. See Edwin C. Webster, "Strophic Patterns in Job 3–28," *Journal for the Study of the Old Testament*, 26 (1983), 33–60.

6. See Shalom M. Paul, "Job 4:15 — A Hair Raising Encounter," *Zeitschrift für die alttestamentliche Wissenschaft*, 95 (1983), 119–21.

7. See Roland E. Murphy, O. Carm., *Wisdom Literature*. Grand Rapids, Mich.: Eerdmans (The Forms of the Old Testament Literature), 1981, pp. 13–45.

8. See Marvin H. Pope, *Job*. Garden City, N.Y.: Doubleday Anchor Bible, 1973, p. 80.

9. See John Briggs Curtis, "On Job's Witness in Heaven," *Journal of Biblical Literature*, 102 (1983), 549–62.

10. See Pope, *Job*, p. 191.

11. See Scott L. Harris, "Wisdom or Creation? A New Interpretation of Job 28:27," *Vetus Testamentum*, 33 (1983), 419–27.

12. See Edwin C. Webster, "Strophic Patterns in Job 29–42," *Journal for the Study of the Old Testament*, 30 (1984), 95–109. See also John C. Holbert, "The Rehabilitation of the Sinner: The Function of Job 29–31," *Zeitschrift für die alttestamentliche Wissenschaft*, 95 (1983), 229–37.

13. See James B. Pritchard, ed., *Ancient Near Eastern Texts Relating to the Old Testament*, 3rd ed. Princeton: Princeton University Press, 1969, pp. 34–35.

14. See Michael Brennan Dick, "Job 31, The Oath of Innocence, and the Sage," *Zeitschrift für die alttestamentliche Wissenschaft*, 95 (1983), 31–53.

15. See Jonas C. Greenfield, "The Language of the Book," in *The Book of Job*. Philadelphia: Jewish Publication Society, 1980, p. xv.

16. See Hedwige Rouillard, "Le sens de Job 33:21," *Revue Biblique*, 91 (1984), 30–50.

17. See Henry Rowold, "Yahweh's Challenge to Rival: The Form and Function of the Yahweh-Speech in Job 38–39," *Catholic Biblical Quarterly*, 47 (1985), 199–211.

18. See John G. Gammie, "Behemoth and Leviathan: On the Didactic and Theological Significance of Job 40:15–41:26," in *Israelite Wisdom*, ed. John G. Gammie et al. Missoula, Mont.: Scholars Press, 1978, pp. 217–31.

19. See Pope, *Job*, pp. xxxii–xl.

20. James L. Crenshaw, *Old Testament Wisdom: An Introduction*. Atlanta: John Knox, 1981, p. 55.

21. See Brevard S. Childs, *Introduction to the Old Testament as Scripture*. Philadelphia: Fortress, 1979, pp. 543–44.

22. For Job's concern with the sufferings of the poor generally, see Gustavo Gutierrez, *On Job*. Maryknoll, N.Y.: Orbis, 1987.

CHAPTER 18

Proverbs

TEXTUAL ANALYSIS

The Book of Proverbs is a collection of poems and sayings, traditionally associated with Solomon, that was probably put together in the late sixth century B.C.E. but may well contain materials that go back to the Solomonic monarchy of 400 years earlier. The present collection may have served as an instruction manual for youth, but traditional assessments of the canonical Hebrew Bible have accounted Proverbs an important piece of wisdom literature.[1] We treat the Book of Proverbs as a binding together of five different subcollections of poems and proverbs:

1:1–9:18	Teacher's Introduction
10:1–22:16	First Collection of Solomonic Sayings
22:17–24:34	Thirty Precepts of the Sages
25:1–29:27	Second Collection of Solomonic Sayings
30:1–31:31	Four Appendices[2]

1:1–9:18 Teacher's Introduction

The Book of Proverbs begins with an attribution to Solomon, who had become the model of wisdom, largely because his rule was considered the most prosperous (and therefore the most sagacious) in Israelite history, and also because he appears to have been a patron of literature. The opening verses provide the purpose for this collection: to help people learn wisdom and the prudential virtues that flow in the train of wisdom. We know from the wisdom psalms of the Psalter and from Job that the predominant conviction of most of the sapiential writers was that virtue leads to blessings and vice leads to sufferings. This is the guiding belief of the Book of Proverbs, so its goal is quite practical: to help people (the nation) know how the world runs (especially the world of human affairs) and thereby merit the blessings of God, which include both material and spiritual benefits.

Verse 1:7 notes that the beginning of wisdom is the fear of the Lord, which suggests a religious attitude that we should not despise. By opening human affairs to divine judgment, the Book of Proverbs situates what people do and know in a context very different from that of the atheist, whose notion of "success" can easily be what produces wealth and power. Verses 1:10–19 are a sober warning about consorting with criminals. The extremity of the actions alluded to here (bloodshed and violence) reminds us that the sapiential writers were not all armchair philosophers, maundering on over port and cigars. The personified cry of Wisdom that we find in verses 1:20–33 is interesting for the feminine persona that it features. No doubt the writer is deliberately contrasting the solicitations of Wisdom with the calls of the streetwalkers who would lead the young soul astray. Wisdom is not sanguine that her cries will be heard. The simple tend to love their simplemindedness, and the scoffers tend to continue to scoff. They will have only themselves to blame for the disasters that Wisdom is sure will fall on their heads. In contrast, those who listen will dwell secure — that is the main plank in the sapiential platform.

Chapter 2 is another discourse on much the same theme. The voice seems to be that of a teacher or sage bent on instructing a youth. The points worth remarking include the hunger for insight that the youth ideally would develop, the teacher's confidence that God will give wisdom to the upright, the depiction of wisdom as a safeguard against vice, and the overtones of Torah that ring in the "paths of the righteous" (verse 2:20).

Chapter 3 provides more orientational guidance, much of it cast in poetic form. The "tablet of your heart" of verse 3:3 recalls the interiorization of the covenant spoken of in Jeremiah 31.[3] The primacy accorded God rather than self is an interesting translation of the fear of the Lord. Note that verse 3:8 thinks of the benefits of such wisdom and fear as quite physical — a reminder of the holism of biblical psychology and ethics, which cannot think of prosperity as either purely spiritual or purely material. Verses 3:11–12 can be interpreted as making Torah like a good parental guidance, which does not mind reproving its immature or recalcitrant children. From verse 3:15 on Wisdom again is given a feminine persona, as though she should be the mother (and perhaps the lover: see verse 3:18) of the young aspirant after success. Verses 3:19–20 introduce the cosmological tone that was so prominent in Job. Wisdom also should serve as an adornment and a source of peace or emotional stability. The rest of the chapter is interesting mainly for the careful dealings with one's neighbor that it recommends.

By the counting of R. B. Y. Scott, these nine introductory chapters contain ten different discourses on wisdom that together provide a full-fledged orientation. Interspersed, as well, are several sapiential poems. Chapters 4 and 5 contain discourses five through nine.[4] In chapter 4 the voice is more paternal than magisterial, although, as we have seen, teacher and parent are conjoined in this work. Verse 4:2 is explicit about the preceptive nature of this wisdom teaching: It moves by discrete sayings rather than sustained philosophical reflections. (As well, it suggests a collector's mentality, rather than the mentality of a creative expositor.) Note in verse 4:7 that getting wisdom, rather than feeling fear of the Lord, is called the beginning of wisdom. We might translate this as, "Desire is the first step." The imagery then turns rather romantic, as though Wisdom were a lovely girl with whom a good-hearted young man might be smitten. Verse 4:10 seems to promise that wisdom should produce long life and easy progress. More negatively, it should keep the young person from the destructive path of sinners (which presumably leads to death and difficulty). This is reminiscent of the Deuteronomic imagery of two ways (Deuteronomy 30:15–20).

Chapter 5 repeats the admonition to attend to the wisdom (words) being offered and so repeats the overtones of divine speech, such as the words given to Moses in the Torah. Opposing the feminine persona of Wisdom is the loose woman, who receives sufficient attention to suggest a parallelism: goddess/whore. If the vice being suggested in chapter 5 is generalized beyond fornication or adultery to waywardness as a whole, the teaching gains in psychological acuity and avoids any stigmatization of sex as the primary domain of sin. The play back and forth between domestic fidelity and wandering afield is also richer if we consider sexual virtue and vice to be symbolic of wider realms. Verse 5:23 summarizes on a note of discipline: Sapiential teaching is a rein, a set of controls. This figure is most apt for youth, and it appears in the ethical discourse of many religious traditions. By maturity, most traditions hope, the discipline will have become interiorized (the Bible would have it inscribed in the heart) and so will not seem burdensome.

Chapter 6 opens with advice about extricating oneself from foolish commitments made to one's neighbors. Then it gives us the less than dazzling figure of the ant, who serves as a lesson in diligent provision. (On the other hand, for the wisdom writers the whole of creation is full of lessons, if we have eyes to see.) A worthless person is portrayed as lacking restraint over physical gestures (being "loose" in several senses). The six and seven things objectionable to the Lord (verse 6:16) sound like a laundry list from elementary instruction. The concrete temper of the biblical wisdom writers shows in the use of various bodily parts to anchor these vicious practices. We hear a repetition of the call to keep one's parents' teachings, and then an extended warning against adultery unfolds. In this passage the specific failing of adultery itself, as well as vice in general, is undoubtedly in question, and we should not forget that the Mosaic code considered this a sufficiently serious sin to prescribe a punishment of death by stoning (for both the adulterer and the adulteress: see Deuteronomy 22:22–24). Here it is interesting that the death penalty is not mentioned. The general attitude that the wife was the property of the husband does continue, however, as we see in the assimilation of adultery to stealing.

Chapter 7 would have the student/child treasure the teacher's commandments and consider Wisdom his sister. That would protect him from the loose woman of vice. The imagery of harlotry that follows is enriched if we recall the prophetic use of harlotry as a figure for false religion. Verse 7:23, which speaks of how adultery may cost a young man his life, can be taken either literally (stoning) or more figuratively (loss of moral integrity and the path to prospering). The imagery used at the end of the chapter is most effective if vice in general is being personified, because surely adultery is not the only house on the way to Sheol.

In chapter 8 Lady Wisdom speaks poetically, and in great contrast to the

Lady Harlotry of chapter 7. Whereas harlotry leads to death, wisdom leads to life. Note that verse 8:1 equates wisdom and understanding. Wisdom promises that her instruction deals in truth and is precious. Verse 8:13 expands on "the fear of the Lord," equating it with hatred of evil. Verses 8:15–16 associate Wisdom with the rule of kings and princes, playing off the idealized figure of the divinely appointed ruler, who would mediate God's Law and Wisdom to the realm. After praising her own various excellences, Wisdom claims an origin at the beginning of creation (verses 8:23–31). This recalls the cosmological aspects of divine intelligence and skill that we found in the wisdom psalms and Job, with the differences that here a personified Wisdom seems to be given a part in the process of creation (verse 8:30), perhaps on the order of the Demi-urge credited by Platonic philosophy with the fashioning of creation. The upshot is that the natural world itself became a source of revelation. The delight mentioned in verses 8:30–31 dovetails with the goodness of creation hymned by Genesis, and it even suggests that God created through an enjoyment of his daughter or even his lover Wisdom who helped him structure the world to all its marvelous beauty. For later Jewish theology, these verses proved that Torah existed before the creation of the world. The final call is from a mother who would have her children prosper by attending at her house.

Chapter 9 describes this house, set on seven pillars.[5] The imagery may reflect the design of ancient Temples, or perhaps the house in question is the whole world, whose pillars are in the depths of the seas. Wisdom is offering a banquet to those with the wit to accept her invitation. In the Book of Proverbs simplicity is not a virtue. Wisdom suggests not wasting one's time on the cynical but concentrating on those who want to learn. The castigation of vice and looseness at the end of chapter 9 leaves us with a clear orientational choice. For the Book of Proverbs, wisdom (instruction) leads to life, and simplicity (stupidity) leads to Sheol.

10:1–22:16 First Collection of Solomonic Sayings

As we noted when dealing with the Book of Job, the wisdom literature of the Bible is usefully set against an international background of similar reflections. Scholars frequently treat this second unit of the Book of Proverbs as possibly derived from training that youths would receive at court, and influenced by similar Egyptian instruction.[6] The materials are attributed to Solomon, which may simply be symbolic, and they comprise discrete maxims or proverbs, most of which come from careful observation of human nature and the attempt to inculcate the prudence necessary to stay out of trouble and be successful.

Chapter 10 opens with a nod to what parents hope from their children, which suggests that the one being addressed is still a student. We immediately encounter the conviction that righteousness brings success, even wealth, whereas wickedness brings thwarting by God — precisely the conviction that Job rejected on empirical grounds. From verse 10:1 to verse 16:7 the basic literary pattern is antithetic: The idea in the second half-verse opposes the thought of the first half-verse. Note how this antithetical structure (virtue X brings such and such benefit, but vice brings the contrary) sharpens their impact. Verse 10:12 has the intriguing comment that love covers all offenses. Verse 10:13 prescribes a beating for the stupid. It is hard to tell how literally we should take verse 10:15, and whether it amounts to a biblical equation of poverty with personal fault. It is probably a simple observation that wealth protects people whereas poverty grinds people down. (In other words, Proverbs is not prophetic — it more observes than tries to change.) Verse 10:23 is shrewd about the pleasure that the wicked can take in wrongdoing and the contrary pleasure that the good can take in doing what is wise. The final verses of the chapter put in almost sing-song fashion the surety that the wisdom writers either have or are trying to bolster up: The Lord makes the wise (the upright) to prosper and brings destruction upon evil-doers.

Chapter 11 continues stringing out maxims. Verse 11:1 gives a nod to social justice: fair measures. Verse 11:2 associates wisdom with humility and makes pride the forerunner of disgrace. In verse 11:4 we find a limitation set on the value of riches: They do not profit on the day of wrath (either the time of divine judgment or the time when human disasters make people seek higher ground). Verse 11:7 is suggestive: Would the righteous have hopes that do not perish at death? Verses 11:12–13 describe the wise person as having a controlled tongue and restraining any babbling. The "violent men" of verse 11:16 might better be described as "vigorous." The beautiful woman who is without discretion (verse 11:22) is fixed indelibly in the memory of most Bible readers. That chapter 11 commends liberality and makes it part of the profile of the wise/righteous loosens the tight self-interest it might otherwise seem to encourage.[7]

On the collection goes, gradually laying out the full portfolio of stocks that are blue chip, in contrast to stocks that are losers. Chapter 12 opens by contrasting a love of discipline with a hatred of reproof. Verse 12:4 is meant to praise the good wife, but it risks suggesting that she simply adorns her husband's status. Many of the succeeding proverbs suggest that those who do not prosper (who lack bread) suffer by their own fault. Note the restraint implied in verse 12:16, where the prudent man ignores an insult. By the end of the chapter we have been led to think of the ideal product of this proverbial education as diligent, restrained in speech, modest in self-presentation, and possessed of a dozen other small-scale, bourgeois virtues. What keeps this profile from pettiness is the assumption that righteousness is pleasing to God and is commanded by the Torah.

In chapter 13 we again notice the importance placed on restraint of speech. This virtue certainly would be useful in all social situations, but perhaps especially so at court, where interactions might be quite sophisticated, gossip might well flourish, and loose speech could have large consequences. Chapter 13 has modest praise for wealth, and it seeks freedom from strife.[8] Verse 13:12 shows some insight into the psychology of coping with the always uncertain future: "Hope deferred makes the heart sick, but a desire fulfilled is a tree of life." From time to time people need success, if they are to keep striving vigorously. Verse 13:13 may well have the Torah in mind, and it operates according to the Deuteronomistic understanding of how righteousness ought to flow into reward. Verse 13:20 is sobering and acute about the influence of one's comrades, especially in the years when character is being formed. We can catch prophetic overtones in verse 13:23, where the fallow ground of the poor is tied to injustice. The use of the rod counseled in verse 13:24 obviously is not a sanction for child beating.

At the outset of chapter 14 Wisdom again is possessed of a house, here one that she is trying to build up. This could be the Temple about which we have speculated, or it could be the family and lineage of those who accept instruction in understanding. Verse 14:4 is rather flat if taken literally, but it becomes amusingly pregnant if we make the oxen symbolic. Verse 14:10 would seem to privatize the struggle after wisdom more than Israelite wisdom generally tends to do. The suspicion of human nature encouraged in verse 14:12 is relatively rare in the Bible. It probably rests on the assumption that without an education that includes considerable discipline people are the prey of their spontaneous desires, many of which are untoward. Note the contrast in verse 14:16 between the caution of the wise and the carelessness of the fool. Does Proverbs even suspect there is a wisdom that is foolishness to the prudent of the world? The contrast set in verse 14:20 between the fate of the poor and the fate of the rich is not calculated to germinate social change. Verse 14:30 might be an insight into the psychology of longevity, and verse 14:31 challengingly associates treatment of the poor with treatment of God.

The opening line of chapter 15 is well known: "A soft answer turns away wrath, but a harsh word stirs up anger." Note in verse 15:3 the divine oversight that supplies a rationale for the sapiential conviction that both the evil and the good do eventually receive just recompense. This thought is repeated in verse 15:11, where even human intentions are made known to God. Verses 15:16–17 echo wisdom from the underside of history: insight into how the havenots can make do. The Lord's maintenance of the widow's boundaries (verse 15:25) strikes a note of prophetic sensitivity. By the end of the chapter we have progressed to a self-effacement that might trumpet the Lord's singular significance: "The fear of the Lord is instruction in wisdom, and humility goes before honor."

The opening advice in chapter 16 suggests experience in prayer, where God can be considered a shaper of conscience and a positive conspirator. After another assurance that the Lord delivers justice, we find the figure of balance, scales, and weights, to suggest that all justice and proportion in the world derive from the creator's wisdom (verse 16:11). The following verses meditate on the significance of the moods of the king, who presumably is God's vice-gerent. Verse 16:18 is probably the source of our popular proverb that pride goes before a fall. The repetition of verse 14:12 in verse 16:25 may suggest a special interest in this thought. Chapter 16 as a whole is another strong endorsement of restrained speech. The last three verses, 16:31–33, suggest the richness that occasionally results from a felicitous pile-up of discrete images. First we get the righteous life resulting in a hoary head. Then we get the primacy of ruling one's own spirit. Last we get the primacy of the divine control of the world. The result might be a spirituality like that reached by Job: giving God a blank check, after one has done one's best to control what lies within human influence.

Chapter 17 offers little that is novel. Quiet, longevity, kindness to the poor, and forgiveness all come in for praise. Note the powerful figure in verse 17:12, where folly becomes worse than the wrath of a she bear. Verse 17:22 repeats homey psychology that we have seen before and seems on the order of the Irish "keep the fair side out." The final verse offers fools a half-way house. If they would but mind their tongues they would be accounted much better than they are.

The figure of deep waters in verse 18:4 is intriguing and perhaps intends the same point as the New Testament proverb that "out of the abundance of the heart the mouth speaks" (Luke 6:45). Verse 18:10 may be encouraging petitionary prayer and the psychological relief of calling upon God. In verse 18:14 we glimpse into the priorities of the biblical anthropology. Although the body and the spirit are inseparable, the afflictions of the spirit are the sorer. Verse 18:18 may be a vestige of ancient practices, when hard decisions were made by lot (as a medium of the divine will). The brothers mentioned in verse 18:19 are well known through Western traditioning of the biblical store of proverbs. Verse 18:22 puts in pithy form the biblical prejudice in favor of marriage.

Chapter 19 opens with a winning boost to the integrity of the poor. Note the astute observation of verse 19:3 that people tend to blame God for misfortunes caused by their own folly. In the background may be the strong conviction we have seen in the Torah and the Prophets that human beings, not God, are the source of disorder and suffering. Verse 19:10 shows some pique that fools might prosper and slaves might rule princes. The figure of dripping rain (verse 19:13) dramatizes contentiousness and tends to stigmatize the unhappy wife as a nagger. Verse 19:16 is clearer than the typical proverb on the coincidence of wisdom and keeping the Torah: "He who keeps the commandment keeps his life; he who despises the word will die." In verse 19:26 lingers some of the horror of not honoring one's father and mother (and perhaps also some of the ancient horror of parricide: killing the source of one's own life).

Chapter 20 opens with a new warning: against wine. In verse 20:5 water again symbolizes the mysteries of human motivation. The lament of verse 20:9 recalls Job's confession that none stands before God as righteous. The waiting upon God for vengeance counseled by verse 20:22 shows a winning trust in the divine judgment, and perhaps as well an appreciation of the fallibility of human judgments. Verse 20:27 contains another hint that some of the sapiential writers knew from prayer the experience of having one's own spirit and the divine spirit coincide.

Chapter 21 cuts the king down to size; even the opening verse makes him easily turned by God. Verse 21:3 takes up the prophetic preference for mercy rather than sacrifice. Note in verse 21:17 the barriers put to hedonism. The contentious (nagging) woman previously symbolized by dripping rain returns twice in this chapter (see verses 21:9, 21:19) for plainer condemnation. Like most of its predecessors, Proverbs 21 stands or falls by the conviction, assumed more than argued or proven, that God causes the evil to fail and rewards the good appropriately.

The last portion of this collection of Solomonic sayings is verses 22:1–16. Verse 22:2 is more forthright about the equality of the rich and the poor before God than many other sapiential sayings are. Verse 22:6 expresses the conviction of many traditional cultures that the tree grows as the twig is bent. The "scoffer" has turned up so frequently in this collection that we may consider this vice as emblematic of the haughty personality closed to wisdom. Verse 22:13 is amusing when read as the extreme to which the lazy will go to avoid work. The conviction with which this collection ends (verse 22:16) seems a pious hope rather than an empirical verity.

22:17–24:34 Thirty Precepts of the Sages

Proverbs 22:17 signals the start of a new collection of traditional proverbial wisdom, and the voice again seems to be that of a teacher trying to instruct youth in the insight that the sages would hand on. Whether these thirty sayings were indeed considered comprehensive is hard to say. In the background may well lie the thirty precepts attributed to the Egyptian pharaoh Amen-em-Opet.[9] Perhaps the "those who sent you" of verse 22:21 are the parents of the student enrolled for instruction.

First comes advice against robbing the poor or crushing the afflicted in court. Second comes advice against befriending the hotheaded. Third, one should not offer collateral for other people's loans. Fourth, one should retain the traditional property boundaries (or the ways of traditional culture in general). Fifth, one should respect craftmanship (which could be extended to virtue of all sorts).

The sixth bit of advice handed on from the sages concerns how to eat with the regal. Seventh, one is warned off from greed. Eighth, one should avoid the company of the stingy, who will begrudge everything they must give. Ninth, one should keep quiet in the hearing of fools, who presumably will only misuse what one says. The tenth precept is against removing an ancient landmark and for seeking learning.

Eleventh, one should be sure to discipline one's children, on the principle that a little pain now can save much suffering later. Twelfth, one should be wise and thereby content. Thirteenth, one should guard against envying sinners. Fourteenth, one should stay clear of drunkards and gluttons, who usually end in poverty and drowsiness or dullwittedness. Precept fifteen is an injunction to buy truth.

The sixteenth precept is a salute to parents, combined with a call to treasure truth and wisdom, so as to make one's parents proud. The seventeenth precept is the warning against harlotry that occurs in verses 23:26–28. The eighteenth precept counsels against drinking, the effects of which, both emotional and physical, are well described. The effects, in fact, are described vividly enough to suggest considerable first-hand experience. Chapter 24 contains another warning against envy of evil-doers, which we can count as precept nineteen. Precept twenty finds wisdom in the skillful building of a house (and so, by implication, in all enterprises that go forward admirably).

The twenty-first precept drawn from the sages proposes the superiority of the wise to the strong on several counts. Precept twenty-two depreciates the fool, who does not understand the wise sayings of good judgment. Precept twenty-three condemns fools and the impious for their ceaseless scheming. The twenty-fourth bit of advice from the sages encourages a show of strength in time of crisis. The twenty-fifth precept occurs in verse 24:11, where the charge is to rescue those heading for death. A modern application could be very sobering: Do something about those being hauled off to the concentration camps, lest your conscience torment you ever after.

The twenty-sixth precept, to eat honey, may well be figurative: Taste and see the goodness of the Lord's counsel. Precept twenty-seven urges letting the wicked come to their natural failure. Twenty-eighth, one should not rejoice at the failure of one's enemies — an ethical advance over the position in many of the psalms. Twenty-ninth, one should trust that the Lord will render justice, and so not fret. According to precept thirty, one should fear both the Lord and the king (whose authority comes from the Lord).

Further sayings of the sages include advice to judge honestly and not skew things in favor of the wicked; to prepare before building one's house, which may be a figure for foresight in general; not to bear witness against neighbor without cause; and not to be zealous to pay back an offender. The final sketch of the sluggard suggests that unless one is energetic in pursuing either a living or a wise life, one will end up destitute.[10]

25:1–29:27 Second Collection of Solomonic Sayings

The thirty precepts of the wise serve as an interlude. We now return to the tatoo of Solomonic sayings, although in this collection the rhythm is not so much antithetical as additive or elaborative: A statement is either simply made, baldly, or made and built upon to intensify the single thought.

Chapter 25 opens with the notice that these proverbs of Solomon were copied by men of King Hezekiah (715 to 687 B.C.E.). Verse 25:2 introduces more mystery than we have hitherto found, suggesting that the depths of divine wisdom lie out of sight. The king is to seek out what divine order he can, but kings themselves share in the divine obscurity. Note the modesty before the king counseled in verse 25:7, which may lie behind Luke 14:7–11. Chapter 25 offers more counsel to prudent speech. Verse 25:16 warns against overindulgence, even when one has found something good. Verses 25:21–22 turn up in Romans 12:20. Verse 25:28 is a strong figure in favor of self-control. The advice in this second collection of Solomonic sayings manifestly comes in stronger images, and even though there is no strict logic to the order in which they occur, together these images paint a quite vivid picture of the way to follow and the way to avoid.

Chapter 26 is concerned with the damage that fools can do. In effect, that is the reverse side of the profit that comes with wisdom. Verse 26:11 is famous for its repulsive concreteness. The sluggard being criticized in this, as in other chapters of Proverbs, perhaps is best understood as the result of boredom or acedia, when the soul is unwilling or unable to put forth the effort that the ethical life demands. Verse 26:20 gives a figure useful in a great many situations, where peace and achievement are undercut by gossip. The description of false speech that follows suggests that deeds, rather than words, should be one's moral criterion. Verse 26:27 puts into more fatalistic, peasant form the lofty notion that God does see to it that evil comes back upon those who initiate evil.

Chapter 27 opens with a firm rebuke to prying into the future and forgetting that all time is in God's hands. Verse 27:4 is intriguing for estimating jealousy as more dangerous than wrath and anger. The hidden love of verse 27:5 is obscure, but the general advice is plain: What is inside should come out, and what is outside should square with what is inside. Verse 27:19 suggests that the mind of a person, though not the whole, is the best indication of the whole. The final verses of chapter 27 introduce a pastoral note, previously rather restrained (no doubt because the majority of the proverbs focus on urban or town life).

Chapter 28 opens with a boost for good conscience, equating it with courage. Verse 28:2 joins wisdom with political stability. The law being praised in verse 28:4 probably is the Torah. Verse 28:5 is provocative: Unless one seeks the Lord, one cannot even understand what justice is, let alone achieve it. Verse 28:8 seems to be condemning usury, and verse 28:9 seems to be exalting hearing Torah over prayer. Verse 28:13 is a rare instance in which Proverbs is concerned with mercy or forgiveness (which takes the prudential calculus of justice to a new level). Verse 28:17 is stern about murder, imposing the punishment of exile. In the remaining observations of chapter 28 riches, wisdom, rebuking, and other familiar themes come in for another treatment, but little changes in the overall advice.

The last chapter of the second collection of Solomonic sayings is as discrete and disparate as the previous chapters. Verse 29:3 is another suggestion that harlotry can stand symbolic duty for folly or vice in general. Verse 29:10 is disturbing: The good provoke the wicked to violence. In verse 29:13 we catch a glimpse of the divine dispassion — light for both the poor and the oppressor — which can hint at the divine transcendence. Verse 29:18 is a rare reference to prophecy, whose relative absence in Proverbs suggests that sages and prophets often traveled different roads. Note, however, that obedience to Torah follows immediately. At the end of this chapter and this second collection, we have the black and white opposition of the righteous and the wicked that has been the foundation throughout. This stark opposition is untrue to most people and most situations, of course, but in a didactic work such as Proverbs we may excuse some oversimplification.[11]

30:1–31:31 Four Appendices

Chapter 30:1–9 appear to be a dialogue between a representative sage (who Agur was is unknown) and a person skeptical of the entire enterprise of trying to acquire wisdom. The skeptic is actually rather shrewd, arguing that all human beings are unequal to the task of discerning the ways of the Holy One who rules from heaven. (Verse 30:4 reminds us of God's speech to Job.) The counter suggested in verses 30:5–6 is that one can rely upon Torah, the words of God (which make the heavenly will present in the midst of human beings). Verses 7–9 may be considered a prayer by the pious respondent, who wants to keep the skepticism of the challenger far from himself.[12] The prayer is interesting for the association it finds between riches *or* poverty and lack of religion. The safest state is a mean between surplus and want.

Verses 30:10–33 list warnings and "numerical proverbs" (advice grouping things, mainly in threes and fours). Slander and cursing are vetoed, as is failure to bless one's mother. Verses 30:13–14 castigate the proud and those who devour the poor. One should avoid greed, of which Sheol is the most striking example. The barren womb is both a symbol of fruitlessness generally and a reminder of pathos of many of the biblical matriarchs, for whom fruitlessness was like a curse from God. The mysteriousness of human love is nicely expressed in verse 30:19, where it ranks among the wonders of nature. The adulteress of verse 30:20 devours the substance of love and feels not the slightest qualm. The disorders mentioned in verses 30:21–23 may reflect the desire of Torah that things from different classes not be mixed. The little people praised in verses 30:24–28 raise affection as well as a good model. The association of the king with the lion, the strutting cock, and the he goat (verse 30:31) no doubt struck the author as ambiguously as it strikes us. The restraint urged at the end of chapter 30 is a good summary of at least half the advice that Proverbs has to offer.[13]

Verses 31:1–9 offer the advice of the mother of Lemuel, king of Massa (Northwest Arabia), who otherwise is unknown. She advises him against committing himself to women, to those who destroy kings, and to wine. (For an entertaining reflection on which of these three is strongest, see the apocryphal book 1 Esdras, chapter 3.) She also advises him to defend the dumb, the desolate, the poor, and the needy, judging righteously: nothing very dazzling, but sober and prudent counsel.

Proverbs ends with an acrostic sketch of, almost a hymn to, the ideal wife (verses 31:10–31). It certainly is intended to bear on actual wives and mothers, but it may also be praise of Lady Wisdom, to whom the sage longed to be espoused. Judaism has made this hymn central to the ideal family life it has sought. The good wife is the first treasure of her husband. She is industrious and provident—a first-rate manager. Vigor and strength dominate her portrait. Because of her work, her husband can sit in the first ranks of the government (verse 31:23). Verse 31:26 associates her with wisdom in her own right. Verse 31:28 is the only mention of her children—she is not just a broodmare. Verse 31:30 is a biblical vote for feminine substance rather than appearance, as well as another indication that fear of the Lord is the quintessential source of wisdom. Thus Proverbs ends praising domestic virtue.[14]

HISTORICAL BACKGROUND

We have already mentioned that the wisdom literature of the Bible partook of a widespread, international search for instruction in the practical intelligence that would make both public affairs and private life prosperous by harmonizing them with the divine order. The "proverb" (mashal) in which bits of such practical intelligence were expressed has the twofold meaning of a similitude and a powerful word.[15] It became regarded as a saying rooted in experience and carrying to those who had ears to hear overtones of the divine intelligence that ran the cosmos. This divine intelligence was the support and the goal of the movement in search of wisdom. The wise person let nature, as well as human behavior, be an instructor. The fool, who becomes in Proverbs the foil off whom wisdom plays, appears in varied garb, but regularly the fool lacks discipline as well as native talent. The different names for the fool thus connote naivete, innate stupidity, obstinacy, persistence in folly, crudeness, brutality or depravity, irrationality, and loose talk.[16] All of these failings prevent one from achieving the self-possession necessary to pay attention, be intelligent, judge rationally, act decisively, and be dominated by fear of the Lord rather than shallow selfishness.

The wisdom movement in Israel also presupposed other philosophical and practical cornerstones, which it shared with its neighbors, such as belief in retribution, education, and discipline. It was a somewhat elitist, what we today might call academic, movement, situated in the upper class or in the royal court. Although it was interested in training youth for public service and the common good, it also sought to instruct the wealthy in how to keep their wealth. As many of the proverbs suggest, it presupposed a talkative, urban environment, where affairs of state and public life were the controlling interest. Thus, some of the proverbs address how the individual may flourish and avoid disaster. In the context of a teacher trying to point youth toward the straight path, the proverbs inevitably were warnings away from companions and character traits that would be destructive. But the overall supposition of Proverbs is a common life that comes into best focus when one loves the wisdom of God and is formed by it from within.

LITERARY INTENT

In treating the canonical intentions of Proverbs, Brevard Childs has stressed the integrity of the wisdom movement from which it is derived.[17] As well, he has read the structure of Proverbs as a sign that the work is not presenting timeless truths as much as offering the wise person stimuli to prudent planning in whatever concrete circumstances arise. As most cultures have appreciated, wisdom in the practical sense of knowing what attitudes and actions will produce survival and prosperity always depends on grasping the common sense of the specific people with whom one is dealing. General precepts are fine, but one has to know how to apply them here and now. If the here and now is Waco, Texas, 1988, c.e., the application may be quite different than it would have been in Bejing, China, 1948, c.e., let alone in Jerusalem, Judea, 448 b.c.e.

Childs thinks that the collection in Proverbs deliberately keeps its distance from the Law, running alongside study of the Law as an alternate religious pathway. This may have been the desire of the editors of some of the subcollections, or even of the canonical editors, but neither the final canonizers nor subsequent Jewish readers of the Bible, shaped by rabbinic interests, kept the Law and wisdom separate. Christian readers thought differently about Law than readers shaped by rabbinic theology, due to the influence of Paul of Tarsus in Christian theology, so wisdom literature such as Proverbs tended to serve Christians as indications of the moral personality that the Spirit of Christ wanted to mold, rather than as a profound expression in the moral realm of the divine wisdom revealed in creation.

We ourselves would stress that the primary intention of most of the people who first collected proverbs of this sort and first directed them toward the instruction of youth was probably to inculcate a sense of how the composed, controlled, mature Israelite might move through the world of human affairs in harmony with the mysterious yet rational order by which God ran creation.

LASTING SIGNIFICANCE

The estimate one makes of the lasting significance of Proverbs depends considerably on one's own sense of religion. This is undoubtedly true for the estimate one makes of any biblical work, but in the case of Proverbs the point seems more acute. Compared to the narratives of the Torah, Proverbs is a rather pallid work, perhaps even somewhat bourgeois. It certainly hints at dark, chaotic recesses of the personality, but neither its evils nor its faith are as dramatic and powerful as those of Abraham, Isaac, and Jacob. The former prophets deal with historical events, political blood and intrigue, and the vicissitudes of the covenanted people so concretely that they too make Proverbs seem the stuff of the drawing room or the retirement home (or the classroom). And the latter prophets, with their emotional flourishes and their poetic heights, inhabit quite a different world. For the latter prophets wisdom is loving God passionately and pursuing justice with all one's might. In comparison, Proverbs seems narrowed, cautious, even self-seeking.

Yet Proverbs has its counter-virtues, and it is pleasant to consider them. First, it avoids the atmosphere of catastrophe or utmost urgency that makes reading the prophets seriatim tantamount to overload. Taken one after another, the prophetic books make religion a matter of constant outcry, lament, and denunciation. Of course there are patches of encouragement and consolation. But few patches suggest a stable status quo, a life whose greatest challenges come from its ordinariness. Proverbs has the asset of dealing with ordinary, comfortable life and the problems of those who are managing fairly well.

Second, Proverbs has the further asset of sharpening readers' wits so that they become aware of the potential in themselves for both prudence and foolishness. Whereas the prophets are sociological, Proverbs is more psychological. Its portraits of the disordered personality sketch in small scale the collective disorders overwhelming a Jeremiah or a Hosea. Proverbs thinks that fear of a somewhat distant God is the paramount virtue, and this proposition can ring very relevant to postmodern ears. Indeed, whenever God has seemed distant, fear of God, in the positive sense that Proverbs attaches to this term, has been a considerable act of trust. Those experiencing the distance of God in worldly terms have been nearly condemned to skepticism or cynicism (perhaps what the Book of Proverbs means by "scoffing"), but those who have feared God have asked for a bigger framework and kept the mysteriousness of ultimate judgments well alive. This in itself can be a great consolation, a way that God speaks eloquently through the simple fact that there are further possibilities.

GLOSSARY

Acedia   Lacking spiritual energy, a state of carelessness and torpor; being dispirited.

Seriatim   In sequence, following along in a series.

Vice-gerent   A representative ruler; one who rules or administers as the deputy of another.

STUDY QUESTIONS

1. Explain the solicitation of Wisdom in Proverbs 1:20–33.
2. How does Proverbs 8 compare with the cosmological arguments of Job?
3. Using verse 11:22 as a case in point, explain the cast of imagination that we find in the Solomonic proverbs.
4. Why does Proverbs attach so much importance to prudent speech?
5. Describe the sense of social justice that prevails in the Book of Proverbs.
6. What would you add to the thirty precepts of the sages to make a comprehensive sketch of the wise person's outlook?
7. What do Proverbs 31:10–31 suggest about the sapiential writers' view of marriage?
8. What arguments could you make against the judgment that Proverbs represents a religious outlook considerably less impressive than that of the latter prophets?

NOTES

1. See Roland E. Murphy, "Proverbs, the," in *Harper's Bible Dictionary*, ed. Paul J. Achtemeier. San Francisco: Harper & Row, 1985, pp. 831–32.

2. See R. B. Y. Scott, *Proverbs, Ecclesiastes*. Garden City, N.Y.: Doubleday Anchor Bible, 1965, pp. vii–viii.

3. See Bernhard Couroyer, "La Tablette du coeur," *Revue Biblique*, 90 (1983), 416–34.

4. See Scott, *Proverbs, Ecclesiastes*, pp. vii–viii.

5. See Bernhard Lang, "Die sieben Säulen der Weisheit (Sprüche ix:1) im Licht israelitischer Architektur," *Vetus Testamentum*, 33 (1983), 488–91.

6. See W. Lee Humphreys, "The Motif of the Wise Courtier in the Book of Proverbs," in *Israelite Wisdom*, ed. John G. Gammie et al. Missoula, Mont.: Scholars Press, 1978, pp. 177–90.

7. See William H. Irwin, "The Metaphor of Prov. 11,30," *Biblica*, 65 (1984), 97–100.

8. See J. A. Emerton, "The Meaning of Proverbs 13:2," *Journal of Theological Studies*, 35 (1984), 91–95.

9. See Scott, *Proverbs, Ecclesiastes*, p. 135. See also James B. Pritchard, ed., *Ancient Near Eastern Texts Relating to the Old Testament*, 3rd. ed. Princeton,: Princeton University Press, 1969, pp. 421–35.

10. We owe this enumeration of the thirty precepts to Scott, *Proverbs, Ecclesiastes*.

11. See Bruce V. Malchow, "A Manual for Future Monarchs," *Catholic Biblical Quarterly*, 47 (1985), 238–45.

12. See Scott, *Proverbs, Ecclesiastes*, p. 176.

13. See Paul Franklin, "The Sayings of Agur in Proverbs 30: Piety or Scepticism?" *Zeitschrift für die alttestamentliche Wissenschaft*, 95 (1983), 239–52.

14. See T. P. McCreesh, O. P., "Wisdom as Wife: Proverbs 31:10–31," *Revue Biblique*, 92 (1985), 25–46.

15. See James L. Crenshaw, *Old Testament Wisdom: An Introduction*. Atlanta: John Knox, 1981, p. 67.

16. See Crenshaw, *Old Testament Wisdom: An Introduction*, p. 81.

17. See Brevard S. Childs, *An Introduction to the Old Testament as Scripture*. Philadelphia: Fortress, 1979, p. 557.

CHAPTER 19

Ruth

TEXTUAL ANALYSIS

Most commentators consider the Book of Ruth an artful short story, perhaps from as early as the tenth to the eighth century B.C.E.[1] It praises the loyalty of a Gentile, the Moabite Ruth, to her Israelite mother-in-law, Naomi, and describes the providential process through which Ruth became the ancestor of King David. The style is reminiscent of the stories about Joseph in Genesis. We may conveniently divide this short book into seven subsections:

1:1–5	Sojourners
1:6–22	Returning Home
2:1–23	Alien Grain?
3:1–18	Encounter at the Threshing Floor
4:1–12	Resolution at the City Gate
4:13–17	The Birth of a Son
4:18–22	Appendix: Genealogy[2]

1:1–5 Sojourners

The opening verses of the Book of Ruth set the scene for the action that is to unfold. First, we learn that the historical period is premonarchical: during the time of the Judges. Second, we learn that it was hard times: famine. A family from Judah, Elimelech and Naomi and their two sons, go, presumably because of the famine, to Moab, a territory east of the Dead Sea. Elimelech dies, as do the two sons, so Naomi is left with only her Moabite daughters-in-law, Orpah and Ruth. The stage is therefore set for the actions that will determine the fate of this unfortunate woman, who as an alien could well fear isolation and abandonment.

1:6–22 Returning Home

Naomi hears that things have improved back in Israel, so she and her daughters-in-law begin the journey to her home. As though it dawns on her that what "home" means to her may be quite different from what it means to the two younger women, she gives them leave to return to their native families, thanking them for the kindness they have shown her and her dead husband and sons. Verse 1:9 reveals much of her motivation: In their own land, the women may remarry (have families, gain security, and enjoy fulfillment). The emotional scene among the three suggests much affection all around, and we probably should take it as a considerable tribute to Naomi that her daughters-in-law did not want to separate from her. Naomi replies with great common sense, even though it saddens her: The younger women have no future with her. In their culture marriage was virtually their only way to security and happiness. Naomi is bitter that fortune ("the hand of the Lord") has gone against her, but she sees things for what they are.

Orpah kisses Naomi and leaves, as everything to this point has led us to think is both her full right and the path of prudence. We should not miss in verse 1:15 the overtones that she is also returning to her native religion. But Ruth clings to Naomi and begs to stay with her. Her entreaty in verses 1:16–17 is eloquent and approaches the force of a holy oath: "for where you go, I will go, and where you lodge, I will lodge; your people shall be my people, and your God my God; where you die I will die, and there will I be buried. May the Lord do so to me and more also if even death parts me from you."[3] Ruth has loved Naomi so much and has come to identify with her husband's family so much that she is like a convert to Israelite faith or a naturalized Israelite citizen.

When the two return to Naomi's native town of Bethlehem, they cause quite a stir. Naomi calls herself Mara, to designate the bitter misfortunes that have come upon her (although Ruth, the agent of her eventual fulfillment, is standing by). The play on full and empty (verse 1:21) sets up an interpretational movement that the good fortune of Ruth later will reverse. "Naomi" has an etymology something like "my pleasant one,"[4] which may explain why the suffering woman rejects her given name. Nothing much is said about Ruth's presence with Naomi. We are left to infer that it was accepted and that the two settled in Bethlehem to comfort one another for their bereavements.

2:1–23 Alien Grain?

The center of the action in chapter 2 is the barley field of Boaz, a relative of Naomi. That the barley harvest was beginning establishes on the plane of nature what is about to happen on the human plane.[5] Ruth's proposal in verse 2:2 that she go to glean in the neighboring fields is mainly a practical plan for getting food, but the "favor" mentioned may suggest as well an effort to attract an eligible man, who might solve the problem the women face. If this second purpose is not plain from the outset, what later happens with Boaz makes it quite plausible. Naomi agrees to the proposal, which leads us to think that it was both fitting and shrewd. The greeting that Boaz gives the reapers (verse 2:4) establishes that he is probably a pious man. Leviticus 19:9–10 formally and legally established the right of the poor to collect what was left after the harvesters had passed through. Boaz notices Ruth, certainly because she was a stranger but perhaps also because he found her attractive. Verse 2:7 further suggests that she had distinguished herself as a hard worker. Boaz speaks kindly and generously to Ruth, no doubt in part because she is the daughter-in-law of his relative Naomi, but probably also because he is a good man and feels some affection for her or some sympathy for the fate that she and Naomi have suffered.

Ruth is touched by this, bows low, and wonders why Boaz should be so kind to her, a foreigner. Boaz then makes it clear that he knows her story and admires or is grateful for her kindness to Naomi. Verse 2:11, echoing Genesis 12:1 (the sojourning of Abraham), suggests that he is also impressed by her willingness to sojourn among an alien people. In verse 2:12 he prays the blessing of God upon her, making it even clearer that he is impressed that she has chosen to shelter under the wings of the God of Israel. This confirms the impression previously given that Ruth's leaving her native people and going to cast her lot with Naomi was something extraordinary. Ruth responds to this blessing with a simple and winning thanks.

Boaz goes further in showing Ruth kindness, providing food for her and easing her way among the reapers, that she may go home with a good portion of food. This only confirms our hunch that he is taken with her. When Ruth hands her gains over to Naomi and they discuss the day, Naomi learns that Boaz has been their benefactor. The fulfillment of the empty Naomi has begun, because she now has both food and grist for hope. This seems to start the wheels turning in Naomi's mind, as she reflects that Boaz is one of her (now their) nearest kin. The advice to take Boaz up on his offer to let Ruth glean in his field is certainly put forward with Ruth's safety and ease of work in mind, but it seems likely that Naomi is also thinking that it will do no harm for Ruth to stay close to this kinsman. The land and produce that initially seemed alien to Ruth have now become more her own. She has taken the first step toward establishing herself as an Israelite, and by the end of the story she will have gained an important place in the lineage of David, the greatest Israelite king.

3:1–18 Encounter at the Threshing Floor

Naomi the mother-in-law has had a little time to consider the future of her daughter-in-law and concoct a bit of matchmaking. She sends Ruth off to pretty herself up with instructions about what Ruth is to do at the threshing floor. These instructions are quite ambiguous, leaving the possibility that Ruth is to make herself available to Boaz, should he desire her. Boaz is feeling no pain, and when he awakens at midnight to find a woman at his feet, he no doubt thinks this a pleasant eventuality. Ruth identifies herself and rather startlingly asks him to take her as his wife, because he is her next of kin (with rights and responsibilities regarding her marrying). Boaz takes this request as a kindness greater than her prior kindness (either in being good to Naomi or in covering his feet — the first obviously is the stronger). Verse 3:10 suggests that Boaz was sensitive to being an older man (probably without a wife) and was flattered by Ruth's request/offer. He promises to do right by Ruth, but there is a problem: Another man is closer kin than he. If that man chooses not to exercise his prior claim to Ruth, Boaz will take her to wife. Meanwhile, he bids her remain with him for the night.

In the morning Ruth leaves the threshing floor while it is still dark, perhaps in order that no taint of scandal should compromise the inquiry to be made of the nearer kinsman. Boaz sends Ruth back to Naomi with a full armload of grain, which seems an earnest on his pledge to do right by her, and which also signals the continuation of the turn of fortune from the side of emptiness toward fullness. Naomi counsels Ruth to wait for the outcome of the inquiry that Boaz will undertake, and she seems confident not only that he will deal with this matter immediately but also that it will turn out well (that he will do his utmost to get Ruth for himself).

4:1–12 Resolution at the City Gate

Boaz takes himself to the city gate, where people did business, and meets the nearer kinsman in question. He takes him aside and gathers a council of elders to formalize the deal he wants to strike. This deal is couched in terms of land: Naomi wants to sell a parcel belonging to Elimelech; the kinsman has prior claim to it; if he does not want to buy it, Boaz wants to exercise his own rights as the second in line and buy it for himself. The use of the term "redeem" to describe this transaction would have seemed to later generations of readers a pregnant invitation to consider it in the context of the Lord's dealings with his people and their land. The nearer kinsman says that he wants to buy the land. Boaz then adds the stipulation that is the real point of the exchange: Ruth goes along with the land (as part of the responsibility to keep it and progeny within the lineage). The nearer kinsman balks at this stipulation, because it will complicate his own bequeathments (presumably he has children by another wife, and how children by Ruth would factor in is uncertain). Therefore, he yields his claim to the land and Ruth, leaving Boaz free. Whether Boaz has carried out this transaction by the book of contemporary legal custom or has slanted things to achieve his own purposes is not clear, because we do not know what customs actually were obtaining at the supposed time of the story. Deuteronomy 25:7–10, which deal with the obligation to wed a dead brother's wife, do not quite meet the whole case that Boaz lays out, because Boaz conjoins wife and land, and Boaz, though a kinsman, is not Ruth's brother-in-law.

At any rate, Boaz accepts the nearer kinsman's offer that Boaz take the land and Ruth for himself, giving the nearer kinsman his sandal, a gesture that the text tells us was the customary way of sealing a transaction (apparently as an altered form of the law in Deuteronomy 25:7–10). Boaz then calls the witnesses to do their job and witness that he is buying Naomi's land from her and is taking Ruth to wife to prolong the inheritance of her dead husband and keep his name alive through offspring. The witnesses notarize this transaction and ask the Lord to bless it with a fertility like that of Rachel and Leah, the wives of Jacob.

4:13–17 The Birth of a Son

Boaz marries Ruth, and they quickly experience the fruits of this blessing. The son that Ruth bears is considered by the female onlookers (women witness both Naomi's emptiness and her fulfillment) a restoration of Naomi to good fortune, because even though death of her (childless) sons had seemed to mean the perishing of her name (she had no chance for the only sort of immortality known then), now she has next of kin and a restoration of life (both happiness and progeny). The fortunate old age to which Naomi can look forward is credited to the love of Ruth, who tellingly is said to be to Naomi "more . . . than seven sons" (verse 4:15). In other words, what Ruth has done for and been to Naomi surpasses the fullness of fecundity and blessing that any Israelite woman could anticipate — high praise indeed, especially when we remember that Ruth was a foreigner and a woman in a small society that was both ethnically self-conscious and strongly patriarchal. Naomi, who identifies with the child to an exceptional degree, becomes his nurse. Indeed, the child, named Obed, comes to be thought of as her own son. The punch line of the story comes in verse 4:17: "He was the father of Jesse, the father of David." By the love of Ruth the Moabite, then, Israel got its greatest king. As in the stories of Genesis about Joseph, divine providence emerges as the true guide of human events, although here this theme is more subtle and tacit.

4:18–22 Appendix: Genealogy

The final verses of the Book of Ruth give us the fuller genealogical context that would have been of great interest to people of both Ruth's time and the times after David. We first met Perez in Genesis 38:29, and from him came a branch of the tribe of Judah that led to David (and, for Matthew 1:3, to Jesus).

HISTORICAL BACKGROUND

Many scholars have noted the similarity between Ruth and such other great heroines of biblical literature as Deborah, Jael, Judith, and Esther. All five saved Israel or Israelites when there was threat of perishing, but none as gently as Ruth.[6] All five took initiative and used their intelligence — Naomi and Ruth quite strikingly in the plan that unfolded at the threshing floor. The supposition of the Book of Ruth therefore includes the tradition of mustering wit to deal with problems, even when one's options seem quite limited, as those of women in the time of the Judges surely seemed. Other suppositions include the trust that God is working through events on behalf of both individuals and the Israelite people as a whole (here the interests of all parties are resolved to everyone's profit), and the conviction that both human beings and God have the obligation and right to fight for life (progeny, continuance) against death (represented by Elimelech and the two sons). Naomi and Ruth have been emptied, but eventually they are fulfilled. And beyond their realization, the small drama of their struggle has played into the greater drama of the rise of the monarchy and the fateful role that David played in all subsequent Israelite history.

LITERARY INTENT

Some interpretations of the Book of Ruth place it quite late, after the return from Babylon, when proscriptions against intermarriage with foreigners were causing hardship in many families. By this reading, the Book of Ruth was praising a foreigner, Ruth, and showing her part in God's providence, to counter the campaign against intermarriage and contact with foreigners. Perhaps Ruth was read this way in the postexilic period, but the archaism of the story itself suggests that it was composed far earlier. Herbert G. May, who favors a date in the postexilic period (fifth or fourth century B.C.E.), describes the primary motivation of the story as follows:

> He [the author] is not a theologian, intent on proclaiming the uniqueness of one God whom all people should worship. He does not envision a future when all peoples will acknowledge Israel's God. He does not condemn Orpah for returning to her gods. . . . His is not a mission of conversion of Gentiles to Judaism. Rather, he writes to answer the question whether it is right and good that a Gentile woman be welcomed through marriage into the community of Israel.[7]

LASTING SIGNIFICANCE

The Book of Ruth is a good example of the biblical humanism that we have praised on more than one occasion. It deals with such central human emotions as loss, love, and trust (both in God and in fellow human beings), but with an admirable restraint. The mood of the story is calm and ordinary. The focus is on three people who certainly are admirable for their intelligence and goodness, but who are enough like the general run of human beings to command our attention. No miracles or hagiography takes the story to a supernatural plane. The main characters seem at home in their world, even though that world has at least as much suffering and trial as occur in most people's lifetimes.

We might also ponder the central if understated role that the story gives to human love. The love of Ruth for Naomi predominates, but the love of Naomi for all the members of her family, dead and living, and the love of Boaz for Ruth are also essential. Most of this love certainly is ordinary, even instinctive, but the story sharpens our focus on it by having it cross ethnic boundaries. We cannot say that the love between Ruth and Naomi was unique, but certainly it stands out for its rooting their bond in a personal affection. Ruth is willing to make Naomi's people her people (some commentators consider her surrendering her Moabite identity and her becoming an Israelite [an ancestor of David] to be the great expression of her love.)

Another point worth noting is the feminist overtones of the love between Naomi and Ruth. In her important book, *God and the Rhetoric of Sexuality*, Phyllis Trible notes that this love promises no reward. Indeed, Naomi warns Ruth that staying with her will only bring disaster. Thus the women here, although they are the main characters, do not function as the strong females that we imagine Deborah and Judith to be. Their doings seem quite natural or ordinary: Ruth gleans, Naomi schemes. Even when they are absent from the principal action, as they are during the scene of the men's settling things at the city gate, they are the principal beneficiaries. All in all, then, we may read the Book of Ruth as an interesting commentary on the "underside" of Israelite history, where the female half of the race lived out its drama with God.[8]

The drama of human affairs thus seems to move on a stage where what people are as individuals means more than the national uniforms they wear. The result is a winning and instructive tolerance, as well as a stimulus to appreciate the universal concern of the biblical God.

GLOSSARY

Hagiography Writing that narrates the life or marvelous deeds of a holy person.
Ideologues Those who are prone to substitute ideas or doctrines for primary reality.

STUDY QUESTIONS

1. What are the main issues involved in the decisions of Orpah and Ruth (verses 1:6–22)?
2. Is Boaz as tolerant of Ruth's foreignness as Naomi?
3. What does the scene at the threshing floor suggest about the biblical view of sex and marriage?
4. What overtones ring in "to perpetuate the name of the dead in his inheritance" (verse 4:10)?
5. Why is the child of Ruth said to have been born to Naomi (verse 4:16)?
6. What is the lasting significance of the love between Ruth and Naomi?

NOTES

1. See Edward F. Campbell and Paul J. Achtemeier, "Ruth, the Book of," in *Harper's Bible Dictionary*, ed. Paul J. Achtemeier. San Francisco: Harper & Row, 1985, p. 886.
2. See Edward F. Campbell, Jr., *Ruth*. Garden City, N.Y.: Doubleday Anchor Bible, 1975, p. xi.
3. See Herbert G. May, "The Book of Ruth," in *Old Testament History*, ed. Charles M. Laymon. Nashville: Abingdon (Interpreter's Concise Commentary), 1983, p. 86.
4. Ibid., p. 84.
5. See D. F. Rauber, "Literary Values in the Book of Ruth," *Journal of Biblical Literature* 89 (1970), 27–37.
6. See Norman K. Gottwald, *The Hebrew Bible: A Socio-Literary Introduction*. Philadelphia: Fortress, 1985, p. 553.
7. See May, "The Book of Ruth," p. 82.
8. See Phyllis Trible, *God and the Rhetoric of Sexuality*. Philadelphia: Fortress, 1978, pp. 166–200.

CHAPTER 20

Song of Songs

TEXTUAL ANALYSIS

The Song of Songs is love poetry, traditionally attributed to King Solomon (perhaps because of his many wives), that was probably written after the Exile, perhaps coming into its present form as late as the third century B.C.E. Scholars debate the date of the work, as well as how to interpret it and whether it is a unity or a collection.[1] What remains relatively undisputed, however, is the provocation latent in the canonical editors' inclusion of this work in the Hebrew Bible. Ever since that decision, both Jewish and Christian readers of the Bible have had to grapple with what appears to be a strong endorsement of erotic love. Although many treatments regard the song as an anthology of love poetry, our analysis of the text, which is indebted to Samuel Terrien, treats it as a highly artful composition in seven parts:

1:2–2:6	Prelude and Reverie
2:7–3:5	First Dream
3:6–5:1	First Tryst
5:2–6:3	Second Dream
6:4–7:9	Second Tryst
7:10–8:5	Commitment
8:6–14	Reverie and Postlude[2]

1:2–2:6 Prelude and Reverie

The first verse of the work calls it the best of songs and attributes it to Solomon. Then we enter on a day-dreaming state in which the voice is that of a young woman expressing her longing for her lover and her memory of prior times with him. The first poetic images evoke the pleasures of the lover's kiss, love, touch, and presence. She imagines the two of them stealing away. From the middle of verse 1:4 the imagery shifts to the nuptials of a king and his bride, and the plural voice suggests the bride in concert with her attendants. Verse 1:5 may be a "travesty," playing on the notion of blackness but not meaning it negatively.[3] The "daughters of Jerusalem" function throughout the Song as a chorus whom the woman addresses when her lover is either absent or sleeping. The "vineyard" of verse 1:6 is susceptible to sexual interpretation, possibly signifying that the woman has not been chaste (a significant statement in the context of the Israelite ideal that the bride be a virgin).[4] The woman's mind roams in search of her lover, and verse 1:8 may be either a response from the chorus or her imagining her lover's reply. In verses 1:9–11 she imagines her lover's praises of her physical beauty, and verses 1:12–14 make most sense as her imagined reciprocation of praise, saying what he means to her. Verses 1:15–17 would then be his further response, as she hears it in her reverie of what their reunion would be like.

Verse 2:1 expresses how the love of her man makes the maiden feel. In verse 2:2 the voice is again that of the man, saying what the woman longingly believes he would say. Verses 2:3–6 express the woman's sense of how her man stands out from all others and how their move to a place where they might make love would go. Verse 2:5 is sweetly melodramatic and hyperbolic: "I am sick with love." At the conclusion of this first part (verse 2:6), she imagines them together to consummate their longing.

2:7–3:5 First Dream

The voice that sounds in this part continues to be that of the young woman. After their love making she sleeps, and in her dream she expresses herself to the daughters of Jerusalem. Verse 2:7 somewhat enigmatically asks that love (now sleeping) only awaken when the time is right. From verse 2:8 the woman is picturing the coming of her lover (here her dream seems less the product of her imagined love making than an expression of her longing for her lover, who in fact is absent from her). He comes like a gazelle, gazes in her window, and speaks words of invitation to go away with him. His call is to go out and enjoy the springtime (when all of nature quickens and flowers). Verse 2:12 is well known: "and the voice of the turtledove is heard in our land." The man speaks of the woman as his own dove, whom he delights in seeing and hearing. The "little foxes" of verse 2:15 remain enigmatic, despite the ingenuity of the allegorists,[5] but the plainest interpretation makes them the nuisances that spoil or distract romantic love. The voice at the end of chapter 2 again is that of the woman, summarizing the mutual belonging that the love of the two entails and describing her lover as a shepherd. May he turn to her, in all the vitality of a gazelle or a young stag. The pastoral imagery here, as throughout, places human love in the context of a fertile, lush nature.

A turtledove, symbol of love.   *(Used with permission of the photographer, Robert L. Cohn)*

The mood shifts abruptly in chapter 3, as the woman finds herself alone in bed in the night. She seeks "him whom my soul loves" (verse 3:1: a prime text for those who have read the Song as an allegory of the love between God and either the individual seeker or God's people), but she cannot find him. So she rises and goes out into the city, her mood more one of longing than one of fear or desperation. We have seen the watchman as a prophetic symbol (for example, in Isaiah 62:6, Ezekiel 33:7–9, Micah 7:4), but here the sense seems to be more literal: those who would be out at night patroling the city. Verse 3:4 exults in a happy finding (pregnant for those interested in the absences and communings of the mystical life), the woman holding on until she can get her lover back to the bedroom (that will no longer be empty). Verse 3:5 repeats verse 2:7 and so marks this second section as a self-enclosed unit.

3:6–5:1 First Tryst

For Terrien, who sees the Song in the broad context of the biblical view of sexual love, verse 3:6 heralds (in the man's voice) the arrival of woman as a wondrous part of the natural order,[6] much as Genesis (2:23–24) implies that her creation was a special blessing. Solomon comes into play, because his wedding processions apparently were a high point in the biblical memory of how romantic love had been bedecked and celebrated. Chapter 4, reminiscent of the *wasf*, an Arabic genre of praise for the physical beauty of a lover, begins a description of the woman's beauty (verses 4:1–7), some of which may be erotically symbolic, but verse 4:7 is the crystal-clear summation: "You are all fair, my love; there is no flaw in you."

From verse 4:8 the woman is the lover's bride, who has completely ravished his heart. We lack the familiarity with the natural allusions necessary for the passage to carry its full poetic force, but certainly we sense that the best of flowers and scents are being pressed into service. The symbol of the garden is layered, suggesting Eden, the choicest preserve of a desert house, and the intimacies of physical love. Verse 4:16 seems to be the voice of the woman, asking the wind (allusive of the divine breath?) to spread the fragrance of the garden (herself, and romantic love), and finishing with a suggestive invitation. Verse 5:1, concluding

Cyclamen, a delicate flower of the land of Israel. *(Used with permission of the photographer, Wolfgang Roth)*

this episode of the first tryst, is a positive response by the man, who comes to the garden (his sister, his bride) to enjoy it himself and celebrate love with his friends. The eating and drinking of verse 5:1 suggest a wedding banquet.

5:2–6:3 Second Dream

The second dream is the bottom and central panel, if we picture the entire Song as a movement down and then back up, as in following a letter U. The first three episodes make the left side of the U. The fourth episode is the bottom curve, where the repetition or parallel of the first three movements begins. So, as in the first dream, we find the woman again sleeping, although her heart was awake (another image that mystics have loved, because it could suggest that even when the mind was asleep or distracted the heart could commune with God). The lover knocks at her door, and he is described as though he has been out in the wet night. Verse 5:3 seems a strange bit of daintiness or distraction, as though the woman were too prettified for her own good. (Perhaps this verse alludes to the frustrations of dreams, where frequently what we are on the verge of accomplishing escapes us.) By the time she gets to the door, her lover has gone. This takes her soul away in panic, and once again she must go in search of him, worrying that they will stay separated.

This time the search goes badly. The woman cannot find her lover or hear him answer her calls. The watchmen beat her and strip away her cloak. She asks the daughters of Jerusalem to communicate to her beloved her dire longing: She is sick with love (verse 5:8 partly repeats verse 2:5, but carrying darker overtones — the illness caused by frustration). The response of the daughters in verse 5:9 moves the speech of the second dream forward. In answering their question (What about her lover stirs her so?), the woman elaborates a description of his physical beauty that parallels the description he gave of her beauty in the first part of chapter 4. (Indeed, it uses many of the same images and so suggests sexual equality.) Once again the referents cannot mean as much to us as they do to the speaker, but we sense that she is employing the richest excellences from her culture's inventory of beauty. In verse 6:1 the daughters again question the woman, asking where her lover has gone. The woman's answer brings back the image of a garden, and her conviction in verse 6:3 that she and her lover belong to one another echoes verse 2:16. Both dreams therefore deal in the coin of romantic union, which may suffer assaults (absences) but carries a fulfillment in its very longing for the beloved.

6:4–7:9 Second Tryst

Even though the second tryst parallels the first, we sense some psychological development. Much of the imagery used in the first description of the woman's beauty recurs, but the force is greater (see verses 6:4–5). She is his dove, and she is flawless (verse 6:9). The imagery of verse 6:10, in which the speaker is wondering at the woman's identity, may exceed the overtones of verse 3:6, in which a similar wonder was displayed. Here the dawn, the moon, and the sun suggest the cosmic force of the divine creativity, love, and wisdom.[7] In verses 6:11–12 the woman seems to be speaking of a descent into the orchard of delights. This imagery, as well as her fanciful sitting in a chariot beside her prince, of course is susceptible to erotic interpretation. Scholars puzzle over verse 6:13, and the "Shulamite" remains obscure. It may refer to one of the names of Ishtar, the Akkadian goddess of love and war, but it may also allude to the dance customary at weddings.[8]

Chapter 7 contains another listing and more praise of the woman's physical charms, this time from the bottom up. The nose "like a tower of Lebanon" in verse 7:4 (stately? straight?) has occasioned much giggling along the student benches, and such other assets as a belly like "a heap of wheat, encircled by lilies" remind us of the cultural distances that separate us from the Israel of perhaps 2400 years ago. In verses 7:8–9 the praiser seems to drop his restraint and make plain the consummation both parties devoutly wish.

7:10–8:5 Commitment

Verse 7:10 repeats verses 2:16 and 6:3. Here the woman belongs to her beloved and his desire is for her. This seems both to set the sexes in balance and to give the woman a basis for her confident repose. She can trust in his love and desire. Once again she would have them go out into the beauties of the fields and the vineyards, and here it is explicit that such an exodus is to make love (verse 7:12). Throughout this passage, nature and human beings move to the same rhythm, which suggests a lovely symbiosis. Verse 7:13 is her promise of a fullness of fragrances and fruits — sensual delights. Although all of this is powerfully erotic, it is also completely forthright and healthy. The woman is speaking in the candid poetry that truly loving sexual intimacy sponsors, and the Song as a whole is a great vote of confidence in the divinely given goodness of such intimacy.

In chapter 8 the man is likened to a brother who nursed with her at her mother's breast. Here, as in the earlier text (verse 4:9), where the man referred to the woman as both sister and bride, the effort manifestly is to use any metaphor that suggests intimacy and sharing. The forthright kissing of verse 8:1 suggests that the relationship of the two would be acknowledged and blessed publicly. As in verse 3:4, the woman would lead her man back to her mother's house and the chamber that conceived her—imagery suggesting both intimacy from birth and renewed love making. Verse 8:3 repeats 2:6 and the imagery of sexual embrace. Verse 8:4 repeats verse 2:7 and would have love sleep on.

In verse 8:5 the identity of the woman is revealed: She is the intimate of, the sojourner with, her beloved man. One interested in a biblical theology that praises heterosexual love and thinks optimistically of the joined fate and passion that the sexes share could make this a key text. The awakening under the apple tree may allude to postcoital sleep, or it may intimate that the woman, who has carried much of the initiative and direction of the love affair, is the one who gives the man his awakening to the full potential of human being. For that he was born, the imagery of travail suggests. The apple tree probably is not the fateful tree of Eden but rather the masculine potential loved by the woman in verse 2:3.

8:6–14 Reverie and Postlude

In Terrien's reading, the Song returns to its starting point, ending where it began, but of course richer by the time of this homecoming (knowing its starting place, the human condition, more fully). Verse 8:6 is probably the most famous line of the Song and is well worth quoting: "Set me as a seal upon your heart, as a seal upon your arm; for love is strong as death, jealousy is cruel as the grave." Many analysts have found correlations between sexual love and death, no doubt ultimately because this primal stratum of human emotions lodges close to our bedrock condition of being mortal. The seals mentioned are not just markers of possession or belonging in the here and now before death, useful to keep outsiders aware of romantic or marital ties. They are also images of shared life and destiny. That is why they immediately conjure up death, for death is the great question mark hanging over all created life and calling its passions into doubt. Here the affirmation is forthright, even defiant. Love is a force capable of contesting death. In profound eros (the love that blazes with desire for the [sometimes apparently unearthly] beauty of the beloved), we hear whispers of immortality. The Greeks were better expositors of this theme than the biblical poets, but here biblical poetry draws close to the channel the Greek lyricists sailed.

The other image, of the fire of jealousy, is ambivalent. On the one hand, it expresses the ardor of love, although in a threatened and possessive way. On the other hand, its "cruelty" (singlemindedness, obduracy, perhaps even inevitability) is as strong as the grave. Verse 8:7 is a powerful, if perhaps somewhat desperate, tribute to love. It can resist all the tides of change and fashion. Compared to it wealth and possessions are but straw. The voice here is less that of the romantic poet who composed the majority of the poem and more that of a sapiential writer. Verses 8:8–10 are rather obscure, but certainly nuptial overtones sound. Perhaps the daughters of Jerusalem are speaking. Verse 8:9 may present a contrast between chastity and looseness.

Verse 8:10 has a lovely conclusion: "Then I was in his eyes as one who brings peace." This peace, no doubt, is not the absence of conflict as much as the positive state of enjoying God's fullness of blessing (something sabbatical, therefore). Verses 8:11–12 seem to contrast the vineyard of this couple with the vineyard of Solomon and find Solomon's possession the lesser treasure. Verse 8:13 sounds like a commendation of love to all who are seeking it: The lover hearing the beloved in the presence of interested companions knows that what all people most deeply are seeking is found in the beloved's voice. The woman's voice prevails at the end, as it prevailed at the beginning, and it repeats the longing for a vital, virile love that has been the driving force of the whole Song.

HISTORICAL BACKGROUND

The date of the composition of the Song of Songs is still debated, and the authorship is unknown. Those who hold for a postexilic final editing can allow that parts of the poem may be from much earlier, perhaps even Solomonic times. Whether we speak of a single authorship, or of fragments from many hands joined through a final editing, largely depends on our interpretation: Does the Song exhibit a thematic and structural integrity? Terrien, who finds great structural and thematic integrity, describes the Song as a "musical masque of love," scripted to be performed (perhaps at the royal court), and intended as a celebration of erotic love. On its own it seems largely secular (not first intended as an allegory of divine love), but it has the effect of counteracting any diminution of sexual love that the alienations described in Genesis might suggest. However, there is no doubt that it entered the canon of the Hebrew Bible because rabbinic interpretation found it profitable when used allegorically[9] (and perhaps also because the rabbis wanted to affirm the value of sexual love).

Israelite poets had examples of love poetry from ancient Egypt and Mesopotamia. They also had stimulating paradigmatic characters from the biblical traditions about the greatest Israelite kings, David and Solomon. David, the great warrior and psalmist, was a notorious lover, as the incident with Bathsheba especially showed. Solomon, the epitome of wisdom, had a harem of legendary proportions. In neither of these cases was erotic love praiseworthy, because it led David to adultery and murder and it led Solomon to idolatry. But in both of these cases it was part of the persona of the biblical hero. Moreover, it was part of the collective persona or corporate personality of Israel itself, because the prophetic probings of the covenantal relationship used the figure of marriage as a central symbol. Passionate, erotic love, therefore, was quite prominent in the biblical inventory of emotions. Some of the songs we find here may have been written for royal weddings or other celebrations of love, so in taking them over the biblical authors in effect moved romance directly into scripture. The canonical editors, if not the original authors, might well have reasoned that if erotic love could be presented artistically and purified of its negative effects, it might well enrich the treasury of literature that instructed Israel in the wonders of its life under God.

LITERARY INTENT

The final reason why the Song of Songs entered the canon may well have been its allegorical potential, but some recent commentators, such as Brevard Childs, speak more of its value as a celebration of the mysteries of human love and marriage.[10] Childs links this value with the interests of the wisdom circles that predominated in decisions about the Writings, suggesting that the Song struck such circles as a fine validation of the unity of religious and secular matters. In terms that we have used previously, the Song expresses the humanistic bent and convictions of the Hebrew Bible. Like the Book of Ruth, it is content to focus on an ordinary human phenomenon (for Ruth, loyalty and daughterly love; for the Song, erotic love) and celebrate its wonders as a creation of God. We can deepen and extend these wonders by adding more explicitly theological or revelational points of view, but the basic goodness and significance of the prime analogate (the ordinary human phenomenon itself) need never be lost.

Wisdom circles, we recall, were especially impressed by the intelligence of God that shone from the conduct of both cosmic and human affairs. Dante captured much of this impress when he spoke of "the love that moves the stars." Human eros, too, is a remarkable tribute and challenge to the creator's intentions. It has such influence in human affairs, both small-scale or familial and world historical, that it must rank as one of the wonders of the world. Indeed, we recall the confession of Proverbs 30:18–19: "Three things are too wonderful for me; four I do not understand: the way of an eagle in the sky, the way of a serpent on a rock, the way of a ship on the high seas, and the way of a man with a maiden." So the way of a man with a maiden (or of a maiden with a man, to give the initiative of the woman of the Song its due) ranks with the wonders of nature. Like them, it calls the sensitive and the religious to contemplate the ways of God, the ultimate mystery, and find still more reasons to bless the holy name.

LASTING SIGNIFICANCE

We mentioned at the outset of this chapter that the Song has always been provocative. Whereas many strands of biblical religion suggest great caution about erotic love, if not downright prudishness, the Song has spoken unabashedly of breasts and embraces, of kisses and delights. Indeed, the more we approach the poetic imagery aware of the double entendre that erotic matters regularly sponsor, the higher the temperature rises. This is a very spicy work, and by that very fact it does wonders for the image of both the biblical deity and the biblical human being. Even when we admit that the rabbis favored allegorical interpretations that made the love a romance between Israel and God, or that Christian theologians saw an allegory of the relationship between the Church and Christ (or between the mystical soul and God), the Song continues to stress the goodness of sexual love.

The prophetic German philosopher-poet Friedrich Nietzsche rejected a God who could not dance and sing. The prophetic German psychoanalyst Sigmund Freud thought that the repressions of nineteenth-century European culture were the great cause of mental illness, and for him the religion at the core of that culture itself was a grand neurosis. These and dozens of similar critiques certainly are themselves liable to criticism as either uncontrolled or generated by a disputable set of first opinions (prejudices). Still, they make the point, shared (though focused differently) by such nineteenth-century critics of religion as Ludwig Feuerbach and Karl Marx, that the interpretation of biblical revelation that became dominant in the West often set humanity and divinity at odds. To praise God, many theologians and preachers went out of their way to denigrate human nature. To sing of the holiness of the creator and the mercy of the redeemer, too many biblical religionists spoke endlessly of the depravities of sinful humanity. The Song suggests that this fault lies less with the Bible than with later generations of Bible readers, who excessively feared the emotions their creator had given them.

The biblical religions have not been unique in their problems with the human body and sexuality, of course. India, China, and Japan all show tensions between prudishness and erotic excess. But the biblical religion that has shaped so much of modern Western (and therefore postmodern world) culture was especially uneasy. Whether we credit this to Victorian repressions, or go farther back to Hellenistic dualism and patriarchal misogynism, the effect remains considerable distortion, guilt, lack of joy, and lack of appreciation for the divine "work" that human beings represent. The Song says that human beings should be passionate and erotic. It says that sexual love is a great treasure and blessing, a joy to be trumpeted rather than a temptation to be denounced.

GLOSSARY

Double entendre A pun or phrase that has double meaning (the second often sexual).

Symbiosis Living together, codwelling.

Travesty A parody or burlesque; a change of clothes and roles (perhaps to bring out new aspects).

STUDY QUESTIONS

1. Why is the inclusion of the Song of Songs in the Bible provocative?
2. Write a brief description of the body and the spirit of the woman who is the main speaker in the Song.
3. How successfully do the dreams depict the sufferings that love endures when the lover is absent?
4. What do the trysts suggest about the equality of woman and man?
5. Why does the Song conjoin the figures of bride, lover, and sibling?
6. What relations does the Song set among love, death, and jealousy?
7. What should the wise learn from the way of a man with a maiden?
8. Explain the predilection both Jewish and Christian writers have had for allegorizing the Song.

NOTES

1. See Marvin H. Pope, *Song of Songs*. Garden City, N. Y.: Doubleday Anchor Bible, 1977, pp. 22–37. See also S. F. Grober, "The Hospitable Lotus: A Cluster of Metaphors. An Inquiry into the Problem of Textual Unity in the Song of Songs," *Semitics*, 9 (1984), 86–112; Cesare Perugini, "Cantico dei Cantici e lirica d'amore sumerica," *Revista Biblica*, 31 (1983), 21–41; Roland E.

Murphy, "Canticle of Canticles," in *The Jerome Biblical Commentary*, ed. R. Brown et al. Englewood Cliffs, N. J.: Prentice-Hall, 1968, Volume 1, p. 507.

2. See Samuel Terrien, *Till the Heart Sings*. Philadelphia: Fortress, 1985, pp. 38–45.

3. See Manfred Görg, " 'Travestie' im Hohen Lied. Eine Kritische Betrachtung am Beispiel von HL 1,5 ff.," *Biblische Notizen*, 21 (1983), 101–15.

4. See Pope, *Song of Songs*, p. 326.

5. Ibid., pp. 402–4.

6. See Terrien, *Till the Heart Sings*, p. 39.

7. Ibid., pp. 41–42.

8. See Robert C. Dentan, "The Song of Solomon," in *Wisdom Literature and Poetry*, ed. Charles M. Laymon. Nashville: Abingdon (Interpreter's Concise Commentary), 1983, pp. 267–68.

9. See Terrien, *Till the Heart Sings*, pp. 45–49. See also John L. McKenzie, *Dictionary of the Bible*. Milwaukee: Bruce, 1965, pp. 833–55.

10. See Brevard Childs, *Introduction to the Old Testament as Scripture*. Philadelphia: Fortress, 1979, pp. 578–79.

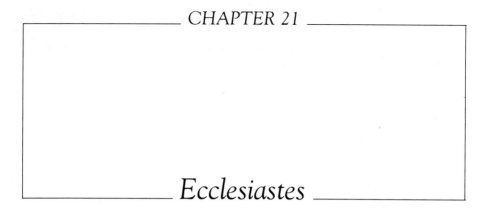

CHAPTER 21

Ecclesiastes

TEXTUAL ANALYSIS

Ecclesiastes, called Qoheleth in Hebrew, represents wisdom's musing in a quite skeptical mood. R. B. V. Scott, in fact, likens it to the voice of the doubter that we found in Proverbs 30:1–4.[1] Scholars remark on the peculiar Hebrew of the text, which contains loan words from Persian and sometimes is colloquial rather than literarily correct, and generally they place it quite late, from the fifth to the third century B.C.E.[2] The present text is but a loosely organized collection of different proverbial sayings and observations, but we may usefully treat it in five unequal parts:

1:1–2	Introduction
1:3–6:12	The Vanity of Life
7:1–9:16	Realistic Advice
9:17–12:8	Concluding Proverbs
12:9–14	Postscripts[3]

1:1–2 Introduction

Ecclesiastes 1:1 tells us that this collection is the words of Qoheleth (perhaps "the Preacher"), whom it identifies as the son of David who ruled in Jerusalem as king—Solomon. The traditional association of wisdom with Solomon undoubtedly occasioned this attribution. Verse 1:2 serves as a motto[4] summarizing the overall

The Western Wall of the Jerusalem Temple Mount, the traditional site of wailing for Israel's sufferings, atop the ancient wall built by Solomon. *(Used with permission of the photographer, Wolfgang Roth)*

message: "Vanity of vanities, says the Preacher, vanity of vanities! All is vanity." The Hebrew word traditionally translated "vanity" (*hebel*: vapor, breath) is perhaps more effectively rendered "futility" (or irony). It denotes fleetingness or emptiness, not excessive self-esteem. From the outset, therefore, the work promises to be sober and testing. Wisdom will have a significant place for challenge and doubt.

1:3–6:12 The Vanity of Life

Having sounded this opening thesis, Ecclesiastes plunges into expatiating upon it. People toil, generations succeed one another, but the Earth remains unchanged. In the foreground is human limitation and mortality, but in the background is the restricted power of the technology of the Preacher's time. We could not get away with this observation today, when atomic and industrial pollutants let loose by one human generation mark both the Earth and all subsequent generations ominously. To verse 1:7, the Preacher is relying on the conviction, staple in the wisdom literature, that the cosmos dwarfs human projects and runs ahead heedless of human concerns. The difference is that whereas other wisdom writers make this a witness to the divine intelligence, the Preacher makes it a strong suggestion that nothing human lasts very long.

In verse 1:8 the mood is surfeit and disillusionment: Nothing sensible gives the human personality the fulfillment it wants. Verse 1:9, with its certainty that there is nothing new under the sun, has become a stock phrase in the storehouse of Western jadedness. The mood of verse 1:11 is that death washes all things away. The counter would be that memory or progeny keep at least a vestige, but the Preacher does not want to hear that. He has his truth, of course: Little of any of us does remain. The burden of this truth is that it can take away our vital spirit.

The benefit is that it can strip us of many trivial preoccupations and force us to confront deeper sources of meaning.

From verses 1:12 to 2:26 the form is autobiographical reflection, as the supposed Solomon (perhaps actually a somewhat bitter old man anxious to share what experience has taught him) thinks back over the experiments he made in pursuit of wisdom. Verse 1:13 seems to make life itself an unhappy business. In verse 1:14 the weary king labels all human striving but the pursuit of wind. Even the vaunted wisdom that this great king acquired, for which he became famous, now seems to him but vexation and the increase of sorrow. Literarily, the author or editor of this collection has considerably increased the impact of its weary skepticism by putting it in the mouth of the man whose name was a synonym for (divinely given) wisdom. If he pronounces all striving after wisdom vain, and calls all gaining of wisdom painful, what hope have lesser mortals that they can find meaning and satisfaction? A sophisticated religious dialectician might use such weariness to make the mind pivot to a "negative" way of finding significance (by the denial that any of the limited things of human experience can be God and the concomitant implication that the true God must be unlimited and transcendent of human experience), but on the simple face of it the passage from verse 12 to verse 16 is terribly pessimistic.

In chapter 2 the kingly sage numbers some of the human qualities he tested and found wanting as sources of permanent or significant satisfaction. He tried pleasure, and it did not do. He tried laughter (levity), and it made no real sense. The same with wine (which stands for all the things that might gladden the body) and even "how to lay hold on folly" (verse 2:3), an enigmatic enterprise (perhaps: studying the way of the fool and acting as though meaning were haphazard). Houses, vineyards, gardens, parks, trees, pools, the services of slaves, possessions, riches, singers, and concubines all proved empty in the final analysis. We think of St. Augustine in the *Confessions*, asking all of creation whether it was God and getting back the answer, "We are not He." The Preacher is not as specific about the goal of his negative experimentation, but he is on the same psychological track. If one tries everything and finds nothing fully satisfying, one meets an oxymoron: pregnant emptiness. What does the vanity, the futility, the irony that pleasure finally fails to please signify? Is it the end of the road or a marker saying that the right path moves on another level?

Chapter 2 continues in this vein, noting how little the wisdom of Solomon actually meant and how little any successor king actually could do to change his predecessor's achievements. In this context verse 2:13 sounds illogical: "Then I saw that wisdom excels folly as light excels darkness." How does an empty wisdom excel a full folly? How does an unilluminating light excel a lightless darkness? Despite his skepticism, the Preacher seems caught in the ordinary preferences that prevail in virtually all cultures. Still, verse 2:14 qualifies the superiority of the wise person to the fool, noting that both are fated to die. Ultimately, then, wisdom may not be superior to folly. Yet the Preacher prefers it for intermediate or penultimate matters, which the administrator (or just the person of common sense) in him realizes are also a part of the human condition with which each of us must come to grips.

The mood becomes especially grim in verse 2:17, for the futility of his ventures has made the Preacher hate life. We would be hard-pressed to find an attitude more starkly opposed to the gratitude for life and creation counseled by Genesis 1, where the refrain is that God saw what he had made and called it good. The Bible, we can only say one more time, truly is a remarkable work. To include attitudes, teachings, apparently diametrically opposed to one another within one housing is to display a stunning tolerance. (Perhaps, as well, it is virtually to force its readers to engage in the debate that the juxtaposition of such opposed viewpoints creates. We might argue, therefore, that the canonical editors of the Bible were like Socratic teachers, trying to force their students to question everything and think for themselves. On that reading, biblical religion is [positively] argumentative to the core and not at all dogmatic or certitudinarian.)

Verses 2:18–19 make it plain that the hatred the Preacher is voicing is an effect of his contemplating the reductions imposed by death. Ironically, some fool may inherit the fruits of the wise person's labors. Death, then, is a great force in the skepticism of this stratum of wisdom literature, and that can make this stratum seem quite modern or existential.[5] Verse 2:21 speaks openly of despair— hopelessness—due to the transiency of wisdom. It cannot be passed on, and where it once worked a fool may easily come to labor. We may count it a muchness that the literary voice of a king, who probably never suffered a callused palm, should go on at such length about toil, but part of what the Preacher is discussing is the toil of the spirit in search of meaning. This, too, can suffer a great weariness, so much so that *acedia* (weariness, loss of heart) became recognized as a central trial of the contemplative life. Qoheleth gains some stature when we place him in this context. If he is worn out from an honest search for treasures safe from moth and worm, he may be less a dissipated cynic and more a valiant, if wearied, soldier.

If a person finds all toil finally bootless, the best remedy or stance to take may be a circumscribed enjoyment of what can be enjoyed on a daily basis: food, drink, the satisfactions of work (when we do not ask it to prove it has ultimate significance). The reference to God in verses 2:24–25 distinguishes this sort of hedonism from the Epicurean "eat, drink, and be merry," considering the pleasure we may find in everyday life a gift from God. This reference should also nudge us to reconsider the skepticism we are being shown. If it assumes as its framework a final trust in God, it is quite different from the foundationally agnostic or atheistic skepticism that calls all such frameworks into question. Verse 2:24 is in the spirit of the more traditional sapiential conviction that God rewards the good and punishes sinners. As such, it is less radical and challenging than what we have previously seen. But verse 2:26, which implies that whatever sinners gather finally is made over to the good, does add another wrinkle to the theme of futility.

Verses 3:1–8 comprise a very famous reflection on the times of human life. The plain meaning is that various experiences turn up as they will, despite what human beings may expect or want. The implication is that people are wise to try to find the rhythm according to which such happenings turn and fit themselves to it. Were we dealing with a typical sapiential writer, we could assume that this pattern was another expression of the guiding divine intelligence, parallel to the expression in the coming of the seasons and the movement of the stars. But Qoheleth is not so simple or trusting a sapiential writer, as verse 3:9, the end of the poem, suggests, and therefore we must be cautious about asserting what the rhythms of the times of life mean to him.

Verses 3:10–15 make up a challenging passage, in which the Preacher reflects

on the significance of the life that God has forced upon human beings. The beauty
of the things of creation lures human beings to ponder it and learn how to harmonize
themselves with it, for best enjoyment. God has even lured human beings beyond
the orbit of temporal alternations, soliciting their contemplation of the transtemporal or eternal realm in which the divinity (as other than creation) must dwell.
Yet, as verse 3:11 insightfully puts it, this contemplation of eternity gains no
resolution, gets no answer to the question it itself is. "God" is mysterious, and the
more that we suspect that the Preacher is deeply impressed by this mysteriousness,
the more we must reckon with the possibility that his descriptions of how meaning
and satisfaction slip out of human beings' hands are calculated, even carefully
wrought.

In this context, verses 3:12–13 are quite beautiful and positive: The mysteriousness or inscrutability of the divine hold on the beginning and end of things
sanctions an enjoyment of the here and now. Were it not for the dangers of eisegesis
(reading-in, here from Christian notions), we might describe this as a wholesome
incarnationalism. Verse 3:14 is a tribute to the divine transcendence and control,
quite in keeping with the wisdom worldview that we have previously seen in Job
and Proverbs. But it has the danger of making God more static and remote than
what the theology of the prophets suggests. Most likely the "fear" mentioned in
verse 3:14 is the "fear of the Lord" so important in Proverbs, which sapiential
writers in general considered the beginning of wisdom. Verse 3:15 is more tribute
to the divine omnipotence and omniscience, which again, as stated, risks theological problems. Here, the problem would be determinism: no innovation or
freedom in creation. The "what has been driven away" of verse 3:15 is obscure.
R. B. Y. Scott translates it for the Anchor Bible as "God will see to what requires
[his] attention."[6]

With verse 3:16 we seem to move to moral futilities, such as those that
distressed Job. Justice and wickedness coincide as the best of human instinct says
they should not do. Verse 3:17 is the staple sapiential response: God will sort it
out (in God's own good time). Verse 3:18 adds the expectable but still provocative
kicker: Suffering evil is a test that God imposes on human beings. The special
note here is that Qoheleth does not specify that the test is for the innocent or the
good, and he makes the lesson to be learned rather harsh: People must learn that
they are but beasts (capable of goring one another?). Like beasts, human beings
die. The breath all animals share is levelingly mortal. The dust of verse 3:20 calls
to mind the account of creation in Genesis. Verse 3:21 challenges any facile
assumption that after death the spirits (breaths) of man and beast go in different
directions (the human spirit to heaven and the beastly spirit to Sheol or back into
the cosmic circuit). The irony is heavy to the point of depression. So chapter 3
ends with a repeat of the cautious humanism and advice voiced previously: The
best thing to do (ultimate matters being so uncertain or mysterious) is to enjoy
one's work and human lot day by day. No one can say what happens after death.
The part of wisdom therefore is to find a way to enjoy or be content with the time
one has to live.

Chapter 4 begins with another mention of oppressions (injustice). The tears
of the oppressed seem to move the Preacher, perhaps even to threaten his stance
and so challenge him either to harden his spirit in a tougher skepticism or find a
perspective from which justice and meaning might become more possible — things

for which he honestly could hope. (The challenge therefore is to think about redemption or salvation, perhaps as the Exile forced some of the prophets to think about these matters.) Verse 4:3 shows the depths of the Preacher's sorrowing and his special talent as a philosopher. Whereas the average sapiential writer in the Bible laments injustice and moves from it to a call upon God, the Preacher goes right to the deepest implications: (Perhaps) it were better never to have been born. The Christian scholastic philosophers dealt with this problem rather simply, asserting that being is always better than nonbeing. That view suggests an ontology well worth pondering, but the Preacher's position here seems the more human and poignant response: If life is going to be mainly oppression, would it not be a mercy never to have been born? (Whether we can validly transfer this attitude to such arenas as the controversies about revolutionary uprisings or abortion is another, quite complicated question, but that the Preacher's musings even suggest it indicates how deeply his ruminations go.)

From verse 4:4 we enter upon a proverbial patch, being warned off from envy, foolishness, unquietness, and asking for whom one toils (or the bell tolls). Verse 4:9 somewhat contradicts verse 4:8, stating that company is better than solitude. (Qoheleth abounds in contradictions, perhaps as another way of suggesting the vanity of thought and life.) If we translate this approval of companionship into "collaboration," "friendship," and "marital love," we see that the Preacher is suggesting defenses against the dark and the cold of futility.[7] Verses 4:13–14 caution that anyone, even the most experienced person, can become foolish and unwilling to take advice. The sense of verses 4:13–16 might be that the succession of rulers (for instance, David standing in the wings and then replacing Saul) is both another stimulus (to the wise) to stay open to how history is moving and another reason to think that no status or achievement is stable enough to defend one against life's general flux and futility. The favor of the people, too, is vanity.

Verse 5:1 contains the first reference to established religion. The Preacher's preferences are for the study or listening of the wisdom schools, rather than the sacrificial activities of the priests. (Priests were involved in sapiential circles, but we catch here a glimpse of the tension between religious study and religious ritual.) It is not clear why the sacrifice of fools is evil, but the Preacher may be thinking that many who sacrifice think they know all about God and what God requires of them. To his more skeptically religious mind, that could ring of idolatry. The following counsel, to keep one's words to God few, is interesting for its rationale: God is in heaven, and the human speaker is on Earth. Qoheleth, we infer, is well aware of what Soren Kierkegaard, the nineteenth-century Danish philosopher, called "the infinite qualitative distinction" between divinity and humanity.

Verses 5:3–6 offer more counsel to restraint and rectitude before God. The advice about vows seems to echo Deuteronomy 23:22. Verse 5:7 has a familiar ring: Fear of God is a good touchstone. In verse 5:8 we hear the sapiential trust and hope that God will render a final judgment, more adequate than the disbursements of goods and privileges that obtain in most societies. The following verses are in the nature of proverbial observations, the general tone of which is skepticism regarding worldly ambitions. Verse 5:15 is nearly identical with Job 1:21, but whereas in Job's mouth it expresses positive resignation to the will of God, here it sounds like a negative comment on life's futility. Verses 5:18–19 repeat the limited hedonism that we have previously seen. Verse 5:20 is a puzzling verse, but certainly it is susceptible to the hopeful interpretation that God can give human beings a joy that makes their days of toil seem of no account.

Chapter 6 opens with further reflections on the vanity of wealth. Verse 6:3 implies that the criterion of a successful life should be (decent) enjoyment of the good things the world offers. Note the association of death with darkness in verse 6:4, and the equation of untimely birth (a miscarriage) with normal death in verse 6:5. Verses 6:7–9 show more of Qoheleth's keen sense of life's vanity. The chapter ends with negative judgments about wordiness and a quite radical doubt that anyone can know what is truly good for human beings, because of the uncertainty that attends everyone's death (verse 6:12).

7:1–9:16 Realistic Advice

Once again we move from prose to poetry, and so we can speak of another textual fold. The proverbs of verses 7:1–13 might occur in the Book of Proverbs, except for their almost morbid negativity. We should note the interest in the fool, which Proverbs also expressed, and the praise of wisdom (which indicates a sus-pension of Qoheleth's more radical perspective, in which death makes the wise person and the fool quite equal). Verse 7:14 is a good counsel to emotional stability. Verse 7:16 gives us another glimpse of the Preacher's idiosyncratic mind: What other biblical writer would warn us against too much righteousness? Like many of the Greeks, Qoheleth thinks that we could find much worse mottoes than "nothing to excess."[8] Verse 7:18 suggests that fear of the Lord is a good anchor for such balance. In verse 7:24 Qoheleth again hints that he has pondered the mysteriousness of the (divine) order in which he finds himself. We suspect that, like Socrates, he thinks his greatest achievement has been to realize he does not understand the most elementary things about himself or his life. The bitter outburst of verse 7:26 against the snaring woman is but one of Qoheleth's several manifestations of misogynism. Verse 7:27 conjures up a man trying to do the sum of the universe and running out of beads on his abacus. Verse 7:29 would be an interesting text from which to ponder the biblical view of the proportions of uprightness and sin that we should think exist in "human nature."

Chapter 8 begins with a teasing challenge: Show me a wise man! The second half of verse 8:1 suggests that genuine wisdom produces light and softness, perhaps because of contentment. Verses 8:2–5, which recall advice from Proverbs about how to deal with kings, stress resignation to authority (both human and divine). Verse 8:7 would derive modesty from the fact that no one knows what the future will bring. The fact that we all die should also restrain our pride, and verse 8:9 suggests that our common mortality is at odds with the way that some lord it over others. Verse 8:11 contains the sobering implication that justice delayed is evil spurred. Verses 8:12–13 have the ring of routine expressions of the sapiential hope that fear of the Lord will make everything turn out well and just. We take verse 8:14 as a reprise of the theme that injustice, the imbalance of the moral scales, is a great source of irony. Enjoyment, good food and drink, once again is the preacher's best counsel. The chapter ends in a religious agnosticism: Human beings will never comprehend the ways of God.

Chapter 9 opens with a positive conclusion from this state of not knowing: All things finally are in God's hands, and whether we should consider a given eventuality an expression of the divine love or the divine hate no one can say with certitude. Verse 9:2 would complicate any easy judgments about people in terms of whether or not they sacrificed to God. Both surely die, and what happens after that none of us can say. The universal evil spoken of in verse 9:3 seems to be death. The figure of verse 9:4 has the tone of a peasant proverb: "for a living dog is better than a dead lion." Qoheleth takes the intractable uncertainty of the human condition as a strong call to live in the present, to appreciate what we can enjoy and we can change, rather than to chase will o'the wisps like invulnerable certainty.

Verse 9:5 offers the sort of certainty with which the Preacher does feel comfortable: The dead know nothing (as far as we know). The following verses are spun out from the Preacher's sense of vanity, but we can read them as a positive, even a religious call to enjoy the situation (of mortality, ignorance, toil, yet limited pleasures) in which God has placed us. Verse 9:9 contradicts Qoheleth's usual misogyny, recognizing the power of love to make life livable. Verse 9:11 takes away any ultimate claims that human excellences or good fortune might make. The parable of the small, besieged city in verse 9:14 may be describing Jerusalem, but this is far from certain.[9] Verse 9:16, the conclusion of this section according to our division, seems to say that even when it is not rewarded or heeded, wisdom is good in itself.

9:17–12:8 Concluding Proverbs

The next verses have the rhythms of traditional proverbs, and their juxta-position of the wise person and the fool shows little we have not seen before. Verses 10:5–7 describe inversions of right order, due to the folly of rulers. The message in verses 10:8–9 appears to be that we cannot avoid being touched by that to which we put our hands. To verse 10:15 we mainly hear more complaints about the damage fools do. Verses 10:16–17 remind us how dependent ancient peoples were on the character and whims of their rulers. Verse 10:19 must be taken in the spirit of the limited hedonism we have previously praised, if they are not to make hash of the preacher's central message of vanity.

Chapter 11 opens with a line that has become famous and is usually under-stood as counseling strong, even adventurous trust in God. The import of the following verses is far from obvious. Perhaps the message is that we should be well aware of the many things in life that are just facts we cannot control, yet not be paralyzed by them. Verse 11:5 speaks of the mystery of conception and prenatal growth as Job might have, making it cause for confessing the transcendence of God. Verses 11:7–8, in their sequence, compose a sermonette on how a good theistic humanist might live. Verse 11:9 offers the same balanced message in slightly different garb: Enjoy, but remember judgment.

Chapter 12 continues in the vein of the end of chapter 11, as though the preacher were also an instructor of youth. The perspective is that of an elderly person recalling the goodness of the vigor of youth and yet knowing almost painfully well its fleetingness and final futility. An old teacher finds little good in old age. The images in verses 12:2–4 are of natural or perhaps military oppression, but they may also be part of an extended metaphor for old age and the approach of death. The key phrase to recall throughout occurs in verse 12:1: "Remember also your

Creator." Verse 12:8 brings us back to our beginning: "Vanity of vanities, says the Preacher; all is vanity."[10] The many images of the decrepitude of old age are final nails banging the main thesis home. We have been round the Preacher's world; the condition that human beings must call home is as futile at the return as it was at the setting out.

12:9–14 Postscripts

In the opinion of Harvey H. Guthrie, Jr., the end of the Book of Ecclesiastes consists of two postscripts.[11] Verses 12:9–11 may be the commendation of one of the disciples of Qoheleth. Note that the province of the Preacher was proverbs — traditional wisdom in maxim form. It is hard to think that the words of the Preacher would have pleased those less radical and able to doubt than he — that is, most of his contemporaries. Verse 12:11 has striking implications: This teacher (shepherd) of wisdom, and perhaps many other teachers, conceived of the teacher's task as furnishing both goads (whips) and nails (secure points, on which one might hang one's behavior).

The second postscript or appendix, verses 12:12–14, appears to be the work of a more pious editor. The second part of verse 12:12 is famous among well-educated students, especially around the time of examinations. In the context of Qoheleth, it implies that even the pursuit of wisdom and learning is futile. Verse 12:13 is more constrained and traditional than the view that has obtained in most of the book. Certainly fear of God has been prominent, but keeping the commandments has barely surfaced. The last verse has the odor of sapiential orthodoxy, and perhaps it was added to soften the skepticism that predominated in the body of the work. The author of the body of the work is far from certain that the rectification promised in verse 12:14 manifestly comes to pass. For the canonical text, however, Torah had to carry that assurance. If the Word of God did not prove to be the reward of the just and the punishment of the wicked, the Law would seem terribly vulnerable. "Exactly," Qoheleth might have said.

HISTORICAL BACKGROUND

For James L. Crenshaw, Qoheleth extends a line of reflection that begins modestly with Proverbs, deepens in Job, and then realizes that more radical questions remain.[12] If the work in fact was collected late, in the period of Persian or even Greek rule, it may well have been influenced by materials such as those we now find in Proverbs and Job. The author certainly deals with a God who is the creator and judge of the world, but little that is distinctively Israelite about this God leaps from the page. We can argue that precisely a background of covenantal theology would make for the skepticism of Ecclesiastes, on the hypothesis that the main voice we hear is of a person who finds little confirmation of the presence of the God of Abraham, Isaac, and Jacob in daily experience. The argument from silence (few references to the God of the covenant), however, is notoriously weak.

Safer, then, is the cosmopolitan background that we have considered when discussing other sapiential works. Qoheleth expresses a probing of human experience that may not have originated in Israelite circles but was considered acceptable there, perhaps because of the stimulus it offered to think more deeply about how divine providence was working, in a time when the Exile was still a vivid memory and dramatic prophets were few. It is clear that "God" provides the Preacher both a way out of the futility he finds in human achievement (although admittedly this is a negative way: God cannot be understood), and a further difficulty: How does "God" square with injustice? At times the negativity of Qoheleth seems to approach mystical maturity, as we noted in commenting on verse 3:11.

Yet on the whole God is rather distant from the main line of reflection, and the basic lesson that the Preacher bequeaths is not to expect very much from human affairs—a rather Stoic bequest.[13] Presumably the audience whom Ecclesiastes had in mind either was familiar with this sort of advice or showed itself especially in need of it. We can find Egyptian proverbial literature that is similarly restrained, and several schools of postclassical (Hellenistic) Greek philosophy took such a view.

LITERARY INTENT

Qoheleth, then, may be witness to a biblical decision to appropriate some of the wisdom of the nations, in an attempt to deepen the Israelite venture in wisdom and probe more fully the implications of human mortality. As well, it probably was written to fill out the insights of the Israelite wisdom writers and take into fuller account the dimension of doubt and skepticism that mature trust in God ought to have sounded. Job left this matter unresolved, not thinking through the wholesale challenges to meaning that the experience of injustice and the delay of divine judgment carry within themselves. Qoheleth adds the reflections of one who has been bent on finding pleasures, satisfactions in work, or just a stance in the world that might evade death and the pall it can cast. As we noted, death is the force that regularly anchors the Preacher's skepticism. Because death washes away all that a person was and accomplished, it raises the question, "Is anything worthwhile?" Equally, death tends to reduce the wise person and the fool, like the rich person and the poor person, to a flat equality. In the grave, or returned to dust, the corpse does not boast of its knowledge or flaunt its silver goblets.

Like Job, Qoheleth finally refers the whole mystery to God. Even if we brush aside the references to divine justice that seemed ritualistic rather than well thought out, we find the Preacher confessing that God is inscrutable (and so perhaps hoping that God has meanings that do not succumb to death). But the reference to God, and the surety that God is in heaven to make all things right in the world, is much more muted and negative than what Job offers. If the problem in Job is the lack of connection between the arguments for God's justice and the charges of experiential injustice that Job makes, the problem in Qoheleth is that the negative way of pointing to God's present, confounding, challenging mystery is so slimly sketched or so tentatively indicated. This way assuredly is present, but only the careful will mark it well and only the religiously mature will be able to make it into a straight path to confidence and joy.

For that reason Qoheleth is a dangerous work and so another tribute to the courage of the canonical editors of the Bible. They were willing to let the enemy come right into their treasury of authoritative writings and make its best case.

Indeed, traditionally Qoheleth was read in the synagogue at the Feast of Booths when temporary dwellings were erected. Again and again reflective readers have found it a canonical challenge to any smugness of religious faith and a salutary challenge to all our images of God.

LASTING SIGNIFICANCE

In this regard, lasting significance of Qoheleth cannot be separated from the lasting necessity for the negative way of approaching God. The Eastern religious traditions, especially the idealistic schools of Hinduism and Mahayana Buddhism, made the negative way their central path. Seeking an ultimate Brahman or Buddhanature, they realized very well that nothing empirical could furnish the unconditionedness and perfection that such realities denoted. So they chanted "neti, neti": "Not this, not that." Whether they pointed to the left or to the right, anything that their eye could behold was not the ultimate.

We find nearly the same language in the (positive) negativity of a Western mystic such as John of the Cross. His "nada" mainly refers to objects of desire — we must strip ourselves so that we do not try to place our security or satisfaction in anything created — but it implies that all finite beings are provisional and relative. Western theology of this sort did not call creation illusory or deceptive, as Eastern philosophy sometimes did. But in both cases a twofold intuition combined to orient the believer away from absorption in the world.

The first portion of the intuition was that nothing worldly can give full satisfaction or can come without bringing pain after it. This is the intuition of Qoheleth, as well as the intuition of the Buddha's first noble truth: All life is suffering. (We might call the Preacher's "vanity" the suffering of the spirit when it realizes that anything it finds attractive soon proves unfulfilling.) The second portion of the central intuition is that creation must have sprung from a source that exceeds human ken, a source whose mystery keeps obscure the question of from where human beings have come, to where they are going, and in what they might find the satisfaction of the best desires apparently built into their minds and hearts: the longings to gain full intellectual light and full emotional warmth.

If we place this warning against absorption in the world in the context of the whole Hebrew Bible, it both does and does not sound familiar. It does sound familiar, inasmuch as the call of Mosaic religion to be faithful to God entailed a rejection of idolatry and worldly ensnarements. Similarly, the prophets called for a depth of religion that would see how mercy and justice rooted in the transpragmatic reality of God. The other wisdom writings, finally, called for bowing before the divine intelligence running the universe and not thinking that any human guile could suffice.

Yet there is also a new note in Qoheleth, a skepticism and insistence on futility that previously were suppressed. Relatedly, there is a call to live in the present, taking what decent pleasure we can, that previously would have been run out of town. Qoheleth bespeaks a greater length of human experience, and a more sophisticated analysis of wealth and power, than either Torah or the Prophets. It is more clear-eyed and emotionally controlled, although also less imaginative and creative. But the final significance of Qoheleth may well lie in its sanctioning a flinty everydayness that few natural or historical thunderstorms could upset. "Remember death," Qoheleth intones (sounding like the late medieval Thomas à Kempis). "Honor the mysterious shroud that death throws around all human enterprises, without ceasing to refer final judgments to God, and you will seldom be unpleasantly surprised."

GLOSSARY

Eisegesis   Reading one's presuppositions into a text.

Hedonism   Devotion to pleasure, carnal satisfaction.

Misogynism   Hatred of women; antifeminism.

Ontology   The study of being or existence.

Oxymoron   A combination of contradictory or incongruous terms — for example, a wise fool.

Transpragmatic   More than simply practical; idealistic.

STUDY QUESTIONS

1. What are the ironies entailed in attributing Qoheleth to King Solomon?
2. What is the most central basis for the Preacher's theme that all is vanity?
3. Is the Preacher's call to enjoy food and drink more praiseworthy or more problematic?
4. Is it legitimate to move from the perception of life's futility to a judgment that it would be better never to have been born?
5. What are the assets and the liabilities in the negative way of treating the divine transcendence?
6. What does verse 6:12 do to the ethicist's project of mapping out the good life?
7. How radically does Qoheleth depart from the theologies of Deuteronomy and Second Isaiah?
8. Why would you like, or not like, to have been apprenticed to King Qoheleth as your teacher?

NOTES

1. See R. B. Y. Scott, *Proverbs, Ecclesiastes*. Garden City, N. Y.: Doubleday Anchor Bible, 1965, p. 165.
2. See James L. Kugel, "Ecclesiastes," in *Harper's Bible Dictionary*, ed. Paul J. Achtemeier. San Francisco: Harper & Row, 1985, pp. 236–37.
3. See Harvey H. Guthrie, Jr., "The Book of Ecclesiastes," in *Wisdom Literature and Poetry*, ed. Charles M. Laymon. Nashville: Abingdon (Interpreter's Concise Commentary), 1983, pp. 249–57.
4. See Roland E. Murphy, O. Carm., *Wisdom Literature*. Grand Rapids, Mich.: Eerdmans (The Forms of the Old Testament Literature), 1981, p. 128.

5. See James L. Crenshaw, "The Shadow of Death in Qoheleth," in *Israelite Wisdom*, ed. John G. Gammie et al. Missoula, Mont.: Scholars Press, 1978, pp. 205–16.

6. Scott, *Proverbs, Ecclesiastes*, p. 221.

7. See Graham S. Ogden, "The Mathematics of Wisdom: Qoheleth iv 1–12," *Vetus Testamentum*, 34 (1984), 446–53.

8 See R. N. Whybray, "Qoheleth the Immoralist? (Qoh 7:16–17)," in *Israelite Wisdom*, pp. 191–204.

9. See Scott, *Proverbs, Ecclesiastes*, p. 247.

10. See Graham S. Ogden, "Qoheleth xi 7–xii B: Qoheleth's Summons to Enjoyment and Reflection," *Vetus Testamentum*, 34 (1984), 27–38.

11. See Guthrie, "The Book of Ecclesiastes," p. 257.

12. See James L. Crenshaw, *Old Testament Wisdom*. Atlanta: John Knox, 1981, p. 126.

13. See John G. Gammie, "Stoicism and Anti-Stoicism in Qoheleth," *Hebrew Annual Review*, 9 (1985), 169–87.

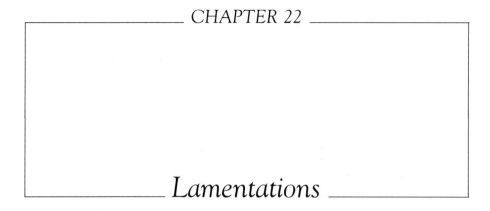

CHAPTER 22

Lamentations

TEXTUAL ANALYSIS

The Book of Lamentations is a series of poetic dirges over the fall of Jerusalem in 586 B.C.E. Traditionally it was attributed to the prophet Jeremiah, but current scholarship disputes this on the ground that the views of Lamentations sometimes conflict with the views expressed in Jeremiah.[1] Still, most scholars relate Lamentations to the period of the fall of Jerusalem, when Jeremiah was active, although the present text probably was written and preserved by survivors in Judah. We treat the book in five parts, following the present chapter division:

1:1–22	"Is There Any Pain Like My Pain?"
2:1–22	"The Lord Became Like an Enemy."
3:1–66	Everyman
4:1–22	The Account of a Survivor
5:1–22	A Prayer[2]

1:1–22 "Is There Any Pain Like My Pain?"

The first four chapters of Lamentations are alphabetical acrostics that use each of the twenty-two letters of the Hebrew alphabet. The style of the whole book suggests dolorous poetry used in religious ceremonies. From the very beginning of the work (in Hebrew it is named from its first line, "Ah, how"), the tone is mournful. Jerusalem after the capture and destruction wrought by the Babylonians is emptied, widowed, reduced to the status of a vassal. Personifying the city as a suffering female, the author imagines her nights as bitter with unconsolable weeping. It is a time when the enemies of Judah are in the ascendant. Where there were festivals, now there is but desolation and suffering.

Verse 1:5 explains this suffering as punishment from God for the multitude of Judah's transgressions. Princes and princesses alike have had to flee. Memory calls to mind how things were before this disaster, but that only increases the taste of wormwood the gloating of the enemy brings. Verses 1:8–9 may refer to idolatrous religious practices, which the prophets regularly symbolized as sexual infidelity and uncleanness, but this is not certain. Verse 1:10 reflects disgust at profanations of the Temple.

Verse 1:11 echoes the physical sufferings that siege and captivity brought. From verse 1:12 the personified city is in a self-pitying mood, making the fall of Jerusalem the worst case of suffering in the annals of human memory. Note that this fate is understood by the personified Jerusalem as punishment from God, who has been angered by Judah's defects. Rather impressively, the city both laments various hardships that came with capture and confesses that the Lord was within his rights to inflict them. The "lovers" of verse 1:19 is metaphorical for the foreign nations with whom Judah sought alliance against Babylon. By verse 1:20 the city has moved from description through confession (verse 18) to direct address to God, and the lamenting has become a petition for help. There is an implicit repentance, and verse 1:21 shows hope that the Lord will one day turn the tables and punish the enemy. (This suggests that the confession that the punishment was well deserved is not the whole story.) The chapter ends with a winningly honest reason why God should come with aid: "for my groans are many and my heart is faint."

2:1–22 "The Lord Became Like an Enemy"

Whereas chapter 1 gives a largely personal, emotional account of the sufferings of captured Jerusalem, chapter 2:1–10 are more objective and descriptive. Once again God is the ultimate source of the destructions visited, coming in hot anger and acting as the prime warrior of the enemy's army, but by now we have a dialogue among several voices trying to come to grips with this fact. Verse 2:5 speaks of palaces destroyed and strongholds laid in ruins. In verse 2:6 the references are to holy places broken and ruined. What had been Zion, the holy mountain where king and priest joined through God's favor, has now become a place where no worship arises. The concern for the demise of sacrificial religion suggests that Lamentations came from priestly circles, and the theological equation of punishment with sin recalls the Deuteronomistic convictions. Verse 2:8 pictures the wrecking of city walls and ramparts. In verse 2:9 gates, bars, rulers, law, and prophets are all broken or inoperative. The picture is of a city and a way of life completely wrecked, as though someone had first thrown sand in a great machine to bring it to a halt and then had carted away its key parts.

Verse 2:11 again shifts gears, moving back from objective description to personal lament. The poet breaks down and weeps. From the scene in verse 2:10 we infer that elders and maidens continued to live in Jerusalem (not all went into Exile), but that their life was sad and desolate. Verse 2:12 suggests a state near famine. In verse 2:13 the poet turns to the city in apostrophe. As in many of the

Psalms, the scorn and derision of Judah's enemies are an especial burden. The long-standing threat of the Lord mentioned in verse 2:17 is vague enough to fit any legal or prophetic sanction that Jerusalem's shortcomings had called forth. Implied in the charge to call upon the Lord (verses 2:18–19) is the possibility that this sort of prayer might bring him to change his mind and work deliverance. Although the poet has seen little comfort for Jerusalem, he has been able to come up with a cause of action: Going to God. Verse 2:20 paints the starkest picture yet: cannibalism and the murder of God's representatives. We should also note the shift of address from Zion to God. The slaughter that the Babylonians effected is depicted in verse 2:21. Chapter 2 thus ends on a note of terror: On the day of God's anger, babes recently dandled on the knee met their end.

3:1–66 Everyman

The middle chapter of Lamentations has the general structure of the two prior chapters, but its individual verses are shorter, and every group of three verses begins with the same letter in alphabetical order. The voice here is mainly in the first person, but the speaker is using his own feelings to epitomize the general desolation. Moreover, this is a new speaker: not the prior poet nor the female city but an individual male mourner. From the outset, the lament is that the Lord has (justly enough, but still painfully) laid on the rod of punishment. Among the memorable images are the bodily wasting and the broken bones of verse 3:4, the imprisonment of verse 3:5, the being like prey to animals of verse 3:6, the teeth grinding on gravel of verse 3:16, and the deprivation of peace and hope in verses 3:17–18. Whereas the focus in verses 2:1–10 was the physical desolation of Zion, here the focus is the personal desolation of an individual victim.

With verse 3:19 the speaker shifts from God the afflictor to God the one who may give deliverance, and he first recalls the pieties he has learned. Note in verse 3:22 the recall of the divine *hesed*, which offers a basis for hope. Verses 3:25–27 could occur in Proverbs or another work from wisdom circles. So could verses 3:28–30, although certainly they are marked by the state of conquest. It is hard to accredit the God of verses 3:31–33, after the prior testimonies to the divine wrath. The assurance of the Lord's passion for justice (verses 3:34–36) seems to veer toward the Babylonians, like a guided missile. The voice in the next three verses is again that of the standard sapiential writer, deep enough in its appreciation of the divine oversight yet, granted the speaker's presumed circumstances, strangely detached. In verses 3:40–42 this reflection bears the fruit of conversion and return to God. Verses 3:43–45 seem not to know whether to praise God for the punishment he has inflicted or to send up reproaches. The same with verses 3:46–48. Yet the tears of the next triad of verses seem genuine enough, and we do not have to get fanciful to lament the fate of maidens captured after a brutal siege. From verses 3:21 to 3:51 a cacophony of voices juxtaposes pieties and the present realities of the city.

The end of the next triad, and then the entire outburst of verses 3:55–57, sounds very much like a psalm of lament. How hope springs from confronting one's depths of desolation is one of the wonders of the spiritual life. In verses 3:61–63 the speaker falls back to complaint and dark spirits. At the end of the chapter, the mood stands midway between depression and peaceful confidence, as the Lord's punishment of Judah's enemies becomes an object enjoyable to contemplate. By this end, however, the man who at the beginning of the chapter could only lick his sores can now face God directly and acknowledge God's response.

4:1–22 The Account of a Survivor

Chapter 4 opens with more images of the wreckage and loss that have overtaken Jerusalem. Many of the figures again point to famine and slaughter—a generation of youth destroyed. Verse 4:6 seems hyperbolic, but the comparison of tragedies is hardly a measured enterprise and certainly the author has plenty of outrages to lament. In verses 4:7–8 the regret is aesthetic as well as civic: Something lovely has perished, thereby afflicting the spirit. The hunger and cannibalism depicted in verses 4:9–10 go far beyond aesthetic repulsiveness, however. Theologically, this extremity does suggest the hot anger of God mentioned in verse 4:11. Verse 4:13 rather pointedly accuses the prophets and the priests of having shed the blood of the righteous and thereby brought down the divine wrath. Presumably these offenders are the ones rejected in verses 4:14–16. The outside help that never came (verse 4:17) probably was expected from Egypt. Part of the shock expressed in verse 4:20 is that such disaster could come upon the people God called his anointed and kept under the shadow of his wings. Verse 4:21 reminds us of the bitter resentment that Edom aroused by joining the Babylonian sack of Jerusalem. Once again, contemplating justice against the enemy allows the author to end a chapter on an upbeat note.

5:1–22 A Prayer

The mental stance of the last chapter of Lamentations is a prayer of petition to God. The movement from chapter 4 to chapter 5 is, once again, from description to direct address to God. The first six verses remind God of the sufferings that the inhabitants of Jerusalem have undergone. This section does not indicate that God imposed such sufferings justly. Verse 5:7, in fact, pushes the guilt off on prior generations. To verse 5:14 the picture is of various outrages and crimes wrought by the captors. Verse 5:15 shows the spiritual consequences: "The joy of our hearts has ceased; our dancing has turned to mourning." Verse 5:16 does link the fall of political sovereignty with the sins that Jerusalem committed. The main theme of chapter 5, from verses 5:1–5:18, however, is lament at present circumstances. The pivot from these circumstances to the unshakable sovereignty of God is interesting. We might say that by walking the negative way of political oppression the author has better appreciated the invulnerable rule of God. Verse 5:20 implies the covenantal relationship and asks God to remember his people. Verse 5:21 starts to get up enthusiasm for renewed intimacy with God (and so renewed prosperity), but this trails off abruptly in the final verse of Lamentations, certainly setting the conclusion on a downbeat: "Or has thou utterly rejected us? Art thou exceedingly angry with us?" The last four verses encapsule the combination of despair, guilt, and hope with which the entire book resounds.

HISTORICAL BACKGROUND

Lamentations obviously presupposes the fall of Jerusalem in 586 B.C.E. and familiarity with the conditions that followed there.[3] It seems to be a book for and by survivors in Judah, rather than exiles in Babylon, and so is evidence of ongoing "Jewish" life in Judah. More religiously, it presupposes the covenantal theology and an understanding of suffering as a punishment for sins. The priests and prophets who failed to keep the people immaculate are accounted most responsible for the disaster. Lamentations assumes that God is well within the divine rights to allow or direct such affliction, yet it retains the right to beg deliverance from God. So even though its reflections on suffering are not the most profound of the Bible, the book does show how many people might have felt and responded. Raising their voices to God, they may well have gained comfort from making sure that God knew their grievances in some detail and was reminded of better times, when both their own performance and the divine steadfast love made the covenantal relationship a thing of joy and material flourishing.

LITERARY INTENT

Lamentations clearly was written to express with full poetic eloquence the desolations felt immediately after the Exile. Psychologically, this allowed people to vent their pains and so perhaps to lessen them. If these dirges served liturgical occasions, they could have enabled people to ceremonialize their sufferings and thereby experience some catharsis. Canonically, this suggests that Lamentations follows on Ecclesiastes, the most skeptical of biblical books, and that its more general neighborhood is the wisdom literature that pondered God's governance of the world. Only certain verses in Lamentations (2:20–22, 3:1–18) explicitly question the divine justice, although many others perhaps do so by implication. The general outlook seems more Deuteronomistic than Jobian. Still, both the event upon which Lamentations focuses and the pain to which it gives voice do raise questions about why Jerusalem should have fallen and what such a comedown of God's fairest city should be taken to signify.

Brevard Childs has interpreted this book as mediating between the specific event of the fall of Jerusalem and the language of faith appropriate for dealing with suffering generally.[4] Norman K. Gottwald has stressed that the fall of Jerusalem was part of the most decisive shift in fortunes, from Israelite autonomy to a subsequent Jewish colonialism (existence largely in subservience and often apart from Judah).[5] Lamentations testifies to the inner correlatives of this outer shift in fortunes. While memories of the fall of Jerusalem were still painfully fresh, its poetic authors gave expression to the shrinking of elan and hope that Conquest had brought. Because the Exile haunted Jewish memory ever after, Lamentations contributed to a perennial appreciation of the sufferings that faith might not be able to avoid.

LASTING SIGNIFICANCE

The lasting significance of Lamentations probably is the stimulus it carries to consider what religious responses to catastrophe are most appropriate. And perhaps Lamentations is effective in carrying this stimulus because it is a poetic outpouring rather than a reasoned theological treatise. Certainly we have seen the value of Psalms from this point of view, and what we find in Lamentations coheres well with what we find in many of the psalms. Israelites felt they had full rights to take their complaints and sufferings to their God, even if turning to face their God might bring back upon themselves accusations of sinfulness and demands for repentance.

This forthright, emotion-laden address to God and so responsibility of listening to the divine response distinguishes Lamentations from most of the wisdom literature that is its canonical context. Certainly Qoheleth does not address God in such a full-bodied way, nor with such overtones of the entire history of the covenantal relationship between God and Israel. Even Job, who is eloquent in venting his grievances, moves in a mood of reflection and talking to himself or to the air (or, in the dialogues, to his unsympathetic friends), more than in a mood of petitionary prayer. Lamentations therefore reminds us of the earlier strata of biblical piety, in which the people are always grumbling and Moses is always having to intercede for them to avert the divine wrath. We do not sense that the authors of Lamentations were, like Moses, the intimates of God, but we do sense that these outbursts were not the first calls upon God that they had ever made.

The issue that Lamentations thus clarifies is whether fully living religion does not have to address God or the ultimate mystery of life in a way that leads to an interpersonal exchange and tests the reality of "God." How to test such a reality rightly can be, of course, a further and difficult issue, but the authors of Lamentations, like most religious people (who are not philosophers), tend to address it "by walking." That is, they tend just to do it: take themselves to God, raise their minds and hearts to heaven or wherever else they think God resides, and speak with God as to a king or a friend or a parent.

Probably even the simpler among such people know that they are talking to deeper parts of themselves, as well as to the mystery of their beginning and their beyond. Probably they are well aware that simply by bowing and singing they are giving their bodies a chance to express their spirits and so comfort them. But there is a further dimension, which too much philosophy of religion does not know how to sound, and that is the sense that such outpourings regularly receive a response. We catch hints of this each time we see the authors of Lamentations moved to express repentance or to take responsibility for their fate. We see it even more clearly in such passages as Lamentations 3:55–66, where hope of help and redress rises from the ashes of despair. We can describe such passages in psychological terms, of course, speaking of instinctive self-help. We can note with the theologians that experience always offers data for both hope and despair. But a fully adequate exposition of the experiences of prayer has to remain open to the possibility that the divinity can and does in fact touch people from within and so heal the rents in their souls, so resurrect their senses of possibility.

GLOSSARY

Apostrophe   Addressing a person (or a personified thing), often one not present.
Catharsis   Purging, letting out one's emotions for the sake of restoring peace.
Liturgical   Pertaining to public, official, ritualized worship.

STUDY QUESTIONS

1. Do the lamentations of chapter 1 seem appropriate to the situation in Jerusalem after the fall to Babylon or excessive?
2. What are the main implications of understanding suffering as a punishment for sin?
3. How are the verses of chapter 3 that express hope related to the verses that depict fearful suffering?
4. Why are the priests and the prophets singled out for special criticism?
5. How significant is it that the final verse of Lamentations asks whether God has utterly rejected his people?
6. What does petitionary prayer show about a people's lived theology?

NOTES

1. See David A. Glatt and Jeffrey H. Tigay, "Lamentations of Jeremiah, the," in *Harper's Bible Dictionary*, ed. Paul J. Achtemeier. San Francisco: Harper & Row, 1985, pp. 544–45.
2. See Delbert R. Hillers, *Lamentations*. Garden City, N.Y.: Doubleday Anchor Bible, 1972, p. ix.
3. See Harvey H. Guthrie, Jr., "The Book of Lamentations," in *The Major Prophets*, ed. Charles M. Laymon. Nashville: Abingdon (Interpreter's Concise Commentary), 1983, pp. 217–18.
4. See Brevard S. Childs, *Introduction to the Old Testament as Scripture*. Philadelphia: Fortress, 1979, p. 596.
5. See Norman K. Gottwald, *The Hebrew Bible: A Socio-Literary Introduction*. Philadelphia: Fortress, 1985, p. 423.

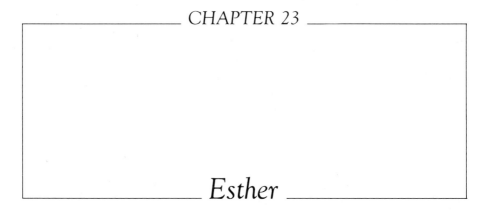

CHAPTER 23

Esther

TEXTUAL ANALYSIS

Scholars tend to regard the Book of Esther as a novella (short, perhaps historical, novel) from the time of Persian rule over Israel—from 400 to 322 B.C.E. The book has been termed a festival legend because it explains the Jewish feast of Purim, which celebrates the deliverance of the Jews of the eastern diaspora from persecution. We schematize the Hebrew text as follows:

1:1–22	Introduction to the Persian Court
2:1–23	Esther Becomes Queen
3:1–4:17	Haman's Wicked Plot
5:1–8:2	Esther Thwarts Haman
8:3–10:3	Happy Ending[1]

1:1–22 Introduction to the Persian Court

The story opens with a description of the historical context: the reign of Ahasuerus (Xerxes I: 485 to 464 B.C.E.), centered in the capital of Susa. It is the third year of this kingship (482 B.C.E.), and the king is giving lavish banquets that demonstrate his great wealth. Verse 1:8, telling us that no one was compelled to drink the royal wine, may defer to Jewish sensibilities about banqueting with pagans. Verse 1:9 suggests that the Persians segregated women from men at social events. The king's desire to exhibit the queen, Vashti, reveals the limitations on any such

THE PERSIAN EMPIRE
550–336 B.C.

THRACE

GREECE
Athens °
Sparta °

CAPHTOR

MEDITERRANEAN SEA

AEGEAN SEA

SCYTHIA

BLACK SEA

Sardis °

LYDIA

CAPPADOCIA

Pteria °

ARMENIA

CASPIAN SEA

MEDIA

L. VAN

L. URMIAH

Ecbatana °

Arbela °

BEHISTUN
ROCK

TIGRIS R.

EUPHRATES R.

ASSYRIA

Haran °

Damascus °

Tyre °
Sidon °
Samaria °
Jerusalem °
Gaza °

CYPRUS
(KITTIM)

Cyrene °

LIBYA

Memphis °

EGYPT

NILE R.

Thebes °

Elephantine °

RED SEA

Elath °

Dumah °

ARABIAN DESERT

Tema °

PROBABLE
ANCIENT
SHORELINE

Nippur °
Babylon °

BABYLON

Opis °
Susiana °
Susa °

PERSIA

Pasargadae °
Persepolis °

PERSIAN GULF

EMPIRE EXTENDS
EAST TO INDIA

363

segregation, and her refusal and the king's subsequent anger afford us a mischievous glimpse of the Persian battle between the sexes. That the king had seven eunuchs as chamberlains fits the ancient Near Eastern pattern, according to which a king kept a royal harem.

The disobedience of Vashti raises the specter of women across the entire Persian realm getting uppity, so the king and his counselors go into heavy conference. Vashti is to be deposed as queen, as an object lesson to all Persian females. Commentators have observed that this opening chapter is both humorous and ironic, because it sets the king up to replace one willful queen only to get another who will manipulate him more skillfully. The chapter plays on the binds into which men get themselves, when too much wine combines with too much ego. It also gives us a sense of the effective system of communications that existed in Persia, so that later decrees of the king may credibly spread across the land. After noting these effects, Carey A. Moore supplies the literary consequence: "But above it all looms the fascinating figure of Xerxes, the mighty king, mastered by wine, defied by his queen, and ill-advised by his friends. Xerxes stands desperately in need of a good consort."[2]

2:1–23 Esther Becomes Queen

Chapter 2 shows us precisely the fulfillment of this need. The word goes out and a sort of beauty pageant is arranged, that the king may obtain a replacement for Vashti. We cut to Mordecai, a Jew deported during the Babylonian captivity, and his orphaned cousin Hadassah (in Persian, Esther). Esther, who is beautiful, gets entered in the competition (how willingly we are not told). She pleases the chief eunuch, who helps her campaign, and Mordecai paces outside the harem, worrying how things will turn out (they have not revealed that Esther is Jewish). Esther wins the contest, because she pleases the king more than any of the other women, and the king sponsors a feast in honor of her succession to Vashti as queen. Esther further gains the king's confidence by bringing him knowledge, gained through Mordecai, of a plot against him, which leads to the hanging of the conspirators. At the end of chapter 2, then, Esther is well established.

3:1–4:17 Haman's Wicked Plot

Ahasuersus (in another display of bad judgment?) appoints Haman as his chief official, before whom all of the king's subjects are to bow. This Mordecai refuses to do, apparently on the grounds that it would violate his religious convictions (that one should express total submission only to God). Infuriated, Haman resolves to destroy all the Jews in the Persian kingdom. He plans a pogrom, designed to eliminate this people who stand apart from the rest of the populace, and he gets the king to agree to his plan. The decree goes out, through the network we have already glimpsed, and the prospect for the Jews is bleak: murder and the confiscation of their property. Looking back from the Nazi holocaust of Jews during World War II, such anti-Semitism seems sickeningly familiar.

Verse 3:15 seems designed to show the irrationality generally perceived in this plan: "And the king and Haman sat down to drink [we already suspect that the king drinks too much, and not with the best companions]; but the city of Susa was perplexed." The casting of lots to determine the day of execution has a patina of religiosity about it, but the deeper effect (wrought by the God of the Jews?) is to delay matters enough to give Mordecai and Esther a chance to work out an escape.

Mordecai, hearing of the decree, dons the garb of mourning and sends up a bitter lament. Everywhere else in the kingdom, other Jews follow suit. Esther begins an investigation of this mourning, and Mordecai makes known to her messenger both the plan of slaughter and the financial profit Haman hopes to reap from it. In Esther's reponse we first learn of a strange custom forbidding, on pain of death, unbidden entrance into the king's inner court (perhaps as a matter of security, but also as a reflection of the sacral status of Persian kings). Mordecai tells Esther that she will have to own up to her Jewish identity. Verse 4:14 is the most theological line in this generally simply human drama: "And who knows whether you have not come to the kingdom for such a time as this?" Esther reminds us of Joseph, given power in the household of a foreign king ruling over Jews, but in the story of Joseph the theme of divine providence is much more explicit.[3] Taking Mordecai's words to heart, Esther proposes a fast, both outside the palace and inside, to dramatize the situation, after which she will risk the king's wrath and death by approaching him unbidden. We may read her resignation — "and if I perish, I perish" (verse 4:16) — as a considerable act of both identification with her people and abandonment of herself to fate (God). Esther's character has thus developed such that she has changed from being a a passive pawn to being a courageous woman (in the line of Deborah, Judith, Naomi, and others) who takes charge.

5:1–8:2 Esther Thwarts Haman

Sandra Beth Berg, among others, has considered the theme of reversal to be a key to the literary build of the Book of Esther.[4] In chapters 5–7 Esther makes Haman's plan turn back upon him. Esther dares to come into the king's presence unbidden, but immediately he pardons this offense, because of the favor she has found "in his sight" (verse 5:2)—an ambiguous phrase that implies that he is smitten with her beauty, but that also hints that she pleases him for more substantial reasons. The king allows Esther any request, and she asks for a dinner to which Haman will come. Her first request seems merely preliminary: A second dinner will be the crucial thing. (The prolonging of dining and drinking both reverses the original situation that led to the king's banishment of Vashti and adds a certain solemnity to the plot, because a royal banquet was a formal and freighted occasion.) Haman interprets his invitation as a mark of the king's favor, but the continued disobedience of Mordecai siphons off his joy. So Haman accepts the counsel of his wife and friends to get the king to have Mordecai hanged (so that Haman may enjoy his dinner in complete contentment—a nice sketch of his character).

Providentially, the king cannot sleep, and in whiling away night time he is reminded of the boon Mordecai did him in uncovering a plot against him. From verse 6:6 the tricky twist on which the reversal of the fortunes of Mordecai (and all the Jews) and Haman depends starts to unfold. Haman, full of himself, assumes that the king's desire to honor someone (in fact, the king's benefactor Mordecai) pertains to himself. So he describes a full course of tributes and benefits. The king then directs Haman to confer all of these honors on Mordecai. Haman complies, but then he hurries home mourning (as Mordecai previously mourned). The wife and friends of Haman, rather strangely, predict that, because Mordecai is Jewish, he is bound to prevail over Haman. Although the Book of Esther is not overtly theological, statements such as this make it plain that a main theme is God's providential care of the Jews, which even the Gentiles can suspect.

Haman goes off to the banquet, but now under a portentous cloud. The king asks Esther to request of him what she will, and she asks for the life of her people and herself (which the plan of Haman threatened). The king turns to wrath when he learns that Haman is the source of this threat (his memory seems bad, because he himself was in on the original plot). Poor Haman, groveling before Esther, is so unlucky (or so sure to be punished by God for his wickedness) that the king takes his posture for an assault on the queen. Verse 7:8 is a peculiarly eloquent line: "As the words left the mouth of the king, they covered Haman's face." Presumably the meaning is that Haman was as good as dead, but the images play off the ancient belief in the sacred power of the words of such officials as kings and priests. Note how this word, carrying death, is contrasted with the prior word of Mordecai that spared the king's life. The gallows that Haman had prepared for Mordecai becomes the site of his own death. The king is restored to good humor, Esther inherits the house of Haman, and Mordecai replaces Haman as the bearer of the king's signet ring (seal of authority). So the reversal has become complete.

8:3–10:3 Happy Ending

It appears, however, that the plan of Haman to liquidate the Jews still has to be dealt with. Esther wins the king's permission to present her plea that the decree to carry out this plan be revoked. In verse 8:8 the king grants this petition, instructing Esther and Mordecai to write an official revocation. The final notion of this verse, that an official edict of the king cannot be revoked, is ambiguous, because it implies both that the new decree is certain to be carried out and that the old decree should have stayed in force. The decree that Mordecai writes and has spread throughout the Persian kingdom is dated to the traditional feast of Purim. Its main provision is that Jews may defend themselves against any who would presume to attack them. Chapter 8 ends with Mordecai's enjoying great status, all the Jews' rejoicing at their new good fortune, and many people's converting to Judaism, because it seems the way that history is favoring.

Chapter 9 shows the Jews getting revenge on their enemies and those who plotted their destruction, again in the time of Purim. Note in verse 9:10 the remark that the Jewish avengers did not plunder their enemies — they were working justice, not excess or new wrongdoing. This remark is repeated in verse 9:15, after the description of the hanging of the ten sons of Haman. (This hanging makes an elevenfold [Haman and the ten sons] reversal of the evil that Haman planned against Mordecai but never got to execute. The very excess shows us the divine favor toward the Jews that the Book of Esther wants to celebrate.) The Jews in the provinces take rich revenge on their enemies, slaying tens of thousands (but also not plundering, see verse 9:16).

Verse 9:19 explicitly connects these military victories with the feast of Purim that now recalls them. The letters of Mordecai to all the Jews in the empire directing them to keep Purim as a feast are said to have explained the purpose of the festival as follows: "They should keep the fourteenth day of the month of Adar and also the fifteen day of the same, year by year, as the days on which the Jews got relief from their enemies, and as the month that had been turned for them from sorrow into gladness and from mourning into a holiday; that they should make them days of feasting and gladness, days for sending choice portions to one another and gifts to the poor" (verses 9:21–22).

Verses 9:24–26 explain the name for the feast, connecting it to the lot (Pur) that Haman had cast to settle the plan to destroy the Jews. The following verses somewhat repetitiously enforce the tradition of celebrating Purim, tying it to the authority of Queen Esther and Mordecai, the chief minister. Chapter 10 testifies to the great power of King Ahasuerus and the great honor of Mordecai, making the Book of Esther end as though it were the Book of Mordecai, the man whose high status in Persia brought honor to all of his people.

HISTORICAL BACKGROUND

Although the general historical situation sketched in the Book of Esther is plausible, such details as the lengthy banquet, the disobedience of Vashti, the letter ordering all Persian men to be masters in their households, the approval of a plan to exterminate the Jews, and the tolerance of the Jews' counter-slaying all seem improbable.[5] Relatedly, the effort to Judaize the feast of Purim may well cover over the non-Jewish origins of this feast, which came to be accepted as a time when heavy drinking was permitted. Current scholarly opinion favors a Persian origin for this festival, but nothing has been definitely proven. We have no record of Mordecai, Esther, Haman, or Vashti from other historical sources, which suggests that although these characters need not violate the general outline of the historical experience of the Jews in the time of the king Xerxes I, they probably are fictional. Finally, this work assumes the existence of the feast of Purim, and probably it assumes as well some memory of victories over enemies in the Persian empire.

LITERARY INTENT

The Book of Esther appears to have been written mainly to explain the rise of Purim and to entertain readers with a rousing story of Jewish triumph over bad fortune during the time of Xerxes I. Later generations undergoing trying times could read this book as a reminder that God is able to bring prosperity out of apparent disaster, as they could read in the story of Joseph in Egypt. Esther and Mordecai are further examples of a heroine and a hero, or even saviors, who served their people by using their talents and wits. Finally, we should not downplay the entertainment value of the plot, all the more so when we place it in the context of celebrating a traditional holiday (whose origins and rationale could have used some shoring up).

In commenting on the apparent goals of the editors who entered Esther in the canon, Brevard Childs has stressed a bracketing of moral judgments, such that the actions of the main characters, whether in gaining influence over the king or in executing revenge on enemies, are neither praised nor condemned. Second, he sees a deliberate fusing of secular and religious dimensions, perhaps as a lesson in how to read contemporary history. Third, small touches, such as associating Purim with generosity to the poor (verse 9:22), appear designed to elevate the feast and improve its overall effect. Last, Childs quotes with approval the theological assessment of Robert Gordis that Esther is concerned to make the preservation of the Jewish people a religious obligation of the first magnitude.[6]

LASTING SIGNIFICANCE

Before we discuss the lasting significance of the Book of Esther, we must consider the opposition that it faced prior to gaining canonical status. First, a potential conflict existed between the feast of Purim whose establishment Esther celebrates and the principle of Leviticus 27:34 that all festivals should have been established by Moses. This principle also did not hold in the case of Hanukkah, however, so apparently it was not hard and fast. Second, overt references to either God or such central features of biblical Judaism as the Temple, sacrifice, and the Law were absent. In addition, the prominence of vengeance made the book unpalatable to many Jews. Third, the rabbinic authorities may have found a way out of these difficulties by understanding Esther as a "historicized wisdom tale." This might have explained the absence of ritualistic features and careful concern for religious law. Last, the book's likeness to Qoheleth (in being relatively secular or humanistic) could have enabled it to ride the coattails of Qoheleth into general acceptance or holy writ.[7]

    In broader context, the lasting significance of Esther no doubt derives from the light it sheds on biblical understandings of providence and from the questions it raises about revenge. The book celebrates a reversal of fortunes through which the chosen people were saved from destruction. Although it does not describe this reversal in terms of dramatic interventions of God, such as had occurred in the Exodus, it does give a positive interpretation of how the initiative of several Jews combined with historical fortune to bring about preservation. The lesson is that providence helps those who help themselves—human beings are the hands of God. Indeed, the message proclaimed by both the Book of Esther and the feast of Purim was that the people had survived and triumphed over their enemies. Because that had happened in the time of Xerxes, later generations might hope that it could happen to them, were they to use their wits and gain influence with the ruling powers.

GLOSSARY

Chosenness   See election (chapter 7). Israel as God's special people.

Diaspora   The dispersion or existence outside Israel that characterized many Jews as exiled.

Pogrom   Murderous attacks, especially of Jews in Gentile environments (for example, in the Polish ghettos).

STUDY QUESTIONS

1. How does the behavior of Vashti suggest satirical intentions in the opening chapter of Esther?
2. What does the plot against the Jews underscore in the characters of the Persians Haman and Ahasuersus?
3. How does the theme of reversal help to unify the story?
4. What is the significance of the fact that a harem queen became a Jewish savior?
5. What are the advantages and the liabilities in celebrating feasts such as Purim?

NOTES

1. See W. Lee Humphreys, "Esther," in *Harper's Bible Dictionary*, ed. Paul J. Achtemeier. San Francisco: Harper & Row, 1985, pp. 280–82.
2. Carey A. Moore, *Esther*. Garden City, N.Y.: Doubleday Anchor Bible, 1971, p. 14.
3. See Sandra Beth Berg, *The Book of Esther*. Missoula, Mont.: Scholars Press, 1979, pp. 123–65.
4. Ibid., pp. 103–13.
5. See Moore, *Esther*, p. xlv.
6. See Brevard Childs, *Introduction to the Old Testament as Scripture*. Philadelphia: Fortress, 1979, p. 606.
7. See Moore, *Esther*, p. xxxiv. Moore also points to Esther's likeness to Job.

CHAPTER 24

Daniel

TEXTUAL ANALYSIS

Scholars now tend to treat the Book of Daniel as "apocalyptic" ("revelatory") literature[1] and to date it to about 165 B.C.E.[2] (The tales in chapters 1–6 may be earlier, perhaps from the third century B.C.E.) The present text is clearly a composite work, because the stories of chapters 1–6 differ in style from the revelatory visions of chapters 7–12. Moreover, whereas chapters 1 and 8–12 are in Hebrew, chapters 2–7 are in Aramaic. Finally, we should note that the Greek (Septuagint) version of Daniel (accepted as canonical by Roman Catholics) includes several incidents missing from the Hebrew Bible. All in all, then, Daniel is a fairly complicated work, and present-day scholars still debate not only the details of its probable composition but even whether we should more regard it as prophecy or as apocalyptic[3] (a genre that developed in the Second Temple period and is represented by the Book of Revelation in the New Testament, as well as by several extracanonical texts, such as the apocalypses of Enoch).

We treat Daniel following its two main divisions:

1:1–6:28   Stories of Daniel
7:1–12:13   Visions of Daniel

1:1–6:28 Stories of Daniel

Drawing on recent studies of folklore by structuralist scholars, John G. Gammie has noted that the six self-contained stories in the first half of the Book of

Daniel all display the same pattern of rewards for fidelity to God. Specifically, each story involves a royal decision threatening to faithful Jews, the resolve of such Jews to cling to their God, trials, a successful outcome, and a new, favorable decision of the king.[4]

The story in chapter 1 deals with the training and testing of youths. The time is said to be the reign of Jehoiakim (606 B.C.E. — few scholars take Daniel 1–6 as accurate history), when Babylon threatened Jerusalem. Along with holy vessels of the Jews, the Babylonian King Nebuchadnezzar has carried back to Shinar (Babylon) some of the elite of the Jewish youths. Among them is Daniel, who will be the hero of this book. (In Ezekiel 14:14 a Daniel is treated with Noah and Job as a paragon of righteousness, and 1 Chronicles 3:1 mentions a Daniel who was the second son of David.) Daniel spurns the good food from the king's table, thinking it would defile him. (He is sensitive to Jewish dietary laws.) Living only on vegetables and water, Daniel and his friends look better than youths served the king's food and so satisfy the chief eunuch, who has become favorably disposed toward them. (Note the parallel to Esther.) Daniel and the others distinguish themselves for wisdom (Daniel, like Joseph, can interpret dreams), so the king prefers them to the magicians of his own court. At the end of the introductory chapter, then, we are primed to think that Daniel will act as an exemplar of Jewish wisdom.

Chapter 2 focuses on a dream of King Nebuchadnezzar that Daniel must interpret. The king challenges his own Chaldean resource people to tell him his dream and interpret it, on pain of death for failure. They claim that this challenge is beyond any human being. Daniel and his companions, being classified as wise men, fall under the king's edict to destroy all supposed wise men, and on learning why the king has issued this decree Daniel asks for an audience with the king, to interpret his dream. After prayer, Daniel receives a vision of what the king has dreamed. Note the sapiential motifs in Daniel's prayer of blessing and thanksgiving (verses 2:20–23): All wisdom comes from God, who can reveal what otherwise is mysterious and hidden.

Brought before the king, Daniel refers his knowledge to God and then gives the king the particulars of the dream, which concerned a frightening image broken and carried away by the wind. Daniel interprets the different parts of the image as kingdoms that will succeed Babylon. (The pattern suggests Babylon, Medea, Persia, Greece, and the Kingdom of God.) The lesson is that all human kingdoms are fragile and will finally crumble, while the reign of God alone is ultimate. By making Babylon the most noble kingdom (gold), however, Daniel is able to flatter Nebuchadnezzar. Because Daniel has known his dream and interpreted it pleasingly, the king falls on his face and honors the God who gave Daniel this wisdom. Daniel becomes a chief ruler over all of Babylon, and his fellow youths also gain high positions. The moral is that trust in the wisdom of God gives both protection and good fortune.

Chapter 3 tells of a trial by fire. Nebuchadnezzar has a great golden image cast and commands all of his people to pay it religious homage, on pain of being cast into a fiery furnace. Three of Daniel's Jewish companions, now occupying high positions, are denounced for disobeying the king's command and failing to worship the golden image (which to them would have been idolatry). They place their trust in God, whom it may please to deliver them from the promised fire.[5] Nebuchadnezzar is enraged and has them cast in. To his astonishment, both the three who disobeyed and a fourth, like a son of the gods (a preserving angel), are preserved in the furnace unharmed. Once again the king bows low to the God of the Jews who has worked such a wonder, forbidding any speech against him and promoting the three who were saved. The Lord can not only deliver wisdom about the dreams of kings and the future course of history, he can also intercede to save his people when they remain faithful to him and refuse to commit idolatry, even to keep their lives.

In chapter 4 King Nebuchadnezzar goes mad, but this too serves to magnify the God of the Jews. Addressing all the peoples of his kingdom, the king praises the most high God (whose kingdom alone is everlasting) and narrates how Daniel alone could interpret his dream. This dream, however, was not of the image described in chapter 2 but of a great tree. Daniel, now the chief of the king's "magicians," heard how the great tree, reaching up to heaven and benefiting all, was fated by the cry of a heavenly "watcher" to be cut down. In verses 4:15–16 the tree becomes a human being sentenced to lose his mind. Verse 4:17 gives the reason for this angelic decree: the manifestation of the power of the Most High over all earthly rulers. Daniel blanches at the meaning of the dream, but, encouraged by the king (and diplomatically making this meaning ill for those who hate the king), he interprets the lofty tree as the king himself, whose realm has grown great. The angelic decree is that Nebuchadnezzar will in fact be brought low, to the demented state of a beast grazing the grass. For a full time decreed by God, the king will need to learn the greater power of God, before his kingdom is restored to him. Note the religious conclusion of verse 4:27, which combines both prophetic and sapiential aspects: "Therefore, O king, let my counsel be acceptable to you; break off your sins by practicing righteousness, and your iniquities by showing mercy to the oppressed, that there may perhaps be a lengthening of your tranquillity."

The fate predicted for the king comes to pass. While he is congratulating himself on the might of the Babylon that he has built up, a voice from heaven announces the departure of the kingdom from him, and he is driven to the fields where he eats grass like an ox. When his reason returns, the king lifts his eyes to heaven and praises the Most High who is the real ruler of all creation. Having so honored right order or the way things truly are, Nebuchadnezzar is restored to his earthly rule. The final verses of chapter 4 suggest the wisdom that he learned through suffering and humiliation: "Now I, Nebuchadnezzar, praise and extol and honor the King of heaven; for all his works are right and his ways are just; and those who walk in pride he is able to abase" (verse 4:37). We see how well these sentiments fit the convictions of the sapiential school that predominates in the Writings.

The story in chapter 5 depicts a feast given by King Belshazzar, son of Nabonidus, the last of the Babylonian monarchs (ruled 556 to 539 B.C.E.). The writer may want to imply that Belshazzar was only standing in for his absent father and threw a big party while he had the chance to play king. Using the vessels taken from Jerusalem was of course offensive to Jews, and verse 5:4 implies that Belshazzar and his friends were crude idolaters. The miraculous writing of the fingers on the wall is in keeping with the dramatic style of the first chapters of Daniel (dreams, fiery furnaces), where God disrupts the natural order of things at a snap. (This is not typical of the sapiential outlook, according to which the regular running of the cosmos displays the divine wisdom.) The Babylonian wise men having failed, the overwrought king is offered the interpretational skills of Daniel, proven since the time of Nebuchadnezzar (three reigns back). Note in verse 5:11 the honorific titles bestowed on Daniel, whom the whole book is presenting as a personification of Jewish wisdom.

In verse 5:17 Daniel dismisses the king's gifts, implying perhaps that wisdom is its own reward, and certainly implying that Belshazzar is a lightweight. Daniel reminds this king of the fate that overcame Nebuchadnezzar, when he puffed himself up. Belshazzar is imitating the folly of his predecessor, praising idols and ignoring the true God ("in whose hand is your breath, and whose are all your ways"; see verse 5:23). Daniel interprets the supernatural writing as a prophecy of the demise of Babylon, because Babylon was found wanting by God. Although the king rewards Daniel for this interpretation, the king is slain and, true to the prophecy, the Medes gain control of Babylon (actually the Persian Cyrus conquered Babylon in 538 B.C.E.). As in his previous discernments of the flux of worldly kingdoms, Daniel here is accredited with insight into how God runs history. We should note both the exclusivity of this knowledge, which only a Jewish wise man possesses, and its ethical dimension: Kingdoms rise and fall in part because of their honoring or failing to honor the true God (an expansion of the Deuteronomistic view of Israel's historical fortunes).

Chapter 6 deals with the famous incident of the lions' den. Daniel is retained by the new regime as a high official, one of three to whom the provincial governors are accountable. Indeed, the king would have raised Daniel to premier rank, and even the enemies of Daniel can find no crack in his wisdom. As a Jew, however, Daniel was vulnerable to the charge of preferring his God to the lordship of the king. Much as enemies of the Jews manipulated Xerxes against them in the Book of Esther, those who resent Daniel get Darius to establish an interdict on petitioning any force other than the Persian king.[6] (On its own terms, Persian theology considered the king the main mediator between heaven and Earth, much as Egyptian theology considered the pharaoh the main mediator or point-of-connection.)

Daniel learns of this decree, but he continues his practice of praying to his own (the true) God in the direction of Jerusalem (the true center of the world). Daniel's enemies denounce his practice of praying three times a day (as a law-abiding Jew should) and call it a violation of the king's decree. (As in Esther, such a decree is irrevocable, in testimony to the sacral effect of the royal word.) Verse 6:16 presents the king as grieved by this outcome and hoping that the God of Daniel may save him from the lions' den. Indeed, in verse 6:18 the king fasts, certainly as an act of mourning and perhaps as an act of petitioning Daniel's safety. Note in verse 6:20 the description of Daniel as servant of the living God (see also verse 6:16). Implied is the contrast between the lifeless divinity of idols and the vital power of the true God.

After time with the lions, Daniel announces that he has been preserved by the angel of God, and this manifestation of his righteousness (he has passed a trial of both his God and himself) gives the king grounds for punishing those who had brought Daniel to such a pass. Needless to say, the lions are not held back in their case and they perish, as wicked infidels should. The decree of Darius is similar to other outpourings of praise for the living, ever-enduring, truly wise God (see Daniel 2:20–23, 4:3, 4:34–35), increasing our impression that a major goal of the first half of the Book of Daniel is to trumpet the superiority of the God of the Jews and the consequent superiority of the wisdom that comes from adhering to this God.

7:1–12:13 Visions of Daniel

The second half of Daniel continues the miraculous motif we have seen in the stories of the first half, but genuine apocalyptic now enters in. The notion is that Daniel receives heavenly information about how history is to unfold and how Jews are to gain relief from their sufferings. Chapter 7 is pivotal, and although scholars debate the unity of the chapter, they agree that much of its imagery comes from the mythology of ancient Ugarit.[7]

Daniel sees in a dream four beasts: lion, bear, leopard, and ten-horned devourer. As in the image dreamed by King Nebuchadnezzar in chapter 2, the point seems to be to present the succession of empires: Babylon, Medea, Persia, and Greece. Often the ten horns are associated with the ten rulers who succeeded Alexander the Great, and the little horn is considered to be Antiochus Epiphanes, who began persecuting the Jews in 168 B.C.E. The "Ancient of days" in verse 7:9 is God, the blinding, deathless holiness that rules everything from heaven. The one in verse 7:13 like "a son of man" who comes before the Ancient of days clearly is to be the representative of heaven who will have dominion on Earth (and so will supplant pagan rulers). The writers of the Christian gospels drew on this tradition to depict Jesus as "the son of man." Most likely the original authors of Daniel had the archangel Michael in mind.[8] Note the promise to Daniel in verse 7:18 that those holy to God (his people, the Jews) will possess the everlasting kingdom (the realm of truth on Earth).

The scene in verse 7:22 of the coming of the Ancient of days to judge for those holy to God delivers the payoff that most apocalyptic writings seek: assurance that the sufferings of the just will end and God will punish the evil-doers. (Anyone who has read the Book of Revelation in the New Testament will have noted both the dependence of Revelation on Daniel and the parallels in psychology.) The general background of this part of Daniel is the upset that produced the revolt of the Maccabees in 167 B.C.E. (although Daniel advocates patient waiting for divine deliverance, rather than military revolution). So the first vision of Daniel promises deliverance by God from the enormities of Antiochus Epiphanes, who was persecuting the Jews and aiming to destroy their faith. Way back at the time of Babylonian rule, when Judah first came under the yoke of pagan oppression, a man of God foresaw the course of history and received divine assurance that God holds all earthly powers in his hand and will not suffer his people to be persecuted forever — that is the literary logic of the vision.

Chapter 8 focuses on a vision that Daniel received in Susa, the Persian capital. He saw a ram and a he-goat, two figures of the Zodiac. The best interpretation of their fight probably is the defeat of the Medes-Persians by Greece. The great horn (verse 8) is Alexander the Great. The little horn (verse 9) again is Antiochus Epiphanes, who desecrated the Temple in Jerusalem (casting the truth of Jewish monotheism down in favor of pagan idolatry). The angelic prediction is that this oppression will last only a stipulated time, until the sanctuary is restored (it was in 164 B.C.E.). Daniel then gets the help of the angel Gabriel and understands that his vision pertains to the end of time, which we perhaps best understand

Herakles, Greek hero. Greek, 480–459 B. C. E. *(The Nelson-Atkins Museum of Art, Kansas City, Missouri [Nelson Fund])*

as the time of God's deliverance of his people from their oppressors (rather than the time when cosmic history as a whole will cease). Gabriel is explicit about the meaning of the vision in verses 8:20–26, but the deeper import is the assurance that time lies in God's hands. Note the implication at the end of the chapter that the vision was a burden to Daniel, as many of the prophets experienced their revelations to be. He is appalled by his vision and does not understand it, which may be the authors' way of warding off any too-literal reading of the symbolism that would try to take away the mysteriousness of the divine plan according to which history unfolds.

Chapter 9 amounts to an interpretation of the prophecy of Jeremiah and a prayer. Daniel is probing the holy books, trying to determine how long the desolations of Jerusalem (which began with the fall to Babylon in 586 B.C.E.) are to last. After reckoning seventy years (perhaps a symbol of a full period), Daniel turns to God in penitential spirit and confesses that Israel has sinned (and so merited the punishments of captivity). Note the place of the Mosaic Law as the standard of proper conduct, and note also the certainty that God has all righteousness on his side. Still, God can, for his own sake, relieve the sufferings of Israel, and Daniel prays that God will. (We have to remember that the audience for the Book of Daniel, living around 165 B.C.E., would have been equating the sufferings of exilic Jerusalem with their own sufferings under Antiochus Epiphanes.)

For his piety, Daniel receives a visit from the angel Gabriel (angels become quite prominent in Second Temple literature, perhaps due to Persian influence, but due as well to a sense that God is more distant and prophets [human intermediaries] are fewer than they were in more prosperous times). Gabriel extends the period of desolation to seventy weeks of years (490), but he implies that this penitential time is due not only to sins but also to the preparations necessary "to bring in everlasting righteousness, to seal both vision and prophet, and to anoint a most holy place" (verse 9:24). Gabriel goes on to predict further troubles, the climax of which probably bears on Antiochus Epiphanes, after which will come the (divinely decreed) end of such abominable desolations as those that Antiochus worked in desecrating the Temple.

The final chapters of the Book of Daniel continue this apocalyptic concern with the last days, when God will liberate his people. Daniel now understands the true word given to him about the conflicts that are to come. The vision by the Tigris is reminiscent of the vision of Ezekiel by the Chebar. The man whom Daniel sees is a celestial being, perhaps Gabriel again, and the imagery about him suggests priestly holiness. The impact upon Daniel conveys the power that "the holy" can exert, when psyches are sensitive to it. Chapter 10 stresses Daniel's acceptance by heaven, which of course enhances the value of his message. Verse 10:13 implies conflict between the angels who represent Persia and the angels of the true God. In this vision the authors take pains to stress the distance between sinful, finite humanity and even the emissaries of the holy God. Generally, the message that Gabriel leaves is that he and Michael are fighting against Persia (and later Greece) on behalf of the Jews.

Chapter 11 is another sketch of the historical unfolding of the pagan kingdoms who conquered Judah. The mighty king of verse 11:3 probably is Alexander the Great. After the death of Alexander in 323 B.C.E., his kingdom divided into a northern realm ruled by the Seleucids and a southern realm ruled by the Ptolemies. The Antiochene rulers were Seleucids, who both battled the Egypt-centered Ptolemies and wrought alliances with them. Verses 11:21–45 appear to concern Antiochus IV Epiphanes, the ruler contemporary with the writing of the Book of Daniel and a great burden to the Jews. Note in verse 11:31 the worst outrage: "Forces from him shall appear and profane the temple and fortress, and shall take away the continual burnt offering. And they shall set up the abomination that makes desolate."

This latter was Antiochus's act of setting up a pagan altar in the Temple of Jerusalem and dedicating the Temple to Zeus Olympius in 167 B.C.E. The prophecy given to Daniel predicts a division among the Jews, some of whom (those who violate the covenant) will be seduced by Antiochus, while wiser others will remain faithful. Once again, we have to realize that Daniel is describing in supposed prospect what was occurring in the 160s through the revolt of the Maccabees (see verses 11:33–35). Antiochus is described as an egomaniac opposed to the true God of the Jews and hell-bent for Hellenization. From verse 11:40 on the predictions look to the future of the rule of Antiochus and, in contrast to the great detail in the descriptions of present happenings, are very sketchy. In fact, they miss the mark: Antiochus did not gain Libya and Ethiopia and then perish.

Chapter 12 foresees Michael's delivering the Jews from a terminal period of trouble. Note in verse 12:1 the figure of a (heavenly) book, which symbolizes divine providence and control of history. Verse 12:2 seems to depict a general resurrection of the dead and final judgment by God — a new notion in the canonical

Jewish books.[9] Chapter 12 therefore is looking beyond the termination of the specific subjugation to Antiochus and speaking of the end of history as a whole. This is "eschatology," concern with the final things, with a vengeance. It is a leap out of history uncharacteristic of prior Israelite theology, and it shows the psychic extremes in which apocalyptic literature flourished. The authors responsible for chapter 12 of Daniel found history so oppressive that they loved to contemplate the end of God's patient experiment with human beings.

In verse 12:5 Daniel meets two more angelic beings along the river (perhaps we are meant to think of the waters of Genesis 2:14). The time that the angel gives until the end is liable to several interpretations, the most literal of which would be three and a half years. What "the shattering of the power of the holy people" in verse 12:7 would be also is debatable. Perhaps the safest interpretation is that when Israel, God's people, is truly in extremis, with its existence or identity in mortal peril, God is bound to terminate history and deliver Israel. Verse 12:8 says that Daniel did not understand these words, and we could take a lesson from that statement. Daniel is to go on his way, trusting that such prophecy is sealed up by God and will become operative when God wishes. Despite all of its itch to foresee an end of Antiochus and a liberation of Israel, then, the Book of Daniel retains a proper respect for the mystery of divine providence. It will not be literal or definitive about how history either will proceed or will end, because that would violate the Bible's own fundamental convictions about the chasm between the creator and human creatures.

Verse 12:10 creates a contrast between the purified and the wicked that draws upon Israel's wisdom traditions and yet is typically apocalyptic. In their warfares, both the canonical and the extracanonical apocalypses tend to create a dualism of saints and the wicked. This is dramatically effective, but it furnishes strong proof that the apocalyptic mentality rather consciously has left ordinary existence, in which sainthood and wickedness stand together cheek by jowl, to dwell in a utopian realm — a "no place" that can instruct us precisely because it does not suffer the complexities and admixtures of any place fully human. The final calculations of the chapter are rather confused, as though when initial predictions of the end were not fulfilled new predictions kept pushing it further into the future. Note that at the conclusion of the Book, Daniel is to go his way, rest, and take his allotted place at the end of the entire scenario: counsel to live matter of factly and let God's plan unfold as it will.

HISTORICAL BACKGROUND

One scholarly interpretation of the literary composition of Daniel speaks of the stories in chapters 2–6 as the oldest materials, perhaps composed in the third century B.C.E. Chapter 7 may well have been composed at the outbreak of the persecutions of Antiochus. These six chapters in Aramaic (an international language of the time) are less nationalistic than the Hebrew chapters 8–12. Chapter 1, which was perhaps translated into Hebrew from Aramaic, serves as an introduction to the whole and may well have been the last part composed.

The most obvious background that Daniel presupposes is the oppressive regime of Antiochus IV Epiphanes. Apparently some Jews felt so threatened by efforts of this ruler (and perhaps even more, by the efforts of Hellenized Jews) to suppress their traditional religious culture and make them participate fully in Hellenistic culture that they thought God would terminate history rather than allow such a disaster. The revolutionary movement spearheaded by the Maccabees put this sentiment into military form: better dead than Hellenized. Daniel speaks for those who prefer to wait upon God's dispositions of history, and perhaps we should associate its more quietistic position with the sectarians of Qumran, who from the mid-second century B.C.E. to the mid-first century C.E. lived apart from the Jewish mainstream and sought by their purity to become worthy of an eschatological age. On the other hand, many Jews were more favorably inclined toward Hellenistic culture, as long as it allowed them to retain their traditional monotheism. John G. Gammie has recently spoken of a Hellenization of Jewish wisdom in the Letter of Aristeas, a well-regarded writing from about 150 B.C.E.[10]

A final presupposition of the Book of Daniel is the traumatic experience of captivity to pagan rule, both Persian and Babylonian. The literary conceit of the book places Daniel in various of the Babylonian and Persian courts. In the first half of the book, this exilic existence is not overly oppressive, for although Daniel and the Jews are threatened by different stupidities of the king or hostile intrigues of their pagan enemies, their wisdom and worth make them indispensable to the king. In the second half of the book, however, foreign rule, in the person of Antiochus Epiphanes, has become intolerable, and this recalls the bitterness of the first, paradigmatic enslavement under Nebuchadnezzar in 586 B.C.E. The mood that we found in the Book of Lamentations plays in the penitential outpourings of Daniel in chapter 9. The original sack of Jerusalem becomes the backdrop for the contemporary despoiling wrought by Antiochus.

LITERARY INTENT

The purpose of the stories of the first half of Daniel seems clear enough. The authors want to extol Jewish wisdom, display the sway of the Jewish God over the foreign kingdoms, and suggest that God will preserve his people from peril, if need be by miracles. All of this, of course, would have been consoling to people trying to make their way under foreign rule and feeling threatened with religious perse-cution. The visions of the second half of Daniel partake of the purposes of apoc-alyptic, which generally are to console those undergoing oppression and promise them that God will soon bring history to an end, vindicate his people, and pass judgment on all evil-doers.

If we study the editorial changes apparently worked to produce the canonical version of Daniel, we can surmise that the final intent was to move beyond concern with the oppressive regime of Antiochus Epiphanes and project into the future a new age that would mean the end of all persecution. In such a projected future, God's elect would be separated from the wicked and a general judgment would be passed.[11] This canonical concern distinguishes Daniel from prior prophets and makes apocalyptic reliance upon God's termination of history a new regulative note. Thereafter, a certain despair about history and reliance upon divine termi-nation became a religious option worth considering. Certainly one could not con-sider it the only option, without blocking out the rest of the Hebrew Bible, but one had to pay the futility of history, the meaninglessness of the flux of worldly empires, its due. Only God stood outside of very fallible human history, and only God could consummate history so as to vindicate his saints.

LASTING SIGNIFICANCE

The spotlight that the Book of Daniel casts on miracles and eschatology remains illuminating today. One who reads the history of religion with attention to the charismatic and millennarian groups is bound to be impressed by both the direct impact that Daniel had in Western religion and the regularity with which the human spirit, East and West, considers trying to leap out of history. For example, what Daniel proposes in its final eschatological scenario seems the psychological equivalent of Indian yoga, insofar as the latter expresses a desire to defeat the time and flux that imprison the human spirit.[12] The Buddhists who awaited the coming of Maitreya, like the Muslims who awaited the Madhi or the hidden Imam, were people despairing about the possibility of altering history by human means, people awaiting a divine alteration.

We could speculate about Marxist and technological equivalents to these religious efforts to transmute history and human nature, and a full historical investigation would certainly call for chapters on alchemy, again both Eastern and Western. The fact is that a dogmatic Marxism, insisting that history is rumbling toward a classless society, is more like a religion that insists God has the future sealed up in a heavenly book of regulative decrees than it is different from such a religion. A dogmatic technology, insisting that behavioralist psychology, or genetic engineering, or nuclear power puts the future into human hands and guarantees deliverance from oppressive crime, sickness, or poverty, labors in the same utopian realms. The Book of Daniel, like the Book of Revelation in the New Testament, is valuable for displaying the hopes and so the truths of the recurrent movement of the human spirit toward transtemporal security, but it is also very dangerous, because this recurrent movement of the human spirit has often proven highly destructive.

Human beings have been most inhumane to one another, have most treated one another like wolves, when they have forgotten their common creaturehood, have forgotten the ineluctible mysteriousness of the genuine God, and have failed to realize that one can never serve the genuine God with murderous means. Because the Bible has texts that might seem to justify these attitudes, we have to read the Bible in the round, making sure that the many other texts that urge just the opposite get the greater weight. Daniel, then, is most significant when we let it tutor us in the twofold conviction that God is greater than history and that we have no warrant from God to alter human affairs by ungodly means.[13]

GLOSSARY

Angel A messenger of God; a heavenly being in the divine service.

Hellenization Process of becoming enculturated by the ideals derived from Alexander the Great.

Quietistic   Peaceful to the point of culpable inactivity.

Son of man   Either simply a human being or the heavenly figure of Daniel 7:13.

STUDY QUESTIONS

1. What are the parallels between the role of Daniel and the role of Esther?
2. Why is the Book of Daniel so interested in the sequence of pagan kingdoms?
3. What is the significance of the praise of the God of the Jews that Nebuchadnezzar comes to confess?
4. How do the stories about Daniel encourage fidelity to Torah?
5. Explain the symbolism of the Ancient of days and his angels.
6. Why is Daniel concerned with the prophecy of Jeremiah?
7. Why is Antiochus Epiphanes so hated?
8. What is the function of the resurrection of the dead treated in chapter 12?
9. Discuss the psychology of apocalyptic literature.
10. In what sense is it irreligious to pray for an end to history? In what sense is it religious?

NOTES

1. See John J. Collins, *Daniel: With an Introduction to Apocalyptic Literature*. Grand Rapids, Mich.: Eerdmans (The Forms of the Old Testament Literature), 1984.
2. See John J. Collins, "Daniel, the Book of," in *Harper's Bible Dictionary*, ed. Paul J. Achtemeier. San Francisco: Harper & Row, 1985, pp. 205–6.
3. See Collins, *Daniel: With an Introduction to Apocalyptic Literature*, pp. 1–24. See also E. W. Nicholson, "Apocalyptic," in *Tradition and Interpretation*, ed. G. W. Anderson. Oxford: Clarendon Press, 1979, pp. 189–213.
4. See John G. Gammie, *Daniel*. Atlanta: John Knox, 1983, p. 9.
5. See James A. Wharton, "Daniel 3:16–18," *Interpretation*, 39 (1985), 170–76.
6. See Shalom Paul, "Dan. 6,8: Aramaic Reflex of Assyrian Legal Terminology," *Biblica*, 65 (1984), 106–10.
7. See Gammie, *Daniel*, p. 71. See also Marc Girard, "Le semblant de fils d'homme de Daniel 7, un personnage du monde d'en haut: approche structurelle," *Science et Esprit*, 35 (1983), 265–96.
8. See Gammie, *Daniel*, p. 76.
9. See Antonio Bonora, "Il linguaggio di risurrezione in Dan. 12, 1–3," *Rivista Biblica*, 30 (1982), 111–25. See also James M. Lindenberger, "Daniel 12:1–4," *Interpretation*, 39 (1985), 181–86.
10. See John G. Gammie, "The Hellenization of Jewish Wisdom in the Letter of Aristeas," *Proceedings of the Ninth World Congress of Jewish Studies*. Jerusalem: World Union of Jewish Studies, 1986, pp. 207–14.
11. See Brevard S. Childs, *Introduction to the Old Testament as Scripture*. Philadelphia: Fortress, 1979, pp. 618–22.
12. See Mircea Eliade, *Yoga*. Princeton: Princeton University Press, 1970.
13. On the political implications, see Eric Voegelin, *The New Science of Politics*. Chicago: University of Chicago Press, 1952.

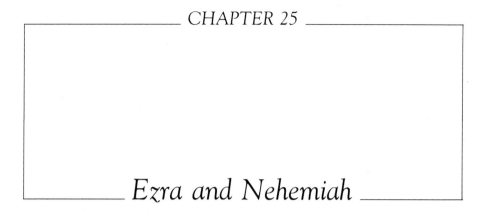

CHAPTER 25

Ezra and Nehemiah

TEXTUAL ANALYSIS

Until the time of the Christian scriptural scholar Origen (third century C.E.), the Books of Ezra and Nehemiah were considered a unit. Today scholars debate such basic questions as precisely when Ezra and Nehemiah worked and precisely what order the presently somewhat disjointed textual parts originally had. The text has passages in Aramaic (verses 4:8–6:18; 7:12–26), and throughout the Hebrew is influenced by Aramaic and Persian. Especially crucial to our view of what the books signify is the influence we accord the person or school responsible for 1 and 2 Chronicles (which precede Ezra and Nehemiah in the Christian Bible). A moderate scholarly view probably would be that although "the Chronicler" played a significant role, essential differences between Chronicles and Ezra-Nehemiah remain and so argue for some separation between the two enterprises.[1] We treat the text according to the following divisions:

Ezra	1:1 – 6:22	The Restoration of the Community
	7:1 – 10:44	The Mission of Ezra
Nehemiah	1:1 – 7:73	The Work of Nehemiah
	8:1 – 10:39	Responses to the Law
	11:1 – 13:31	Organizing the Community[2]

Ezra 1:1–6:22 The Restoration of the Community

If the proclamation of Cyrus occurred during his first year in control of Babylon, where the Jewish community was in exile, we may date it to 538 B.C.E. From the outset of the Book of Ezra, the rebuilding of the Temple in Jerusalem was considered to be ordered and guided by God. Note the theme that what Nebuchadnezzar had pillaged from the Israelites was now to be restored. Precisely who Sheshbazzar was and what he did as "prince of Judah" remain obscure.

Chapter 2 offers a census of those who returned from Babylon to Jerusalem. The reason for this listing remains unclear.[3] Certainly the general purpose of Ezra-Nehemiah is to narrate how the Israelites returned from Exile and rebuilt the center of their national life. Perhaps this census is meant to liken the project of returning and rebuilding the Temple to such other great movements as the Exodus and the Conquest of the promised land, which also entailed enumerations of the personnel involved (Numbers 1, Joshua 13–19). Note that several of the groups mentioned (priests, levites, temple servants) were connected with the Temple.

Chapter 3 describes the beginning of restoring the altar and the Temple. The atmosphere is religious and festive, as though the returnees were delighted to get back to their Mosaic obligations and resume the sort of worship that the psalms of David epitomized. The book of Haggai also deals with this time.

The conflicts described in chapter 4 probably reflect the antagonisms between those who had not gone into Exile and the returnees. Whereas Haggai focuses on the defects of the returnees, Ezra attributes the delays in rebuilding the Temple to the opposition of the "people of the land." (Many of those exiled had been from the upper classes, so a social clash may have existed between peasants and aristocrats.) The returnees considered this opposition party tainted by contact with foreigners and so less than fully Israelite.[4] Textual criticism suggests that verses 4:7–23 would better fit in Ezra 10 or Nehemiah 1. In heeding the advice of the informers and forbidding the work of rebuilding the Temple, Artaxerxes contradicts the decree of Cyrus and the Jeremian word of God with which the Book of Ezra began. The impression given is that, like most rulers, Artaxerxes was much swayed by the specter of discord among his subjects or dilution of his power. Verse 4:24 poses chronological problems, in that the Darius in whose reign Haggai and Zechariah worked preceded Artaxerxes.

Chapter 5 describes both the resumption of the rebuilding the Temple and the objections of the Persian provincial governors. In effect, it recapitulates the setting of the stage with which the book began. In chapter 6 Darius finds the original decree, reaffirms it, and agrees to underwrite the costs of the restoration from the treasury of the officials who had complained. The personal benefit that Darius foresees appears in verse 6:10: "that they may offer pleasing sacrifices to the God of heaven, and pray for the life of the king and his sons." Ezra presents Darius as a good man who appreciates the power and rights of the true God. In verse 6:14 Artaxerxes confusingly is listed among the Persian kings who sponsored the reconstruction. The date given in verse 6:15 for the completion of the Temple would be 516 B.C.E. The description of the celebration emphasizes the people's return to a Mosaic purity.

Model of the Second Temple and the city of Jerusalem at the Holyland Hotel, Jerusalem.
(Used with permission of the photographer, Robert L. Cohn)

Ezra 7:1–10:44 The Mission of Ezra

The story of the scribe Ezra would fit more coherently between chapters 7 and 8 of Nehemiah. In the present ordering, the effect is both to make the restoration of the Temple the backdrop for the work of Ezra and to make this portion of Ezra's career preliminary to the work he does associated with Nehemiah in Nehemiah 7–13. We are probably dealing with a text more interested in religious paradigms than straightforward history. Note that his genealogy links Ezra with Aaron and so with high priestly prestige. The seventh year of Artaxerxes (see verse 7:7) would be 458 B.C.E. If Artaxerxes II is meant, the date would be 398 B.C.E. Either way, the gap between the completion of the Temple and the work of Ezra is considerable. Ezra is presented as both skilled in the Law and loving to study and teach it. The letter of Artaxerxes frees Ezra to go from Babylon to Jerusalem and enrich the Temple. Verse 7:23 suggests that the king feared the wrath of the God of heaven and so was generous. The king gives Ezra sweeping authority in Syro-Palestine (the province beyond the river). The final verses of chapter 7 present Ezra's thanks to God for such providential help.

In chapter 8 we read of those who went with Ezra from Babylon to Jerusalem. Note in verses 8:21–23 the petition of God's protection, with the implication that this was a sacred exodus not relying on human arms. Ezra gives the priests charge of the gold and other treasures intended for the Temple. The returnees arrive successfully and greatly enrich the Temple.

When Ezra learns of the defilement of the Israelite community, both rank and file, through intermingling with the surrounding pagan peoples, he is appalled. Verse 9:4 judges the prior returnees (those who left Babylon shortly after 538 B.C.E.) to have proven faithless. The prayer of Ezra links this infidelity to the prior failures that caused Israel to fall into the hands of its enemies. Note the interest in a pure remnant expressed in verse 9:8. Recalling prior legislation against inter-marriage with impure foreigners (Leviticus 18:24–30, Deuteronomy 7:3), Ezra reaches the conclusion that the remnant given a new chance in his day must not repeat the sins of their forebears but keep themselves apart and pure.

Chapter 10 shows the people's embracing this conclusion and asking Ezra to guide them in a covenant to put away their foreign wives and children and re-dedicate themselves to God. The Book concludes with a description of how Ezra oversaw this purification and a list of the various Israelites who put away their foreign wives and children. The overtones are of the people's recovenanting with the holy God and making themselves again worthy of being his people.

Nehemiah 1:1–7:73 The Work of Nehemiah

H. G. M. Williamson views the scholarship about Nehemiah as follows: "It has long been recognized—and is today universally agreed—that substantial parts of the Book of Nehemiah go back to a first-person account by Nehemiah himself (or someone writing under his immediate direction). Broadly speaking, this material is to be found in Neh 1–7; parts of 12:27–43, and 13:4–31."[5]

Nehemiah 1:1 suggests that the year when Nehemiah learned of the sorry state of Jerusalem and those returned there from Exile was 445 B.C.E.[6] The prayer that Nehemiah offers is a remarkable specimen of postexilic piety that shows how love of the God of the covenant could combine with great sensitivity to infidelity to the Law and its supposed effects. Deuteronomy 30:1–5 is perhaps the text closest to the "word" mentioned in 1:8. As cupbearer to the king of Persia, Nehemiah would have been a servant of considerable status.

Like Joseph, Daniel, Esther, and other Israelites who gained favor and in-fluence at foreign courts, Nehemiah uses the royal power on behalf of his people. He will go with the king's letters of passage to rebuild Jerusalem. Verse 2:10 mentions the displeasure felt by non-Jewish subjects of the Persian king in the area around Jerusalem at the prospect of restoring the city. Ezra-Nehemiah feels com-pelled to buttress its program of separation from foreigners with evidences of such foreigners' hostility. After inspecting the wall of Jerusalem, Nehemiah tells the leaders of the Jewish community of the reconstruction he feels inspired by God to carry out and of the blessing given by king Artaxerxes. The non-Jewish opposition derides the project, justifying the judgment of verse 2:20 that they have no rights in Jerusalem.

The description in chapter 3 of the various rebuildings of walls carried out by different groups suggests that the people took to this work with some of the enthusiasm that went into the original construction of Jerusalem and the Temple. Sanballat (verse 4:1) is described in extrabiblical sources as the governor of Samaria. The prayer of Nehemiah in verses 4:4–6 is reminiscent of the curses and prayers for vengeance that we find in the prophetic literature and the psalms. The threats of their non-Jewish neighbors forces Nehemiah to organize his workers as soldiers as well as laborers. The God of his prayers takes on the lines of the old warrior God who was the first champion of the people (see verse 4:20). Rebuilding even the walls of the holy city has become a sacred cause.

Chapter 5 discloses both the economic difficulties of this period and the social injustices that had arisen. Nehemiah's wrath flames at the irony that Jews bought back from Exile and slavery should now be the victims of fellow-Jewish usurers. As in the Levitical sense that people have inalienable rights to their land and the prophetic sense that mercy is more important than economic profit, Nehemiah's analysis depends on an awareness that all rights come from God and that people should feel a solidarity more basic than the privileges that distinguish them. Note that in verse 5:15 Nehemiah attributes his feeling the need to give good example in this regard to fear of the Lord (a sapiential motif). His commission to rebuild the wall has expanded into a commission to care for the people of Jerusalem.

The stratagem of Sanballat and the other enemies shifts in chapter 6. Whereas previously they had tried to inhibit the work of rebuilding by ridicule and threats of attack, now they accuse Nehemiah of planning rebellion against the king of Persia. Nehemiah prays that God will strengthen his hands. He turns aside the scheme of the traitor Shemaiah, protesting that as a layperson (and perhaps, as a high servant of the Persian king, a eunuch) he could not fittingly enter the Temple.[7] Shemaiah and his cohorts are then shown to be but the latest in the long line of false prophets. The wall is completed, to great praise of God, but Nehemiah's enemies and their allies within the Jewish camp continue to threaten him.

Chapter 7 first sketches the discipline that Nehemiah proposes for safeguarding the restored Jerusalem and then gives another account ("genealogy") of those who had returned from Exile. Note in verses 7:64–65 the problem of authenticating dubious claims to rightful membership in the people. The chapter draws to a close with suggestions that the work of restoration had been rounded off: In the seventh month all were in their allotted places.

Nehemiah 8:1–10:39 Responses to the Law

Ezra reappears in chapter 8 (this section probably originally followed on Ezra 7–10). The scene suggests a reconsecration of the people to the Mosaic Law. Verses 8:9–12 are instructive: The people are told to rejoice in the hearing of the Law, not weep (when reminded of their failings or their recent inabilities to live as a people formed by the Law). Hearing that the Feast of Booths had been commanded for the seventh month, in which they now found themselves, the people renew the observance of Booths, which verse 8:17 says had long fallen into disuse. The whole reading of the Torah becomes a week of rededication and rejoicing, as at a new birth.[8] Chapter 9 renews the public confession of sins, perhaps on the model of the Day of Atonement. Note the positive tone of blessing God (verse 9:5). The prayer of Ezra blends praise of the creator of the natural world with remembrance of the history of salvation that God had worked, from the very beginnings of the people with Abraham and Sarah. The Exodus gets full remembrance, and although Ezra recalls the people's sins and hardness of heart (perhaps using an old synagogue prayer), the stronger motif is of God's steadfast love (verse 9:17). After recalling

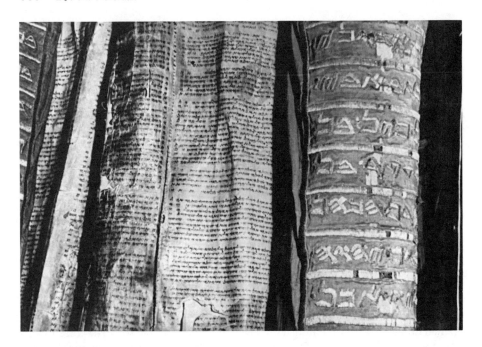

A revered Torah scroll of the Samaritans.   *(Used with permission of the photographer, Wolfgang Roth)*

the Conquest of the promised land, Ezra offers an epitome of the period of the kings and the prophets, when a pattern of apostasy, punishment, and regeneration obtained. All that the people suffered was justified by their wrongdoing, yet in verses 9:36–37 the scribe asks God to see the present plight of his people and act on their behalf. The covenant mentioned at the end of the chapter is apparently motivated by the conviction that if the people renew their fidelity their lot will improve.

Chapter 10 first lists the leaders who pledged themselves to this covenant and then suggests the terms to which the entire people pledged themselves. Having put away foreign wives and children, they agreed under curse and oath to observe the Mosaic Law. In addition to separation from foreigners, the key provisions were keeping the Sabbath, following the prescriptions for the seventh year (see Exodus 23:11 and Deuteronomy 15:1–3), and agreeing to support the Temple and those who serve it, by offering first fruits and tithes.

Nehemiah 11:1–13:31 Organizing the Community

Chapter 11 tells us that Jerusalem was reestablished as the practical capital and that measures were taken to assure it a sufficient population. The listing of specific people confirms our impression that Ezra-Nehemiah thinks of the reestablishment of Jerusalem and the people genealogically, as though it were another key phrase in the "generations" first treasured by Genesis. Chapter 12 continues this enumerating, summing up at verse 26 with the governorship of Nehemiah and the religious governance of the priest/scribe Ezra, as though this joint leadership were the seal. The dedication of the new walls occurs with great celebration, as befitted a refounding of a people. The liturgical refrains heard here and previously, along with the recall of David, suggest hopes for a return to the golden age when Jerusalem was the splendidly holy city that centered the chosen people of God. The willingness to detail the gates manifests the pride and love the rebuilding had occasioned. Verse 12:47 explicitly likens the time of Nehemiah to the time of David, perhaps because both sponsored liturgical music and splendid divine praise.

Chapter 13 brings the narrative to conclusion on the theme of separation and purification. The text in mind at the outset may be Deuteronomy 23:3–5, and the attitude exhibited is a striking fundamentalism. The offense of Eliashib was to give Tobiah, a foreigner, a place in the holy Temple. Nehemiah orders the place recleansed. In the absence of their zealous leader, the people have held back from the full generosity toward the Temple that they had pledged. Nehemiah's prayer in verse 13:14 that God reward him for the good deeds he has done on behalf of the Temple has the ring of a fighter grown weary. He has to chasten those who continue to profane the Sabbath, warning them that they risk the renewal of God's wrath. Verses 13:19–22 describe the practical steps Nehemiah took to safeguard the Sabbath (including threatening physical punishment [v. 21]), and this work, too, becomes a platform from which the reformer can ask God's remembrance and mercy.

As he had monitored the purity of the Temple and the observance of the Sabbath, so Nehemiah checks on the separation of the people from foreigners. Once again he finds backsliding and has to mete out punishments. Note how Solomon, the exemplar of kingly wisdom, has become the stock example of the evils to which mingling with foreigners can lead. The mentality behind Nehemiah's purifications is clearly expressed in verse 13:29: "Remember them, O my God, because they have defiled the priesthood and the covenant of the priesthood and the Levites." The reconstituted people are to focus themselves as a holy assembly that can properly worship and sacrifice to the awesomely holy God. The book ends with Nehemiah's proud claim that he cleansed the people of everything foreign, which he hopes will lead to God's remembering him for good.

HISTORICAL BACKGROUND

As mentioned, the historical background of Ezra-Nehemiah is somewhat obscure, so scholars still debate such matters as precisely when Ezra and Nehemiah worked, who preceded whom, and whether or not they overlapped. This relates to debates about the original structure of the text, which now seems disjointed. Particularly galling is our inability to establish a clear chronology and sequence for the two figures, scribe and reformer, that would enable us to understand their interaction.

Still, F. Charles Fensham has noted that Ezra-Nehemiah does shed some light on the period when Xerxes and Artaxerxes I ruled Persia (ca. 485 to 424 B.C.E.). He understands the work to be especially interested in showing the Samaritan (partly kindred, partly foreign) opposition to the rebuilding of the Temple and reconstitution of the Israelite people. Nonetheless, at least three hypotheses for the chronological relationship between the leading figures Ezra and Nehemiah retain support. The first and most traditional has Ezra arriving in Jerusalem in 458 and Nehemiah arriving in 445. One problem with this scenario is that Nehemiah says nothing in his memoirs about the reforms that Ezra the scribe carried out (Ezra 7–10) in 458. So, for example, the separation from foreign women described in Ezra 10 was apparently not effective in Nehemiah's time, for he considered inter-marriage a problem still to be solved. One solution to this difficulty with the traditional chronology is to posit that Ezra returned to Persia after his reforms, so that when Nehemiah arrived thirteen years later the problems had regrown. Ezra would then have returned to Jerusalem and helped Nehemiah during the latter's twelve years of governance and reform.

A second chronological hypothesis has Ezra arriving in Jerusalem in 428, during the second term of Nehemiah's governance. Proponents of this view tend to consider Ezra 7:8 a textual error and rewrite it as the thirty-seventh, rather than the seventh, year of the reign of Artaxerxes. Although this would make the association of Ezra and Nehemiah smoother, it implies that both Ezra 7–10 and the whole of Nehemiah should be reorganized. Another problem is that Nehemiah 13, which describes the second term of Nehemiah, makes no mention of Ezra.

A third hypothesis separates Ezra and Nehemiah completely, placing Ezra's arrival in Jerusalem in 398, during the reign of Artaxerxes II. Nehemiah would still have arrived in 445. The great problem with this hypothesis is that it renders the mention of Ezra in the memoirs of Nehemiah (Nehemiah 8–9) completely mistaken.

Fensham's own sketch of the historical background of Ezra-Nehemiah stresses the international politics of the period. He emphasizes the devastation of Jerusalem wrought by Nebuchadnezzar in 586, which both demolished the cult that had been the people's center and laid low the economy. The members of the community varied in their reactions to this situation, as they had varied in the time of Jeremiah on how to respond to the Babylonian threat. The conquest of Babylon by Persia, whose rulers appear to have been quite tolerant of ethnic diversity, allowed the Jewish exiles a chance to return, but only some of them seized it. Those who did return apparently received financial assistance from prosperous compatriots who remained in Babylon and Egypt, but their lives were still poor. This would explain the delays in rebuilding the Temple and the city. Ezra-Nehemiah would seem to concentrate on the situation after 519, when Darius of Persia was in charge and was willing to honor the edict of his predecessor Cyrus that had given the Jews the right to rebuild the Temple (see Ezra 5–6). Darius's motive would have been to develop loyal subjects close to Egypt, a land conquered in 523 but not fully secured. The work of Nehemiah might well have been allowed later by king Artaxerxes for similar reasons, because he needed loyal supporters in his struggles with Egypt, Greece, and dissidents in his own realm.[9]

Norman K. Gottwald has also stressed the international politics of the period of Ezra and Nehemiah — for instance, by interpreting the refortification and re-population of Jerusalem accomplished by Nehemiah as an enhancement of the Persian imperial administration and trade. He also suggests that Nehemiah's pro-gram against intermarriage with foreigners and for greater economic justice would have most benefited the impoverished local landholders whose unrest posed the greatest threats to the stability of Persian rule. This group would have been com-posed mainly of those who had not gone into exile, and they would have resented the wealthier returnees who were in a position to exploit them. The returnees would have had the greatest opportunity to marry non-Jews, so Nehemiah's two-pronged attack on them (banning intermarriage and demanding economic relief for those in debt to them) would have made him popular with the lower classes.[10] Opposed to this theory may be the text's own statements that resistance to the work of reconstruction came largely from the people of the land, who may have been nonexiles as well as Samaritans and others of mixed lineage.

Gottwald admits that the chronology of the missions of Ezra and Nehemiah is baffling, and his tendency is to separate the work of the two and view the text as an untidy welding of two separate literary traditions. He thinks that more coherence comes when the work of Ezra is placed after that of Nehemiah, and he would explain the different order of the canonical text as the sort of chronological error quite frequent when ancient historians worked with imperfect records. He admits, however, that the traditional order, in which Ezra precedes Nehemiah, recently has found a resurgence of support.[11]

Peter R. Ackroyd, a specialist in the historical books of the Bible,[12] also seems to favor separating the work of Ezra and Nehemiah and placing Ezra after Nehemiah, although he admits that there is no certainty in this matter. He notes that Ezra gained considerable prominence in later Jewish tradition, being credited with dictating some ninety-four books that were meant to replace scriptures lost during the Exile. Some of these entered the canon, but others were kept secret. The overall effect of this reputation was to liken Ezra to Moses and make him a major link in the chain that passed the Torah from its origins to the great rabbis who came after the postexilic period. The hostility to Ezra shown in the Samaritan literature suggests a memory of him as leading the postexilic Jewish community and spearheading its reforms in ways irksome to the Samaritans.[13]

LITERARY INTENT

The shape of the canonical books of Ezra and Nehemiah shows such a clear disregard of chronological and narrative order that interpreters such as Brevard Childs find it easy to concentrate instead on theological themes.[14] Among those that Childs treats is the theme that God uses foreign rulers for the sake of Israel. Thus Cyrus, Darius, and Artaxerxes all act benevolently toward the Jews out of respect for their God. In contrast, the people of the land contest the work of both Ezra and Nehemiah. The result is some nuance in the question of pagan or outsiders' treatment of the Jews. Genuine foreigners may be more helpful, more appreciative of the rights of the sole God, than half-foreigners like the neighboring Samaritans.

The third theme that Childs emphasizes is the separation of the Jews from foreigners in the name of religious purity. This goes hand in hand with the reestablishment of Jerusalem and the recovenanting of the people to God. Childs downplays the theme that the return from Exile is a new exodus, reserving any strong impact of this theme for Chronicles. He also downplays the separation of Ezra and Nehemiah that some scholars propose, because he finds that the canonical text goes out of its way to link the two men. The result of this linkage is a doubled leadership and force for reconsecrating Israel. Childs believes that, for all its stress on reinvigorating the community's adherence to the Mosaic Law, Ezra-Nehemiah has the reformation of the community precede the reading and joyous affirmation of the Law. As we noted, the liturgical overtones to Ezra's proclamation of the Law are heavy and obvious. This suggests that we should hear in the word "Law" celebration and worship even more than ethical obedience. The community that Ezra-Nehemiah wishes to place before its readers will above all be a people holy enough to function as a priestly party fit to worship the true God.

In a theological evaluation of Ezra-Nehemiah, H. G. M. Williamson is stimulated by certain features of the narrative. He notes that the story presented in the texts suffers manifest chronological gaps and so infers that the authors have used theological significance as their criterion for including and correlating the events they report. The message of the first large textual unit, Ezra 1–6, would be that divine providence arranged for Ezra to return from exile, triumph over local opposition, and supervise the rebuilding of the Temple. Similarly, Ezra is able to triumph over both external and internal opposition and reinvigorate the reception of Torah. Nehemiah works in a similar pattern, getting a providential permission, overcoming opposition, and succeeding in reforming the city and the people in ways that justify joyous celebration. Williamson thinks the books want to provide their audience assurance that the postexilic community stands in continuity with the preexilic community as law abiding. Related to this is an assurance that Jews can indeed find it possible to live a life of fidelity despite being subjected to foreign rule. The prayers of Nehemiah offer models of how to live with the tension between spiritual freedom rooted in covenant with God and earthly subjugation. The conclusion of Nehemiah (chapter 13) does not gloss over the partiality of what Nehemiah's reforms have achieved and so suggests that imperfection is bearable.[15]

More generally, Ezra-Nehemiah tells its readers that God has not left them without resources. Ezra and Nehemiah serve as examples of leaders whom God is willing to raise up, and the Mosaic Torah again comes into focus as the main source of the people's prosperity. When Jews are willing to hear those who would repristinate their fidelity to Torah, they are at least in sight of the path that brings life and prosperity. Certainly Jerusalem emerges as the ideal center for this life, and a vigorous liturgy in the restored Temple is strongly desirable. That both Ezra and Nehemiah kept a vigorous faith alive in Exile argues, however, that religion may survive in less than ideal circumstances. Indeed, back in the chosen land fidelity has not necessarily been more vigorous than it was in Exile. So although the ideal certainly would be worship and justice emanating from Jerusalem, conditions less than ideal can be endured.

The last intent worth noting are the calls for social justice and observance of the Sabbath that dovetail with the call for separation from foreigners. The "argument" of Ezra-Nehemiah is that if the Jews are to be what God and their own best traditions say they should be, they must comport themselves as a people set apart for a special measure of fair dealing, reverence for God, and abhorrence of defilements incompatible with the divine purity.

LASTING SIGNIFICANCE

We have noted the reputation that Ezra gained as a mediator of Torah and so a bridge between preexilic Israel and the Israel led by the rabbis from the time of the Second Temple into Post-Second Temple times. Ezra-Nehemiah helped to justify the centrality of Torah that Judaism has always stressed. Indeed, with Ezra the "Law of Moses" (Nehemiah 8:1) is introduced to the people for the first time as the law of the land backed by the Persian authorities. Until then the Law had been largely the private domain of the priest. But, in contrast to the other ancient Near Eastern cults, here the Law is publicly proclaimed and made clear to all (Nehemiah 8:3). Torah, we might say, comes out of the closet to become the foundation of Jewish life. For the first time, adherence to Torah defines the Jewish group (against "people of the land" and others who become dissidents). That both Ezra and Nehemiah support this innovation, despite their different orientations as scribe and layperson, enables it to succeed.

Ezra-Nehemiah also helped to justify movements toward separation from foreign influences. The major significance of the book, however, may lie in its presentation of divine providence. Even though Jews were either in bondage to foreign rulers or suffering great deprivations in their native land, God kept faith alive in strong personages like Ezra and Nehemiah and through them worked salvation (help, restoration) for the chosen people. The obvious message of this work is that things of moment did occur. The Temple was restored, the city was rebuilt, the Torah was given, and the people were reconsecrated to their God and their better selves. The imperfections in these achievements not withstanding, God acted on the people's behalf.

One interested in a theology of action or political responsibility can find useful markers here. There is implicit advice, for instance, to cooperate with even alien rulers of good will and see what helps they can provide. There is quite explicit suggestion that no matter how pure or unobjectionable one's purposes, one is nearly certain to encounter opposition. Indeed, perhaps the greatest irony of Ezra-Nehemiah is that the reforms proposed by its two heroes were abetted by foreigners and resisted by compatriots or neighbors close to home. This can qualify the call to purification from contact with foreigners, even after we have admitted that the liturgical community idealized by Ezra-Nehemiah shows a strong dose of xenophobia. Indeed, Ezra-Nehemiah is only being faithful to its predecessor works of scripture in exhibiting ambiguity about what chosenness means. On the one hand, it means separation from all other peoples for a special relation to the one holy God. On the other hand, it means serving a God who is also Lord of the nations and can be better honored by foreigners such as Cyrus than members of his special people.

GLOSSARY

Divine providence   God's oversight of history and care for human beings.

Samaritans   Inhabitants of the district of Samaria (who only accepted the five books of Moses and preferred Mount Gerizim to Mount Zion).

STUDY QUESTIONS

1. What role do the kings of Persia play in the drama of Ezra-Nehemiah?
2. Why does the text provide so many lists of people who participated in the reconstructions and reforms?

3. What are the main problems of chronology and textual arrangement that scholars enumerate?

4. What tactics do the opponents of Nehemiah use?

5. Using the prayers of Nehemiah, give a sketch of his personal religion.

6. What place does liturgy have in the recovenanting of the people?

7. Taking the part of a wife or child put aside as "foreign," write a brief argument against the reforms that Ezra and Nehemiah demanded.

8. What are the main requisites for a mature theology or philosophy of political action?

NOTES

1. See Brevard S. Childs, *Introduction to the Old Testament as Scripture*. Philadelphia: Fortress, 1979, pp. 624–37. See also F. Charles Fensham, *The Books of Ezra and Nehemiah*. Grand Rapids, Mich.: William Eerdmans (The New International Commentary on the Old Testament), 1982, pp. 1–19. Fensham offers a fine bibliography on pp. 30–37.

2. See Peter R. Ackroyd, "Ezra" and "Nehemiah," in *Harper's Bible Dictionary*, ed. Paul J. Achtemeier. San Francisco: Harper & Row, 1985, pp. 295–96 and 694–95.

3. Jacob M. Myers, *Ezra-Nehemiah*. Garden City, N.Y.: Doubleday Anchor Bible, 1965, p. 14.

4. See Celine Mangan, *1–2 Chronicles, Ezra, Nehemiah*. Wilmington, Del.: Michael Glazier (Old Testament Message), 1982, p. 159.

5. H. G. M. Williamson, *Ezra, Nehemiah*. Waco, Tex.: Word Books (Word Biblical Commentary), 1985, p. xxiv.

6. See J. G. McConville, *Ezra, Nehemiah, and Esther*. Philadelphia: Westminster (The Daily Study Bible), 1985, p. 74.

7. See Fensham, *The Books of Ezra and Nehemiah*, p. 204.

8. On the different significances of "Law" in Nehemiah 8 and Ezra 7, see Rolf Rendtorff, "Ezra und das 'Gesetz,' " *Zeitschrift für die Alttestamentliche Wissenschaft*, 96 (1984), 165–84.

9. See Fensham, *The Books of Ezra and Nehemiah*, pp. 5–16.

10. See Norman K. Gottwald, *The Hebrew Bible: A Socio-Literary Introduction*. Philadelphia: Fortress, 1985, pp. 432–33.

11. Gottwald cites Shemaryahu Talmon, "Ezra and Nehemiah (Books and Men)," *The Interpreter's Dictionary of the Bible, Supplementary Volume*. Nashville: Abingdon, 1976, pp. 317–28.

12. See Peter R. Ackroyd, "The Historical Literature," in *The Hebrew Bible and Its Modern Interpreters*, ed. Douglas A. Knight and Gene M. Tucker. Philadelphia: Fortress, 1985, pp. 297–323.

13. See Ackroyd, "Ezra," p. 296.

14. See Childs, *Introduction to the Old Testament as Scripture*, pp. 630–37.

15. See Williamson, *Ezra, Nehemiah*, pp. xlvii–lii.

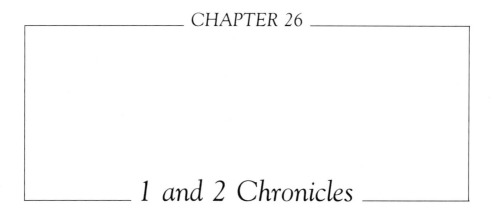

CHAPTER 26

1 and 2 Chronicles

TEXTUAL ANALYSIS

Virtually all commentators link 1 and 2 Chronicles with Ezra and Nehemiah. Some scholars hold that the four books should be considered a single historical project, but the mainstream of present-day expert opinion seems to distance Ezra and Nehemiah from 1 and 2 Chronicles sufficiently to make the "Chronicler" something less than a single author who composed one unified work. Indeed, the sweep of 1-2 Chronicles (like Ezra-Nehemiah, the two books were originally considered one) is so much broader than Ezra-Nehemiah that even when we speak of a similar date of composition (fourth century B.C.E.), similar interests, and similar religious convictions, we have to acknowledge different sources and a different scale. We treat 1-2 Chronicles in four textual parts:

1 Chronicles	1:1 – 9:44	From Adam to Saul
	10:1 – 29:30	The Kingship of David
2 Chronicles	1:1 – 9:31	The Kingship of Solomon
	10:1 – 36:23	The Davidic Line to the Exile[1]

1 Chronicles 1:1–9:44 From Adam to Saul

The materials we find in 1 and 2 Chronicles are historical, in the sense that they purport to explain what happened in Israel's past. Like most of the Bible's historiography, however, 1 and 2 Chronicles are shaped by theological convictions about what ought to have been and what patterns of meaning God was providentially providing. We are warned of this at the outset, when the Chronicler begins with Adam and tips us off that this work will be an interpretation of how Israel got from the genesis of humanity to its present postexilic state and of what lessons that long span of experience ought to have inculcated. After pointing out that the genealogies of the first nine chapters serve to validate the position of David, who is for the Chronicler what Moses is for the Deuteronomist, Jacob M. Myers comments:

> But the new situation [of the Israelite community reconstituted after the return from Exile] faced by the Chronicler called for a new method of approach in which he follows that of the priestly writer who introduces his work by referring to the generations of the heavens and the earth. . . . The Chronicler's lists read like sermon notes to be filled in by the speaker as he pointed out their relevance to his subject. Little attention is paid to side lines or other details because he wants to get to the main point of his argument as quickly as possible — the new messianic implications centering in David and his line on the one hand and on the other the direct and connected line of the descent behind the Israel of his day.[2]

The first chapter suggests the place that Abraham and his descendants held among all the nations who descended from Adam and Eve, the primal couple. Note in verse 1:34 the use of "Israel" rather than "Jacob." As Ezra-Nehemiah was interested in the lists of people who took part in the reconstitution of the community after the Exile, Chronicles is interested in the full backdrop of this event.

Chapter 2, which deals mainly with the descendants of Judah, draws on materials now found in Genesis (chapters 35, 38, and 46), Numbers (chapters 1 and 32), Joshua (chapters 7 and 14), Ruth (chapter 4), and 1 Samuel (chapter 27). Generally commentators point out that the Chronicler must have had access to large amounts of what later became the canonical scriptural material, especially the historical materials that we now find in the books of Samuel and Kings. Indeed, a primary interest of current scholars is how these materials were harmonized, supplemented, or treated selectively.[3] Only someone deeply convinced that the genealogical line running through Abraham, Israel, and David was of earth-shaking importance would have bothered to trot out so many nearly faceless names.

Whereas chapter 3 concentrates on the Davidic line, listing the offspring of David and then Solomon, chapter 4 is interested in the preexilic descendants of Judah (and Simeon). The different logics employed in relating these blocks of material suggests that the Chronicler was trying to harmonize his own interests in the Davidic line with the independent interests of the sources he was using.

Chapter 5 concentrates on the lineage of the tribes who remained east of the Jordan and so fell outside the main axis of covenantal history. The descendants of Levi no doubt get special mention because of their relations with the priesthood and the Temple. As we saw in Ezra-Nehemiah and see again in Chronicles, the Temple and its worship are the central delight of the postexilic theology we find at the end of the Hebrew Bible. Note, for example, the interests displayed in verses 6:31–32: "These are the men whom David put in charge of the service of song in the house of the Lord, after the ark rested there. They ministered with song before the tabernacle of the tent of meeting, until Solomon had built the house of the

Lord in Jerusalem; and they performed their service in due order." More than simple reportage runs through these lines. There is considerable esteem as well. See also verse 6:49, in which Aaron and his sons are singled out similarly. The later listings of the chapter include mention of the lands that different families received, which should remind us that traditions, blood, and territory all merged in the Chronicler's sense of "Israel."

The description of the northern line in chapter 7 is comparatively brief, and the stress on military matters seems to come from an interest in the relation of these people to David (verse 7:2). Chapter 8 deals with the Benjaminites, whose main claim on the Chronicler's interest was probably their connection to Jerusalem and Saul (verses 8:28, 33).

Chapter 9 gives the Chronicler's main source for these genealogies, the "Book of the Kings of Israel." Although this should not simply be equated with the present scriptural books of Samuel and Kings, certainly it contained much of the material they now present. Note in verse 9:1 the Chronicler's summary understanding of why the Exile to Babylon occurred: because of Judah's unfaithfulness. The description of post-exilic "Israel" that follows assumes that after the fall of the Northern Kingdom to Assyria "Israel" lay in the Southern Kingdom (Judah), which remained free. Verses 9:2–16 roughly parallel Nehemiah 11:3–19, where the author lists the inhabitants at the time that Jerusalem was restored. Verses 9:17–34 show that the paradigm the Chronicler has in mind when he treats of the postexilic community, Temple, and worship is the pattern he associates with David (who here is helped by the seer Samuel). The covenant with David, somewhat in contrast to the covenant with Moses, offers the Chronicler his basic sense of how the postexilic community ought to understand itself.

1 Chronicles 10:1–29:30 The Kingship of David

Chapter 10 concludes the story of Saul, the predecessor of David (see 1 Samuel 31:1–13). The Chronicler mainly sees Saul as the unfaithful predecessor and antagonist who sets David in a fine light: "So Saul died for his unfaithfulness; he was unfaithful to the Lord in that he did not keep the command of the Lord, and also consulted a medium, seeking guidance, and did not seek guidance from the Lord. Therefore the Lord slew him, and turned the kingdom over to David the son of Jesse" (verses 10:13–14). For the Chronicler faithfulness means relying on God for one's victories and prizing only the divine guidance (available in Torah, which includes prophetic as well as legal inspiration).

Whereas 2 Samuel 1–4 suggest that David had to struggle to consolidate his succession to Saul, the Chronicler has David anointed king without challenge. Note in verse 11:2 the joining of "shepherd" and "prince." The first thing David does is conquer Zion and build there "the city of David" (Jerusalem). This is another indication of the historical interests that the Chronicler is pursuing. The center of his story is the cultic community that God established for worship at Jerusalem. The rest of chapter 11, dealing with the chiefs of David's army, draws on 2 Samuel 23 but adds a few new features. The chiefs are rather heroic, as befits the men of the model king.

Chapter 12 continues in this vein, showing David's ability to attract valorous followers and also idealizing him. Note in verses 12:16–17 the combination of goodheartedness, realism, and faith, as David offers the Benjaminites and Judahites friendship but trusts in God to punish any wicked intents on their part. Another theme is that Saul's own kin quickly offered loyalty to David. Verse 12:38 stresses the singlemindedness of all Israel in making David king.

Established as king, David swiftly moves to the cultic work for which the Chronicler so venerates him. Thus chapter 13 shows David's assembling all Israel around the ark—unifying the many tribes through a common focus on the presence of their God. The rest of the chapter quite remarkably describes the mixture of joy and fear that the holy presence of God elicited. The Chronicler makes David's fear of the mortal power of God the reason he did not take the ark home to Jerusalem.

The special note of chapter 14 is the guidance that David received from God in his battles with the Philistines. Established in Jerusalem, with his house and many wives and children, David remained the warrior king who championed the chosen people. The Chronicler stresses that God continued to be the people's main warrior, and it is significant that he makes David a charismatic fighter (somewhat like Saul) who sought divine approval for any movement into battle.

Chapter 15 stresses that David set the Levites their particular role in carrying the ark and ministering to God, although verse 15:15 links his prescriptions with the prior commands of Moses. The Chronicler's interest in religious song again appears, as David arranges for musicians. The ark is brought to Jerusalem with rejoicing and festival song, but (as in 2 Samuel 6:16) Michal, the daughter of Saul, despises David for his display of dancing and merrymaking. The implication is that the line of Saul did not appreciate the joy that true fidelity and worship arouse.

David functions like a priest in chapter 16, distributing portions of the sacrifice to the people. The psalm that dominates the chapter memorializes Asaph, a leading composer, and is compiled from various present biblical psalms (96, 105, 106). Note the motifs of pure thanksgiving and praise of God, reciting the history of God's saving (covenantal) deeds on behalf of his people, and calling nature into the praise and glorification of God. The overall effect is to paint David as having wonderfully established what proper worship should be.

The word of God given to the prophet Nathan in chapter 17 mainly serves to extol the bond between God and the house of David, although it is also interesting as an expression of the strain of Israelite theology that considered any housing of God unfitting. David's response magnifies the goodness of God, wonders at the uniqueness of Israel as God's beneficiary, and prays that the promises made to him and his line be fully accomplished. We must note, however, that the Chronicler makes no mention of the personal events narrated in 2 Samuel 9–20, where the prophet Nathan rebukes David for his adultery with Bathsheba and his murder of Uriah the Hittite. As a result, this David is considerably more ideal and considerably less human than the one we find in 2 Samuel (a highpoint of biblical narrative).

Chapter 18 describes more of David's military victories and assures us that he "administered justice and equity to all his people" (verse 18:14). In chapter 19 Joab functions as David's general, gaining vengeance against Ammonites and Syrians who have treated Israelites badly, but the king himself comes to lead the final battles and secure the victory. The first lines of chapter 20 come from 2 Samuel 11, and the fact that the Chronicler cites them and then omits the story of Bathsheba and Uriah confirms the impression that his idealization of David is deliberate. David is functioning in his story as the sort of ruler whom Israel should have in the golden future that the Chronicler hopes will appear for the postexilic community. Chapter 20 therefore only details more victories.

We see some blemishes in chapter 21, however, where Satan incites David to perform a census. (In 2 Samuel 24 the divine anger prompts this arrogation of divine prerogatives. In the centuries between the two accounts, "Satan" has arisen to personify what troubles the relation between God and human beings.) Celine Mangan describes the Chronicler's motivation here as follows: "Up to this point, the Chronicler avoided recounting any of the earlier stories which portrayed David as a sinner but, at last, he is forced into doing so because the story of David's taking a census of the people provides the backdrop for the acquiring of the land on which the Temple was to be built."[4] Here Joab represents the better religious instinct and opposes David, but the king's will prevails. As soon as he experiences God's displeasure, however, David repents, and by his choosing to let God determine his punishment he wins God's relenting. David both sees the avenging angel (a tribute to his spiritual powers) and offers himself in place of the people, as an ideal king (shepherd—note the "sheep" of verse 21:17) would. The threshing floor of Ornan where this takes places becomes the site of the Temple.

Whereas 1 Kings makes Solomon the architect of the Temple, the Chronicler feels this most important construction must be credited to David. So David gets things under way, and verse 22:5 shunts Solomon to the side as too young and inexperienced to supervise such an undertaking. Yet the strength of the Solomonic tradition was such that the Chronicler could not contradict it without losing credibility. His compromise is to have David pass the commission on to Solomon, on the grounds that Solomon is innocent of the sort of bloodshed that David had to commit and so will bring cleaner hands to the task. David retains the honors of the commissioner. In fact, he becomes the counselor of Solomon (verses 22:11–16) and so may be credited for the wisdom that the tradition came to attribute to Solomon. Finally, it is due to David that the leaders of Israel help Solomon execute the great work of building the Temple.

Verse 23:1 is explicit that David passed the kingship on to Solomon, implying that the aged king arranged for a smooth transition. The main accomplishment narrated in the chapter, however, is the assignment of the duties of the Levites. Note the stress on cleanliness and praise (verses 23:28–30). The parallel activity recorded in chapter 24 is David's organization of the priests. The two chapters therefore make David the source of religious order in Israel, which puts him on a par with Moses (if not indeed above Moses). The musicians are cared for in chapter 25, and the gatekeepers, treasurers, and other functionaries in chapter 26. The paradigmatic work of the ideal king is comprehensive. Most likely the Chronicler instinctively held some form of the ancient Near Eastern myth of divine kingship, even the mild versions of which had the head of the human community as the mediator of divine power to the whole group. As Ezra-Nehemiah goes out of its way to tie the reestablishment of the Temple and Jerusalem to the edicts of the Persian kings (godfearing and so used by the one true God), so Chronicles goes out of its way to make David the source of the sacral-social order it thinks God wants for the postexilic community. (Note that even the prophets and seers have functioned as adjuncts of the king, rather than as a countervailing source of divine guidance.)

In chapter 27 David puts military and civil matters in shape, and in chapter 28 he provides for the final plans for the Temple. This chapter somewhat overlaps with chapter 22, and it rather cleverly skirts the viewpoint expressed in chapter 17, where God made Nathan the mouthpiece for the view that the divinity ought not to dwell in any house (a view associated with the God of the Exodus, who wandered with the people), by passing the actual execution of this work over to Solomon. David is disqualified for having shed blood, but Nathan's revelation is ignored rather than superseded. That the Chronicler, who passionately believed in the Temple, felt compelled to mention that the transcendent God wanted no Temple probably testifies to the strength (and perhaps to the antiquity) of that viewpoint. David bids the people to observe and seek out all the commandments of the Lord (verse 28:8), and he bids Solomon to seek the God who has chosen him to build a sacred house, promising him God's help.

In chapter 29 David explains his bequests to the Temple, as though he were publicizing his last will and testament. This stimulates the people to match his generosity and themselves donate to the Temple lavishly. Verses 29:10–13 comprise a beautiful and famous prayer, but it seems significant that it makes no mention of an afterlife. The continuance of David's farewell prayer stresses that all good things come from God and that God stays close to those who seek him with pure hearts. The chapter ends with an exemplary worship of God, as Solomon succeeds to David's kingship and David dies to consummate a nearly perfect rule of Israel.[5]

2 Chronicles 1:1–9:31 The Kingship of Solomon

For the Chronicler Solomon represents a slight decline from the heights of ideal monarchy, but he is nonetheless an admirable continuance of the Davidic line, in great part because he carried out the work of constructing the Temple. So 2 Chronicles 1:1 gets the narrative off on a positive note by judging that "the Lord his God was with him and made him exceedingly great." The first scene places Solomon at the head of Israel and worshiping at the bronze altar and tent of meeting — archaic sites of God. The new king prays, according to the counsel of David, for wisdom, and the Lord is pleased to grant this high-minded request. At the end of the chapter he has already begun to enrich Jerusalem and make it prosper as never before.

Chapter 2, which describes the beginnings of the king's construction of the Temple and the royal palace, parallels 1 Kings 5. Note that the king of Tyre responds favorably because of God's manifest blessing in giving Israel David and his son. The census that Solomon conducts at the end of the chapter brings no displeasure from God, perhaps because it concerns aliens, and the king's assignment of these aliens to hard labor for his building projects should remind us that conscription of foreigners, if not outright slavery, sat lightly on the Chronicler's conscience.

The measurements given for the house of the Lord in chapter 3 seem exaggerated, perhaps in an effort to increase the impressiveness of the construction. Most of chapter 4 parallels 1 Kings 7, and like the account of the construction of the Temple in 1 Kings, it stresses the splendor of the fittings and the sacredness of their purpose.

Chapter 5 describes bringing the ark of the covenant into the Temple, stressing the joy of the whole proceeding. The main difference between the account of the Chronicler and that of 1 Kings 8 is the Chronicler's mention of the priests and singers. Note also the mention of the tables of the Mosaic Law (verse 5:10) and the cloud that symbolized the divine presence and glory. Clearly, the Chronicler loved to contemplate anything associated with the establishment of the divine worship that he considered the heartbeat of his people. The speech that opens chapter 6 also comes from 1 Kings 8, and in the Chronicler's narrative it serves to underscore how the construction of the Temple fulfilled the divine promises to David. The worship that Solomon performs probably is meant to be exemplary, showing all Israelites how to praise God and recall his fidelity to the covenant. Note in verses 6:15–17 that God's fidelity is to promises made to David rather than Moses. The Chronicler nicely finesses the problem of the divine unwillingness to be contained by having Solomon acknowledge it yet ask God to condescend to take note of what goes on in the Temple. A list of the community affairs that can be settled in the Temple follows, which reminds us that in biblical Israel all aspects of life bore a religious significance. Especially important are the occasions when people sin or suffer hardship. At those times the Temple will serve as the place where they may find forgiveness and renewal—spiritual experiences whose significance is hard to overestimate.

Of the response that Solomon received to the prayer of chapter 6 Jacob M. Myers has written: "The response of Yahweh to Solomon's dedication of the temple was a gigantic holocaust ignited by fire from heaven, which confirmed his acceptance of both temple and offerings that had been waiting."[6] The Chronicler stresses the thickness of the glory of the Lord that filled the Temple, as well as the people's worshipful thanks for this manifestation of the divine goodness. Solomon leads a week's worth of sacrifices, songs, and feasting, all part of the solemn dedication of the Temple. To confirm the completion of Solomon's work, the Lord appears to him in a dream and promises to make the Temple a place that he will take note of and bless with the presence of his name, his eyes, and his heart for all time (verse 7:16). Because the divine name, eyes, and heart could be equivalent to the divine substance or self, the Chronicler has gone about as far as he could in affirming that the Temple will house the Lord of heaven and Earth without making outright assertions that would compromise the divine transcendence and so court blasphemy. The personal advice that the Lord gives Solomon is somewhat ominous, in that tradition portrayed him precisely as having gone after false gods. Verse 7:20 promises that such infidelity would bring the Temple itself into disfavor. The Chronicler follows the Deuteronomistic theology of reward for fidelity and punishment for infidelity, so he may be previewing the reasons why Israel had to suffer the punishments of Exile and why the Temple was desecrated. By the end of chapter 7 this implication has shed any cloaking and has become an explicit prophecy of what happened in 586 B.C.E.

Chapter 8 follows 1 Kings 9 in detailing further activities of King Solomon. It mainly concerns foreign relations and repeats that Solomon put aliens into forced labor (verse 8:8). It does give the assurance that Solomon enslaved no Israelites (verse 8:9), and in verse 8:11 the Chronicler seems to make Solomon aware that his marrying an Egyptian princess was in conflict with the holiness of Israelite kingship. His worship and appointment of priests and Levites seem in good order, so the foreign marriage is the only sour note.

Chapter 9 borrows quite directly from 1 Kings 10. The first effect of the visit of the Queen of Sheba is to exalt the wisdom of Solomon, and then to exalt the God of Israel who so blessed his people in bestowing such wisdom on their leader. Whether advertently or not, the Chronicler certainly would have pleased devotees of wisdom literature through this passage. The spices and riches that the Queen of Sheba brought are a mixed blessing. On the one hand, they contribute to a sense of opulence that makes the reign of Solomon a high-water mark of Israelite success and so favor from God. On the other hand, they suggest an overripeness or excess that portends forgetfulness of God and the simpler religious virtues. This is as close as the Chronicler comes to reporting the dark side of Solomon's reign. On the whole his presentation of the construction of the Temple and the prosperity of the kingdom makes that time a golden chapter. It is left to the following chapters, in which the division of the kingdom and the evils of the southern line are described, to suggest that perhaps all was not perfect in the founding dyad of David and Solomon. The Chronicler himself does not want to admit this possibility, but his own history of Judah, as well as his deliberate omissions of facts well known from Kings, makes considering it inevitable.[7]

2 Chronicles 10:1—36:23 The Davidic Line to the Exile

Chapter 10 follows 1 Kings 12 in describing the split between Rehoboam, the son of Solomon, and Jeroboam, leader of the North. The account is slightly sanitized, to protect the image of the South, but we are allowed to wonder why Solomon forced Jeroboam into flight into Egypt. Rehoboam is portrayed as foolish in treating the North harshly, but he seems to be following his father Solomon's policy, which gives us further reason to wonder about Solomon's practical wisdom. The Chronicler admits in this chapter that "Israel" was the proper name for the North, but verse 10:17 shows that he thinks the true Israel now resided in Judah. The final verse of the chapter is the tipoff: The North has "been in rebellion against the house of David to this day."

Chapter 11 repeats much of what we find in 1 Kings 12, although verses 5–11 are additions that improve the image of Judah. Jeroboam is portrayed as idolatrous (verse 11:15) and the priests and Levites as flocking to Judah, where true worship was possible. Rehoboam seems to prosper, ruling wisely and providing well for his growing household. In chapter 12, however, things go downhill, for the apostasy of Rehoboam (unspecified forsaking of the divine law) begets the punishment of invasion by Egypt (see 1 Kings 14). Rehoboam's repentence brings mitigation of this punishment (the Chronicler seems sensitive to what contrition can accomplish), and his reign overall is not judged too harshly: "conditions were good in Judah" (verse 12:12). The conflict between North and South that began with Jeroboam and Rehoboam and suggested irreligion on the part of both continues under Rehoboam's son Abijah. Two motifs of chapter 13 are that the North is in rebellion against the rule that God gave to David, and that the North has turned idolatrous. That is the reason God fights for Judah and gives it the victory.

Expanding on the meager account available in 1 Kings 15, the Chronicler devotes chapters 14–16 to the reign of Asa, who imitated David through most of his kingship. He eliminated idolatrous cults, fortified Judah, and gained a period of peace. When he had to do battle, as against the Ethiopians, he called upon the

Lord and was heard because of his piety, gaining the victory. Azariah, a spokesperson for the spirit of God, urges Asa to persevere in his piety, equating it with good times for Israel. So Asa leads Israel in more turning from idolatry and in genuine worship from the heart. In chapter 16, however, Asa fails and turns from God to earthly sources of security, placing Judah in league with Syria to oppose the North. Asa will not hear the judgment of the seer Hanani against him and sets his spirit in rebellion against God. For this reason he dies diseased.

Jehoshaphat, son of Asa, also makes a good beginning but then comes to grief. While he avoided the baals and followed the ways of the Lord he and Judah prospered. Their enemies feared God and left them alone. But when Jehoshaphat struck an alliance with Ahab, the Northern king (see 1 Kings 22), he started to close his soul to genuine guidance such as that offered by the true prophet Micaiah. (Note the Chronicler's use of Northern material here — a rare occurrence. Perhaps he was impressed by the discussion of the conflict between true and false prophecy.) The result was an ill-advised battle and the ironic death of Ahab. However, as we see in chapter 19, Jehoshaphat learned from this error and on returning to Judah ruled wisely, following the counsel of Hanani and demanding just verdicts of his judges — a major indication of genuine religion in the land. In chapter 20 Jehoshaphat recurs to God in face of the threat coming from the Moabites and the Ammonites, great enemies of proper cult, and the Lord rewards the piety of the people with victory. The final verses dealing with Jehoshaphat note, however, that he did not take away the high places where idolatries flourished, and that at the end he joined Ahaziah of Israel in ventures displeasing to God.

Jehoram, eldest son of Jehoshaphat, proves rotten from the start, killing his brothers and other princes of Israel (Judah). The Chronicler implies that his marriage to a daughter of Ahab was a major reason for his wickedness and notes that God only withheld full punishment for the sake of David. Elijah is used, despite the historical unlikelihood that he was living at that time, to express God's judgments on Jehoram. Jehoram dies of intestinal miseries and "he departed with no one's regret" (verse 21:20).

The kingdom passes to a different Ahaziah, who shows that the Davidic line is now badly tainted, following the idolatrous ways of his Northern kin (see 2 Kings 8). His death occasions the accession of the Queen Mother Athaliah, who consolidates her power by trying to destroy all the royal house of Judah (verse 22:10). She finally is overthrown, mainly (according to the Chronicler) through the efforts of the Levites and singers — personnel of the Temple. The priest Jehoiada leads the people in renewing their covenantal bond with God and God's king (verse 23:16). With joy they reassert the true religion of the house of David. The new king Joash begins well by ordering the Levites to restore God's house. After the death of Jehoiada, however, he proves unable to control the idolatrous trend of many of the princes of Judah. (The Chronicler departs from 2 Kings 12 in adding this detail.) Indeed, he himself kills Zechariah, the son of Jehoiada, and so opens the gate to the downfall of conquest by a puny band of Syrians. His successor Amaziah follows the by now established pattern of beginning well but then falling into apostasy. Note the reflection in verse 25:4 on individual responsibility.[8] Although Amaziah follows the counsel of the man of God sent to advise him about battle, he has done wrong in depending on Northern (impure) troops and so Judah suffers. He then compounds his evil by worshiping false gods and rejecting the advice of his prophetic counselor. He thus suffers defeat at the hands of another Joash, king of Israel, and the Temple is pillaged. After his death at the hands of disgruntled subjects, his son Uzziah follows him in beginning piously but ending badly. At first Judah prospers (note verse 26:10: Uzziah loved the soil), but then Uzziah's military victories and works of construction go to his head. He thinks he can enter the Temple and play the role of a priest, despite the falseness (verse 26:16) in him that soon breaks out as leprosy. He is punished by isolation, and his son Jotham takes over the kingship.

Chapter 27, reporting the good reign of Jotham, draws on 2 Kings 15. The typical view of the Chronicler sounds in verse 27:6: "So Jotham became mighty, because he ordered his ways before the Lord his God." Ahaz, the son of Jotham, dramatically does not order his ways rightly. Following the idolatrous ways of the Northerners and people driven out of Judah, he leads his people into disastrous defeat at the hands of the Syrians and the Israelites and is responsible for great slaughter. The brave intervention of the prophet Oded saves many prisoners (note the appeal to the conscience of the Israelites in verse 28:10). Ahaz tries to recoup by petitioning help from Assyria, but this only brings more affliction, which drives him to further idolatries and sacrileges (verse 28:24), so the Chronicler's final judgment on him is wholly negative.

Chapters 29–33 detail with considerable praise the reforms of King Hezekiah. Note in verse 29:2 the leitmotif: "according to all that David his father had done." To bring back the favor of God, Hezekiah has the priests and Levites spearhead a repair and cleansing of the Temple and a renewal of proper worship. He also arranges for a massive sacrifice to atone for the people's sins. As has been true previously, the Chronicler stresses the music and joy with which the sacred actions went forward. All of Israel and Judah are invited to return to the true God and celebrate the passover. Note in verse 30:9 the assurance that those who do return will find the Lord gracious and merciful. The Northerners do not respond, but Judah gives a generous hearing and celebrates the passover well. This brings great joy, "for since the time of Solomon the son of David king of Israel there had been nothing like this in Jerusalem" (verse 30:26). Hezekiah then supervises the destruction of heathen shrines and a reordering of the priests and Levites. The people resume their generous support of the priests and Levites with tithes, making the reign of Hezekiah pleasing to God and prosperous.

Chapter 32 gives the Chronicler's version of how Hezekiah dealt with Sennacherib of Assyria (see 2 Kings 18–20). The information about preparations for siege is new, and the speech about trusting in God (as one's main warrior) is a pure translation of the Chronicler's theology. Hezekiah and the prophet Isaiah have to contend with a strong Assyrian campaign of propaganda against their faith. Both their victory and the death of Sennacherib are presented as signs that they served the true God. The Chronicler notes Hezekiah's slight dip into pride (verse 32:25), but otherwise he considers this king one of the greatest in the Davidic line.

Manasseh, in contrast, does evil to the point of sacrificing his own sons (verse 33:6) and polluting the Temple. (Note the fusion of Davidic and Mosaic motifs in verses 33:7–8). Even wicked Manasseh can receive the divine aid, however, if he is willing to repent (verse 33:13). Amon, though, only does evil and so occasions great strife in the land.

Josiah, the next king, outstrips even Hezekiah in doing good. His main benefactions are the usual: stopping the idolatrous cults and upbuilding the Temple. The Chronicler parallels 2 Kings 22 in recounting the finding of the book of the Law. The new purifications occasioned by this, and by the interpretation of the prophetess Huldah, merely redouble the attacks on idolatry that the Chronicler finds so admirable. As more closely associated with the Mosaic (Deuteronomic) Law, however, they fuse the Davidic and Mosaic traditions. Josiah also reinvigorates the celebration of Passover (an especially Mosaic feast), setting a new standard for solemnity (verse 35:18). It is not clear whether Josiah's death in battle stems from a prideful unwillingness to hear the Egyptian Neco's claim to be following God. By the Chronicler's usual equation of success with fidelity we may suspect that Josiah should have heard these words as prophetic. Still, the king dies praised and lamented, as even the great prophet Jeremiah mourns his passing.

Jehoahaz/Jehoiakim is the sorry ruler in whose time the accumulation of Judah's infidelities comes home to roost. First he is deposed by the Egyptians and carried away to their land. Then (contrary to 2 Kings 24:6) he is taken off to Babylon by Nebuchadnezzar. The rest of the description of the conquest by Babylon stresses the corruption of the people that justified it. The Chronicler calls on Jeremiah to buttress this judgment (verse 36:21). For "seventy years" (a full time) the land lay desolate. The final note of Chronicles is positive, however, as Cyrus of Persia, who has conquered Babylon, becomes the means for fulfilling Jeremiah's prophecies of restoration and offers the exiles a chance to return and rebuild their nation around the house of their God.

HISTORICAL BACKGROUND AND LITERARY INTENT

We sketched the general backdrop for the writing of 1–2 Chronicles in the previous chapter, because Ezra-Nehemiah and 1–2 Chronicles appeared at about the same time (fourth century B.C.E.) and from the same postexilic circles. The dramatic event of being allowed to return from Exile and rebuild their nation stimulated the postexilic theologians to reconsider what their past had been. If they were to face the future wisely, they ought to grasp firmly what "Israel" ought to connote and where history told them the path to prosperity lay.

The Chronicler shares with the author of Ezra-Nehemiah a conviction that proper worship, in the Temple of Jerusalem and according to Mosaic prescriptions, is the crux of Israelite identity. He is also concerned, however, to rethink from where the Temple and proper worship came. This leads him to concentrate on the Davidic line, with special stress on David and Solomon, that determined how the people's possession of Judah had gone. The main basis for assigning praise and blame is a given king's support of pure worship in the Temple. In the aftermath of Israel's having been abused by foreign powers, the Chronicler concentrates nearly obsessively on the God of the covenant, thinking that God a much surer source of protection than either military arms or foreign deities. The history that the Chronicler retells from the sources available thus concentrates on the Davidic line and gilds the theme of worship in God's own house. He is more interested in the contributions of priests and Levites than his predecessors were, and more concerned to guarantee that if leaders had repented of their infidelities and returned to the true God they could have averted disaster.

Dealing more precisely with the social circumstances of the Chronicler's own day, Jacob Myers has stressed the failure of religious institutions that we find decried in the postexilic prophet Malachai, speaking of "a breakdown of morality and common decency." The returnees from Exile were in bad economic straits and on the verge of being absorbed into the socio-political structures of peoples neighbor to them. The leadership, both political and religious, seemed incapable of preserving the people, so when reformers such as Ezra, Nehemiah, and the group for whom the Chronicler spoke went to work they had to be ruthless in their determination to bring the people back to what had made them "Israel":

> The postexilic writers sometimes leave us cold and unresponsive because we fail to grasp the importance of institutions that are strong and vigorous enough to offset those [disruptive] pressures in difficult times. There is a certain analogy between medieval monasticism and the separatist movement of Ezra-Nehemiah. Both were a bulwark against forces that could easily have wrecked what they stood for and what they regarded as essential for themselves and the world of their time.[9]

LASTING SIGNIFICANCE

We might begin a reflection on the lasting significance of 1–2 Chronicles with the observation that in fact Israel was preserved and Jewish faith has survived down to the present day, often by relying on ideas laid out in these last books of the Hebrew Bible. This could lead to the further reflection that the identity of traditional peoples above all lay in what they found when they repeated the forms of worship handed down to them. We need not agree with the particular superstructure of Temple, Davidic kingship, Mosaic Law, ethnic separatism, and the rest (or with the new focus on the study of Torah that came in rabbinic Judaism) to be impressed by the Jewish instance of the common religious pattern, any more than we need agree with the superstructures that Christians, Muslims, Hindus, Buddhists, or others have used. Inevitably there will be some superstructure, with specific debts to the historical experience of the group in question. "Worship" never occurs in the abstract or as a suprahistorical activity. Yet when we reflect on the role that worship has played in peoples' self-definition, the particulars do fall to the side and global impressions of the central importance of facing the mysteriousness of creation and salvation do take center stage. Let us reflect on this fact.

The difference between worship and reflection on where we have come from and where we are going is slight to the point of nearly forcing us to equate the life of prayer and the life that is examined. Worship merely articulates, usually in the plural voice, the "Thanks!" and "Help!" that any reflection on the beauty and fragility of life seems bound to summon. The Chronicler is saying that people come to know who they are and where their best future lies by expressing such praise and petition together, coloring them by the specific story of how past generations of the tribe managed to survive.

It will work out, of course, that in offering their thanks, expressing their petitions, and remembering their forebears people will stumble into the part of their tradition that tells them they have to manage their workaday affairs responsibly. Thus Ezra-Nehemiah tells its contemporaries that they have to restore social justice and Chronicles tells them that they have to maintain a pure cult in a well-kept Temple. Later Jewish theologians would stress the study of Torah and the maintenance of good morals. Worship therefore is not the enemy of human responsibility and initiative.

Worship is, however, the enemy of both human pretensions to self-sufficiency and human temptations to despair. For one and the same reason, it opposes the extremes in the swing of the human psyche between mania and depression. The single reason is that worship inevitably ushers the personality out of narrow, insufficient perspectives and toward the darkness and silence of ultimacy. Faced with the unanswerable question of where life came from, or where life is going, or why there is so much beauty, or why there is so much evil, the personality is forced to confess that it does not know, that it lives in the midst of mystery. Such a confession immediately takes from its sails the wind that would puff it with pride and tempt it to strut as though it were all powerful. Far from being all powerful, all of us are very ignorant, limited, and mortal.

GLOSSARY

Divine kingship   The concept, common to many ancient societies, that the monarch so mediates between the people and ultimate reality that he should be considered a god.

Worship   Prayer, cult, devotion to God that honors the divine holiness.

STUDY QUESTIONS

1. Why does the Chronicler begin his work with a genealogy that runs from Adam to Saul?
2. What makes David the ideal king?
3. How does the history of Judah reveal the goodness of God?
4. Compare Hezekiah and Josiah.
5. Explain the psychology of the Chronicler's concern that worship be joyous.
6. How could rallying around the Temple have revivified postexilic life?
7. What seems necessary to turn reflection into worship?
8. How does worship tend to blend a people's encounter with mystery and its tales of times past?
9. How can reflection fight depression?

NOTES

1. See Peter R. Ackroyd, "Chronicles, the First and Second Books of the," in *Harper's Bible Dictionary*, ed. Paul J. Achtemeier. San Francisco: Harper & Row, 1985, p. 165.
2. Jacob M. Myers, *I Chronicles*. Garden City, N.Y.: Doubleday Anchor Bible, 1965, pp. 6–7.
3. See Brevard S. Childs, *Introduction to the Old Testament as Scripture*. Philadelphia: Fortress, 1979, pp. 645–53.

4. Celine Mangan, *1–2 Chronicles, Ezra, Nehemiah.* Wilmington, Del.: Michael Glazier (Old Testament Message), 1982, p. 53.

5. See Vladimir Peterca, "Die Vendung des Verbs BHR für Salomo in den Buchern der Chronik," *Biblische Zeitschrift*, 29 (1985), 94–96.

6. Jacob M. Myers, *II Chronicles.* Garden City, N.Y.: Doubleday Anchor Bible, 1965, p. 40.

7. See Raymond B. Dillard, "The Literary Structure of the Chronicler's Solomon Narrative," *Journal for the Study of the Old Testament*, 30 (1984), 85–93.

8. See Joel P. Weinberg, "Der Mensch im Weltbild der Chronisten: seine Psyche," *Vetus Testamentum*, 33 (1983), 298–316.

9. Myers, *I Chronicles*, p. xxxvii.

CHAPTER 27

The World View of
the Hebrew Bible

To conclude our study of the Hebrew Bible, it may be most profitable for us to reflect on the "world view," the sense of how things hang together, that the different books, taken as a whole, project. We must say immediately, of course, that the books vary considerably in what they say about the key topics that any world view must consider. We might in fact justifiably speak of the world views of the Hebrew Bible. Yet both Jews and Christians have believed that the Hebrew Bible or Old Testament comprises something unified. After admitting its considerable range of interests and topics, both groups still have found the Bible whole or harmonious. Our studies of the individual books should have provided sufficient experience of the biblical range of interests and topics, so our concluding study deals with themes that bring biblical religion into focus as a significant unity.

If we treat the world view of the Hebrew Bible on its own terms, not forcing it to fit a framework shaped by modern, secular convictions, it quickly becomes apparent that we must speak of biblical theology. All of the major terms in the lexicon of the biblical world view bear a reference to God. Thus the academic study called "biblical theology" is a vigorous enterprise, even though those who now perform it seem unable to agree about precisely what it ought to mean and how it ought to focus itself.[1] Sufficient for our purposes, however, is the advice that we can glean from such recent judgments as that of Paul D. Hanson that the factor unifying the different strands is the divine-human relationship,[2] and that of George W. Coats that Israelite theology came from the conviction that God had communicated knowledge about the divine nature (and, no doubt, about the nature of Israel itself) through historical actions on Israel's behalf.[3] Our treatment therefore has three major foci, through which we can hope to suggest the whole of the biblical world view: the covenanted people, the biblical God, and the dynamics of historical revelation.

THE COVENANTED PEOPLE

Analyzing the term "covenant" (*berith*), Johannes Schildenberger has claimed that in Daniel 11:28, 30, " 'the holy covenant' comes to mean the same thing as the religion of Israel."[4] As our prior studies should have made plain, the religious leaders of Israel constantly worried about the relationship between this people and their God. Certainly the relationship that Moses came to personify and to speak for was the most influential version of the covenantal bond, but the Bible also interpreted Israelite existence on the model of such other relationships as the covenants thought to have been struck with Adam, Noah, Abraham, and David.

What these covenants held in common far outweighed what they implied distinctively. All assumed the existence of God, a creative and directive force ultimately responsible for nature and human history, and all confessed a trust that God had pledged support and good will sufficient to make life both meaningful and good. All of the covenants carried the implication that God was making available sufficient instruction or guidance (Torah) to show the human partners how to prosper. The general result was a good feeling about Israel's place in the world. What happened in nature or human history occurred with the knowledge and control of a God who had pledged support, protection, and love. Indeed, Israel felt that this pledge was unique: Although God cared for all creatures and guided all nations, Israel was the apple of his eye. From such a feeling came the customs, institutions, and responsibilities that gave Israel a unique corporate existence.

We have seen the prominence given to religious cult or worship at the end of the canonical Bible, where the Chronicler recasts the history of the people largely in terms of the success or failure of the kings of the Davidic line to achieve a proper celebration of the cult. If we wish, we can interpret this literary fact as a desire on the part of the final editors to have the story or instruction conclude with a strong call to proper worship. With echoes of Deuteronomy, the Chronicler might be read as having been arranged to have the final word ring out, "Do this [worship your God in purity and joy] and you will live!" Such worship clearly was related to the Chronicler's conviction that false cult had been the major reason for Israel's historical losses and sufferings. The stress on the covenant with David did not erase the Deuteronomist's interpretation of the covenant with Moses, according to which fidelity to Torah would bring success and infidelity would bring disaster. If anything, the Chronicler's reading of Davidic history strengthened the legitimacy of that theological position. By its equal stress on the need for joy and song, however, the Chronicler's understanding of worship linked up with what we find in many of the psalms: a desire to praise God purely, for the splendor that divinity has even apart from its blessings on Israel.

The Israelite cult used the covenantal traditions, and the covenantal action called "sacrifice," to make these emotions and convictions vivid. As we have seen, book after book of the Hebrew Bible refers to the traditions of the Exodus and the Conquest of the promised land. In short formulas or longer recitals, the high points of God's past provision for Israel become warrants for believing that God will be good to Israel in the future, if only Israel will again turn to God, repent of its misdeeds, and rededicate itself to the holiness that God by nature demands. The key events in effect become paradigms by which covenantal trust can orient itself. Through sacrifices according to long-hallowed forms, the people would act out such a rededication, trying both to externalize the guilt they wanted to be quit of and offer God something precious that would token their praise.

The holiness and goodness of God, which we consider more fully in the next section, are the reason the Bible itself gives for the worship that Israel ought to carry out.[5] By the wondrous, inexplicable fact that the holy God had chosen Israel for a relationship as intimate and pervasive as a marriage, Israel had incurred the obligation (and the privilege) of striving to be as holy — as removed from corruption, as just and good — as it could be. The great prophets were especially sensitive to this theme, and we have seen in the Isaiahs, Jeremiah, and Ezekiel its many permutations. Ezekiel, like the Chronicler, is thoroughly shaped by a priestly reading of what holiness requires. For him proper sacrifice in a properly holy Temple is the major task to which Israel is called. Other prophets make more of economic justice and compassion for the unfortunate, but they too are shaped by Israel's call to holiness. It follows that the ethical prescriptions of the Hebrew Bible have to be read as guidance for the covenantal call to holiness. Be it legislation for how to treat the land, how to carry out marriage and family life, how to transfer property, or how to punish murderers, adulterers, and thieves, the call to holiness always frames the discussion and furnishes the ultimate rationale.

From the call to holiness came a twofold minimalism. First, Israelites wanted the material necessities. At times, of course, the biblical writers clearly want more than necessities: Luxuries would be quite welcome. But most of the authors, if pressed, would settle for decent food, clothing, family life, economics, and politics, where "decent" could mean "spare but sufficient" (see Proverbs 30:7–9). The biblical writers give little evidence that they ever expected hard work, sickness, death, and other trials to vacate the human scene. Apart, perhaps, from a few apocalyptic and messianic passages, the Bible wastes little energy on utopianism. Quite enough usually would be the promised land, flowing with milk and honey. Quite enough would be seeing one's children's children and feeling that the people had a rich future.

The second aspect of what we are calling the minimalism of the Israelite notion of the good life (of the justification for walking the ways of Torah) is the enjoyment of God. Keeping the laws of the covenant and carrying out the prescribed worship certainly had a theme of doing good so as to secure good fortune, but the deeper theme we find is that living by Torah is virtually its own reward, because it brings an enjoyment of God. Playing a semantic game, we might note that this phrase can carry at least two significances. The obvious significance is that Israelites would find the pleasure of spiritual peace and joy, the pleasure of feeling their lives to be supremely meaningful because properly ordered. A subtler possibility is that the phrase could also signify giving joy to God, pleasing the divinity. This possibility runs into some theological questions, most of which boil down to the insoluble problem of anthropomorphism. Yet it also opens the door to the intriguing thought that the covenant, as the marital symbolism of an Hosea or an Ezekiel suggests, could bring Creator and creature into a glow that pleased them both.

THE BIBLICAL GOD

Scholars may dispute the desirability of working with a biblical category called "election,"[6] but they can only deny Israel's sense of uniqueness at the price of falsifying the biblical record. Equally, they may point to correlations between the conception of God that we find in the Hebrew Bible and the conception we find in other classics of world-wide religion, but they can only contradict the Bible's own preference for monotheism by deafening themselves to its inmost message. The Shema (Deuteronomy 6:4) put it for all generations: "Hear, O Israel: The Lord our God is one Lord." Whether one understands this as a rejection of the many deities to which Israel's neighbors gave fealty, or as a call to rivet one's soul to the single mysterious source of creation and time, the result is a cleared psyche, a ruthless simplification. Israelite life, in all its folds and crannies, was to have only one foundation. Every speck of ultimate significance was to derive from the Lord.

The biblical God was Lord of both creation (physical nature) and history (time). The latter Lordship was more significant to Israel, and the paradigmatic center of Israelite history was the Mosaic period that included the Exodus from Egypt, wandering in the desert, receiving of the Torah at Sinai, and entrance on the promised land. A secondary, but very important, paradigm lay in the kingship of David and Solomon, when the people enjoyed their richest prosperity and built the Temple that sacrosummarized their life. Both of these colored the Israelite monotheism, in ways that we might label redemptive and establishing.[7]

The God revealed in Mosaic history (the episode at the burning bush as well as the Exodus and covenanting) was a redeemer, a liberator, from bondage. There was bondage in Egypt, from which this God led the people out. There was bondage to the elements in the desert, from which God freed the people by providing water from the rock, manna from heaven, cloud and pillar of fire that gave guidance and security. There was bondage to human weakness, from which the commitments of the covenant and the instructions of its Torah gave freedom. There was bondage to homelessness, rootlessness, alienation, from which the land that God gave through Joshua provided relief. And finally there was bondage to many spiritual powers, many finite baals, from which the God who could only be the sole deity gave release.

These dramatic events, which in the Bible have become an inseparable blend of history (memory of actual experiences) and myth (story of how things make most sense), suggested that the one God could free Israelites from any enslavements that might befall them. Thus, one could, one should, call upon him when foreign captors descended. One could and should call upon him when flood or famine threatened. If wrongdoing had led to heaping up guilt, the way down and out was to ask God for forgiveness and the strength to make proper restitution.[8] If barrenness, or sickness, or even death was the oppressive factor, the God of the Exodus offered powers that were stronger. No constraint, suffering, or evil that Israel could experience lay beyond the possibility that God could liberate Israel from it. Consequently, nothing that Israel could experience could take away its quite specific, quite historically accredited reasons for hoping that things would improve and God's establishment of Israel again would be obvious.

We could say of course that Israel was established through the pact made on

Sinai. We could say that Israel was established in the loins of Abraham and Sarah, through God's singular promise and its miraculous fulfillment. Each time that a judge like Deborah or a prophet like Samuel arose, Israel could think that God was at work establishing or confirming or repairing the construction he had begun with Abraham. Indeed, we could say that from the uttermost beginnings, with Adam and Eve, God had been minded to establish his special people, through which all the others might learn of his true character. "Establishment" therefore proves as flexible a notion as "redemption." It is no more limited to the Davidic monarchy than redemption is limited to what God did through Moses and Sinai. Whatever built the chosen people up and strengthened them to live as Torah encouraged was illumined by the metaphor of the Davidic monarchy, but certainly the priesthood, the wisdom schools, and above all the Torah itself established powers outside the sweep of that metaphor.

If redemption/liberation and establishment express some of the main work that Israel associated with its God and call to mind some of the key paradigms by which the Bible organized its overall narrative, "wisdom" and "order" suggest some of the overtones that God's work in nature came to bear. These overtones are perhaps clearest in the wisdom schools that developed relatively late in biblical history, but even the ancestral sagas clearly assume that the one who was guiding Abraham, Isaac, and Jacob was the fashioner and controller of natural phenomena. So God shuts or opens the wombs of the matriarchs, just as God had controlled

Intimations of the impersonal divinity of Asia. "Ink Bamboo" *Mo-chu* by Li K'an. *(The Nelson-Atkins Museum of Art, Kansas City, Missouri [Nelson Fund])*

the skies in the days of Noah. The later imagery of Second Isaiah, like the imagery of Psalms, depicts God moving the stars and the seas, the lion and the lamb.

Interestingly, Job, the book that most explicitly contends with the problems of evil and injustice, deals more with the God who is the creator of nature (which of course includes human beings) than with the God who had proven himself Lord of history through his interventions on Israel's behalf. Whatever the original provenance of Job, its reception into the Hebrew Bible gave canonical status to that theological option. Job, the literary character, suspects that this framework is not adequate, because he rejects the calls of the "comforters" to submit himself to the inscrutable ways of the one who set the seas their boundaries. But the speculation that flourished after the Exile, when the degradations of bondage seem to have left more impression than any joys of restoration to Jerusalem, was slow to take up the possibility that God himself suffers evil and fights alongside humanity as one who knows injustice as a personal hurt.[9] The suffering servant of the Lord imagined by Second Isaiah had richer suggestions, but after the return from Exile prophecy was a bear market and most Israelites felt the spirit of God had been quenched.

The result is that the portions of the Bible that most seek and praise the divine wisdom that orders the universe do not coordinate creation and redemption as skillfully as they might. It is left to Genesis to stand out as a better example, and quite likely the two stories of creation that were merged in the canonical account of the beginning represent a deliberate effort to effect such a coordination. In Genesis God is both the maker of everything that human beings know, including themselves, and the one who puts up with human weakness and guilt. The primal man and woman are punished for their disobedience but, far from abandoning them, God clothes their nakedness and continues to speak to their line. We cannot say that the God of Genesis positively wished the disobedience of Adam and Eve, planning it as a rite of passage to maturity and knowing evil from bitter personal experience of doing it. Even more, we cannot say that the God of Genesis came to consider human nature depraved and so expected human beings to lash themselves with guilt and make their first reaction to one another suspicion. The Hebrew Bible is much less enamored of "original sin" than Western Christian theology came to be. What Genesis suggests is that the one God both gave all that has life its breath and shows himself to be a marvelous parent, able to harmonize the task of forcing human beings to honor the truth (to grow conscientious and responsible) and the task of promising them that their weakness, or even their failure, would not cut off the divine-human relationship or staunch the flow of divine love.

THE DYNAMICS OF HISTORICAL REVELATION

Having dealt with the self-conception that Israel developed, the heart of which seems to have lain in its sense of being covenanted to the one God, and having elaborated some of the Israelite convictions about the nature of that one God, we now turn to the mode in which Israel and its God lived together. This invites us to contemplate such topics as "history," "revelation," and the "biblical humanism" that we have already extolled on numerous occasions.

"History," to be sure, has numerous connotations, and recent hermeneutics (studies of interpretation) have only widened and enriched them. Even though we may abstract a notion that would make the past like a video recorded without a director, simply giving us what occurred everywhere, this notion bears little relation to what peoples actually have done in their historiographies and so is of only speculative use. Consistently, peoples have interpreted their past, selecting certain happenings as central and organizing while relegating other happenings to the margins. This certainly was true of the biblical historians. What we read in the Pentateuch and the former prophets is a highly select and tendential narrative of Israel's past. The writers have very little, if any, interest in simply chatting up the old news. Consistently they are at work to press forward paradigms, privileged symbols and patterns, through which their readers might meaningfully, indeed consolingly, bring the past down into their present and launch themselves successfully into the future.

The assumption of the biblical historians is that who or what Israel is may be found in what Israel has been, and that the core of what Israel has been lies in the intrigue and challenge of its bond with the divine mystery. We could show analogies in the historical sensibilities of other peoples, from the Egyptians to the ancient Chinese, but in such other cases the accent on meaning being revealed through the linear flow of the people's collective experience of time would not be so sharp. The divinity that centered the worlds of ancient Egypt, China, and other peoples that we would want to survey in any comprehensive comparison set those worlds slowly revolving in recurrent, circular patterns. By its own stability and status as the fontal source of being and order, the divinity typical of the ancient civilizations made the time, and so the cultural experience, of such civilizations like a stately dance — a minuet in which the main melodies and steps repeated year after year, generation after generation. In fact there was considerable change in the people who danced through such minuets, but the debts of the divinity typical of ancient civilizations to the regularities of the natural world meant that what went on here below was thought to mirror what went on in heaven above, where little was innovative and most was eternally predictable. Israelite history was shaped by a more mysterious and less predictable divinity. It was shaped ,as well by the people's sense that God had erupted into their time, grabbed them by the scruff of the neck, and set them marching forward, into a future they could never know, a future they had to trust.

"Revelation" is essentially this experience and conviction that time can break open new meanings. If we think of the typical ancient divinity as serenely enthroned behind a veil, revelation conjures up a slashing of that veil, by a word or an act of energetic self-disclosure. Because of its especially acute appreciation of the divine mysteriousness, of the basal fact that the source of being and life cannot be controlled by human beings, Israel heard special overtones in the inner words of the acts of understanding of its elite. When a patriarch, a matriarch, a judge, a king, a prophet, a priest, or a wise person who stood out for excellence in her or his order caught on to what was happening, understood the signs of the times, the Israelite appreciation of how time mediated divinity, of how God was partnered to Israel's experience, made this understanding a word from God. Rightly enough, and with convictions that continue defensible even in our psychologically more sophisticated time, Israel could depict this "word" as spoken by God directly, on the order of the express production of meaningful sounds that constitutes typical human communications. But admitting this need not keep us from thinking that the core of biblical revelation occurred as the people's (divinely guided and encouraged) interpretation of the theological significance of their experiences in battle, in cultic sacrifice, in economic exchanges, in marital beds, in wrangles with their children—in all of life, from wondrous sunrise to wondrous sunset.

Still, Israelite revelation had more definition than what this claim that it could be coextensive with striking human experience and understanding suggests. Because certain narratives gained paradigmatic, "constitutional" status, the revelational flux was channeled along definite lines. This meant that Moses and Sinai had more influence than Ezekiel and Chebar, to say nothing of the thousands of candidates for revelatory significance that never made it into the canonical reckoning. It meant that David and Solomon counted for more, revealed more, than Ahab and Jezebel. Abraham encapsuled, served as a cipher for, more significance, more disclosure of meaning by the divine mystery, than Cain or Noah or Caleb. As in any story, some characters and their plots were more important than others. Throughout there was selection, arrangement, interpretation. Throughout revelation was a most human enterprise, because the divinity had been merciful enough, intriguing enough, to accept the limitations entailed in embarking on an intercourse with a collective partner both finite and mottled.

Anchored in such hope, the biblical appreciation of the human condition flowered handsomely. This led to the "humanism," the shrewd and positive eval-

Reason's Sleep Gives Birth to Monsters (Los Caprichos), by Francisco Goya y Lucientes, shows problems with modernity.   *(The Nelson-Atkins Museum of Art, Kansas City, Missouri [Nelson Fund])*

uation of human actualities and potentialities, that we have consistently praised. The shrewdness comes through in the Bible's tendency to account all people, even its heroes, afflicted with bits of clay and straw that keep them considerably less than the angels. So Moses grumbles and does not believe, disqualifying himself for the triumphant procession into the promised land. David commits adultery with Bathsheba and murders Uriah, making his heartful repentance fully necessary. Solomon is led astray by foreign wives, Jeremiah is something of a complainer, Abraham is not above hiding behind the skirts of Sarah, and Sarah mocks God's promise to fill her empty womb. Even Adam and Eve, the source of the staggering profusion and drama we call humanity, are far from ideal. The biblical appreciation of humanity is clear-eyed and unblinking. The more human beings puff themselves up with pretensions, acting as though they were little gods, the more the Bible sticks a pin in them. Human pridefulness is comic, as well as destructive. Human foibles and sins must strike a living God as reason for going tenderly, all the while that a living God has to render just judgment.

Many passages in the Hebrew Bible boil with resentment at sin and suffering, just as many passages run on and on with lamentation. The writers and editors are as imperfect as the characters they present. And, on the whole, this makes the Bible as human and lovable in its own literary character as in the Davids and Sarahs it presents. The self-knowledge, the irony, the playfulness, the willingness to bare its soul and not disguise its doubts — all these make the Bible a book by and for people just like ourselves. Its characters, its authors, and its editors all suffered the confusions, indeed the outright pains, of living in a time that was out of joint more often than it was healthy. That, despite this complete sharing in human imperfection and folly, the Bible still can open vistas of trust and hope, still can linger over dazzlingly poetic appreciations of natural beauty and human potential, raises it above most other literature and justifies its claim to be itself revelation from God.

Treatments of suffering, even eloquent ones, are a dime a dozen. Expositions of human hope, even nonutopian, realistic ones, are nearly as numerous. What is rare is a comprehensive vision of human experience that embraces both suffering and hope and raises both to a higher power by riveting them onto the foundational mystery of the divine love. This love is the best "reason" human beings have mustered for why there should be something rather than nothing. It is the best resource human beings have found for thinking that suffering and defeat may not have the last word. It has given countless generations a basis for obeying the ethical precepts of their society and worshiping its source in joy. It is what mothers and fathers have finally mediated to their children, when they have said through their hugs and their sacrifices and their other expressions of concern and goodness that one can go on, that tomorrow is worth facing.

If the Bible were only a slim collection of precepts to the effect that tomorrow is worth facing, it would have lain on the shelf little used. Because it is a large collection of varied narratives and poems to this effect and much more, it has been the foundational book of Western culture. For the Bible, tomorrow follows tomorrow and the covenant is something processive. For the Bible, God is historical, and God reveals what he will of the ultimate mysteries dynamically, through the clashes that move human beings almost despite themselves. From "In the beginning God created the heavens and the earth," to "Whoever is among you of all his people, may the Lord his God be with him. Let him go up," the Bible uses yesterday to keep today good and tomorrow open. Is that not enough to make it Torah: blessed guidance in the way?

GLOSSARY

Cult Worship, usually in the sense of a formal, perhaps compulsory set of ceremonies or rituals.

Deism The tendency to regard God as a remote source of the world who now takes little part or interest in it.

Elusive presence A paradoxical way of summarizing the biblical view of God: here, but mysterious.

Fealty Obedience, loyalty, owed to an overlord.

STUDY QUESTIONS

1. Explain the tension between world view and world views in the Hebrew Bible.
2. What are the distinctive qualities of the main covenants that the Bible describes?
3. What motive does the Bible give for God's having chosen to walk with Israel through its time?
4. How does the "liberation" or freeing worked by the biblical God relate to "salvation" or radical healing?
5. Suggest some of the biblical descriptions that make the divine personality parental.
6. How do the prime paradigms of biblical history prove revelatory of the divine nature?
7. How does the biblical interpretation of yesterday lay open a hopeful tomorrow?
8. What are the main deficiencies of the biblical view of human nature, when the task is a self-understanding sufficient to give human beings a year 2100 c.e. rich in peace and justice?

NOTES

1. See *Horizons in Biblical Theology*, 6 (1984), iii–80, for a series of articles by distinguished scriptural scholars on the future of biblical theology.
2. See Paul D. Hanson, "Theology, Old Testament," in *Harper's Bible Dictionary*, ed. Paul J. Achtemeier. San Francisco: Harper & Row, 1985, p. 1062.
3. See George W. Coats, "Theology of the Hebrew Bible," in *The Hebrew Bible and Its Modern Interpreters*, ed. Douglas A. Knight and Gene M. Tucker. Philadelphia: Fortress, 1985, p. 257. See also Gerhard F. Hasel, "Major Recent Trends in Old Testament Theology 1978–1983," *Journal for the Study of the Old Testament*, 31 (1985), 31–53, and John Goldingay, "Diversity and Unity in Old Testament Theology," *Vetus Testamentum*, 34 (1984), 153–68.
4. Johannes Schildenberger, "Covenant," in *Encyclopedia of Biblical Theology*, ed. J. B. Bauer. New York: Crossroad, 1981, p. 140.

5. See Elpidius Pax, "Holy," ibid., pp. 372–75.

6. See Jeremy Cott, "The Biblical Problem of Election," *Journal of Ecumenical Studies*, 21 (1984), 199–228.

7. See Elizabeth A. Johnson, "The Incomprehensibility of God and the Image of God as Male and Female," *Theological Studies*, 45 (1984), 441–65. See also Norbert Lohfink, "Das Alte Testament und sein Monotheismus," in *Der eine Gott und der dreieine Gott*, ed. Karl Rahner. Munich: Schnell & Steiner, 1983, pp. 28–47.

8. See John H. Hayes, "Restitution, Forgiveness, and the Victim in Old Testament Law," *Trinity University Studies in Religion*. 11 (1982), 1–21.

9. See Edmond Jacob, "Le Dieu souffrant, un thème théologique veterotestamentaire," *Zeitschrift für die alttestamentliche Wissenschaft*, 95 (1983), 1–8.

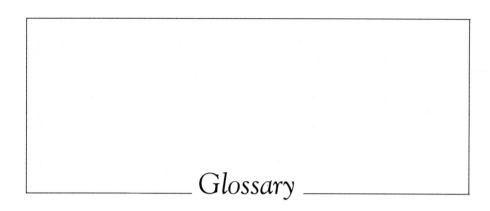

Glossary

Acedia Lacking spiritual energy, a state of carelessness and torpor; being dispirited.

Acrostic An arrangement in which stipulated letters (for example, the first) of the words in question (often of a poem or psalm) themselves form a word or regular pattern.

Agape The sort of love that can be predicated of God — selfless, pure, willing to suffer.

Aggiornamento Pope John XXIII's Italian word for bringing Roman Catholicism up to date.

Agnosticism Not knowing one's position, especially on ultimate matters such as the existence of God.

Allegory A literary form that makes point-by-point correspondences between two different situations.

Anamnesis Recollection, remembrance, deliberately making the past inform present consciousness.

Angel A messenger of God; a heavenly being in the divine service.

Anthropomorphic Personifying; treating something nonhuman as though it were human.

Anthropomorphism Personification; treating something nonhuman as though it were human.

Apocalyptic A supposed revelation about the end of the world or God's coming to render justice; the sort of literature that purports to derive from heavenly visions and usually offers a view of the future consoling to those who suffer for the faith.

Apocrypha Books or parts of books not found in the Hebrew Bible but included in the Christian Old Testament.

Apostasy Renouncing one's faith or professed allegiance.

Apostrophe Addressing a person (or a personified thing), often one not present.

Ark (of the covenant) A container or chest, principally used to carry the two tablets of the Mosaic Law; not to be confused with the tabernacle, a larger portable sanctuary within which the ark would be placed for worship services.

Baal A general Canaanite name for "lord," "owner," "husband," as well as for "god." Also the name of a specific Canaanite god (of the storm).

Biblical humanism The appreciation of human existence — grandeur, depravity — we find in the Bible.

Booths See Sukkot. Festival commemorating life in the wilderness.

Canaanite religion The polytheistic cult of Israel's most important neighbors. It was greatly concerned with fertility.

Canon A list or body of writings that is considered scriptural.

Canonical Officially accredited or authoritative; entered on the list of approved and directive documents.

Canonization Process of drawing up a list of officially approved writings.

Carte blanche A blank check, free rein.

Catharsis Purging, letting out one's emotions for the sake of restoring peace.

Charismatic Gifted; possessed of (divine or divinely given) powers or talents.

Chosenness See election. Israel as God's special people.

Classic A work that later generations use as a measure of their humanity.

Cosmological myth The notion that the whole of reality is an ordered (usually living) unity composed finally of a single stuff.

Covenant The semicontractual bond between Israel and Yahweh such that Israel would be his people and he would be their God.

Covenant Code The teaching that lays out the behavioral implications of the covenant.

Covenanted Bonded; refers to the solemn, almost legal bond between God and Israel.

Critical Passing judgment or sifting evidence so as to arrive at a reasoned stance about the matter in question.

Cult Worship, usually in the sense of a formal, perhaps compulsory set of ceremonies or rituals.

Deism The tendency to regard God as a remote source of the world who now takes little part or interest in it.

Deutero-canonical See Apocrypha. Books included in the Septuagint but not in the Hebrew Bible.

Deuteronomist (D)   Concerning the history or theology of the Book of Deuteronomy.

Deuteronomistic history   The narrative that spans from the Book of Joshua through the Books of Kings.

Diaspora   The dispersion or existence outside Israel that characterized many Jews as exiled.

Didactic   Teaching, lecturing, explaining.

Dies irae   The day of wrath (judgment), especially as contemplated liturgically.

Differentiated   Separated, developed. For example, a differentiated consciousness distinguishes myth from history and history from philosophy (without isolating them).

Divination   Art of discerning future events or God's intentions.

Divine kingship   The concept, common to many ancient societies, that the monarch so mediates between the people and ultimate reality that he should be considered a god.

Divine providence   God's oversight of history and care for human beings.

Dogmatic   Pertaining to official doctrine, set forth by a religious group's duly constituted authorities, that is considered binding on all orthodox members.

Double entendre   A pun or phrase that has double meaning (the second often sexual).

Doxology   An expression of praise and giving glory.

Eisegesis   Reading one's presuppositions into a text.

Election   Selection to special status (as the unique people of God).

Elohist (E)   The source, found in Genesis through Numbers, that calls God Elohim. The Elohist stems from the eighth or ninth century B.C.E. and supplements the Yahwist in the light of pre-Mosaic theology.

Elusive presence   A paradoxical way of summarizing the biblical view of God: here, but mysterious.

Enlightenment   Eighteenth-century European movement that stressed the untrammeled use of reason.

Eschatological   Pertaining to the last things (end of world, judgment, heaven, hell) or final age.

Etiological myths   Stories that employ nonordinary agents or circumstances to explain the origins of something.

Eucharistic   Pertaining to the Christian sacrament of thanksgiving that recalls the death and resurrection of Christ and offers believers communion with him through consecrated bread and wine.

Exorcism   The process of trying to cast out evil spirits thought to have possessed a person.

Faith   Belief; wholehearted commitment or assent beyond factual surety or proof.

Fealty   Obedience, loyalty, owed to an overlord.

Form criticism   Historical and literary analysis that concentrates on the structure and use that isolatable textual units probably had before being set into their present larger context.

Genealogy   A listing of descendants, to establish lineage and personal history.

Godfearers   Gentiles who accepted the biblical God and the biblical ethics and perhaps were considering conversion.

Grace   Divine favor, help, blessing, benevolence.

Grundlage (G)   A source common to J and E and so called (in German) the foundation.

Hagiography   Writing that narrates the life and/or marvelous deeds of a holy person.

Halakhah   Jewish legal tradition, talmudic law.

Hedonism   Devotion to pleasure, carnal satisfaction.

Hegemony   Preponderant influence or authority; leadership.

Heilsgeschichte   Salvation-history (history interpreted as the drama of divine interventions on human beings' behalf).

Hellenism   The cultural ideals, derived from Alexander the Great, that dominated the Near East and Eastern Europe in the late centuries B.C.E. and the early centuries C.E.

Hellenization   Process of becoming enculturated by the ideals derived from Alexander the Great.

Hesed   Steadfast kindness and love, the key attribute of the God of the covenant.

Hierodules   Slaves attached to temples; sacred prostitutes.

Historicity   The quality of existing in time, developing in epochs, and being liable to narrative description.

Historiography   The writing of history; narrative reconstruction of the past.

Hodayot   Songs of praise used at Qumran (the Essene community of separatists) at the end of the biblical period.

Holiness Code   Chapters 17–27 of Leviticus, which detail the laws for ensuring, protecting, and promoting holiness (nonordinariness, specialness, sacredness).

Holocaust   A form of sacrifice in which the victim/gift is burned to symbolize complete giving to God.

Holy War   War sanctioned by God, often supposedly led by God (the prime warrior), and sometimes requiring complete slaughter of the enemy.

Ideologues   Those who are prone to substitute ideas or doctrines for primary reality.

Ideology   Positively, ideas or doctrines that strongly influence or shape behavior; negatively, such ideas or doctrines that substitute for primary reality and commonsensical honesty.

Immanent   Existing or being present within (for example, God is immanent to the world or human experience as well as transcendent); part of Israel's experience of God's action in history.

"Israel"   The people descended from Jacob; the Northern Kingdom.

Jingoism   Belligerent chauvinism, aggressive nationalism or ethnocentricity.

Jubilee   The fiftieth year (after seven cycles of seven years) when all land was to return to its ancestral owners and slaves were to be freed—a super-Sabbath.

Kohathites   A Levitical family who had the important function of transporting the Holy of Holies.

Levirate law   (see Deuteronomy 25:5–10) The law that the brother of a man who died without a son had the obligation to marry the widow and try to give her a son in the dead man's name.

Levites   Members of the tribe of Levi (the third son of Jacob) who had priestly duties of both sacrificing and administering the divine law.

Liminality   State of in-between existence, experienced at such times as initiation and pilgrimage, when ordinary patterns fall away and people experience a foretaste of the freer community implied by their ideals. Israel's time in the wilderness has liminal ("threshold") characteristics.

Liturgical   Pertaining to public, official, ritualized worship.

Mandala   Visual form, often of wholeness, useful for meditation.

Menorah   A lampstand, usually made of gold, holding seven candles, and used in the cult.

Merkabah   The divine chariot featured in the vision of Ezekiel (verses 1:22–28) that became a central symbol in Jewish mysticism.

Mezuzah   The doorpost, and so the container affixed to the doorpost that holds scriptural passages (see Deuteronomy 6:9).

Millennial movements   Tendencies to expect the end of the world or Judgment Day after 1000 years or at the turn of a millennium.

Mis en scène   Stage setting; context for a given action or speech.

Mishnah   Code of Jewish law (interpretations of the oral Torah) formally promulgated around 200 c.e.

Misogynism   Hatred of women; antifeminism.

Mystery   A surplus or excess of meaning; something that has not been explained or cannot be explained.

Mysticism   Experience of or direct communion with ultimate reality.

Nazirite vow   A consecration to God requiring abstaining from wine and other intoxicants, not having one's hair shorn, and not going near a dead body.

Noahite covenant   The bond between God and Noah (who came to stand for all Gentiles) established after the flood (see Genesis 9).

Numinous   Concerning the divine or sacred.

Ontological   Concerning being, existential status, essential makeup.

Ontology   The study of being or existence.

Oracle   An expression of divine revelation, usually enigmatic and given through a prophet or diviner.

Oxymoron   A combination of contradictory or incongruous terms—for example, a wise fool.

Paradigmatic   Providing a template, a normative pattern.

Parallelism, semantic   Symmetry of meaning, repetition of denotation.

Parallelism, static   A duplication or mirroring with little movement of thought or imagery.

Passover   The commemoration of the flight from Egypt and escape into freedom.

Pogrom   Murderous attacks, especially on Jews in Gentile environments (for example, in the Polish ghettos).

Priestly (P)   The source in Genesis through Numbers that is most interested in law and ritual.

Quietistic   Peaceful to the point of culpable inactivity.

Qur'an   Muslim scripture; Muhammad's "Recital."

Redaction   Editing; reworking.

Relativism   The view that there are no binding norms, that all insights and truths are confined to the perspectives that generated them.

Religious   That which pertains to communion with, service of, or concern for ultimate reality.

Remnant   The portion left over after a part has been removed; the portion of the covenant community that would remain after defection and chastisement.

Revelation   Disclosure of sacred truth (usually by God).

Righteous Gentile   A non-Jew who lives a good life and honors God; applied to non-Jews who helped Jews during the Nazi era.

Sabbath   The Jewish day of worship, fashioned in conjunction with the picture of God's rest after creation (Genesis 2:2–3).

Sabbaticals   Times of rest and renewal; seventh days or seventh years considered dedicated to God.

Samaritans   Inhabitants of the district of Samaria (who only accepted the five books of Moses and preferred Mount Gerizim to Mount Zion).

Sapiential   Concerning wisdom.

Second Temple   The temple rebuilt upon return from Exile in 520 to 515 B.C.E. The Babylonians had destroyed the first Temple, built by Solomon.

Secular   Worldly view of life that sometimes tends to depreciate religion.

Seriatim   In sequence, following along in a series.

Shavuot   The Feast of Weeks (Pentecost in Greek) seven weeks after Passover, originally for the wheat harvest but later for the giving of the law on Sinai.

Shekinah   The glorious divine presence (considered feminine); seen in the cloud that accompanied the marchers in the wilderness.

Sheol   The shadowy underworld to which the departed spirits of the dead go (See Amos 9:2, Proverbs 9:18).

Shibboleth   Catchword or slogan thought to distinguish true adherents (native speakers) of a tradition.

Son of man   Either simply a human being or the heavenly figure of Daniel 7:13.

Spirit The divine breath, animating force, power that gives life, courage, creativity, holiness.

Sukkot (Feast of Booths or Tabernacles) Autumn harvest festival when huts of branches are erected in memory of the time in the wilderness.

Suzerain An overlord to whom vassals owe fealty.

Symbiosis Living together, codwelling.

Tabernacle The portable sanctuary supposedly used in the wilderness (see Exodus 25–30); a rectangular enclosure housing the Holy of Holies, the Ark, the Altar of Incense, the Menorah, and the table for the bread of the presence. The full description of the tabernacle has been influenced by the appearance of Solomon's Temple and probably does not apply to the tent of meeting used in the wilderness.

Talmud Primary source of Jewish law and rabbinic learning; Mishnah plus Gemara (debates on the Mishnah).

Talmudic Concerning the Talmud or main collection of postbiblical Jewish wisdom.

Tanak The Law-Prophets-Writings that constitute the Hebrew Bible.

Tefillin Phylacteries; a pair of small black boxes that contain scriptural passages in parchment and are wrapped by straps around the upper left arm and forehead during morning prayer.

Teleological Concerning ends, goals, final products, ultimate patterns.

Tent of meeting A simple form of the tabernacle probably actually used in the wilderness.

Tetrateuch The books Genesis through Numbers.

Theocentricity God-centeredness.

Theodicy The attempt to justify God in the face of evil.

Theophanous Manifesting or bearing God.

Theophany A manifestation of the divine.

Toledot The "generations" used in Genesis as a way of periodizing early biblical history.

Torah Jewish term for Teaching, Divine Guidance, Law.

Tradition Teaching and practice that have been handed down as authoritative and helpful.

Transcendence State of going beyond the usual limits, often going out to the divine.

Transpragmatic More than simply practical; idealistic.

Travesty A parody or burlesque; a change of clothes and roles (perhaps to bring out new aspects).

Type-scene A term from literary criticism used to describe situations that recur with new actors (for example, how Isaac and Jacob get their wives Rebekah and Rachel).

Usury Charging interest on money loaned.

Utopianism   The tendency to project ideal states in which one's hopes and convictions may be contemplated as though realized.

Vice-gerent   A representative ruler; one who rules or administers as the deputy of another.

Wars of the Lord   Religious battles, supposedly fought by or for God; a source quoted in Numbers 21:14–15.

Weeks   See Shavuot. The Feast of Pentecost.

Worship   Prayer, cult, devotion to God that honors the divine holiness.

Xenophobia   Fear of foreigners, usually to the point of hostility.

Yahweh   The most important personal name for God in the Hebrew Bible. Usually it was represented by the four consonants YHWH but in speech was replaced by Adonai (Lord).

Yahwist (J)   The oldest source in the books Genesis through Numbers, characterized by its use of the name Yahweh (Jahweh in German) for God and dating to the tenth century B.C.E.

Zionism   Jewish movement to secure a state in Palestine; centralizing focus on Mount Zion as the holiest place (site of the Temple) in the holiest city (Jerusalem).

Bibliography

NOTE: Entries marked with an asterisk (*) are suitable for undergraduates.

TORAH

*BURNS, RITA J. *Exodus, Leviticus, Numbers.* Wilmington, Del.: Michael Glazier, 1983.

CASSUTO, U. *The Documentary Hypothesis and the Composition of the Pentateuch.* Jerusalem: Magnes, 1961.

CLINES, DAVID J. A. *The Theme of the Pentateuch.* Sheffield, England: Department of Biblical Studies, University of Sheffield, 1978.

*COATS, GEORGE W. *Genesis with an Introduction to Narrative Literature.* Grand Rapids: Eerdmans, 1984.

*CRAIGIE, PETER C. *The Book of Deuteronomy.* Grand Rapids: Eerdmans, 1976.

CROSS, FRANK M. *Canaanite Myth and Hebrew Epic: Essays in the History of the Religion of Israel.* Cambridge, Mass.: Harvard University Press, 1973.

*ELLIS, PETER F. *The Yahwist: The Bible's First Theologian.* Collegeville, Minn.: Liturgical Press, 1968.

JENKS, ALAN W. *The Elohist and North Israelite Traditions.* Missoula, Mont.: Scholars Press, 1977.

JOHNSON, MARSHALL D. *The Purpose of the Biblical Genealogies.* Cambridge: Cambridge University Press, 1969.

KAUFMANN, YEHEZKEL. *The Religion of Israel: From Its Beginnings to the Babylonian Exile.* New York: Schocken Books, 1960.

*LEVENSON, JON D.   *Sinai and Zion: An Entry into the Jewish Bible.* Minneapolis: Winston, 1985.

*L'HEUREUX, CONRAD E.   *In and Out of Paradise.* New York: Paulist Press, 1983.

MAYES, A. D. H.   *Deuteronomy.* London: Oliphants, 1979.

MCCONVILLE, J. G.   *Law and Theology in Deuteronomy.* Sheffield, England: JSOT Press, 1985.

MCEVENUE, SEAN E.   *The Narrative Style of the Priestly Writer.* Rome: Biblical Institute Press, 1971.

MENDENHALL, GEORGE E.   *Law and Covenant in Israel and the Ancient Near East.* Pittsburgh: Biblical Colloquium, 1955.

NICHOLSON, E. W.   *Deuteronomy and Tradition.* Philadelphia: Fortress, 1967.

NIDITCH, SUSAN.   *Chaos to Cosmos: Studies in the Biblical Patterns of Creation.* Chico, Calif.: Scholars, 1985.

*PLAUT, H. GUNTHER, ed.   *The Torah: A Modern Commentary.* New York: Union of American Hebrew Congregation, 1981.

POLZIN, ROBERT.   *Moses and the Deuteronomist.* New York: Seabury, 1980.

RAD, GERHARD VON.   *Studies in Deuteronomy.* London: SCM, 1947.

*RIGGANS, WALTER.   *Numbers.* Philadelphia: Westminster, 1983.

*SARNA, NAHUM N.   *Understanding Genesis.* New York: Schocken, 1966.

THOMPSON, THOMAS L.   *The Historicity of the Patriarchal Narratives.* Berlin: Walter de Gruyter, 1974.

VAN SETERS, JOHN.   *Abraham in History and Tradition.* New Haven: Yale University Press, 1975.

WEINFELD, MOSHE.   *Deuteronomy and the Deuteronomic School.* Oxford: Oxford University Press, 1972.

*WESTERMANN, CLAUS.   *Genesis 1–11.* Minneapolis: Augsburg Publishing House, 1984.

PROPHETS

*ACKROYD, PETER RUNHAM.   *Exile and Restoration.* London: SCM; Philadelphia: Westminster, 1968.

BERGEN, RICHARD V.   *The Prophets and the Law.* Cincinnati: Hebrew Union College–Jewish Institute of Religion, 1974.

BIRCH, BRUCE C.   *The Rise of Israelite Monarchy: The Growth and Development of 1 Samuel 7–15.* Missoula, Mont.: Scholars Press, 1976.

*BLENKINSOPP, JOSEPH.   *A History of Prophecy in Israel from the Settlement in the Land to the Hellenistic Period.* Philadelphia: Westminster, 1983.

———.   *Prophecy and Canon: A Contribution to the Study of Jewish Origins.* Notre Dame: University of Notre Dame Press, 1977.

BOLING, ROBERT G.   *Judges.* Garden City, N.Y.: Doubleday, 1975.

*BRUEGGEMANN, WALTER.   *Tradition for Crisis: A Study in Hosea.* Richmond: John Knox, 1968.

CARLSON, R. A.   *David, the Chosen King: A Traditio-Historical Approach to the Second Book of Samuel.* Stockholm: Almqvist & Wicksell, 1964.

CARROLL, ROBERT P.   *When Prophecy Failed: Cognitive Dissonance in the Prophetic Traditions of the Old Testament.* New York: Seabury, 1979.

CLEMENTS, RONALD E.   *Isaiah and the Deliverance of Jerusalem: A Study of the Interpretations of Prophecy in the Old Testament.* Sheffield, England: JSOT, 1980.

*———.   *Prophecy and Tradition.* Atlanta: John Knox, 1975.

*CLIFFORD, RICHARD J.   *Fair Spoken and Persuading: An Interpretation of Second Isaiah.* New York: Paulist, 1984.

*CODY, AELRED.   *Ezekiel.* Wilmington, Del.: Michael Glazier, 1984.

CONROY, C.   *Absalom Absalom! Narrative and Language in 2 Samuel 13–20.* Rome: Biblical Institute Press, 1978.

*———.   *1–2 Samuel, 1–2 Kings.* Wilmington, Del.: Michael Glazier, 1983.

*CRAIGIE, PETER C.   *Ezekiel.* Philadelphia: Westminster, 1983.

*———.   *Twelve Prophets,* Volume 1. Philadelphia: Westminster, 1984.

CRENSHAW, JAMES L.   *Prophetic Conflict.* Berlin and New York: Walter de Gruyter, 1971.

———.   *Samson: A Secret Betrayed, a Vow Ignored.* Atlanta: John Knox; London: SPCK, 1978.

*DAVIDSON, ROBERT.   *Jeremiah,* Volume 1. Philadelphia: Westminster, 1983.

EMMERSON, GRACE I.   *Hosea: An Israelite Prophet in Judean Perspective.* Sheffield, England: JSOT Press, 1984.

ENGNELL, IVAN.   *Studies in Divine Kingship,* 2d ed. Oxford: Blackwell, 1967.

*FRETHEIM, TERENCE E.   *The Message of Jonah: A Theological Commentary.* Minneapolis: Augsburg, 1977.

GORDON, R. P.   *1 and 2 Samuel.* Sheffield, England: JSOT Press, 1984.

GOTTWALD, NORMAN K.   *The Tribes of Yahweh: A Sociology of the Religion of Liberated Israel 1250–1050 B.C.E.* Maryknoll, N.Y.: Orbis Books, 1979.

GRAY, JOHN.   *Joshua, Judges and Ruth.* London: Nelson, 1967.

———.   *I and II Kings.* London: SCM, 1970; Philadelphia: Westminster, 3d rev. ed., 1977.

GREENBERG, MOSHE.   *Ezekiel 1–20.* New York: Doubleday, 1983.

GUNN, DAVID M.   *The Fate of King Saul: An Interpretation of a Biblical Story.* Sheffield, England: JSOT, 1980.

———.   *The Story of King David: Genre and Interpretation.* Sheffield, England: JSOT, 1978.

*HAMLIN, E. JOHN.   *Inheriting the Land: A Commentary on the Book of Joshua.* Grand Rapids: Eerdmans; Edinburgh: The Handsel Press, 1984.

*HESCHEL, ABRAHAM.   *The Prophets.* New York: Harper & Row, 1962.

HILLERS, DELBERT R.   *Micah.* Philadelphia: Fortress, 1984.

JAGERSMA, HENK.   *A History of Israel in the Old Testament Period.* Philadelphia: Fortress, 1983.

*JENSEN, JOSEPH.   *Isaiah 1–39.* Wilmington, Del.: Michael Glazier, 1984.

———.   *The Use of Torah by Isaiah.* Washington, D. C.: Catholic Biblical Association of America, 1973.

JONES, GWILYM H.   *1 and 2 Kings,* Volume 1. Grand Rapids: Eerdmans, 1984.

———.   *1 and 2 Kings,* Volume 2. Grand Rapids: Eerdmans, 1984.

KAISER, OTTO.   *Isaiah 1–12.* Philadelphia: Westminster, 1983.

KNIGHT, GEORGE A. F. *Isaiah 40–55: Servant Theology*. Grand Rapids: Eerdmans, 1984.

KOCH, KLAUS. *The Prophets, Volume Two: The Babylonian and Persian Periods*. Philadelphia: Fortress, 1984.

LIEBERMAN, DAVID. *The Eternal Torah, Part Two: Joshua, Judges, Samuel One, Samuel Two*. New York: Ktav, 1983.

LINDBLOM, JOHANNES. *Prophecy in Ancient Israel*. Philadelphia: Muhlenberg, 1962.

McCARTER, P. KYLE. *I Samuel*. Garden City, N.Y.: Doubleday, 1980.

———. *II Samuel*. New York: Doubleday, 1984.

MONTGOMERY, JAMES A., and HENRY SNYDER GEHMAN. *The Books of Kings*. Edinburgh: T. & T. Clark, 1951.

NIELSEN, KIRSTEN. *Yahweh as Prosecutor and Judge: An Investigation of the Prophetic Lawsuit*. Sheffield, England: JSOT, 1979.

NOTH, MARTIN. *The Deuteronomistic History*, trans. from German by J. Doull et al., 1967. *Journal for the Study of the Old Testament*, Supplement Series 15 (1981).

OVERHOLT, THOMAS W. *The Threat of Falsehood: A Study in the Theology of the Book of Jeremiah*. Naperville, Ill.: Alec R. Allenson, 1970.

PERDUE, LEO G., and BRIAN W. KOVACS, eds. *A Prophet to the Nations*. Winona Lake, Ind.: Eisenbrauns, 1984.

*PETERSEN, DAVID. *Haggai and Zechariah 1–8*. Philadelphia: Westminster, 1984.

POLK, TIMOTHY. *The Prophetic Persona: Jeremiah and the Language of the Self*. Sheffield, England: The University, 1984.

*RAD, GERHARD VON. *The Message of the Prophets*. New York: Harper & Row, 1965.

*SAWYER, JOHN F. A. *Isaiah*, Volume 1. Philadelphia: Westminster, 1984.

SIMPSON, CUTHBERT AIKMAN. *Composition of the Book of Judges*. Oxford: Blackwell, 1957.

SOGGIN, JUAN ALBERTO. *Joshua: A Commentary*. London: SCM; Philadelphia: Westminster, 1970.

———. *Judges: A Commentary*. London: SCM; Philadelphia: Westminster, 1981.

WHEDBEE, J. WILLIAM. *Isaiah and Wisdom*. Nashville: Abingdon, 1971.

WHYBRAY, ROGER N. *The Succession Narrative*. London: SCM, 1968.

*———. *The Second Isaiah*. Sheffield, England: JSOT Press, 1983.

WILSON, ROBERT R. *Prophecy and Society in Ancient Israel*. Philadelphia: Fortress, 1980.

ZIMMERLI, WALTER. *Ezekiel 2*. Philadelphia: Fortress, 1983.

WRITINGS

*ANDERSON, BERNHARD W. *Out of the Depths: The Psalms Speak for Us Today*. Philadelphia: Westminster, 1983.

*———. *Signs and Wonders: A Commentary on the Book of Daniel*. Grand Rapids: Eerdmans, 1984.

BELLINGER, W. H. *Psalmody and Prophecy*. Sheffield, England: JSOT Press, 1984.

BERG, SANDRA BETH. *The Book of Esther: Motifs, Themes and Structure*. Missoula, Mont.: Scholars Press, 1979.

*BERGANT, DIANNE. *What Are They Saying About Wisdom Literature?* New York: Paulist, 1984.

BROCKINGTON, LEONARD HERBERT. *Ezra, Nehemiah and Esther*. London: Nelson, 1969.

*BRUEGGEMANN, WALTER A. *In Man We Trust*. Richmond: John Knox, 1972.

BRYCE, GLENDON E. *A Legacy of Wisdom: The Egyptian Contribution to the Wisdom of Israel*. Lewisburg and London: Bucknell University and Associated University Press, 1979.

*CLINES, D. J. A. *Ezra, Nehemiah, Esther*. Grand Rapids: Eerdmans, 1984.

*COLLINS, JOHN J. *Daniel with an Introduction to Apocalyptic Literature*. Grand Rapids: Eerdmans, 1984.

———— *The Apocalyptic Vision of the Book of Daniel*. Missoula, Mont.: Scholars Press, 1977.

COX, DERMOT. *The Triumph of Impotence: Job and the Tradition of the Absurd*. Rome: Universita Gregoriana Editrice, 1978.

*CRENSHAW, JAMES L. *Old Testament Wisdom, an Introduction*. Atlanta: John Knox, 1981.

————, ed. *Studies in Ancient Israelite Wisdom*. New York: Ktav, 1976.

————. *Theodicy in the Old Testament*. Philadelphia: Fortress, 1983.

CROSS, FRANK M., JR., and DAVID N. FREEDMAN. *Studies in Ancient Yahwistic Poetry*. Missoula, Mont.: Scholars Press, 1975.

DAHOOD, MITCHELL. *Psalms* (3 volumes). Garden City, N.Y.: Doubleday, 1965, 1968, 1970.

*DRYBURGH, B. *Lessons for Lovers in the Song of Solomon*. New Canaan, Conn.: Keats, 1975.

FUERST, WESLEY J. *The Books of Ruth, Esther, Ecclesiastes, The Song of Songs, Lamentations*. Cambridge: Cambridge University Press, 1975.

*GLATZER, NAHUM N. *The Dimensions of Job*. New York: Schocken Books, 1969.

GORDIS, ROBERT. *The Book of Job: Commentary, New Translation and Special Studies*. New York: The Jewish Theological Seminary of America, 1978.

HALS, RONALD M. *The Theology of the Book of Ruth*. Philadelphia: Fortress, 1969.

*HAMMER, RAYMOND. *The Book of Daniel*. Cambridge: Cambridge University Press, 1976.

HANSON, PAUL D. *The Dawn of Apocalyptic: The Historical and Sociological Roots of Jewish Apocalyptic Eschatology*. Philadelphia: Fortress, 1975.

HARTMAN, LOUIS F., and ALEXANDER A. DiLELLA. *The Book of Daniel*. Garden City, N.Y.: Doubleday, 1978.

HEATON, E. W. *The Book of Daniel: Introduction and Commentary*. London: SCM, 1956.

HILLERS, DELBERT R. *Lamentations*. Garden City, N.Y.: Doubleday, 1972.

JAPHET, SARA. *Ideology of the Book of Chronicles and Its Place in Biblical Thought*. Jerusalem: Hebrew University, 1973.

KAHN, JACK H. *Job's Illness: Loss, Grief, and Integration*. Oxford and New York: Pergamon, 1975.

KALUGILA, LEONIDAS. *The Wise King*. Lund: Gleerup, 1980.

KNIGHT, GEORGE A. F. *Psalms*, Volume 2. Philadelphia: Westminster, 1983.

LACOCQUE, ANDRE. *The Book of Daniel*. Atlanta: John Knox, 1979.

LANDY, FRANCIS. *Paradoxes of Paradise: Identity and Difference in the Song of Songs*. Sheffield, England: Almond, 1983.

*McCONVILLE, J. G. *I & II Chronicles*. Philadelphia: Westminster, 1984.

*McKANE, WILLIAM. *Proverbs*. Philadelphia: Westminster, 1970.

MOORE, CAREY A. *Esther*. Garden City, N. Y.: Doubleday, 1971.

*Morgan, Donn F.   *Wisdom in the Old Testament Traditions.* Atlanta: John Knox, 1981.

Mowinckel, Sigmund.   *The Psalms in Israel's Worship* (2 volumes). Nashville: Abingdon, 1962.

*Murphy, Roland E.   *Wisdom Literature and Psalms.* Nashville: Abingdon, 1983.

*———.   *Wisdom Literature: Job, Proverbs, Ruth, Canticles, Ecclesiastes, Esther.* Grand Rapids: Eerdmans, 1981.

Myers, Jacob M.   *I Chronicles, II Chronicles, Ezra, Nehemiah.* Garden City, N.Y.: Doubleday, 1965.

Perdue, Leo G.   *Wisdom and Cult.* Missoula, Mont.: Scholars Press, 1977.

Pope, Marvin H.   *Job.* Garden City, N.Y.: Doubleday, 1973.

———.   *Song of Songs.* Garden City, N.Y.: Doubleday, 1977.

*Rad, Gerhard von.   *Wisdom in Israel.* Nashville and New York: Abingdon, 1972.

*Reese, James M.   *The Book of Wisdom, Song of Songs.* Wilmington, Del.: Michael Glazier, 1983.

*Ringgren, Helmer.   *The Faith of the Psalmists.* Philadelphia: Fortress, 1974.

*Russell, D. S.   *Apocalyptic: Ancient and Modern.* Philadelphia: Fortress, 1978.

Sasson, Jack M.   *Ruth: A New Translation with a Philological Commentary and a Formalist Interpretation.* Baltimore: Johns Hopkins University Press, 1979.

Scott, R. B. Y.   *Proverbs, Ecclesiastes.* Garden City, N.Y.: Doubleday, 1965.

*———.   *The Way of Wisdom in the Old Testament.* New York: Macmillan, 1971.

Sheppard, Gerry T.   *Wisdom as a Hermeneutical Construct.* Berlin and New York: Walter de Gruyter, 1980.

*Stuhlmueller, Carroll.   *The Psalms.* Wilmington, Del.: Michael Glazier, 1983.

*Towner, W. Sibley.   *Daniel.* Atlanta: Knox, 1984.

Urbach, Ephraim E.   *The Sages: Their Concepts and Beliefs,* Volumes 1 and 2. Jerusalem: Magnes, 1975.

*Vawter, Bruce.   *Job and Jonah: Questioning the Hidden God.* New York and Ramsey: Paulist, 1983.

*Westermann, Claus.   *The Psalms: Structure, Content and Message.* Minneapolis: Augsburg, 1980.

Whybray, Roger N.   *The Intellectual Tradition in the Old Testament.* Berlin and New York: Walter de Gruyter, 1974.

———.   *Wisdom in Proverbs.* London: SCM, 1965.

Williams, James G.   *Those Who Ponder Proverbs: Aphoristic Thinking and Biblical Literature.* Sheffield, England: Almond, 1981.

Williamson, Hugh G. M.   *Israel in the Books of Chronicles.* Cambridge: Cambridge University Press, 1977.

Zerafa, Peter Paul.   *The Wisdom of God in the Book of Job.* Rome: Herder, 1978.

Zimmermann, Frank.   *The Inner World of Qohelet.* New York: Ktav, 1973.

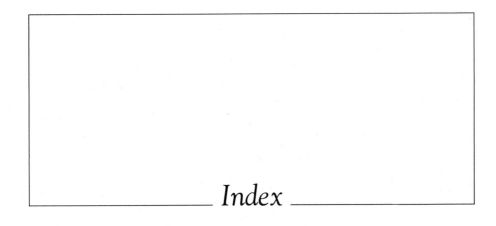

Index

Aaron, 54, 60-61, 75, 87, 89
  budding rod of, 90
  covenant of "salt," 91
  death of, 91, 93
  fusion with other Levitical
    people, 86
  lineage of, 67
Abel, woman of, 151
Abel and Cain, 28
Abiathar, 161
Abigail, 145
Abijam, 163
Abimelech, 35, 37
  kingship of, 132
Abiram, rebellion of, 90
Abishag, 161
Abner, murder of, 146
Abram/Abraham, 12, 32-36,
    394
  advance of the promise to,
    35-36
  call of, 32
  covenants and offspring of,
    33-34
  genealogy of, 31
  testing of, 35
Absalom, 149-50
  death of, 150-51
Achish, 145

Achsah, incident of, 125
Ackroyd, Peter R., 389
Acrostics, alphabetical, 355
Action, theology of, 391
Adam, genealogy of, 26-29
Admonition, prophetic oracles
    of (psalm genre), 267,
    275
Adonijah, 160-61
Adultery
  Hosea on, 228
  Israel's infidelities as, 206-7
Advent, Christian liturgy for,
    183
Afterlife, 115
Agag, 142-43
Agur, 320
Ahab (Northern king), 164,
    165, 166, 401
Ahasuerus (Xerxes I), reign of,
    362-67
Ahaz, King, 168, 177, 402
Ahijah (prophet), 163
Ahikam, 197
Ahithophel, 150
Ai, 122
Akkadians, 10
Alexander the Great, 14, 254,
    374, 376

Alter, Robert, 34, 199, 284
Amalek, 57, 142
Amaziah, 168, 401-2
Amen-em-Opet, 317
Ammonites, 34, 216, 249
  Jephthah and, 132
  Jeremiah's oracle against, 201
Amnon, 149
Amon (god of Thebes), 200
Amon (son of Manasseh), 169
Amorites, 123
Amos, Book of, 12, 19, 232-36
Ancestors, period of, 31-43
Angel
  Jacob's wrestling with, 48
  Samson's encounter with, 133
  Zechariah's vision of, 252
Animal sacrifice, 33
  regulations on, 77-78
Antigonus II, 14
Antiochus Epiphanes, 374, 378
Antiochus IV Epiphanes, 14,
    376-77
Apis, the divine Egyptian bull,
    200
Apocalyptic (revelatory)
    literature, 223, 370
Apocrypha, 7

Archetype (heavenly pattern),
   60
Ark of the covenant, 60, 62,
   120, 396, 398-99
   capture by Philistines, 139-40
   coming to Jerusalem of,
      153-54
   David's dancing before, 148
Artaxerxes II, 383
Asa, reign of, 164, 400-401
Asaph, psalms credited to, 271
Ashurbanipal, King, 203
Assyria, 179, 180-81, 187, 240,
   241, 249
   conquest of Northern
      Kingdom, 168-69
   as Lord's "rod of anger, staff
      of fury," 178
   Nahum on, 245-46
   threats to Judah (734 to
      701), 176, 177
Athaliah, Queen Mother, 168,
   401
Atonement, Day of, 77, 79, 90
Augustine, St., 344
Authors, biblical
   chauvinism of, 128
   historicity and, 156
   purpose of, 5
Azariah, 168, 401
Azazel, 77

Baals, cult of, 164-65
Baasha, 164
Babel, Tower of, 30-31
Babylon, 178, 187, 200
   fall of, 201, 202
   fall of Judah to, 181
   as hammer of God, 202
   Isaiah on, 179
   Jeremiah's oracle against, 201
   Persian conquest of, 388
   punishment of, 183
   Zedekiah's revolt against,
      203-4
   See also Exile, Babylonian
Balaam's ass, incident of, 91-92
Banhadad, death of, 167
Banias, 108
Baruch, 197, 199
Bashan, 91
Bathsheba, 148-49, 161
Bedouins, 216
Behemoth, 304
Bellah, Robert, 3
Belshazzar, King, 372-73
Benhadad, 165
Benjamin, 39, 41
   justice done to, 134

Benjaminites, 146
Berg, Sandra Beth, 365
Bestiality, 78
Bethel, 37, 39
Bethlehem, 243
Biblical humanism, 48-49,
   155-56, 414-16
Biblical theology, 407
   arguments for, 2-3
   See also World view of
      Hebrew Bible
Bildad the Shuhite, 295, 297,
   299
Bilhah, 38, 39
Bisexuality of humanity,
   Yahwist view of, 26
Bland, K. P., 223
Blessings, 282
Blood
   as polluter, 93
   as symbol of life, 28, 29
Blood vengeance, 149, 151
Boadt, Lawrence, 88
Boaz, 326-28
Boling, Robert, 127-28, 131
Bones, vision of the dry, 219,
   224
"Book of the Kings of Israel,"
   395
Booths, Feast of, 79, 86, 256
Bread, liturgical significance of,
   33
Breastplate of judgment, 61
Breath of life, 26
Buddhism, Mahayana, 352

Cain and Abel, 28
Caleb, 89-90, 123-25
Calf, incident of golden, 61
Canaan
   Conquest, 10-11, 44, 45, 91,
      119, 120, 120-23
   allotting land gained from,
      123-25
   boundaries established
      from, 93
   limited success of, 123-25,
      130-31
   mobilization and invasion,
      120-21
   religious ideology of, 122
   warfare, 121-23
   Egypt contrasted with, 101
   expedition to reconnoiter, 89
   false report about, 89, 90
   See also Joshua
Canaanite religion, 102
Canonization
   effects of, 111-12

of Pentateuch, 67
of Scriptures, 21
Census(es), 92
   by David, 152
   Levitical, 86, 87
   by Moses, 85-86
Ceremonial songs, 268
   royal, 274, 277-80, 282
Chaos before Creation, 25
Character, moral, 3-4
Chariot and cherubim,
   symbolism of, 222
Chariots, Zechariah's vision of,
   253
Chemosh, 200
Childbirth, purification required
   after, 76
Childs, Brevard, 31, 67, 111,
   128, 205, 222, 244, 307,
   322, 338-39, 359,
   367-68, 389-90
Child sacrifice, 169
Chosenness, issue of, 69
Christianity
   effects on Torah, 114-15
   priesthood and, 57-58
   Protestant, 4
   Sunday morning and, 1-2
1 and 2 Chronicles, 20,
   393-406
   historical background, 403-4
   lasting significance, 404-5
   literary intent, 403-4
   textual analysis, 393-403
      from Adam to Saul, 393-95
      Davidic line to the Exile,
         400-403
      kingship of David, 395-98
      kingship of Solomon,
         398-400
Circumcision, 33-34
   prenuptial, 54
   spiritual, 192
Cities of refuge, prescription
   for, 125
City-dwellers, Cain as ancestor
   of, 28
Civil religion, 128
Clan vengeance, 93
Classical status of the Bible,
   156-57
Cloud of incense, 76
Coats, George W., 407
Commandments, 58-59, 67,
   100
   Israel's existence and, 107
   See also Deuteronomy; Mosaic
      covenant

Communal lament, psalms of, 267, 270, 273, 275-79, 281, 282, 283
Communication, problems of religious, 189
Commutation of votive gifts, 80-81
Confessions of Jeremiah, 194
Confidence, psalms of, 266-67, 268, 273-74
  communal, 280-82
  individual, 281
Coniah (Jehoiachin), 196
Conquest of Canaan, 10-11, 44, 45, 91, 119, 120, 120-23
  allotting land gained from, 123-25
  boundaries established from, 93
  limited success of, 123-25, 130-31
  mobilization and invasion, 120-21
  religious ideology of, 122
  warfare, 121-23
  See also Joshua
Conquest of the Babylonians, 106
Covenant Code, 59, 67
Covenanted people, Israel as, 408-9
Creation
  Near Eastern accounts of, 25
  priestly account of, 25-26
  Western sense of, 47
  Yahwist account of, 26-29
Crenshaw, James L., 306-7, 350
Criticism, form and historical, 16
Crusades, Christian, 127
Cult, 408
  of the Baals, 164-65
  Canaanite, 122
  ethics and, 74, 78, 82
  Israelite, establishment of, 62
  See also Deuteronomy
Culture
  secularism of Western, 288
  Sumerian, 10
Cup of the wine of the Lord's wrath, imagery of, 196
Curses for disobeying law, 105-6
Cushan-rishathaim, 131
Cynicism about integrity or unity of Bible, 5-6
Cyrus of Persia, 181, 182-83
  proclamation of, 382

Dahood, Mitchell, 268, 286
Damascus, 201, 233

oracle against, 178
Daniel, 20-21, 370-80
  historical background, 377-78
  lasting significance, 379
  literary intent, 378-79
  textual analysis, 370-77
  stories of Daniel, 370-74
  visions of Daniel, 374-77
Danites, 133
Dan (Joseph's brother), 39
Darius, King, 251
Dathan, rebellion of, 90
David, King, 11, 12, 40, 160, 329
  Bathsheba and, 148-49
  census of, 152
  Chronicles on kinship of, 395-98
  covenant with, 408
  dying counsel to Solomon, 161
  Goliath and, 143
  Jonathan and, 142, 144, 146
  line of, 400-403
  as paradigm of love poetry, 338
  Philistines and, 144, 146-48
  psychological interest story cycle, 154
  reign of, 146-51
  rise of, 143-46
  song of, 152
  succession of, 142
Day of Atonement, 77, 79, 90
Death, Ecclesiastes on, 351
Deborah (prophetess), 131
Decalogue. *See* Ten commandments
Declarative praise, psalms of, 267, 274, 277, 278
Delilah, 133
Descriptive praise, hymns of, 266, 277, 278
Desert, Israel's wandering in, 56-57, 65, 90
Determinism, 346
Deuteronomist, the, 17, 56
Deuteronomistic history, 17-18
  anti-monarchical strain of, 131-32
  conclusion of, 160
  Exodus and, 67
  priestly interests in, 168
Deuteronomy, 18, 24, 98-117, 172, 384
  cultic character of, 110
  discovery of, 169
  historical background, 109-10
  lasting significance, 112-15

literary intent, 110-12
neo-Assyrian politics and, 109-10
as part of larger historical writing, 17-18
problem of evil and, 112-13
textual analysis, 98-109
  fifth discourse or blessing and leaving, 109
  first discourse or prologue, 99
  fourth discourse or final appeal, 106-9
  second discourse, 99-101
  third discourse, 101-6
theology of, 173
"Devoted thing," 80
Dharma, 114
Diaspora, 231
Dinah, rape of, 39
Disasters, human failings and, 113
Discharges, genital, 76
Discipline, parental, 100
Disease
  hygiene and, 75
  of skin, regulations for dealing with, 76
Divinatio, 142
Divine jealousy, Zechariah on, 254
Divine justice, Habakkuk on, 246-47
Divine mystery, steadfast love as nature of, 244
Divine presence (theophany), 188
Divine providence, theme of, 38, 40, 43
Divinity
  history and, 189
  humanity's distinction from, 347
Divorce, 105
Doctrine of grace, 100
Documentary Hypothesis, 16
Doeg, 144
Dome of the Rock, 77
Dream(s)
  of "Jacob's Ladder," 37
  Joseph's interpretation of, 40-41

Ebedmelech, 200
Eber, children of, 30
Ebla, 100
Ecclesiastes, 15, 20, 342-54
  historical background, 350-51
  lasting significance, 352-53

 ⌐2
 42-50
 .overbs,

 .ion, 342-43
 .pts, 350
 .tic advice, 348-49
 .ity of life, 343-48
 , 26
 ,m and Edomites, 91
 betrayal by, 237
 Jeremiah's oracle against, 201
 Obadiah on, 236-37
Egypt, 203-4
 civil turmoil predicted for (in
  Isaiah), 179
 contrasted with Canaan, 101
 dependence upon (Isaiah on),
  180
 Ezekiel on, 217-18
 governmental system, 122
 Jacob in, 41-42
 Joseph's slavery in, 40
 liberation from. See Exodus
 during period of Abraham, 10
Ehud, 131
Eisegesis, 346
Elah, 164
Elam, 201
Elders, tribal, 122
Eleazar, 91, 93
Eli, 139
 sons of, 139
Eliakim, 179
Eliashib, 387
Elihu, discourses of, 300-303
Elijah (prophet), 12, 164-67,
 189, 401
Elimelech, 325-26, 328
Eliphaz the Temanite, 294,
 296-97, 298, 306
Elisha, 165-68
Elohistic strains of Exodus, 67
Elohist tradition, 44, 111
Enlightenment (European), 4
Enoch, 28-29
Entrance and processional
 liturgies (psalm genre),
 267, 268
Environment, pollution of, 81
Ephod, 61
Ephraim, 41, 132, 180
 Jacob's blessing of, 42
 war with Syria (734-733),
  176, 177
 See also Northern Kingdom
Esau, 37, 237
 Jacob and, 28, 36-39

 traditions about, 39
Eschatology, 377
Establishment, notion of, 411
Esther, 20, 362-69
 historical background, 367
 as "historicized wisdom tale,"
  368
 lasting significance, 368
 literary intent, 367-68
 textual analysis, 362-67
  Esther becomes queen, 364
  Esther thwarts Haman,
   365-66
  Haman's wicked plot,
   364-65
  happy ending, 366-67
  introduction to the Persian
   court, 362-64
 works of, 15
Ethics
 Amos on, 236
 crux of, 272
 cult and, 74, 78, 82
Ethiopia, 249
Ethnic separatism, 39, 389-90,
 391
Evil, Deuteronomy and problem
 of, 112-13
Excommunication, 78
Exile, Babylonian, 14-15, 170,
 171, 181, 182, 183
 Chronicles on, 400-403
 Job and, 306
 restoration from, 198
 as transitional, 184
Exodus, 10, 11, 44, 45, 52-72
 canonical shaping of, 67
 cultic regulations of, 69-70
 historical background, 63-66
 holy war and, 69
 lasting significance, 68-70
 Liberation Theology in,
  68-69
 literary intent, 66-68
 textual analysis, 52-63
  apostasy and renewal,
   61-62
  building the tabernacle,
   62-63
  Exodus from Egypt, 52-56
  instructions for the
   tabernacle, 60-61
  Israel in the desert, 56-57
  making the covenant,
   59-60
Experience, religious, 48
Ezekiel, 211-26, 409
 call from God, 211-12
 development of, 18

 historical background, 221
 imagery of harlotry, 222
 lasting significance, 222-25
 literary intent, 221-22
 textual analysis, 211-20
  oracles of judgment on
   Judah and Jerusalem,
   211-16
  oracles on the restoration
   of Judah, 216-20
 works of, 15
Ezra, 14, 381-91
 historical background, 387-89
 lasting significance, 390-91
 literary intent, 389-90
 memoirs of, 20
 reforms of, 111
 textual analysis, 381-84
  mission of Ezra, 383-84
  restoration of the
   community, 382

Fasting, Zechariah on, 254
Fatherhood, motif of, 41
Fear of the Lord, 312, 346
Feast of Booths, 256
Feminist overtones in Ruth, 330
Fensham, F. Charles, 387-88
Fertile Crescent, the, 53
Fertility, 29
 deities of, 178
 religion, 26-27
Festivals, religious, 79
 legislation for, 103
Fire, divine presence and, 33
First-born, 86
Firstlings, 86
Flood, Noah and the, 29-30
Foreigners, separation from, 39,
 389-90, 391
Form criticism, 16
Framework poem, 293
Fratricide, 134
Futilities, moral, 346

Gabriel (angel), 374-75
Gad, 93, 125-26
Gammie, John G., 370-71, 378
Gan ha-Sheloshah, 135
Gedaliah, 171, 200
Generations (toledot), 86
Genesis, 3, 24-51, 412
 founding of Israel and, 44
 historical background, 43-45
 lasting significance, 46-49
 literary intent, 45-46
 textual analysis, 24-43
  period of the Ancestors
   (11:27–50:26), 31-43

primeval history
(1:1–11:26), 25-31
Gentile nations. *See* Nations,
the
Gibeonites, 122-23, 151
Gideon, 131-32, 135
Gifts, commutation of votive,
80-81
Gilead (northeastern Israel),
233
Gilgamesh, Seal of, 30
God
biblical, 410-12
culpable ignorance about,
177, 179
fidelity to, 102-3
hiddenness of, 183
jealousy of, 92, 94-95, 100
Job's dialogues with, 303-5
as king and partner of Israel,
81
maternal figure for, 183
mystery of, 48
negative way of approaching,
352
of Numbers, 94
"servant" of, 182
See also Lord, the; YHWH
Golden calf, incident of, 61
Goliath, David and, 143
Gomorrah, Sodom and, 33, 34
Good Friday, 242
Good life, minimalist notion of,
409
Gordis, Robert, 368
Gottwald, Norman K., 10, 17,
43-44, 121-22, 204, 205,
268, 270, 277, 359,
388-89
Government
Egyptian, 122
pollution of, 81
"G" process, 44
Grace, doctrine of, 100
Grant, Michael, 10
Greenberg, Moshe, 139
Greenstein, Edward L., 81
Guilt offering vs. sin offering,
74
Gunkel, Herman, 264, 285
Guthrie, Harvey H., Jr., 350

Habakkuk, 19, 246-48
Habits, of the heart (moral
character), 3-4
Hadassah. *See* Esther
Haddad, 162
Hagar, 33, 34-35
Haggai, 19, 250-52

Ham, 30
Haman, 364-66
Hamor, 39
Hanamel, 198
Hanani, 401
Hannah, 139
Hanson, Paul D., 407
Harlotry
Ezekiel's imagery of, 222
Hosea on, 228, 229
Hasmonean rule, 14
Hawking, Stephen, 47
Hazael, 165, 167
Hazor, 201
Heavenly pattern (archetype),
60
Heifer, ritual involving the
ashes of the red, 91
Hellenism, 14
Hellenized Jews, 378
Herakles, 375
Herod the Great, 14
Hezekiah, King, 14, 102, 169,
181
Hinduism, 352
Hiram of Tyre, King, 162
Historical criticism, 16
Historical psalms, 275, 278, 289
Historical revelation, dynamics
of, 412-16
Historicity, biblical authors and,
156
History
Bible and, 4-5
connotations of term, 412-13
deuteronomistic, 17-18
divinity and, 189
of Israel, 9-23
from 3000 B. C. E. to 922
B. C. E., 9-12
from 922 B. C. E. to 90 C.
E., 12-15
division of, 12-14
Hellenization, 14
paradigms of, 410
Prophets and, 17-19
Roman rule, 14
Southern Kingdom, 12-14
Torah and, 15-17
Writings and, 19-21
See also Conquest of
Canaan; Exile,
Babylonian; Exodus
primeval, 25-31
theology of, 173-74
Hobab, 88
Holiness, treatment in
Leviticus, 83
Holiness Code, 17, 77-80

"Holy of Holies," 77
Holy war, 92, 249
concept and rules for, 126
Conquest of Canaan as, 12
difficulties raised by doctrine
of, 128
Exodus and, 69
Muslim (jihads), 127
Numbers and, 94
regulations for, 120
Homosexuality, 78
Hophra, Pharaoh, 200
Horeb, 54
rock of, 57
Horns, Zechariah's vision of,
252
Hosea, 12, 19, 207, 227-30
Huldah (prophetess), 169, 403
Humanism, biblical, 48-49,
155-56, 414-16
Humanity
awakening to shame of, 27
bisexuality of, Yahwist view
of, 26
creation of, 26
divinity's distinction from,
347
Human nature, depiction in
Genesis of, 47-48
Human sacrifice, 35
Humility, Zephaniah's counsel
to, 249, 250
Hushai, 150
Hygiene, disease and, 75
Hymn(s), 269
of kingship of God, 277
of praise or thanksgiving
(psalm genre), 264, 267,
273, 277, 280, 281, 282,
283-84, 289
descriptive, 266, 277, 278
of Zion, 270-71, 275, 276,
281
See also Psalms; Songs

Ichabod, birth of, 139
Identity of Israel, proper
worship as crux of, 403,
404-5
Idolatry, 102
Ezekiel on, 214
Isaiah on, 178-79, 182
in Israel, 162-64
of political and military
power, 187
Idols, nothingness of, 194
Ignorance, culpable, 177, 179
Imagination, prophetic
of postexilic times, 256-57

37

...ont.)

...77 regarding,

...ents, psalms of,
.0, 273-79, 282,

...mous, 269
...ual psalms of confidence,
281
.delity, 102
marital, procedure for dealing
with, 87
religious, 106-8
Inheritance, laws concerning
family, 92
Injustice, 346-47
social injustice, 185, 204-5,
390
Amos on, 236
Micah on, 241, 243-44
Innocence, oaths of, 300
Intertribal warfare (fratricide),
134
Isaac, 12, 34, 36-43
binding of, 35
blessing of, 37
threats to, 34-35
Isaiah, 169, 176-90
development of, 18
historical background, 186-87
lasting significance, 188-89
literary intent, 187-88
textual analysis, 176-86
First Isaiah, 176-81
Second Isaiah, 181-84
Third Isaiah, 184-86
Ishbosheth, 146
Ishmael, 33, 35, 171
Ishmaelites, 40
Ishtar (Akkadian goddess), 336
Israel
advent of kingship in, 140-43
ambivalence about building
Temple of Jerusalem,
148
Amos's indictment of, 233,
234
commandments and existence
of, 107
conflict with Judah, 146
corruption and decadence in
premonarchical period,
133-34, 138-39
defection from religious
beginnings, 192
in the desert, 56-57, 65, 90

disregard of prophets, 193-94
end of kingdom of, 168
Genesis and founding of, 44
history of, 9-23
from 3000 B. C. E. to 922
B. C. E., 9-12
from 922 B. C. E. to 90 C.
E., 12-15
division of, 12-14
Hellenization, 14
paradigms of, 410
Prophets and, 17-19
Roman rule, 14
Southern Kingdom, 12-14
Torah and, 15-17
Writings and, 19-21
See also Conquest of
Canaan; Exile,
Babylonian; Exodus
idolatry in, 162-64
infidelities as adultery, 206-7
liberation by Judges, 131-32
paganism and, 131-32
postexilic restoration of,
382-83
rise of kingship in, 152
senselessness of, 193
wisdom movement in, 20,
321, 322
See also Jacob; Judges
Israelites
cult of, establishment of, 62
ideal, 264
identity of, proper worship as
crux of, 403, 404-5
reconstitution of, 386-88
"Is There Any Pain Like My
Pain?" (Lamentation),
355-56

Jacob, 12, 36, 36-43, 237
blessing of Ephraim, 42
blessing of Manasseh, 42
in Egypt, 41-42
Esau and, 28, 36-39
reencounter of, 38-39
traditions about, 39
funeral of, 43
journey of, 37
Laban and, 38
last testament, 42-43
Rachel and, 37-38
wrestling with the angel, 48
See also Israel
"Jacob's Ladder," dream of, 37
Jamnia, 14
Japheth, 30
Jealousy
of God, 92, 94-95, 100

Zechariah on, 254
image of fire of, 337
Jebel Musa, 64
Jehoahaz/Jehoiakim, King, 168,
171, 196, 197, 203, 403
Jehoash, 168
Jehoiachin, King, 171, 214-15,
221
Jehoiada (priest), 168, 401
Jehoram, 401
Jehoshaphat, 166, 401
Jehu, 165, 168
dynasty of, 12
Jephthah, 132
Jeremiah, 191-210
confessions of, 194
Daniel's interpretation of
prophecy of, 375
development of, 18
historical background, 203-4
lasting significance, 206-8
literary intent, 204-6
textual analysis, 191-203
historical appendix, 202-3
prophecies against the
nations, 200-202
speeches and stories,
196-200
visions, judgments, and
personal laments, 191-96
Jericho, 120
fall of, 121
Jeroboam, 162, 163, 168
Rehoboam's split with, 400
Jeroboam I, 12
Jeroboam II, 235
Jerusalem, 155
ark of the covenant coming
to, 153-54
Ezekiel's oracles on, 211-16
fall of, dirges over. *See*
Lamentations
Haggai on post-Exilic, 250-52
Isaiah's oracles against, 180
Jeremiah's prophecy on, 193
Micah's oracles on, 241-42
restoration of, 183
siege of, 212, 242
sufferings of captured, 356
Zechariah's visions about,
252-57
Zephaniah's oracles against,
249-50
See also Zion
Jerusalem Temple. *See* Temple
of Jerusalem
JE strand of Numbers, 85, 93-94
Jezebel, 164, 165
Jihads (Muslim holy wars), 127

Joab, 146, 149, 150-51, 397
  murder of, 161
Joash (Israelite king), 402
Joash (Northern king), 401-2
Job, 292-310, 412
  development of, 20
  historical background, 306-7
  lasting significance, 308
  literary intent, 307-8
  textual analysis, 292-306
    dialogues with friends,
      293-300
    dialogues with God, 303-5
    epilogue, 306
    monologues, 300-303
    opening monologue, 293
    prologue, 292-93
Joel, 19, 230-32
Johanan, 200
John of the Cross, 352
Jonah, 19, 238-40
Jonathan (Saul's son), David
  and, 142, 144, 146
Jordan river, crossing of, 120-21
Joseph, 38, 39-43
  brothers revisited by, 41
  death of, 43
  interpretation of dreams,
    40-41
  J story of, 40
  sale into slavery in Egypt, 40
  success and misfortune of, 40
  traditions about, 43-44
Joshua, 57, 61, 89-90, 93,
  118-29
  historical background, 126-27
  lasting significance, 128
  literary intent, 127-28
  succession of, 92, 107
  textual analysis, 118-26
    allotting inheritance,
      123-25
    keeping the peace, 125-26
    mobilization and invasion,
      120-21
    testament of Joshua, 126
    warfare, 121-23
  theme of the land in, 128
  traditions about, 43
  Zechariah's vision and, 253
Josiah, King, 14, 169-70, 191,
  203, 402-3
  reform of Southern Kingdom,
    111
  reign of, 107
Jotham, 402
  parable of, 132
Jubilee, 79-80
Judah, 40, 163, 169-71

Assyrian threats to
  (734-701), 176, 177
conflict with Israel, 146
descendants of, 394
Ezekiel's oracles
  on judgment of, 211-16
  on restoration of, 216-20
fall of, 181, 203
Jeremiah on, 195, 196
Malachai's oracles against,
  257-60
restoration of, 243
Judges, 12, 130-37
  historical background, 134
  lasting significance, 135-36
  literary intent, 134-35
  textual analysis, 130-34
Judgment
  breastplate of, 61
  Joel on day of, 231
  prophetic oracles of (psalm
    genre), 267, 275
  Zechariah's oracles of coming,
    255-56
Justice
  divine, Habakkuk on, 246-47
  human, Job and, 308

Kedar, 201
1 and 2 Kings, 118, 160-75
  historical background, 171-72
  lasting significance, 173-74
  literary intent, 172-73
  textual analysis, 160-71
    divided monarchy, 163-69
    kingdom of Judah, 169-71
    reign of Solomon, 160-63
Kingship
  priority of prophecy over,
    163, 165
  rights and duties of, 141
  rise in Israel of, 152
  Saul and advent of, 140-43
  See also Monarchy, Israelite
Knowledge
  of the Lord, 198
  tree of, 26
Kohathites, 87
Korah, rebellion of, 90
Korahites, 270

Laban, 37, 38
Lament(s)
  communal, 267, 270, 273,
    275-79, 281, 282, 283
  individual, 264-70, 273-79,
    282, 283
  in acrostic form, 268
  anonymous, 269

Lamentations, 355-61
  historical background, 359
  lasting significance, 360
  literary intent, 359
  textual analysis, 355-58
    account of a survivor, 358
    Everyman, 357-58
    "Is There Any Pain Like
      My Pain?," 355-56
    "The Lord Became Like an
      Enemy," 356-57
    a prayer, 358
Lampstand, Zechariah's vision
  of sevenfold, 253
Land, theme in Joshua of, 128
Law, book of. *See* Deuteronomy
Law, the
  Nehemiah's responses to,
    385-86
  Proverbs and, 322
  public proclamation of, 391
  See also Torah
Law(s)
  concerning family
    inheritance, 92
  curses for disobeying, 105-6
  forbidding sexual intercourse,
    76
  levirate, 105
  religious, 69-70
  of uncleanness, 75-76
Leadership, question of, 134-36
Leah, 36, 37, 38
Lebanon, 255
Legislation, 81. *See also*
  Leviticus
Leprosy, 76
Levi, 39. *See also* Levites
Leviathan (Canaanite monster
  of the sea), 179, 239,
  305
Levirate ("husband's brother")
  law, 105
Levites, 60-61, 220, 394, 396
  benefits of, 91
  inheritance for, 93
  land inheritance of, 125
  Moses' cleansing of, 87-88
Leviticus, 73-84
  historical background, 81
  lasting significance, 82-83
  literary intent, 81-82
  priestly tradition and, 73
  textual analysis, 73-82
    commutation of votive
      gifts, 80-81
    Holiness Code, 77-80
    inaugural services at the
      sanctuary, 74-75

_anness, 75-76
_ of the
_ary and nation,
_
_ncial system, 73-74
_on/redemption, notion
of, 411
_iblical calls to, 112
theology in Exodus of, 68-69
Life
blood as symbol of, 28, 29
breath of, 26
minimalist notion of good,
409
vanity of, 343-48
Lions den, incident of, 373-74
Literalism, 4-6
Literature
apocalyptic (revelatory), 223,
370
biblical, 5-6
as linear view of human
time, 46
Liturgical procession, 274
Liturgy(ies)
for Advent, Christian, 183
entrance and processional,
267, 268
Locusts, plague of, 231, 232
Loincloth, symbolism of, 194
Lord, the
fear of, 312, 346
knowledge of, 198
silence of, 185
wrath of, 196
"Lord Became Like an Enemy,
The" (Lamentation),
356-57
Lot, 32-33, 34
Love
erotic, 332
nature of divine mystery and,
244
Ruth and, 330
See also Song of Songs

Maccabees, 14, 378
Machpelah, cave of, 36
"Magnificat" of Mary, 139
Mahayana Buddhism, 352
Malachai, 19, 257-60, 404
Manasseh, 41, 92, 93, 125-26,
169, 402
Jacob's blessing of, 42
Mangan, Celine, 397
Manna, 56-57
Mara (Naomi), 326

Marriage, 26
imagery of, 184, 192, 207
in Hosea, 230
infidelity in, procedure for
dealing with, 87
Mary, "Magnificat" of, 139
May, Herbert G., 330
Medes, 178, 201
Meeting, tent of, 61, 62-63
Melchizedek, 33
Mendenhall, George, 44
Menorah, 60
Merkabah ("chariot") mysticism,
223
Mezuzah ("doorpost"), 100
Micah, 19, 133, 197, 241-44
Micaiah (prophet), 166, 401
Michal, 146, 148
Midianites, 40, 88
Milgrom, Jacob, 73
Military power, idolatry of, 187
Minimalism of Israelite notion
of good life, 409
Miriam (prophetess), 56, 89
Mizpah, ceremony at, 141
Moab, 200, 216
Amos on, 233
degradation of, 167
events at, 91-93
journey from Sinai to, 88-91
Moabites, 34, 249
Monarchy, Israelite
divided, 161-69
establishment of, 127
as providential, 153-54
See also Kingship
Monotheism, 100, 410
Moore, Carey A., 364
Moral character, 3-4
Moral futilities, 346
Mordecai, 364-65
Moreh, oak of, 32
Mosaic covenant, 57-60, 172,
408. See also
Deuteronomy
Moses, 12
census conducted by, 85-86
cleansing of Levites, 87-88
death of, 109
lineage of, 67
meekness of, 89
murmurings of people and, 89
Pharaoh and, 54-55
position and work of, 53-54
primacy in prophetship of,
104
traditions about, 43
See also Exodus
Mount Sinai (Horeb), 63

Mowinckel, Sigmund, 264, 279,
280, 285-86
Myers, Jacob M., 394, 399, 404
Mystery, steadfast love as nature
of divine, 244
Mystery of God, 48
Mysticism, merkabah ("chariot")
and rabbinic, 223

Naaman, 167
Nabal, 145
Nadab, 164
Nahum, 19, 244-46
Naomi, 325-31
Naphtali, 39
Nathan (prophet), 148, 161,
396, 398
parable of, 149
Nations, the, 200
judgment coming upon,
249-50
oracles against, 233, 254
Jeremiah's, 200-202
Table of, 30, 32
Nazirite vow, 87
Nebuchadnezzar, King, 171,
198, 202, 203, 214-15
dream of, 371-72
fall of, 372
trial by fire, 371-72
Nebuzaradan, 200
Neco, 403
Nehemiah, 14, 381-92
historical background, 387-89
lasting significance, 390-91
literary intent, 389-90
memoirs of, 20
reforms of, 111
textual analysis, 384-87
organizing the community,
386-87
responses to the Law,
385-86
work of Nehemiah, 384-85
New Testament, 280
New Year, 79
Nietzsche, Friedrich, 339
Nineveh
Jonah's preaching to, 238
Nahum's oracles against,
244-46
Noachite covenant, 29-30
Northern Kingdom
Assyrian conquest of, 168-69
collapse of, 111
traditionists (keepers of
tradition), 110-11
See also Ephraim
Noth, Martin, 44

Numbers, 85-97
God of, 94
historical background, 93-94
holy war and, 94
JE sources of, 85, 93-94
lasting significance, 94-95
literary intent, 94
military ferocity and, 94
P sources of, 85, 94
textual analysis, 85-93
in the desert at Sinai, 85-88
events at Moab, 91-93
journey from Sinai to Moab, 88-91
view of women in, 95
Numerical proverbs, 320

Oak of Moreh, 32
Oaths of innocence, 300
Obad, book of, 19
Obadiah, 164, 236-37
Oded (prophet), 402
Oholah, 216
Oholibah, 216
Old Testament, 7
Omri, 164
dynasty of, 12, 168
Oppressions, 346-47
Ordaining of priests, 61, 75
Order, 411-12
Origen, 381
Original sin, 412
Orpah, 326
Othniel, 131

Paganism, 131-32. See also Idolatry
Palestine during period of Abraham, 10
Paltiel, 146
Parallelism, semantic, 284
Parental disciplining, 100
Parental preference, theme of, 48
Pashur, 196
Passover, 55, 60, 79, 88, 171
Paul of Tarsus, 322
Peniel, 48
Pentateuch, 7, 21, 24
canonization of the, 67
diversity in sources of, 16
P stratum, 17
See also Deuteronomy; Exodus; Genesis; Leviticus; Numbers
Perez, 40, 329
Persia, 14, 201

conquest of Babylon, 388
Persian Empire, 363
Pethuel, 231
Pharaoh, 54
Moses and, 54-55
See also Exodus
Pharisees, 14
Philistines, 152-53, 200, 216
capture of ark of the covenent by, 139-40
David and, 144, 146-48
oracle against, 178
Samson and, 133
Phinehas, 67
Phylacteries, 100
Plague(s)
episode of the ten, 67
of locusts, 231, 232
Poem, framework, 293
Political power, idolatry of, 187
Political responsibility, 391
Politics
neo-Assyrian, Deuteronomy and, 109-10
power, 113
Pollution
blood and, 93
of environment and government, 81
Pompey, 14
Pope, Marvin, 299
Potiphar's wife, 40
Poverty, 103
Power
idolatry of, 187
politics, 113
Praise, hymns of, 264, 267, 268, 273, 277, 280-84, 289
declarative, 267, 274, 277, 278
descriptive, 266, 277, 278
Praxis, prayer and, 83
Prayers, 83, 289
royal, 276
Preacher, the. See Ecclesiastes
Priesthood
Christian notion of, 57-58
compilation of Leviticus and, 81-82
function of, 75
Leviticus and, 73
prophecy's primacy over, 74-75
tribe of Levi and, 60-61
Priests, 79
Aaronic, 90-91
interest in Deuteronomistic history, 168

Malachai on, 257-59
ordaining, 61, 75
of Zadok, 220
Primeval history, Genesis on, 25-31
Prophecy
contest between false and true, 166
as inheritor of Mosaic power and authority, 166
primacy over kingship, 163, 165
primacy over priesthood, 74-75
Prophetic imagination
of postexilic times, 256-57
utilities of, 207-8
Prophetic oracles of judgment or admonition (psalm genre), 267, 275
Prophets, 7, 14, 113
false, Micah on, 241
former, 17
goal of, 173
history of Israel and, 17-19
latter, 17
theology of, 208
the Twelve, 18-19, 227-62
Amos, 12, 19, 232-36
Habakkuk, 19, 246-48
Haggai, 19, 250-52
Hosea, 12, 19, 207, 227-30
Joel, 19, 230-32
Jonah, 19, 238-40
Malachai, 19, 257-60, 404
Micah, 19, 133, 197, 241-44
Nahum, 19, 244-46
Obadiah, 164, 236-37
Zechariah, 252-57
Zephaniah, 19, 248-50
Prosperity, ideal of biblical, 293
Protestant Christian religious beliefs, 4
Proverbs, 19, 20, 311-25
guiding belief of, 312
historical background, 321
lasting significance, 322-23
Law and, 322
literary intent, 322
numerical, 320
textual analysis, 311-21
appendices, 320-21
first collection of Solomonic sayings, 314-17
second collection of Solomonic sayings, 319-20

.nt.)
.er's introduction,
,11-14
.iirty precepts of the sages,
317-18
alms, 19, 20, 263-91
of confidence, 266 67, 268,
273-74
communal, 280, 281-82
individual, 281
entrance and processional
liturgies, 267, 268
historical, 275, 278, 289
historical background, 285-86
hymns of praise or
thanksgiving, 264, 267,
268, 273, 277, 280-84,
289
anonymous individual, 269
communal, 274, 278
descriptive, 266, 277, 278
hymns of Zion, 270-71, 275,
276, 281
laments
communal, 267, 270, 273,
275-79, 281, 282, 283
individual, 264-70, 273-79,
282, 283
lasting significance, 287-89
literary intent, 286-87
prophetic oracles of judgment
or admonition, 267, 275
royal, 264, 289
ceremonial songs, 268,
274, 277-80, 282
prayers, 276
thanksgiving songs or
declarative praise, 267
wedding songs, 270
sapiential, 281, 282
textual analysis, 264-85
1–41, 264-70
42–72, 270-74
73–89, 274-76
90–106, 276-78
107–150, 278-85
wisdom, 264, 267, 274, 277,
280, 283
Psammetichus II, pharaoh, 215
P sources, 17
Genesis materials and
perspectives of, 67
of Numbers, 85, 94
of Pentateuch, 17
Ptolemies, 14, 376
Purification
after childbirth, 76
from foreign influences,
theme of, 39, 389-90, 391

of sanctuary and nation, 76-77
Purim, feast of, 362

Qoheleth. See Ecclesiastes
Qur'an, 2, 114

Raamses II, Pharaoh, 11
Rabbah, battle at, 149
Rabbinic mysticism, 223
Rabshakeh, 169, 180-81
Rachel, 39
Jacob and, 37-38
securing of, 36
Rahab the harlot, 120
Rape, punishment for, 104-5
Rebekah, 36, 37
Rechabites, 199
Redemption/liberation, notion
of, 411
biblical calls to, 112
theology of, 68-69
Reed Sea, crossing of, 121
Rehoboam, 12, 163, 400
Religion
civil, 128
fertility, 26-27
Religious experience, 48
Responsibility, political, 391
Reuben, 39, 40, 93, 125-26
Revelation, dynamics of
historical, 412-16
Revelatory (apocalyptic)
literature, 370
Reversal, theme of, 365
Rite of the bronze serpent, 91
Ritual involving the ashes of
the red heifer, 91
Ritual uncleanness, 216
Rivalry, sibling, 28, 36, 40, 48
Rizpah, 151
Rock, imagery of, 108
Rock of Horeb, 57
Roman rule of Israel, 14
Royal ceremonial songs, 268,
274, 277-80, 282
Royal prayers, 276
Royal psalms, 264, 289
Royal thanksgiving songs, 267
Royal wedding songs, 270
Ruth, 19-20, 325-31
feminist overtones in, 330
historical background, 329
human love and, 330
lasting significance, 330-31
literary intent, 329-30
textual analysis, 325-29
alien grain?, 326-27
birth of son, 328-29
encounter at the threshing

floor, 327-38
genealogy, 329
resolution at the city gate,
328
returning home, 326
sojourners, 325-26

Sabbath, 1, 26, 79-80
observance of, 390
reinstitution of, 61
Sacred scripture, notion of,
264-65
Sacrifice(s), 79, 408-9
animal, 33
child, 169
human, 35
in Leviticus, 73-74
prescriptions for, 59
regulations for, 92
ritualistic, 70
Sages, thirty precepts of the,
317-18
Samaria, 216
Samaritans, 169
Samson, 132-33
1 and 2 Samuel, 11, 138-59
historical background, 152-53
lasting significance, 154-57
literary intent, 153-54
textual analysis, 138-52
miscellaneous materials,
151-52
reign of David, 146-51
rise of David, 143-46
Saul and advent of
kingship, 140-43
story of Samuel, 138-40
Sanballat, 384-85
Sanctuary
inaugural services at, 74-75
purification of, 76-77
Santa Katerina monastery, 64
Sapiential psalms, 281, 282
Sarah, 32-36
burial of, 35-36
threats to, 34-35
Satan, 293, 397
Zechariah's vision and, 253
Saul, 11, 12
advent of kingship and,
140-43
Chronicles on, 395
David and, 144-45
death of, 145-46
Schildenberger, Johannes, 408
Scott, R. B. Y., 312, 342, 346
Scripture, 14
canonization of last portion, 21
notion of, 264-65

Scroll, Zechariah's vision of
flying, 253
Secularism of modern Western
culture, 288
Seir, Mount (Edom), Ezekiel's
oracle against, 218-19
Seleucids, 14, 376
Self-criticism, religious, 218
Self-definition, worship and,
403, 404-5
Semantic parallelism, 284
Semitic peoples, 30
Sennacherib of Assyria, 402
Separatism, ethnic, 39, 389-90,
391
Septuagint, 7, 15
Serpent
in garden of Eden, 26-27
rite of the bronze, 91
"Servant" of God, 182
Sesostris III, 55
Seth, 28
Sexual intercourse, laws
forbidding, 76
Shame, awakening of humanity
to, 27
Shamgar, 131
Shavuot, 60
Shearjashub, 177
Sheba, 151
Sheba, Queen of, 162
Shebna, steward of Hezekiah,
179
Shechem, 32, 39, 125
Shem, 30
Shema, 100, 410
Shemaiah, 163
Sheol, 90, 218, 320
Sheshbazzar, 382
Shiloh, destruction of, 193
Shimei, 150, 161
Shinar, 31
Shishak of Egypt, 163
Sibling rivalry, 28, 36, 40, 48
Sidon, fall of, 179, 217
Silence of the Lord, 185
Simeon, 92
landlessness of the tribes of,
39
Sin
consciousness in Psalm 51 of,
272
original, 412
Sinai, journey to Moab from,
88-91
Sin offering vs. guilt offering,
74
Skin diseases, regulations for
dealing with, 76

Slavery
Joseph's sale into, 40
regulations about, 59
Slaves, freeing of, 103, 199
Smiths, Zechariah's vision of,
252
Social injustice, 185, 204-5,
390
Amos on, 236
Micah on, 241, 243-44
Sodom and Gomorrah, 33, 34
Solomon, King, 11, 12, 149,
311, 332-34, 342, 344
alliance with Pharaoh, 161
Chronicles on, 397-400
as paradigm of love poetry,
338
reign of, 160-63
Solomonic sayings
first collection of, 314-17
second collection of, 319-20
Solomon's Temple, 219-20
Song of David, 152
Song of Deborah, 18
Song of Hannah, 139
Song of Songs, 15, 332-41
allegorical potential, 338
historical background, 338
lasting significance, 339-40
literary intent, 338-39
textual analysis, 332-38
commitment, 336-37
first dream, 333-34
first tryst, 334-35
prelude and reverie, 333
reverie and postlude,
337-38
second dream, 335-36
second tryst, 336
Songs
royal
ceremonial, 268, 274,
277-80, 282
thanksgiving, 267
wedding, 270
of thanksgiving or declarative
praise, 264, 268, 273,
277, 282, 283, 289
anonymous individual, 269
communal, 274, 278
See also Hymn(s)
Southern Kingdom, 12-14
fall of, 203
Josiah's reform of, 111
Speech, restraint of, 315
Speiser, E. A., 30
Sternberg, Meir, 148
Stone, symbolic meaning of, 105
Stoning, 79

Strength of Hebrew women,
52-53
Suffering, Job and, 307
Sukkot, 60
Sumerian culture, 10
Syria during period of Abraham,
10
Syro-Ephramite war (734 to
733), 176, 177

Tabernacle
building of, 62-63
holiness of the area around,
86
instructions for, 60-61
Table of the Nations, 30, 32
Tabor, Mount, 133
Tamar, 40
rape of, 149
Tammuz, 213
Tanak, 7
Teacher, image of, 180
Tefillin ("phylacteries"), 100
Tekoa, incident of the woman
of, 149
Tel Beth Shean, 123
Teleology, 47
Temple of Jerusalem, 14, 63,
77, 171, 232
building of, 161
Israelite ambivalence
about, 148
Chronicles on, 394-95,
397-98
dedication of, 161-62
defilement of, 213
rebuilding of, 382-84
delays in, 388
Haggai on, 250-52
ruin of, 162
Western Wall of, 343
Temple Sermon, 193, 197
Ten commandments, 58-59, 67,
100
Israel's existence and, 107
See also Deuteronomy; Mosaic
covenant
Tent of meeting, 61, 62-63
Terrien, Samuel, 26, 27, 332,
337, 338
Thanksgiving, songs of, 264,
268, 273, 277, 282, 283,
289
anonymous individual, 269
communal, 274, 278
Theodicy
of Habakkuk, 247-48
Job and, 308

...91
...07. *See also* World
...w of Hebrew Bible
...tory, 173-74
...ration/redemption, 68-69
... Prophets, 208
...heophany (divine presence),
    188
"Therapeutic" language, 3
Thongs, symbolism of, 197
Tibni, 164
Time
  biblical literature as linear
      view of, 46
  common experience of, 1
Tirzah, 164
Tocqueville, Alexis de, 3-4
Torah, 7, 18, 98
  Christianity's effects on,
      114-15
  focuses of, 44-45
  God's free communication of,
      114
  heartbeat of, 80
  history of Israel and, 15-17
  as revelation and
      jurisprudence, 114
  Yahwist stratum in, 16
  See also Deuteronomy;
      Exodus; Genesis; Law,
      the; Leviticus; Numbers
Tree of knowledge, 26
Tribal elders, 122
Tribes, twelve
  encampment of, 86
  Ezekiel on, 220
Tribes of Yahweh, The
    (Gottwald), 121
Twelve, the, 18-19, 227-62
  Amos, 12, 19, 232-36
  Habakkuk, 19, 246-48
  Haggai, 19, 250-52
  Hosea, 12, 19, 207, 227-30
  Joel, 19, 230-32
  Jonah, 19, 238-40
  Malachai, 19, 257-60, 404
  Micah, 19, 133, 197, 241-44
  Nahum, 19, 244-46
  Obadiah, 164, 236-37
  Zechariah, 252-57
  Zephaniah, 19, 248-50
Type-scene, 36
Tyre, fall of, 179, 217

Uncleanness
  laws of, 75-76
  ritual, 216

Understanding, wisdom and,
    314
Uriah the Hittite, murder of,
    145, 148-49
Uzzah, death of, 148
Uzziah, 402

Valley of slaughter, 196
Vanity of life, 343-48
Vashti, queen, 362-64
Vengeance, clan, 93
Virginity, 104-5
Visionaries, problem faced by,
    188-89
von Rad, Gerhard, 31, 127-28
Vow(s)
  in Leviticus, 80-81
  Nazirite, 87
  of women, 92

Wadi Firan, 65
Wandering in the desert, 56-57,
    65, 90
War, 121-23
  Deuteronomic view of, 104
  holy, 92, 249
    Muslim (jihads), 127
  intertribal (fratricide), 134
  See also Conquest of Canaan
Wealth, vanity of, 348
Wedding songs, royal, 270
Weeks, Feast of, 79
Westerman, Claus, 31
Western culture, secularism of,
    288
Western Wall of Jerusalem
    Temple Mount, 343
Wife swapping, 105
Williamson, H. G. M., 384,
    390
Wine, liturgical significance, 33
Wisdom, 411-12
  beginning of, 312, 346
  personae of, 313-14
  transiency of, 345
  understanding and, 314
  See also Job; Proverbs
Wisdom movement, 20, 321,
    322
Wisdom psalms, 264, 267, 274,
    277, 280, 283
Wisdom tale, Esther as, 368
Witch of Endor, 145
Women
  status of, Exodus and, 59
  strength of, 52-53
  view in Numbers of, 95

vows of, 92
World view of Hebrew Bible,
    407-17
  biblical God, 410-12
  covenanted people, 408-9
  historical revelation, 412-16
Worship, 408
  beginning of true, 28
  human fulfillment and, 70
  Israelite self-definition
      (identity) and, 403,
      404-5
  significance of, 265
  See also Cult
Writings, the, 7, 17, 263
  history of Israel and, 19-21
  literary genres in, 19

Xenophanes, 246
Xerxes I (Ahasuerus), reign of,
    362-67

Yahwist religion, 44, 56
  account of creation, 26-29
  Exodus materials of, 66
  first phases of, 32
  in Torah, 16
  view of bisexuality of
      humanity, 26
YHWH, 12, 16
Yoke bars, symbolism of, 197
Yom Kippur (Day of
    Atonement), 77, 79, 90

Zadok, priests of, 220
Zalmunna, 131
Zebah, 131
Zechariah, 19, 252-57, 401
Zedekiah, King, 171, 196-200,
    202, 215
  revolt against Babylon, 203-4
Zephaniah, 19, 248-50
Zerubbabel, 251
Ziba, 150
Zilpah, 38
Zimri, 164
Zion
  capture of, 146
  hymns of, 270-71, 275, 276,
      281
  restoration of, 183
  See also Jerusalem
Zion, Mount, 232
Zionism, 107
Zophar the Naamathite,
    295-96, 298